Mozambique

the Bradt Travel Guide

Philip Briggs

edition 5

www.bradtguides.com

Bradt Travel Guides Ltd, UK
The Globe Pequot Press Inc, USA

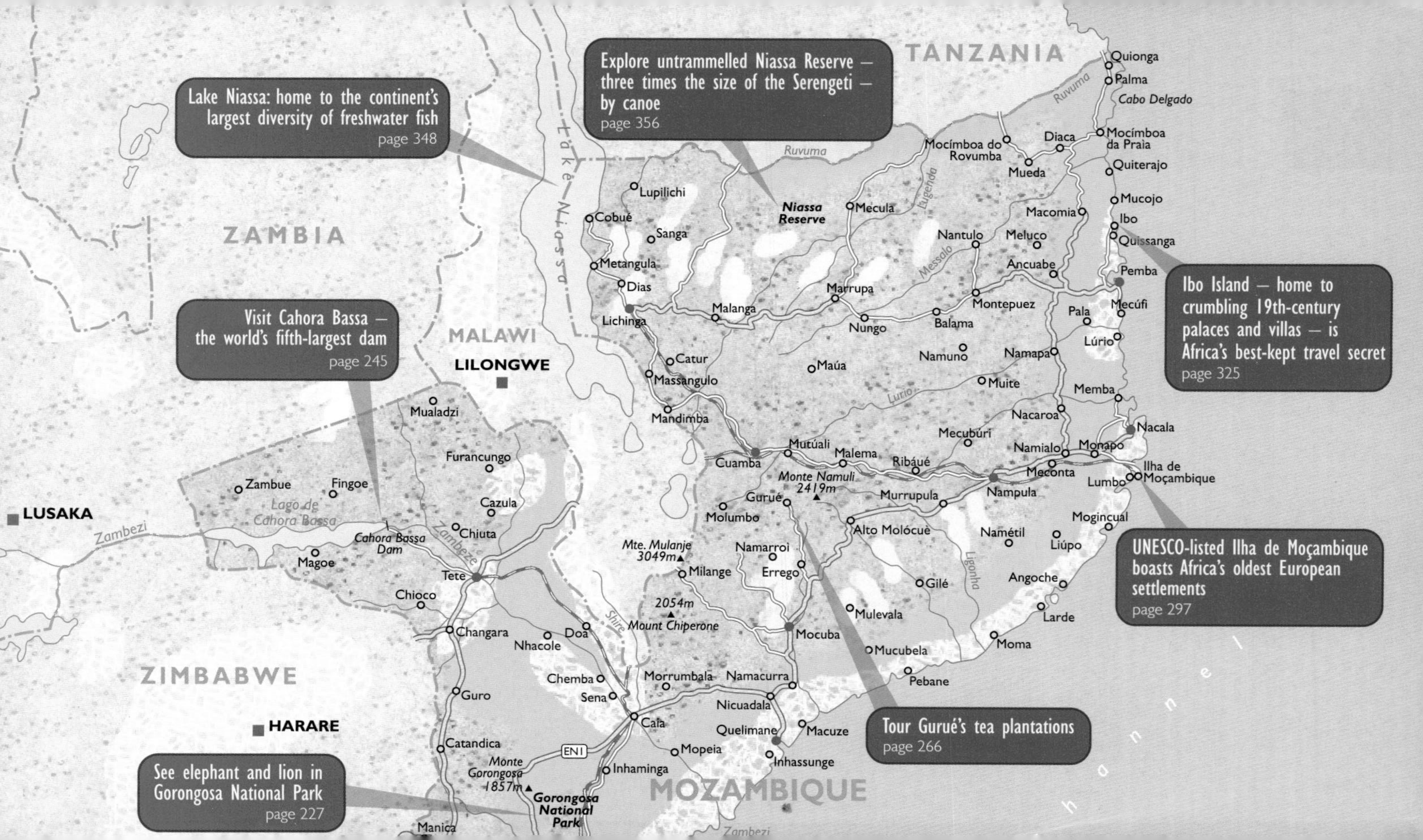
Lake Niassa: home to the continent's largest diversity of freshwater fish
page 348
Explore untrammelled Niassa Reserve – three times the size of the Serengeti – by canoe
page 356
Visit Cahora Bassa – the world's fifth-largest dam
page 245
Ibo Island – home to crumbling 19th-century palaces and villas – is Africa's best-kept travel secret
page 325
UNESCO-listed Ilha de Moçambique boasts Africa's oldest European settlements
page 297
Tour Gurué's tea plantations
page 266
See elephant and lion in Gorongosa National Park
page 227
TANZANIA
ZAMBIA
MALAWI
ZIMBABWE
MOZAMBIQUE
LUSAKA
LILONGWE
HARARE
Lake Niassa
Niassa Reserve
Gorongosa National Park
Lago de Cahora Bassa
Cahora Bassa Dam
Zambezi
Zambeze
Ruvuma
Lugenda
Messalo
Lúrio
Ligonha
Shire
Cabo Delgado
Quionga
Palma
Mocímboa da Praia
Quiterajo
Mucojo
Ibo
Quissanga
Pemba
Mecúfi
Lúrio
Pala
Memba
Nacala
Monapo
Ilha de Moçambique
Lumbo
Mogincual
Liúpo
Angoche
Larde
Moma
Pebane
Mucubela
Mulevala
Gilé
Namétil
Nampula
Meconta
Namialo
Nacaroa
Namapa
Mecubúri
Ribáuè
Malema
Murrupula
Alto Molócuè
Monte Namuli 2419m
Mutúali
Cuamba
Gurué
Molumbo
Namarroi
Errego
Mocuba
Namacurra
Nicuadala
Quelimane
Macuze
Inhassunge
Mopeia
Inhaminga
Morrumbala
Caia
Sena
Chemba
Doa
Nhacole
Mount Chiperone
2054m
Mte. Mulanje 3049m
Milange
Mandimba
Massangulo
Catur
Lichinga
Malanga
Marrupa
Nungo
Balama
Montepuez
Nantulo
Meluco
Ancuabe
Macomia
Mueda
Diaca
Mocímboa do Rovumba
Mecula
Maúa
Namuno
Muite
Lupilichi
Cobué
Sanga
Metangula
Dias
Mualadzi
Furancungo
Cazula
Chiuta
Zambue
Fingoe
Magoe
Tete
Chioco
Changara
Guro
Catandica
Monte Gorongosa 1857m
Manica
EN1
Channel

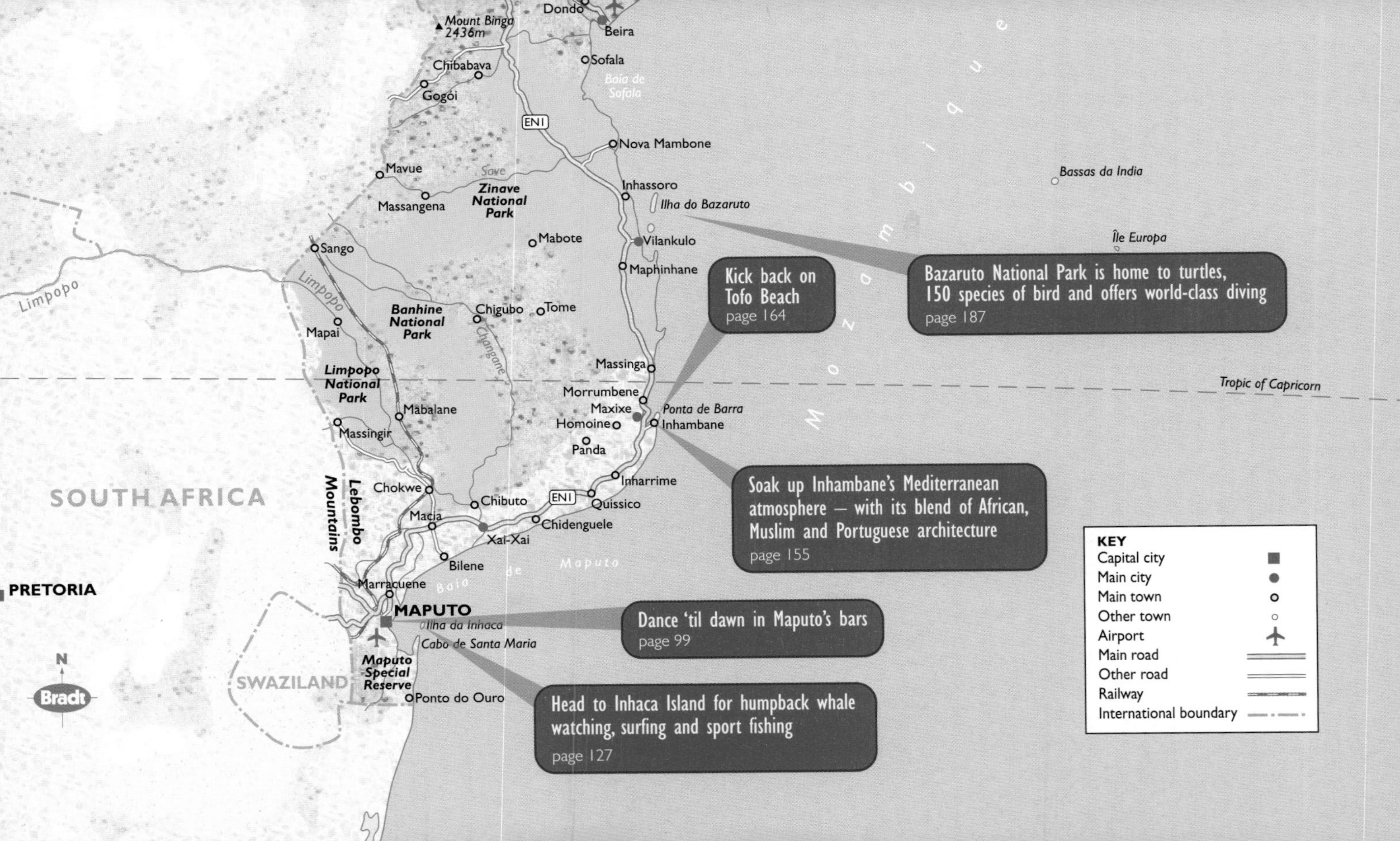
Bazaruto National Park is home to turtles, 150 species of bird and offers world-class diving
page 187
Kick back on Tofo Beach
page 164
Soak up Inhambane's Mediterranean atmosphere – with its blend of African, Muslim and Portuguese architecture
page 155
Dance 'til dawn in Maputo's bars
page 99
Head to Inhaca Island for humpback whale watching, surfing and sport fishing
page 127
KEY
Capital city
Main city
Main town
Other town
Airport
Main road
Other road
Railway
International boundary
Mozambique
Tropic of Capricorn
Bassas da India
Île Europa
Dondo
Beira
Sofala
Baia de Sofala
Mount Binga 2436m
Chibabava
Gogoi
EN1
Nova Mambone
Mavue
Save
Massangena
Zinave National Park
Inhassoro
Ilha do Bazaruto
Vilankulo
Maphinhane
Mabote
Sango
Limpopo
Banhine National Park
Chigubo
Tome
Mapai
Changane
Limpopo National Park
Massinga
Morrumbene
Maxixe
Ponta de Barra
Inhambane
Homoine
Panda
Mabalane
Massingir
Inharrime
Chokwe
Chibuto
Quissico
Lebombo Mountains
SOUTH AFRICA
Macia
Xai-Xai
Chidenguele
Bilene
Baia de Maputo
Marracuene
PRETORIA
MAPUTO
Ilha da Inhaca
Cabo de Santa Maria
N
Bradt
SWAZILAND
Maputo Special Reserve
Ponto do Ouro

Mozambique Don't miss...

World-class diving and snorkelling
Scuba diver and crescent-tailed bigeyes, Tofo beach
(WF) page 85

Maputo
The city's oldest mosque
AVZ) page 99

Beira's Art Deco architecture
Corner shop
(AVZ) page 197

Deserted beaches
Matemo Island, Quirimbas Archipelago
(IB/FLPA) page 334

Sailing on a handmade *dhow*
Benguerra Island, Bazaruto Archipelago
(AVZ) page 189

above **Tea picker at work, Gurué** (AVZ) page 266

below **Rural homestead, Gurué** (AVZ) page 266

above **Horse riding on Tofo beach** (AVZ) page 164

below **Canoeing on Lugenda River in Niassa Reserve** (AVZ) page 356

above Bottles of *piri-piri* – a Mozambican speciality – for sale near Inhambane (AVZ) page 62

below Mozambique's lengthy coastline and rich waters mean there's always plenty of fresh seafood on offer (IB/FLPA) page 62

AUTHOR

Philip Briggs has been exploring the highways, byways and backwaters of Africa since 1986, when he spent several months backpacking on a shoestring from Nairobi to Cape Town. In 1991, he wrote *South Africa: The Bradt Travel Guide*, the first such guidebook to be published internationally after the release of Nelson Mandela. Over the rest of the 1990s, Philip wrote a series of pioneering Bradt guides to destinations that were then – and in some cases still are – otherwise practically uncharted by the travel publishing industry. These included the first dedicated guidebooks to Tanzania, Uganda, Ethiopia, Malawi, Mozambique, Ghana and Rwanda (co-authored with Janice Booth), all now in their fourth–sixth edition. Philip has visited more than two dozen African countries in total and written about most of them for specialist travel and wildlife magazines including *Africa Birds & Birding*, *Africa Geographic*, *BBC Wildlife*, *Travel Africa* and *Wanderlust*. He still spends at least four months on the road every year, usually accompanied by his wife, the travel photographer Ariadne Van Zandbergen, and spends the rest of his time battering away at a keyboard in the sleepy village of Bergville, in the uKhahlamba-Drakensberg region of South Africa.

AUTHOR'S STORY

In 1996, Hilary Bradt asked me to update the southern half of what was then an 88-page 'No Frills Guide to Mozambique', written by Bernard Skrodzki in the immediate aftermath of the civil war. Naturally, I said yes, and with an insouciance that eludes me today, my soon-to-be wife Ariadne and I left our Johannesburg home in our 15 year-old 1.3-litre Toyota Corolla, and spent the next few weeks puttering it along the spectacularly potholed '4x4 only' EN1 from Maputo to Beira. By then, however, it was clear that the real adventures lay further north, so we flew to Pemba, and from there bumped our way to the remote likes of Ilha de Moçambique and Lago Niassa on buses that were abysmal even by the unexacting standards of mid-1990s Africa. Based on this adventure, Bradt was able to publish the first full-length guidebook to this then-emergent tourist destination, and its wonderful array of beaches, reefs and crumbling old colonial cities.

In 2010, driving a more appropriate vehicle, we returned to Mozambique to research the fifth edition of the same guide. It was both strange and wonderful to revisit towns and beaches we hadn't seen in 15 years, and see what had changed (the facilities, invariably for the better) and what hadn't (the people, charming and hospitable as ever). Even more of a thrill to reach a host of alluring places that had been inaccessible first time round, among then the revitalised Gorongosa National Park and Niassa Reserve. The result, I believe, is the most thorough and detailed guidebook to Mozambique yet published, a full 100 pages longer than any previous edition, and we only hope that our readers enjoy using it half as much as we did putting it together!

PUBLISHER'S FOREWORD

Adrian Phillips, Publishing Director

Philip Briggs is Bradt's most prolific author, and knows much of Africa inside out. He has taken the opportunity to completely overhaul this fifth edition of *Mozambique* – including restructuring the content to make it more user-friendly, significantly increasing the wildlife coverage and re-drawing the majority of maps from scratch. This book allows travellers to explore not only the sandy beaches of the south but the little-visited north of the country. Philip's thorough research and honest reviews do the Bradt name proud. You have a treat ahead of you, both in reading about and travelling around this lovely, welcoming country.

Fifth edition published April 2011 First published in 1997

Bradt Travel Guides Ltd, IDC House, The Vale, Chalfont St Peter, Bucks SL9 9RZ, England
www.bradtguides.com
Published in the USA by The Globe Pequot Press Inc, 246 Goose Lane, PO Box 480, Guilford, Connecticut 06437-0480

Project Manager: Emma Thomson

ISBN-13: 978 1 84162 342 9

British Library Cataloguing in Publication Data
A catalogue record for this book is available from the British Library

Photographers Ariadne Van Zandbergen (AVZ), Flip Nicklin/Minden Pictures/FLPA (FN/MP/FLPA), ImageBroker/FLPA (IB/FLPA), SuperStock (SS), WaterFrame (WF)
Front cover People loading up *dhow* taxi near Fortaleza de São Sebastião, Ilha de Moçambique (SS)
Back cover Aerial view of island in the Quirimbas Archipelago (AVZ), Makonde mask (AVZ)
Title page Makua girl with white facemask, Ibo Island (AVZ); Mural depicting a popular beer, Maputo (AVZ); Beach, Bazaruto Island (AVZ)

Maps David McCutcheon
Illustrations Annabel Milne

Typeset from the author's disc by Wakewing
Production managed by Jellyfish Print Solutions and manufactured in India

Acknowledgements

Many people have provided help and support during the gestation of this guidebook, not the least of them being Ross Velton and Danny Edmunds, updaters for the third and fourth editions respectively, whose excellent work made my job so much easier when tackling this expanded fifth edition. I'm also grateful to my wife and photographic collaborator Ariadne Van Zandbergen, who shared driving duties on the 10,000km trip that was required to update this fifth edition, and the usual suspects at Bradt Travel Guides – Adrian Phillips, Hilary Bradt and project manager Emma Thomson.

Thanks also, and in particular order, to following for their assistance with planning or on the ground: Mike 'Mozman' Slater, Kerry Butler of Mozaic Travel, Arianna Fogelman, Marjaana Kohtamaki, Roger Diski, Derek Schuurman, Natalie Bockel, Branda Dickenson, Debbi Jackson and Marc Veldhaus, Uwe Reichelt of Ruby Backpackers, Vasco Galante and Hendrik Pott at Gorongosa National Park, Peter-Jan Hulsebosch, Val Cuzen, Rob and Jocelyn Janisch of Explore Gorongosa, Marcia Baloyi of LAM, Michele Abraham and the staff and management of various Rani Resorts, Maya Litscher, Anita Pieterse of Zavora Lodge, Anja Mann of the Pink Papaya, Fernando Mateus, Fiona Record & the staff at Ibo Island Lodge, Ian and Joanne Martin, Christelle at the Honeypot, Fátima Vieira of Fátima's Place, Sabrina at Zombie Cucumber, Elize Hulster, Gabriele Melazzi, Elize Scheepers, the Oosthuizen family at Dugong Lodge, Div de Villiers of Tofo Beach Cotttages, Anna McGinn of Indigo Bay, Carlo Macchiarulo, Carla Antoniazzi, Marie Klagsbrun and the management and staff of Marlin Lodge, the staff and management of Bamboozi Lodge … and the many other people who helped us along the way.

UPDATES WEBSITE AND FEEDBACK

For the latest travel news about Mozambique, please visit the update page on Bradt's website: updates.bradtguides.com. This page supplements the printed information in the Bradt guidebook and provides an online space where both author updates and reader feedback can be shared.

If you have any comments, queries, grumbles, insights, news or other feedback please contact us on: 01753 893444; info@bradtguides.com. Alternatively, contact Philip direct at philari@hixnet.co.za. The best and most useful comments will be posted on our website.

Contents

Introduction VII

PART ONE GENERAL INFORMATION 1

Chapter 1 **Background Information** 3
Geography 3, Climate 4, History 4, Government and politics 18, Economy 18, People 21, Language 22, Religion 23, Culture 23

Chapter 2 **Natural History** 25
Vegetation 25, Mammals 26, Birds 30, Reptiles 32, Marine life 34

Chapter 3 **Practical Information** 39
When to visit 39, Highlights 39, Tourist information 40, Tour operators 40, Red tape 42, Getting there and away 43, Crime and safety 46, Focus on specific groups 49, What to take 50, Money 53, Budgeting 54, Getting around 55, Accommodation 59, Eating and drinking 61, Public holidays 62, Shopping 63, Photography 65, Media and communications 66, Responsible tourism 67, Travelling positively 68

Chapter 4 **Health** 71
Preparations 71, Medical facilities 77, Common medical problems 77

Chapter 5 **Diving and Snorkelling** 85
Choosing an operator 85, Preparations before diving 85, During the dive 89, Snorkelling 92

PART TWO SOUTHERN MOZAMBIQUE 95

Chapter 6 **Maputo** 99
History 102, Getting there and away 104, Getting around 105, Where to stay 107, Where to eat 110, Nightlife 114, Safety and hassles 115, Entertainment 115, Shopping 117, Other practicalities 118, What to see and do 120, City walks 122, Day trips from Maputo 124

Chapter 7	**Maputaland** Inhaca Island 127, Catembe 131, Bella Vista and Salamanga 132, Maputo Special Reserve 134, Ponta Mamoli and Malongane 135, Ponto do Oro 136	**127**
Chapter 8	**The Limpopo Valley and Coast South of Inhambane** Marracuene and surrounds 141, Bilene 142, Limpopo National Park 144, Xai-Xai 148, Beaches around Xai-Xai 152, Northeast of Xai-Xai 153	**141**
Chapter 9	**Inhambane and Surrounds** Inhambane 155, Maxixe 162, Beaches around Inhambane 164, North of Inhambane 173	**155**
Chapter 10	**Vilankulo, Inhassoro and Bazaruto National Park** Vilankulo 175, Inhassoro 184, Bazaruto National Park 187	**175**
PART THREE	**CENTRAL MOZAMBIQUE**	**193**
Chapter 11	**Beira** History 197, Getting there and away 198, Orientation and getting around 200, Where to stay 200, Where to eat and drink 202, Other practicalities 203, What to see and do 206	**197**
Chapter 12	**Chimoio and the Manica Highlands** Chimoio 212, Lake Chicamba 217, Manica 217, Penhalonga 221, Chimanimani National Reserve 223	**211**
Chapter 13	**Gorongosa and the Caia Road** Gorongosa National Park 227, Mount Gorongosa 232, The EN1 from Inchope to Caia 234	**227**
Chapter 14	**Tete** Tete 241, Around Tete 245	**239**
PART FOUR	**NORTHERN MOZAMBIQUE**	**251**
Chapter 15	**Zambézia** Quelimane 255, The Quelimane–Nampula Road 261, The Western Highlands 266	**255**
Chapter 16	**Nampula** Getting there and away 275, Where to stay 276, Where to eat and drink 277, Other practicalities 278, What to see and do 278, Around Nampula 279	**275**
Chapter 17	**Ilha de Moçambique and Surrounds** History 286, Getting there and away 288, Where to stay 288, Where to eat 290, Shopping 291, Other practicalities 291, Exploring Ilha de Moçambique 292, Mossuril Bay 298, Nacala 302	**285**

Chapter 18	**Pemba and the Northeast** Pemba 308, Montepuez 316, Towards Tanzania 317	**307**
Chapter 19	**The Quirimbas** History 324, Ibo 325, Other islands of the Quirimbas 333, The Quirimbas mainland 337, Pangane 340	**323**
Chapter 20	**Niassa Province** Cuamba 341, Mandimba and Massangulo 343, Lichinga 344, Lago Niassa (Lake Malawi) 347, Niassa Reserve 356	**341**
Appendix 1	**Language**	**363**
Appendix 2	**Further Information**	**367**
Index		**373**

LIST OF MAPS

Alto Molócué 265
Angoche 280
Bazaruto archipelago 176
Beira, orientation 199
Beira, centre 204–5
Bilene 143
Chimoio 214
Chimoio & Manica Highlands 210
Cóbuè 355
Cuamba 343
Gorongosa National Park 226
Gurué 267
Ibo 329
Ilha de Moçambique 284
Ilha de Moçambique, Stone Town 294
Inhambane 159
Inhambane & surrounds 156
Inhassoro 185
Lichinga 346
Macomia 318
Mandimba 344
Manica 219
Maputaland & Maputo Special Reserve 128
Maputo, Baixa 113
Maputo, orientation 100–1
Maputo, Polana 106
Maxixe 163
Metangula 352
Milange 273
Mocuba 263
Montepuez 316
Mossuril Bay 300
Mueda 320
Nacala 304
Namialo 283
Nampula 274
Mozambique, central 194–5
Mozambique, northern 252–3
Mozambique, southern 96–7
Pemba & Wimbe Beach, orientation 306
Pemba, centre 311
Ponta do Ouro 137
Quelimane 258
Quirimbas, south 324
Tete 240
Tofo & Tofinho 166
Vilankulo 179
Xai-Xai 150

Introduction

Visit Mozambique today, and you'll find it difficult to imagine that it once attracted a larger number of tourists than South Africa and Rhodesia. Equally incredible, for that matter, is the realisation that, over the 15 years prior to 1992, this beguiling country was embroiled in an all-consuming civil war that claimed the lives of almost one million people, and caused the displacement of five times more.

Fortunately, the war is long over, and Mozambique is now preparing to celebrate 20 years of political stability, economic growth and progressive governance. Indeed, one of the most notable things when talking to Mozambicans about their recent history is how much more interested they are in making the most of the future rather than sliding back into the arguments of the past.

Recent figures suggest that, of all the countries in the world, nowhere is tourism developing as quickly as it is in Mozambique today. True, this statistic is to some extent reflective of the tiny base from which tourism has grown since the early 1990s. Equally, during South African and Zimbabwean school vacations, the resorts that line the coast between Maputo and Beira are bursting with cross-border holidaymakers, to the extent that in some resorts you'll hear more English and Afrikaans spoken than Portuguese or any indigenous language.

So far as tourists are concerned, Mozambique might almost as well be two countries. Linked only by a solitary new bridge that spans the mighty Zambezi River at Caia, and divided by the more than 1,000km of road connecting Beira and Nampula, southern Mozambique and northern Mozambique offer entirely different experiences to visitors. The two parts of the country have in common the widespread use of Portuguese and a quite startlingly beautiful coastline. The difference is that the south coast of Mozambique is already established as a tourist destination, with rapidly improving facilities and a ready-made market in the form of its eastern neighbours. The north, by contrast, has few facilities for tourists, and getting to those that exist takes determination and either time or money, although once you reach them they are the equal of anything in the region, and in some cases the world.

The majority of people who buy this guide will probably confine their travels to southern Mozambique. Not only does this part of the country offer good roads, reasonable public transport, some exceptional restaurants, and any number of beach resorts suitable for all tastes and budgets, but it is within a day's drive of Johannesburg, the subcontinent's largest city and major international transport hub. The south coast of Mozambique is exceptionally beautiful – truly the archetype of palm-lined tropical-beach nirvana – as well as boasting snorkelling, diving and game fishing to rank with the very best in the world. Add to this Maputo and Beira, two of Africa's most attractive cities, not to mention the old-world gem that is Inhambane town, and you are looking at a stretch of coast as varied and attractive as any in Africa.

Any honest description of travel conditions on Mozambique's northern mainland – serious linguistic barriers to non-Portuguese speakers, humidity levels that reach intolerable proportions in summer, relatively high costs and a public transport system that in places defies rational comprehension – is bound to ring alarm bells with anybody seeking comfort, predictability or packaged entertainment. Equally, it is likely to whet the appetite of travellers looking for an adventurous trip through one of southern Africa's least-explored regions. The northern provinces of Zambézia, Niassa, Nampula and Cabo Delgado have a remote, isolated and self-contained feel – not surprising when you consider that they are collectively bordered by the undeveloped southeast quarter of Tanzania to the north, and by the vast watery expanses of the Indian Ocean and Lago Niassa to the east and west.

That said, northern Mozambique now boasts several upmarket resorts – mostly on the Quirimbas and the mainland around Pemba – that meet world-class standards, making the area highly attractive to fly-in visitors who are able to foot the rather hefty bills associated with these idyllic examples of 'barefoot luxury'. And while backpackers will find that much of northern Mozambique feels like travel for its own sake (a great deal of bumpy motion with relatively few highlights), the area does boasts two historical attractions of quite compelling singularity, namely the former Portuguese capital on Ilha de Moçambique and the ancient island town of Ibo.

A recent development in Mozambique is the upgrading and opening up of several national parks and other potential safari destinations that suffered heavy losses to poaching during the years of civil war. Foremost among these is the newly refurbished Gorongosa National Park, which is showing the potential to become as important an attraction in the future as it was in the colonial era, when it was known as the Serengeti of southern Africa. Other important reserves with recently improved facilities include Limpopo National Park (which combines with South Africa's Kruger National Park and Zimbabwe's Gonarezhou National Park to form the Great Limpopo Transfrontier Park), the Maputo Special Reserve (home to several hundred elephant) and the inconceivably vast Niassa Reserve in the far north.

Mozambique may not be the easiest country in which to travel; in the northeast it can be downright frustrating. But this will change. And as this stands, it is not the least of Mozambique's attractions that it still offers ample scope for genuinely exploratory travel, offering adventurous travellers the opportunity to experience it entirely for themselves, without the distorting medium of a developed tourist industry.

MAP REFERENCES

Several maps use grid lines to allow easy location of sites. Map grid references are listed in square brackets after listings in the text, with page number followed by grid number, eg: [118–19 C3].

Part One

GENERAL INFORMATION

MOZAMBIQUE AT A GLANCE

Location Mozambique extends for 2,500km along the east coast of Africa, between latitudes 11° and 26°S and longitudes 30° and 40°E
Neighbouring countries Tanzania, Malawi, Zambia, Zimbabwe, South Africa, Swaziland
Area 799,380km^2, of which 13,000km^2 is water. It is the 16th-largest country in Africa, roughly two-thirds the size of the neighbouring Republic of South Africa, about three times the size of Great Britain and slightly larger than the state of Texas.
Climate Almost all the country is below 2,000m, and covered in a mixture of subtropical scrub. The south tends to be cooler and drier than the north.
Status Multi-party republic
Population 23 million (2010 estimate)
Life expectancy 48
Capital Maputo (population around 1.9 million including Matola)
Other main towns Nampula (535,000); Beira (450,000); Chimoio (260,000); Nacala (220,000); Quelimane (205,000)
Economy Predominantly subsistence agriculture, although this is changing as exploitation of mineral resources increases.
GDP US$900 per capita (2009); annual growth 2000–2008 around 2.5%
Languages The official language, Portuguese, is mother tongue to only 3% of the population. Some 40 indigenous languages are all classified in the Bantu linguistic group, the most widely spoken being Macua (24% of the population), Sena (11%) and Tsonga (11%). English and Swahili are widely understood in some border areas.
Religion About 52% of the population is Christian, with Catholicism dominating, and 28% is Muslim. The remainder hold traditional or profess no religious beliefs.
Currency Metical (Mt, plural meticais)
Exchange rates US$1 = Mt32; £1 = Mt51; €1 = Mt43 (Feb 2011)
National airline Linhas Aéreas de Moçambique (LAM). Airports with scheduled direct international connections are in Maputo, Vilankulo and Pemba.
International telephone code +258
Time GMT +2
Electrical voltage 220V, 50Hz
Weights and measures Metric
Flag Three horizontal bands: from top, green, white-edged black and yellow. There is a red triangle on hoist side, centred around a yellow star bearing an open white book on which are depicted a crossed AK47 and a hoe in black.
National sports Football, basketball
Public holidays Mozambique has 12 national public holidays (see pages 62–3).

Background Information

GEOGRAPHY

The topography of eastern Mozambique is dominated by a low-lying coastal belt that widens from north to south to account for almost half of the country's surface area. The coastal plain rises gradually towards the west to meet a high plateau of 500m to 1,000m. Mozambique is generally characterised by relatively flat terrain, though much of the northwest is mountainous and several areas of the western plateaux are dotted with isolated granite inselbergs known in southern Africa as *koppies*.

In the areas bordering Malawi and Zimbabwe, there are a few mountains that rise to an altitude of more than 1,800m. Mount Binga in the Chimanimani Range on the Zimbabwean border is Mozambique's highest peak at 2,436m. Other notable mountains include the massive inselberg of Gorongosa (1,862m) in Sofala Province; Mount Domue (2,095m) near Bragança in Tete Province; Mount Chiperone (2,052m) near Milange and Mount Namuli (2,419m) near Gurué in Zambézia; and Mount Txitonga (1,848m) and Mount Jeci (1,836m) on the Rift Valley escarpment north of Lichinga in Niassa Province.

Mozambique is traversed by several major river systems, all of which flow eastwards into the Indian Ocean. The mouths of these rivers have played a significant role in Mozambican history: many of the country's older towns are situated on large river mouths, and the rivers themselves often formed important trade routes into the interior. The Zambezi is Africa's fourth-largest river and the Limpopo its tenth largest. The Zambezi basin, at 1,330,000km², is the third-largest drainage system

MOZAMBIQUE: PROVINCE BY PROVINCE

Province	Capital	Area (km²)	Population (2006 census)
Cabo Delgado	Pemba	82,625	1,650,270
Gaza	Xai-Xai	75,709	1,333,106
Inhambane	Inhambane	68,615	1,412.349
Manica	Chimoio	61,661	1,359,923
Maputo City	Maputo	300	1,244,227
Maputo	Matola	26,058	1,072,086
Nampula	Nampula	81,606	3,767,114
Niassa	Lichinga	129,056	1,027,037
Sofala	Beira	68,018	1,676,131
Tete	Tete	100,724	1,551,949
Zambézia	Quelimane	105,008	3,794,509

MOZAMBIQUE'S CLIMATE

		Temp	Rainfall	Humidity
January	Maputo	21–30°C	130mm	73%
	Beira	24–32°C	270mm	75%
July	Maputo	13–25°C	15mm	73%
	Beira	16–25°C	30mm	79%

in Africa (after the Zaïre and the Nile) and the 13th largest in the world. Of the 820km-long Mozambican section of the Zambezi, 460km are navigable.

Other main river systems are the Ruvuma on the Tanzanian border; the Lúrio on the border of Cabo Delgado and Nampula provinces; the Save on the border of Sofala and Inhambane provinces; and the Limpopo in the south of the country.

Roughly 200km of the eastern shore of Africa's third-largest freshwater body, Lake Malawi, lies in Mozambique, where it is known as Lago Niassa. Further south, the lake formed by the Cahora Bassa Dam is one of the 15 largest in Africa, its exact ranking depending on the effects of rainy seasons and swamp flooding at three other lakes.

Mozambique is divided into ten provinces. Each province is divided into districts, further subdivided into administrative areas and civil parishes. Zambézia and Nampula provinces in the northern half of the country contain the richest agricultural land and 40% of the population, whereas the three southern provinces of Gaza, Inhambane and Maputo are mostly arid and previously served as labour reserves for Mozambique's industries and for mines and farms in South Africa.

CLIMATE

The climate in most of Mozambique is tropical and warm with a dry cooler season from April until September and a wet hot season with temperatures of around 28°C at the coast from October until April. In winter the weather at the coast is sunny and pleasantly warm (the average temperature in Maputo in June and July is 19°C). The dry and relatively cool winter months between April and September offer the most comfortable and easy travel conditions.

Temperatures and rainfall figures vary widely across the country. Hottest and most humid are the northeastern coast and the upper Zambezi Valley, while the coolest areas are those at higher altitudes, such as the highlands of Niassa and Nampula provinces. Most of northeastern and central Mozambique has an annual average rainfall in excess of 1,000mm, with the wettest part of the country being the highlands east of Malawi, where several areas experience almost 2,000mm of rain annually. The south is generally much drier, with coastal regions south of Beira generally receiving around 900mm of rain and some parts of the interior of Gaza Province dropping to an average of below 500mm annually. The rainy season in the south runs from October to March, while north of the Zambezi it tends to start and end a month or two later.

HISTORY

EARLY HISTORY

The interior It is widely agreed that humans evolved in east Africa. Mozambique itself has yielded few notable hominid fossils, but it is nevertheless reasonable to assume that it has supported human life for millions of years. Southeast Africa has incurred two major population influxes from west Africa in the last few millennia. The first occurred roughly 3,000 years ago, when the lightly built Batwa hunter-gatherers – similar in appearance and culture to the modern Bushmen of Namibia – spread throughout the region. Roughly 1,000 years later, the Bantu-speakers who still occupy most of the region started to expand into eastern Africa, reaching the Indian Ocean coast in about AD400, an influx which broadly coincided with the spread of Iron Age culture in the region. Although there is little concrete evidence of the mechanisms of this so-called Bantu migration, the records of early Portuguese adventurers leave us with a good idea of the main Bantu-speaking groupings of the southeast African interior at around AD1500.

The low-lying, dry and disease-prone Mozambican lowveld was then, as it is now, relatively thinly populated, with the dominant ethnolinguistic groupings being the Macua north of the Zambezi River, the Tonga between the Zambezi and the Inhambane area, and the Nguni south of Inhambane into modern-day South Africa. The three main ethnolinguistic groups of the lowveld had discrete social and economic systems: the Macua had a matrilineal social structure as opposed to the patrilineal system favoured further south, while the Nguni had a cattle-based economy and the Tonga a mixed farming economy supplemented by revenue from the trade routes passing through their territory.

What the people of the lowveld had in common was a decentralised political structure, based around fragmented local chieftaincies. In direct contrast, the Karanga (or Shona) who occupied the highveld of what is now Zimbabwe had a highly centralised political structure with an ancient tradition of stone building that evidently dates to around AD1000. At the centre of this region stood the extensive and magnificent city of Great Zimbabwe, which is thought to have had a population of more than 10,000 at its peak. The economy of Karangaland was probably based around cattle ownership, but its external relations were shaped by the coastal trade in gold, which has been mined in the Zimbabwean highlands since around AD900.

Karangaland appears to have gone through a major political upheaval in the second half of the 15th century. Great Zimbabwe was abandoned in roughly 1450, for reasons that remain a matter of speculation, but which are probably linked to local environmental degradation or a secession struggle. Whatever the cause, the abandonment of Great Zimbabwe coincided with a northerly reorientation of the highland kingdoms and a corresponding shift in the main trade routes. During the 15th century, the trade routes fanning from the Zambezi assumed greater importance, while the established route inland of Sofala along the Buzi River appears to have diminished in use. It is highly probable that the Karanga kingdoms known to the earliest Portuguese explorers were relatively new creations resulting from the upheavals of the late 15th century.

By 1500, the three main kingdoms of the highveld were Butua, in what is now the Bulawayo area of Zimbabwe; Monomotapa, in what is now central Zimbabwe; and Manica, in the highlands of what is now the Zimbabwe–Mozambique border area. The upheavals also resulted in two Karanga chieftaincies being established in what had formerly been Tonga territory: Barue in the lowveld south of the Zambezi and west of Sena, and Kiteve in the lowveld between the Pungue and Buzi rivers. Of these five main kingdoms, Butua was the only one to retain the stone-building tradition, while Monomotapa established itself as the paramount dynasty in the region.

The coast The east African coast has long been a centre of international trade. Starting in around 2,500BC, the ancient Egyptians evidently entered into spasmodic trade with an east African port they knew as Punt. From about 600BC, the Phoenicians and Romans are known to have traded with an east African port called Rhapta. The location of Punt remains a matter of pure speculation, but detailed references to Rhapta in Ptolemy's 4th-century *Geography* and in an older Phoenician document *Periplus of the Ancient Sea* point to a location somewhere in present-day Tanzania, possibly near the mouth of the Pangani River.

The collapse of the Roman Empire signalled a temporary end to maritime trade with the east African coast, and it presumably forced the closure of any contemporary trade routes into the African interior. Ptolemy claims that a Greek explorer called Diogenes saw two snow-capped mountains 25 days upriver from Rhapta and that he was told by other traders of vast lakes further inland, which indicates that 4th-century trade routes must have penetrated the interior as far as Mounts Kenya and Kilimanjaro, and possibly also Lakes Victoria and Tanganyika.

The rise of Islam in the 7th century AD revived the maritime trade with east Africa. The writings of Ali Masudi in AD947 make it clear that Arab mariners had by this time entered into regular trade with Madagascar and that they were aware that the main source of Africa's gold was Sofala, near the mouth of the Buzi River in what is now central Mozambique. The presence of 9th-century Islamic ruins on Manda Island off the Kenyan coast indicates that Arabic traders started settling in east Africa at a very early point in this era of trade. The 12th-century geographer Al Idrisi refers to Sofala as an important source of iron, gold and animal skins, and he indicates that by this time China and India were both trading with east Africa. By the 13th century, the coast between Somalia and central Mozambique was dotted with some 30 or 40 Swahili city-states, among the most important of which were Mogadishu, Malindi, Mombasa, Pangani, Zanzibar, Kilwa and Sofala.

Although many of these ancient Swahili cities have survived into the modern era, our best idea of what they must have looked like comes from the extensive ruins of those that haven't – notably Kilwa in southern Tanzania and Gedi in Kenya. The impressive rag coral architecture and overwhelming Muslim influence of such places has led many popular accounts to treat them as little more than Arabic implants. However, most modern historians are agreed that this is an outdated interpretation, and that there was a high level of integration between Arabic settlers and the indigenous peoples of the coast. It is true that the Islamic religion was adopted all along the coast, but then so was the Swahili language, which is self-evidently Bantu in origin, and which adopted elements of Arabic vocabulary only after the arrival of the Omani Arabs in the 18th century.

Several modern Mozambican ports have been built over medieval Swahili trade settlements – most notably Ilha de Moçambique, but also Angoche, Ibo and possibly Inhambane. However, the most important port south of Kilwa in medieval times, Sofala, is no longer in existence. The port of Sofala is thought to have been founded as a trading post in the 9th century, as a result of an Arabic ship being blown off course to hit land south of the Zambezi. Sofala is said to have had a population of around 10,000 by the 15th century. The absence of suitable building material meant that the medieval cities of Mozambique were never built as durably as those located further north, so little physical evidence of Sofala remains. Even if Sofala had been a stone city, it would now be submerged off the ever-mutating sandy shoreline south of the Buzi River.

Despite the absence of tangible ruins at Sofala, one should not underestimate its importance in medieval times, when it formed the pivotal link between the gold mines of Karangaland and Manica and the port of Kilwa. Sofala was best known to Arabs as the source of Kilwa's gold, but it was also an important trade centre in its own right, with direct maritime links to Madagascar and indirect links via Madagascar to India and Indonesia. Sofala's main exports, apart from gold, were worked iron, copper, ivory and cotton – the last grown as far south as Inhambane by the 15th century.

There is strong evidence to suggest that Arabic vessels explored the Zambezi as far inland as Cahora Bassa. It also seems highly probable that Muslim traders settled along the Zambezi long before the arrival of the Portuguese. Despite the oft-repeated assertion that Portugal founded the river ports at Sena and Tete in 1531, the greater probability is that Portuguese traders occupied existing Muslim settlements at these locations. Particularly compelling evidence of this comes from a 12th-century Arab document that refers to a town called Seyouna located near the confluence of two large rivers and a large mountain – the similarity in name and the geographical details would point to Seyouna and Sena being one and the same place. It has also been suggested that a town referred to as Dendema in a 14th-century document was in the same locality as present-day Tete.

PORTUGUESE OCCUPATION OF EAST AFRICA 1488–1530 The well-established trade links that bonded east Africa to the Gulf and to Asia were to alter dramatically in the 16th century following the arrival of the Portuguese on the Indian Ocean. Throughout the 15th century, Portugal attempted to find a route around Africa, with the main impetus of establishing direct control over the eastern spice trade. After Portugal captured the Moroccan port of Ceuta in 1415, it also became conscious of the fact that somewhere in Africa lay the source of the gold traded in that city. Furthermore, the Portuguese Crown was eager to establish the whereabouts of the legendary kingdom of Prester John (the name by which they knew Ethiopia) and to forge links with this isolated Christian empire.

It took Portugal almost a century to circumnavigate Africa, quite simply because they underestimated the continent's size. Nevertheless, Portuguese explorers had sailed as far south as Senegal by 1444; they reached the Gambia River in 1446; Sierra Leone in 1460; and São Tomé in 1474. In 1485, under King João II, an expedition led by Cão sailed up the Congo River as far as it was navigable, then continued south as far as Cape Cross in present-day Namibia. Cão died near Cape Cross, but when the survivors of his journey returned to Portugal, King João ordered Bartholomew Diaz to continue where he left off. Diaz set sail in August 1487, and in early 1488 he unwittingly rounded the Cape of Good Hope into the Indian Ocean, eventually sailing to roughly 50km past where the city of Port Elizabeth stands today. At the same time as Diaz was exploring the route via west Africa, another Portuguese explorer, Pero da Covilham, made his way overland and along the east African coastline to Kilwa and Sofala. The two routes of exploration finally connected in 1498, when Vasco da Gama sailed around Africa, stopping at Mozambique Island before continuing as far north as Malindi and, with the help of a Swahili navigator, crossing the Indian Ocean to India.

In 1505, the Portuguese decided to occupy the east African coast. In July, Kilwa was captured and a friendly sheikh installed on its throne. Two months after that, a Portuguese boat landed at Sofala and was given permission by the local sheikh to erect a fort and trading factory – however, the sheikh and his allies attacked the Portuguese stockade within a year of its foundation, resulting in the sheikh being killed and replaced by a Portuguese puppet. In 1507, a permanent Portuguese settlement was established on Mozambique Island, which so rapidly became the centre of Portuguese operations that Kilwa was abandoned by its colonisers in 1513.

Portugal also set about attacking rival Muslim centres of commerce: Oja, Bravo and Socatra on the north coast were sacked in 1507, and the islands of Mafia, Pemba and Zanzibar followed in 1509. Several Muslims from Mozambique Island and Sofala were forced to relocate to Angoche and Querimba Island, where they started a clandestine trade which was temporarily halted when Portugal razed Angoche in 1511 and Querimba in 1522. By 1530, practically the whole east African coast north of Sofala was under Portuguese control.

THE EAST AFRICAN COAST 1530–1600 The boundaries of modern Mozambique were in many instances shaped by events during the first four centuries of the Portuguese occupation of the coast, but Mozambique as we know it is in essence a 20th-century entity. The expansions and contractions of Portuguese influence between 1500 and 1890 don't really reflect a considered policy, but rather a haphazard sequence of largely unsuccessful attempts at formal expansion from a few coastal strongholds.

The Portuguese presence in east Africa was characterised by a high level of disunity. The interests of the Crown and the appointed Captain of Mozambique (who prior to 1670 ran the 'colony' as a private trade enterprise) were often in conflict, as were those of the many Portuguese deserters who fled from the few formal Portuguese settlements to intermarry with locals and form a distinct group of mixed-race *mazungos*. Contrary to popular perception, Mozambique prior to 1890 was not so much a Portuguese territory as it was a patchwork of endlessly mutating and fragmenting fiefdoms, some of which were under the nominal or real rule of the Portuguese Crown, but the greater number of which were lorded over by self-appointed despots, be they renegade *mazungos*, indigenous chiefs or Muslim sheikhs.

In the early years of the Portuguese occupation, the kingdom of Monomotapa (more accurately transcribed as Mwene Mutapa, that is the state of the Mutapa dynasty) took on legendary proportions in the mind of its would-be conquerors. For centuries, it has been assumed that Monomotapa was a vast and all-powerful homogeneous empire covering most of modern-day Zimbabwe as well as parts of Botswana and Mozambique. Modern academics, however, believe that the kingdom's size and importance were exaggerated by Portugal, and that the Mutapa dynasty ruled over what was merely one of many loosely defined Karanga kingdoms. Quite how Monomotapa's mythical status arose is an open question, but it is fairly certain that it would have suited Portuguese interests to perpetuate the myth that the whole interior was one vast centralised kingdom – especially after 1607, when Portugal signed a treaty with the Mutapa giving it full access to all gold, copper and silver mines in his kingdom.

The earliest sanctioned exploration of the Mozambican interior was made by António Fernandes, who reported on the main gold trade routes over three journeys between 1511 and 1513, and who was probably the first Portuguese to visit the capital of Monomotapa in the Cahora Bassa Region. However, Fernandes's findings did not result in the official occupation of the interior – on the contrary, the Portuguese Crown appears to have been content to trade with local chiefs from its coastal fortresses. The disruption caused to the gold trade by the upheavals in Karangaland and the clandestine approach of the Muslim gold traders at places like Angoche forced the Portuguese to turn their attention to ivory, which by 1530 had replaced gold as the main item of export. The Portuguese fortresses on the coast also required large amounts of food, which created a secondary trade network between the representatives of the Crown and established chiefs. Despite initial tensions, the market for food and ivory eventually created a mutual dependency and stable relations.

Once Portugal realised that it would be unable to wrest control of the elusive gold trade from the Muslim traders by force, it attempted to take control of the routes to the interior by occupying the existing Muslim settlements at Tete, Sena and Quelimane in 1531.

The only concerted effort made by the Crown to conquer Monomotapa in the 16th century was an expedition of 1,000 men led by Francisco Barreto, which arrived at Sena in December 1571. Hundreds of Barreto's men had died of fever along the way and – ignorant of tsetse fly and mosquito-borne diseases – Barreto blamed his losses on the black magic of the Muslims at Sena. The Portuguese troops attacked Sena, killing most of its Muslim population and capturing the 19 men they identified as their leaders, who were then tortured to death at the rate of two a day. In July 1572, Barreto marched towards Tete with 650 men, but before he could reach his destination, his troops were attacked by a force of 16,000 Africans led by a Maravi king known as Mambo. Barreto's men were forced to turn back after killing some 4,000 of their attackers. Only 180 of the men who left Sena returned there alive, and Barreto himself died of fever on the way. Two years later, another group of soldiers marched 450km inland, defeating the Kiteve capital but achieving little else before they returned to the coast with their numbers reduced to a third by malaria.

The Portuguese occupation of Mozambique should not be seen as colonisation in the way we understand it today. Most of the infiltration of the interior and the coast away from the fortress towns was the work of Afro-Portuguese *mazungos*, many of whom were refugees from the Crown. Armed with muskets, many of these refugees married into local communities and assumed the role of surrogate chiefs, building up their own private armies and trade empires. During the 16th century, not only did various *mazungos* establish themselves at practically every port and island along the coast, but they also settled along the southern bank of the Zambezi as far as Tete, setting up what were in effect minor chieftaincies over the local Tonga.

Ironically, it could be argued that the most successful expansionists in 16th-century Mozambique were not of European but African origin. Probably as a result of a drought, cannibalistic Zimba warbands from the Maravi kingdom of the Shire Highlands (in Malawi) swept into Mozambique in the late 1560s. The Zimba attacked Tete in the 1560s, halted Barreto's progress in 1572, and then continued northwards, razing Kilwa and Mombasa and eating many of their occupants. The Zimba were eventually defeated near Malindi in 1587, but the survivors returned southwards to settle in the area between the Rovuma and Zambezi rivers, practically all of which was ruled over by one or other Maravi chieftaincy at the beginning of the 17th century.

Towards the end of the century, Portugal's dominance in the region was threatened by Turks, for which reason the fortifications of Mozambique Island and Mombasa were vastly improved and the coast was divided into two administrative regions with Cabo Delgado as the boundary. This border has remained significant ever since and now separates Tanzania from Mozambique.

THE EAST AFRICAN COAST 1600–1800 In the early 17th century, Portugal experienced the first serious rivalry to its status as the dominant European power in the Indian Ocean. In 1602, barely a decade after the first Dutch and British ships had rounded the Cape of Good Hope, the Dutch East India Company (VOC) was formed with the intent of taking over Portugal's Indian Ocean trade. In 1607, the Dutch made a concerted effort to capture the Portuguese capital on Mozambique Island, a six-week siege which failed only because the invaders were unable to take the Portuguese fortress. After a second attempt at ousting Portugal in 1608, the Dutch fleets left Mozambique Island alone, but in alliance with English ships they captured several other Portuguese territories in the Indian Ocean. This period of instability ended in the late 1630s, when treaties were signed between the three countries.

The beginning of the 17th century also saw Karangaland fall into an extended period of instability following the death of the Monomotapa in 1597. The succeeding Monomotapa, Gatse Lucere, became dependent on the protection of the *mazungo* Diego Madeira's armies to retain control over his kingdom, which Madeira saw as more or less an invitation to take over Karangaland following the signing of a mineral rights treaty in 1607. Gatse Lucere died in 1623, to be succeeded by Inhamba, who in 1628 murdered the Portuguese envoy to his capital, prompting a full-scale war with Portugal. Inhamba was driven from his capital, and a baptised Mutapa was installed in his place. However, this puppet ruler had little support, and in 1631 Inhamba led an uprising in which he recaptured the Crown and killed several hundreds of Portuguese and their supporters. Meanwhile, the Maravi took advantage of the chaos in Monomotapa to capture Quelimane.

In 1632, Portugal had one of its few successful military forays in the Mozambican interior. Under the leadership of Sousa de Menesis, 2,000 troops landed at Quelimane, where they booted out the Maravi, then marched to Karangaland, destroyed Inhamba's army and installed a vassal Monomotapa. So began a 60-year period in which Portugal was to have its only sustained control of Karangaland. During this time, major Portuguese settlements grew up around the various gold fairs of the interior, notably Dambarare (near modern-day Harare) and Masekesa (on the site of Manica town).

The Crown's tenuous supremacy in Karangaland ended in 1693, when a Changamire chief called Dombo attacked Dambarare and killed all its Portuguese inhabitants. Other Portuguese settlements in Karangaland were evacuated and the Changamire proceeded to attack all the gold fairs in Manica. As things settled down, the Changamire took effective control of the highlands to found the Rozvi Kingdom, while the Portuguese kept control of the lowveld. This boundary is reflected in the modern one between Mozambique and Zimbabwe.

Events on the coast in the late 17th century reinforced what was eventually to become the northern border of modern Mozambique. In 1650, Muscat was captured by Omani Arabs and used as a base from which to launch an attack on the east African coast. Omani ships attacked Zanzibar in 1652 and Mombasa in 1661. Ten years later, Mozambique Island was looted by Omani sailors, and once again it was only the fortress of São Sebastão that prevented Portugal being ousted from their east African capital. The Omani never again attempted to attack Portuguese settlements in what is now Mozambique, but in 1698 they captured Mombasa. The coast north of Cabo Delgado was lost to Portugal forever.

The period between 1650 and 1800 saw the informal *mazungo* chieftaincies of the Zambezi Valley formalised into a network of *prazo* estates – large tracts of land granted to settlers and wealthy traders by the Portuguese Crown. The *prazo* leases were good for three generations, and they were inherited by females, presumably as a way of encouraging wealthy Portuguese to settle in the Zambezi Valley. In theory, no person was allowed to own more than one *prazo*, but in reality large blocks of *prazos* were linked by marriage. The holders of the leases, known as *prazeros*, ruled over their estates with absolute authority. In effect, the *prazos* were run as small feudal empires, and the *prazeros* derived most of their income by forcing tributes from people living on their estate rather than by developing the estate for agriculture.

MOZAMBIQUE IN THE 19TH CENTURY The early part of the 19th century was a time of great hardship in southeastern Africa, as the region was gripped by severe droughts between 1794 and 1802 and again between 1817 and 1832. These droughts were to have far-reaching effects on Mozambique and many other parts of southeast Africa, most significantly among the Nguni people of southern Mozambique and the east coast of South Africa. During the first years of the drought, the Nguni became increasingly dependent on cattle raids to support themselves, which led to a high degree of militarisation and eventually to the centralisation of the Nguni into three main kingdoms: the Zulu, Swazi and Ndandwe. The Zulus, who emerged as the most powerful of these kingdoms under the leadership of Shaka, raided and looted surrounding territories, causing vast tracts of the South African highveld to become depopulated and forcing many people to migrate to other areas.

In 1819, the Zulus conquered the Ndandwe Kingdom, causing the survivors to emigrate from the area in a number of large warbands which grew in size as they raided and plundered the villages that they passed through. The warband that was to have the greatest effect on Mozambique was that led by Nxaba, who attacked Inhambane in 1824 and conquered many of the chieftaincies of Manica in 1827. In the early 1830s, with the drought at its peak, Nxaba was based around the Gorongosa area, and in 1836 he plundered Sofala. Following a Nguni leadership battle in 1837, Nxaba and his followers were forced to flee Mozambique, while the victor, Shoshangane, founded the Gaza Kingdom, which covered most of Mozambique south of the Zambezi between 1840 and its conquest by Portugal in 1895.

Elsewhere, the Rozvi Empire of the Zimbabwean highlands was destroyed and the Changamire killed by a Nguni warband, and eastern Zimbabwe was eventually settled by the Matabele, another Nguni offshoot. Within Mozambique, a Nguni leader called Maseko established a kingdom north of Tete, while another called Gwangwara established himself along what is now the Tanzanian border. The Nguni invasion made travel in the interior unsafe, and Nguni warbands destroyed many of the gold fairs, practically forcing the closure of the gold trade.

Another significant feature of the first half of the 19th century, one that was not entirely unrelated to the drop in the gold trade, was a rapid increase in slave trading along the east African coast. Prior to the mid-18th century, slaves formed only a small part of the Indian Ocean trade network, but this started to change after the 1770s with the emergence of clandestine trade between the Muslims of Ibo and the French sugar plantations of the Indian Ocean islands. In the 1770s, the number of slaves being exported from Mozambique was still relatively low – fewer than 2,000 annually – but as increasing restrictions were imposed on the trade out of west Africa, prices rose and so did the number of slaves being exported from the ports of east Africa. Between 1825 and 1830, around 20,000 slaves were shipped out of Mozambique annually, to destinations as far afield as the USA and Brazil. It has been estimated that more than a million Africans were shipped out of the ports of Mozambique in the 19th century.

Britain persuaded Portugal to abolish the slave trade in 1836, in effect driving it underground – the number of slaves shipped out in the 1850s probably exceeded that in the 1830s. Public attention was drawn to this clandestine trade when the Scottish missionary David Livingstone published reports of his Zambezi expedition of 1858–64. Following Livingstone's death in 1875, several Scottish missions were established in the Shire Highlands (a part of modern-day Malawi that would otherwise almost certainly have been incorporated in Mozambique later in the century).

The great droughts undermined the agricultural base of the Zambezi Valley, forcing many *prazeros* to abandon their estates. By the mid-19th century, power in this important area had become consolidated under five large feudal fiefdoms ruled over by powerful *mazungo* families or other settlers. The Zambezi Valley became a lawless zone, characterised by inter-family feuds and mini-wars, starting in 1840 with an unsuccessful attack on the Pereira family by the Portuguese authorities, and reaching a peak in 1867–69 with four abortive and bloody attempts to capture the Da Cruz family stockade at Massangano. The Zambezi Valley was only fully brought under government control in 1887, when Massangano was captured by the Governor of Manica.

An important feature of 19th-century Mozambique was the strong British influence on the east African coast following its successful takeover of the Cape Colony in 1806 and Mauritius in 1810. In 1820, the British flag was raised on the southern part of Delagoa Bay, initiating a protracted period of disputes between Britain, Portugal and the Boer Republic of the Transvaal over the control of this strategic possession. This dispute was only resolved in 1875, when French arbitrators gave the whole bay to Mozambique. Meanwhile, as the so-called Scramble for Africa approached its climax, the Beira Corridor area became something of a battleground between the British imperialist and founder of Rhodesia, Cecil Rhodes, and his Portuguese counterpart Paiva de Andrada.

After a couple of years of haggling over boundaries and disputed territories, Britain and Portugal signed a treaty in May 1891 and Mozambique took its modern shape. The northern boundary with German East Africa (Tanzania) simply followed the border established centuries before between the administrative regions of Mombasa and Mozambique Island. The northwestern borders were more keenly contested, but they were basically settled in favour of the power that had the higher presence in each area – hence northern Mozambique was bisected by the Scottish-settled area that is now southern Malawi. The southwestern borders followed well-established divides: the border with Zimbabwe was similar to the one that separated the Rozvi and Portuguese spheres of influence between around 1700 and 1840; the western borders with the Transvaal followed the one agreed to in the Boer–Portuguese treaty of 1869; and the southern border with the British colony of Natal had been determined by French arbitration in 1875.

THE COLONIAL PERIOD 1890–1975 Mozambique is less arbitrarily delineated than many other countries in Africa. Nevertheless, it was anything but a cohesive entity at the time its boundaries were defined, and parts of the country remained entirely independent of Portugal as late as 1914. As an indication of the weakness of Portuguese colonial rule during the closing decade of the 19th century, it is interesting to note that Britain and Germany signed a secret treaty determining how Mozambique and Angola should be divided in the event of their being abandoned by Portugal.

Only four of Mozambique's ten modern-day provinces were directly administered by the colonial authorities. The area south of the Save River – basically the modern provinces of Maputo, Inhambane and Gaza – was given a reasonable degree of political coherence by the Gaza monarchy, who were conquered by Portugal between 1895 and 1897. The other part of the country that fell under direct colonial rule was the area around Mozambique Island (modern-day Nampula Province), but the Portuguese presence in much of this area was rather tenuous until around the time of the outbreak of World War I. In 1904, the Portuguese in this area were attacked by a collection of Muslim and African chiefs, and forced to take refuge on Mozambique Island.

The rest of the country fell under indirect rule. The present-day provinces of Niassa and Cabo Delgado were leased to the Niassa Company between 1894 and 1929. The Niassa Company was almost totally ineffective until 1908, when it was taken over by a South African company and started to make its presence felt in the northern interior. The Yoa capital at Mwende was captured by the Niassa Company in 1912, but the Makonde Plateau remained independent until after World War I. Meanwhile, most of what are now Tete and Zambézia provinces were controlled by *prazeros*, while the area now incorporated into the provinces of Sofala and Manica was leased to the Mozambique Company from 1891 to 1941.

A significant trend in the first decade of formal colonialism was the rising economic importance of southern Mozambique. This was directly due to the proximity of Lourenço Marques to the gold mines of the Witwatersrand in South Africa. Following the completion of the rail link to the Witwatersrand in 1894, the port at Lourenço Marques exported roughly a third of this wealthy area's minerals.

No less significant was the volume of migrant labour from southern Mozambique to the mines of Witwatersrand. The Witwatersrand Native Labour Association employed between 50,000 and 100,000 Mozambicans annually between the end of the Boer War and the start of World War II. In some years, the tax contributed by the migrant workers of southern Mozambique amounted to more than half of the total revenue raised by the colonial government.

At around the turn of the 20th century, Lourenço Marques was made the official capital of Mozambique, replacing the former capital of Mozambique Island after almost four centuries (strangely, various sources give an array of different dates for when the capital was transferred, the main contenders being 1886, 1897, 1898, 1902 or 1907 – though the year 1898, as quoted by the official Lourenço Marques city guide published in 1964, seems most plausible).

Migrant labour had been an important factor in the Mozambican economy even before 1890, but the volume of workers increased dramatically following the Colonial Labour Law of 1899. Not only did this decree divide Mozambicans into two classes, indigenous and non-indigenous, but it also required that all indigenous males and females aged between 14 and 60 had to work and had to pay hut tax. It can be argued that the Labour Law rescued Mozambique from the bleak economic future that many had predicted at the time of its formal colonisation, but it is equally true that by imposing the obligation to work on the indigenous population it allowed them to be exploited in a manner that was little better than slavery. Paradoxically, it was the people who lived in the *prazos* and company concessions who were most ruthlessly exploited – until the 1930s, people in these areas were regularly press-ganged into 'employment'. The migrant labour of southern Mozambique was socially disruptive, but it also meant better wages and a lower cost of living, so that even as late as 1967, roughly half a million Mozambicans (out of a total population of eight million) were working in South Africa or Rhodesia.

In 1926, Portugal's Republican government was overthrown in a military coup, leading to the so-called 'New State', a dictatorship dominated by António Salazar, prime minister from 1932 to 1968. Salazar envisaged a future wherein Portugal and its colonies would form a self-sufficient closed economy with the mother country serving as the industrial core and the dependencies providing the agricultural produce and raw materials. Salazar outlawed the company concessions and *prazos* which had until then practically ruled two-thirds of Mozambique, and was largely successful in his efforts to create a more unitary administration. Forced labour was replaced by forced agricultural schemes, leading to a tenfold increase in Mozambique's cotton and rice production between 1930 and 1950. As a result, Mozambique enjoyed something of an economic boom, particularly during World War II when Portugal's neutral stance allowed Mozambique to concentrate on food production and benefit from a 500% increase in the value of its exports. However, the war also meant a decrease in the activity of the mines of South Africa and Rhodesia, and the return of large numbers of migrant labourers, one result of which was the introduction of population control rulings that mimicked the South African Pass Laws.

The post-war period saw greater economic diversification in Mozambique, with the development of secondary industries, particularly in Lourenço Marques and Beira, and a boom in incoming tourism from South Africa and Rhodesia. The outcome of the war encouraged Salazar to drop his more fascist policies and to enter NATO in 1949, one result of which was the admittedly rather semantic change in Mozambique's status from a colony to an overseas province.

After World War II, almost all of Europe's African colonies experienced a vociferous and sometimes violent campaign for independence. Generally, these calls for liberation were initiated by African soldiers who had fought for democracy in Europe and then returned home to find that they remained second-class citizens in the country of their birth. That no significant liberation movement existed in Mozambique prior to 1960 can probably be attributed to Portugal's neutrality during the war. Nevertheless, following a violent uprising in Angola in February 1961, the ever-astute Salazar decided to try to forestall the inevitable, firstly by allowing Portugal's overseas provinces to be represented in the Lisbon government, and secondly by bestowing full citizenship on the indigenous population. In December of that year, Portugal's three colonial enclaves in Asia were reclaimed by India, and Salazar decided to oppose similar calls from his African colonies with force.

Mozambique's first broad-based liberation movement was formed in exile in 1963, when President Nyerere of Tanzania persuaded a number of small-time liberation groups to amalgamate into an organisation called the Front for the Liberation of Mozambique (Frelimo), held together by the powerful leadership of Eduardo Mondlane, a Mozambican academic living in the USA. In 1964, Frelimo decided on a militant policy, and by the end of 1965 it had captured much of Cabo Delgado and Niassa provinces. Portugal responded by arresting 1,500 Frelimo agents in southern Mozambique, effectively destroying the organisation in this part of the country. Meanwhile, Frelimo started to factionalise in the north, with the educated leadership on the one side and the traditionalist chiefs on the other. In 1968, the Frelimo offices in Dar es Salaam were raided by traditionalists, and rioting in the Frelimo-run school there forced its closure. In February 1969, Mondlane was assassinated using a letter bomb. The ensuing power struggle forced out the traditionalists and saw the military commander, Samora Machel, take over the party presidency in May 1970.

Machel faced an immediate challenge in the form of 35,000 troops sent by the government to clear Frelimo out of northern Mozambique and attack its bases in Tanzania. Instead of fighting, Frelimo evacuated the north, slipped through Malawi, and relocated its centre of internal operations to the area north of Tete. With the support of the local Chewa people, Frelimo attempted to destabilise the Tete and Beira corridors and to disrupt the construction of the Cahora Bassa Dam, a policy that culminated in the derailing of trains to Beira in 1974.

The extent to which Frelimo's limited attacks influenced Mozambique's eventual independence is debatable. At least as significant were the concurrent political changes in Portugal. Upon entering the European Common Market in 1970, Portugal was forced to dismantle its rigid trade agreements with Mozambique. The result was an almost immediate realignment of the Mozambican economy towards South Africa – by 1974, South Africa had already become the main investor in Mozambique, as well as its principal trading partner. Even more critical to Mozambique's future was the left-wing coup that took place in Lisbon in April

1974. Within two months, the new government of Portugal had entered into negotiations with Frelimo. In September 1974, the two sides signed the Lusaka Accord: Mozambique would be granted independence after a mere nine months of interim government, and power would transfer to Frelimo without even the pretence of a referendum or election.

INDEPENDENT MOZAMBIQUE Three factors were to prove critical in shaping Mozambique during the first two decades of independence: the mess left behind by the colonisers, the leadership of Frelimo, and the destabilising policies of South Africa's nationalist government.

It would be easy enough to see the first 15 years of Frelimo government as typical of the sort of Marxist dictatorship that has characterised post-independence Africa. It would also be rather simplistic. Frelimo assumed a dictatorial role through circumstance as much as intent – there simply *was* no viable opposition in the decade following independence – and its progressive, humanitarian ideals were a far cry from the self-serving, repressive policies enacted by many of its peers. Frelimo's undeniable failures can be attributed partly to unfortunate circumstance, but most of all to its intellectual and interventionist policies – idealistic grand schemes which failed to take into account the importance of ethnicity, tradition and religion in rural African societies, and which ultimately alienated the peasantry.

The party's most notable successes were on the social front. In the first few years of independence, primary school attendance doubled and enrolment at secondary schools increased sevenfold. The new government attempted to combat the appalling literacy rate of less than 5% at the time of independence by initiating an adult literacy scheme that benefited hundreds of thousands of Mozambicans, and sought to undermine the problem of ethnicity by spreading the use of Portuguese as a common language. Despite there being fewer than 100 trained doctors in the country in 1975, Frelimo launched an ambitious programme of immunisations, praised by the World Health Organization (WHO) as one of the most successful ever initiated in Africa. The scheme reached 90% of the population in the first five years of Frelimo rule, resulting in a 20% drop in infant mortality. Frelimo's emphasis on sexual equality was underscored by the fact that 28% of the people elected to popular assemblies in 1977 were women – a higher figure than almost anywhere else in the world.

Frelimo's critical failing was on the economic front which, while caused partly by its own policies, was undoubtedly exacerbated by the situation in which the newly independent country found itself. Mozambique's economy, never the most developed in southern Africa, was further damaged by emerging in the middle of the global depression following the 1973 oil crisis. The crisis not only damaged Mozambican businesses but also led to the South African gold mines laying off two-thirds of their Mozambican workers in 1976, with a resultant loss of significant foreign earnings.

Portuguese settlers, faced with a choice between immediate repatriation or enforced Mozambican citizenship, chose mass exodus, stripping assets as they went. The loss of capital and expertise caused the collapse of many of the country's secondary industries, most of which remain moribund. Frelimo attempted to abate this outflow by nationalising a number of industries, but at a pace that only caused the situation to spiral, and which gave many Portuguese settlers a pretext for destroying anything that they couldn't take out of the country. Meanwhile Frelimo's ambitious agricultural schemes were obstructed by climatic factors: disastrous floods hit the main agricultural areas in the summer of 1977/78, followed by four years of nationwide drought.

Lastly, Mozambique was surrounded by hostile countries. South Africa and Zimbabwe (then Rhodesia) were still white-ruled and feared independence movements that had proved so effective in neighbouring countries springing up in their own backyards. Malawi, while nominally independent, adopted a heavily pro-Western approach and actively supported the activities of the white minority governments.

Shortly after Mozambique became independent, the Rhodesian Special Branch – aided by former members of the Portuguese Security Police – set up a guerrilla organisation called the Mozambican National Resistance (Renamo), At that time, the Frelimo government was allowing Zimbabwean liberation movements to operate out of Manica, and Renamo was conceived as a fifth column to attack strategic bases in Mozambique. After Zimbabwe achieved independence in 1980, the South African Defence Force (SADF) took over the organisation and retrained its soldiers at Phalaborwa in northern Transvaal. With SADF backing, Renamo enjoyed considerable success – most notably by blowing up the Zambezi rail bridge in 1983 – and boosted its ranks by kidnapping young boys in rural areas. Assisted by various anti-Marxist American groups, South Africa managed to give its sponsored outlaws some sort of credibility by establishing Renamo offices in several capital cities, most of them manned by non-Africans. However, it has to be emphasised that Renamo did not have a coherent political philosophy until after the 1994 peace accord – it existed solely as South Africa's destabilisation arm.

On 16 March 1984, Mozambique and South Africa signed the Nkomati Accord, an agreement that neither country would support elements hostile to the other. Mozambique abided by the accord, but the SADF continued to give clandestine and possibly unofficial support to Renamo, helped by Malawi's President Banda, who allowed the organisation to operate out of his country. In September 1986, President Samora Machel of Mozambique, along with the presidents of Zimbabwe and Zambia, held a summit with Banda in Malawi and persuaded him to boot out Renamo. On the return flight to Maputo, Machel's plane was diverted by a South African radio signal and crashed in South African territory, killing everybody on board. Conspiracy theories abound, the most likely being that of South African sabotage. Indeed, after an inquiry launched in May 1998, South Africa's Truth and Reconciliation Committee decided that the incident raised questions that merited further investigation by an appropriate body.

In December 1986, Malawi signed a mutual security agreement with Mozambique's newly installed President Joaquim Chissano. Left with nowhere else to run, Renamo was forced to base itself permanently in Mozambique, where it took on a life of its own. Formerly, Renamo had limited its activities to occasional raids on strategic targets. From 1987 onwards, Renamo warbands roamed through the Mozambican countryside, supporting themselves with random raids on rural villages in what an official of the US State Department described as 'one of the most brutal holocausts against ordinary human beings since World War II'. By 1990, Frelimo's control barely extended beyond the main towns. It has been estimated that Renamo killed 100,000 Mozambicans during this period, and that as many as one-third of Mozambique's human population was displaced or forced into exile by the raiding warbands. The country's economic infrastructure, already crippled by the post-independence withdrawal of skills and funds, then by years of misplaced Marxist policies, was practically destroyed. Frelimo's social achievements were reduced to cinders along with roughly 2,500 primary schools and 800 clinics and hospitals. Teachers, doctors and educated administrative staff who hadn't managed to flee the country in time were systematically executed by Renamo.

In November 1990, pressured by overseas aid donors, Frelimo unveiled a new constitution denouncing its former Marxist policies and allowing for multi-party elections. However, the civil war continued into 1992, when the Rome Conference in October resulted in a ceasefire being signed by President Chissano and the Renamo leader Afonso Dhlakama. Mozambique's first democratic elections, which achieved an 85% turnout, were held in October 1994, with Chissano obtaining 53% of the presidential vote and Dhlakama 34%. Neither party achieved an absolute majority in the parliamentary elections, with Frelimo picking up 44% of the vote to Renamo's 38%. The strongest Renamo support came from the central provinces of Nampula, Zambézia, Sofala, Manica and Tete, where it attained a majority of parliamentary seats, while the northern and southern provinces went to Frelimo. Renamo's relative success in the election came as a surprise to many, considering its history and the fact that it had no real policies other than being anti-Frelimo. The good showing was probably due to Frelimo's low-key campaigning and failure to connect with the populace at grassroots level rather than any inherent virtues seen to be attached to Renamo.

The remainder of the 1990s was characterised by an uneasy peace and the jostling for political power that invariably follows a protracted civil war. After the 1994 parliamentary election, Renamo asserted the right to the governorships in the provinces where it had won majorities, a claim that was swiftly rejected by Chissano. Frelimo further bolstered its authority in the May 1998 local elections – boycotted by Renamo and 16 other opposition parties – in which it won almost everything up for grabs. It came as little surprise, then, that in general elections held in December 1999, Chissano was re-elected president for a further five-year term, Frelimo won an outright majority of parliamentary seats, and Renamo contested the result on the basis that the voting had been fraudulent. Although international monitors declared that the election had been free and fair, Renamo threatened unilaterally to establish a parallel government in the central and northern regions unless the vote was recounted or new elections held. As Mozambique moved into the new century, however, it continued to be governed by a single authority which, although by no means perfect, could at least claim to exercise effective and legitimate control in a country where such a feat has never been easy to achieve.

THE 21ST CENTURY In February 2000, attention was detracted from the Frelimo/Renamo soap opera by the worst flooding in Mozambique for nearly 50 years. After weeks of heavy rains and a wet and windy cyclone, rivers in southern and central parts of the country burst their banks. In the resulting floods, hundreds lost their lives and thousands more their homes and livelihoods. Television sets the world over broadcast the unforgettably tragic images of families hanging from treetops, their homes submerged under muddy waters, as helicopters tried to save what was left of their broken lives. The rainy season the following year caused similar damage, although on a slightly lesser scale.

The main areas of flooding were in the valleys of the Zambezi and Limpopo rivers, which had burst their banks after the combined effects of weeks of torrential rain and the 260km/h winds of Cyclone Eline. Floodplains along these two rivers were, at some points, 5km wide, and the water level was 7m higher than usual. The waters began to recede in the beginning of March, leaving the country to count the costs. Some 700 people had died and 500,000 more had been made homeless. There was also colossal material and infrastructural damage. Roads, bridges and railway lines had been destroyed, an estimated quarter of the country's agriculture had been damaged, and 80% of the livestock in Mozambique had perished. The floodwaters had also dislodged land mines laid during the civil war, re-depositing them elsewhere.

Meanwhile President Chissano remained in power. In September 2004, having declared that he would not stand for a third term, he made a farewell tour of all the country's ten provinces, by which time over nine million people had registered to vote in the forthcoming election. In the national elections of December 2004, the Frelimo candidate Armando Guebuza was elected president with 64% of the vote, exactly twice as many as his Renamo rival Afonso Dhlakama. Guebuza was inaugurated as president in February 2005 and three months later his predecessor Chissano was named the UN's top official for Guinea Bissau. Renamo lost further ground in the 2009 presidential elections, in which Guebuza garnered 75% of the vote and 8.6% went to the Democratic Movement of Mozambique (MDM), which splintered from Renamo in March 2009 under the leadership of the relatively young Mayor of Beira Daviz Simango, leaving Dhlakama with a mere 16.4% of electoral support.

Although Mozambique has enjoyed a high level of stability since the civil war ended, the peace has been punctuated by episodes of localised violence, such as the rioting that broke out in Montepuez and elsewhere in Cabo Delgado in November 2000 in response to allegations of Frelimo vote-rigging in the previous year's election. More recently, in September 2010, Maputo experienced a two-day standstill after police opened fire on a mass protest against an official rise in bread prices, leading to widespread vandalism and looting, and at least 14 deaths. The riot did encourage the government to announce a subsidy on bread prices, and Maputo had all but returned to normal within 48 hours of the riot's starting. Nevertheless, growing public dissatisfaction at rising living costs seems inevitable in a country where 90% of the population lives on less than US$2 a day, unemployment stands at 60%, food production has yet to reach subsistence levels since the agricultural sector collapsed in the civil war, and the currency has depreciated against that of its major trading partner (South Africa) to the order of 50% in 12 months.

GOVERNMENT AND POLITICS

Mozambique is a multi-party democracy led by an elected president. In practice, it has been a two-party state for most of the post-civil war period, dominated by the struggle between Frelimo and Renamo. The former, which has held power since independence in 1975, has increased its stranglehold on power over the course of the four elections since 1994, squeezing through with slightly more than 50% of the vote in 1994 and 1999, but gaining 64% of the vote in 2004 and 75% in 2009.

A political force that shouldn't be ignored is that of the traditional chiefs, many of whom still wield considerable clout. Indeed in rural areas it's not unknown for the traditional chief to be the de facto power of his area, with the local political appointees being largely ignored.

ECONOMY

Mozambique is a country with tremendous economic potential. There is no shortage of arable land, water resources or woodland. Extensive tracts of tropical hardwoods still exist in many places which, if managed responsibly, offer economic possibilities. The country has considerable mineral reserves, and modern ports linked to a rail network constructed for the transportation of goods to and from the states of southern central Africa. The sea has plentiful supplies of fish, and the islands and coastline are ideally suited to tourism. This economic potential has never been developed to the full, either in Portuguese colonial times or since.

During the civil war, Mozambique's economic development was predictably sluggish, and a shortage of skilled labour combined with Frelimo's rigid, centrally planned economic policies didn't exactly help the situation. Since the ceasefire in 1992, however, agricultural production has been increasing gradually, and Frelimo has instigated market-orientated reforms, including privatisation in several important industrial sectors. In June 1999, the International Monetary Fund (IMF) and World Bank agreed to reduce Mozambique's public debt by two-thirds, which, along with other debt-relief programmes, augured well for the country's continued economic improvement. Then came the floods in February 2000 (see *The 21st Century*, page 17), which washed away over 100,000ha of crops, killed more than 40,000 cattle and caused considerable infrastructural damage.

The extent to which the country's economic recovery will continue following this setback is dependent on the foreign assistance made available to repair the damage.

The Mozambican economy in 2008 was dominated by commerce and services, accounting for 46%. Next was industry, with 30.5%, followed by agriculture at 23.5%. In practice, however, agriculture is the main preoccupation of most Mozambicans. An estimated 80% of Mozambique's population relies on subsistence agriculture and fishing to survive, although the enduring effects of the war, droughts and floods continue to hinder the country's efforts to regain self-sufficiency in food production. The main export crops are shrimps, prawns, cotton, cashew nuts, sugar cane and copra, while the principal subsistence crops are cassava, corn and wet rice grown in the floodplains of the country's many rivers.

The second major contributor to the economy is industry, primarily food processing, beverages, tobacco, textiles, edible oils, soaps and other consumer goods. During Portuguese times, Mozambique was the fourth industrial power in Africa, although, considering the relatively low rate of industrialisation of the continent, this is no great claim. In the first ten years after independence the country's industrial sector slowed at an alarming pace, primarily because most whites had fled the country in fear of Frelimo and the uncertainty of its policies during the transitional phase to independence. Companies were deserted by their owners, machinery often destroyed.

The exodus of the settler population meant the loss of management expertise, skilled workers and capital, and by the end of the 1980s industry had ground to an almost complete halt. Frelimo embarked on a policy of privatisation after the end of the civil war in an attempt to kick-start the industrial sector, and during the 1990s hundreds of enterprises were bought by private investors. Past problems have doomed some of these privatisations to failure; others – particularly those backed by foreign investment – have been more successful.

A particular growth area at the moment is mining and heavy industry. Several billion dollar projects have been set up over the past five years – the Mozal aluminium smelter project in Maputo, the Heavy Sands ore extraction project in Nampula Province and the coal mines in Tete are all major projects with significant levels of foreign investment, predominantly from South Africa. Another sector showing considerable growth is the provision of electricity to neighbouring countries from the generators of Cahora Bassa (also in Tete). There is some debate about the long-term value of such projects to the economy as a whole, and it has been suggested that they may stifle the development of other sectors by pushing up the exchange rate and sucking huge amounts of the country's limited resources.

FOREIGN INVESTMENT The Mozambican economy is dependent on foreign investment, and the government is trying hard to improve conditions and attract foreign money. In Maputo there is a chamber of commerce:

Câmara de Comércio de Moçambique (*452 R Mateus Sansão Mathemba, CP 1836, Maputo;* ☎ *+258 21 492904; www.ccmusa.co.mz*) Private banks, both local and foreign, are now permitted to operate in the country and private farmland that was brought under state control during the revolutionary years is now being returned to its Portuguese and South African owners. There are 'industrial free zones' in Maputo, Beira, Mocuba and Nacala intended to encourage investors to come to the country. In these zones, certain taxes and duties are waived in favour of a small royalty on sales.

Certain businesses, previously state-owned, have been offered for sale by tender. In 1994, for instance, a short list of about a dozen enterprises covered a range of industries from plastics to pasta, from transport to tea – over US$60 million of sales turnover. Arguably the largest carrots for foreign investors are the transportation 'corridors' linking the landlocked countries of southern Africa to the Mozambican ports of Maputo, Beira and Nacala (see box *Corridors of power* on page 57). In January 2000, for example, a consortium led by South African, Portuguese and US companies was granted a concession to manage the port of Nacala and the Malawi–Nacala railway; and negotiations for similar concessions for the Maputo and Beira corridors were also under way. Inevitably, fears have been expressed in the country of a sell-out of Mozambican resources to foreign countries. But without foreign investment Mozambique will have very little chance of ever getting back on its feet economically.

Without doubt, the most influential of all Mozambique's trading partners is South Africa, whose businesspeople seem to be buying up everything – factories, mines, breweries, hotels, transport concerns and so on.

FOREIGN EXCHANGE During Portuguese colonial times the main sources of foreign exchange were the export of agricultural produce; rail transport and provision of ports for South Africa, Northern Rhodesia (Zambia), Southern Rhodesia (Zimbabwe), Nyasaland (Malawi) and Swaziland; income from the supply of manpower to South African and Rhodesian mines and plantations; and tourism from South Africa and Rhodesia.

Except for agricultural exports, these sources of income have since more or less disappeared, although tourism is slowly beginning to re-emerge, particularly south of Beira. Rail transportation to neighbouring countries is now only possible on a small scale as a result of the civil war. After the government's severing of trade links with South Africa at the beginning of the 1980s, South Africa terminated the existing agreement on the employment of Mozambican workers by the South African mines. This agreement between Portugal and South Africa, dating from 1928, had been particularly lucrative for Mozambique since it meant that 60% of the salaries were paid at a fixed gold price.

Nowadays, since the rehabilitation of the Cahora Bassa hydro-electric plant in 1997 and the beginning of construction of a new plant some 70km downstream of Cahora Bassa, Mozambique is beginning to earn a considerable amount of its foreign exchange from the export of electricity to neighbouring countries.

NATURAL RESOURCES During colonial times there was almost no exploitation of the country's large mineral deposits; it is estimated that more geological investigations were conducted in Mozambique between 1977 and 1983 than during the entire colonial period. In the course of these investigations, rich deposits of coal, salt, iron ore and phosphate, as well as gold, tantalum, chromium, copper, bauxite, nickel and many other minerals, were discovered. At present, only coal and salt are mined in significant quantities, although bauxite and graphite are starting to be exploited at commercially viable levels. Other resources with potential include titanium, the world's largest reserve of which was discovered in Gaza Province in 1999, and gas, found principally in Inhambane Province. Once again, the exploitation of these natural resources is dependent on large amounts of foreign investment.

FACIM TRADE FAIR Mozambique's window on the world, economically speaking, is the Feira Internacional de Maputo, or FACIM. It is the only real trade fair in Mozambique and attracts considerable international participation. It is held in Maputo annually towards the end of August. For further information, contact **FACIM/Maputo Trade Fair** (*Av 10 de Novembro, Maputo; +258 21 427 151*).

TOURISM Prior to independence, Mozambique was one of the most popular tourist destinations in southern Africa. In those days, thousands of Rhodesians and South Africans flocked to the beaches and offshore islands in the south, and Gorongosa National Park was one of the region's major attractions. The bottom fell out of the tourism industry after independence, and the outbreak of civil war hardly helped to bring the tourists back. The statistics speak for themselves: in 1972, 292,000 people visited Mozambique; by 1981, this number had fallen to just 1,000. It was never in much doubt, however, that once a semblance of stability had returned to the country, tourism would once again play an important economic role. Sure enough, by the end of the 1990s, tourism was the fastest-growing sector of the Mozambican economy, and it is still growing rapidly today.

As an indication of the importance attached to encouraging this industry, the post of Minister for Tourism was created following the 1999 election. Then came the National Policy of Tourism, outlining the way in which the government would like to see tourism develop in the near future. The areas prioritised for immediate 'exploration' were, predictably, the beach resorts near Maputo and Beira.

The national parks are gradually being developed, with most activity at the time of writing being based around Limpopo and Bazaruto in the south, Gorongosa in the middle of the country, and Niassa and the Quirimba in the north.

PEOPLE

Over 98% of the people in Mozambique are African, which stands to reason. The remainder is made up of Europeans (mainly Portuguese), Indians, east Asians and *mestiços* (people of mixed African–European ancestry). As in most of Africa, the tribes living in Mozambique share cultural and linguistic similarities with their counterparts in neighbouring states.

The basic tribal pattern in Mozambique is a result of pre-19th-century migrations from the north and west, and the fleeing of people in the early 19th century from the violent Zulu Kingdom in South Africa. This has left a north–south split, with the Zambezi River as the dividing line. The tribes north of the Zambezi are predominantly agriculturists and have matrilineal societies. The two largest tribes, the Macua and the Lomwe, who are concentrated in Zambézia, Nampula, Niassa and Cabo Delgado provinces, together make up about 35% of the total Mozambican population. Another northern tribe worth knowing is the

Makonde, famous for its art and its wooden statues and masks, who live on both the Mozambican and Tanzanian sides of the Rovuma River. The tribes south of the Zambezi River are mainly cattle-rearing and have patrilineal societies. The most important is the Thonga, the country's second-largest ethnic group, who are concentrated in the area south of the Save River and make up around 23% of the population. The majority of Africans in Maputo are Thonga. Meanwhile, most of Sofala and Manica provinces are inhabited by Shona, a tribe whose numbers have grown due to migrations into Mozambique of Shona from Zimbabwe and South Africa. In addition to the tribal differences north and south of the Zambezi River, a third distinct region is formed by the Zambezi Valley itself, which has historically been influenced by the Portuguese and Arabs who used the river to access the interior.

The population of Mozambique was estimated at 23 million in 2010, and is expected to exceed 30 million by 2020. The average life expectancy is around 48 years. Approximately 60% of the population live in rural areas, but there is an ongoing trend of gravitation to the cities.

Mozambique has one of the lowest population densities in southern and eastern Africa, currently standing at roughly 28.5 inhabitants per km^2. Excluding the desert countries of Namibia and Botswana, Zambia is the only country in the region more thinly populated than Mozambique. It has been suggested that the low population density was due to the protracted civil war. In fact, the interior of Mozambique has always been sparsely populated, and the population has grown by more than 50% in the 20 years since independence. The most densely populated provinces are Zambézia, Nampula and Maputo.

Minority population groups include Indians and Pakistanis, particularly around Nampula, and Portuguese, who are concentrated in the cities of Maputo and Beira.

LANGUAGE

Portuguese is the official language of Mozambique, but it is generally only spoken by the 45% or thereabouts of the population who have been to school. This creates serious problems: the economic, business and legal language is Portuguese; tuition in high schools, colleges and universities is exclusively in Portuguese and thus debars the many who have had no chance to learn it in primary education; many of the younger people grew up in refugee camps and have had little formal education, let alone in what is essentially a foreign tongue, and slightly over 50% of the population are illiterate, despite considerable efforts by themselves and by the government. The problems with education, both in languages and in general, have become so acute that some schools have started to work a shift system: children of one age group go to school every day for a few hours in the morning, children of another in the afternoon.

All of Mozambique's indigenous languages belong to the Bantu family. The root Bantu language is thought to have spread through eastern and southern Africa during the first half of the first millennium AD, since when it has diversified into many linguistic subfamilies and several hundred languages and closely related dialects. Roughly 40 distinct languages and dialects are spoken in Mozambique. The various dialects of Macua-Lomwe are spoken only north of the Zambezi, but they nevertheless account for the home language of around 40% of the total population of Mozambique. In the south, the majority of people speak dialects of Tsonga, a language also spoken in South Africa. Various Tsonga and Shona dialects are spoken in central Mozambique.

In northern coastal regions, some people speak KiSwahili, a variant Bantu language with some Arabic influences that became the lingua franca of coastal trading centres between Mogadishu and Sofala in medieval times.

Visitors who are unfamiliar with Portuguese and Bantu languages will find that most Mozambicans are extremely helpful and will do what they can to overcome your language barrier. The mixing of the people during the war has made them adept at getting along and making themselves understood in a variety of communication forms: a bit of gesturing and drawing in the dirt with a stick can overcome many barriers. Often, people will simply lead you to where you want to go. For practical information on speaking Portuguese, see *Appendix 1, Language*, page 361.

Concern has recently been expressed in Lisbon that the end of apartheid and the democratisation of South Africa will lead to the anglicisation of Mozambique. Since Portuguese is not an indigenous language and all of Mozambique's neighbours and SADCC partners (Angola excepted) use English as an official language, as do most donor countries, there would be a certain logic to displacing Portuguese with English as the main language of education and government. In recognition of the importance of English to furthering international trade, English is now being taught a few years earlier at school than it has been in the past, but all official government business is still conducted in Portuguese.

RELIGION

Slightly more than 50% of Mozambicans are Christian, with Catholicism being followed by 33% of the population and various Protestant denominations by 18%. About 28% of the population are Muslim. Christianity is more common in urban areas while the Muslim faith is predominantly confined to the north. Many Mozambicans either adhere to traditional beliefs or have a dualistic faith that integrates Christian/Muslim beliefs with traditional animism or pantheism. Traditional faiths and medicines were suppressed as backward and unscientific during the communist era, but are now enjoying something of a resurgence, encouraged by the resumption of authority of many local chiefs in the absence of any other effective management. Traditional healers are also enjoying a comeback as part of this cultural renaissance.

CULTURE

ART Maputo was a hotbed of artistic creativity in the decade following independence, a scene centred upon Centro de Estudos Culturais. Artistic activity was stifled during the long years of war that followed, and it has never picked up in quite the same way again, though the best of the Makonde influenced artworks sold at craft markets throughout the country are in a league above the tourist tack available in most African countries. There are also many quality murtals in the country's larger towns and cities, often depicting events from the liberation or civil wars. It will be interesting to see whether the 2010 opening of a new National School of Visual Arts (ENAV), built with US$750,000 of Chinese finance, will stimulate the arts scene.

Visitors interested in the visual arts should visit the Museu Nacional des Artes, Centre, the Cultural Franco-Mozambicain and Núcleo de Arte in Maputo, as well as the house of the late Alberto Chissano in nearby Matola. Born in 1934, Alberto Chissano is arguably the finest sculptor to have worked in Mozambique, a former soldier and miner who first exhibited at the Núcleo de Arte in 1964 and won several awards for his wood and stone sculptures prior to his death in 1994. His contemporary Malangatana Ngwenya, a politicised painter and poet who mostly exhibited under his first name only, was born in the far south of the country in 1964 and studied art in Lisbon in 1971 following 18 months imprisonment by the colonial secret police for his involvement in Frelimo. Malangatana painted several of the war murals that adorn Mozambique's, and in more recent years he was the founder of the Mozambican Peace Movement and several cultural institutions prior to his death in Portugal in January 2011.

FICTION Naturally the bulk of Mozambican fiction has been written in Portuguese, and until recently comparatively little has been available in English. This is now starting to change.

The Mozambican writer Mia Couto is an international literary star whose books have been published in more than 20 countries. Several of his novels, including *Under the Frangipani, A River Called Time, The Last Flight of the Flamingo* and *Sleepwalking Land*, are available in excellent English translations by David Brookshaw from Serpent's Tail in London. Couto's novels are essential reading for anyone planning to visit Mozambique. *Neighbours: The Story of a Murder* by the highly regarded, if less famous, Lilia Momplé is also available in English from Penguin Classics.

Paulina Chiziane was the first Mozambican woman to publish a novel. She has been translated into numerous languages and is well known in both Europe and parts of Asia. Her comic novel *Niketche: A Story of Polygamy* was finally published in an English translation in 2010.

Several of Luis Bernado Honwana's stories have been translated and included in anthologies, and another name to look out for is Nelson Saute, translations of whose work can't be far off.

Mozambican poets José Craveirinha and Rui Knopfli have an international reputation, and their anthologies shouldn't be hard to track down.

There are also foreign writers who live in Mozambique, including the Swedish novelist Henning Mankell, whose novel about Maputo street children, *Chronicler of the Winds*, is easily obtainable in English. His two novels *Secrets in the Fire* and *Playing with Fire* are based on the true story of a young girl growing up during the war who is disabled by a landmine.

The Nigerian Noble Laureate Wole Soyinka wrote a poem *Ogun Abibiman* based on Samora Machel's 1976 declaration putting Mozambique on a war footing with white Rhodesia.

Meet me in Mozambique by Montserrat author E A Markham is partially set in the idealism of pre-revolutionary Mozambique.

The British author Lisa St Aubin de Terán lives in rural Nampula Province running an NGO. Her book *Mozambique Mysteries*, a memoir of the culture of that region, was published in September 2007 by Virago.

You should be able to get most of the above from any good bookshop, but an excellent source is the Africa Book Centre which (as the name suggests) covers the whole continent. A browse of their website (*www.africabookcentre*.com) is recommended.

MUSIC There are a couple of useful websites for exploring the contemporary Mozambican music scene. The best is www.mozambique-music.com which lists artists ranging from traditional Afrobeat-influenced styles to more modern hip-hop and blues influences. They have links enabling you to buy albums and try 30-second clips before you buy.

There's less content, but www.afromix.org/html/musique/pays/mozambique/index.en.html gives a few more artists worth checking out.

2

Natural History

Unlike most other countries in sub-equatorial Africa, Mozambique is not primarily or even secondarily a safari destination. Although more than 10% of the country has been designated as some form of protected area, little of this land is readily accessible to visitors, and the once abundant wildlife was severely depleted during the long years of civil war and associated poaching (the elephant population, for instance, dropped from around 65,000 to 15,000 between 1970 and 1995, though it has increased steadily in subsequent years).

Today, the country has six national parks, of which Quirimba and Bazaruto are primarily marine reserves, while Zinave and Banhine have very limited facilities and support little wildlife. There are also eight national or special reserves, but again most of these are remote and poorly developed. However, facilities in certain reserves and parks have improved greatly in the past few years, and Mozambique does now offer a few decent wildlife-viewing opportunities, most notably at the rehabilitated and relatively accessible Gorongosa National Park. Also worth considering are the immense Niassa Reserve, the recently proclaimed Limpopo National Park (a Mozambican extension of South Africa's famous Kruger Park), the Maputo Special Reserve south of the capital, and (especially for backpackers) the Chimanimani National Reserve.

VEGETATION

Most of Mozambique is covered in savanna, a loosely applied term that can be used to cover practically any wooded habitat that doesn't have a closed canopy. Characteristically, the Mozambican savanna is much more densely wooded than similar habitats in Zimbabwe and South Africa, and the trees are much taller. Brachystegia woodland, named after the most common tree, is the main savanna type throughout northern Mozambique, in the Zimbabwe and Zambia border areas, and along the coastal belt north of the Limpopo. In total, it covers about 70% of the country, but is replaced by mopane woodland in drier areas such as Tete Province south of the Zambezi and the interior of Gaza Province, and by acacia woodland in parts of the south and along the main watercourses of the north.

The coastal beaches are typically coverered in dense, scrubby thickets and palm groves, the latter particularly impressive around Inhambane and Quelimane. The floodplains of major rivers such as the Limpopo, Zambezi and Pungue, and the area near Lake Chilwa on the Malawian border, are covered in alluvial grasslands and marshes. The largest alluvial plain in Mozambique is the Zambezi Delta, a vast marshy area of thick grassland and borassus palms that stretches for 120km along the coast and covers an area of roughly 8,000km^2.

Only a tiny portion of Mozambique is covered in true forest. There are rainforests on the upper slopes of a few mountains, notably Mount Gorongosa in Sofala, the Chimanimani and Inyanga highlands on the Zimbabwean border, and Mount Murrumbala, Namuli, Mabu and Chiperone in western Zambézia. Dry lowland forest occurs in patches in some coastal areas, notably in northern Cabo Delgado and around Dondo near Beira, while several rivers support thin belts of riparian forest.

MAMMALS

Several useful field guides to African mammals are available for the purpose of identification. What most such guides lack is detailed distribution details for individual countries, so the following notes should be seen as a Mozambique-specific supplement to a regional or continental field guide.

PREDATORS A firm safari favourite, the **lion**, Africa's largest cat, is a sociable animal that lives in family prides of up to 15 animals and tends to hunt by night, favouring large and medium-sized antelopes. Though widespread in Mozambique (a recent survey suggests a national population in excess of 2,000), it is likely to be seen by visitors only in Gorongosa National Park and to a lesser extent the Niassa Reserve. The smaller, solitary and more secretive **leopard**, with its distinctive black-on-gold rosetted coat, is also still widespread in Mozambique, and far more numerous than the lion, but sightings are very uncommon. So far as we are aware, the more streamlined **cheetah**, a plains dweller with distinctive black 'tear marks' running down its face, is more or less extinct in Mozambique. Several smaller species of cat, such as **caracal**, **serval** and **African wild cat**, occur in Mozambique, but they are rarely seen on account of their nocturnal habits.

Leopard

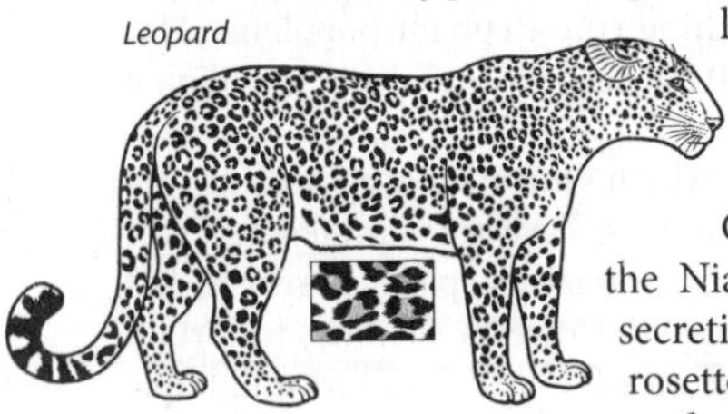

Cheetah

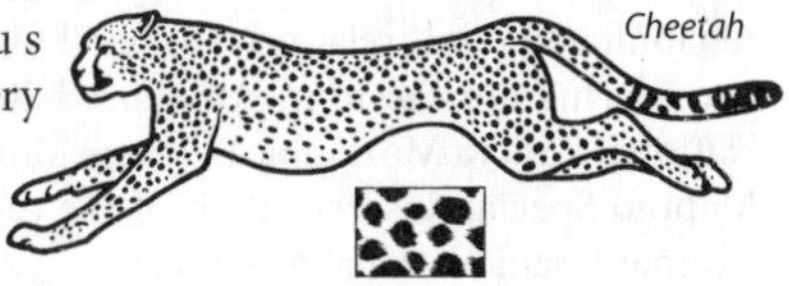

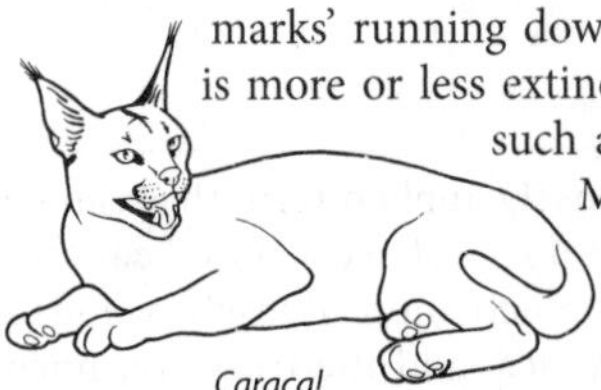

Caracal

The largest indigenous canine species, the **African hunting dog**, is unmistakable on account of its blotchy black, brown and cream coat. Hunting dogs live and hunt in packs, normally about ten animals strong. The introduction to Africa of canine diseases such as rabies has caused a severe decline in hunting dog numbers in recent years, and this endangered species has been on the IUCN Red List of Threatened Animals since 1984. Mozambique is one on the most important strongholds for this rare creature, which is still quite numerous in the northerly Niassa Reserve and Quirimba National Park. The more lightly built **side-striped** and **black-backed jackals**, mostly nocturnal in habit and are generally seen singly or in pairs, are widespread in brachystegia and acacia habitats respectively.

African hunting dog

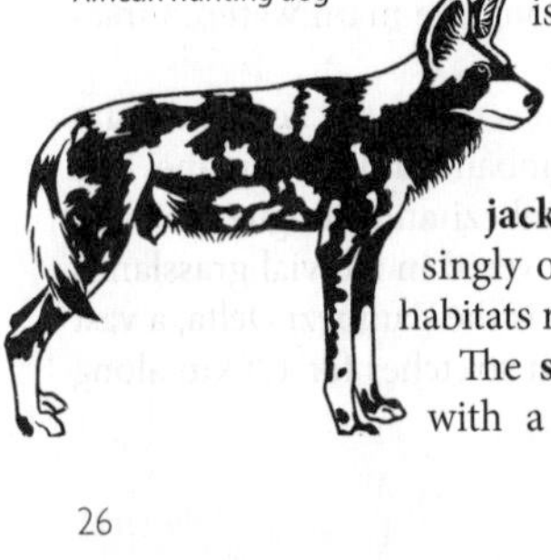

The **spotted hyena** is a large, bulky, widespread predator with a sloping back, black-on-brown lightly spotted coat

Spotted hyena

and dog-like face. Contrary to popular myth, it is not a type of dog, nor is it exclusively a scavenger, nor is it hermaphroditic. The *Viverridae* is a group of small predators that includes **mongooses** and the cat-like **civets** and **genets**. At least ten mongoose species have been recorded in Mozambique, most of which can be readily observed in the right habitat. The African civet, tree civet and large-spotted genet are all present too, but they are rarely seen except on night drives in Gorongosa National Park or the Niassa Reserve. Four representatives of the *Mustelidae* occur: the **honey-badger**, **Cape clawless otter**, **spotted necked otter** and **striped polecat**.

PRIMATES The most common primate in Mozambique is probably the **vervet monkey**, a small, grey animal with a black face and, in the male, blue genitals. Vervet monkeys live in large troupes in most habitats except desert and evergreen forest. The closely related **samango** or **blue monkey** is a less common and more cryptically marked species associated with evergreen and riverine forests, as well as coastal thicket. The **yellow baboon** is common in northern Mozambique, while the greyer **chacma baboon** occurs in the south, with the population in Gorongosa possibly representing an intermediate form. The wide-eyed bushbaby, a small nocturnal primate that is heard more often than seen, can often be located at night by tracing its distinctive, piercing call to a tree and then using a flashlight to pick up its eyes.

Vervet monkey

Samango monkey

Bushbaby

ANTELOPE A number of large antelope species occur in Mozambique, with the greatest variety in Gorongosa, Niassa and Maputo Special Reserve. These include the **eland**, Africa's largest antelope, and the handsomely marked **greater kudu**, immediately recognisable by the male's immense spiralling horns. Gorongosa is one of the best places in Africa to see the striking **sable antelope**, the male of which has large, backward-curving horns and a glossy black coat. Easily seen near water in several reserves, the **common waterbuck** has a shaggy coat and a distinctive white horseshoe on its rump. Other large antelope associated mainly with the northern reserves are the closely related and equally doleful looking **Niassa wildebeest** and paler and more lightly built **Lichtenstein's hartebeest**. The most widespread medium-sized antelope

Eland

Greater kudu

DANGEROUS ANIMALS

Contrary to popular belief, most wild animals fear us more than we fear them, and their normal response to human contact is to flee. That said, a number of fatalities have been caused by such incidents.

The need for caution is greatest near water. Hippos are responsible for more human fatalities than any other large mammal, not because they are aggressive but because they panic when something comes between them and the safety of the water. Never walk between a hippo and water, and never walk along riverbanks or through reed beds, especially in overcast weather or at dusk or dawn, when hippos are grazing.

Watch out, too, for crocodiles. Only a very large crocodile is likely to attack a person, and then only in the water or right on the shore. Near settlements, you can be fairly sure any such beast will have been consigned to its maker, so the risk is greatest away from human habitation. It is also near water that you might unwittingly come upon a bushbuck; though normally placid, it has a reputation as the most dangerous African antelope when cornered.

There are areas where hikers may still stumble across an elephant or a buffalo, the most dangerous of Africa's terrestrial herbivores. Elephants almost invariably mock charge and indulge in some trumpeting before attacking in earnest. Provided you back off at the first sign, they are unlikely to take further notice of you. If you see them before they see you, give them a wide berth.

If an animal charges you, the safest course of action is to climb the nearest tree. Black rhinos are prone to charge without apparent provocation, but they're too rare in Mozambique to be much cause for concern. Elephants are the only animals to pose a danger to a vehicle – if an elephant doesn't want you to pass, back off and wait until it has moved away before you try again. Leave your engine running

is the thicket and forest-associated **bushbuck**. The male has a dark chestnut coat marked with white stripes and spots, while the female is lighter with similar markings, giving it an appearance much like a European deer. The closely related **nyala** is a southern African species that might be seen in well-wooded habitats as far north as Gorongosa. The **impala**, a gregarious, gazelle-like antelope that is numerous in savanna, has a bright chestnut coat, distinctive white and black stripes on its rump, and (male only) large lyre-shaped horns. The **southern reedbuck**, a lightly coloured, somewhat nondescript antelope almost always associated with water, is particularly common in Maputo Special Reserve.

Common reedbuck

Impala

Smaller antelope include the **klipspringer**, which has a grey, bristly coat and lives exclusively on rocky outcrops where it displays a goat-like ability to jump and climb up almost vertical rock faces. The grassland-dwelling **oribi** is a tan-coloured antelope with a white belly, black tail and a diagnostic black patch beneath its ears. **Livingstone's suni** is a tiny grey antelope that lives in coastal scrub. The **grey** or **common duiker**, a greyish antelope with a white belly and a tuft

when close to an elephant, and avoid letting yourself be boxed in between an elephant and another vehicle.

Vervet monkeys and baboons have become pests at some campsites. Feeding them is highly irresponsible, since it encourages them to scavenge and may lead to their being shot. Vervet monkeys are too small to be more than a nuisance, but baboons have killed children and maimed adults with their teeth. Do not tease or underestimate them. If primates are hanging around a campsite and you wander off leaving fruit in your tent, don't expect the tent to be standing when you return.

Most large predators stay clear of humans and are only likely to kill accidentally or in self-defence. Lions are arguably the exception. Should you encounter one on foot, don't run, since this is likely to trigger the instinct to give chase. Of the other cats, cheetahs represent no threat and leopards only really attack when cornered. Hyenas are potentially dangerous, but in practice are more likely to slink off into the shadows when disturbed.

A slight but real danger when sleeping in the bush without a tent is that a passing hyena or lion might investigate a hairy object sticking out of a sleeping bag, and decapitate you out of predatorial curiosity. In areas where large predators are common, a sealed tent practically guarantees your safety – but don't sleep with your head sticking out and don't put meat in the tent.

All manner of venomous snakes occur in Mozambique, but they generally slither away when they sense the vibrations of a person walking. For more details see the *Snakes* section in *Health*, pages 82–3.

When all is said and done, the most dangerous animal in Africa, exponentially a greater threat than everything mentioned above, is the anopheles mosquito, which carries the malaria parasite. Humans – particularly behind a steering wheel – run them a close second!

between its small horns, is widespread, while the smaller and more beautiful **Natal red duiker** and **blue duiker** are confined almost exclusively to forest interiors.

Klipspringer

Natal red duiker

Other ungulates Despite the heavy poaching of the war years, the **African elephant** is still reasonably common in the Gorongosa, Limpopo and Quirimba national parks as well as the Niassa and Maputo special reserves. **Black** and **white rhinos** are officially extinct, but as fences between the Limpopo and Kruger national parks become more pregnable (they will eventually drop altogether) it seems likely that some individual will cross into the Mozambican part of this transfrontier park. **Hippos** have also suffered from poaching, but they are easily seen in the Niassa and Maputo Special Reserve, as well as in Gorongosa. **African buffalo**, **Burchell's zebra** and **southern giraffe** are also present in some reserves. Two swine species are common: the duirnal and easily seen **warthog**, which has a uniform bristly grey coat and the distinctive habit of holding its tail erect when it runs, and the more secretive and nocturnal **bushpig**.

Black rhino

The exact number of birds recorded in Mozambique is open to debate, with various sources listing between 750 and 800 species, a discrepancy attributable to various controversial taxonomic splits as well as one's acceptance of vagrant and uncorroborated records. A useful checklist can be found online at www.birdlist.org/mozambique and a good field guide will help identify most of the birds you see. This list includes one full endemic, the *Namuli apalis*, along with the olive-headed weaver, which of all the bird species resident in southern Africa has possibly been seen by the fewest birdwatchers (a patch of tall brachystegia woodland just south of the town of Panda, 60km inland of Inharrime in Inhambane Province, is the only locality in the region where the birder has a chance of seeing it).

Mozambique is an important destination for southern African birders. Of the 850-odd bird species that are resident in or regular migrants to Africa south of the Zambezi, roughly 30 have been recorded only in Mozambique or else have their main concentration there. Some of the birds fitting into one of these categories are the Madagascar squacco heron, eastern saw-wing swallow, Bohm's bee-eater, palmnut vulture, silvery-cheeked hornbill, green tinkerbird, green-backed woodpecker, green-headed oriole, tiny greenbul, stripe-cheeked greenbul, white-chested alethe, Swynnerton's robin, East Coast akalat (Gunning's robin), Chirinda apalis, black-headed apalis, moustached grass warbler, Robert's warbler, mashona hylotia, yellow-breasted hylotia, black-and-white flycatcher, Woodward's batis, pale batis, Livingstone's flycatcher, Achieta's tchagra, chestnut-fronted helmet-shrike, red-headed quelea, cardinal quelea, olive-headed weaver, lesser seedcracker, yellow-bellied waxbill and lemon-breasted canary.

Visitors to southern Mozambique seldom stray far inland. Among the exciting birds to be found along the coast are crab plovers, which are seen regularly in and around the Bazaruto Archipelago in summer, and occasionally as far south as Inhaca Island near Maputo. One of the rarest raptors in the world, Eleanora's falcon, has been seen at Vilanculos and Pomene. Vast flocks of migrant waders include bar-tailed godwit, terek sandpiper and greater sandplover. The rarely seen gull-billed tern has recently been spotted at freshwater lakes in three localities. Indigenous woodland is scarce along the coast, having been largely replaced by exotic coconut palms and cashew trees. However, the red-throated twinspot, Livingstone's turaco and brown scrub-robin can still be found near Xai-Xai and in Maputaland.

Other exciting birds to be seen in the brachystegia woodlands of the Mozambican interior south of the Save River include chestnut-fronted helmet shrike, racket-tailed roller, mottled spinetail, Rudd's apalis, Livingstone's flycatcher, plain-backed sunbird, Neergard's sunbird and pink-throated twinspot. In central Mozambique, two localities of great interest to birders are Gorongosa Mountain (near Gorongosa National Park) and the forests north of Dondo. Species that cannot be seen elsewhere in southern Africa include green-headed oriole and East Coast akalat.

Northern Mozambique is particularly alluring to birders, since many areas have yet to be thoroughly explored and birdwatchers are likely to find species new to the Mozambique list – and possibly even new to science. Birders in northern Mozambique will certainly encounter species that are not included in southern African field guides, so they will need to refer to a second field guide (see *Appendix 2, Further Information*, page 366). Some of the birds that are known to occur in northern Mozambique but not in southern Africa are pale-billed hornbill; brown-breasted barbet; mountain, little, grey-olive, Fischer's and Cabanis's greenbuls; Thyolo alethe; central bearded scrub-robin; evergreen and red-capped forest

BIRDING EQUIPMENT *Keith Barnes and Josh Engel*

OPTICAL EQUIPMENT A sealed and waterproof pair of binoculars is the most essential piece of equipment. Someone who has been thrifty on binoculars will soon realise that they have wasted their time and money, because once your bins fill with water or mist, they become useless. In the rainforest 8x32 magnification is normally the safest bet as this tends to gather more light and pinning down the bird in your viewfinder is easier. In open areas such as savanna, 10x40s are more useful as the image is larger. Telescopes can be useful, particularly in the savannas, or when watching waterbirds on an open lake. In the forest a telescope is of limited use and cumbersome to carry.

RAINGEAR The only thing worse than your binoculars being filled with water is being soaking wet yourself. Be sure to get sturdy waterproof boots, ponchos and rainproof trousers. Boots also double as protection from ant swarms, and ponchos make excellent makeshift hides. Peak or broad-brimmed hats keep rainwater out of your eyes and binoculars.

SOUND GEAR Much forest birding depends on your ability to recognise, follow, locate and reproduce bird sounds. These days, mp3 players with an attached amplified speaker are the norm. Southern Africa has a superb set of bird sounds in the form of Guy Gibbons's *Southern African Bird Sounds* CDs available from Wildsounds (*www.wildsounds.co.uk*).

GPS These units are extremely useful both for finding your way and marking locations for future birders. Their compass and altitude features are also very helpful, but be warned that signals may not be available under forest canopy. Also be sure to seek local advice before wandering off the beaten track, as landmines are a serious issue.

FLASHLIGHT A powerful flashlight will help you find night birds. As much birding in Mozambique requires camping, this will be particularly rewarding.

BOOKS A good field guide is essential; see page 368 for recommendations.

warblers; Kretchmar's longbill; white-winged apalis, long-billed tailorbird; white-tailed blue flycatcher, mountain babbler, red-and-blue and eastern double-collared sunbirds; Bertram's weaver; Zanzibar red bishop; African citril and stripe-breasted canary.

IBAs (*Keith Barnes and Josh Engel*)

What are IBAs? Put simply, IBAs (Important Bird Areas) are sites, either protected or unprotected, that are vital for bird conservation. Because IBAs target specific categories of birds, normally threatened, rare or range-restricted birds, they often double as some of the finest birding destinations, particularly for those birders seeking more elusive species. Mount Gorongosa and Gorongosa National Park, Maputo Special Reserve, Mount Namuli and the Zambezi River Delta are all IBAs.

What makes them IBAs is that they are well-defined sites with boundaries – making it possible to demarcate and conserve them – and that they each hold one or more of a particular set of special birds worthy of conservation attention. Also, because IBAs are selected using identical and standardised criteria, an IBA in Mozambique is the same as an IBA in South Africa, Malawi, Thailand or England; as a result they form a global conservation currency. Mozambique holds 15 IBAs that support an excellent cross-section of the country's threatened and unique avifauna. Often these sites double as key birdwatching areas, with ecotourism-based initiatives alongside them.

How are IBAs protected? Selecting IBAs according to the criteria is probably the easiest part of the process. The publication of the directories documenting the sites is only a beginning. The directories serve to highlight certain areas requiring additional conservation attention, as an alarming proportion of the sites fall outside the official protected area network. The most difficult job is to get people to sit up and listen. Unfortunately, Mozambique lacks a BirdLife partnership. These partnerships have been most influential in this regard, liaising with government officials, international conservation bodies and key global decision-makers to further the ends of the programme.

Mozambique's national IBA programme stands to benefit from concerned individuals taking an interest in their local IBAs, as volunteers or custodians. If you would like to become involved, please contact the **BirdLife International Secretariat** (*Wellbrooke Ct, Girton Rd, Cambridge CB3 0NA;* ✆ *01223 279800;* e *birdlife@birdlife.org.uk; www.birdlife.net*).

REPTILES

NILE CROCODILE The order Crocodilia dates back at least 150 million years, and fossil forms that lived contemporaneously with dinosaurs are remarkably similar to their modern counterparts. The Nile crocodile is the largest living reptile, regularly growing to lengths of up to 6m. Widespread throughout Africa, it was once common in most large rivers and lakes, but it has been exterminated in many areas over the past century – hunted professionally for its skin as well as by vengeful local villagers. Contrary to popular legend, Nile crocodiles feed mostly on fish, at least where densities are sufficient. They will also prey on drinking or swimming mammals when the opportunity presents itself, dragging their victim underwater until it drowns, then storing it under a submerged log or tree until it has decomposed sufficiently for them to eat. A large crocodile is capable of killing a lion or wildebeest, or an adult human for that matter. Today, large specimens are mostly confined to protected areas, and are especially common along the rivers through the Niassa Reserve.

SNAKES A wide variety of snakes occurs in Mozambique, though – fortunately, most would agree – they are typically shy and unlikely to be seen unless actively sought. One of the snakes most likely to be seen on safari is Africa's largest, the rock python, which has a gold-on-black mottled skin and regularly grows to lengths exceeding 5m. Non-venomous, pythons kill their prey by strangulation, wrapping their muscular bodies around it until it cannot breathe, then swallowing it whole and dozing off for a couple of months while it is digested. Pythons feed mainly on small antelopes, large rodents and similar. They are harmless to adult humans, but could conceivably kill a small child.

Of the venomous snakes, one of the most commonly encountered is the puff adder, a large, thick resident of savanna and rocky habitats. Several cobra species are present, most with characteristic hoods that they raise when about to strike, though they are seldom seen. Another widespread family is the mambas, of which the black mamba – which will only attack when cornered, despite an unfounded reputation for unprovoked aggression – is the largest venomous snake in Africa, measuring up to 3.5m long. Theoretically, the most toxic of Africa's snakes is the boomslang, a variably coloured and largely arboreal snake, but it is back-fanged and very passive, and the only human fatalities recorded involve snake handlers.

Most snakes are non-venomous and harmless to any living creature much bigger than a rat. One common species is the green tree snake (sometimes mistaken for a boomslang, though the latter is never as green and more often brown), which feeds mostly on amphibians. The mole snake is a common grey-brown savanna resident that grows up to 2m long and feeds on moles and other rodents. The remarkable egg-eating snake lives exclusively on bird eggs, dislocating its jaws to swallow the egg whole, then eventually regurgitating the crushed shell in a neat little package. Many snakes will take eggs opportunistically, for which reason large-scale agitation among birds in a tree is often a good indication that a snake (or small bird of prey) is around.

LIZARDS All African lizards are harmless to humans, with the arguable exception of the giant monitor lizards, which could in theory inflict a nasty bite if cornered. Two species occur in Mozambique, the water and the savanna monitor, the latter growing up to 2.2m long and occasionally seen in the vicinity of termite mounds, the former slightly smaller but far more regularly observed by tourists. Their size alone might make it possible to fleetingly mistake a monitor for a small crocodile, but their more colourful yellow-dappled skin precludes sustained confusion. Both species are predatorial, feeding on anything from bird eggs to smaller reptiles and mammals, but will also eat carrion opportunistically.

The common house gecko is an endearing bug-eyed, translucent white lizard that inhabits most houses as well as lodge rooms, scampering up walls and upside-down on the ceiling in pursuit of pesky insects attracted to the lights. Also very common in some areas are various agama species, distinguished from other common lizards by their relatively large size of around 20–25cm, basking habits, and almost plastic-looking scaling – depending on the species, a combination of blue, purple, orange or red, with the flattened head generally a different colour from the torso. Another common family is the skinks: small, long-tailed lizards, most of which are quite dark and have a few thin black stripes running from head to tail. The most charismatic of all lizard groups, the swivel-eyed, colour-changing chameleons, are also well represented in Mozambique.

TORTOISES AND TERRAPINS These peculiar reptiles are unique in being protected by a prototypal suit of armour formed by their heavy exoskeleton. The most common of the terrestrial tortoises in the region is the leopard tortoise, which is named after its gold-and-black mottled shell, can weigh up to 30kg, and has been known to live for more than 50 years in captivity. It is often seen motoring along in the slow lane of game reserve roads. Three species of terrapin – essentially the freshwater equivalent of turtles – are resident in Mozambique, all somewhat flatter in shape than the tortoises, and generally with a plainer brown shell. They might be seen sunning on rocks close to water or peering out from roadside puddles.

MARINE LIFE

Uniquely in southern and eastern Africa, Mozambique is better known and more often visited for its wealth of marine wildlife than for the terrestrial creatures that roam its relatively underutilised game reserves. For much of its 2,470km length, Mozambique's Indian Ocean coastline is protected by a succession of offshore coral reefs that offer sublime conditions for snorkelling and diving, along with dozens of small islands such as those that make up the Bazaruto and Qurimba Archipelagos, both of which are protected within national parks.

There are dozens of established dive and snorkel sites along the coast, and many more that remain undeveloped for tourism, but the main centres for viewing marine life are Ponta Do Ouro (known for reef fish and ragged-tooth sharks), the coast around Inhambane, Tofo and Závora (where ocean safaris offer snorkelers and divers the opportunity to swim with marine giants such as whale-shark, manta ray and dolphins), Vilankulo and the nearby Bazaruto Archipelago (a huge diversity of reef fish and the one place where snorkelers regularly encounter turtles, also with very occasional dugong sightings) and the Quirimbas (superb for reef fish but less good for larger marine creatures). A brief overview of some of the marine wildlife likely to be seen along the Mozambican coast follows:

MARINE MAMMALS At least ten species of cetacean (whales and dolphins) are resident along, or seasonal visitors to, the Mozambican coast. These remarkable mammals have a similar body temperature to humans, and are as dependent on atmospheric oxygen as any terrestrial creature, yet they lead a totally aquatic existence, often in water so cold it would induce fatal hypothermia in most other mammals. Some species can spend up to an hour below water without surfacing, thanks to their large lungs, capacity to replenish 90 percent of their air supply in one breath, and the ability to store oxygen in their muscles, while a dense subcutaneous layer of insulating blubber protects them from the cold. Unfortunately, the commercial value of this blubber has also led to their persecution by the lucrative whaling industry - the global population of the blue whale, for instance, is now fewer than 5,000 after at least 300,000 individuals were harpooned in the 20th century.

Cetaceans are divided into two distinct groups, based on their feeding anatomy. Baleen whales are named for the comb-like baleen upper-jaw plates that are used to sieve plankton, other tiny invertebrates and small pelagic fish from the water as they swim. Surprisingly perhaps, the largest creature ever to inhabit our planet, the blue whale – at up to 180 tons, some 20–30 times heavier than an African elephant – feeds on near-microscopic organisms in this somewhat passive manner. Blue whales are extremely rare off the coast of Mozambique, but the 40-tonne humpback whale is seasonally very common, and it is often seen on ocean safaris out of Tofo over June to December. The slightly bulkier southern right whale is often seen in the far south of Mozambique at the same time as year, while the southern minke whale, the smallest of the baleen whales, is resident throughout the year, often feeding in small groups in bays.

The other main group, comprising dolphins, porpoises and toothed whales, are the odontocetic cetaceans: active hunters whose dental structure resembles that of the terrestrial carnivores. Eight families are recognised, all of which feed mainly on large invertebrates and fish. Quite commonly seen from boats off Mozambique, the spinner dolphin is named for its occasional habit of pirouetting longitudinally when it leaps out of the water. Also present are the false killer whale, Blainville's whale, spinner dolphin, spotted dolphin, common dolphin and humpback dolphin.

Commonest in Mozambique's warm to temperate waters, however, is the bottlenose dolphin, which is the most globally abundant and widespread cetacean. Named for the elongated upper and lower jaws that create its characteristic smiling expression, it is dark grey above and paler below, grows to a length of up to four metres, weighs up to 650kg, and typically lives in pods of 3–12 individuals. Known for its friendly character and curiosity about humans, the bottlenose is often seen playing in the surf or swimming in the wake of a boat. It sometimes places a marine sponge on its beak as protection when it forages in the sandy sea bottom, the only known instance of tool use in a marine mammal.

The Bazaruto Archipelago is one of the last few strongholds for the dugong, a bulky (up to 1,000kg) marine mammal that feeds mainly on sea-grass and is placed alongside the manatee of the Atlantic Ocean in the family *Sirinia*, whose closest terrestrial relatives are elephants and hyraxes. The name *Sirinia*, a reference to the Sirens of Greek legend, has been given to this family of marine animals because they are considered the most likely source of the mermaid myth. Dugongs used to be abundant throughout the Indo-Pacific region, and as recently as the early 1970s groups of four to five were commonly seen in places like Inhambane, Angoche and even near Maputo. Unfortunately, they have suffered a drastic population decrease in the past few decades, probably because so many are trapped in fish nets. IUCN listed as Vulnerable, the dugong is now threatened with extinction except in the seas around northern Australia and the Arabian Gulf.

TURTLES The Mozambican coastline is one of the most regions globally for marine turtles, representatives of conservative reptilian lineage that first appeared in the fossil record more than 100 million years ago and had evidently evolved into distinctive modern genera some 60 million years back. Five marine turtle species are resident or regular visitors to the Mozambican coast, including the soft-shelled leatherback, which is the world's bulkiest marine reptile, the largest on record having measured about three metres long and weighed 916kg. More common, however, are the breeding green and loggerhead turtles, while other species that visit with varying degrees of regularity are the olive ridley and hawksbill.

Marine turtles remained common to abundant throughout their natural range until the late-19th century, since when the combination of hunting (for food, skin, and tortoiseshell), accidental trapping, habitat destruction and pollution has resulted in a serious decline in numbers. Indeed, of the seven recognized species, all but one is listed on the IUCN Red Data List, with eventual extinction being a distinct possibility for three Critically Endangered species (Kemp's ridley, hawksbill and leatherback).

The life cycle of marine turtles is unusual. Their full lifespan remains a matter of speculation, but most species reach sexual maturity in their twenties or later, and many individuals probably live for longer than a century. The main breeding season in Mozambique is between October and February, when male and female turtles converge offshore to mate. Once the eggs are ripe – usually on a moonlit night – the female crawls onto the beach to dig a 50cm-deep hole, lays up to 120 eggs, and covers them with sand, leaving them to hatch about two months later. Oddly, water temperature affects the sex of the hatchlings - a balance between male and female is to be expected at 28°C, but males will predominate on cooler waters, and females in warmer water.

FISH Although exact figures are unavailable, it is estimated that more than 2,000 species of marine fish, including 17 endemics, occur along the Mozambican coastline (a national tally boosted by around 350 freshwater species, including another 11 endemics, most of which are associated exclusively with Lago Niassa). For visitors, the most interesting marine fish fall into three broad categories. Most prolific among these are a kaleidoscopic miscellany of hundreds colourful reef fish, several dozen of which might be encountered on a single snorkelling or diving session. Less numerous but arguably more exciting are cartilaginous marine giants such as sharks and rays, which are something of a speciality of the coast around Tofo and Inhambane. Finally, there are the game fish – marlins, sailfish, barracuda and such – that attract dedicated fisherman (see box on page 189).

Among the cartilaginous fishes most eagerly sought by divers are the whale-shark, the world's largest fish, and the equally impressive manta ray, both of which employ similar filter-feeding methods to the baleen whales (see box on page 165 for more details). Many more actively predatory shark species occur off the Mozambican coast, among them the legendarily aggressive great white shark, which can grow up to eight metres long, and more docile ragged-toothed shark, the latter often seen by divers in the far south of the country. The region is also a stronghold for the Zambezi bull shark, a 300kg marine species that can live for long periods in freshwater, where it frequently attacks unsuspecting villagers as they bathe or do their laundry. Snorkelers and divers may also encounter several of the region's species of stingray, most of which have a 'wingspan' of around 75cm to 1.5 metres and tend to swim close to the sandy ocean floor.

Some of the world's finest and best preserved coral reefs lie off the shore of Mozambique, all the way from Ponta do Ouro on the South African border to the Quirimba Archipelago in the far north. These spectacular multihued natural aquaria form the focal point of most diving and snorkelling excursions in Mozambique, and support a total of about 800 reef fish species, with biodiversity increasing as you head further north. When exploring these reefs, one visual sweep of your surrounds might reveal a selection of a dozen or more species, whose memorable names reflect an extraordinary range of shapes and colours. There are the closely related devil's firefish and red lionfish, whose gaudy pattern and poisonous spines have the appearance of psychedelic marine porcupines. Other memorable genera and species include the brilliantly colourful sweet-lips, angelfishes, butterfly fishes and wrasses, the predatory honeycomb eel and scalloped hammerhead, and the elongated needlefish and outsized rock cods.

The oceanic waters off Mozambique are also home to the coelacanth, a peculiar two-metre long fish that was known only from fossils – and thought to have been extinct for more than 60 million years – prior to the discovery of the first living specimen of the southeast coast of South Africa in 1938. Now regarded to be the world's oldest surviving vertebrate species, the coelacanth is known to inhabits the underwater canyons carved into the continental shelf offshore the Mozambique/South African border area, where the first documentary footage of these extraordinary 'living fossils' was captured in the year 2000.

OTHER MARINE CREATURES The oceanic waters off Mozambique support a diversity of invertebrate species more remarkable even than its fish. For instance, coral, contrary to its rocklike appearances, is an organic entity comprising the limestone exoskeleton of colonial polyps that are related to sea anemones and feed mainly on photosynthetic algae, which thrive at a depth of up to 15 metres in warm aerated water along the continental shelf. One single reef might be composed of more than 50 different coral species, and as you examine the reefs closely, you see it is studded with studded with sea anemones, spiky predatory polyps that often possess a nasty sting. There are also thousands of sea molluscs, crustaceans and other creatures with shells or exoskeletons, among them crabs and crayfish, and rock-loving invertebrates such as mussels, oysters, barnacles and periwinkles, which are often associated with intertidal rock pools. Several islands off the north of Mozambique are home to the giant coconut crab, which can weigh up to 5kg, making it the world's largest terrestrial crustacean (see box on page 337).

3

Practical Information

WHEN TO VISIT

The coastal regions of Mozambique are best visited in the dry winter months of May through to October, when daytime temperatures are generally around 20–25°C. There is no major obstacle to visiting Mozambique during the summer months of November to April, except that climatic conditions are oppressively hot and humid at this time of year, especially along the north coast. Because most of the country's rain falls during the summer months, there is also an increased risk of contracting malaria and of dirt roads being washed out.

Unless you are a South African with children at school, it is emphatically worth avoiding the south coast of Mozambique during South African school holidays, when campsites as far north as Vilankulo tend to be very crowded and hotels are often fully booked. The exact dates of South African school holidays vary slightly on a provincial basis, but the main ones to avoid are those for Gauteng (the province that includes Johannesburg, South Africa's most populous city and only a day's drive from Maputo). To give a rough idea of the periods to avoid, there are four annual school holidays in Gauteng: a three-week holiday that starts in the last week of March and ends in the middle of April, a month-long holiday running from late June to late July, a two-week holiday starting in late September, and a six-week holiday from early December to mid January (for exact dates, check www.schoolguide.co.za/school_holidays.html or ask a South African embassy). If you do visit southern Mozambique during school holidays, then you should make reservations for all the hotels and campsites at which you plan to stay.

School holidays in landlocked Zimbabwe see a substantial influx of Zimbabwean tourists into southern Mozambique, so that most resorts between Beira and Xai-Xai are more crowded than usual. Provided that you have a tent, you shouldn't get stuck during these periods.

Few South Africans or Zimbabweans currently venture north of the Beira Corridor (the road and railway line linking Beira to the Zimbabwean border town of Mutare), so school holidays have no notable effect on tourist patterns in northern Mozambique.

HIGHLIGHTS

DESERTED BEACHES Most people who visit Mozambique, whether they're from South Africa, Zimbabwe or farther afield, do so for the country's coastal attractions. Indeed, there are few other countries in the world with such an extensive, beautiful and largely undeveloped coastline. This means that travellers will find truly deserted beaches, many of which stretch for kilometres on end, even at the more built-up resorts. The top upmarket beach destinations in Mozambique are the Bazaruto and

Quirimba archipelagos, while more affordable mainland options include Ponta do Ouro, Tofo (near Inhambane) and Vilankulo.

DIVING AND FISHING Once you have made the effort to get to these beaches, the opportunities for diving and fishing are among the best in southern Africa. Once again, the infrastructure underpinning these activities is still in its infancy, which means that dive sites are uncrowded and the fish varied and plentiful.

WHALES Another attraction of the southern Mozambican coastline is the very high probability of seeing humpback whales between September and the middle of November as they head north with their newly born calves, and Tofo has a reputation as being one of the best places in the world to see manta rays.

BIRDWATCHING Nature lovers, especially birdwatchers, will find plenty to see on dry land provided that they are prepared to make the effort to get to the country's national parks and reserves, the most accessible being Limpopo and Gorongosa national parks, both of which have seen considerable development in recent years. Animals are less numerous here than in the well-stocked parks of neighbouring countries, but the atmosphere is 100% wild.

HISTORIC TOWNS And then there are the towns. Sleepy, historic **Inhambane** would be a highlight on any African itinerary, and should not be missed by travellers to Mozambique. **Ilha de Moçambique** and **Ibo Island** are no less historic and even more compelling, although it will take slightly more effort to get to them. **Maputo**, meanwhile, is as clean and safe a city as you'll find in Africa; and with an increasing number of quality hotels, restaurants and other facilities, it's the perfect base for a trip around Mozambique.

THE PEOPLE However, the main highlight of a trip to Mozambique is the people. Generally unassuming, helpful, funny and honest, the Mozambicans are what really makes Mozambique one of the greatest travel destinations in Africa.

TOURIST INFORMATION

Resources are limited. Most tourist-orientated hotels will have a certain amount of tourist information available, although it's not always particularly up to date, and (certainly in the backpackers' hostels in Maputo) may well cover South Africa rather than Mozambique. There are also a couple of privately run tourist information offices in Mozambique, notably the tourist office in Vilankulo and Kaskazini in Pemba. The Pink Papaya in Chimoio and Ruby Backpackers on Ilha de Moçambique are both run by well-informed and helpful owner-managers. A growing body of useful websites is headed by Mike Slater's estimable www.mozguide.com and the excellent www.ofroadandsea.com. Useful sources of non-travel information include www.ilhademo.net (a website chock-full of information about Ilha de Moçambique) and www.poptel.org.uk/mozambique-news (the English version of the Mozambican news agency).

TOUR OPERATORS

UK

Aardvark Safaris 01980 849160 or 01578 760222; e mail@aardvarksafaris.com; www.aardvarksafaris.com. Offers tailor-made safaris using small, owner-run camps. ATOL protected.

Africa Explorer www.africa-explorer.co.uk. Specialist in tailor-made safaris across southern Africa.

Africa Travel 0845 450 1520; f 0207 7383 7512; e info@africatravel.co.uk; www.africatravel.co.uk. Tailor-made specialist with 25 years' experience; offers beach resorts, island retreats, city hotels & flights.

Audley Travel 01993 838500; www.audleytravel.com. Award-winning UK operator with top-notch selection of Mozambican itineraries.

Baobab Travel Ltd 0121 314 6011; e info@baobabtravel.com; www.baobabtravel.com. UK-based tour operator specialising in tailor-made African holidays promoting a form of responsible tourism.

Bridge & Wickers 020 7483 6575; e africa@bridgeandwickers.com; www.bridgeandwickers.co.uk. A knowledgeable team of Mozambique specialists (they've all visited several times) & particular expertise in the best places to dive.

Definitive Africa & Indian Ocean 0161 9292 5151; e enquiry@definitive-indianocean.com; www.definitive-africa.com or www.definitive-indianocean.com. Small independent tour operator specialising in tailor-made itineraries throughout east & southern Africa.

Expert Africa 020 8232 9777; e info@expertafrica.com; www.expertafrica.com. Knowledgeable African safari company offering an unusually wide choice of options on Mozambique's islands.

Explore Worldwide 0845 013 1537; e info@explore.co.uk; www.explore.co.uk. Offers small-group adventure holidays with the emphasis on responsible tourism.

Imagine Africa 020 7622 5114; e info@imagineafrica.co.uk; www.imagineafrica.co.uk Has 25 years of travel experience of luxury safari & beach holidays to Africa & the Indian Ocean, including Mozambique.

J & C Voyageurs Ltd 01373 832111; e info@jandcvoyageurs.com; www.jandcvoyageurs.com. Individually tailored holidays, specialising in small exclusive beach & safari properties.

Mozambique Odyssey 020 7471 8780; e info@mozambiqueodyssey.com; www.mozambiqueodyssey.com. Tailor-made itineraries in Mozambique including the island archipelagos of Quirimba & Bazaruto.

Okavango Tours & Safaris 020 8347 4030; e info@okavango.com; www.okavango.com. Individually tailored safaris combined with barefoot luxury on beaches.

Rainbow Tours 020 7226 1004; e info@rainbowtours.co.uk; www.rainbowtours.co.uk. Award-winning UK-based tour operator offering tailor-made beach & safari holidays, especially to Bazaruto & the Quirimbas.

Steppes Travel 01285 880980; e enquiry@steppestravel.co.uk; www.steppestravel.co.uk. Steppes Travel offers luxury tailor-made holidays to both southern & northern Mozambique.

Tim Best Travel 020 7591 0300; e info@timbesttravel.com; www.timbesttravel.com. Specialises in tailor-made safaris, family holidays & honeymoons.

Time for...Travel 01798 867750; e sales@timefortravel.co.uk; www.timefortravel.co.uk. Tailor-made holidays to Africa & the Indian Ocean islands.

Trailfinders 0845 058 5858; www.trailfinders.com. Over 20 offices around the UK. Includes Mozambique among the 10 African countries it visits.

Travelbag 0870 703 4698; www.travelbag.co.uk. Various offices around the UK; specialises in package tours worldwide, including Mozambique.

World Odyssey 01905 731373; e info@world-odyssey.com; www.world-odyssey.com. Arranges tailor-made holidays to the Bazaruto & Quirimba archipelagos in Mozambique.

Zambezi Safari & Travel Co Ltd 01548 830059; e info@zambezi.com; www.zambezi.com. UK- & Africa-based safari specialists operating through east & southern Africa. ATOL protected.

US

Ker & Downey 6703 Highway Bd, Katy, TX 77494; toll-free US & Canada +1 800 423 4236; e safari@kerdowney.com; kerdowney.com. Upmarket southern African safaris with beach extensions to Bazaruto & the Quirimbas.

Tropical Birding 1 409 515 0514; e info@tropicalbirding.com; www.tropicalbirding.com. Offers small-group custom tours focused on birding in numerous countries, including Mozambique.

AFRICA

Dana Tours Lda ☎ +258 214 95514; e natalie@danatours.net; www.danatours.net. Small, efficient Maputo-based company offering tailor-made itineraries.

Kaskazini m +258 82 309 6990; e info@kaskazani.com; www.kaskazini.com. Based in Pemba, these helpful folk are the acknowledged on-the-ground experts in travel in the northern provinces of Niassa, Nampula & Cabo Delgado.

Mozaic Travel ☎ +258 21 451380; m 82 328 0520; e mozaictravel@gmail.com; www.mozaictravel.com. Excellent Maputo-based owner-managed company specialising in safaris & beach holidays countrywide.

Mozambique Connection PO Box 2861, Rivonia 212; ☎ +27 11 803 4185; f +27 11803 3861; e bookings@mozcon.com; www.mozcon.com

Mozambique Travel ☎ + 27 21 702 0285; e admin@mozambiquetravel.com; www.mozambiquetravel.com. Based in Cape Town, this specialist Mozambique operator has hands-on managers who know the country backwards & can put together everything from honeymoon trips & beach holidays to birding trips & safaris. It also operates a website advertising special offers (*www.mozambiquespecials.com*).

Pulse Africa Johannesburg; ☎ +27 11 325 2290; e info@pulseafrica.com; www.pulseafrica.com. Booking agent for flights & beach packages to Mozambique.

Rani Resorts ☎ +258 213 01618; e enquiries@raniresorts.com; www.raniresorts.com. Tailor-made fly-in itineraries to the Niassa Reserve & some of the country's top beach retreats.

Unusual Destinations ☎ +27 11 706 1991; e info@unusualdestinations.com; www.unusualdestinations.com

GLOBAL

Flight Centre www.flightcentre.com. Offices in Australia, Canada, New Zealand, South Africa, the UK & the US.

STA Travel www.statravel.com. Operates in more than 20 countries.

RED TAPE

A valid passport is required to enter Mozambique. The date of expiry should be at least six months after you intend to end your travels; if it is likely to expire before that, get a new passport.

VISAS

South Africans If you are travelling on a South African passport (or one from another neighbouring country) you no longer need a visa to enter Mozambique – when you turn up at the border you will be given a free entry permit valid for up to 30 days. However, these permits cannot be extended in Mozambique itself – if you intend staying longer then you will either need to get a single-entry visa valid for the required period in advance, or you must leave and re-enter Mozambique before that month expires.

All other nationalities Visas are required by everyone else. In the past you had to go to an embassy in advance, but these days you can buy a single-entry visa valid for 30 days at all normal ports of entry (international airports and major overland borders). This costs US$50 at most borders but the price can vary. Multiple-entry visas or single-entry visas valid for longer than 30 days must be bought in advance at a Mozambican embassy or consulate. Note that the immigration office in Chimoio is currently something of an exception insofar as it will usually extend a 30-day visa bought at the border (check with Pink Papaya for details of how to go about this).

CUSTOMS Vigorous steps have been taken recently to eradicate corruption in the Mozambique customs service. New staff have been recruited and trained, and there is even a special authority to deal with officials who attempt to solicit bribes during the course of their duties. Those who have a legitimate complaint should contact the Internal Irregularities Unit in Maputo (☎ *+258 21 308 584*), taking note of the fact that offering or paying a bribe is also a criminal offence.

Import limits

Groceries	US$50 per person (for which you may need to provide receipts)
Alcohol	2.25l of wine and 1l of spirits
Tobacco	400 cigarettes or 100 small cigars or 50 big cigars or 250g loose tobacco
Perfume	50ml
Medication	Reasonable quantities for personal use
Firearms	Only permitted with special licence

Narcotics and **pornography** are prohibited

Currency controls You are not permitted to take more than 50,000 meticais (about US$1,450) out of the country. Quite what you'd do with 50,000 meticais once you've left is another question.

EMBASSIES, CONSULATES AND HIGH COMMISSIONS A full list of Mozambican embassies and consulates outside the country can be found at www.embassiesabroad.com/embassies-of/Mozambique. A selection of those most likely to be useful to readers is as follows:

Belgium 97 Bd Saint Michel, B-1040 Brussels; ☎ +32 2 736 0096/2564; e mozambiqueembassy@yahoo.com
France 82 Rue Laugier, 75017 Paris; ☎ +33 1 47 64 91 32; e embamocparis@compuserve.com
Germany Strom Strasse 47, 10551 Berlin; ☎ +49 30 398 76500/1/2; e emoza@aol.com
Malawi Lilongwe ☎ +265 1784100; e mozambique@malawi.net; Blantyre ☎ +265 1643189 e mozamcons@malawi.net
Portugal Av de Berna 71050, Lisbon; ☎ +351 21 797 1994; e embamoc.portugal@minec.gov.mz
South Africa Pretoria ☎ +27 12 401 0300; Johannesburg ☎ +27 11 325 5714; e cgeral@intekom.co.za; Cape Town ☎ +27 21 426 2944/5, e mozcpt@kingsley.co.za; Durban ☎ +27 31 304 0200, e mozamcom@mweb.co.za; Nelspruit ☎ +27 13 752 7396
Swaziland Highlands View, Princess Drive Rd, Mbabane; ☎ +268 404 1296; e moz.high-swd@africaonline.co.sz
Tanzania 25 Garden Av, PO Box 9370, Dar es Salaam; ☎ +255 22 211 6502; e embamoc@africaonline.co.tz
UK 21 Fitzroy Sq, London W1T 6EL; ☎ 020 7383 3800; www.mozambiquehighcommission.org.uk
US 1990 M St, NW Suite 570, Washington, DC 20036; ☎ +1 202 293 7146; www.embamoc-usa.org
Zambia 9592 Kacha Rd, Northmead, Lusaka; ☎ +260 1 239 135; e mozhclsk@zamnet.zm
Zimbabwe 152 Herbert Chitepo Av, Harare; ☎ +263 4 253 871; e embamoc@embamoc.org.zw

GETTING THERE AND AWAY

BY AIR The only airlines with direct flights to/from Europe are the national carrier LAM (*www.lam.co.mz*) and TAP Air Portugal (*www.flytap.com*). In both instances this will involve routing through Lisbon (unless that is where you are flying from anyway). Another reasonably direct option from certain European cities, including London, is Kenya Airways (*www.kenya-airways.com*), routing through Nairobi.

It is more common for European and other intercontinental visitors to fly to Johannesburg (South Africa) and transfer to Mozambique from there. LAM and South African Airways (*www.flysaa.com*) operate plenty of flights daily between Johannesburg and Maputo, and the former also flies from Maputo to all provincial capitals in Mozambique. Other options are Pelican Air (*www.pelicanair.co.za*) from Johannesburg to Maputo; SA Airlink (*www.saairlink.co.za*) from Durban to Maputo or from Johannesburg to Beira, Tete or Pemba; or ETA Travelmax (*www.etatravelmax.co.za*) from Johannesburg to Vilankulo or Inhambane.

Provided that you have a valid passport and visa, and a return ticket, you should whizz through the entrance formalities at Mozambique's international airports with a minimum of fuss.

BY LAND Provided you arrive at the border with a visa, you should have no problem entering Mozambique overland, nor is there a serious likelihood of being asked about onward tickets, funds or vaccination certificates. About the worst you can expect at customs is a cursory search of your luggage (see *Customs*, page 42).

If you have a car ... Things are a little more complex, although not outrageously. You'll need a 'temporary export document' (signed by immigration authorities) from whichever country you are coming from before you can pass through the exit gate at the border post. Both need to be taken to the customs officials on the Mozambican side who'll stamp them and charge you a nominal fee, payable in meticais. Before you leave them check the expiry date of the export documents – they may not be the same as the expiry date on your visa. You will also need to buy third-party insurance, which will cost around US$20 for a car and a further US$10 if you have a trailer as well. If you do have a trailer then you have to have a little triangular blue-and-orange sign on the front of your car and the back of your trailer. Once you have your stamped export document and insurance papers, take them to a third official who will sign off your gate pass and check your vehicle. Don't forget to get your passport stamped too! More advice on driving in Mozambique starts on page 56.

CHANGING MONEY AT BORDERS

At most land borders there is nowhere to change money legally, which means that you may have to change money with a private individual. Although this is not always strictly legal, the trade is conducted perfectly openly at most borders – though obviously it is wise to be discreet in the presence of officialdom. Generally, the rates you get at borders are lower than they would be elsewhere, because the moneychangers need to make a profit on transactions in both directions. At some borders, there's a lot of hustle attached to changing money privately, and especially along the Beira Corridor there is a real risk of being conned.

One solution would be to arrange in advance to be carrying money for the country you are entering – ask travellers coming in the opposite direction if they have any leftover cash to swap. If you can't do this, try to carry a small surplus of the currency from the country you are leaving (say around US$20) and to change this at the border rather than using up your hard currency. Whatever else you do, try to establish the rough exchange rate in advance and avoid changing significantly more than you will need until you can get to a bank. It is a good idea to keep the money you intend to change separate from the rest of your hard currency and/or travellers' cheques.

Overland routes into Mozambique Mozambique has land borders with an unusually large number of other countries: South Africa, Swaziland, Zimbabwe, Zambia, Malawi and Tanzania.

South Africa

Ponta do Ouro: Kosi Bay (🕘 *08.00–17.00*) This border on the southern coast is normally used to get to and from Ponta do Ouro and the other resorts in the deep south of the country. Road links to Maputo (and hence the rest of the country) are poor and you'll need a 4x4.

Ressano Garcia: Komatipoort (🕘 *07.00–20.00, although apparently it's open 24 hours during the busy December holiday period*) The most-used border between South Africa and Mozambique; the road links to Maputo and further north are good-quality tarmac. If you're travelling by public transport, there is a daily train to Maputo from Ressano Garcia and plenty of buses on both sides.

Giriyondo (*Oct–Mar 08.00–16.00; 08.00–15.00 at other times. Visas are issued in 10mins*) The main crossing within the Greater Limpopo Transfrontier Park is 95km from Phalaborwa via Letaba Rest Camp, and about 450km from Maputo. A vehicle with good ground clearance is recommended, but a 4x4 is not essential.

Pafuri: Pafuri (🕘 *08.00–16.00*) This little-used crossing is way up at the northern end of Greater Limpopo Transfrontier Park. 4x4 essential.

Swaziland

Namaacha: Namaacha (🕘 *07.00–20.00*) This busy crossing is up in the Swazi Mountains. A quieter alternative for self-drivers is the Goba border post a short distance further south.

Zimbabwe

Espungabera: Mount Selina (🕘 *06.00–18.00*) Little known and little used in the Chimanimani Mountains, this is probably only for those with their own transport and a hankering for roughing it.

Machipanda: Mutare (🕘 *06.00–18.00*) The western end of the Beira Corridor and a major route both for trade goods and Zimbabwean holidaymakers. The road is good-quality tarmac all the way to the Indian Ocean.

Nyamapanda (🕘 *06.00–18.00*) The western end of the Tete Corridor between Zimbabwe and Malawi and a well-trodden route for both tourists and freight. The road is good-quality tarmac all the way to Malawi.

Mucumbura: Mukumbura (🕘 *06.00–18.00*) Far less well known.

Zambia

Zumbo: Luangwa (🕘 *08.00–15.00*) One of the most intriguing crossings but also one of the most remote. The border is reputedly crossable only by dugout canoe.

Cassacatiza (🕘 *06.00–18.00*) The major trade route between Zambia and Mozambique, though still pretty minor by other standards.

Malawi

Calómuè: Dedza (🕘 *06.00–18.00*) Less used than the Zobue crossing further south, this is the most direct route to Lilongwe. It is about 125km further on from Zobue though, so if you're transiting from Zimbabwe to Malawi you'd probably end up spending a night in Mozambique if you try to use this border.

Zóbuè: Mwanza (🕘 *06.00–18.00*) The eastern end of the Tete Corridor and the most common route for travellers.

Milange: Muloza (🕘 *06.00–18.00*) A busy trade border, but little used by travellers.

Entre Lagos: Nayuchi (🕘 *06.00–18.00*) Formerly one of the more popular routes for tourists, but not since trains stopped running through here.

Mandimba: Chiponde (🕘 *06.00–18.00*) The road from Mandimba runs down to Mangochi at the bottom end of Lake Malawi and is really rather attractive. This crossing links in with the passenger train service from Cuamba to Nampula (for Ilha de Moçambique or Pemba).

Cóbùe: Likoma The Likoma Islands are in Mozambican waters but are Malawian territory. See pages 353–5 for further details on this crossing.

Tanzania

Namuiranga: Mwambo (🕘 *08.00–16.00*) The Ruvuma River is one of the tougher crossings, not so much for the river itself but because of the effort it takes to get to there in the first place. The new Unity Bridge further west is the better option for self-drivers. See page 319 for more details.

CRIME AND SAFETY

THEFT AND VIOLENCE Bearing in mind that no country in the world is totally free of crime, and that tourists to so-called developing nations are always conspicuously wealthy targets, Mozambique is a relatively low-risk country so far as crime is concerned. Compared with parts of Kenya and South Africa, mugging is rare, and the sort of con tricks that abound in Nairobi and Dar es Salaam even rarer. Petty theft such as pickpocketing and bag-snatching is a risk in markets and other crowded places, but on a scale that should prompt caution rather than paranoia. Walking around large towns at night feels safe enough, though it would be tempting fate to wander alone along unlit streets or to carry large sums of money or valuables. On the basis that it is preferable to err on the side of caution, here are a few tips that apply to travelling anywhere in Africa:

- Most casual thieves operate in busy markets and bus stations. Keep a close watch on your possessions in such places, and avoid having valuables or large amounts of money loose in your daypack or pocket.
- Keep all your valuables and the bulk of your money in a hidden money belt. Never show this money belt in public. Keep any spare cash you need elsewhere on your person.
- A buttoned-up pocket on the front of the shirt is one of the most secure places as money cannot be snatched from it without the thief coming into your view. It is also advisable to keep a small amount of hard currency (ideally cash)

REPORTING A CRIME

Danny Edmunds

If you're unlucky enough to be robbed while you're in Mozambique then you will need to report this to the police for insurance purposes. The process is very different from what we are used to in Europe, so here are my experiences of the process.

I had a daypack stolen from a pensão in Nampula. The door wasn't damaged and I had the key in my pocket – you can come to your own conclusions about how the thieves got into my room. In order to report the crime I had to visit one of the police stations. The desk officer called over a sergeant who took basic details and dispatched another officer back to the pensão with me. The officer spoke to the pensão staff but showed no interest in seeing the room, checking for fingerprints, or any of the sort of forensic examination I'd expect in the UK. After an hour, we went back to the police station where he spoke to the sergeant who told me and three of the members of staff to return the next morning to give statements.

The statements were taken in public in front of the staff in a small open booth with me sitting on one side and the three staff sitting on the other. It took place in Portuguese, with the result that much of what was being said went over my head, but after around two hours I did get a copy of the statement from the officer, although they didn't have a photocopier in the station so we had to go elsewhere and make the copy there. I was then given a crime number and asked to return in a few days' time.

On my return I was directed to the Criminal Investigations Department where, after a certain amount of looking through the ledgers of crimes on their desk, I was given a second crime number and somewhat to my surprise asked to go to the tribunal the next morning. The tribunal wasn't the court I was expecting, but a large room crammed with desks covered in paper. After an hour's fruitless looking through the piles of papers, they took my details and said that they'd ring me back. Needless to say no phone call ever arrived.

Just to add insult to injury, the insurance company have turned down my claim on the grounds that no damage was caused to the door of the room I was staying in – best check your policies to see if they're likely to try the same trick on you.

hidden away in your luggage so that, should you lose your money belt, you have something to fall back on.

- Where the choice exists between carrying valuables on your person or leaving them in a locked room, the latter option is generally safer, though obviously you should use your judgement and be sure the room is absolutely secure. Some travellers' cheque companies will not refund cheques stolen from a room, or might reject the claim on a technicality, for instance if the door wasn't damaged during the robbery.
- Leave any jewellery of financial or sentimental value at home.

BANDITRY Mozambique has a long history of banditry. During the civil war, a significant risk of being held up at gunpoint was attached to driving practically anywhere in the country. This risk has abated in the past few years, but it still exists, though it is probably only of concern to people driving themselves through Mozambique, and seems to be confined to the south coast. Incidents are probably fairly random, and they appear to be related to the car-hijacking syndicates that are rife in South Africa, which means that new minibuses, pick-up trucks and 4x4s are probably at greater risk of being hijacked than are older vehicles and saloon cars. For South Africans, the risk of armed hijacking is probably less than it would be in Johannesburg.

There are certainly a few precautions you can take against hijacking. The first and most obvious is never to drive at night, and to set off travelling as early as possible so that you have the maximum available time to deal with unexpected car problems during daylight hours. In Johannesburg, most people now drive around with doors permanently locked and windows raised high enough so that nobody can reach in and open the lock – an obvious precaution in an urban context, perhaps less so in rural Mozambique, but one that can do no harm.

BRIBERY, FINES AND BUREAUCRACY Corruption is widespread, though as a tourist you are most likely to see it at roadblocks, when the driver of your *chapa* will slip the traffic policeman something to ease the journey. If you are driving your own vehicle, then you are a little more vulnerable (see page 56). If you are fined for any reason, then you should be given a receipt for the payment – this will usually entail going to a police station. If the officer seems reluctant to go to a police station, there is a good chance that he is trying to bump up his income.

One thing that has to be stated is that offering or paying a bribe is a criminal offence in Mozambique, and there is an established anti-corruption programme, though it is not clear whether any local pays it a blind bit of notice (see *Customs*, page 42).

If you do happen to get caught in an extended attempt to extract a bribe, taking out your mobile phone and saying you're going to ring your embassy can make a distinct difference (although for obvious reasons it only works in an area where you have reception). The British embassy maintains a record of bribe attempts that it passes to the Mozambican government on a regular basis, and other embassies may also do this. If you are forced to go to this extreme, get the officer's name and number– all police officers are required to carry ID papers while on duty and produce them when requested.

There is a tendency to portray African bureaucrats as difficult and inefficient in their dealings with tourists. As a rule, this reputation says more about Western prejudices than it does about Mozambique. Sure, you come across the odd unhelpful official, but that's the nature of the beast everywhere in the world and the vast majority of officials encountered in Africa have been courteous and helpful in their dealings with tourists, often to a degree that is almost embarrassing. The most frustrating aspect of Mozambican officialdom is the length of time that it seems to take to do anything. Once you accept that, it is usually quite straightforward to deal with them.

The biggest factor in determining the response you receive from African officials will be your own attitude. If you walk into every official encounter with an aggressive, paranoid approach, you are quite likely to kindle the feeling held by many Africans that Europeans are arrogant and offhand in their dealings with other races. Instead, try to be friendly and patient, and to accept that the person to whom you are talking probably doesn't speak English. Treat people with respect rather than disdain, and they'll tend to treat you in the same way.

LAND MINES The de-mining programme in Mozambique is co-ordinated by Instituto Nacional de Desminagem (IND), a branch of the Mozambican government, and they will be able to give you up-to-date information on the current land-mine situation across the country. The IND is based in Maputo (*1746 R da Resistência; +258 21 410 400; www.ind.gov.mz*), and its public relations officer is Mr Benjamin Sitoe (*bsitoe@ind.gov.mz*). These days, however, the situation in Mozambique is far better than it is generally portrayed. At the end of the civil war, there were estimates of over two million land mines in the country, many in poorly marked locations, and de-mining operations were given a high priority. It now appears that these estimates were somewhat over-pessimistic, and much of what was there has now been cleared, leaving most of the country safe for travel. In practice, there is nothing to worry about, unless you are travelling way off the beaten track, in which case tapping into local knowledge will prove invaluable.

FOCUS ON SPECIFIC GROUPS

WOMEN TRAVELLERS Women travellers generally regard sub-equatorial Africa as one of the safest places to travel alone anywhere in the world. Mozambique in particular poses few if any risks specific to female travellers. It is reasonable to expect a fair bit of flirting and the odd direct proposition, especially if you mingle in local bars, but a firm 'no' should be enough to defuse any potential situation. To be fair to Mozambican men, you can expect the same sort of thing in any country, and – probably with a far greater degree of persistence – from many male travellers.

Presumably as a result of Frelimo's pro-feminist leanings, Mozambican women tend to dress and behave far less conservatively than their counterparts in neighbouring countries. You will often see evidently 'respectable' women drinking in bars and smoking on the street, behaviour that is seen as the preserve of males and prostitutes in many other parts of east and southern Africa. As for dress codes, Muslims in Mozambique seem far less orthodox than in some other African countries, but overly revealing clothes will undoubtedly attract the attention of males.

Tampons are not readily available in smaller towns, though you should be able to locate them in Beira and Maputo. If you're travelling in out-of-the-way places, it's advisable to carry enough to see you through to the next time you'll be in a large city, bearing in mind that travelling in the tropics can sometimes cause women to have heavier or more regular periods than they would at home.

GAY TRAVELLERS In common with many African countries, male homosexuality is illegal in Mozambique, and while the law makes no specific reference to lesbianism, this should probably be viewed as a token of judicial denial rather than tolerance. In practice, however, there is little if any legal persecution of gays, social taboos are not nearly as strong as in the likes of Uganda, and a gay rights movement called the Mozambique Association for Sexual Minority Rights (LAMBDA) has been active in the country (albeit unregistered) since 2006. As such, while gay travellers are unlikely to encounter any problems in Mozambique, unless perhaps they make a point of drawing attention to their sexual orientation, there is to the best of our knowledge nothing, not even in Maputo, that could be described as a gay scene.

TRAVELLING WITH CHILDREN The south coast has several resort areas – Bilene, Ponta do Ouro, Xai-Xai, Tofo and Vilankulo among them – whose main high season clientele comprises South African families containing children of all ages. However, while there is no obstacle to visiting these places with children, it should be noted that most South African visitors focus strongly on fishing and other marine activities, usually bringing all their own gear, and there are few public facilities aimed at

TRAVELLERS WITH DISABILITIES

Gordon Rattray (www.able-travel.com)

Mozambique's idyllic coastal resorts and stunning colonial architecture are, by their very nature, relatively inaccessible. Soft sand, potholed pavements and steep stone stairways are certain wheelchair stoppers, and will challenge even those with fewer mobility problems. However, if you are well organised, prepared to compromise, and can put up with some hardship, then a rewarding visit is quite possible.

ACCOMMODATION I have yet to hear of accommodation in Mozambique that has made serious efforts to include people with disabilities. Occasionally (more by accident than design) bathrooms will be reachable in a wheelchair, but where this is not the case you should be prepared to improvise.

The more upmarket the hotel, the greater the chance that the rooms will be spacious and have conveniences (essential for some people) such as bedside telephones. Research your options thoroughly in advance; most good tour operators will take time to listen to your needs. If you prefer to travel independently, many establishments can be found and contacted directly using the internet.

TRANSPORT

By air For people with mobility problems, entering and exiting aircraft will not be as slick a procedure as you may be used to. It is unlikely that there will be an aisle chair or wheelchairs in the airport, especially in smaller domestic terminals, and staff might not be used to handling disabled travellers.

By bus These are often crowded, with no facilities for wheelchairs, and getting off and on can be a hectic affair. You may need to ask fellow passengers to help you to your seat, though this will rarely be a problem.

By car Unless you use local taxis, most vehicles will be 4x4s or minibuses, which are higher than normal cars. For some people, this is easier; for others, more difficult. Although drivers and guides are normally happy to help, they are not trained in this skill. Thoroughly explain your needs before transferring, and stay in control of the situation. Distances are great and roads can be bumpy, so people prone to skin damage need to take extra care. It may be a good idea to place your own pressure-relieving cushion on top of the original car seat and pad your knees and elbows if necessary.

HEALTH AND INSURANCE Doctors will know about everyday illnesses, but you must understand and be able to explain your particular medical requirements. African hospitals are often basic, so if possible, take all less-common medication and

youngsters. The rest of Mozambique offers quite challenging travel conditions, and lacks child-specific facilities, so it should only be attempted with children who have experienced (and enjoyed) travel in more mainstream destinations.

WHAT TO TAKE

LUGGAGE If you intend using public transport or doing much hiking, it's best to carry your luggage on your back. There are three ways of doing this: with a purpose-made backpack, with a suitcase that converts to a rucksack, or with a large daypack.

equipment with you. It is advisable to pack this in your hand luggage during flights in case your main luggage gets lost, though liquid medications may be better kept in checked luggage due to security restrictions on liquids.

Mozambique can be hot. If this is a problem for you, be careful to book accommodation with fans or air conditioning. A useful cooling aid is a plant-spray bottle.

Travel insurance can be purchased in the UK from Age UK (*0845 600 3348; www.ageuk.org.uk*), who have no upper age limit, and Free Spirit (*0845 230 5000; www.free-spirit.com*), who cater for people with pre-existing medical conditions. most insurance companies will insure disabled travellers, but it is essential that they are made aware of your disability.

SECURITY For anyone following the usual security precautions (see page 46) the chances of robbery are greatly reduced. In fact, as a disabled person I often feel more noticed in public places, and therefore a less attractive target for thieves. But the opposite may also apply, so do stay aware of where your bags are and who is around you, especially during car transfers and similar activities.

SPECIALIST OPERATORS

Endeavour Safaris 23 Lark Crescent, 7441 Table View, Flamingo Vlei, Cape Town, South Africa; +27 (0)21 556 6114; e info@endeavour-safaris.com; www.endeavour-safaris.com. Specialists in accessible travel for people with disabilities.

FURTHER INFORMATION

Books Bradt Travel Guides' new title *Access Africa – Safaris for People with Limited Mobility* is packed with useful advice and resources for disabled adventure travellers.

Online

www.able-travel.com A regularly updated website with both worldwide and country-specific info.

www.globalaccessnews.com A searchable database of disability travel information.

www.rollingrains.com A searchable website advocating disability travel.

www.youreable.com A UK-based general resource for disability information, with an active forum.

www.apparelyzed.com A site dedicated to spinal injury, but containing info that people with other disabilities will also find useful. It also hosts a hugely popular forum.

The choice between a convertible suitcase or a purpose-built backpack rests mainly on your style of travel. If you intend doing a lot of hiking, you're definitely best off with a proper backpack. However, if you carry everything in a smaller 35–45-litre day pack, the advantages are manifold on public transport and in terms of overall mobility.

CAMPING GEAR Accommodation in Mozambique isn't as cheap as it used to be, so you can make a significant saving by carrying camping gear – a lightweight tent, a bedroll and a sleeping bag. For most purposes, a light sheet sleeping bag is as useful as the real thing, performing the important role of enclosing and insulating your body, and your tent should be as light as possible. Camping gear probably won't squeeze into a daypack, in which case a sensible compromise is to carry a large daypack in your rucksack. That way, you can carry a tent and other camping equipment when you need it, but at other times you can reduce your luggage to fit into a daypack and leave what you're not using in storage.

MONEY BELT It is advisable to carry all your hard currency and credit cards, as well as your passport and other important documentation, in a money belt. The ideal money belt for Africa can be hidden beneath your clothing, as externally worn money belts are as good as telling thieves that all your valuables are there for the taking. Use a money belt made of cotton or another natural fabric, though bearing in mind that such fabrics tend to soak up a lot of sweat, you will need to wrap plastic around everything inside the money belt.

CLOTHING If you're carrying your luggage on your back, restrict your clothes to the minimum, ie: one or two pairs of trousers and/or skirts, one pair of shorts, three shirts or T-shirts, at least one sweater (or similar) depending on when and where you are visiting, enough socks and underwear to last a week, one pair of solid shoes and one of flip-flops or sandals.

Ideally, bring light cotton or microfibre trousers. Jeans are also great for durability, but they can be uncomfortable in hot weather and slow to dry after washing. Skirts, like trousers, are best made of a light fabric, and should reach below the knee (short skirts will cause needless offence to some Muslim Mozambicans and may be perceived as provocative). Any fast-drying, lightweight shirts are good, but pack at least one with long sleeves for sun protection. For general purposes, one warm sweater or fleece should be adequate. During the rainy season, it's worth carrying a light waterproof jacket or an umbrella.

Socks and underwear must be made from natural fabrics, and bear in mind that re-using them when sweaty will encourage fungal infections such as athlete's foot, as well as prickly heat in the groin. Socks and underpants are light and compact enough to make it worth bringing a week's supply. As for shoes, bulky hiking boots are probably over the top for most people, but a good pair of walking shoes, preferably with some ankle support, is recommended. It's also useful to carry sandals, flip-flops or other light shoes.

OTHER USEFUL ITEMS A mobile phone (unlocked or get it unlocked in any city) will be useful. You can buy a local SIM card for next to nothing and top-up cards are readily available and inexpensive. This also doubles as your alarm clock for any early starts.

Binoculars are essential for close-up views of wildlife, especially birds. Compact binoculars are more backpack-friendly, but their restricted field of vision compared with that of traditional binoculars can make it difficult to pick up animals in thick bush. For most purposes, 7x magnification is fine, but birdwatchers might find a 10x magnification more useful.

If you stay in local hotels, carry a padlock, as many places don't supply them. You should also carry a towel, soap, shampoo, toilet paper and any other toiletries you need (all of which are now available in Shoprite and some other supermarkets, including tampons). A torch is essential as electricity is never guaranteed. Another perennial favourite is a Swiss Army knife or multi-purpose tool.

Secondhand English-language novels can often be exchanged at beach resorts or backpackers, but you won't find them on sale in many places, so it's a good idea to bring a few with you.

If travelling in your own vehicle, make sure you have a good set of tools, a selection of wire, string and rope, your driver's licence and the vehicle's registration papers (and a letter of permission to use the vehicle if it is not registered in your name). Depending on how far, where and when you're driving, you might also consider spare engine oil, a jerrycan for fuel, a fan belt, spare fuses and a fluorescent light that plugs into the cigarette lighter.

Medical kits and other health-related subjects are discussed in *Chapter 4, Health*, but do note that contact lens solutions may not be available, so bring enough to last the whole trip – and bring glasses in case the intense sun and dry climate irritates your eyes.

ELECTRICAL Electricity is 220V AC at 50Hz cycles and available in most towns and cities across the country. You're less likely to find it in rural areas or the remoter towns in the north. Two-pin plugs are in use and there is no earthing wire. Stabilisers are required for sensitive devices and adaptors for appliances using 110V. AA and D batteries sold on the street are made in China and mostly of very poor quality. You can get higher-quality Western batteries in Maputo, Beira and Nampula, but expect to pay a premium. If you need any other type of battery, you're strongly advised to bring them with you. With rechargeable batteries, your charger should work perfectly well all over the country.

MAPS Backpackers and other travellers who need a good map of Mozambique for hitching or driving purposes have a few choices. Arguably the most useful is the German *Reise Know How Mosambik & Malawi* (*www.reise-know-how.de*), which is up to date and accurate, and contains a wealth of information without being cluttered. It's also waterproof and claims to be tear-proof, something you hopefully won't need to put to the test. Also recommended is the Map Studio's *Mozambique Road Atlas* (*www.mapstudio.com*), which has lots of town plans and regional maps, but tends to be less accurate.

DOCUMENTATION You are legally required to carry identification papers with you at all times, which in practice means your passport. If this gives you the willies, then a notarised copy is acceptable. There are photocopy shops in all the provincial capitals and you should be able to find a lawyer permitted to notarise those photocopies as well.

$ MONEY

The Mozambican unit of currency, the metical (Mt, plural meticais) used to be one of those slightly daft African currencies where you have to work in tens of thousands to buy anything (the exchange rate in January 2007, for instance, was around Mt26,000 to US$1). Since then, however, the currency has been redenominated by a factor of 1,000, so that Mt5,000 is now Mt5. Old notes ceased to be street legal on 31 December 2006, but should you happen to end up with some old currency it can be exchanged for new currency in the banks until the end of 2012.

In some places you may find it easier to use foreign currency than meticais. South African rand (ZAR) can be used at many South African-owned resorts in the south of the country, many of which price themselves in ZAR rather than Mt.

Up on the shores of Lake Malawi, Malawian kwacha are easier to use than meticais, predominantly because of the greater availability of change for kwacha.

TRAVELLERS' CHEQUES Travellers' cheques are not as useful as they used to be, and an exorbitant commission is charged at the few outlets that accept them. These days, the ATM network is so good that it has to be the preferred method of accessing currency.

CASH You won't have any problems changing foreign currency in banks or cambios anywhere in Mozambique, although at a bank you may have to queue (an experience in itself). There doesn't seem to be a huge variation in rates, so it's down to you how much time you're willing to spend hunting for the best deal. It is worth having a rough idea of the current rate before you change money – ask around or visit the website www.xe.com, which has a currency converter that covers every world currency. Changing money on the streets is possible, and it may be necessary at some border crossings or if you arrive from another country after banking hours, but otherwise it carries more risks than benefits.

CREDIT CARDS It is staggering quite how good the ATM (Auto Teller Machine) network is. All the provincial capitals have several different ATMs available, and most of the smaller towns will have at least one. However, most ATMS accept Visa cards only, though BIM Millennium and Standard Bank also accept MasterCard. There doesn't appear to be anywhere that takes American Express. Most ATMs have a daily withdrawal limit of Mt3,000 (about US$85) but Barclays and Standard Bank have a more useful daily limit of Mt10,000.

CHANGE Most visitors to Africa will have had problems getting change for large banknotes every now and again, one of those slightly charming little quirks that can just be laughed off as local colour. But it is noticeably worse (and significantly more annoying) in Mozambique, particularly once you get north of the Zambezi and out into rural areas. It is worth stocking up on change when you are in any town, and resolutely holding on to any change that does happen to come your way.

BUDGETING

Day-to-day expenses tend to be quite high and often poor value for money – what might be described as African standards at Western prices. The cheap-and-cheerful, few-dollars-a-night African-style lodges that exist in neighbouring countries (especially Malawi) are few and far between in Mozambique. As elsewhere,

A NOTE ON PRICES

All prices in the guide were collected in late 2010 and are quoted in US dollars, but might originally have been in meticais, US dollars or South African rand (ZAR). They are based on a rough exchange rate of Mt35/ ZAR7 to the US dollar. Given the current volatility of the dollar these rates will almost certainly have changed by the time you read this. The biggest increases tend to be with the cost of accommodation – as a very rough estimate you might expect to pay 10% more than the quoted price for each calendar year after they were collected.

any budget will depend greatly on how and where you travel, but the following guidelines may be useful to people trying to keep costs to a minimum.

If you travel widely in Mozambique, it will be difficult to keep your basic travel expenses (food, transport, accommodation and drink) to much below US$35 per day for one person or US$50 per day for a couple. Your main expense will probably be accommodation: in many towns, you'll be lucky to find a double room for less than US$20, and there are plenty of places where camping costs around US$10 per person. A meal in a restaurant will typically cost US$8–10 per head, though you can save considerably by putting together your own food or eating at market stalls. Transport costs will probably work out at around US$3–4 daily, assuming that you're on the move every other day or thereabouts. It is possible to travel more cheaply if you carry a tent, are selective about where you visit, and stay put in cheaper places for a few days.

GETTING AROUND

BY AIR Given Mozambique's size, and the variable conditions of some of the roads, internal flights can be an attractive option. The provincial capitals all have their own airports and most have regular scheduled flights. Prices tend to be high, however, a situation that dates back to when the national airline, LAM, had a monopoly on internal flights. This is beginning to change, and you an often pick up competitive flight prices on their website (*www.flylam.co.za*). Alternatively, pop into the airline office or a travel agency to make a booking. Airports tend to be somewhat chaotic, and the usual rules about not leaving baggage lying around apply.

BY BOAT There are regular ferries between Maputo and Catembe. Boats must also be used to get between Vilankulo or Inhassoro and the islands of the Bazaruto Archipelago, to Ibo Island in northern Mozambique, and to cross some of the country's main rivers and inland waterways (the Zambezi River, Ruvuma River and Lake Niassa, for instance). If travelling by sea is your thing, you may be able to find the odd trawler plying the coast between Beira and Quelimane; in the far north near the Tanzanian border, private fishing dhows are a legitimate alternative to travelling by road.

BY RAIL There are only two passenger routes that would interest travellers, between Maputo and the South African border at Ressano Garcia, and between Nampula and Cuamba. The rest of the network is either out of action or only used for freight trains, and while you may be able to hitch a lift on one, travelling by road will be quicker and easier.

BY ROAD The road network in Mozambique has historically suffered from underinvestment. In the days of the Portuguese, the railways were the dominant means of getting around the country, and little investment was available for the roads during the civil war. Since the end of the war there has been an increase in civil projects (often funded by foreign aid packages) aimed at improving the major roads, and this is gradually bearing fruit despite setbacks caused by flooding during the rainy season.

As a general rule, roads in Mozambique fall into three main categories, tarmac, graded dirt and ungraded dirt, and (as you'd expect) are somewhat variable in quality. Details of the major roads in each province are included in the relevant chapters. However it does need to be stressed that the combination of the weather and the road repair programme will change things. Good maps are hard to come by in the country, so best buy one before you travel (see page 53).

Driving in Mozambique Mozambique (like neighbouring countries) drives on the left hand side of the road, at least where potholes permit it. As a general rule you won't have any problems travelling in a saloon car on major roads until you get north of Pemba, with the exception of the road between Nampula and Cuamba. The main hazard to your vehicle on Mozambican roads comes from pot-holes. You are advised to keep your eyes glued to the road ahead and to slow down for oncoming traffic, since a vehicle passing in the opposite direction will impede your ability to manoeuvre around an unexpected pot-hole. If you're travelling off the major roads then you'd be strongly recommended to use a high-clearance 4x4. Livestock and pedestrians frequently wander into the middle of the road, and motorists tend to be more reckless, not to mention inebriated, than in Europe, so drive more defensively than you would at home. Driving at night is inadvisable, partly for security reasons, but also because the general chaos on the road is exacerbated by vehicles lacking headlights.

Another source of chaos and possible damage is the lack of warning triangles. While there is a legal requirement for all vehicles to carry one, this is more honoured in the breach than the observance (and lack thereof is dealt with by bribing the relevant officer). The alternative used is to pop into the bush, hack off some branches and lay them behind the broken-down vehicle, so if you do see a series of branches lying on one side of the road, slow down and be prepared. This method also seems to be used for roadworks.

Finally, be aware of cyclists – bicycles are a common form of local transport. They won't necessarily be aware of your presence so you'll have to be aware of theirs.

At the moment petrol in Mozambique costs around US$1.50 per litre, although given the current fluctuations in petrol prices, the odds on it staying there long are slim.

Traffic police Police in Mozambique come in two flavours: civic police (who dress in grey uniforms) and traffic police (who dress in white uniforms). Traffic police are the only ones who can officially stop vehicles and there should be one at every roadblock. They will want to see your vehicle documents, whereas civic police should only ask to see your personal ID. In our experience (about 10,000km driving in Mozambique), traffic police will only create problems if you break the law, or are perceived to, in which they can occasionally become extremely difficult and unpleasant in the hope of levering you into paying a bribe.

Documents You should always have the following with you:

- Personal ID (your passport or a notarised copy thereof)
- Driving licence (an international one)
- Vehicle registration and ownership documents
- Third-party insurance (the one you bought at the border)
- Temporary import certificate (again, the one you got at the border)

Indicating If you are stopped, then always indicate as you pull into the side of the road, and put your hazards on while stopped.

Speed limits Usually 50km/h in towns, 100km/h outside, although if you see a different limit on a sign make sure you stick to that. There are at least two mobile speed traps operating on the EN1, there may be others elsewhere, and officers favour setting up the traps on the outskirts of villages where an incongruously low speed limit is often indicated on a sign. A standard speeding fine of Mt1,000 is charged whether you are caught driving 1km/h or 50km/h above the limit; it's up to you whether you take advantage of the negotiable clemency offered to motorists who don't require a receipt.

Reflective jackets and warning breakdown triangles You are legally obliged to have at a warning triangle in your vehicle, although you may be better off having two – the lack of a second is frequently used as leverage for a bribe by traffic police. It is also required to carry an orange reflective jacket slung on the back of the driver's seat. Both are available at the border coming from Komatipoort in South Africa.

Trailer signs If you are towing a trailer, you should display blue-and-orange triangular signs on the front of your vehicle and the rear of the trailer.

Seat belts Must be worn at all times.

Sunglasses While there doesn't seem to be any legal basis, you hear occasional reports of traffic police stopping and trying to fine people who wear sunglasses while driving, usually on the grounds that their driving licence doesn't state that they need correction to their vision. This appears to be a scam, and the threat of contacting the anti-corruption campaign and/or your embassy should see you on your way.

If you suspect that you're being scammed The first thing to do is ask the official for his name and number and note it down. If he refuses to give them and he's on a motorbike or in a car, take the registration number of that. If the fine is

CORRIDORS OF POWER

While misfortune has hit Mozambique hard in recent years (civil war, droughts, floods, etc), the country can claim one big advantage over its neighbours: its location. For Mozambique is the southern African middleman, providing a vital outlet for landlocked countries such as Swaziland, Zimbabwe, Malawi, Zambia and even the Democratic Republic of Congo, while South Africa, although it boasts the continent's longest coastline, also relies heavily on Mozambican ports. To facilitate the movement of goods from these countries to the Indian Ocean, several transportation corridors exist in Mozambique. The Maputo Corridor serves mainly South Africa and Swaziland; the Beira Corridor links Zimbabwe and Zambia to the port of Beira; the Limpopo Corridor links Zimbabwe to the port of Maputo; and the Nacala Corridor is for Malawi. All of these corridors have railway lines, and the ports of Maputo, Beira and Nacala are the country's three most important. Middlemen always make money, and Mozambique has earned some vital hard currency by selling concessions to foreign investors to manage the railway lines along these corridors, as well as the ports at the end of them. Another vital transportation route, and a popular one with travellers, is the Tete Corridor, which links Zimbabwe to Malawi via the Mozambican town of Tete.

genuine he is legally obliged to give you a receipt. If he is reluctant to do this then it could be an indication of a scam.

Parking It is illegal to park on the side of the road that faces oncoming traffic – in other words, except on one-way streets, you must always park on the left side of the road in relation to the direction you are driving, never on the right.

Hiring a vehicle Having a 4x4 vehicle at your disposal is a definite luxury, permitting you to forget the hassles of public transport and navigate the more difficult tracks to out-of-the-way places. This luxury, however, comes at a hefty price. A 4x4, for example, rarely costs much less than US$100 per day, and quite often considerably more. The larger hotels and most travel agents can arrange car hire. Alternatively, go directly to the car-rental agencies, most of which are based at the country's larger airports (ie: Maputo, Beira and Nampula). If using one of the smaller car-hire firms, be warned that we've had iffy reports of some of them: one or two people have had their hire cars impounded by the police. These three are only indicative – there are other options: **Avis** (*www.avis.com*), **Europcar** (*www.europcar.com*), **Hertz** (*www.hertz.com*).

Buses If you're planning on using public transport, there are two words that you'll need to become very familiar with – *machimbombo* and *chapa*. Both are forms of buses, but machimbombo refers only to coaches. Chapa has much wider application and can pretty much apply to any other form of public transport, up to and including lorries. You should be aware that, regardless of what form of vehicle you end up in, it is very unlikely that it would pass a European safety test. Most chapas are in better condition, but it's still not comfortable being crammed into the back seat of one with three other people bouncing along a rough track. The most common form of chapa is the minibus. These are the workhorses of the Mozambican public transport system and you'll see them everywhere. They are, almost without exception, packed, and if you have a long journey they can make for a very uncomfortable ride, particularly if you get stuck at the back. The best seats in a minibus are the two at the front, next to the driver.

Small lorries are almost as common as minibuses in the north of the country. While lorry rides often entail sitting on your rucksack or a bag of dried fish and hanging on for dear life, an advantage over minibuses is that you do at least have the sun on your back and the wind in your hair. It is unusual for lorries to offer any shade (although a few have a tarpaulin cover), and with journey times of up to six hours there's a strong risk of sunburn, so you'd be well advised to have a hat with a chinstrap to hold it on. Hats without chinstraps have a tendency to disappear over the side early in the journey, and the likelihood of the driver noticing and stopping is slim to none. Suntan lotion is a must.

Chapas obey the usual African laws of leaving when they are full – there is no schedule, and a good chance that the chapa you are travelling in will be hanging around for some time after you get into it while the crew (driver and conductor) get more passengers together. Machimbombos may leave at a set time, although this is really limited to the big transport groups such as Oliveira's or Grupo Mecula. And be aware that on many routes, most or all transport leaves very early in the morning – typically around 05.00 or earlier – so when in doubt, if you absolutely need to get somewhere on any given day, an early start is always recommended.

Costs of chapas are not (in comparison with accommodation) expensive in Mozambique. As a very general rule of thumb, expect to pay around US$1–1.50

per hour of travel. Costs are listed at relevant points in this guide, but there's no substitute for going down to the chapa terminal and asking the other passengers. Doing this also means that you can work out how much time you need to allow for the walk from your hotel to the chapa terminal, which may grant you an extra half-hour in bed. It's not unknown for you to be charged for baggage that goes in the hold or on the roof. The latter cost may be in the region of US$1.50 and seems to be charged across the board, rather than just to foreigners. It seems to be more common in the south of the country than it is north of the Zambezi.

Hitching Hitching is a viable option south of Vilankulo, where there is a fair amount of private transport, and on the roads between Tete, Chimoio and Beira. It is generally slower in northern Mozambique, and the line between hitching and public transport is rather blurred here as elsewhere in Africa: most truck drivers will informally carry passengers for the same fee charged by buses and chapas, so expect to pay for any lift offered by a Mozambican.

ACCOMMODATION

As a rule, accommodation at the budget end of the scale is overpriced for what you get by almost any standards, but smarter rooms can be better value. Tourism in Mozambique is still a developing industry and the network of Western-orientated hotels is smaller than that elsewhere, so you may occasionally need to bite the bullet and take a room somewhere that is less comfortable than you would normally accept – needless to say the further you travel from the established tourist destinations, the more likely this is. There is a variety of different types of accommodation, some of which require a little explanation:

PENSÃO This is the Portuguese word for a guesthouse and is widely used throughout the country. It can be anything from a room in a family house to a fully fledged hotel. Generally speaking they won't be organised for travellers, but can be very good value.

POUSADA Literally means 'inn' but is interchangeable with pensão.

COMPLEXO TURÍSTICO Normally a compound with a restaurant, bar, parking and rooms for hire. May also have a disco on site.

BOMA Camping specific, this refers to a pitch surrounded by a fence of wood or reeds to provide some privacy from the rest of the campsite.

BARRACA Also camping specific, this is a large bivouac beneath which you can pitch tents.

Detailed accommodation listings for specific places are given in the regional part of the guide and graded into five categories: exclusive/luxury, upmarket, moderate, budget and shoestring. The purpose of this categorisation is twofold: to break up long hotel listings that span a wide price range, and to help readers isolate the range of hotels that will best suit their budget and taste. The application of categories is not rigid. Aside from an inevitable element of subjectivity, it is based as much on the feel of a hotel as its rates (which are quoted anyway) and placement may also be influenced by the standard of other accommodation in the same place. Room rates in this guide are in accordance with the normal way the specific establishment charges, that is B&B for bed and breakfast, DB&B for dinner, bed and breakfast, FB for full-board (all meals included) or all inclusive (which usually means activities are included along with all meals). Where none of the above is indicated, the rate is bed only.

EXCLUSIVE/LUXURY This category embraces a handful of international four- and five-star luxury hotels, as well as a few select smaller lodges and resorts notable less for their luxury than for offering a genuinely exclusive experience. Rates are typically upwards of US$300 for a double. This is the category to look at if you want the best and/or most characterful accommodation and have few financial restrictions.

UPMARKET This category includes most Western-style hotels, lodges and resorts that cater mainly to international tourist or business travellers but lack the special something that might elevate them into the luxury or exclusive category. Hotels in this range would typically be accorded a two- to three-star ranking elsewhere, and they offer smart en-suite accommodation with a good selection of facilities. Rates are typically around US$100–200 for a double, dependent on quality and location. Most package tours and privately booked safaris use accommodation in this range.

MID-RANGE This is the most nebulous category, essentially consisting of hotels which couldn't really be classified as upmarket, but are a notch or two above the budget category in terms of price and/or quality. In cities, expect unpretentious en-suite accommodation with hot water and possibly television, a decent restaurant and efficient English-speaking staff. In more resort-like areas, a lot of the accommodation in this category comprises the self-catering units favoured by South Africans. Prices are generally in the US$50–80 range. This is the category to look at if you are travelling privately on a limited or low budget and expect a reasonably high but not luxurious standard of accommodation.

BUDGET Accommodation in this category falls into two broad types. There are hotels aimed largely at the local market that don't approach international standards, but are still reasonably clean and comfortable, with a decent restaurant attached, and en-suite rooms with running cold or possibly hot water. Then there are the more Westernised but equally affordable backpacker hostels and beach resorts that form the accommodation mainstay for many independent travellers to Mozambique. Expect to pay around US$20–50 for a double, depending on the location, or less to pitch a tent or stay in a dorm. This is the category to look at if you are on a limited budget, but want to avoid total squalor.

SHOESTRING This is the very bottom end of the market, usually small local guesthouses with simple rooms and common showers and toilets. Running the gamut from pleasantly clean to decidedly squalid, hotels in the category typically cost around US$10–20 for a room. It is the category for those to whom keeping down costs is the main imperative.

CAMPING Many backpacker hostels and beach resorts allows camping, typically at a cost of around US$3–5 per person. Campsites are split across the accommodation categories but would most often be associated with the budget range.

EATING AND DRINKING

FOOD Mozambique's lack of infrastructure and general easy-going attitude mean that restaurants tend to adopt a rather laissez-faire attitude towards both menus and opening hours. The further you are from the city centres, the more flexible you'll need to be. As a very general guideline, the more Westernised restaurants in the biggest cities (Maputo, Beira and to a lesser extent Nampula) will be open between around 10.00–20.00/21.00 and will have most of their menus available. As you go into the hinterland it becomes more important that you check with the establishment in question whether they will be open that evening and what they'll have on the menu. It may well be worth placing an order in advance and agreeing a time when you'll arrive.

In remote rural areas, food will by and large be limited to *ncima* and meat, chicken, fish, beans or similar. Meat (if you're offered it) will be goat – beef is very rarely available outside the major towns, or if you are (for whatever reason) an honoured guest. *Ncima* (which is also known as *ugi*, *ugali*, *sadza* or *pap*) is a form of porridge made by mixing ground maize with water and boiling it until it forms a starchy paste. It can either then be eaten as a hot porridge or left to set and eaten cold in chunks. Many foreigners are indifferent to the stodgy result, but Africans by and large love it – so much so that if offered a choice between *ncima* and a more Western staple such as potatoes or rice, they will choose the *ncima*.

In the bigger towns, menus tend to be either chips or rice with a side salad (usually heavy on tomatoes and onions) and fish (or some other form of seafood), chicken or beef. Chicken and fish will tend to be grilled or fried, while beef will almost always be a variant on a Portuguese dish called a *prego*. A *prego* is essentially a minute steak, usually boiled with a sauce that tastes a little like a toned-down Worcestershire sauce. The classic *prego no prato* (literally *prego* on a plate) will be served with a portion of rice, a portion of chips, the side salad and a fried egg on top. A common snack is the *prego no pão*, a *prego* in a bread roll. Many of the dishes that you'll see in the swankier restaurants will be variants on the *prego no prato*, sometimes with added ingredients (chorizo sausage, for instance).

FOOD VOCABULARY

cheese	*queijo*
chips	*batatas fritas*
crab	*caranguejo*
egg	*ovo*
fish	*peixe*
lobster	*langosta*
meat	*carne* (note that this may be either beef or goat)
octopus	*polvo*
Portuguese spicy sausage	*chouriço*
potato	*batata*
prawn	*camarão*
rice	*arroz*
sandwiches/snacks	*petiscos*
squid	*lula*

Given the length of the coastline, it would be surprising if the Mozambican seafood wasn't outstanding, and Mozambican prawns d have a global reputation, but the crab, lobster, crayfish and octopus are equally good.

These are some other dishes that you might come across:

Matapa or *mu-kwame*	A paste made of shredded cassava leaves, ground peanuts and coconut
Lomino	Coconut milk-based curry
Caldeirada	A stew with a mixture of different fish/seafood in a potato, onion and tomato sauce
Kitole	Rice and beans with fish and a tomato and onion sauce
Xicontombuilo	A mixture of cassava and beans
Makuchoho	Crushed maize and coconut milk
Piri-piri	Chilli sauce which can vary from merely piquant to mouth-roaringly hot. There are a few other flavours (garlic and lemon is very nice).

DRINKS Coca-Cola is the undisputed champion of the cola wars in Mozambique, being available virtually everywhere across the country, along with various flavours of Fanta (its stablemate). Sparletta, another range of soft drinks, is also universally available – the lemon-twist flavour is quite refreshing. They will almost always be brought to you sealed and opened in front of you. You can buy fruit juices in the Shoprite supermarkets, and you should be able to get the mixed fruit juice called Santal in most of the larger towns. Bottled water is ubiquitous but again make sure it's sealed.

The most widespread beers are 2M (named after a Frenchman called Mac-Mahon – you can read more about him in the introduction to Tete Province, see page 239), Laurentina (which comes in two styles, a Continental-style lager and a stout) and Manica. You can also get South African brands like Castle and Lion.

Wine is imported, mostly from South Africa but also from Portugal. You can get it in bottles as normal, or (if you're willing to risk it) in 5-litre containers with a plastic raffia-style handle. The wine in the latter is undoubtedly an acquired taste.

PUBLIC HOLIDAYS

In addition to the following fixed public holidays, Good Friday and Easter Monday are recognised as public holidays in Mozambique. Many of these days will be marked by heavily orchestrated public demonstrations and marches.

1 January	New Year's Day
3 February	Heroes' Day
7 April	Women's Day
1 May	Labour Day
25 June	National Day (Independence Day)
7 September	Lusaka Accord Day
25 September	Armed Forces Day
25 December	Family Day

There are also marked commemorative days:

25 May	Day of African Unity
1 June	International Children's Day
16 June	Resistance Day
20 September	Assumption of Power by Transitional Government

In addition, Maputo has a public holiday on 10 November.

SHOPPING

The north of the country has a craft industry, primarily making wooden furniture of simple but handsome appearance. Other crafts include the well-known Makonde carvings. The Makonde are centred on Mueda in the northeast, and here you can get representative items of their work very cheaply. Other places where you might find selections are Nampula, Nacala and Pemba.

Apart from in Maputo, where there are shops specialising in arts and crafts, most of the souvenirs that you'll find on your travels will be sold on the street outside hotels, restaurants and other places frequented by tourists. Even this is a relatively recent development; a few years ago it was difficult to find souvenirs of any description sold anywhere. As elsewhere in Africa, bargaining for souvenirs is expected, although you should conduct such negotiations in a respectful and responsible manner (see below for further details).

If you are in Nampula or Cabo Delgado, keep an eye open for cashew nuts being sold on the street.

BARGAINING AND OVERCHARGING The emphasis that some tourists (both package and independent) place on bargaining can be a little over the top. Bargaining has its place but the common assumption that every individual you come across will quote inflated prices to tourists is nonsensical. Hotels, pensões, restaurants and supermarkets will display prices for their wares, so bargaining is of no value. In the off-season, some of the more expensive hotels may have special rates that will be worth asking about, but that's not a bargaining situation as such.

Buses and taxis also tend to operate standard rates, but it is harder to find out what these are. The best way is just to ask a few people what a fair price is from X to Y – the consensus will give you a good guide. There may be some flexibility with taxis but it's highly unlikely with buses.

Fruit and vegetable markets and stalls are a different proposition. Hang about any market for a short while and you will see bargaining going on between locals, so this is a situation where bargaining is acceptable. As ever the better informed you are at the start of the process, the more likely you are to be able to come to a mutually satisfying agreement, so it's worth asking at a few stalls to see what the norm is before starting your bargaining. In addition you'll find that stallholders will be far more amenable if you are buying a range of produce rather than just one or two items. The longer you spend in a town, the easier you will find it to gauge what is a fair price for the items you are buying there.

Similarly arts and crafts have scope for a degree of bargaining, and in fact the vendors would probably be hugely surprised if you didn't haggle to some extent. Again it will be easier to gain a reduction if you are buying a range of items rather than just the one. In some places (notably the Makonde carving collectives in Nampula and Pemba) the carvings are all individually priced using sticky labels.

The key thing when bargaining is to be relaxed about the whole business. Adopting an aggressive posture is only likely to irritate the other party and lowers the likelihood of a successful conclusion to the whole business.

Above all it's crucial to retain a sense of proportion. Regardless of how poor you are in Western terms, you will have far more money than the person you're dealing with. Temper your desire for a bargain with some generosity and you will find that you get a better deal as a result.

PHOTOGRAPHIC TIPS

Ariadne Van Zandbergen

EQUIPMENT Although with some thought and an eye for composition you can take reasonable photos with a 'point-and-shoot' camera, you need an SLR camera if you are at all serious about photography. Modern SLRs tend to be very clever, with automatic programmes for almost every possible situation, but remember that these programmes are limited in the sense that the camera cannot think, but only make calculations. Every starting amateur photographer should read a photographic manual for beginners and get to grips with such basics as the relationship between aperture and shutter speed.

Always buy the best lens you can afford. The lens determines the quality of your photo more than the camera body. Fixed fast lenses are ideal, but very costly. A zoom lens makes it easier to change composition without changing lenses the whole time. If you carry only one lens, a 28–70mm (digital 17–55mm) or similar zoom should be ideal. For a second lens, a lightweight 80–200mm or 70–300mm (digital 55–200mm) or similar will be excellent for candid shots and varying your composition. Wildlife photography will be very frustrating if you don't have at least a 300mm lens. For a small loss of quality, tele-converters are a cheap and compact way to increase magnification: a 300 lens with a 1.4x converter becomes 420mm, and with a 2x it becomes 600mm. Note, however, that 1.4x and 2x tele-converters reduce the speed of your lens by 1.4 and 2 stops respectively.

For photography from a vehicle, a solid beanbag, which you can make yourself very cheaply, will be necessary to avoid blurred images, and is more useful than a tripod. A clamp with a tripod head screwed onto it can be attached to the vehicle as well. Modern dedicated flash units are easy to use; aside from the obvious need to flash when you photograph at night, you can improve a lot of photos in difficult 'high contrast' or very dull light with some fill-in flash. It pays to have a proper flash unit as opposed to a built-in camera flash.

DIGITAL/FILM Digital photography is now the preference of most amateur and professional photographers, with the resolution of digital cameras improving the whole time. For ordinary prints a 6 megapixel camera is fine. For better results and the possibility to enlarge images and for professional reproduction, higher resolution is available up to 24 megapixels.

Memory space is important. The number of pictures you can fit on a memory card depends on the quality you choose. Calculate in advance how many pictures you can fit on a card and either take enough cards to last for your trip, or take a storage drive onto which you can download the content. A laptop gives the advantage that you can see your pictures properly at the end of each day and edit and delete rejects, but a storage device is lighter and less bulky.

Bear in mind that digital camera batteries, computers and other storage devices need charging, so make sure you have all the chargers, cables and converters with

PHOTOGRAPHY

Taking photographs is part and parcel of travelling, but it needs to be done with sensitivity. Taking wildlife photographs and scenic views is fine, but you do need to be a little more circumspect when taking photographs of buildings and people. It is illegal to take photographs of any public buildings in Maputo, and there is a danger of being fined if you are caught doing so. Similarly if you are caught taking

you. Most hotels have charging points, but do enquire about this in advance. When camping you might have to rely on charging from the car battery; a spare battery is invaluable.

If you are shooting film, 100 to 200 ISO print film and 50 to 100 ISO slide film are ideal. Low ISO film is slow but fine grained and gives the best colour saturation, but will need more light, so support in the form of a tripod or monopod is important. You can also bring a few 'fast' 400 ISO films for low-light situations where a tripod or flash is no option.

DUST AND HEAT Dust and heat are often a problem. Keep your equipment in a sealed bag, stow films in an airtight container (eg: a small cooler bag) and avoid exposing equipment and film to the sun. Digital cameras are prone to collecting dust particles on the sensor, which results in spots on the image. The dirt mostly enters the camera when changing lenses, so be careful when doing this. To some extent photos can be 'cleaned' up afterwards in Photoshop, but this is time-consuming. You can have your camera sensor professionally cleaned, or you can do this yourself with special brushes and swabs made for the purpose, but note that touching the sensor might cause damage and should only be done with the greatest care.

LIGHT The most striking outdoor photographs are often taken during the hour or two of 'golden light' after dawn and before sunset. Shooting in low light may enforce the use of very low shutter speeds, in which case a tripod will be required to avoid camera shake.

With careful handling, side lighting and back lighting can produce stunning effects, especially in soft light and at sunrise or sunset. Generally, however, it is best to shoot with the sun behind you. When photographing animals or people in the harsh midday sun, images taken in light but even shade are likely to be more effective than those taken in direct sunlight or patchy shade, since the latter conditions create too much contrast.

PROTOCOL In some countries, it is unacceptable to photograph local people without permission, and many people will refuse to pose or will ask for a donation. In such circumstances, don't try to sneak photographs as you might get yourself into trouble. Even the most willing subject will often pose stiffly when a camera is pointed at them; relax them by making a joke, and take a few shots in quick succession to improve the odds of capturing a natural pose.

Ariadne Van Zandbergen is a professional travel and wildlife photographer specialising in Africa. She runs The Africa Image Library. For photo requests, visit www.africaimagelibrary.co.za or contact her on ariadne@hixnet.co.za.

photographs of military or government buildings anywhere in the country you may be in for a bumpy ride.

When taking photographs of specific individuals it is vital that you ask their permission first. Like many African countries, Mozambique is socially a little more conservative than the West, and pointing a camera at someone without asking can cause offence. One of the most common reactions of people who do not want to be photographed is to turn their face away from the camera or hide behind their hand – if you see this reaction then point your camera in a different direction. It may seem silly to us, but appearing to continue photographing them will cause grave offence. At best it will just reinforce the stereotype of tourists being rude, at worst it may lead to a public altercation.

Although it's impossible to ask everyone in a street scene, you should watch for similar reactions there. If it's clear that a significant number of people are disturbed by your camera, put it away.

The above does make it sound as though people in Mozambique are generally averse to having their photographs taken, but this isn't the case – the majority will be more than happy to have you snap them, providing you ask first. With children it's not unknown for a scrum to develop as everyone tries to get themselves in shot. If you are shooting digital, it's well worth showing them the resultant photographs – the overwhelming reaction is paroxysms of delight.

MEDIA AND COMMUNICATIONS

NEWSPAPERS The main daily newspapers are *Noticias* (Maputo), which supports the government, and *Diario* (Beira). The main weeklies are *Savana*, *Domingo* (coming out on Sundays) and the magazine *Tempo*. If you are craving an English-language news fix, South African newspapers are also available in a very few places in Maputo, normally a day or two old and at a very high price.

TELEVISION AND RADIO Radio Mozambique broadcasts on three channels in Portuguese as well as several local languages. Since 1981 there has been experimental television, TV Mozambique, which broadcasts imported Portuguese and Brazilian programmes alongside Mozambican programmes. There is also an independent station, RTK Television, with an English-language bias. Many upmarket hotels pick up DSTV, a South African service offering a varied bouquet of international satellite sports, news, movie and other channels.

TELEPHONE The international telephone code for Mozambique is +258, and the internal telephone system is surprisingly efficient. The national backbone is reasonably extensive and stable; if you're dialling in-country, just knock the +258 off the front. Mobile phones have really taken off in Mozambique, and the coverage is already extensive and continues to grow. The two major networks are the home-grown mCel (numbers beginning with 82) and the South African Vodacom (numbers beginning with 84). For both networks, phone numbers have nine digits, and you'll have no problems buying SIM cards or top-up vouchers in places where there is coverage. Both networks have coverage in all the provincial capitals, and along most of the major roads south of the Zambezi. North of the river, things are more patchy and in the very far north you won't have coverage outside of the larger towns. On the shores of Lake Malawi, you may find it easier to connect to a Malawian network than a Mozambican one. All fixed and mobile numbers in Mozambique used to have a leading 0, but this was ditched a few years ago, reputedly only as a temporary measure, although no-one seems in a rush to reinstate them.

POST Post from Mozambique is cheap and reasonably reliable, but it is often very slow. Postcards are difficult to find in Mozambique, and when you do find them they are often very expensive and usually not even of Mozambique.

EMAIL AND INTERNET The network of internet cafés is not as wide, or as cheap or as fast as in the rest of the world, but it does at least exist. In the larger towns. Most of the time. The national telecommunications company TDM has a good network with an office in most towns, and its connections are usually solid if not spectacularly fast. You will find privately run internet cafés, which vary a bit more in quality and cost, listed at relevant points in this guide. If you need regular internet access, the easiest solution by far is to buy a mobile phone with an internet facility, and get somebody in a Vodacom or mCel office to rig it up to browse using a local SIM card– this takes five minutes to set up, and gives you seriously inexpensive internet access wherever there is mobile reception.

RESPONSIBLE TOURISM

BEFORE YOU LEAVE If you want to swot up beforehand on what it means to be a responsible tourist, a UK-based source of information is **Tourism Concern** (*020 7753 3330; f 020 7753 3331; e info@tourismconcern.org.uk; www.tourismconcern.org.uk*). It's also good to do some research about the country you're about to visit – not just its weather and its costs and its hotels, but also what makes it tick: its history, culture, achievements, failures and so on. It can help to break the ice with local people if you know something (anything!) about their country and way of life.

CARBON EMISSIONS If you'd like to offset the carbon footprint of your flight, try www.carbonneutral.com, run by a UK organisation. The website has an easy-to-use emissions calculator and a range of offset programmes.

IN MOZAMBIQUE Fancy terms such as 'cultural sensitivity' and 'low-impact tourism' just boil down to good old-fashioned respect and common sense. As a visitor, you should be willing to adapt to and respect local customs and traditions. For example, learn a bit of the local language, seek the permission of the community leader before roaming through villages, and ask before you take photographs. In conservative rural areas, note how the local people dress and don't expose parts of yourself that they keep hidden. Of course pick up your litter or don't drop it in the first place – and don't uproot plants and flowers. Also be careful to use energy resources such as water and electricity efficiently, not to wash in lakes or rivers (regardless of local practices, because of pollution) or get too close to the wildlife.

Shop locally and use the services of local people whenever possible. Buy souvenirs from the craftspeople who made them rather than via middlemen who will siphon off profits, and patronise small street vendors rather than big supermarkets. Don't bargain unreasonably; the difference may be the cost of a drink to you but a whole family meal to the vendor. Use the services of a local guide, or a child who wants to help, and pay a fair rate.

If you have spent time in a village and become friendly with its inhabitants, why not consider donating pens, crayons and notebooks to the local primary school? It's easy to buy stationery in local markets. Ask to meet the schoolteacher, so that

PECULIAR CUSTOMS

Danny Edmunds

As you travel around Mozambique, you may find odd customs every now and again. Here are some of those I've come across along with the places I first noticed them.

BAGS OF WATER (MAPUTO) If you look carefully, you'll see little plastic bags of water hanging from the rafters in restaurants, particularly outdoor ones. These are there to repel flies. I've asked scientists about this, and they tell me that when the fly gets close to the bag, it sees itself reflected but because of the curvature, much, much bigger. This frightens the fly and it goes elsewhere for its dinner. Apparently it works very well…

FREE PAPER HANKIES (BEIRA) In several of the supermarkets in Beira, I was given little packets of paper hankies, even when I only popped in to ask directions. I have no idea why this happened, but all the shops it happened in were owned and run by Muslims, so it may be due to something in the Islamic code. If anyone has any idea why, please get in touch – I'd be fascinated to know the background.

DRIED LEAVES (INHAMBANE) Many of the shops in Inhambane have strings of dried leaves hanging over the door. This is a Hindu custom, a sign of welcome and believed to bring good luck.

he/she can receive and officially distribute the gift. Offer to spend some time in the school, being questioned by the children about your home country.

A warning: travellers often collect up pens/biros at home beforehand and bring them over to donate – but, in this case, *please* check that they work and have plenty of ink before handing them over. To an impoverished rural child, a new pen is a huge and thrilling gift. He/she is so proud and happy – and then so bitterly disappointed when it stops working after only a few hours. And do bear in mind the damage you can do by giving little gifts (coins, sweets, pens, cookies or whatever) to a child or youngster who comes up and begs, however cutely. If the begging bears fruit (and if the gift isn't immediately grabbed by a bigger child), he/she will start to pester all visitors. Or begging may appear more profitable than going to school.

TRAVELLING POSITIVELY *with Janice Booth*

Don't lose sight of the fact that you contribue to a country's economy simply by being there. Every time you travel by public transport, eat in a restaurant, buy a paper from a street vendor or give a few coins to a local guide you are providing a very real benefit to them and their families. But there are ways in which you can help more. Some of the lodges have established well-thought-out development programmes – with the best of these the programmes would have been a major part of the original plan and will have evolved as the lodge developed. Particularly good examples are mentioned in the text. If this is something you'd like to encourage, then ask your lodge in advance about community programmes it is involved with. If you like what you hear, then stay there, and if you don't then try one of the other places listed.

After you've returned home, try to be an ambassador. Share your experiences, and keep in touch with the people you've met on your travels. Mozambique's international image has been rather negative in recent years, and simply by talking about the country's beauty and many other positive aspects you can help to dispel misconceptions.

If you've enjoyed Mozambique and feel that you'd like to stay in touch with the country or to put something back into it, here are a few suggestions. If you ask around on the spot, you'll certainly find others.

If you'd like to return as a **volunteer** and have some relevant skills, check out **Voluntary Service Overseas** (*www.vso.org.uk*). They also welcome donations, from small amounts up to the cost of maintaining a volunteer in a developing country. Also worth checking out is **Travel People and Places** (*www.travel-peopleandplaces.co.uk*) and **International Voluntary Service** (*www.ivsgb.org.uk*).

A way to volunteer without leaving home is via the **Online Volunteering Service** (*www.onlinevolunteering.org*); it's managed by the United Nations Volunteers Programme (UNV), which is the volunteer arm of the UN. Volunteers need reliable access to a computer and the internet, and some relevant skill or experience.

It's sometimes hard to remember that the work of the massive international **charities** reaches down to benefit the poorest, and that they need our small donations. But it does, and they do. For making a general donation you could do far worse. Check which come closest to your interests. If it's wildlife that appeals to you, then you'll already know about the **Worldwide Fund for Nature** (*www.wwf.org*) which has a big presence in Mozambique and particularly in the new Quirimba National Park (see page 326). Below are some others.

PRACTICAL ACTION (*www.practicalaction.org*) Formerly the Independent Technology Group (*www.itdg.org*), founded in 1966 by the radical economist Dr E F Schumacher, Practical Action works to show that correctly chosen technologies can help people to find lasting, appropriate solutions to poverty, and that a small-scale approach can bring results that benefit whole communities long into the future. It enables poor communities to discover how new technologies, adapted in the right way, can improve their lives.

BOOK AID INTERNATIONAL (*www.bookaid.org*) This is another organisation well worth supporting. A UK-based charity, established in the 1950s, it works in 17 sub-Saharan African countries. The majority of its partners are urban and rural libraries that are free for use by all, but it also works with schools throughout the region. Book Aid prides itself on ensuring that the books it sends out are of genuine educational value and covering as wide a range of subjects as possible.

SAVE THE CHILDREN (*www.savethechildren.org.uk*) One of the bigger charities, it started work in Mozambique in 1984. Its aim is to improve the lives of children and young people and to ensure that they have access to good-quality basic services. It works in partnership with the government, donors, local and international NGOs and local communities.

SOS CHILDREN'S VILLAGES (*www.soschildrensvillages.org.uk*) This organisation constructed its first community in Mozambique in 1987, in Tete, for children who had lost their parents in the war. Since then it has opened villages and/or centres in Maputo and Pemba. These include schools, medical centres and vocational training. Contact details for SOS Children's Villages in Mozambique are on the website.

WATERAID (*www.wateraid.org.uk*) This much-praised charity is dedicated to the provision of safe domestic water, sanitation and hygiene education to the world's

STUFF YOUR RUCKSACK – AND MAKE A DIFFERENCE

www.stuffyourrucksack.com is a website set up by TV's Kate Humble which enables travellers to give direct help to small charities, schools or other organisations in the country they are visiting. Maybe a local school needs books, a map or pencils, or an orphanage needs children's clothes or toys - all things that can easily be 'stuffed in a rucksack' before departure. The charities get exactly what they need and travellers have the chance to meet local people and see how and where their gifts will be used.

The website describes organisations that need your help and lists the items they most need. Check what's needed in Mozambique, contact the organisation to say you're coming and bring not only the much-needed goods but an extra dimension to your travels and the knowledge that in a small way you have made a difference.

poorest people. In Mozambique, it has already helped more than 270,000 people to access clean water. WaterAid's partner in Mozambique, ESTAMOS, has won the Mozambique Development Prize for its work in ecological sanitation.

Local organisations worth checking out include the **Manda Wilderness Community Trust** at Nkwichi Lodge (*www.mandawilderness.org*) and **Happy Africa Foundation** in Vilanculos (*www.happyafricafoundation.org*).

4

Health

with Dr Felicity Nicholson

People new to exotic travel often worry about tropical diseases, but it is accidents that are most likely to carry you off. Road accidents are very common in many parts of Mozambique so be aware and do what you can to reduce risks: try to travel during daylight hours, always wear a seatbelt and refuse to be driven by anyone who has been drinking. Listen to local advice about areas where violent crime is rife too. It is imperative to have appropriate and good quality travel insurance that covers the activities you intend to pursue and is adequate for your health needs. You would be advised to read the small print to ensure that you are covered for vaccine preventable diseases if you decide not to take the vaccines assuming you have enough time.

PREPARATIONS

Preparations to ensure a healthy trip to Mozambique require checks on your immunisation status: it is wise to be up to date on tetanus, polio and diphtheria (now given as an all-in-one vaccine, Revaxis, that lasts for ten years), and hepatitis A. Immunisations against meningococcus and rabies may also be recommended. Proof of vaccination against **yellow fever** is needed for entry into Mozambique if you are coming from another yellow fever endemic area. If the vaccine is not suitable for you then obtain an exemption certificate from your GP or a travel clinic although there is no guarantee that the Mozambique border guards will accept this. Immunisation against cholera may be recommended during outbreaks or if you have a long term medical condition that puts you more at risk. The vaccine (Dukoral) is given as a drink in two doses at least one week apart for those aged six or over, and as three doses for those aged two–five.

A single dose of **hepatitis A** vaccine (eg: Havrix Monodose, Avaxim) provides cover for a year and can be administered close to the time of departure. A second dose given at least six months after the first dose will extend protection to around 25 years. The two doses cost in the region of £100, but may be available free of charge on the NHS.

Hepatitis B vaccination should be considered for longer trips (two months or more) or for those working with children or in situations where contact with blood is likely. Three injections are needed for the best protection and can be given over a three-week period if time is short for those aged 16 or over. Longer schedules give more sustained protection and are therefore preferred if time allows. Hepatitis A vaccine can also be given as a combination with hepatitis B as 'Twinrix', though two doses are needed at least seven days apart to be effective for the hepatitis A

LONG-HAUL FLIGHTS, CLOTS AND DVT

Any prolonged immobility including travel by land or air can result in deep vein thrombosis (DVT) with the risk of embolus to the lungs. Certain factors can increase the risk and these include:

- Previous clot or close relative with a history
- Being over 40 with greater risk over 80 years
- Recent major operation or varicose veins surgery
- Cancer
- Stroke
- Heart disease
- Obesity
- Pregnancy
- Hormone therapy
- Heavy smoking
- Severe varicose veins
- Being very tall (over 6ft/1.8m) or short (under 5ft/1.5m)

A deep vein thrombosis (DVT) causes painful swelling and redness of the calf or sometimes the thigh. It is only dangerous if a clot travels to the lungs (pulmonary embolus). Symptoms of a pulmonary embolus (PE) include chest pain, shortness of breath, and sometimes coughing up small amounts of blood and commonly start three to ten days after a long flight. Anyone who thinks that they might have a DVT needs to see a doctor immediately.

PREVENTION OF DVT

- Keep mobile before and during the flight; move around every couple of hours
- Drink plenty of fluids during the flight
- Avoid taking sleeping pills and excessive tea, coffee and alcohol
- Consider wearing flight socks or support stockings (see www.legshealth.com)

If you think you are at increased risk of a clot, ask your doctor if it is safe to travel.

component, and three doses are needed for the hepatitis B. Again this schedule is only suitable for those aged 16 or over.

The newer injectable **typhoid** vaccines (eg: Typhim Vi) last for three years and are about 85% effective. Oral capsules (Vivotif) may also be available for those aged six and over. Three capsules over five days lasts for approximately three years but may be less effective than the injectable forms They should be encouraged unless the traveller is leaving within a few days for a trip of a week or less, when the vaccine would not be effective in time. Meningitis vaccine containing strains A, C, W and Y is ideally recommended for all travellers, especially for trips of more than four weeks (see *Meningitis*, page 81). Vaccinations for rabies are ideally advised for everyone, but are especially important for travellers visiting more remote areas, especially if you are more than 24 hours from medical help and definitely if you will be working with animals (see *Rabies* page 81).

Experts differ over whether a BCG vaccination against tuberculosis (TB) is useful in adults: discuss this with your travel clinic.

In addition to the various vaccinations recommended above, it is important that travellers should be properly protected against malaria. For detailed advice, see below.

Ideally you should visit your own doctor or a specialist travel clinic (see pages 75–6) to discuss your requirements if possible at least eight weeks before you plan to travel.

PROTECTION FROM THE SUN Give some thought to packing suncream. The incidence of skin cancer is rocketing as Caucasians are travelling more and spending more time exposing themselves to the sun. Keep out of the sun during the middle of the day and, if you must expose yourself to the sun, build up gradually from 20 minutes per day. Be especially careful of exposure in the middle of the day and of sun reflected off water, and wear a T-shirt and lots of waterproof suncream (at least SPF15) when swimming. Sun exposure ages the skin, makes people prematurely wrinkly; and increases the risk of skin cancer .Cover up with long, loose clothes and wear a hat when you can. The glare and the dust can be hard on the eyes, too, so bring UV-protecting sunglasses and, perhaps, a soothing eyebath.

MALARIA Along with road accidents, malaria poses the single biggest serious threat to the health of travellers in most parts of tropical Africa, Mozambique included. It is unwise to travel in malarial parts of Africa whilst pregnant or with children: the risk of malaria in many parts is considerable and these travellers are likely to succumb rapidly to the disease. The risk of malaria above 1,800m above sea level is low.

Malaria in Mozambique The *Anopheles* mosquito that transmits the parasite is found throughout the country all year round.

Malaria prevention There is not yet a vaccine against malaria that gives enough protection to be useful for travellers, but there are other ways to avoid it; since most of Africa is very high risk for malaria, travellers must plan their malaria protection properly. Seek current advice on the best antimalarials to take: usually mefloquine, Malarone or doxycycline. If mefloquine (Lariam) is suggested, start this two-and-a-half weeks (three doses) before departure to check that it suits you; stop it immediately if it seems to cause depression or anxiety, visual or hearing disturbances, severe headaches, fits or changes in heart rhythm. Side effects such as nightmares or dizziness are not medical reasons for stopping unless they are sufficiently debilitating or annoying. Anyone who has been treated for depression or psychiatric problems, has diabetes controlled by oral therapy or who is epileptic (or who has suffered fits in the past) or has a close blood relative who is epileptic, should probably avoid mefloquine.

In the past doctors were nervous about prescribing mefloquine to pregnant women, but experience has shown that it is relatively safe and certainly safer than the risk of malaria. That said, there are other issues, so if you are travelling to Mozambique whilst pregnant, seek expert advice before departure.

Malarone (proguanil and atovaquone) is as effective as mefloquine. It has the advantage of having few side effects and need only be continued for one week after returning. However, it is expensive and because of this tends to be reserved for shorter trips. Malarone may not be suitable for everybody, so advice should be taken from a doctor. The licence in the UK has been extended for up to three months' use and a paediatric form of tablet is also available, prescribed on a weight basis.

Another alternative is the antibiotic doxycycline (100mg daily). Like Malarone it can be started one day before arrival. Unlike mefloquine, it may also be used in travellers with epilepsy, although certain anti-epileptic medication may make it less effective. In perhaps 1–3% of people there is the possibility of allergic skin reactions developing in sunlight; the drug should be stopped if this happens. Women using the oral contraceptive should use an additional method of protection for the first four weeks when using doxycycline. It is also unsuitable in pregnancy or for children under 12 years.

Chloroquine and proguanil are no longer considered to be effective enough for Mozambique but may be considered as a last resort if nothing else is deemed suitable.

All tablets should be taken with or after the evening meal, washed down with plenty of fluid and, with the exception of Malarone (see above), continued for four weeks after leaving.

Despite all these precautions, it is important to be aware that no anti-malarial drug is 100% protective, although those on prophylactics who are unlucky enough to catch malaria are less likely to get rapidly into serious trouble. In addition to taking anti-malarials, it is therefore important to avoid mosquito bites between dusk and dawn (see box *Avoiding insect bites*, page 80).

There is unfortunately the occasional traveller who prefers to 'acquire resistance' to malaria rather than take preventive tablets, or who takes homeopathic prophylactics thinking these are effective against killer disease. Homeopathy theory dictates treating like with like so there is no place for prophylaxis or immunisation in a well person; bone fide homoeopathists do not advocate it. It takes at least 18 months residing in a holoendemic area for someone to get some immunity to malaria so travellers to Africa will not acquire any effective resistance to malaria. The best way is to prevent mosquito bites in the first place and to take a suitable prophylactic agent.

Malaria diagnosis and treatment Even those who take their malaria tablets meticulously and do everything possible to avoid mosquito bites may contract a strain of malaria that is resistant to prophylactic drugs. Untreated malaria is likely to be fatal, but even strains resistant to prophylaxis respond well to prompt treatment. Because of this, your immediate priority upon displaying possible malaria symptoms – including a rapid rise in temperature (over 38°C), and any combination of a headache, flu-like aches and pains, a general sense of disorientation, and possibly even nausea and diarrhoea – is to establish whether you have malaria, ideally by visiting a clinic.

Diagnosing malaria is not easy, which is why consulting a doctor is sensible: there are other dangerous causes of fever in Africa, which require different treatments. Even if you test negative, it would be wise to stay within reach of a laboratory until the symptoms clear up, and to test again after a day or two if they don't. It's worth noting that if you have a fever and the malaria test is negative, you may have typhoid or paratyphoid, which should also receive immediate treatment.

Travellers to remote parts of Mozambique would be wise to carry a course of treatment to cure malaria, and a rapid test kit. With malaria, it is normal enough to go from feeling healthy to having a high fever in the space of a few hours (and it is possible to die from falciparum malaria within 24 hours of the first symptoms). In such circumstances, assume that you have malaria and act accordingly – whatever risks are attached to taking an unnecessary cure are outweighed by the dangers of untreated malaria. Experts differ on the costs and benefits of self-treatment, but agree that it leads to over-treatment and to many people taking drugs they do not need; yet treatment may save your life. There is also some division about the best treatment for malaria, but either Malarone or Coarthemeter are the current treatments of choice. Discuss your trip with a specialist either at home or in Mozambique.

TRAVEL CLINICS AND HEALTH INFORMATION A full list of current travel clinic websites worldwide is available on www.istm.org/. For other journey preparation information, consult www.nathnac.org/ds/map_world.aspx. Information about various medications may be found on www.netdoctor.co.uk/travel.

UK

Berkeley Travel Clinic 32 Berkeley St, London W1J 8EL (near Green Park tube station); 020 7629 6233; 10.00–18.00 Mon–Fri; 10.00–15.00 Sat

The Travel Clinic Ltd, Cambridge 41 Hills Rd, Cambridge CB2 1NT; 01223 367362; e enquiries@travelclinic.ltd.uk; www.travelcliniccambridge.co.uk; 10.00–16.00 Mon, Tue & Sat, 12.00–19.00 Wed & Thu, 11.00–18.00 Fri

The Travel Clinic Ltd, Ipswich Gilmour Piper, 10 Fonnereau Rd, Ipswich IP1 3JP; 01223 367362; 09.00–19.00 Wed, 09.00–13.00 Sat

Edinburgh Travel Health Clinic 14 East Preston St, Newington, Edinburgh EH8 9QA; 0131 667 1030; www.edinburghtravelhealthclinic.co.uk; 09.00–19.00 Mon–Wed, 09.00–18.00 Thu & Fri. Travel vaccinations & advice on all aspects of malaria prevention. All current UK prescribed anti-malaria tablets in stock.

Fleet Street Travel Clinic 29 Fleet St, London EC4Y 1AA; 020 7353 5678; e info@fleetstreetclinic.com; www.fleetstreetclinic.com; 08.45–17.30 Mon–Fri. Injections, travel products & latest advice.

Hospital for Tropical Diseases Travel Clinic Mortimer Market Centre, Capper St (off Tottenham Ct Rd), London WC1E 6JB; 020 7388 9600; www.thehtd.org; 13.00–17.00 Wed & 09.00–13.00 Fri. Consultations are by appointment only & are only offered to those with more complex problems. Check the website for inclusions. Runs a Travellers' Healthline Advisory Service (*020 7950 7799*) for country-specific information & health hazards. Also stocks nets, water purification equipment & personal protection measures. Travellers who have returned from the tropics & are unwell, with fever or bloody diarrhoea, can attend the walk-in emergency clinic at the Hospital without an appointment.

InterHealth Travel Clinic 111 Westminster Bridge Rd, London SE1 7HR, 020 7902 9000; e info@interhealth.org.uk; www.interhealth.org.uk; 08.30–17.30 Mon–Fri. Competitively priced, one-stop travel health service by appointment only.

MASTA (Medical Advisory Service for Travellers Abroad) At the London School of Hygiene & Tropical Medicine, Keppel St, London WC1E 7HT; 09068 224100 (this is a premium-line number, charged at 60p per minute); e enquiries@masta.org ; www.masta-travel-health.com. For a fee, they will provide an individually tailored health brief, with up-to-date information on how to stay healthy, inoculations & what to take.

MASTA pre-travel clinics 01276 685040; http://www.masta-travel-health.com/travel-clinic.aspx. Call or check the website for the nearest; there are currently 50 in Britain. They also sell malaria prophylaxis, memory cards, treatment kits, bednets, net treatment kits, etc.

NHS travel websites www.fitfortravel.nhs.uk or www.fitfortravel.scot.nhs.uk . Provide country-by-country advice on immunisation & malaria prevention, plus details of recent developments, & a list of relevant health organisations.

Nomad Travel Clinics Flagship store: 3–4 Wellington Terrace, Turnpike Lane, London N8 0PX; 020 8889 7014; e turnpike@nomadtravel.co.uk; www.nomadtravel.co.uk; walk in or appointments 09.15–17.00 every day with late night Thu. Also has clinics in west & central London, Bristol, Southampton & Manchester – see website for further information. As well as dispensing health advice, Nomad stocks mosquito nets & other anti-bug devices, & an

excellent range of adventure travel gear. Runs a Travel Health Advice line on ☎ 0906 863 3414.
Trailfinders Immunisation Centre 194 Kensington High St, London W8 7RG; ☎ 020 7938 3999; www.trailfinders.com/travelessentials/travelclinic.htm; ⏲ 09.00–17.00 Mon, Tue, Wed & Fri, 09.00–18.00 Thu, 10.00–17.15 Sat. No appointment necessary.
Travelpharm www.travelpharm.com. The Travelpharm website offers up-to-date guidance on travel-related health & has a range of medications available through its online mini-pharmacy.

Irish Republic

Tropical Medical Bureau 54 Grafton St, Dublin 2; ☎ +353 1 2715200; e graftonstreet@tmb.ie; www.tmb.ie; ⏲ until 20.00 Mon–Fri & Sat mornings. For other clinic locations, & useful information specific to tropical destinations, check their website.

USA

Centers for Disease Control 1600 Clifton Rd, Atlanta, GA 30333; ☎ (800) 232 4636 or (800) 232 6348; e cdcinfo@cdc.gov; www.cdc.gov/travel. The central source of travel information in the USA. Each summer they publish the invaluable *Health Information for International Travel.*

IAMAT (International Association for Medical Assistance to Travelers) 1623 Military Rd, #279 Niagara Falls, NY 14304-1745; ☎ 716 754 4883; e info@iamat.org; www.iamat.org. A non-profit organisation with free membership that provides lists of English-speaking doctors abroad.

Canada

IAMAT (International Association for Medical Assistance to Travellers) Suite 10, 1287 St Clair Street West, Toronto, Ontario M6E 1B8; ☎ 416 652 0137; www.iamat.org

TMVC Suite 314, 1030 W Georgia St, Vancouver, BC V6E 2Y3; ☎ (604) 681 5656; e vancouver@tmvc.com; www.tmvc.com. One-stop medical clinic for all your international travel health & vaccination needs.

Australia and New Zealand

TMVC (Travel Doctors Group) ☎ 1300 65 88 44; www.tmvc.com.au. 30 clinics in Australia & New Zealand, including: *Auckland* Canterbury Arcade, 174 Queen St, Auckland 1010, New Zealand; ☎ (64) 9 373 3531; e auckland@traveldoctor.co.nz; *Brisbane* 75a Astor Terrace, Spring Hill, Brisbane, QLD 4000, Australia; ☎ (07) 3815 6900; e brisbane@traveldoctor.com.au; *Melbourne* 393 Little Bourke St, Melbourne, Vic 3000, Australia; ☎ (03) 9935 8100; e melbourne@traveldoctor.com.au; *Sydney* 428 George St, Sydney, NSW 2000, Australia; ☎ (2) 9221 7133; e sydney@traveldoctor.com.au
IAMAT (International Association for Medical Assistance to Travellers) 206 Papanui Rd, Christchurch 5, New Zealand; www.iamat.org

South Africa

SAA-Netcare Travel Clinics ☎ 011 802 0059; e travelinfo@netcare.co.za; www.travelclinic.co.za. 11 clinics throughout South Africa.

TMVC NHC Health Centre, Cnr Beyers Naude & Waugh Northcliff; ☎ 0861 300 911; e info@traveldoctor.co.za; www.traveldoctor.co.za. Consult the website for clinic locations.

PERSONAL FIRST-AID KIT A minimal kit contains:

- A good drying antiseptic, eg: iodine or potassium permanganate (don't take antiseptic cream)
- A few small dressings (Band-Aids)
- Suncream
- Insect repellent; anti-malarial tablets; impregnated bed-net or permethrin spray
- Aspirin or paracetamol

- Antifungal cream (eg: Canesten)
- Ciprofloxacin or norfloxacin, for severe diarrhoea
- Tinidazole for giardia or amoebic dysentery (see below for regime)
- Antibiotic eye drops, for sore, 'gritty', stuck-together eyes (conjunctivitis)
- A pair of fine pointed tweezers (to remove hairy caterpillar hairs, thorns, splinters, coral, etc)
- Alcohol-based hand rub or bar of soap in plastic box
- Condoms or femidoms
- A digital thermometer

MEDICAL FACILITIES

In Mozambique there are private clinics, hospitals and pharmacies in most large towns, but unless you speak Portuguese you may have difficulty communicating your needs beyond relatively straightforward requests such as a malaria test – try to find somebody bilingual to visit the hospital with you. Consultation fees and laboratory tests are remarkably inexpensive when compared with those in the West, so if you do fall sick it would be absurd to let financial considerations dissuade you from seeking medical help.

You should be able to buy such commonly required medicines as broad-spectrum antibiotics and Flagyl at any sizeable town. If you are wandering off the beaten track, it might be worth carrying the obvious with you. As for malaria tablets, whether for prophylaxis or treatment you would be wise to get them before you go as not all tablets are available readily.

If you are on any medication prior to departure, or you have specific needs relating to a known medical condition (for instance, if you are allergic to bee stings or you are prone to attacks of asthma), then you are strongly advised to bring any related drugs and devices with you. Take the informational leaflets with me just in case you're challenged.

WATER STERILISATION You can fall ill from drinking contaminated water so try to drink from safe sources eg: bottled water where available. If you are away from shops such as half way up the Ruwenzori and your bottled water runs out, make tea, pour the remaining boiled water into a clean container and use it for drinking. Alternatively, water should be passed through a good bacteriological filter or purified with iodine or the less-effective chlorine tablets (eg: Puritabs).

COMMON MEDICAL PROBLEMS

TRAVELLERS' DIARRHOEA Travelling in Mozambique carries a fairly high risk of getting a dose of travellers' diarrhoea; perhaps half of all visitors will suffer and the newer you are to exotic travel, the more likely you will be to suffer. By taking precautions against travellers' diarrhoea you will also avoid typhoid, paratyphoid, cholera, hepatitis, dysentery, worms, etc. Travellers' diarrhoea and the other faecal-oral diseases come from getting other peoples' faeces in your mouth. This most often happens from cooks not washing their hands after a trip to the toilet, but even if the restaurant cook does not understand basic hygiene you will be safe if your food has been properly cooked and arrives piping hot. The most important prevention strategy is to wash your hands before eating anything. You can pick up salmonella and shigella from toilet door handles and possibly bank notes. The maxim to remind you what you can safely eat is:

PEEL IT, BOIL IT, COOK IT OR FORGET IT.

TREATING TRAVELLERS' DIARRHOEA

Dr Jane Wilson-Howarth

It is dehydration that makes you feel awful during a bout of diarrhoea and the most important part of treatment is drinking lots of clear fluids. Sachets of oral rehydration salts give the perfect biochemical mix to replace all that is pouring out of your bottom but other recipes taste nicer. Any dilute mixture of sugar and salt in water will do you good: try Coke or orange squash with a three-finger pinch of salt added to each glass (if you are salt-depleted you won't taste the salt). Otherwise make a solution of a four-finger scoop of sugar with a three-finger pinch of salt in a 500 ml glass. Or add eight level teaspoons of sugar (18g) and one level teaspoon of salt (3g) to one litre (five cups) of safe water. A squeeze of lemon or orange juice improves the taste and adds potassium, which is also lost in diarrhoea. Drink two large glasses after every bowel action, and more if you are thirsty. These solutions are still absorbed well if you are vomiting, but you will need to take sips at a time. If you are not eating you need to drink three litres a day plus whatever is pouring into the toilet. If you feel like eating, take a bland, high carbohydrate diet. Heavy greasy foods will probably give you cramps.

If the diarrhoea is bad, or you are passing blood or slime, or you have a fever, you will almost certainly need antibiotics in addition to fluid replacement. A dose of norfloxacin or ciprofloxacin repeated twice a day until better may be appropriate (if you are planning to take an antibiotic with you, note that both norfloxacin and ciprofloxacin are available only on prescription in the UK).If the diarrhoea is greasy and bulky and is accompanied by sulphurous (eggy) burps, one likely cause is giardia. This is best treated with Tinidazole (four x 500mg in one dose, repeated seven days later if symptoms persist).

This means that fruit you have washed and peeled yourself, and hot foods, should be safe but raw foods, cold cooked foods, salads, fruit salads which have been prepared by others, ice cream and ice are all risky, and foods kept lukewarm in hotel buffets are often dangerous. That said, plenty of travellers and expatriates enjoy fruit and vegetables, so do keep a sense of perspective: food served in a fairly decent hotel in a large town or a place regularly frequented by expatriates is likely to be safe. If you are struck, see box above for treatment.

EYE PROBLEMS Bacterial conjunctivitis (pink eye) is a common infection in Africa; people who wear contact lenses are most open to this irritating problem. The eyes feel sore and gritty and they will often be stuck together in the mornings. They will need treatment with antibiotic drops or ointment. Lesser eye irritation should settle with bathing in salt water and keeping the eyes shaded. If an insect flies into your eye, extract it with great care, ensuring you do not crush or damage it otherwise you may get a nastily inflamed eye from toxins secreted by the creature. Small elongated red-and-black blister beetles carry warning colouration to tell you not to crush them anywhere against your skin.

PRICKLY HEAT A fine pimply rash on the trunk is likely to be heat rash; cool showers, dabbing dry, and talc will help. Treat the problem by slowing down to a relaxed schedule, wearing only loose, baggy, 100%-cotton clothes and sleeping naked under a fan; if it's bad you may need to check into an air-conditioned hotel room for a while.

SKIN INFECTIONS Any mosquito bite or small nick in the skin gives an opportunity for bacteria to foil the body's usually excellent defences; it will surprise many travellers how quickly skin infections start in warm humid climates and it is essential to clean and cover even the slightest wound. Creams are not as effective as a good drying antiseptic such as dilute iodine, potassium permanganate (a few crystals in half a cup of water), or crystal (or gentian) violet. One of these should be available in most towns. If the wound starts to throb, or becomes red and the redness starts to spread, or the wound oozes, and especially if you develop a fever, antibiotics will probably be needed: flucloxacillin (250mg four times a day) or cloxacillin (500mg four times a day). For those allergic to penicillin, erythromycin (500mg twice a day) for five days should help. See a doctor if the symptoms do not start to improve within 48 hours.

Fungal infections also get a hold easily in hot, moist climates so wear 100%-cotton socks and underwear and shower frequently. An itchy rash in the groin or flaking between the toes is likely to be a fungal infection. This needs treatment with an antifungal cream such as Canesten (clotrimazole); if this is not available try Whitfield's ointment (compound benzoic acid ointment) or crystal violet (although this will turn you purple!).

OTHER INSECT-BORNE DISEASES Malaria is by no means the only insect-borne disease to which the traveller may succumb. Others include sleeping sickness and river blindness (see box, *Avoiding insect bites*, page 80). Dengue fever is not common in Mozambique but there are many other similar arboviruses. These mosquito-borne diseases may mimic malaria but there is no prophylactic medication against them. The mosquitoes that carry dengue fever viruses bite during the daytime, so it is worth applying repellent if you see any mosquitoes around. Symptoms include strong headaches, rashes and excruciating joint and muscle pains and high fever. Viral fevers usually last about a week or so and are not usually fatal. Complete rest and paracetamol are the usual treatment; plenty of fluids also help. Some patients are given an intravenous drip to keep them from dehydrating. It is especially important to protect yourself if you have had dengue fever before, since a second infection with a different strain can result in the potentially fatal dengue haemorrhagic fever.

BILHARZIA OR SCHISTOSOMIASIS (*with thanks to Dr Vaughan Southgate of the Natural History Museum, London, and Dr Dick Stockley, The Surgery, Kampala*) Bilharzia or schistosomiasis is a disease that commonly afflicts the rural poor of the tropics. Two types exist in sub-Saharan Africa – Schistosoma mansoni and Schistosoma haematobium. It is an unpleasant problem that is worth avoiding, though can be treated if you do get it. This parasite is common in almost all water sources in [country], even places advertised as 'bilharzia free'. The most risky shores will be close to places where infected people use water, wash clothes, etc.

It is easier to understand how to diagnose it, treat it and prevent it if you know a little about the life cycle. Contaminated faeces are washed into the lake, the eggs hatch and the larva infects certain species of snail. The snails then produce about 10,000 cercariae a day for the rest of their lives. The parasites can digest their way through your skin when you wade, or bathe in infested fresh water.

Winds disperse the snails and cercariae. The snails in particular can drift a long way, especially on windblown weed, so nowhere is really safe. However, deep water and running water are safer, while shallow water presents the greatest risk. The cercariae penetrate intact skin, and find their way to the liver. There male and female meet and spend the rest of their lives in permanent copulation. No wonder you feel tired! Most finish up in the wall of the lower bowel, but others can get lost and can cause damage to many different organs. *Schistosoma haematobium* goes mostly to the bladder.

AVOIDING INSECT BITES

As the sun is going down, don long clothes and apply a 50–55% DEET based insect repellent on any exposed flesh. You also need either a permethrin-impregnated bednet or a permethrin spray so that you can 'treat' bednets in hotels though taking your own is still the best option. Permethrin treatment makes even very tatty nets protective and prevents mosquitoes from biting through the impregnated net when you roll against it; it also deters other biters. Otherwise retire to an air-conditioned room or burn mosquito or sleep under a fan. Coils and fans reduce rather than eliminate bites. Travel clinics usually sell a good range of nets, treatment kits and repellents.

Mosquitoes and many other insects are attracted to light. If you are camping, never put a lamp near the opening of your tent, or you will have a swarm of biters waiting to join you when you retire. In hotel rooms, be aware that the longer your light is on, the greater the number of insects will be sharing your accommodation.

Aside from avoiding mosquito bites between dusk and dawn, which will protect you from elephantiasis and a range of nasty insect-borne viruses, as well as malaria (see page 73), it is important to take precautions against other insect bites. During the day it is wise to wear long, loose (preferably 100% cotton) clothes if you are pushing through scrubby country; this will keep off ticks and also tsetse and day-biting *Aedes* mosquitoes which may spread viral fevers, including yellow fever.

Tsetse flies hurt when they bite and it is said that they are attracted to the colour blue; locals will advise on where they are a problem and where they transmit sleeping sickness.

Minute pestilential biting blackflies spread river blindness in some parts of Africa between 19°N and 17°S; the disease is caught close to fast-flowing rivers since flies breed there and the larvae live in rapids. The flies bite during the day but long trousers tucked into socks will help keep them off. Citronella-based natural repellents (eg: Mosi-guard) do not work against them.

Tumbu flies or putsi, often called mango flies in Mozambique are a problem where the climate is hot and humid. The adult fly lays her eggs on the soil or on drying laundry and when the eggs come into contact with human flesh (when you put on clothes or lie on a bed) they hatch and bury themselves under the skin. Here they form a crop of 'boils' each with a maggot inside. Smear a little Vaseline over the hole, and they will push their noses out to breathe. It may be possible to squeeze them out but it depends if they are ready to do so as the larvae have spines that help them to hold on.

In putsi areas either dry your clothes and sheets within a screened house, or dry them in direct sunshine until they are crisp, or iron them.

Jiggers or sandfleas are another flesh-feaster, which can be best avoided by wearing shoes. They latch on if you walk barefoot in contaminated places, and set up home under the skin of the foot, usually at the side of a toenail where they cause a painful, boil-like swelling. They need picking out by a local expert.

Although the adults do not cause any harm in themselves, after about 4–6 weeks they start to lay eggs, which cause an intense but usually ineffective immune reaction, including fever, cough, abdominal pain, and a fleeting, itching rash called 'safari itch'. The absence of early symptoms does not necessarily mean there is no infection. Later symptoms can be more localised and more severe, but the general symptoms settle down fairly quickly and eventually you are just tired. 'Tired all the time' is one of the most common symptoms among expats in Africa, and bilharzia, giardia, amoeba and intestinal yeast are the most common culprits.

Although bilharzia is difficult to diagnose, it can be tested at specialist travel clinics. Ideally tests need to be done at least six weeks after likely exposure and will determine whether you need treatment. Fortunately it is easy to treat at present.

Avoiding bilharzia If you are bathing, swimming, paddling or wading in fresh water which you think may carry a bilharzia risk, try to get out of the water within ten minutes.

- Avoid bathing or paddling on shores within 200m of villages or places where people use the water a great deal, especially reedy shores or where there is lots of water weed.
- Dry off thoroughly with a towel; rub vigorously.
- If your bathing water comes from a risky source try to ensure that the water is taken from the lake in the early morning and stored snail-free, otherwise it should be filtered or Dettol or Cresol added.
- Bathing early in the morning is safer than bathing in the last half of the day.
- Cover yourself with DEET insect repellent before swimming: it may offer some protection.

HIV/AIDS The risks of sexually transmitted infection are extremely high in Mozambique, whether you sleep with fellow travellers or locals. About 80% of HIV infections in British heterosexuals are acquired abroad. If you must indulge, use condoms or femidoms, which help reduce the risk of transmission. If you notice any genital ulcers or discharge, get treatment promptly since these increase the risk of acquiring HIV. If you do have unprotected sex, visit a clinic as soon as possible; this should be within 24 hours, or no later than 72 hours, for post-exposure prophylaxis.

MENINGITIS This is a particularly nasty disease as it can kill within hours of the first symptoms appearing. The tell-tale symptoms are a combination of a blinding headache (light sensitivity), a blotchy rash and a high fever. Immunisation protects against the most serious bacterial form of meningitis and the conjugate tetravalent vaccine ACWY (Menveo) may be recommended for Mozambique by British travel clinics.

Although other forms of meningitis exist (usually viral), there are no vaccines for these. Local papers normally report localised outbreaks. A severe headache and fever should make you run to a doctor immediately. There are also other causes of headache and fever; one of which is typhoid, which occurs in travellers to Mozambique. Seek medical help if you are ill for more than a few days.

RABIES Rabies is carried by all mammals (beware the village dogs and small monkeys that are used to being fed in the parks) and is passed on to man through a bite, scratch or a lick of an open wound. You must always assume any animal is rabid, and seek medical help as soon as possible. Meanwhile scrub the wound with soap under a running tap or while pouring water from a jug. Find a reasonably clear-looking source of water (but at this stage the quality of the water is not important), then pour on a strong iodine or alcohol solution of gin, whisky or rum. This helps stop the rabies virus entering the body and will guard against wound infections, including tetanus.

Pre-exposure vaccinations for rabies is ideally advised for everyone, but is particularly important if you intend to have contact with animals and/or are likely to be more than 24 hours away from medical help. Ideally three doses should be taken over a minimum of 21 days, though even taking one or two doses of vaccine is better than none at all. Contrary to popular belief these vaccinations are relatively painless.

If you are bitten, scratched or licked over an open wound by a sick animal, then post-exposure prophylaxis should be given as soon as possible, though it is never too late to seek help, as the incubation period for rabies can be very long. Those who have not been immunised will need rabies immunoglobulin (RIG) and a full course of rabies vaccine. RIG is often hard to come by and is very expensive – another good reason to get pre-exposure vaccines before you go. If there is no RIG available then you should get your insurance to evacuate to South Africa. Tell the doctor if you have had pre-exposure vaccine, as this will change the treatment you receive. You will no longer need RIG and you will only need two further doses of vaccine given three days apart. This is usually available in Mozambique so will avert the need for evacuation in most cases. And remember that, if you do contract rabies, mortality is 100% and death from rabies is probably one of the worst ways to go.

TICKBITE FEVER African ticks are not the rampant disease transmitters they are in the Americas, but they may spread tickbite fever and a few dangerous rarities in Mozambique Tickbite fever is a flu-like illness that can easily be treated with doxycycline, but as there can be some serious complications it is important to visit a doctor.

Ticks should ideally be removed as soon as possible as leaving them on the body increases the chance of infection. They should be removed with special tick tweezers that can be bought in good travel shops. Failing that you can use your finger nails: grasp the tick as close to your body as possible and pull steadily and firmly away at right angles to your skin. The tick will then come away complete, as long as you do not jerk or twist. If possible douse the wound with alcohol (any spirit will do) or iodine. Irritants (eg: Olbas oil) or lit cigarettes are to be discouraged since they can cause the ticks to regurgitate and therefore increase the risk of disease. It is best to get a travelling companion to check you for ticks; if you are travelling with small children, remember to check their heads, and particularly behind the ears.

Spreading redness around the bite and/or fever and/or aching joints after a tick bite imply that you have an infection that requires antibiotic treatment, so seek advice.

SNAKEBITE Snakes rarely attack unless provoked, and bites in travellers are unusual. You are less likely to get bitten if you wear stout shoes and long trousers when in the bush. Most snakes are harmless and even venomous species will dispense venom in only about half of their bites. If bitten, then, you are unlikely to have received venom; keeping this fact in mind may help you to stay calm. Many so-called first-aid techniques do more harm than good: cutting into the wound is harmful; tourniquets are dangerous; suction and electrical inactivation devices do not work. The only treatment is antivenom. In case of a bite that you fear may have been from a venomous snake:

- Try to keep calm – it is likely that no venom has been dispensed.
- Prevent movement of the bitten limb by applying a splint.
- Keep the bitten limb BELOW heart height to slow the spread of any venom.
- If you have a crêpe bandage, wrap it around the whole limb (eg: all the way from the toes to the thigh), as tight as you would for a sprained ankle or a muscle pull.
- Evacuate to a hospital that has antivenom. At the time of writing this is only known to be available in Kampala. Many centres have an Indian antivenom that does not include the most common biting snakes in Mozambique

And remember:

- NEVER give aspirin; you may take paracetamol, which is safe.
- NEVER cut or suck the wound.
- DO NOT apply ice packs.
- DO NOT apply potassium permanganate.

If the offending snake can be captured without risk of someone else being bitten, take this to show the doctor – but beware since even a decapitated head is able to bite.

5

Diving and Snorkelling

Danny Edmunds

The diving in Mozambique is as good as you'll find anywhere along the east African coastline south of the Equator, but the remoteness of the location and comparative lack of diving-specific medical facilities mean that you need to be savvy. Most of the following applies to divers, so a separate section on snorkelling is included at the end.

CHOOSING AN OPERATOR

Dive operators are opening up all the way along the coastline, and the vast majority are affiliated to PADI (Professional Association of Diving Instructors) or another internationally recognised training and certification organisation. In addition there are a few operators who don't have affiliation to any of the dive associations. It would be unfair to label the latter as bad a priori, but it does mean that they don't operate to the same level of inspection as an affiliated operator.

If you can't see the logo for your preferred association, then ask – if affiliated they should be able to produce the relevant certificate. However, certification is only one indicator you should look for – the section below also gives some pointers.

If you're faced with a plethora of operators, it's worth asking other divers and locals their opinions.

PREPARATIONS BEFORE DIVING

QUALIFICATIONS Any reputable operator should check both your qualification level (as shown on your C-card) and your recent dive history. They should then tailor the dive to the ability level of the least-qualified diver, and if this isn't feasible, split the group.

KIT In remote places, kit will almost certainly be serviced on site. It may look worn and faded but providing it's been well maintained it will be reliable. Personally I always put together any kit that I am going to use myself, and I check the following:

Regulators

- Does it have an octopus? Do both sets of regulators breathe easily on the surface, with no evidence of juddering?
- Is the contents gauge showing zero before the regulators are connected to the tank? Does it show the correct pressure once the regulators are pressurised? Turn the tank off again and breathe through the regulator – the needle should move down smoothly.

- When the regulators are pressurised, can you detect any leakages from the hoses? If possible dunk the pressurised set in the water before you get on the boat – can you see any obvious leakages? If you can't dunk it while on the shore, do a check once you are in the water *before* leaving the surface.
- Check the hoses connecting the first stage to the second stage for cracking or other damage.
- If there is a depth gauge on the unit, check that the marker needle is moved back to zero before you get in the water. Keep an eye on it as you descend through the first few metres of water – it should clearly indicate the depth change.

Stab/BC

- Does it fit properly? If it's too big or too small, get another one.
- What is the condition of the clips that hold it together? They should fit securely enough to hold during normal use and yet still be breakable should you need to dump the kit in a hurry.
- Does the inflator valve connect properly to the hose? Always test the inflator before leaving the shore to make sure that you can fully inflate the stab. It should not deflate when dunked in water. In particular check the seams of the stab for leaks.
- Do all the dump valves work properly? Make sure you are familiar with their location on the kit and that you can work them easily while wearing the kit.

Tank

- Check the condition of the tank for signs of rust and external damage, and also check the condition of the pillar valve – it should take a little effort to open and close (thus ensuring that it's not going to close accidentally during the dive). If there is any visible damage to the pillar valve or it appears to stick, get a replacement tank.
- Is there enough air in the tank for the dive you are intending to do? Does it taste clean and dry when you test the regulators?
- Look for evidence of testing on the cylinders. This can be tricky in Mozambique, but the standard in the UK is for each tank to have the date and type of its last test stamped into it. If you're unsure then ask for clarification on precisely when, where and how the tanks were last tested.

Fins and booties You will probably be offered a choice between separate booties with rear-entry fins (where you put the booties on like shoes and then slip into the fins) or slipper fins (where the booties and fins are combined into one unit). I'd only recommend the latter if you know for sure that you'll be able to walk across clean sand to the boat. If you have any doubt or are going to have to wade to the boat or the dive site, take separate booties and fins. Much of the coastline of Mozambique is made up of a combination of coral rag and sand infested with sea urchins and other nasties: you'll need the protection.

- Check the fit of the booties and fins before you leave the shop – too loose and you risk losing them during your dive; too tight and you'll get cramp and blisters and may find yourself unable to fin.

Weight belt

- Weight is carried to compensate for the air lost during the dive, so the ideal amount of weight to carry is enough to enable you to hover comfortably at 5m with only 50 bar remaining for a few minutes. You should know how much weight you need from the details in your logbook.

- Check the weight belt fabric – it should be strong with little fraying or cuts.
- Check the buckle – it should hold in any position but still be undoable in an emergency. Bear in mind that during the dive it will become looser as your wetsuit compresses, so you may need to readjust it occasionally. The belt should be tight enough to stay in position without restricting your breathing.
- Check the fixing of the weights. They should be secured so that they don't move around during the dive. Needless to say they should not be capable of falling off during the dive.

Clothing

- The surface temperature of the seas in Mozambique is likely to be in the region of 23–28°C depending on the time of year. You may feel that this is warm enough to dive wearing only a T-shirt and shorts but bear in mind that thermoclines can occur where you'll lose up to 5°C, so a wetsuit covering at least your torso is highly recommended.
- Wetsuits will also protect you from jellies, hydroids and other stinging things.

Masks

- It is crucial that the mask fits your face, and the best way of checking this is to put the mask on your face so that it seals around your eyes and nose. Breathe in through your nose and hold your breath – the mask should stay attached to your face with no leakages. If it loosens or drops off then try another mask.
- Check the skirt (the latex seal) around the mask – it should be reasonably flexible with no damage or tears.
- Check the side clips holding the mask-strap onto the mask – they should be sound and secure.
- Check the strap – it should be in good condition with some slack in it when you are wearing it. It's important that you don't have the strap too tight.
- If you need prescription lenses, then I'd strongly recommend that you take your own mask with you.

Computers/dive watches It's highly unlikely that you'll be given a computer or dive watch as part of the basic kit. However, it is crucial that you have a means of measuring both the length of time you have been underwater and the depth you're at (see the section on *Decompression illness*, page 89). Personally, I carry my dive computer with me when I travel somewhere I might be diving.

OTHER DIVERS It's extremely likely that you'll be lumped in with other divers of whom you will almost certainly know nothing.

- One of the best ways of assessing other divers is to watch them put their kit together. If they seem hesitant or slapdash you may want to reconsider diving with them. It's also worth talking to them – find out who they are, how many dives they've done, what qualification they hold and so on.
- One of the most important people to find out about is the leader of the dive. Discover what qualification they hold (at the very minimum they should be a PADI divemaster or equivalent), how familiar they are with the site, how much experience they have.

- How many divers will there be on the dive? The ratio should be as low as possible and certainly no more than six paying divers to every divemaster. On any dive where there are more than three paying divers I would expect there to be at least two divemasters, one leading from the front and one bringing up the rear.
- Are you being formally buddied up with another diver? If not, find out why not and what the established procedure is should you have a problem during the dive. If you are being formally buddied, have a good chat with your buddy and find out their interests, experience and intentions – these should more or less match your own. It is essential that you establish these guidelines and perform a thorough buddy check – this is the person you are relying on to help you out if you get into trouble.
- One particular bugbear is photographers. I'm an underwater photographer myself and I have no hesitation in saying unequivocally that the most considerate, careful buddy in the world turns into a nightmare when given a camera. If you are a non-photographer diving in a group with a large number of photographers, make a beeline for any other competent non-photographer in the group and stick to them like glue. If you are a photographer then it's crucial that you put aside that suicidal determination to get the shot and make strenuous efforts to dive as a buddy first and a photographer second.

DIVE BRIEFING This should be accurate and reasonably concise. At the very minimum I would expect the following to be adequately covered:

- Site orientation, including a map giving the general lie of the site, clear waypoints, tidal direction and likely strength, entry and exit points (if a shore dive), boat position (if a boat dive) and danger points (downward rip currents, disorientating holes, areas of entanglement).
- Emergency and problem procedures, which should include clear instructions on signals to be used. It should also give clear indications of what is expected by the boat crew and the help that they will be able to give you in the event of an emergency.
- Depth and time plans, including any decompression stops. You should have some method of checking and recording this for reference during the dive. Check the tables before getting on the boat to see how much leeway there is in the plan, bearing in mind that the closer you are to 'no stop' limits the higher the risk of running short of air and ending up with excessive nitrogen in your bloodstream. If you feel that the dive is too long or too deep, then ask for the plan to be revised. Make a note of the plan and the fallback if you go slightly deeper or stay slightly longer than intended.
- If you have any questions, make sure that you ask them – if you aren't happy with the answers then ask again. Remember that you are paying for the dive and the operator has a duty to keep you safe and satisfied.

THE DIVE BOAT As a bare minimum the boat should have oxygen, a radio, life jackets, a first-aid kit, an engine and alternate means of propulsion. However, this is where the very nature of Mozambique requires a degree of compromise. A radio is only of any use if there is going to be someone listening out for a call. In addition none of the dive operators I saw carried oxygen – they should do, but didn't while I was there (for more on this see the section on *Decompression illness*, opposite).

Drivers should be trained and competent in diver pick-up, and if you are diving from a hard boat or one with high sides, a solid (ie: not rope) ladder should be provided for climbing aboard.

DURING THE DIVE

- Watch where you are in relation to your buddy and the rest of the group. You should under no circumstances stray more than a few metres from any other diver – remember that if your air fails without warning then you have to cover that distance, almost certainly without any air in your lungs. Don't rely on your buddy (or nearest diver) realising what's going on – there's a strong likelihood that they'll be looking at the pretty fish rather than you. This is particularly the case with photographers: I've seen photographers who spent so long lining up a shot that they failed to realise that the rest of the group left them five minutes ago.
- Keep an eye on the divers around you. If everyone is keeping an eye on everyone else then problems should be spotted early and resolved before they become dangerous.
- Keep an eye on your depth gauge and watch or your computer and air contents gauge. You should be checking these once a minute at the very minimum. Inform the dive leader when you reach the predetermined quantity of air left and make sure that the message is received and understood.
- If you are separated from the rest of the group, *do not* continue the dive alone. Look around for between 30 seconds and one minute (certainly no longer) and then ascend to 6m. Unless there is some other major problem (for instance you're out of air), carry out the planned decompression (if any) between 5 and 6m and then take one minute to continue to the surface. Always try to add a three-minute safety stop on top of any planned decompression. It's possible that on surfacing you'll work out where the group are – *under no circumstances should you attempt to rejoin them under the water.*
- Try to avoid touching the reef. Not only is this likely to harm the coral and other animals living there, but the reef contains organisms that will sting or bite you. Do not pick anything up – again, it's damaging to the reef, and there are one or two animals that are quite capable of killing you (see *Nasties*, page 91).

DECOMPRESSION ILLNESS There isn't space here for an in-depth section on decompression, so I will give an overview and concentrate on avoidance and treatment. Any decent dive course book will give a good basic understanding of the physical and biological actions that lead to decompression illness (DCI), colloquially known as 'the bends'.

During any dive nitrogen from the compressed air we breathe is absorbed into our tissues at rates higher than we experience on the surface, and the amount of nitrogen absorbed (the 'nitrogen loading') is directly related to the length of time we spend underwater and the depths we have visited. As we rise from the deepest part of our dive, the absorbed nitrogen starts to come out of solution and form bubbles within the body. Providing these bubbles are small enough they are carried to the bloodstream and thence to the lungs to be exhaled. If we rise too fast the bubbles get too big to be transported in this manner, and there is a risk that they will get stuck somewhere in the body. This is what causes DCI.

It needs to be stated upfront: there is no way to avoid nitrogen uptake and release during a dive, so the key is to ensure that the nitrogen is released slowly enough to pass to the lungs safely. Algorithms have been developed over the decades to help measure this, and these algorithms form the basis of all dive tables and dive computers, which is why it is so important that we dive within the limits prescribed by them.

However, diving within the limits set by tables or your computer is not going to eliminate the risk of a bend developing – it will merely reduce the risk to acceptable levels. It is perfectly possible for an individual to dive well within their tables and perfectly sensibly and still end up with a bend. It also needs to be stated that neither tables nor dive computers are intended to bring you back to the surface completely decompressed – the process of nitrogen release will continue for some hours after the end of any dive. This becomes important when considering flights.

One major factor in many bends is dehydration, often (if not exclusively) linked to excessive drinking. The precise mechanism is not understood, but there is a clear linkage between excessive alcohol consumption and the likelihood of a bend, so if you are intending to dive, it's best to limit yourself to one or two the night before.

The only cure for a serious bend is recompression in a hyperbaric chamber to push the bubbles back into solution in a controlled manner. The decompression process can then be carried out under controlled circumstances with proper medical supervision. The closest chambers to Mozambique are in Durban or Johannesburg in South Africa. They are a very long way away from the Mozambican coast and any evacuation for a major bend will involve a flight.

For minor bends administration of 100% oxygen can prove useful, but this is not a cure and is entirely inappropriate with a bend affecting any of the major organs or the central nervous system. However, I came across no dive operators that had oxygen available during my travels around Mozambique. While there may be understandable reasons for this (the difficulty of maintaining supplies of oxygen in the country) it is a factor that all those considering diving in Mozambique need to bear in mind.

Flying involves a degree of depressurisation and it should be obvious that this presents further danger of DCI in those who have recently dived. The various diving associations give different times that should be observed between the end of the last dive and take-off, but the consensus seems to be in the region of 16 hours. Personally I always allow 24 hours between the end of my last dive and my flight home.

The only time when this should be broken is with medical evacuations. If you have to be medically evacuated after a dive (regardless of the reason) then it must be emphasised to the pilot that under no circumstances should the flight be higher than 500m above sea level. While I was in Mozambique there was an incident when a diver was airlifted from the coast suffering from a major bend. The pilot took her to the Johannesburg chamber. Johannesburg is at an altitude of around 1,700m above sea level and the diver died *en route*. Had she been taken to Durban (which is on the coast and so can be reached without breaking 500m) she might have survived. The same is true of land evacuations – in the event of a major DCI, the diver must be kept below 500m above sea level and got to a chamber as soon as possible.

Medical evacuation and chamber treatment is fearsomely expensive (the bill can come to tens of thousands of US dollars) so it is important to check the terms of your medical insurance and not stray outside those. The freephone helplines that are so often touted may be of limited use in cases of DCI, so it may help to speak to someone with specialist knowledge of diving. The Divers Alert Network (*www.dan.org*) isn't bad, but their knowledge of facilities outside the USA is limited. Personally I'd contact the London Diving Chamber (*www.londondivingchamber.co.uk*) – officially they deal only with members (as do DAN), but they will never turn away someone in trouble and have done a lot of pro bono work back in the UK. Lastly, be aware that some chambers may well be reluctant to provide treatment (I've heard a few horror stories of divers with major bends being told to treat themselves with vitamin B12 or that 'it's too late to treat'): if this should happen to you, ring the London Diving Chamber's emergency line and get them to talk to the chamber in question.

Hopefully you can see why it is important to dive extremely conservatively in Mozambique – the medical facilities are far below those available in many dive locations so you have to dive defensively. The golden rule with DCI is that any abnormal symptoms that exist after a dive should be regarded as DCI until proven otherwise.

NASTIES In all my time diving in tropical waters, the worst injuries I've had have been coral cuts and sea urchin spines. There are numerous things that might bite or sting you out of fear, curiosity or just plain accident, but only around 2% of diving incidents are caused by marine wildlife – you're much more at risk from your fellow divers.

Jellyfish There are plenty of jellyfish in Mozambican waters but none of them are regarded as life-threatening to a healthy adult (which doesn't rule out the risk of severe allergic reaction). Portuguese men-of-war (*Physalia physalia*) are fairly common at certain times of year, as are purple stingers (*Pelagia noctiluca*), and both of these can give nasty stings which are on very rare occasions fatal.

If you are stung by a jellyfish, pour vinegar (or in the absence of vinegar, urine) over the affected area – the venom from the vast majority of jellyfish is alkaline and will be neutralised by the acid. Try and remove any remaining stinging cells from the skin with a stick (not your fingers). If this fails, dust the area with flour and scrape the resulting gloop off with a blunt knife. Treat any swelling with a mild steroid cream (such as hydrocortisone). In the event of allergic reaction it's vital to get to medical aid as soon as possible.

Coral stings There are thousands of different coral species, the identification of most of which involves microscopic examination of the polyps, so generally corals are referred to by the forms their colonies grow into. The only coral form you need to be actively aware of is the fire coral, which classically has a bright yellow margin running along its crown. The sting is in itself not fatal but may hurt. As with the jellyfish there is the possibility of allergic reaction. Treatment is the same as for jellyfish stings, but if the skin is broken you'll need to treat for cuts and scrapes (see below).

Cuts and scrapes The coastal islands of Mozambique are all based on a hard core of coral rag overlain with sand. Coral rag is a concrete mixture of coral skeleton, sand and shell, cemented and hardened by the actions of the wind and waves. It's surprisingly brittle but can cut very deeply, so if you are ever walking on coral rag, you must wear some form of foot protection. The biggest risk with a coral cut is that minute particles of the rag break off inside the cut. These particles will be laden with bacteria, algae and coral polyps that will merrily begin to grow inside the cut. It's vital that you thoroughly wash out any cut as soon as possible, then treat it with antiseptic and cover. Check it on a regular basis – one of the peculiarities of tiny cuts in marine tropical environments is that they very quickly form abscesses which can take a surprisingly long time to heal. My personal record is a couple of mosquito bites that I scratched – the resulting abscesses didn't heal properly until three months after I returned to the UK, and the scars are over an inch in diameter.

Animals that can cause cuts and scrapes range from members of the shark family (obviously the teeth can inflict cuts, but the skin also presents a risk, being covered in tiny scales called denticles that act as a form of sandpaper), surgeonfish (which have tiny blades at the base of their tails), lobsters, crabs and other crustaceans, moray eels, barracuda and titan triggerfish.

The best way to avoid getting bitten is not to irritate the animal in question – the vast majority of fish would rather steer well clear of you and will only attack when cornered. However, the titan triggerfish (*Balistoides viridescens*) is highly territorial and there are many recorded incidents of attacks on divers who have accidentally or deliberately strayed into a nesting zone.

Sharks have, in my opinion, been given a bad rap over the years, but it's undeniable that some species, including several regularly found in Mozambican waters, will attack humans. Reading shark behaviour is complex and best left to the experts, so ask your dive guides what sharks are likely to be present, whether they are dangerous and what the warning signs are. That having been said, providing sharks are not provoked, they are highly unlikely to attack you.

Venom Many of the animals in the coastal waters of Mozambique have venom, either as protection from hunters or to help hunt for food. This venom can give an extremely painful sting but is only in itself fatal in a very few species. The treatment for the venom from virtually all of these animals is to immerse the sting site in water as hot as possible – the heat breaks the toxins down. This basic treatment will cover the vast majority of stinging animals from sea urchins and fire worms through to sea snakes and striped catfish (*Plotosus lineatus*) to the various members of the scorpionfish family (including lionfish, devilfish and stonefish). Of this last group the worst is unquestionably the stonefish, the sting of which has been implicated in several deaths, although it's unclear whether the venom was directly fatal or whether the victim died of some other problem brought on by the pain caused by that venom. At any rate all of them have venom that can be broken down by heat.

The most important exception to the hot water treatment is the cone shell. Two species of cone shell – the textile cone (*Conus textile*) and the geographic cone (*Conus geographus*) – are found on the Mozambican coastline and both have been responsible for fatalities. There is anti-venom but it is absolutely crucial that the affected area be immobilised and the victim transported to medical care immediately. It has to be restated that it is highly unlikely that a normal medical centre on the coast of Mozambique will carry the anti-venom as a matter of course, and the more sensible approach is not to get stung in the first place – in other words, don't touch anything.

Spines The coastal area of Mozambique is littered with various species of black spiny sea urchins, the spines of which are often coated with a venomous mucus. Puncture wounds from these often contain the tips of spines and will readily abscess. Removal of tips trapped in the skin should only be done by qualified medics. There are several species of spiny starfish that have similar spines and should be treated in the same manner, and there have also been occasions where the stinging spines of scorpionfish and catfish have broken off in the wound.

SNORKELLING

Much of the diving section also applies to snorkelling – while you don't need to worry about DCI, the nasties won't make the distinction between divers and snorkellers (or indeed those just splashing around in the surf).

ADDITIONAL KIT Mask and fin fitting are as important for snorkellers as for divers. The snorkel should fit comfortably in your mouth and be easily replaceable if it happens to come out. Some snorkels have clearance valves on them and these can be useful if you can't muster the puff to clear the tube in the traditional manner. A less helpful tweak is a flexible tube between the main body of the snorkel and the mouthpiece – the theory behind them is that they provide a more comfortable fit, but I've found that they tend to fall away from your mouth at the wrong moment. You may also want to ask for a buoyancy device – this is a little like a waistcoat filled with buoyant material that will prevent you sinking to the bottom of the ocean.

BRIEFINGS These are as crucial to snorkellers as they are to divers and should contain much the same sort of information, particularly with regard to surface currents. You also need to know where the lookout is going to be sited – they may be your only means of communication with the shore. Check to see whether there will be a cover boat to pick you up if you do get out of your depth. When I'm running snorkelling operations I try to have at least one strong staff swimmer in the water with the snorkellers, usually with a life-ring to hold onto while being towed (if towing is required).

SAFETY TIPS

Beware sunburn You're far more susceptible to sunburn while snorkelling than while diving or just sitting on the beach. Avoidance tactics include wearing a T-shirt to protect your back, and a hat to protect the top of your head (make sure it has a chinstrap). You may want to invest in one of the Lycra bodysuits which will keep you warm and protect you from sunburn and jellyfish stings. Any bits that aren't covered need to be liberally coated in a good high-factor sunblock – as a guide I'd suggest a minimum of factor 40 – which must be waterproof. From personal experience I'd suggest applying a thick layer to the backs of the ears.

Beware cold It may seem stupid but you can lose sufficient core body temperature during a long snorkel session (particularly when there's a bit of wind) to bring you into danger of shock. Lycra bodysuits can protect against this, or just pop out every now and again to warm up a bit.

Don't go out of sight Always bear in mind that if you can't see the lookout, they can't see you, and if you've wandered off from the main group searching for peace and quiet, remember that it's the group they will be watching.

Keep an ear open for the warning signal While there aren't any formal beach lifeguards in Mozambique, it's likely that any snorkel operator will have an established system of signalling (usually blasts on a whistle) for the lookout to communicate with the snorkellers. It's vital that you keep an ear open for this and that you make a clear response when you hear it.

Part Two

SOUTHERN MOZAMBIQUE

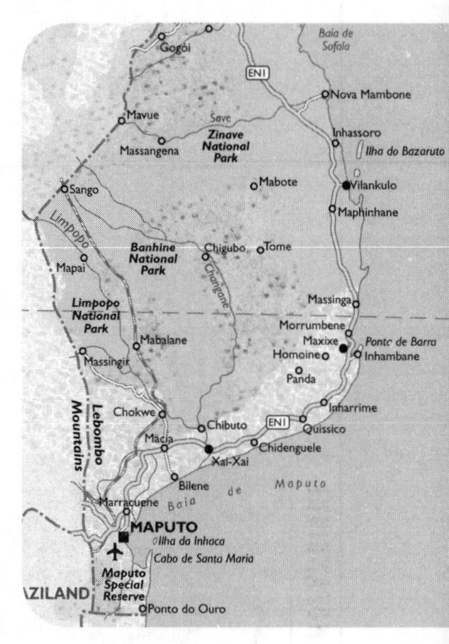

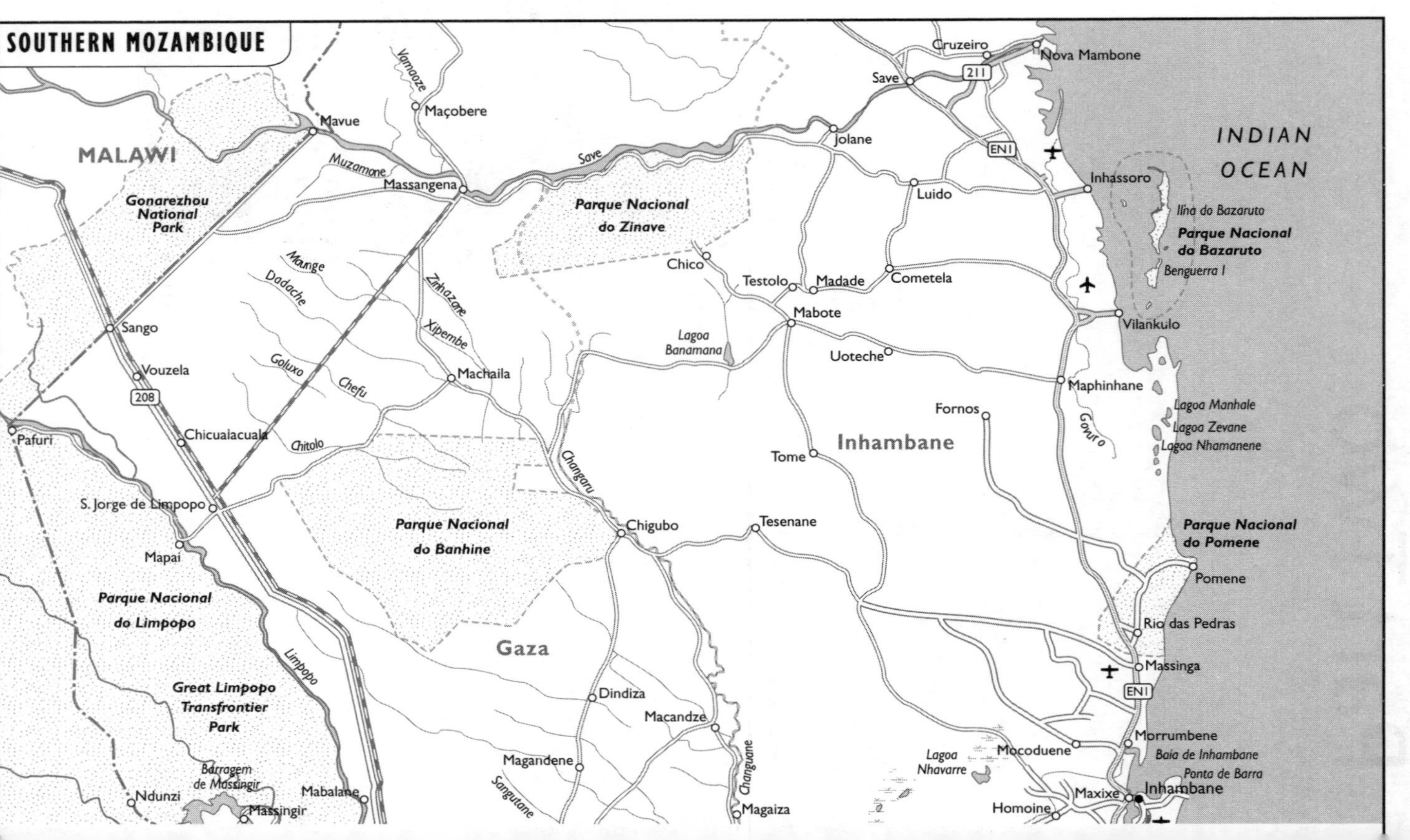
SOUTHERN MOZAMBIQUE
INDIAN OCEAN
Ilha do Bazaruto
Parque Nacional do Bazaruto
Benguerra I
Nova Mambone
Cruzeiro
211
Save
EN1
Inhassoro
Vilankulo
Maphinhane
Govuro
Lagoa Manhale
Lagoa Zevane
Lagoa Nhamanene
Parque Nacional do Pomene
Pomene
Rio das Pedras
Massinga
Morrumbene
Baía de Inhambane
Ponta de Barra
Inhambane
Maxixe
Homoine
Mocoduene
Lagoa Nhavarre
Jolane
Luido
Cometela
Madade
Testolo
Chico
Mabote
Uoteche
Fornos
Inhambane
Tome
Tesenane
Lagoa Banamana
Parque Nacional do Zinave
Mavue
Maçobere
Vamaoze
Muzamone
Massangena
Save
MALAWI
Gonarezhou National Park
Maunge
Dadache
Zinhazane
Xipembe
Machaila
Goluxo
Chefu
Chitolo
Sango
Vouzela
208
Chicualacuala
Pafuri
Changaru
Chigubo
S. Jorge de Limpopo
Mapai
Parque Nacional do Banhine
Parque Nacional do Limpopo
Limpopo
Gaza
Great Limpopo Transfrontier Park
Dindiza
Macandze
Magandene
Sangutane
Changane
Magaiza
Barragem de Massingir
Ndunzi
Mabalane
Massingir

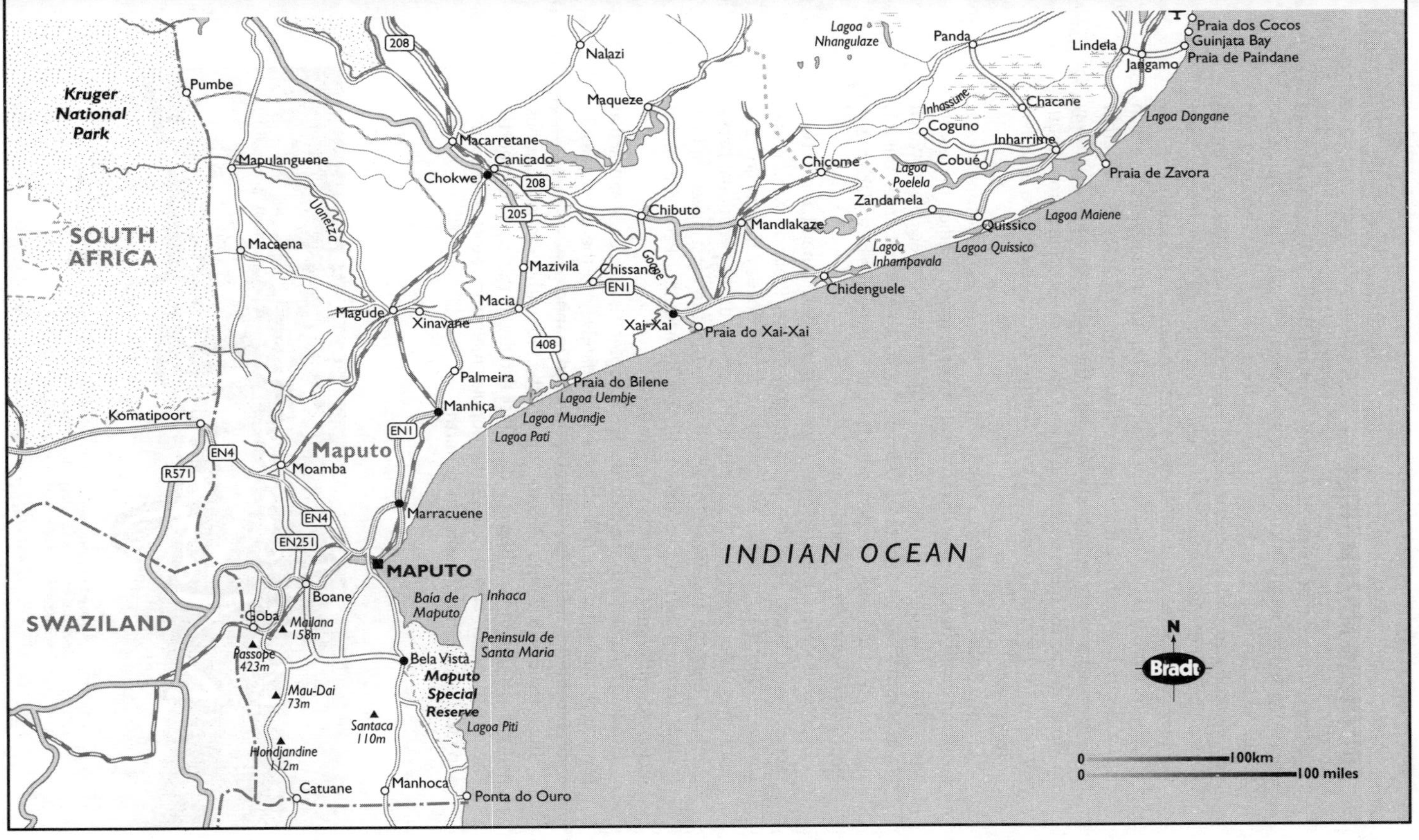

Kruger National Park
Pumbe
208
Nalazi
Lagoa Nhangulaze
Panda
Lindela
Praia dos Cocos
Guinjata Bay
Praia de Paindane
Jangamo
Maqueze
Inhassune
Chacane
Coguno
Lagoa Dongane
Macarretane
Inharrime
Mapulanguene
Canicado
Chicome
Lagoa Poelela
Cobué
Praia de Zavora
Chokwe
208
Zandamela
205
Chibuto
Mandlakaze
Quissico
Lagoa Maiene
Uanetza
SOUTH AFRICA
Macaena
Lagoa Inhampavala
Lagoa Quissico
Mazivila
Chissano
Gaza
EN1
Chidenguele
Macia
Magude
Xinavane
Xai-Xai
Praia do Xai-Xai
408
Palmeira
Praia do Bilene
Lagoa Uembje
Manhiça
Lagoa Muandje
Komatipoort
EN1
Lagoa Pati
EN4
Maputo
R571
Moamba
Marracuene
EN4
EN251
INDIAN OCEAN
MAPUTO
Boane
Baía de Maputo
Inhaca
SWAZILAND
Goba
Mailana 158m
Peninsula de Santa Maria
Passope 423m
Bela Vista
Maputo Special Reserve
Mau-Dai 73m
Santaca 110m
Lagoa Piti
Hondjandine 112m
Catuane
Manhoca
Ponta do Ouro
N
Bradt
0 100km
0 100 miles

SOUTHERN MOZAMBIQUE

The five chapters that follow cover the southern third of Mozambique, an area bounded by South Africa in the far southwest, Swaziland and Zimbabwe to the west, and the Save River to the north. It is the most developed and heavily touristed part of Mozambique, boasting around 1,000km of Indian Ocean shoreline and several of the country's most popular resorts, from Ponta Do Ouro in the south to Vilankulo and Inhassoro in the north.

Chapter 6 focuses on Maputo, the country's capital and largest city, which has a distinctive and likeable Afro-Mediterranean character but is rather lacking in major tourist attractions. Maputo is the main international gateway to Mozambique for business travellers and backpackers coming from South Africa, but is frequently bypassed by self-drive visitors and leisure travellers arriving by air.

Chapter 7 covers the wildly attractive mosaic of forested dunes, freshwater lakes and idyllic beaches that lies to the south of Maputo, a region frequently referred to as Maputaland. Its best-known attractions are Inhaca Island, which lies in Maputo Bay, and Ponta Do Ouro on the South African border, but it is also the site of the underrated Maputo Special Reserve, the best place to see elephants in southern Mozambique.

Chapter 8 covers the coast between Maputo and Inhambane, whose succession of beach resorts – most notably Bilene, Praia do Xai-Xai and Závora – cater mainly to the South African family-holiday market and can feel rather abandoned out of season. It also covers a trio of national parks, Limpopo, Banhine and Zinave, of which the first is the most developed for tourists, forming part of the Great Limpopo Transfrontier Park, which also includes South Africa's legendary Kruger Park.

Heading further north, the focal point of Chapter 9 is the sleepily attractive town of Inhambane, which is also the main gateway to the other seaside resorts covered in this chapter, notably Tofo and Tofinho.

The offshore Bazaruto Archipelago, protected within an eponymous national park, is the centrepiece of tourist activity in the area covered by Chapter 10, which also describes the popular mainland resort of Vilankulo and rapidly growing Inhassoro to its north.

6

Maputo

The largest urban centre in Mozambique, Maputo is a bustling and attractive port city that has served as the national capital since 1898, when it was known as Lourenço Marques (LM for short). It lies on the Gulf of Maputo (formerly Delagoa Bay), in the far south of Mozambique, within 100km of the South African and Swaziland borders. As such, it often feels more strongly connected to South Africa than to the rest of Mozambique, a circumstance reflected in a popular saying that likens Mozambique to a funnel – all the money flows down south!

Maputo was formerly the administrative capital of a province of the same name, which extended all the way south to the borders with South Africa and Swaziland. In 1998, the city became a separate administrative entity called Maputo Cidade, which is by far the smallest and most densely populated of Mozambique's 11 provinces, while the satellite city of Matola was made capital of the more rural Maputo Province. The actual population of Maputo almost certainly outstrips the official figure of 1.25 million, and may be as high as 1.75 million. In practical terms, this figure is further boosted by the estimated 750,000 residents of Matola, technically the second-largest city in Mozambique but more sensibly treated as part of a greater urban conglomeration centred on Maputo.

Outside images of post-civil war Maputo, like those of Mozambique itself, have been dominated by stereotypes relating to its intense poverty, flagrant corruption and run-down architecture. There is a small – and ever decreasing – element of truth to these stereotypes, but overall Maputo comes across as an intensely agreeable city, whose charms tend to grow on visitors the longer they stay. No longer severely potholed, the avenidas of the city centre are wide and tree lined, sloping down towards an attractive seafront and harbour, and for every faded architectural gem there are two others that are well maintained and smart. The streets and markets are busy and energetic, and drivers tend to be courteous and somewhat less manic than in many other parts of Africa. Furthermore, while it would disingenuous to claim Maputo is entirely bereft of poverty, its more shanty-like suburbs are no slummier than their counterparts in, say, Nairobi, Lilongwe or (dare it be said) Johannesburg.

Arrive in Maputo without prejudice and it is, quite simply, a most likeable city – as safe as any in Africa, and with a good deal more character than most. The jacaranda-, flame tree- and palm-lined avenidas with their numerous street cafés have a relaxed, hassle-free, Afro-Mediterranean atmosphere that is distinctively Mozambican. And they are flanked by any number of attractive old colonial buildings in various states of renovation and disrepair, ranging in style from pre-World War I classical to later Art Deco, all dwarfed in places by various incongruous high-rise relics of the 1950s and 1960s, when the city was something of a laboratory for devotees of the Bauhaus architectural style. Add to these a new crop of office buildings, shopping complexes, hotels and condominiums – with

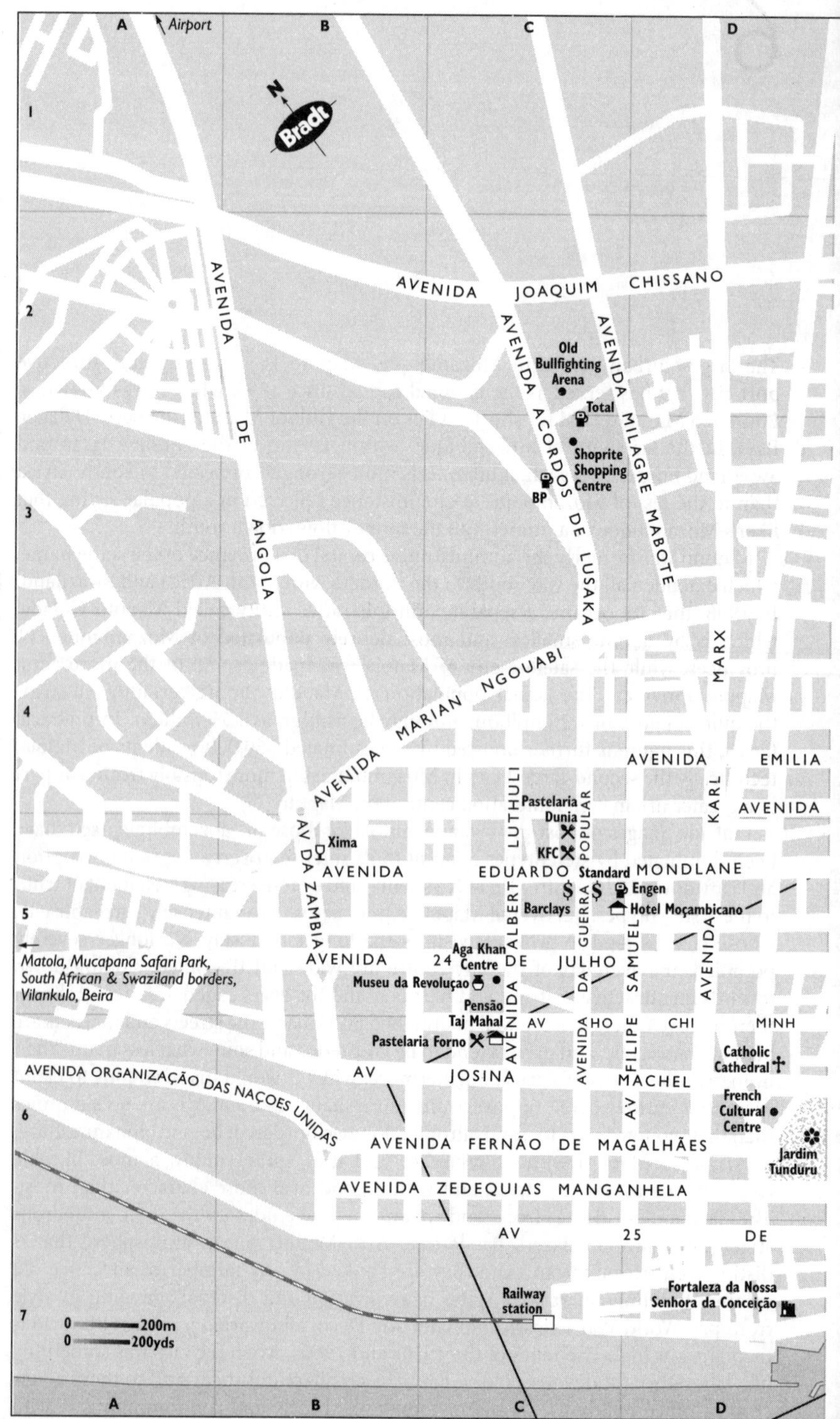
Airport
Bradt
AVENIDA JOAQUIM CHISSANO
AVENIDA DE ANGOLA
AVENIDA ACORDOS DE LUSAKA
AVENIDA MILAGRE MABOTE
Old Bullfighting Arena
Total
Shoprite Shopping Centre
BP
AVENIDA MARIAN NGOUABI
KARL MARX
AVENIDA EMILIA
AVENIDA
AVENIDA
Pastelaria Dunia
KFC
Xima
AV DA ZAMBIA
AVENIDA EDUARDO MONDLANE
AVENIDA ALBERT LUTHULI
AVENIDA DA GUERRA POPULAR
Standard
Engen
Barclays
Hotel Moçambicano
Matola, Mucapana Safari Park, South African & Swaziland borders, Vilankulo, Beira
AVENIDA 24 DE JULHO
Aga Khan Centre
Museu da Revoluçao
AV FILIPE SAMUEL
Pensão Taj Mahal
AV HO CHI MINH
Pastelaria Forno
Catholic Cathedral
AVENIDA ORGANIZAÇÃO DAS NAÇOES UNIDAS
AV JOSINA MACHEL
French Cultural Centre
Jardim Tunduru
AVENIDA FERNÃO DE MAGALHÃES
AVENIDA ZEDEQUIAS MANGANHELA
AV 25 DE
Railway station
Fortaleza da Nossa Senhora da Conceição
0 200m
0 200yds

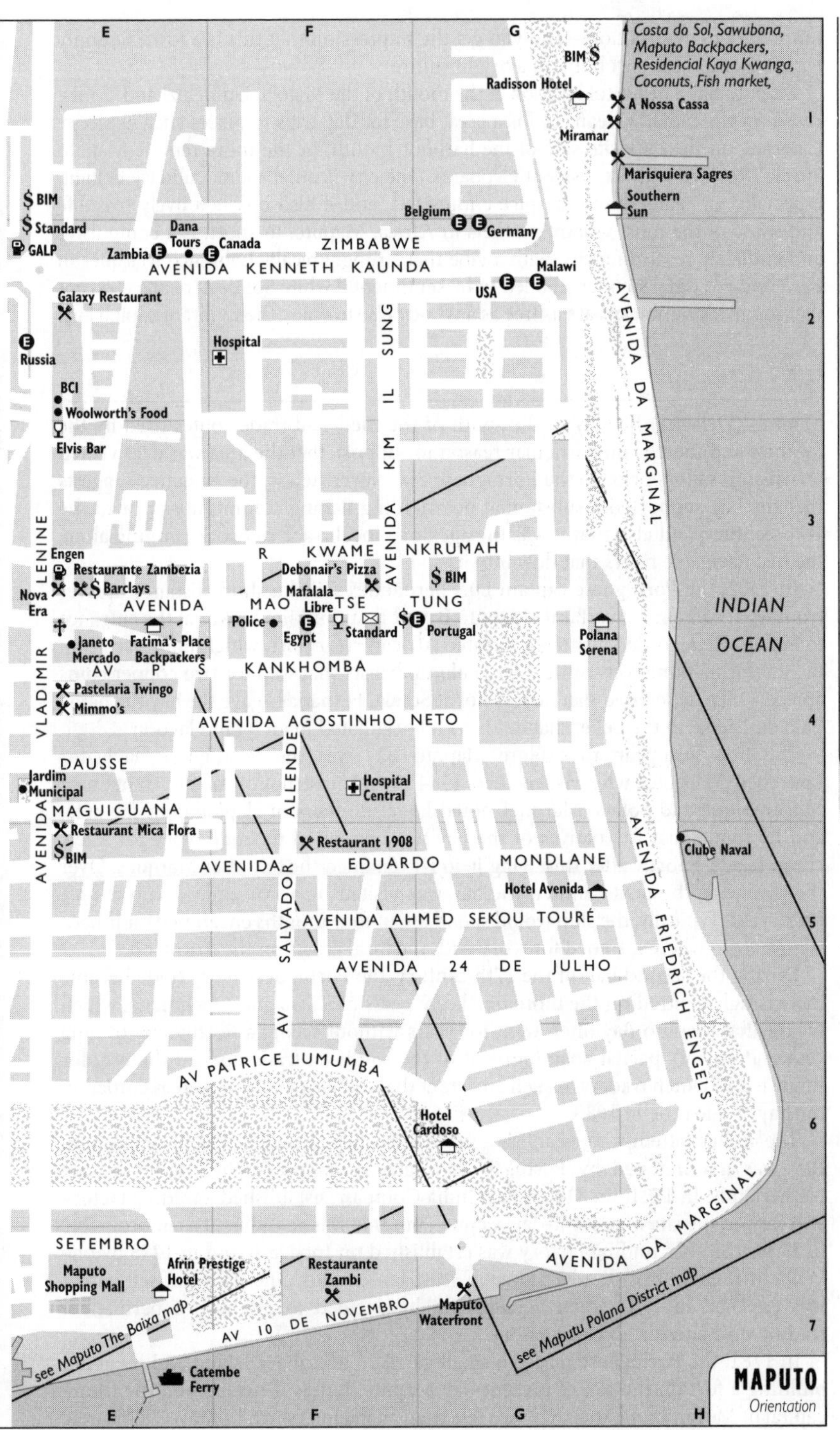
MAPUTO
Orientation
Costa do Sol, Sawubona, Maputo Backpackers, Residencial Kaya Kwanga, Coconuts, Fish market,
BIM
Radisson Hotel
A Nossa Cassa
Miramar
Marisquiera Sagres
Southern Sun
Belgium
Germany
Malawi
USA
ZIMBABWE
AVENIDA KENNETH KAUNDA
Zambia
Dana Tours
Canada
BIM
Standard
GALP
Galaxy Restaurant
Russia
Hospital
BCI
Woolworth's Food
Elvis Bar
AVENIDA KIM IL SUNG
AVENIDA DA MARGINAL
R KWAME NKRUMAH
Engen
Restaurante Zambezia
Barclays
Nova Era
Debonair's Pizza
Mafalala Libre
AVENIDA MAO TSE TUNG
Police
Egypt
Standard
Portugal
Polana Serena
INDIAN OCEAN
Janeto Mercado
Fatima's Place Backpackers
AV P S KANKHOMBA
Pastelaria Twingo
Mimmo's
AVENIDA AGOSTINHO NETO
AVENIDA VLADIMIR LENINE
DAUSSE
Jardim Municipal
MAGUIGUANA
ALLENDE
Hospital Central
Restaurant Mica Flora
BIM
Restaurant 1908
AVENIDA EDUARDO MONDLANE
Clube Naval
Hotel Avenida
AV SALVADOR
AVENIDA AHMED SEKOU TOURÉ
AVENIDA 24 DE JULHO
AVENIDA FRIEDRICH ENGELS
AV PATRICE LUMUMBA
Hotel Cardoso
AVENIDA DA MARGINAL
SETEMBRO
Maputo Shopping Mall
Afrin Prestige Hotel
Restaurante Zambi
Maputo Waterfront
AV 10 DE NOVEMBRO
see Maputo The Baixa map
see Maputu Polana District map
Catembe Ferry
E
F
G
H
1
2
3
4
5
6
7

Maputo 6

more under construction – and you get the impression that this is a town not only with a memorable past but also a bright future.

Maputo has a beautiful location at the mouth of the Matola, Umbeluzi and Tembe rivers on the Indian Ocean, and is a great base for day trips to places such as sleepy Catembe on the opposite side of the harbour mouth, or the more remote Maputo Special Reserve with its resident elephants. The city is an absolute culinary delight, especially for seafood and/or spice enthusiasts, and it also boasts a lively nightlife and some of the most vibrant markets in Africa. Maputo, in short, is a compulsive and endlessly rewarding city, with a vibe that strongly recalls Lourenço Marques in the 'good old days' so often alluded to by sentimental white South Africans – except that today Mozambicans are as free as anybody else to enjoy their vibrant capital city.

HISTORY

Maputo (Delagoa) Bay lay to the south of the medieval trade routes used by the Swahili, and there is no particular reason to suppose that the area was ever visited by Muslim sailors prior to the Portuguese era. Nevertheless, the evidence suggests that the bay supported a substantial ocean-going fishing community prior to the 16th century, and also that it was the apex of a local trade network running along the five navigable rivers that flow into it.

In 1502, the Portuguese captain Luis Fernandes sailed a short distance upriver from what was almost certainly Maputo Bay, at first thinking he was at the entrance to Sofala. He recorded visiting a sizeable African river port, which impressed him mostly for its numerous cattle – large plump beasts that sold for two copper coins apiece. Once he realised that he was not at Sofala, Fernandes gave the bay the name Baía da Lagoa, in the belief that its rivers all originated in an inland lagoon.

The first European to explore Maputo Bay was the Portuguese navigator Lourenço Marques, who visited it in 1544 on the instruction of the Captain of Moçambique and Sofala. Marques noted large numbers of elephants in the area, and he found that the natives of the bay were prepared to trade ivory for a few cheap beads. Shortly after this, King João III renamed the bay after Marques. Over the course of the next century, the bay was visited by a Portuguese ship almost every year. Typically, the ship would spend about four months encamped on Inhaca Island, from where it traded for ivory with the local chiefs on the mainland.

During the second half of the 17th century, the Portuguese ivory trade became increasingly centred on the more northerly ports of Kilwa and Quelimane, which meant that Maputo Bay often went for years without seeing a Portuguese trading vessel. Portugal's partial abandonment of the southern trade opened the way for English and Dutch traders to such an extent that five British ships were recorded in the bay at one time in 1685.

The earliest attempt to establish a permanent European settlement on Maputo Bay was not initiated by Portugal, as might be supposed, but rather by the Netherlands. In 1721, the Dutch East India Company established a trading factory and fort on the site of present-day Maputo, but this was abandoned as unprofitable in 1730. Another trading factory was established on Inhaca Island in 1778 by one William Bolts, a British adventurer in Austrian employ. The Austrian settlement was expelled in 1781 when Portugal finally decided to establish a permanent trading post and fort at Delagoa Bay.

In 1781, the Portuguese placed a small garrison on Inhaca Island and set about building a fort on the site of present-day Maputo, but as it turned out, the future capital of Mozambique was to have a less than auspicious start. In May 1782, barely a month after the fort had been completed, the entire settlement burned to the ground. It was quickly rebuilt, but an argument between the newly appointed Governor of Lourenço Marques and local chiefs forced Portugal to evacuate it in 1783. The settlement was reoccupied under a new governor in 1784, and a stronger fortress was built on the site of the modern one, but the garrison of 80 men was plagued by fever and so when three French gunboats arrived in the harbour in October 1796, the Portuguese settlers fled inland. The fortress was reoccupied in 1800, after which time Portugal retained a permanent presence on the bay.

In the early 19th century, Lourenço Marques was a modest and unremarkable trading outpost; in 1825, the only permanent building apart from the fort was a solitary corrugated-iron homestead. Nevertheless, the settlement stood at the centre of a vast trading network that spread along the rivers into the present-day South African provinces of Mpumalanga and KwaZulu-Natal. These inland trade routes to Maputo Bay were fiercely contested by various local chieftaincies, especially after the great drought of the 1790s initiated an unprecedented and highly militant phase of empire building among the Nguni peoples of the lowveld. In 1833, Lourenço Marques was razed and its governor killed by Dingane's Zulu army. After 1838, when the Boers defeated the Zulu army at Blood River, the trade routes to Lourenço Marques became the focus of an ongoing battle between the Swazi and Gaza kingdoms.

In terms of the development of southern Mozambique in general and Lourenço Marques in particular, the most portentous event of 1838 was the arrival at Delagoa Bay of the Boer leader Louis Trichardt. The Boers of the Transvaal were eager to open an export route to Delagoa Bay, not only because it was the closest port to the Boer Republic, but also because it would put an end to their dependency on British ports such as Cape Town and Durban. Trichardt died of malaria in Delagoa Bay, but his visit there signalled the beginning of a protracted three-way dispute over the control of what is arguably southeast Africa's finest natural harbour.

The competition for control of Maputo Bay increased after the discovery of diamonds at Kimberley in 1867 and gold at Lydenberg in 1869. In 1868, the government of the Transvaal claimed that its frontier extended to the coast, a claim that was immediately contested by Britain and Portugal. As a result, the Transvaal and Portugal signed a treaty that not only delineated the modern border between Mozambique and South Africa north of Swaziland, but also, and no less significantly, provided for the joint construction of a road between the Transvaal and Lourenço Marques.

Unwilling to see the Transvaal establish links with a Portuguese port, Britain immediately and unilaterally annexed the southern part of Delagoa Bay and Inhaca Island to their Natal Colony. Portugal called on France to arbitrate over the territorial dispute, and in 1875 it was awarded the entire bay. This was a major blow to the British policy of keeping indirect economic control over the Boer Republic – so much so that Britain annexed the Transvaal to its Cape Colony between 1877 and 1881, thereby stalling the development of transport links to Lourenço Marques.

Following the discovery of gold on the Witwatersrand in 1886, Portugal and the Transvaal decided to build a railway line between Pretoria and Lourenço Marques. It was the completion of this line in 1894 that prompted the modern growth of the city. In 1870, Lourenço Marques was a tiny, stagnant trading centre protected by an unimpressive fort. By the turn of the century, the city centre had taken on its modern shape, the port handled roughly one-third of exports and imports from the Transvaal, and the railway line carried over 80,000 passengers annually. On 12 November 1898, Lourenço Marques formally replaced Ilha de Moçambique as the capital of Portugal's east African colony. After independence, the city was renamed after the Rio Maputo.

GETTING THERE AND AWAY

BY AIR Maputo International Airport [100–1 A1] is about 5km northwest of the city centre, up at the end of Avenida Accordos de Zambia. **LAM** (*www.flylam.co.za*) flies to/from Maputo from all provincial capitals north of Xai-Xai and also operates several international flights daily to/from Johannesburg and less regular flights to/from Lisbon, Luanda (Angola) and Dar es Salaam (Tanzania). Other international carriers to Maputo include **TAP** (the Portuguese national carrier; *www.flytap.com*), **SAA** (*www.flysaa.com*) and a smaller South African operator called **1time** (*www.1time.aero*). There is no public transport from the city centre to the airport, though some chapas do run to within about 1km of it. It's not walkable (unless you're really into your urban hiking), though taxis are readily available and cost around US$10–15.

BY RAIL There is a daily train to/from Maputo to Ressano Garcia on the border with South Africa. It leaves Maputo at 07.45 daily and starts the return leg at around 12.00. Tickets are very inexpensive but it takes up to four hours in either direction, as opposed to about an hour by car to cover the same route.

BY ROAD

To/from South Africa See *Overland routes to Mozambique*, pages 44–6 for details of arriving in Maputo by bus from South Africa and Swaziland. There's an air-conditioned luxury **TCO (Transportes Carlos Oliveira**) coach between Johannesburg and Maputo thrice weekly, leaving Maputo at 07.00 on Monday, Wednesday and Friday and returning from Johannesburg at the same time on Tuesday, Thursday and Saturday; one-way tickets cost around US$25 and bookings can be made at their Maputo (*21 300634*) or Johannesburg (*+27 11 452 1771; m +27 72 563 8648*) offices. Other reliable South African-based coach services include **Intercape** (*www.intercape.co.za*), **Translux** (*www.translux.co.za*) and **Greyhound** (*www.greyhound.co.za*), which operate affordable daily services between Pretoria and Maputo stopping at Midrand, Johannesburg, Nelspruit and Komatipoort. Tickets from Johannesburg to Maputo cost around US$35, credit

YOUR FIRST HALF-HOUR: ARRIVING AT MAPUTO AIRPORT

Maputo is one of the easier international airports. Immigration and customs are simple and reasonably fast, and you won't be hassled by taxi drivers as soon as you step through the doors. There are the usual facilities – a bank, a *cambio*, a snack bar, car-rental agencies and an ATM that takes Visa. These can all be found in the departures terminal, a few yards from arrivals.

Taxis are clearly marked and will cost you about US$10–15 for the ride to the city. If you are staying at one of the more upmarket hotels there will be a courtesy bus waiting for you, and the three backpacker hostels will also pick you up if you let them know when you are arriving. As a last resort, chapas leave from the roundabout at the end of Avenida dos Accordos de Lusaka heading towards the Baixa – but unless you're travelling with minimal luggage a taxi is preferable.

card bookings can be made online or by phone, and the websites contain full details of pick-up and drop-off points. Alternatively, chapa-style minibuses for Johannesburg leave from Avenida Albert Luthuli next to the stadium and cost in the region of US$20. Be aware that it is very unlikely that your large rucksack will be put inside the minibus with you unless you are willing to pay a carriage charge. Like all chapas, they leave when they are full enough to make it worthwhile.

In Mozambique If your first stop out of Maputo is Inhambane, Tofo or any place along the EN1 south of that, then there's a lot to be said for using the daily **shuttle service** linking Maputo to Tofo. This leaves Maputo at 05.30 daily, stopping right outside Fatima's Place [100–1 E4] and Base Backpackers [113 F3]. Tickets, which cost around US$17, can be booked at the reception desk of either hostel. The most reliable service for places north of Inhambane is the **TCO** air-conditioned coach to Beira (*21 300634*), which leaves at 04.00 in either direction daily except Sunday, and takes about 16 hours, with stops at Vilankulo and Maxixe (for Inhambane and Tofo), though the full fare of around US$40 is charged wherever you disembark. This also connects to a thrice-weekly TCO service further north to Quelimane and Nampula. The TCO depot is way out past the Praça 16 de Junho at the end of Avenida 24 de Julho, and you'll need to get there by taxi.

All other long-distance buses start from a place outside the city centre called Junta, which is the closest Maputo has to a bus terminal. Getting there isn't difficult as many internal chapa routes run through there (if in doubt, ask the people on the bus with you). Once you're there, simply wander around until you find a bus heading in the direction you're going. You'll definitely get buses to Beira and Chimoio, and will probably find them going as far as Tete if you are there on the right day. The chapa fare from the town centre to Junta will be less than US$1, while a taxi will cost around US$8.

GETTING AROUND

BY TAXI Taxis are more numerous than they used to be, and you can usually rely on there being some at the airport taxi rank, outside the central market [113 B2], anywhere along Avenida Julius Nyerere, and outside upmarket hotels such as the Cardoso [106 C4] and Polana [106 D2]. Taxi fares are negotiable, but you can expect to pay around US$5 for a ride within the city centre and up to US$15 between the city centre and the airport.

BY CHAPA Minibus chapas travel the length and breadth of the city, with major bus stands in front of the Natural History Museum [106 A5] (described simply as 'museu' on the front of buses) and the large markets. You will probably have absolutely no idea where most of these buses are going at first, so the best advice is to stay on the main thoroughfares and be prepared to take more than one to get to your final destination. Fares are typically around US$0.25.

TOURS Also worth looking at is **Mozambique City Tours** (*21 333531;* m *82 316 1160;* e *info@mozambiquecitytours.com*), a new hop-on hop-off bus service that runs several times daily between the railway station [113 A3], the Southern Sun Hotel [100–1 H1] and various points in between. Full details can be obtained from their website (*www.mozambiquecitytours.com*) and tickets can be obtained from their booking office at the railway station or the front desk at the Polana, Southern Sun or Cardoso hotels.

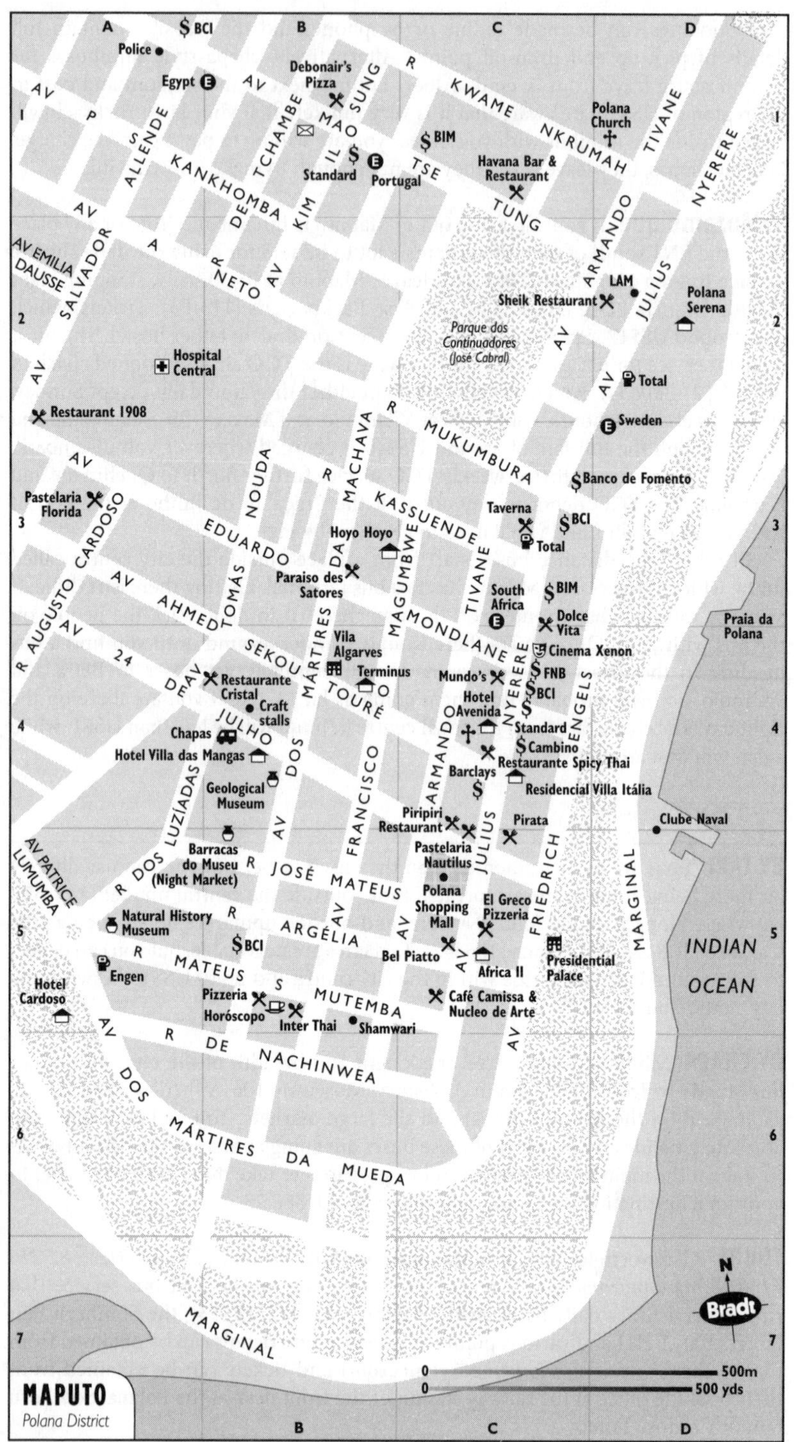
MAPUTO
Polana District
A
B
C
D
1
2
3
4
5
6
7
BCI
Police
Egypt
Debonair's Pizza
Standard
Portugal
BIM
Havana Bar & Restaurant
Polana Church
AV KWAME NKRUMAH
R KWAME NKRUMAH
AV MAO TSE TUNG
AV KIM IL SUNG
AV P S ALLENDE
AV KANKHOMBA
R DE TCHAMBE
AV A NETO
AV EMILIA DAUSSE
AV SALVADOR ALLENDE
AV JULIUS NYERERE
AV ARMANDO TIVANE
LAM
Sheik Restaurant
Polana Serena
Parque dos Continuadores (José Cabral)
Hospital Central
Total
Sweden
Restaurant 1908
R MUKUMBURA
R MACHAVA
R KASSUENDE
Banco de Fomento
Pastelaria Florida
AV EDUARDO MONDLANE
TOMÁS NOUDA
Taverna
BCI
Total
Hoyo Hoyo
Paraiso des Satores
South Africa
BIM
Dolce Vita
R AUGUSTO CARDOSO
AV AHMED SEKOU TOURÉ
AV 24 DE JULHO
R DA MAGUMBWE
TIVANE
Cinema Xenon
Vila Algarves
Terminus
Mundo's
FNB
BCI
Restaurante Cristal
Craft stalls
Hotel Avenida
Standard
Chapas
Cambino
Hotel Villa das Mangas
Restaurante Spicy Thai
Barclays
Residencial Villa Itália
Geological Museum
AV MÁRTIRES DOS
AV FRANCISCO O
ARMANDO
JULIUS NYERERE
FRIEDRICH ENGELS
Piripiri Restaurant
Pirata
Clube Naval
Praia da Polana
Barracas do Museu (Night Market)
R DOS LUZÍADAS
AV PATRICE LUMUMBA
R JOSÉ MATEUS
Pastelaria Nautilus
Polana Shopping Mall
El Greco Pizzeria
MARGINAL
Natural History Museum
R ARGÉLIA
AV
BCI
Bel Piatto
Africa II
Presidential Palace
INDIAN OCEAN
Engen
R MATEUS S MUTEMBA
Hotel Cardoso
Pizzeria Horóscopo
Inter Thai
Shamwari
Café Camissa & Nucleo de Arte
R DE NACHINWEA
AV DOS MÁRTIRES DA MUEDA
MARGINAL
N
Bradt
0
500m
0
500 yds

WHERE TO STAY

Nowhere is Maputo's current prosperity more evident than in the number of high-quality hotels that can now be found in the city. Generally speaking, the upper-range hotels in Maputo are the best value for money you'll find in Mozambique, and if you feel like spoiling yourself, these are the places to do it. If these are a trifle above your budget there are plenty of three-star hotels to choose from, and if your budget is lower still a range of places offer cheap, safe and clean accommodation, although only three of these are really geared to backpackers.

LUXURY

Polana Serena [106 D2] (55 rooms) Av Julius Nyerere; 21 241700; e reservations@serenahotels.co.za; www.serenahotels.com. Sited on a low cliff overlooking the Indian Ocean, Maputo's most prestigious hotel since it opened in 1922 has only gained in stature following a takeover by the highly regarded Kenya-based Serena chain & extensive renovations completed in late 2010. Although it fell into a state of neglect during the civil war, it has since reclaimed its status as one of the most elegant & well-run hotels in Africa, combining Edwardian grace with modern luxuries such as DSTV, free Wi-Fi & AC in all rooms, internet access, a gymnasium, a gourmet restaurant & coffee shop, & one of the most attractive swimming pools on the continent. *US$240/265 sgl/dbl; US$285/325 exec sgl/dbl; all rates B&B.*

Southern Sun [100–1 H1] (158 rooms) 4016 Av Marginal; 21 495050; e maputo@southernsun.com; www.southernsun.com. Formerly the Holiday Inn, this is probably the best overall value for money in this range, lacking the character of the Polana but compensating with its more resort-like beachfront setting less than 1km from the city centre. The comfortable rooms are pleasantly decorated in colourful contemporary style & have similar facilities to the Polana. Other facilities include a gift shop, infinity pool, business centre & good restaurant, & it is also well placed to eat at the cluster of restaurants running along the Av Marginal just 200m further north. *US$225/255 sgl/dbl; US$245/276 sea-facing sgl/dbl; suites from US$450; all rates B&B.*

Hotel Avenida [106 C4] (159 rooms) 627 Av Julius Nyerere; 21 484400; e bookings@hotelavenida.co.mz; www.htdhotels.pt. This well-established hotel a few blocks further south along the same road as the Polana lacks its neighbour's intimacy, Edwardian grace & direct sea views, but otherwise the comfortable & well-equipped rooms are much on a par, with DTSV, AC, Wi-Fi & mini-bar. There is a rooftop swimming pool, a remarkable piano bar & a good restaurant & it is well placed for eating out in the heart of Maputo. Maybe a touch overpriced compared to the above. *US$277/309 sgl/dbl; US$330/363 exec sgl/dbl; suites from US$513; all rates B&B.*

Afrin Prestige [100–1 E7] Rua Ngungunyana; 21 358900; m 82 358 0001; e prestige.hotel@afrinhotels.co.mz; www.afrinhotels.co.mz (website under construction). Warmly praised by several people who've stayed there, this recent addition to Maputo's hotel scene is situated right next to the Maputo Shopping Centre, a stone's throw from the Catembe ferry & within easy walking distance of most places in the city centre. Somewhat less staid than its more established competitors, it combines comfortable furnishings & all the expected facilities with a light airy ambience enhanced by the liberal placement of contemporary African artworks around the reception areas. *US$220/245 sgl/dbl; US$255/295 exec sgl/dbl; suites from US$420.*

UPMARKET

Girassol Bahia [113 E3] (84 rooms) 737 Av Patrice Lumumba; 21 360360; e girassolbahiahotel@visabeiramoz.co.mz; www.girassolhoteis.co.mz. This relatively new hotel, set in a quiet part of the city centre, offers a commanding view of the bay across to Catembe from the bar/restaurant area as well as from the sea-facing rooms at the back. The spacious rooms come with DSTV & AC, & the hotel is within walking distance of a good selection of shops

& restaurants. *US$175/199 sgl/dbl; suites from US$250; all rates B&B.*

Hotel Cardoso [106 A5] (130 rooms) 707 Av Mártires de Mueda; 21 491071; e info@hotelcardoso.co.mz; www.hotelcardoso.co.mz. Part of the highly regarded international Lonrho group, the Cardoso is another Maputo institution, situated in a quiet corner of town opposite the Natural History Museum on a cliff offering a view over the city centre to the harbour & Catembe. The large tiled rooms are decorated with sedate good taste & come with DTSV, AC & Wi-Fi. *US$175/195 sgl/dbl with city view; US$195/215 with sea view; suites from US$295; all rates B&B.*

Pestana Rovuma [113 D2] (117 rooms) 114 R da Sé; 21 305000; f 21 305305; e reservas.africa@pestana.com; www.pestana.com. One of the finest hotels in the Baixa area – along with the cathedral it dominates the eastern edge of the Praça Independência. Its main selling point is its location right in the heart of Maputo, a 5min walk to the shops, restaurants & bars on & around the Av 25 de Setembro & only about 15mins by foot from the Polana district. Rooms have DSTV, AC & internet connection, & other facilities include a swimming pool, gym, sauna & business centre. Good value at *US$155/172 sgl/dbl; suites from US$197/218; all rates B&B.*

MID-RANGE

Hotel Villa das Mangas [106 B4] (21 rooms) 401 Av 24 Julho; 21 497507; m 82 873 2474; e arabias@hipchichotels.com. One of the few Mozambican hotels to which the adjective 'boutique' could be added with a straight face, this small, characterful place in the Polana district stands in an old house alongside the Geological Museum. The compact en-suite rooms & suites, clustered around a pretty little garden with a swimming pool, all have DTSV & AC, & are decorated in funky African style. A decent restaurant is attached. *Around US$90/100 sgl/dbl B&B.*

Residencial Palmeiras [113 E2] (6 rooms) Av Patrice Lumumba; 21 300199; m 82 306 9200; e carlos.pereira@tvcabo.co.mz; www.palmeiras-guesthouse.com. This pleasant small guesthouse, set in an old funkily decorated double-storey building along the same road as the Cardoso, provides an agreeable & characterful alternative to the more institutional large hotels that dominate its price range. *US$65–85 dbl B&B.*

Hotel Turismo [113 C3] (165 rooms) Av 25 de Setembro; 21 352200; e reservas@hturismo.com; www.hturismo.com. This new & impeccably central multi-storey hotel might be a little short on character, but the en-suite rooms are very comfortable, brightly decorated, & come with DTSV, AC & Wi-Fi. Great value at *US$60/70 B&B sgl/dbl or US$75 exec dbl.*

Residencial Kaya Kwanga [100–1 H1] (44 rooms) Av Marginal; 21 492706; e miramar.kayakwanga@tvcabo.co.mz; www.kayakwanga.co.mz. The least urbanised hotel in Maputo, this sprawling chalet complex lies about 1km north of the Southern Sun along the beachfront road to the Casta da Sol. There is a large swimming pool, pretty green gardens scattered with indigenous trees, a salon & nursery, as well as a good restaurant within the complex. Rooms have AC, DTSV, barbecue facilities & private parking. *US$65/70 B&B sgl/dbl; US$120 suite.*

Terminus [106 B4] (45 rooms) 587 Av Francisco Orlando Magumbwe; 21 491333; f 21 491 284; e info@terminus.co.mz; www.terminus.co.mz. Set on a quiet street in the Polana district, the Terminus advertises itself as a '5-star hotel at 3-star prices', which is a bit of a stretch, but it does boast most of the facilities of the bigger fish above, an extremely friendly staff & good value rack rates. *US$65/95 sgl/dbl; suites from US$130; all rates B&B.*

Monte Carlo [113 F3] (58 rooms) 620 Av Patrice Lumumba; 21 304048; e info@montecarlo.net; www.montecarlo.co.mz. This sister hotel to the Terminus shares its older & slightly pricier sibling's slogan, & offers much the same ambience (or lack thereof) & value for money. *US$60/80 sgl/dbl.*

Hotel Moçambicano [100–1 C5] (63 rooms) 961 Av Filipe Samuel Magaia; 21 310600; m 82 305 2890; e info@hotelmocambicano.com; www.hotelmocambicano.com. The contemporary decor, though a little bombastic for some tastes, sets this comfortable, central hotel apart, & it is centred around a green courtyard with a swimming pool. There's free 24hr internet & a 24hr lobby bar, & clean en-suite rooms with DTSV & AC. *US$57/70 sgl/dbl B&B.*

BUDGET

Pensão Martins [113 F2] (26 rooms) 1098 Av 24 Julho; 21 301429; e pensaomartens@gmail.com. This small but nicely laid-out & quite trendily decorated hotel offers good-value en-suite accommodation in bright but small rooms with parquet floor, DSTV & AC, & it lies close to the heart of Maputo's main dining-out area. *US$50/65 sgl/dbl.*

Hoyo Hoyo [106 B3] (37 rooms) 837 Av Francisco Orlando Magumbwe; 21 490701; e hotelhoyohoyo@tvcabo.co.mz; www.hoyohoyo.odline.com. One of the best-value hotels in Maputo, offering accommodation in comfortable en-suite rooms with AC & DSTV, usefully located within walking distance of numerous restaurants. *US$48/55 sgl/dbl; US$75 suite.*

Escola Andalucia [113 F3] (56 rooms) 508 Av Patrice Lumumba; 21 322460. The training school for Mozambique's hoteliers, the Escola has a reputation for excellent service – which perhaps stands to reason. The rooms are pleasant enough, although some of the sgls are a little cramped. *US$40/65/70 sgl/dbl/suite.*

Santa Cruz [113 F3] (75 rooms) 1417 Av 24 Julho; 21 303004; e hsantacruz@teledata.mz. An adequate if rather timeworn option offering reasonably priced rooms with AC & TV. *US$33/40 sgl/dbl.*

SHOESTRING

Fátima's Place Backpackers [100–1 E4] (13 rooms, 5 dorms) 1321 Av Mao Tse Tung; 21 302994; m 82 307 0870; e fatimas@tvcabo.co.mz; www.mozambiquebackpackers.com; reception 07.00–22.00. Under the same hands-on owner-manager since it opened its doors in 1992, Fátima's is the most established backpackers in Maputo, & the best run. Assets include the clued-up English-speaking staff, lively decor, a chilled sociable atmosphere, well-equipped kitchen, plenty of outdoor seating, safe parking, laundry, baggage storage, mosquito netting on all beds & free pick-up from the airport (or elsewhere in Maputo) during daylight hours. The staff, noticeboard & website are useful sources of information about Maputo and elsewhere in Mozambique, as – usually – are the other travellers you will meet there. Expect an internet & TV room to be operational by 2011. There is limited camping space too. Advance booking is strongly recommended. The pricing system is somewhat Byzantine, but put simply you are looking at *US$15 pp for a dorm bed except over the Christmas period, & US$30/35 for a sgl/dbl using shared facilities or US$35/55 for an en-suite sgl/dbl (rising to US$35/45 or US$45/60 over Easter and June-Sep, and higher still over the Christmas period).*

The Base Backpackers [113 F3] (2 rooms; 3 dorms) 545 Av Patrice Lumumba; 21 302723; m 82 820 7673. Cheaper, quieter & slightly more downmarket than Fatima's, this small central backpackers overlooking the bay has a self-catering kitchen, laundry service, internet access & a great location for exploring the city centre. Mosquito nets not supplied. *US$10 pp dorm or US$26 dbl using shared ablutions.*

Maputo Backpackers [100–1 H1] (9 rooms & dorms) Rua do Palmeiras; 21 451213; m 82 467 2230; e maputobp@gmail.com. Situated off the Av Marginal about 5km north of the city centre, a couple of mins' walk from the beach, this place has a variety of dorms & smaller rooms spread over 3 storeys of a residential property. Facilities include a lounge with DTSV, a self-catering kitchen, a nice garden, free pick-up from the city centre & a nightly drop-off at any restaurant in town. Chapas between Costa do Sol & central Maputo pass within 100m of the hostel & cost around US$0.25. *US$15–20 pp.*

Pensão Central [113 D1] (24 rooms) 1957 Av 24 Julho; 21 324476. This basic, reasonably priced pensão is clean and has staff who are eager to please. The perfectly acceptable, en-suite rooms have ceiling fans but don't include mosquito nets. *US$14/20/30 sgl/dbl/tpl.*

Pensão da Baixa [113 B2] (28 rooms) Av Filipe Samuel Magaia; 21 308190; m 82 757 0617. Another adequate central option with clean rooms & fans but no nets & shared ablutions only. A touch overpriced at *US$23/35 dbl/twin.*

Pensão Taj Mahal [100–1 C6] (30 rooms) Av Ho Chi Min; 21 402350. An extremely popular option, well run & worth a look, particularly if you need to be near the buses, but vacant rooms are often in short supply. *US$14/17 sgl/dbl without AC or US$21/28 with AC.*

WHERE TO EAT

One thing you'll never have to worry about in Maputo is finding a decent meal – there are restaurants everywhere catering to all tastes and budgets. The emphasis is on seafood and Portuguese dishes such as the ubiquitous chicken piri-piri, but there are also a good number of specialised places ranging from pizzerias and steakhouses to Indian and oriental restaurants.

FEIRA POPULAR [113 D4] (*Av 25 de Setembro*) If you aren't sure what you feel like, or just want to browse a bit without stretching the legs too much, then this is an excellent place to start. In addition to the fairground rides, the Feira hosts over a dozen eateries serving far beyond the burger 'n' chips combos that might be expected, and you have the possibility of wandering from one to the next clutching a beer until you find something that takes your fancy.

Lua Cryptically named but excellent Chinese restaurant sited close to the main entrance.

Restaurante Coqueiros Specialises in food from the Mozambican province of Zambézia.

Restaurante Escorpião Lays claim to being the most popular eating place in Maputo & does mainly Portuguese dishes, reasonably priced & more than generous.

Restaurante Bamboo Inexpensive but good Vietnamese dishes.

BAIXA

Restaurant 1908 [106 A2] Cnr Av Eduardo Mondlane & Salvador Allende; 21 304428; restaurante1908@hotmail.com; 08.00–22.00 Mon–Sat. Set in a beautiful colonial house complete with period furnishing, this is one of the most outstanding purveyors of traditional Mozambican cuisine in Maputo, with the choice of eating formally indoors or in the shady gardens. The formal menu isn't bad value at all, *with most dishes costing around US$10, but the significantly cheaper informal menu (for outdoor diners only) is exceptional.*

Maputo Waterfront [100–1 G7] Av 10 de Novembro; 21 301408; 09.00–23.00 Mon-Sat, 09.00–17.00 Sun. Arguably the best location in all Maputo, overlooking the harbour and Catembe, this highly rated & often very busy sports-bar-cum-restaurant is a great spot for sundowners. It also boasts a swimming pool (looking uninvitingly green on last inspection) & live jazz on Wed, Fri & Sat (no cover charge but a minimum consumption equivalent to about US$6 pp is imposed on music nights). *The menu includes a selection of pizzas (US$5), salads (US$6–8) & a huge variety of seafood dishes & combos (US$12–18).*

Centre Cultural Franco-Mozambicain [113 C2] Av Samora Machel; 21 314590; 82 301 8000; www.ccfmoz.com; 12.00–19.00 Mon, 10.00–19.00 Tue–Sat. The café at this trendy arts centre serves a selection of filled focaccia & other light meals. Service can be slow, but if you are not in a hurry, the ambience compensates. *Around US$6.*

Restaurante Zambi [100–1 F7] Av 10 de Novembro; 21 328557; restaurantezambi@gmail.com; 12.00–24.00 daily. Facing the waterfront looking across to Catembe, this has a large breezy terrace, formal indoor seating, & a *highly rated menu of seafood, steaks & salads in the US$10–20 range.*

Khana Khazana [113 F3] Av Patrice Lumumba; 21 313872; 11.30–15.00 & 18.30–23.00 daily. Directly opposite the Base Backpackers, this quality Indian restaurant offers a wide range of tandoori dishes & curries, including an extensive vegetarian selection, with a few Chinese dishes to keep things interesting. Alcohol is served. *Mains are typically around US$7–8.*

Restaurant Kitos [113 B1] Cnr Av 24 de Julho & Vladimir Lenine; 21 426783; 10.30–22.30 daily. This unpretentious eatery, set in an old corner building, serves large portions of adequate but not exceptional Chinese food; the sizzling meat & chicken are recommended & there is plenty for vegetarians. *Mains in the US$5–7 range.*

✕ **Restaurante Impala** [113 C2] Cnr Av Karl Marx & Av Josina Machel; ☎ 21 302384. This long-serving central eatery serves a range of Pakistani, Indian & Portuguese meals, & damn fine mango lassi. One portion of rice & a main dish is more than enough for all but the hungriest eaters. Alcohol isn't served. *Mains are US$4–6.*

✕ **Great Wall** [113 D2] Av Patrice Lumumba; ☎ 21 431642; m 82 605 5060; ⏲ 10.00–22.00 daily. This no-frills Chinese eatery has the usual extensive menu supplemented by a few Mozambican favourites. *Mains cost around US$6 but it is worth looking first at the daily 2-course specials for around US$4.*

✕ **Cafe-Bar Radio Mozambique** [113 D2] R do Radio Clube. Situated at the northern end of the botanical gardens, this has a nice terrace but feels a little run-down indoors. Still, the Mozambican fare is pretty good & well priced. *Petiscos for around US$4 & mains at US$4–6.*

POLANA

✕ **Restaurante Cristal** [106 B4] Praça Travessa do Zambeze; m 82 281 5180; e restaurantecristal@hotmail.com; ⏲ 06.00–03.00 daily. Maintaining the longest opening hours of any Maputo restaurant, this place is also highly rated for its tasty but reasonably priced seafood & traditional Mozambican dishes. With indoor & outdoor seating, it's a great spot for b/fast or an early hours nightcap. *Mains mostly US$10–12.*

✕ **Pirata** [106 C5] Cnr Av Julius Nyerere & 24 de Julho ☎ 84 433 7984; ⏲ 11.00–23.00 daily. One of the better-value eateries along Av Julius Nyerere, this informal Italian and seafood restaurant, set on an enclosed patio, serves tasty pastas, grills, burgers, salads & filled pittas. The daily special is often a bargain. There's MTV on the big screen. *US$6–11.*

✕ **Mundo's** [106 C4] Cnr Av Julius Nyerere & Eduardo Mondlane; ☎ 21 494080; m 84 468 6367; ⏲ 08.00–01.00. The business card describes it as a 'restaurant, pub & everything', & it's difficult to quibble with that: divided into 4 indoor and outdoor areas of varying informality. It's also a popular drinking hole with expats, with a selection of beers on tap, & large screens that draw crowds for major sporting events. *Light meals for US$7–8, pizzas for around US$10, & seafood & meat grills for US$14–18.*

✕ **Bel Piatto** [106 C5] Cnr Av Julius Nyerere & Argelia; ☎ 21 491130; m 84 457 3747; ⏲ 12.00–14.30 Mon–Fri, 13.00–16.00 Sun, 19.00–22.30 daily. About as formal as it gets in Maputo, this stylishly swanky Italian restaurant serves pastas & grills. *US$13–20.*

✕ **Inter Thai** [106 B5] Av Mateus S Muthemba; m 82 760 9080; ⏲ 11.30–22.30 Tue–Sun. Set in a suburban garden at the south end of the Polana district, this is probably the best Thai eatery in the city. *Most mains at around US$10.*

✕ **Taverna** [106 C3] Av Julius Nyerere; m 84 444 5550; e restaurante.taverna.moz@gmail.com; ⏲ 12.00–15.00 & 18.00–22.000 daily. This smart Portuguese restaurant has an extensive menu, with an impressive selection of Portuguese & Cape wines. *Meat, chicken & seafood dishes in the US$13–17 range.*

✕ **PiriPiri Restaurant** [106 C4] Cnr Av 24 de Julho & Julius Nyerere; ☎ 21 492379; e rest.piripiri@tvcabo.co.mz; ⏲ 11.00–24.00 daily. Best known for its curries but also strong on chicken piri-piri and seafood, this is a popular place to hang out while recuperating from those Sun afternoon hangovers. *Most mains around US$6.*

✕ **Milano Grill House** [113 G2] Cnr Av 24 Julho & Salvador Allende; ☎ 21 328377; ⏲ 10.00–23.00 daily. With plenty of indoor seating as well as a wide balcony for people-watching, this relaxed,informal Italian eatery combines a steakhouse ambience with a menu dominated by pizzas, seafood & an unusually varied choice of salads. *Mains are mostly in the US$5–10 range.*

✕ **Dolce Vita** [106 C4] Av Julius Nyerere; ⏲ 08.00–02.00 daily. Good for b/fast, lunch, a last late round, or sundowners from the extensive cocktail menu, this trendy café serves salads, brochettes & light meals. *US$6–8.*

✕ **Restaurante Spicy Thai** [106 C4] Av Julius Nyerere; ☎ 21 497644; ⏲ 10.00–22.00 daily. A refreshing change from the Continental and Mozambican fare that dominates in Maputo, this serves a varied selection. *Meat, vegetarian green & red curries, stir-fries & salads in the US$7–9 range; seafood dishes are mostly around US$15.*

☕ **Shamwari** [106 B5] Av Mateus S Muthemba; ⏲ 08.00–18.00 daily. This popular café at the south end of the Polana district with indoor & outdoor seating serves delicious pastries, inexpensive filled rolls & salads, invigorating espressos. *A few meals of the day in the US$6–8 range.*

Horoscopo [106 B5] Av Mateus S Muthemba; 07.00–23.00 Mon–Sat. Choose from deli-style light meals or more substantial meat & seafood grills at this popular café. *Most dishes clock in at well under US$10.*

Mimmo's [113 G2] Cnr Av 24 Julho & Salvador Allende; m 82 948 7420; www.mimmos.co.za; opening hours and prices as for the branch on Av Vladimir Lenine (see below).

NORTH OF THE CITY CENTRE

Mimmo's [100–1 E4] Av Vladimir Lenine; 21 333463; m 82 307 0420; 11.00–23.00 daily; www.mimmos.co.za. This popular South African franchise, a 5min walk from Fatima's Place, is best known for its pizzas & pastas, but also has an extensive selection of more expensive steaks & seafood grills & a good selection of everyday Cape wines for around US$10 per bottle. There is large-screen DSTV for major sporting events. *US$4–12.*

Pastelaria Twingo [100–1 E4] Av Vladimir Lenine; 21 313492; 07.00–21.00 daily. This excellent pastelaria, situated on the same block as Mimmo's, serves sandwiches, burgers, pizzas & Mozambican dishes, & a selection of pastries as well as espresso. An internet café is attached. *US$1–4.*

Restaurante Zambezia [100–1 E3] Av Mao Tse Tung; until late daily. Catering mainly to the local market, the closest eatery to Fatima's Place serves decent no-frills Mozambican fare, as well as possibly the cheapest beers in this part of town. *US$4–6.*

Miramar [100–1 G1] Av Marginal; m 82 319 3950 or 82 303 0690; 09.00–late daily. A Maputo institution, this seafront bar-restaurant near the Southern Sun Hotel is all about seafood, which is usually excellent. *US$10 upwards for a main.*

Marisqueira Sagres [100–1 G1] Av Marginal; 21 492501; 11.00–23.00 daily except Tue. This highly regarded eatery combines a great seafront location (near the Southern Sun) with a tasty & sensibly priced menu dominated by but not restricted to seafood – the seafood rice dishes are especially recommended. *Mains are in the US$8–14 range.*

A Nossa Casa [100–1 G1] Av Marginal; m 84 317 9590; 9.00–23.00 daily except Mon. The most affordable of the trio of seafront restaurants near the Southern Sun, this has a good reputation for seafood, but pizzas & salads are also prominent on the menu. A popular place to watch big rugby matches & other sports events on large-screen TV. *Mains are in the US$7–10 range.*

Sawubona [100–1 H1] Av Marginal; 11.00–late daily. Aimed firmly at locals, with prices to match, this stilted wooden construction with a decent sea view about halfway between the Southern Sun and Costa do Sol specialises in charcoal-grilled chicken & seafood. *Portions are generous, most dishes are in the US$5–8 range.*

Costa do Sol [100–1 H1] Av Marginal; 21 450115; e rcs@teledata.mz; lunch & dinner daily. The grande dame of Maputo eateries lies about 7km out of town on beach also known as Costa do Sol, & is recommended for its seafood dishes, including prawns & calamari. If going at the weekend, book to be sure of a table. *Mains are around US$10.*

JUNK FOOD If you're desperate for good old-fashioned junk food then next to the Hotel VIP on Avenida 25 de Setembro is a block of South African fast-food joints. **Steers**, **Debonair Pizza**, **Nando's** and **Kentucky Fried Chicken** are all waiting to take your order. A similar and even more varied selection of snack bars and fast-food outlets can be found in the courtyard of the **Maputo Shopping Centre** near the Catembe ferry pier. In addition there is a **Pizza Hut** on Avenida Mao Tse Tung opposite the Parque dos Continuadores. Strangest of all in this category is a **Domino's Pizza** on Avenida 24 Julho just down from **Mimmo's**. To all intents and purposes it is a corner shop selling all the usual things a corner shop does sell, but it also has what appears to be a legitimate Domino's take-away licence. Eat on the tables outside, take it away with you, and you can even phone your order in (*21 313 702*), although they don't seem to have a delivery service.

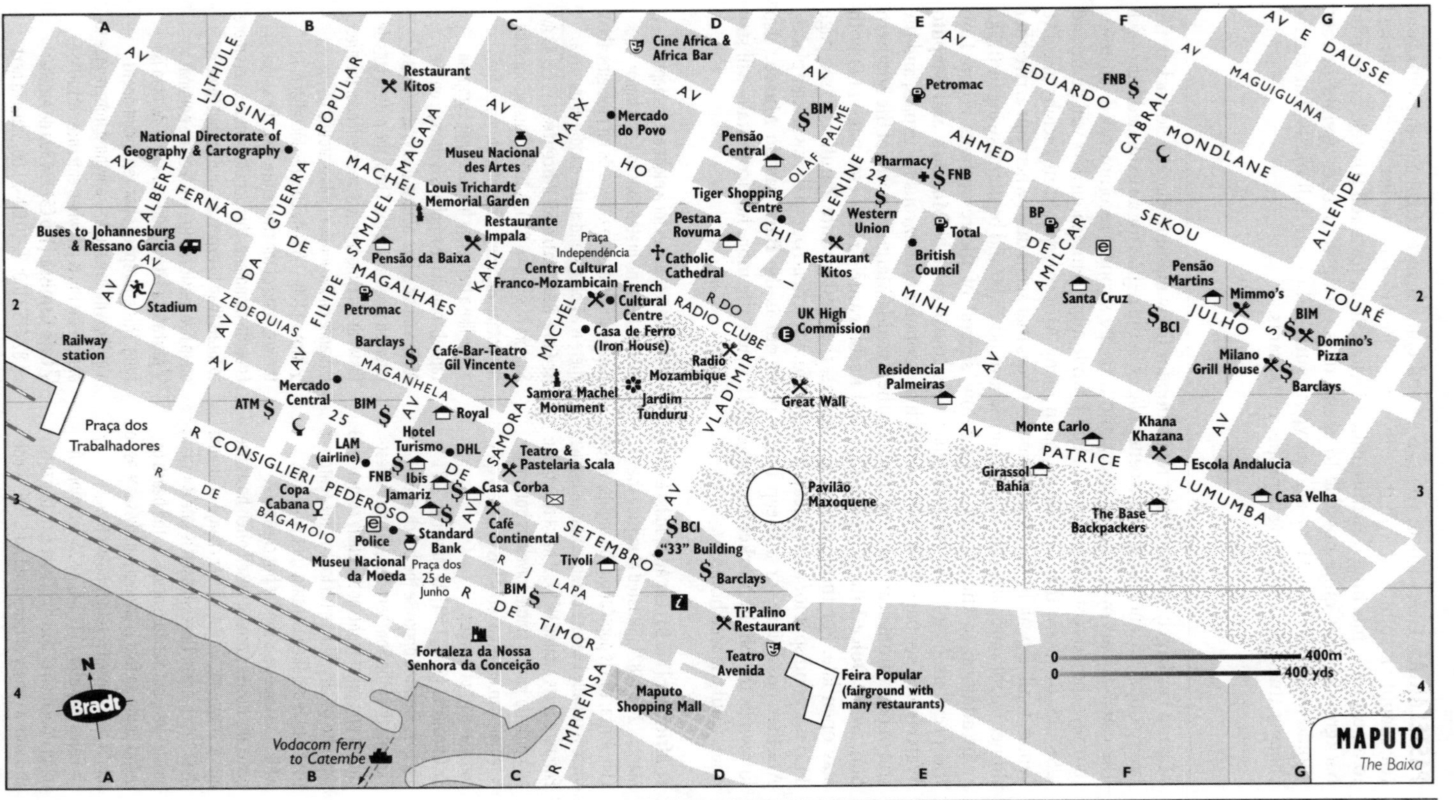
MAPUTO
The Baixa
Restaurant Kitos
National Directorate of Geography & Cartography
Museu Nacional des Artes
Louis Trichardt Memorial Garden
Buses to Johannesburg & Ressano Garcia
Stadium
Restaurante Impala
Pensão da Baixa
Praça Independência
Centre Cultural Franco-Mozambicain
French Cultural Centre
Casa de Ferro (Iron House)
Petromac
Barclays
Café-Bar-Teatro Gil Vincente
Railway station
Mercado Central
ATM
BIM
Royal
Samora Machel Monument
Jardim Tunduru
Radio Mozambique
Praça dos Trabalhadores
LAM (airline)
Hotel Turismo
DHL
FNB
Ibis
Jamariz
Teatro & Pastelaria Scala
Casa Corba
Copa Cabana
Police
Standard Bank
Café Continental
Museu Nacional da Moeda
Praça dos 25 de Junho
Tivoli
"33" Building
BCI
Barclays
Ti'Palino Restaurant
Fortaleza da Nossa Senhora da Conceição
Teatro Avenida
Maputo Shopping Mall
Feira Popular (fairground with many restaurants)
Vodacom ferry to Catembe
Cine Africa & Africa Bar
Mercado do Povo
Pensão Central
Tiger Shopping Centre
Pestana Rovuma
Catholic Cathedral
Restaurant Kitos
UK High Commission
Great Wall
Pavilão Maxoquene
BIM
Petromac
Pharmacy
FNB
Western Union
Total
British Council
Residencial Palmeiras
FNB
BP
Santa Cruz
Pensão Martins
Mimmo's
BCI
BIM
Domino's Pizza
Milano Grill House
Barclays
Monte Carlo
Khana Khazana
Escola Andalucia
Girassol Bahia
The Base Backpackers
Casa Velha
AV LITHULE
AV JOSINA MACHEL
AV ALBERT FERNÃO DE MAGALHAES
AV GUERRA POPULAR
AV SAMUEL MAGAIA
AV DA FILIPE
AV ZEDEQUIAS MAGANHELA
AV 25 DE SETEMBRO
R CONSIGLIERI PEDEROSO
R DE BAGAMOIO
AV KARL MARX
AV SAMORA MACHEL
AV HO CHI MINH
R DO RADIO CLUBE
AV VLADIMIR I LENINE
OLAF PALME
AV 24 DE JULHO
AV AHMED SEKOU TOURÉ
AV EDUARDO MONDLANE
AV AMILCAR CABRAL
AV ALLENDE
AV MAGUIGUANA
AV E DAUSSE
AV PATRICE LUMUMBA
R J LAPA
R DE TIMOR
R IMPRENSA
0 400m
0 400 yds
N
Bradt
A B C D E F G
1 2 3 4

PASTELARIAS Cafés where you can sit and enjoy a slice of cake along with your tea; Maputo is so littered with these that there are too many to list. Many are linked to an espresso machine franchise called Delta – look for a red triangle on a green background. It is quite possible to spend days eating your body weight in cake should you so desire. Many also serve savoury dishes and full meals that are far cheaper than the same thing at proper restaurants.

NIGHTLIFE

Maputo has largely reclaimed the reputation for lively nightlife that it held back in the late colonial era, and is one of the better places in the region for an extended bar crawl. The usual caveats over security apply, and taxis are strongly recommended: 'in-town' journeys should cost in the region of US$4, while more remote journeys will be around US$7.50. Be aware that in Maputo, as in many African capitals, nightclubs and live venues tend to peak in the small hours, so places that seem dead when you arrive after dinner might start gathering momentum at around 23.00 and be in full swing by 01.00.

In addition to the venues listed below, several of the restaurants covered on the previous pages also have popular bars, most notably **Mundo's** and **Maputo Waterfront** (see page 110), both of which are popular rendezvous for expats, and the trio of beachfront seafood restaurants on the Avenida Marginal north of the Southern Sun, while **Dolce Vita** (see page 111) and **Restaurante Cristal** (see page 111) both stay open late. For those staying at Fatima's, the **Restaurante Zambezia** (see page 112) is a good spot for a few cheap rounds before you head out to the swankier places. Another possibility for a cheap boozy night out is the **Barracas do Museu**, also known as the **Night Market** (see page 117), where the more hardcore stalls will stay open until the wee hours.

☆ **Africa Bar** [113 D1] Cnr Av 24 Julho & Karl Marx; ☎ 21 314821. Situated alongside the Cine Africa, this is popular on Thu nights, when there is usually live jazz or Mozambican music. Entrance costs around US$7. It has a reputation as a pick-up joint & single travellers both male & female can expect a lot of hassle unless they come as part of a group.

☆ **Coconuts** [100–1 H1] Av Marginal; ☎ 21 322217. Situated opposite the beach about 1km north of the Southern Sun, Maputo's best-known upmarket nightspot actually comprises 3 separate venues. The swish Ice Lounge (entrance US$8 pp) is a chilled dancing spot with a DJ, while The Lounge is similar but cheaper & generally busier. Coconuts itself often hosts live music at w/ends, when a cover charge of around US$17 is charged. The club itself is safe & usually hassle-free, but walking across to the beach or going home on foot is strongly inadvisable as you might be followed – rather take a taxi.

☆ **Feira Popular** [113 D4] Av 25 Setembro. A conglomeration of dozens of bars & restaurants, also with a variety of fairground rides, this is one of the liveliest places for a night out in Maputo, though it has no pretensions to being hip or happening in any way. If you do hit problems, then there is a police stand in the middle of the area.

☆ **Café-Bar-Teatro Gil Vincente** [113 C2] 43 Av Samora Machel; m 82 153 1020. Situated opposite the botanical gardens, this intimate venue feels a little like a transplant from a trendy European capital, though the emphasis is strongly on live African music & jazz, almost always at w/ends & often on week nights too. Check the posters outside for what's playing here & at the next-door theatre. Entrance on live music nights is around US$6.

🍸 **Xima** [100–1 B5] Av Eduardo Mondlane. At the west end of the city centre neat the statue of Eduardo Mondlane, this popular venue caters more to locals than to expats or tourists, but there is often live music & entrance fees are nominal.

🍸 **Mafalala Libre** [100–1 F4] 911 Av Mao Tse Tung. This atmospheric bar-restaurant opens nightly, with live music – anything from reggae to blues – on Thu & Fri, when entrance costs US$6.

🍸 **Café Camissa** [106 C5] 194 Rua de Argélia; m 82 415 3100; ⏰ 10.00–21.00. Situated next to the Núcleo de Arte, this trendy café attracts a cosmopolitan arty crowd & often hosts live music. It's more of an early evening venue than a real nightspot, but it often stays open long past the official closing time.

Copa Cabana [113 B3] Rua do Bagamoio. The best known of the half-dozen or so strip & other clubs that line Maputo's seedy 'Street of Trouble', an area best avoided after dark unless you're with a group or prepared for a lot of hassle.

SAFETY AND HASSLES

Maputo is no more dangerous than any other large city; indeed, crime levels are very low compared with Nairobi, Lagos and Johannesburg, and violent crime against tourists is highly unusual. It's certainly very safe to walk around the city by day – pickpockets, con artists and the like are few and far between, and the occasional hawker tends to be far less persistent than is the case in many other cities in the continent. Crowded places, particularly the markets, should be approached with mild caution – stash valuables out of reach of wandering hands, and don't display flashy jewellery, bulging wallets or expensive cameras. It's also a good idea to carry some ready cash (a few low-value notes and some coinage, which makes a distracting noise when shaken) in a small accessible wallet or pocket, and to use that throughout the day, keeping your main stash of cash tucked out of sight.

There's no great risk associated with walking along the main streets in the early evening – they are reasonably lit and there are plenty of other pedestrians around – but the alleys and back ways should be avoided. Later in the evening it's probably advisable to use taxis for all your journeys. Two places which have seen several muggings by day and night, and should be steered clear of at all times, are the winding roads connecting Avenida Friedrich Engels and Avenida da Marginal, and the overgrown escarpment between the Baixa and Polana districts.

There does appear to be a fair amount of property crime in Maputo, particularly against motor vehicles – car parts aren't readily available and so they are subject to a growing shady market. If you are carrying stuff in the back of a pick-up truck, be careful in traffic jams or at traffic lights, as you may be distracted in some way by a couple of people while their friends help themselves to anything that's not secured. You also hear stories, possibly apocryphal, of people grabbing accessories like hubcaps and indicator light covers off cars while they're stalled at traffic lights. It is definitely unsafe to leave a car parked on the street overnight; don't stay at a hotel unless it can offer you somewhere safe to park.

Drugs are not tolerated – if you do get caught carrying them then prepare either to pay a hefty bribe or spend longer than you expected in the country in distinctly less salubrious surroundings than you paid for. Knives are also not tolerated – if you are stopped carrying them then they will be confiscated and the very least you will get is a stiff talking to in Portuguese.

ENTERTAINMENT

Nowadays, there are enough facilities in Maputo to make it possible to indulge most pastimes.

TENNIS CLUB [113 D2] In the botanical garden, with six courts and changing rooms. Non-members can play for around US$5 per hour.

SWIMMING POOLS Found at all of the capital's major hotels and some of the lesser ones, most can be used by non-residents on payment of a fee, though the Polana

POLICE AND PASSPORTS

The biggest hassle most travellers face in Maputo comes not from lawbreakers but law enforcers. Mozambican law requires that people carry valid identification on them at all times, which in the case of foreign travellers means their passport. And there are plenty of police in Maputo who take great delight in enforcing this law – or, more accurately, in using it as a pretext to stop travellers in the street in the hope of extracting a bribe.

If this happens, and you are not carrying your passport, the normal drill is for the police to threaten to take you to a police station to pay a fine, and if that doesn't leave you looking suitably intimidated, they might also threaten to detain you overnight on some logistical pretext (for instance, the guy who makes out the invoices has knocked off for the day). And even if you are carrying a passport, they may decide you have committed some other offence, for instance not stopping in time, and either way the conversation will lead to your paying them a bribe in exchange for your freedom.

However the scenario builds up, the one thing that needs to be stressed is that the police in Maputo are generally as unenthusiastic as you when it comes to laying a formal charge of this sort. All they want is a bribe, and the moment they sense that this won't be forthcoming, they will lose interest. So just play it cool, be friendly, smile a lot, and generally convey the impression that a visit to the police station, or even an overnight stay there, is absolutely good with you, and it is almost certain they will let you go after ten minutes or so.

That said, the whole thing can be an irritating waste of time, so if you will be staying in Maputo a while and are disinclined to expose your passport to pickpockets et al, a notarised copy of the document costs next to nothing to make, and it will do just as well. There is a good notary around the corner from Fatima's Place on Avenida Vladimir Lenine, but there are several others dotted around the city and any hotel will be able to point you to one nearby.

now restricts use to hotel residents. One of the best pools – Olympic size and right on the seafront – is at the Clube Naval [100–1 H5], which charges around US$3 per person and lies on Avenida da Marginal south of the Southern Sun.

FOOTBALL MATCHES Stadiums are at Costa do Sol, Desportivo, Machava and Maxaquene.

CINEMAS AND THEATRES There are a few dotted around the city centre, mostly showing the usual mix of dubbed or subtitled Hollywood films. You may find more arty stuff at some of the arts foundations. Theatrical productions are mostly in Portuguese.

Centre Cultural Franco-Mozambicain [113 C2] Av Samora Machel; 21 314590; m 82 301 8000; www.ccfmoz.com. This arty venue, set in an 1898 building abutting the botanical garden, has a busy programme of live performances, ranging from contemporary music to theatre. The website contains full details of up-and-coming events (in Portuguese & French only).

Cinema Gil Vincente [113 C2] 45 Av Samora Machel; 21 308768; part of the café-bar of the same name, with occasional live performances.

Cinema Xenon [106 C4] 776 Av Julius Nyerere; ☎ 21 497 256

Teatro Avenida [113 D4] On Av 25 de Setembro just down from the Hotel Tivoli, this has occasional theatrical & operatic performances, most often at w/ends – check the posters outside for forthcoming attractions.

SHOPPING

MARKETS

Barracas do Museu [106 B5] Rua dos Lusiados. The so-called Night Market does open at night, but sells nothing but drink. A warren-like conglomeration of perhaps 100 bars, this is one of the most extraordinary places to drink anywhere in Africa, & is highly recommended provided that you don't carry vast sums of money or valuables on your person.

Fish market [100–1 H1] Av Marginal, opposite the Club Maritimo, along the road to the Costa do Sol about 1.5km north of the Southern Sun. In addition to being the cheapest place to buy fresh fish, it is of interest to amateur ichthyologists for the variety of tropical ocean fish that can be seen (even if they are out of their natural habitat).

Mercado Artesanato [113 C3] Praça 25 de Junho. Held every Saturday morning, this is a particularly good place to buy batiks, woodcarvings & items crafted from semi-precious stones such as malachite. In recent years, arts & crafts salesmen have responded to the increase in tourist traffic by setting up shop outside the main hotels & other points where tourists tend to congregate. Consequently, the best selection of crafts & curios can be found outside places such as the Hotel Polana, the Hotel Cardoso, the Costa do Sol, the Hotel VIP & the Polana Shopping Centre. All manner of basket work, ranging from reed chairs to bookshelves, can be bought from street vendors along the Av Marginal & Av Julius Nyerere north of the Hotel Polana.

Mercado Central [113 B2] Av 25 de Setembro. Housed in an impressive building dating from 1901, this is a good place to buy a variety of fresh & frozen fish as well as other fresh produce. It's the prettiest market in Maputo: lively, African & colourful. In addition to vegetables, fruit & everyday household goods, carvings, baskets & other souvenirs are available at the back right-hand side.

Mercado do Povo [113 C1] Cnr Av Karl Marx & Av Ho Chi Minh. It reputedly sells a variety of groceries & vegetables & large numbers of chickens, which are tucked away at night when the market becomes one of the liveliest places for a cheap, informal beer in the city centre.

Mercado Janeta [100–1 E4] Behind the church near the intersection of Av Vladimir Lenine & Av Mao Tse Tung. A good place for fruit & vegetables & for a cheap meal of chicken or fish with rice, and conveniently close for those staying at Fátima's Place. Get there early-ish in the morning and take your pick from the finest selections of produce you'll see in the country.

Xipamanine Market This huge warren of tiny shops & alleyways is known for its traditional medicines & associated items. It's located outside the city centre in the Alte Mae district, so you'll need to take a bus to get there. Look for anything heading to Xipamanine – they all stop right outside the market. The journey should cost around US$0.20. You may share your return journey with chickens.

Makonde Art Co-op [100–1 H1] Av Marginal. About 1.5km north of the Southern Sun, shortly after the junction for the fish market, this is the best place in Maputo to buy the intricate Makonde carvings and paintings that derive from the northern part of the country.

SUPERMARKETS AND MALLS There are dozens of supermarkets in the city, some more tucked away than others. **Woolworths Food** [100–1 E2] at the north end of Avenida Vladimir Lenine is a good bet. If you want a Western-style supermarket, then the biggest is **Shoprite** [100–1 C3], which lies in the Shoprite Mall on Avenida Accordos dos Lusaka about 1km north of the city centre, along with a collection of banks and ATMs, a CNA news agency, large clothing shops and a Woolworths. If you visit this mall, check out the monumental Praça do Taurus (Bullfight Arena) immediately north of it; if it looks familiar that's probably because it is the setting of a scene in the film *The Interpreter* starring Sean Penn and Nicole Kidman.

Two large new malls can be found in the city centre. The **Polana Shopping Centre** [106 C5] on Avenida Julius Nyerere has several banks and ATMs, a superb deli, and a selection of stylish upmarket boutiques, salons and outlets for upmarket brands (Lacoste, Swatch) familiar even to this fashion-illiterate writer. The **Maputo Shopping Mall** [113 D4] on Avenida Ngungunyana, near the Catembe ferry jetty, is a four-storey building containing more than 100 different shops, ranging from a dedicated tobacconist and gaming shop to cosmetics, baby clothing and shoe shops. There is also a large hypermarket, a vast outlet of the South African clothes chain Mr Price, and a food courtyard with at least a dozen pastelarias, fast-food outlets and other affordable eateries.

HANDICRAFTS Look no further than the banks of stalls that line Avenida Julius Nyerere and the first block or two of the main roads running west from it. There must be at least 50 stalls in this area selling everything from batiks and Makonde paintings to woodcarvings, cheap jewellery and other ornaments. Friendly bargaining is the order of the day here, and it is worth looking at a few stalls to get a feel for prices and quality before you actually part with any cash.

OTHER PRACTICALITIES

AIRLINES The main **LAM** office [113 B3] is on Avenida Karl Marx, just off Avenida 25 de Setembro in the heart of downtown Maputo with a subsidiary office near the Polana Hotel on the corner of Avenida Mao Tse Tung and Julius Nyerere (*21 326001 or 465074; www.flylam.co.za*). Other airlines represented in Maputo include **SAA** (*Av do Zimbabwe; 21 488970; www.flysaa.com*) and **TAP Air Portugal** (*Pestana Rovuma Hotel; 21 303927; www.flytap.com*).

COMMUNICATIONS AND MEDIA

Post The main post office [113 C3] occupies an impressive colonial building on Avenida 25 de Setembro complete with decorative mosaics at the front. (Its sister building, the National Library just down the street, is in a worse state of repair.)

Phone You can make telephone calls (local, national and international) at the post office or from any one of a number of telephone bureaux dotted around the city. SIM cards for your mobile can be bought and topped up from dozens of places, and text messages are very cheap to send all around the globe.

Internet At first glance internet cafés are not easy to find, as they are either tucked away in corners of shopping centres or disguised as the front rooms of private houses, but they are there. Reasonable (if not fast) connection speeds and decent-quality PCs to run them with are the norm. Among the better places to browse online are the Pastelaria Twingo [100–1 E4], Mundo's [106 C4], Cafe Nautilus [106 C5] (next to Restaurante PiriPiri) and Dolce Vita [106 C4] (see page 111). Most upmarket and luxury hotels also have internet, though it tends to be costly for non-residents, and Fatima's Place [100–1 E4] will install it by 2011. For anybody spending time in Maputo, a better option than using internet cafés would be to buy a local SIM card direct from a Vodacom or mCel shop and ask the staff to set up your phone to get satellite internet access (which is so cheap it's as good as free) or, if you have a laptop, to buy a Vodacom satellite modem for it.

The post office also has an internet facility, at least in theory, but it is closed more often than not. Dedicated Mac users are out of luck – Bill Gates rules in Maputo!

Books Only a small selection of English-language newspapers (mostly from South Africa) and magazines is ever available at the kiosks at the tourist-class hotels. English-language books and novels, meanwhile, are even more difficult to come by. There is a very small selection of English-language books (predominantly coffee-table photo books) at the bookshop on Avenida Julius Nyerere [106 C4] opposite the South African High Commission and you may find some others if you hike around the *livrarias*.

Maps All in all it's best to get your maps before you arrive. For detailed 1:50,000 maps, there is a helpful map sales office in the **National Directorate of Geography and Cartography** [113 B1] (DINAGECA; *21 300 486*) on Avenida Josina Machel, a block west of Avenida Guerra Popular. Individual sheets cost US$2–3 and there is a facility to download some maps at www.cenacarta.com.

FOREIGN EMBASSIES Office hours are usually 07.30–12.30 and 14.00–17.30 Monday to Thursday, 07.30–12.30 and 14.00–17.00 Friday. It's not unknown for embassies to change their phone numbers, so it may be worth checking when you arrive in the country.

- **Belgium** [100–1 G1] 470 Av Kenneth Kaunda; 21 492009
- **Canada** 1138 Av Kenneth Kaunda; 21 492623
- **Eire** 3332 Av Julius Nyerere; 21 482700
- **France** 94 Av Ahmed S Touré; 21 484600
- **Germany** [100–1 G1]506 R Damião Góis; 21 492714
- **Malawi** [100–1 G2] 75 Av Kenneth Kaunda; 21 492676
- **Netherlands** 324 R Kwame Nkrumah; 21 490031
- **Norway** 1162 Av Julius Nyerere; 21 480100
- **Portugal** [106 B1] 720 Av Julius Nyerere; 21 490316
- **South Africa** [106 C3] 41 Av Eduardo Mondlane; 21 490059
- **Spain** 347 R Damião Góis; 21 492025
- **Swaziland** Par 141/A Av Zimbabwe; 21 491601
- **Sweden** 1128 Av Julius Nyerere; 21 480300
- **Switzerland** 1213 Av Julius Nyerere; 21 492744
- **Tanzania** 852 Av Mártires Machava; 21 490110
- **UK** [113 D2] 310 Av Vladimir Lenine; 21 356000
- **USA** [100–1 G2] 107 Av Kenneth Kaunda; 21 492797
- **Zambia** 1286 Av Kenneth Kaunda; 21 492452
- **Zimbabwe** 242 R Damião Góis; 21 490499

Be aware that your embassy may charge you for their time if you need to call on them for trivial matters.

MEDICAL

Hospitals There are four in Maputo, but the most central one lies on the corner of Avenida Eduardo Mondlane and Augustinho Neto (*21 325000*). The others are on Avenida Agostinho Neto, Avenida Salvador Allende and Avenida Tomas Nduda.

Medical centres There are a number of these dotted around the city and it's probably best to ask your hotel/hostel for the nearest, or failing that head straight for the hospital.

Pharmacy There is a 24-hour pharmacy [113 E1] on Avenida 24 do Julho just down from the corner with Avenida Amilcar Cabral. Right next to it is an ATM that takes Visa.

MONEY

Travellers' cheques The only place that will now take travellers' cheques is the Polana Serena Hotel [106 D2]. You may get lucky and find a cambio somewhere that will change them, but expect to pay an exorbitant commission.

Cash The streets of Maputo are lined with cambios willing to take your hard currency in exchange for meticais. You could spend years going from one to the next trying to find the best rate. There doesn't seem to be a huge difference in the rate offered by banks as opposed to cambios. Beware of the rate offered by the hotels and pensões – in the more expensive ones you will probably get a reasonable rate, but the cheaper ones (and this includes the backpacker hostels) seem to be somewhat lax in updating their rates so if you're not careful you may end up out of pocket.

You can change money on the black market if you choose, but you won't get a significantly better rate. If you do decide to do this, the place where the minibuses leave for Johannesburg [113 A2] would be a good place to start. The Mercado Central [113 B2] has also been suggested as a possible location, but it's a little too crowded and busy for comfort. The police seem to take a relaxed view of black-market deals, but that cuts both ways – they may not be all that proactive if you do get ripped off.

Credit cards ATMs taking credit cards can be found all over central Maputo (indeed it is unusual to walk more than two blocks without encountering one), and this is by far the best option for accessing your currency. Visa is far and away the most useful brand of card in Maputo (as elsewhere in Mozambique), and it is accepted at practically all ATMS. MasterCard and Maestro are very poor seconds, accepted at some ATMs, and American Express and other more obscure brands are as good as useless. If you decide to pay for goods and accommodation using a card, it will almost certainly have to be a Visa card, and you may have a small percentage added to your bill (in which case you might prefer to pop round the corner to draw cash from an ATM before paying your bill).

POLICE The police can be contacted on ☎ 21 325031. Police stations can be found at:

Av Eduardo Mondlane Between Av Karl Marx & Rua de Redondo
Av Amilcar Cabral Between Av Mao Tse Tung & Rua Kwame Nkrumah
Av Marian Ngoudai Cnr with Av Accordos de Lusaka
Av de Zambia Between Av Ahmed Sekou Touré & Av Eduardo Mondlane
Av Julius Nyerere At the junction with Rua Mateus S Mutemba

In addition there are also police stands in the **Feira Popular** and in the **Mercado Central.**

WHAT TO SEE AND DO

MUSEUMS AND GALLERIES

Natural History Museum [106 A5] (*104 Praça da Travessia do Zambeze, opposite the Hotel Cardoso;* ☎ *21 491145;* f *21 490879;* ⏲ *09.00–15.30 Tue–Fri, 10.00–17.00*

Sat & Sun; entry fee US$1.50) Housed in one of the finest buildings in Maputo, a palace built in the Manueline style (a sort of Portuguese Gothic), decorated with wonderfully ornamental plasterwork. The collections are somewhat dusty and dilapidated, but there has been some attempt to keep them scientifically up to date – one of the more bizarre exhibits is a display on genetics and heredity, including the ideas of dominance and recession, although there is no text accompanying the diagrams. Also on display is a series showing the development during gestation of elephant embryos, proudly announced as the only such display in the world.

Geological Museum [106 B4] *(Cnr Av 24 Julho & Av Dos Mártires da Machava; 21 315508; 09.00–16.00 Tue–Fri, 09.00–14.00 Sat & 14.00–16.00 Sun; entrance free)* Housed in what used to be Maputo's synagogue, this recently renovated museum has an interesting collection of geological exhibits from around the country.

Museu Nacional da Moeda [113 B3] *(Praça 25 de Junho; 21 320290; 09.00–12.00 & 14.00–17.00 Tue–Thu & Sat, 09.00–12.00 Fri, 14.00–17.00 Sun; entrance free)* The potentially dry 'money museum' is actually surprisingly worthwhile, displaying currency from across the world, with the most interesting items dating back to before the arrival of the Portuguese. It is housed in one of the oldest buildings in Maputo, the Casa Amarela ('Yellow House'), which dates to the 1860s.

Museu da Revoluçao [100–1 C5] *(Av 24 Julho; formerly 09.00–12.00 & 14.00–18.00 w/days (except Wed), 14.00–18.00 Sat, 09.00–12.00 & 15.00–18.00 Sun; entry fee US$0.40)* For those interested in the history of Mozambique's revolution, this is also surprisingly interesting, with many of the accompanying texts having a distinct whiff of Cold War rhetoric. It was closed for renovations in late 2010 but should have reopened by the time you read this.

Museu Nacional des Artes [113 C1] *(Av Ho Chi Min; 11.00–18.00 Tue–Fri, 14.00–16.00 Sat & Sun; nominal entrance fee)* Dedicated to paintings and sculptures by some of Mozambique's better-known artists, it also holds other exhibitions which are listed on posters at the entrance.

Núcleo de Arte [106 C5] *(R da Argélia, off Av Julius Nyerere; 21 492523)* A collective where artists can work and display their pieces, this also has a rather good café, internet access and occasional exhibitions. It has recently been involved in a project to make sculptures from old AK47 guns, land mines and other weapons associated with the civil war, and several of the results of this experiment are on display.

Fortalezada Nossa Senhora da Conceição [113 C4] *(Praça 25 de Junho; 09.00-17.00 daily; entrance free)* This burnished waterfront fortress encloses an area of 3,000m^2 and was constructed between 1851 and 1867 on the site of a smaller fort built in 1791 (see the plaque above the main entrance). Architecturally, it is a classic Portuguese fort of its era, built of red sandstone in a rough square topped with battlements. Inside there is a display of old cannons in the courtyard and on the battlements. Owned by Eduardo Mondlane University, the whole structure is in remarkably good condition, and the courtyard contains some interesting artworks, including some larger-than-life cast-iron statues of Portuguese colonial bigwigs on horseback, and murals depicting the 19th-century battles between the Portuguese settlers at Maputo and the local Gaza Kingdom.

CITY WALKS

Maputo lends itself to casual exploration on foot, with several interesting colonial buildings and a buzzing street life. Walking around the Polana district is particularly pleasant on a Sunday when the streets are quiet and most of the hawkers are sleeping off the previous night's revelries. In addition to the two walks described below, it's very pleasant to walk along the seafront along the Avenida da Marginal which is usually pretty quiet, with just a few anglers and other promenaders, and a nice breeze through the palms. Don't be tempted to cut off the road, though – there have been several muggings in the bush area around there.

POLANA Start from the **Polana Serena** (formerly the Hotel Polana) [106 D2], for decades the showpiece of Maputo's hotels, situated on a rise high above the Bay of Maputo in the quarter of the same name, east of the city centre on Avenida Julius Nyerere. Built in 1922, it was designed by the celebrated architect Sir Herbert Baker, who also created Cape Town's iconic Mount Nelson Hotel and the Union Buildings in Pretoria, where Nelson Mandela was inaugurated as President of South Africa in 1994. The Polana survived the revolution in a somewhat run-down condition, but was refurbished by a South African hotel chain in the early 1990s and is now restored to its former glory.

Heading south from the Polana, turn off Avenida Julius Nyerere into the first street to the left and walk along Avenida Friedrich Engels, which runs high above the coast. This shady road is lined with trees, bougainvillaea-draped lookout points and well-maintained benches, and the view extends over the Club Naval beyond the Bay of Maputo to the island of Inhaca. One can walk along Avenida Friedrich Engels almost as far as the **Presidential Palace** [106 C5] (be very careful when taking photographs) and then turn right into the Avenida Dos Mártires de Mueda, perhaps enjoying a coffee in the **Hotel Cardoso** [106 A5] with its fine views of the wide river estuary and the harbour. The open ground next to the hotel has a good view over the city centre.

Near the Hotel Cardosa, on the Praça da Travessia do Zambeze, lies the **Natural History Museum** [106 A5]. One block further on the Avenida Tomás Nduda is the old Maputo synagogue [106 B4] (now the **Geological Museum**). On the Avenida Patrice Lumumba, the **Casa Velha**, with adjoining amphitheatre for open-air performances, is well worth seeing.

If you like tumbledown buildings then there's a gorgeous old colonial house called **Vila Algarve** [106 B4] on the corner of Avenida Ahmed Sekou Toure and Avenida dos Mártires da Machava (next door to the Hotel Terminus). Covered in intricate mosaics, it's a beautiful building, though your admiration may be tempered by the realisation it that it was the centre for the security police in latter colonial times, and a byword for torture and murder. It appeared to be under restoration in late 2010.

THE BAIXA The best place to begin a walking tour of the city centre is at the intersection of the Avenida 25 de Setembro and the Avenida Samora Machel, with the **Café Continental** on one corner and the Scala Restaurant and Cinema Scala, built in 1931, on the other. Walk down the Avenida 25 de Setembro in a westerly direction (away from the Feira Popular) – you'll pass the utterly enchanting **Casa Coimbra** [113 C3], an Art Deco-style building, the ground floor of which was a department store, but is now very closed.

After the next street to the right (Avenida Karl Marx) you reach the **Mercado Central** [113 B2]. The surrounding streets have several Asian-owned shops with a decent selection of imported hardware items (flashlights, lanterns, tools, etc). Continue along the Avenida 25 de Setembro and walk down the Avenida Guerra Popular which brings you to the **Praça dos Trabalhadores** [113 A3], at the centre of which lies a large, rather ugly memorial to the Portuguese soldiers killed in World War I.

On the western side of the square is the palatial green-and-white **railway station** [113 A2], built in 1910 following a design by the architect Gustave Eiffel (of Eiffel Tower fame) and notable for its plethora of marble pillars and wrought-iron detail. Once the terminus of the most important railway line in southern Africa, the shortest coastal connection from the industrial areas and gold mines of the Witwatersrand and Johannesburg and the mines of southern Zimbabwe, the opulent, Victorian-style station is little used these days, which gives it a rather sad appearance but does not detract from its importance as an architectural monument. *Newsweek* magazine recently named it as one of the world's ten most impressive railway stations, the only African selection in the list.

Close to the railway station, lies the entrance to the **harbour** [113 B4]. During colonial times, Maputo harbour was more important to southern Africa than even Durban, a status it seems unlikely to reclaim in the foreseeable future. From the quay, with its huge cranes, there is a view of the ships anchored in the Bay of Maputo.

Between the station forecourt and the Avenida Samora Machel is the **Old Town**. Most of the buildings constructed in the late 19th century are quite run-down but they still have a certain charm. Many are still graced by wood or iron filigree and covered balconies, reminiscent of the Creole style of Mauritius and Réunion, and a few have been restored in recent years. It's worth poking around these streets, taking in the variety of buildings, and in particular taking a look at the **Jumma Masjid** [113 B3], a large, well-kept and much-frequented mosque. As usual with religious buildings, be respectful – the mosque doesn't seem to allow visitors and it's probably best not to push the point.

East of the station, Rua de Bagamoio – formerly known as the 'Street of Trouble' by sailors who frequented its many bars – is still not the most peaceful or salubrious of places, indeed it pretty much serves as Maputo's red light district, with its numerous down-at-heel bars and strip clubs, though there is little evidence of this in daylight hours. Rua do Bagamoio terminates at the **Praça dos 25 de Junho** [113 C3], whose Saturday curio market is the place to buy some of the finest batiks on offer in Mozambique. The **Fortalezada Nossa Senhora da Conceição** and **Museu Nacional da Moeda** (see page 121) both stand on this square.

Immediately opposite the fort is the **Ministério da Indústrio e Comércio,** a strong contender for the title of 'ugliest building in Maputo'. It's a large Stalinesque concrete slab with an utterly bizarre tower that seems to have been based on a German alpine castle. The overall effect is to make it look like a nightmarish experiment. Some of the cannons in the fort are pointing directly at it, and it's tempting to think that the only reason it's still standing is that they are waiting for the right calibre ammunition to arrive.

Next to the money museum is a police station and next to that is the new Banco de Moçambique with a stylish glass-and-steel frontage. Take the street heading north opposite the bank to Avenida 25 de Setembro and walk back towards the crossroads with Avenida Samora Machel, then turn north towards the **Jardim Tunduru** (Botanical Gardens) [113 D2], a public park with many large shady trees. It's particularly pleasant towards the end of the day as the lowering sun casts yellowing stripes on the grass. You'll have to share the park with many courting couples.

LOUIS TRICHARDT MEMORIAL GARDEN

Situated on the alleged spot where the famous great trek leader Louis Trichardt died of malaria in October 1838, this large memorial garden [113 C2] consists of a stone frieze reminiscent of Pretoria's Voortrekker Monument and a circular pond, at the base of which is a ceramic map depicting Trichardt's route from the Cape to Maputo, complete with stylised mosaics of African chiefs in headdress and Bushmen bearing bows and arrows. Alongside the frieze, under the inscription 'They Harnessed the Wilds', the story of Trichardt's trek is told in the sort of messianic tones you might expect of a monument opened in 1968 by the South African Nationalist Party's Minister of Education, one J De Klerk. Odd enough to find this anachronistic and rather culture-bound slice of apartheid chic still exists in 21st-century Maputo; odder still that it has been maintained with meticulous care throughout the last 35 years of civil war, socialism and democracy.

To the left of the main entrance gate, on the Praça de Independência, is a **statue of Samora Machel** [113 C2], the country's first president. Donated by Kim Il-Sung of North Korea, the statue of Machel bears a strange and inaccurate resemblance to Chairman Mao. Just up from there is the **Casa de Ferro** (Iron House) [113 C2], a construction of prefabricated metal parts designed by the French engineer Eiffel. Opposite, on the east side of the Tunduru gardens, is the palace in which Paul Kruger, President of the South African Republic, resided after fleeing from British troops at the end of the 19th century. This old building now houses the **Centre Cultural Franco-Mozambicain** [113 C2], which has a pleasant semi-outdoor café, regular art exhibitions and a funky little shop selling locally made handicrafts and clothing.

Continuing up the Avenida Samora Machel brings you to the imposing **town hall**. On its right is the glistening white **Catholic cathedral** [113 D2], a boldly unattractive structure that was completed in 1944. From the cathedral, cross the Praça de Independência and walk along Avenida Josina Machel for 1½ blocks. On the southern side of the road is perhaps the most surprising monument in the Baixa, the **Louis Trichardt Memorial Garden** (see box above), which lies on Avenida Josina Machel immediately west of Avenida Karl Marx, and is worth seeing if only because it is so incongruous. Finish off your walk by going back along the Avenida Josina Machel to the crossroads with Avenida Karl Marx, and pop into the **Restaurante Impala** [113 C2] for a mango lassi, watching the passers-by as the sun goes down.

DAY TRIPS FROM MAPUTO

The opportunities for exploring around Maputo are limited, and if you are dependent on public transport, the most intriguing possibility is a day trip across the harbour to Catembe, which can easily be twinned with a walking tour of the main sights in the Baixa. Further afield, the private Mucapana Park north of town is a pleasant enough goal for a day of low-key game viewing, birdwatching and stylish dining. For business travellers with a day or two to spare, more serious day and overnight game-viewing excursions to Maputo Special Reserve and across the border to the Kruger National Park are a possibility, or you could arrange to take a day or overnight trip to Inhaca Island. Note that Catembe, Inhaca and Maputo Special Reserve are covered in the next chapter.

Recommended operators for day trips out of Maputo include **Mozaic Travel** (*21 451380; m 82 328 0520; e mozaictravel@gmail.com; www.mozaictravel.com)* and **Dana Tours** (*21 497483; e info@danatours.net; www.danatours.net*).

ILHA DA XEFINA This island, slightly to the north of Maputo, was once a leper colony and still has the remains of one of the old Portuguese forts on it, complete with disused cannon. There is no accommodation on the island but it is possible to do it as a day trip from Maputo. **NAU Tours** (*21 380 010/34; m 82 78 58 030/82 31 58 860; f 21 380 034; e nautours@teledata.mz; www.nautours.co.mz*) has a boat that can be chartered for the day.

COSTA DO SOL The best way to enjoy the sea close to the city is to take a trip up to the Costa do Sol Restaurant. It's too far to walk, so head for the upper end of Avenida Julius Nyerere and look for buses heading to Costa do Sol – the ride will cost US$0.20. From Maputo onwards, one casuarina tree-lined beach after the other lines the coastline. The seabed is very flat, however, and one must wade out a long way to be able to swim. The water is also often cloudy and brown as a result of the river mouth nearby. In the Costa do Sol Restaurant at the end of the street, you can eat well and at a reasonable price, although the road is lined with little drinks booths, some of which also serve food. One or two of them even have tables and chairs on the beach where you can enjoy your drink while the chickens that feature on the menu peck the sand at your feet.

MATOLA It has to be said that Matola is most definitely not a tourist destination, but it will give you a taste of the 'real Mozambique' that seems to be so popular. Situated a little way to the southwest of Maputo, Matola is a pleasant, quiet, tree-lined town – if you are still labouring under the illusion that Mozambique is a land of run-down buildings handicapped by intense poverty then Matola will set you straight: it's as close as you'll get to suburban Mozambique, clearly well off and well kept with a quiet but discernible civic pride in itself and its country.

Technically this is the industrial zone of Maputo. At the end of the Portuguese colonial period, Mozambique was the fourth most industrialised country in Africa. Most of the industries did not withstand the first years of the socialist People's Republic, and few still function properly. The policy of economic reconstruction begun in the late 1980s is intended to change this. You can experience something of the scenery and atmosphere of southern Mozambique if you cross the Matola River from the town. Matola lay outside the army's protective cordon during the war and consequently suffered significant damage, so that much of the land is now turned over to agriculture.

Matola is the site of the home and burial place of the sculptor Alberto Chissano, one of Mozambique's leading artists (see pages 23–4), who committed suicide in 1994. His home on Rua Torre de Vale now functions as the **Galleria Chissano** (*09.00–12.00 & 15.00–17.00 daily except Mon*) and displays a selection of his work alongside that of other Mozambican artists.

To get to Matola, catch a chapa marked 'C Matola-Museu'. It'll cost you around US$0.25.

MUCAPANA SAFARI PARK This private park 35km north of Maputo hosts a variety of introduced game, including giraffe, ostrich, zebra and various antelopes, and is also home to a rich birdlife. It opens at weekends only and can be visited as an organised day trip including a large buffet lunch of traditional African cuisine

KRUGER DAY TRIPS

The Crocodile Bridge entrance gate to South Africa's legendary Kruger National Park is little more than an hour's drive west of Maputo, ideally with the earliest possible start, via the Komatipoort/Ressano Garcia border post, and it makes for a superb day or overnight excursion from the capital for anybody stuck there on business over a weekend. No less so because the part of Kruger closest to Maputo is among the finest for game viewing, with white rhino especially common along the road connecting Crocodile Bridge to Lower Sabie Rest Camp, which lies in an area famed for its concentrations of lion, elephant and buffalo. As with any large African game reserve, the Kruger offers no guarantees about what might be seen where on any given day, but day trippers from Maputo might reasonably hope to see three of the Big Five in the course of a day, and an overnight stay would greatly boost your chances of a full house. Either way, the scenery along the Sabie River in particular is riveting, and the birdlife can be utterly spectacular. A recommended operator for Kruger day and overnight trips (or longer trips embracing the Mozambican sector of the Greater Limpopo Transfrontier Park, see page 125) is Mozaic Travels.

and seafood overlooking a waterhole where animals come to drink. It lacks the authenticity of the larger parks further north, but nevertheless it makes for an enjoyable day out in the bush for anybody stuck in the city over a weekend. Tours run on Saturday and Sunday, departing Maputo at around 09.00, returning at 18.00, and cost US$80. Bookings can be made through any tour operator in Maputo, as well as through most upmarket hotels and at the reception of Fátima's Place (see page 109).

7

Maputaland

The small block of Mozambican territory that lies to the south of Maputo has a very different feel from the rest of the country, and much of it is more accessible – or at least more commonly visited – from South Africa than from the capital, the notable exception being Inhaca Island. Often referred to as Maputaland, it is a wild and thinly populated region, whose utterly beautiful coastline hems in a hinterland of tall vegetated dunes, shallow lakes, dense coastal forests and grassy slopes inhabited by what is surely the most southerly free-ranging elephant population in Africa. The more popular beaches retain a pristine quality often lacking in their counterparts further north. No higher tribute can be paid to this fascinating area than to say that it is so very reminiscent of South Africa's bordering iSimangaliso (formerly Greater St Lucia) Wetland Park, a UNESCO World Heritage Site.

The main beach resorts in this area are Inhaca Island, which lies in Maputo Bay and is easily visited from the capital, as well as Ponta do Ouro and Ponta Malongane, close to the South African border and renowned for their diving and snorkeling. The other potential tourist attraction is the Maputo Special Reserve, home to several hundred elephants and a variety of other wildlife. It has been the subject of some big plans for development over the years, and though none has come to fruition thus far, this must surely change one day. Birdwatching is superb throughout the region, and several archaeological sites, currently closed to the public, have potential for development. Much of the region requires a 4x4 to explore properly, but this may also change if plans to surface the main road between Catembe and the border ever come to anything,

INHACA ISLAND

Situated about 35km from central Maputo, Inhaca is a dislocated extension of the narrow peninsula that runs northward from Maputo Special Reserve to Cabo Santa Maria, from which it is separated by a shallow channel just 500m wide. Effectively forming the shore of Maputo Bay, Inhaca is among the most accessible of Mozambique's many offshore islands, and ideally situated for a short break from the capital. It luxuriates in an archetypal tropical island atmosphere, with a couple of good beaches, a mangrove-lined north coast and brightly coloured reefs off the west coast. The main tourist focus is Inhaca village, a tiny settlement dominated by a centre crammed with bars. The beach directly in front of the lodges is an interesting place to sit and watch the boats as the sun goes down. Away from the village, the beaches on both the western side of the island (facing Maputo) and its eastern side (facing the Indian Ocean are utterly deserted, and offer mile after mile of sun-kissed, wave-swept sand. The reefs of Inhaca are among the most southerly in Africa, and as the water in the gulf is five degrees warmer than elsewhere at this

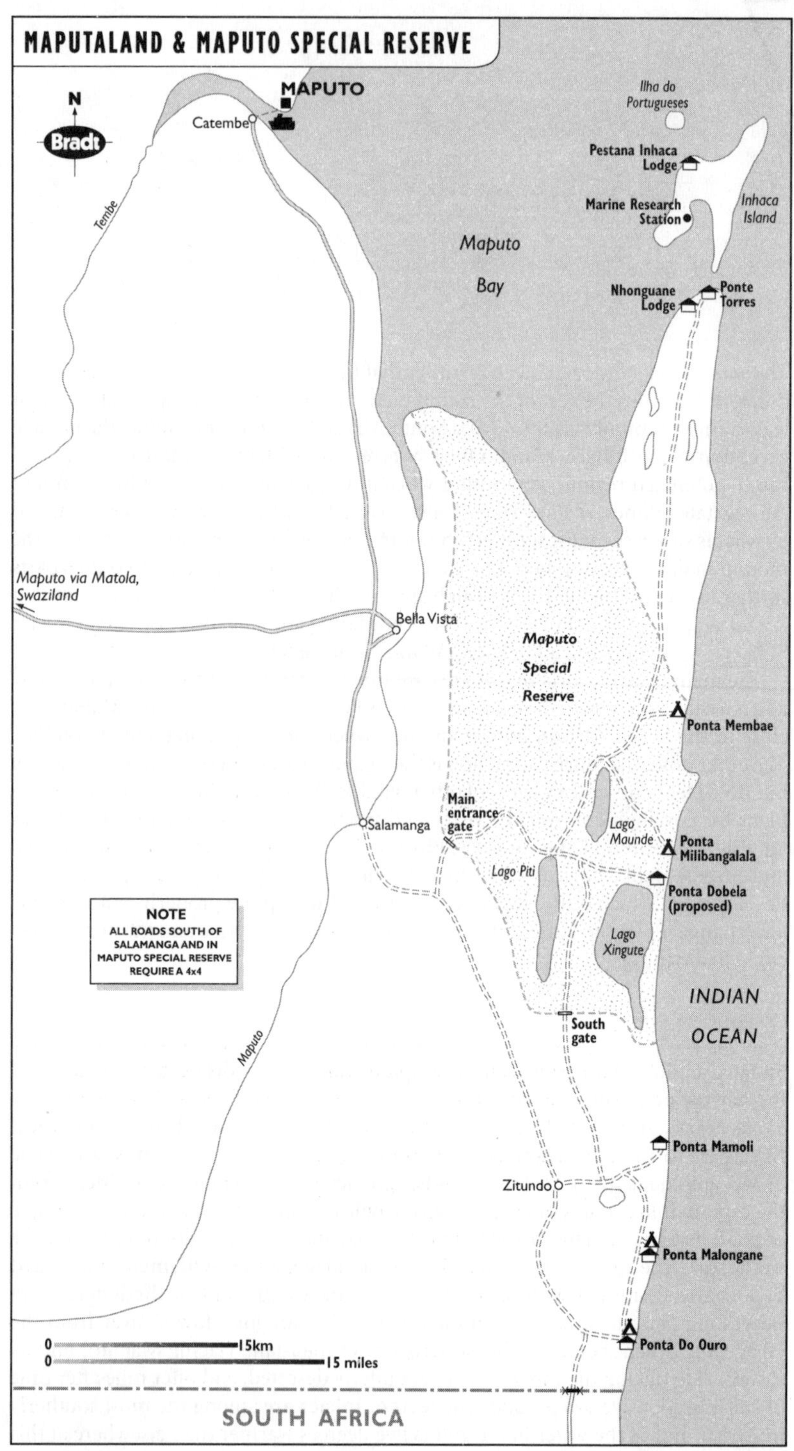
MAPUTALAND & MAPUTO SPECIAL RESERVE
MAPUTO
N
Bradt
Catembe
Tembe
Ilha do Portugueses
Pestana Inhaca Lodge
Marine Research Station
Inhaca Island
Maputo Bay
Nhonguane Lodge
Ponte Torres
Maputo via Matola, Swaziland
Bella Vista
Maputo Special Reserve
Ponta Membae
Main entrance gate
Salamanga
Lago Maunde
Ponta Milibangalala
Lago Piti
Ponta Dobela (proposed)
NOTE
ALL ROADS SOUTH OF SALAMANGA AND IN MAPUTO SPECIAL RESERVE REQUIRE A 4x4
Lago Xingute
INDIAN OCEAN
South gate
Maputo
Ponta Mamoli
Zitundo
Ponta Malongane
Ponta Do Ouro
0 15km
0 15 miles
SOUTH AFRICA

latitude, the island has been a centre of scientific research for over 50 years. If you're looking for diving the outer reefs are well worth visiting, and a large number of the region's diveable wrecks are scattered among the islands. There's good humpback whale watching between September and November, while back on terra firma, butterflies and dragonflies seem to swarm from every bush in summer.

There is also a nascent surfing scene, with the reef crest between the north end of Inhaca and Ilha Portuguesa becoming increasingly well known in the community. If you are interested in sport fishing, Inhaca has some of the finest opportunities south of Beira. Every May, the Inhaca Challenge brings fishermen from all over the region to compete against one another. Two international sailing challenges start from here – the Inhaca Race (to Richards Bay) at Easter and the Vasco da Gama Race (*www.vascodagama.co.za*) in July. Add to the mix the marine reserves, the deserted beaches, the relaxed feel of the island and the fact that it's within three hours of Maputo Airport, and it's surprising that Inhaca hasn't become a much more popular destination.

A park entrance fee equivalent to around US$6 is charged to all visitors to Inhaca.

HISTORY The island is named for the Inhaca chieftaincy, the dominant power on the southern mainland of the Gulf of Maputo in the 16th century. Chief Inhaca offered a hospitable welcome to the Portuguese trader Lourenço Marques, and frequently came to the assistance of shipwrecked Portuguese sailors. From about 1550 onwards, a Portuguese ship would set up camp on Inhaca Island for a few months annually to trade ivory with the chief's town on the mainland. In 1593, one Portuguese navigator settled on the island for a year before he was murdered and his ship looted by a rival chieftaincy. After 1621, Inhaca fell out of favour with the Portuguese: the ships relocated their annual encampment to Xefina Island and obtained their ivory from the Tembe chieftaincy on the northern part of the bay.

GETTING THERE AND AWAY

By boat/ferry There are two regular **boat services** between Maputo and Inhaca, a government-run slow ferry and a privately owned, much faster catamaran known as the *Vodacom* after its advertising deal. The *Vodacom* (m *82 338 9055;* e *mozguide@yebo.co.mz; www.inhacaferry.co.za*) makes the return trip from the fishing port on Praça 25 de Junho on Saturdays and Sundays throughout the year, as well as on Wednesdays from November to April, when the normal single/return/day return fare of around US$30/45/50 increases to US$40/50/60. The boat leaves Maputo at 08.00, returning the same day at 15.00 from the Inhaca jetty, and the crossing takes up to two hours in either direction. The boat has a bar on board should you fancy a drink as the sun drops over the yardarm. The day return includes a drop-off on Ilha Portuguesa, collecting you later in the day.

The **government ferry** leaves from the end of the jetty on Avenida 10 de Novembro every Tuesday, Thursday, Saturday and Sunday at around 07.30 but you're strongly recommended to get there early as this can depend on the tide. It returns later the same day from the jetty at Inhaca at around 15.00, again tide dependent. The journey takes around three hours, weather permitting. If you're returning to Maputo on the Sunday afternoon be warned that you may be accompanied by a number of individuals who have over-indulged – it can be an unpleasantly messy trip. One-way tickets cost US$10 and can be bought from the ticket office at the entrance to the jetty for the out-bound journey and on the ferry itself for the return leg.

By air Alternatively, **TransAirways** (*www.iba-vet.co.mz*) flights from Maputo to Inhaca Island take around 15 minutes and cost US$50 plus airport tax of US$10. Reservations can be made online or at any travel agent in Maputo.

WHERE TO STAY AND EAT It should be pointed out that at certain times of year – notably the Christmas period and during the Inhaca Challenge and the two yacht races – Inhaca becomes very busy. The costs listed below will rise and you may have trouble finding accommodation. In the village there are several bars and small local restaurants, all serving much the same fare.

Pestana Inhaca Lodge t 21 760005; f 21 760010; e inhaca.lodge@pestana.com; www.pestana.com. Sited at the end of the jetty, this is the most established of the lodges, with a mixture of chalets & rooms, a large central swimming pool & tennis court & an excellent restaurant. If you are staying at another Pestana hotel or lodge, check to see if there are any deals for guests. *From US$153/250 sgl/dbl HB.*

Inhacazul Lodge t +27 (0)78 701 6510 (South Africa); e andyaccrue@gemail.com; www.inhacazullodge.itgo.com. This hidden treasure consists of a mixture of well-equipped chalets & cabins, with a beach bar, restaurant & small shop, while a deal allows guests to use the Inhaca Lodge's facilities. The restaurant is good for Mozambican dishes (the piri-piri chicken is well worth trying) but it's wise to let them know in advance if you intend to eat there. *There is a sliding scale of charging depending on how many people are staying, beginning at around US$50 for someone on their own.*

Marine Research Station t 21 760009. Located to the south of Inhaca village, the research station may take visitors if there is space, although priority is given to researchers rather than the public, so ring ahead. *Rooms cost around US$12 pp.*

Ross Ramos Camp m +27 82 925 9065 (South Africa); www.accommodationmozambique.co.za. Sited next to the airport, the camp is a tightly packed but well-maintained collection of chalets & tents. *US$35 for a log cabins (sleeping 2) or rondawel (sleeping 4); US$23 standing tent (sleeping 2).*

Lucas Restaurante Right in the heart of the village, Lucas Restaurante is easily the best on the island, specialising in seafood, but not cheap. The crayfish is quite superb. At busy times let them know you'll be eating there. *Mains US$8–12.*

WHAT TO SEE AND DO

Marine station Inhaca has been a centre of scientific research for 65 years. An interesting marine research station lies to the south of Inhaca village, along with a well-kept **museum of natural history**. For those with a strong interest in the island's ecology, it's worth trying to get hold of a copy of *The Natural History of Inhaca Island* (edited by Margaret Kalk, Wits University Press, Johannesburg), a 395-page book that includes comprehensive species descriptions of the fauna and flora as well as line drawings depicting the more common species. The station can be reached either by walking along the road or by the western beaches.

Gone Fishing The only charter company currently running on the island, Gone Fishing are sited at the entrance to the Inhaca Lodge at the end of the jetty. They do a variety of excursions including diving, fishing and whale watching in season. Some of the options do not include the fuel used to get to the site, so check before agreeing a deal. They will run you around the island in their Land Rover for a price. Prices for snorkelling start at US$15 per person, scuba US$35 per person per dive and fishing US$150 for a half day. These prices do not include fuel costs.

The northern lighthouse Another good walk (around three hours each way), through grassland, local fields, salt flats and mangroves. Take the road south of the airport and keep checking with the people you meet – asking '*O camino para faro*?' and pointing should do the trick. You must take water. If you're interested in riding the surf, you'll need to head here, but given the distance you might prefer to take a ride on the Gone Fishing pick-up, which charges US$15. Alternatively Maurice (m *82 766 4770*) in the village will take you there for US$13. Arrange to be collected again.

The west beaches You can walk all the way around the island should you wish, but a good alternative is to take the west side from the jetty down to the marine station – mile after mile of perfect deserted beach. It's worth stopping every now and again just to listen to the waves on the shore and the wind in the palm trees. It's almost impossible to believe that you're only a short distance from Maputo, until you look to the horizon where you can see the buildings gleaming in the sunlight. The walk takes between 1½ and two hours each way, and check the state of the tide – it may not be passable at high spring tides, and there are one or two places where you'll need to scramble over rocks, so sandals are a good idea.

Birdwatching With more than 200 species recorded in an area of only $40km^2$, Inhaca offers some very good birding, with a variety of marine species alongside those more associated with coastal thickets and scrub. Among the most striking or beautiful species associated with vegetated habitats are the African fish eagle, trumpeter hornbill, green pigeon, Narina trogon, African hoopoe and green twinspot, while the sandy shores of the island often host large mixed groups of migrant and resident waders, ranging from the localised crab plover and bulky curlew to diminutive sandpipers and stints. Pelicans and cormorants are common around the bay, while offshore birds, most likely to be seen in flight, include half a dozen species of tern (including the localised black-naped tern), three types of skua, Cape gannet and Pintado petrel.

Ilha Portuguesa A small island to the north of Inhaca itself, this island is now a nature reserve. In Portuguese colonial times it was a leper colony, and there are supposedly some ruins from those days, although they haven't been found again since the 1960s. The beaches tend to be very flat with large sandbanks at low tide. If the tide is particularly low, you can cross the channel between the two islands on foot, although you must take a guide and be aware that the tide may rise faster than you think. It's safer to take a boat from Inhaca – ask at the lodges or speak to the skipper of *Vodacom* (see page 129). The best swimming beach is the one facing Inhaca, but it is dangerous to swim out too far as the current is very strong. You can walk round the Ilha Portuguesa in approximately 1½ hours.

CATEMBE

Situated on the southern bank of Maputo Bay, directly opposite Maputo city centre, the little fishing village of Catembe is both a popular goal for a day trip out of the capital and the main domestic gateway to all destinations further south in Maputaland, including Maputo Special Reserve and Ponta do Ouro. There is no direct road link between Maputo and Catembe, only a ferry service, so that the village retains a very different and distinctly more rustic vibe than its vast, sprawling neighbour. Indeed, were it not for the high-rise skyline to the north, Catembe would have little to distinguish it from hundreds of other small fishing villages along the Mozambican coastline.

As you walk along the landing quay (where there are a couple of basic restaurants), check out the dilapidated jetty to the right, and its gradually disintegrating old ferry. A little way along the beach, fishing vessels land their catch at the end of the day. The fish are sold at the small market lining the left-hand side of the jetty – but be aware that untreated sewage is pumped into Maputo Bay, so you may think twice before buying any. The village and surrounding beaches are well worth exploring, and the many bars that line the waterfront are pleasant places to sit and people-watch. Large banknotes may not be appreciated here.

GETTING THERE AND AWAY The ferry to Catembe usually runs from dawn to dusk daily, with boats typically leaving in either direction every 15–20 minutes. The terminal is located at the west end of Avenida 10 de Novembro. The journey itself takes around ten minutes, but loading the ferries (particularly the car ferry) takes significantly longer, and can cause huge amusement. Tickets can be bought at the little hut next to the jetty and cost next to nothing to foot passengers. Vehicles must pay US$7.50. Regular chapas to Bella Vista and more occasional ones to Ponta do Ouro leave from the end of the Catembe pier.

WHERE TO STAY AND EAT

Catembe Gallery Hotel 21 380050/51; m 82 228 3623; e reception@catambe.net; www.catembe.net. The view over the water to Maputo is extremely pretty, & the accommodation is good, as the restaurant. *Rooms from US$60.*

Restaurante Diogo About 500m from the ferry jetty, this place is legendary for its good but inexpensive seafood, in particular prawns. *Mains are in the US$4–5 range.*

BELLA VISTA AND SALAMANGA

The largest town in Maputaland, Bella Vista stands on the west bank of the Rio Maputo some 42km south of the Catembe ferry. It has an isolated and rather spaced-out feel, more like an unfinished plan than an actual town, centred on a misproportioned praça that could embrace several football fields. The only real attraction in the town itself is the river views from the jetty at the end of the main road, but there is also a large market. Bella Vista would be a useful base for earlyish game drives in nearby Maputo Special Sanctuary. About 15km past the town, the road south crosses the Rio Maputo at Salamanga, where there is a rather officious police roadblock and, right alongside it, the elaborate Shree Ram Hindu Temple. Constructed in 1908, this is one of the largest such shrines anywhere in Mozambique, despite its remote location, and arguably the most beautiful. Visitors are welcomed.

GETTING THERE AND AWAY Coming from Maputo, you must first cross the Catembe ferry, from where it is 42km south to Bella Vista and another 15km to Salamanga along a well-maintained murram (and in places tar) road, on which you should maintain a speed of around 60–70km/h, though it can be slippery in parts when wet. Bella Vista itself lies a couple of kilometres east of the main road along a tarred feeder road. There are plenty of chapas between Catembe and Bella Vista, which continue to Salamanga along the road to Ponto do Ouro and the South African border. There are two other possible approaches to Bella Vista: the 70km EN202 from the quiet Goba border post with Swaziland, and the 90km EN3 from Maputo via Matola and Boane (which joins the EN202 30km before Bella Vista). Both are in fair condition and can be travelled in a sturdy saloon car.

WHERE TO STAY AND EAT

Complexo Quinto Mila (16 rooms) 21 620027; m 82 320 4500; e quinta.mila@gmail.com. This unexpectedly pleasant little hotel, set in green grounds overlooking the riverbank, has a decent restaurant serving typical Mozambican mains for around US$5. All rooms are en suite. *US$17/23 sgl/dbl; US$43 dbl with TV & AC; US$50 suite.*

MAPUTO SPECIAL RESERVE

This little-known 750km² reserve extends over a lushly scenic, lake-studded tract of coastal bush and grassland running for about 50km south from the Bay of Maputo to within 10km of Ponta Mamoli. It is one of the oldest conservation areas in Mozambique, established in 1932 as the Maputo Elephant Reserve (not, incidentally, after the city then known as Lourenço Marques, but after the Rio Maputo, which runs along part of its western boundary), and now forms a disjunct part of the Ndumo-Tembe-Futi Transfrontier Conservation Area, which otherwise lies mainly within South Africa and is connected to it by an ancient elephant migration corridor along the Futi Channel. Although the reserve supports a few farming and fishing communities, fewer than 1,000 people in total, their activities are monitored by the authorities and most of it remains ecologically pristine.

The special reserve has had a chequered history in terms of conservation and tourist development. As with most other Mozambican reserves, it was heavily poached during the war years: the 65 white rhinos that were introduced from South Africa in the 1960s were killed, many other large mammal species including cheetah and buffalo became locally extinct, and the elephant population plummeted from 350 in 1970 to fewer than 60 in 1994. In the late 1990s, the reserve was earmarked for development as a major tourist destination, a project that would have involved intensive restocking and the construction of upmarket accommodation, but this fell though after the death of the main investor, an American called James Blanchard. As a result, although the reserve is officially open to visitors, facilities remain severely limited at the time of writing, though this may well change during the lifespan of this edition.

Today, the special reserve is well worth a slight diversion for the opportunity to see elephants (probably about 50/50 on a day trip) and highly recommended as a scenic destination and for its superb birdwatching. However, the majority of visitors are there for the lovely swimming beaches, the superb fishing and challenging 4x4-only roads, which means that the campsites tend to be quite busy over long weekends and South African school holidays. At other times, you would most likely have the reserve practically to yourself.

An entrance fee equivalent to around US$6 per adult, US$3 per child and US$6 per vehicle must be paid at the entrance gate.

GETTING THERE AND AWAY The main entrance gate is about one hour's drive from Catembe, a couple of kilometres north of the main road towards Ponta do Ouro, along a turn-off that is clearly signposted about 5km past Salamanga. A saloon car could easily make it as far as the entrance gate in dry conditions, but the roads within the reserve are strictly 4x4 only. Mozaic Travel (see page 125) runs regular day trips to the special reserve from Maputo city centre, and longer trips can be arranged.

WHERE TO STAY The main **campsite** is at Ponta Milibangalala about 25km from the entrance gate. It lies in thick coastal scrub above a pretty beach and has room for around 15 parties. Facilities are limited to a basic pit latrine and a well producing slightly brackish water. A proper ablution block with showers is planned. A second beachfront campsite about 10km further north at Ponta Membae has room for about three parties only, and the only facility is a freshwater well. Camping costs US$6 per person. All campers should be self-sufficient in terms of food, drinks, cooking facilities and fuel.

Camping aside, there are no overnight facilities in the reserve at the time of writing. However, it can easily be visited as a day trip from Bella Vista, about 25km from the entrance gate, as well as from Maputo (ideally catching the first ferry to Catembe) or Ponta do Ouro. On the Santa Maria Peninsula immediately north of the reserve, accessible only by 4x4, are two remote and low-key self-catering complexes, **Ponte Torres** (*+27 11 791 0519 (South Africa); www.africastay.com/ponta-torres-camp.html*) and **Nhonguane Lodge** (m *84 555 0822 or 82 252 4670;* e *info@africaafrica.co.za; www.nhonguanelodge.co.za*). Both charge around US$50 per person. In addition, it seems likely that an upmarket concession will open during the lifespan of this edition, most likely at Ponta Dobela in the south of the reserve, under **Barra Resorts** (*www.barraresorts.com*).

GAME VIEWING The reserve today offers a mixed bag when it comes to the large stuff. Elephants, the only confirmed member of the so-called Big Five, have largely recovered from the poaching of the 1980s, and the population is now thought to stand at around 300. They remain shy and aggressive following years of persecution, however, so sightings tend to be sporadic and fleeting, and the matriarchs in particular should be treated with respect. The reserve supports an estimated population of around 1,150 common reedbuck, which is the most visible antelope, usually seen singly or in small parties in relatively open habitats. Grey duiker, red duiker and nyala are all quite common too, and greater kudu, common waterbuck, impala, bushbuck, suni and steenbok occur in small numbers. It is unclear whether leopards survive, but side-striped jackal and various smaller predators are present. The lakes support an estimated 180 hippos, and small pods are almost guaranteed where the road to Ponta Milibangalala passes the northern end of Lagoa Xingute and northwest shore of Lagoa Maunda. Turtles nest on some of the beaches and might be observed in the breeding season, and whales also come past seasonally.

Though relatively small in area, Maputo Special Reserve supports a wide diversity of habitats, including mangroves, freshwater wetlands, dune and riparian forest, open grassland and thick acacia and albizia woodland. Thanks to this, it has an astonishingly varied avifauna, with some 350 species recorded to date. An excellent spot for freshwater birds is the northern floodplain of Lagoa Xingute, which supports large numbers of waders and shorebirds, with Caspian tern, pied avocet, African spoonbill and various sandpipers, storks, herons and egrets all likely, while African fish eagles are resident in the forested floodplain edge. Elsewhere, ponds with lily pads often have African pygmy-goose and lesser jacana among more common waterbirds.

The various wooded habitats support several birds with restricted ranges, or that are eagerly sought by birders, among them palm-nut vulture, grey crowned crane, green coucal, spotted ground thrush, brown robin, Rudd's apalis, Woodward's batis, Neergaard's sunbird and pink-throated twinspot. The grasslands around the reserve have a number of uncommon species, including Denham's bustard, Senegal lapwing, black coucal (seasonal) and the localised rosy-breasted longclaw. Overall, this is probably the single most exciting birding destination in southern Mozambique, and well worth giving a few days if you want to see all the local specialities. See also the detailed booklet *Birds of the Maputo Special Reserve, Mozambique*, which can be bough online at www.nhbs.com.

PONTA MAMOLI AND MALONGANE

Less well known than the more southerly Ponta do Ouro, these two isolated resorts retain a genuine bush feel, dominated by coastal scrub and dune forested inhabited by a rich array of birds and plentiful vervet and blue monkeys. The diving and snorkelling are comparable to Ponto do Ouro, though the choice of operators is more limited, but the reward is one of the most wildly beautiful beach destinations anywhere in the country. Ponta Mamoli is the more isolated and undeveloped of the two, while Ponta Malongane has better facilities for budget and mid-range travellers and campers, and its one upmarket lodge, Tartaruga Maritima, is a forest-swathed delight.

GETTING THERE AND AWAY Both resorts are ideally accessed by 4x4 only, though a powerful 2x4 pick-up with diff-lock and heavily deflated tyres should also get through. Coming from South Africa, as most visitors do, follow the same directions as for Ponta do Ouro, from where a signposted track that more or less demands 4x4 leads north through the coastal scrub, arriving at Ponta Mamoli after about 20km and passing through Ponta Malongane roughly halfway. Coming from Maputo, follow the main road south from Catembe towards the South African border as far as Zitundo, which lies 36km past Salamanga, along a road that gradually deteriorates to become a sandpit for the last 5km – whatever else you do along these intersecting tracks try to avoid losing momentum!

At Zitundo, instead of following the road signposted for the border, turn left onto an adequate tar road that leads to Ponta Mamoli after 11km. If you are heading to Ponta Malongane, follow this road for about 7km out of Zitundo until you see a papyrus-fringed lake to your right; immediately after passing it, turn right onto a sandy track that leads through a follow-your-nose network of other criss-crossing tracks that bring you where you need to be after about 20 minutes (it may help you orientate to know that the hillside aerials you see in the distance behind the lake are at Ponta Malongane).

WHERE TO STAY

Upmarket

Tartaruga Maritima (8 units) m 82 773 0067; e tartaruga@mweb.co.za; www.tartaruga.co.za. Named after the turtles that sometimes nest on the beach below, this nature-lovers' paradise is carved into a patch of dense coastal dune forest alive with birds & monkeys, & leads to a quiet and idyllic swimming beach. The bush-meets-beach feel is typified by rustic but well-equipped standing tents on tall stilted timber bases, with private balconies, ceiling fans, mosquito netting & en-suite shower. Instead of a restaurant, there is a large common lounge with loads of fridge space & well-equipped self-catering facilities; alternatively you can eat at Parque de Malongane or one of the nearby local places. There is also a swimming pool & TV lounge with DSTV. For activities, visit the dive centre at Parque de Malongane. *US$105/175/210 sgl/dbl/trpl rising by about 20% w/ends & public holidays.*

Ponta Mamoli Resort (15 units) +27 35 592 8100/01 (South Africa); e bookings@pontamamoli.com; www.pontamamoli.com. Set on a tall forested dune about 20km up the coast from Ponta do Ouro, this isolated resort has a stunning location overlooking a fine beach. Standard chalets, connected to the main building by stilted wooden walkways, have king-size or twin beds with nets, en-suite showers, fans, & a shaded sea-facing veranda. Facilities include an open-air seafood restaurant & swimming pool, while an on-site dive centre arranges fishing, diving, horseriding, whale-watching & other excursions. Family & luxury chalets are also available. *From US$130/190 sgl/dbl low season; US$150/250 peak season.*

Budget and camping

Parque de Malongane Resort (about 80 units) +27 13 741 1975 (South Africa); f +27 13 741 3730 (South Africa); e reservations@malongane.co.za; www.parquedemalongane.com. Next door to Tartaruga &, like its more upmarket neighbour, carved attractively into the thick coastal scrub, though with far more vegetation cleared, this sprawling resort caters mainly to the South African fishing market, so occupation is highly seasonal. It has its own activities centre offering a variety of diving, snorkelling, dolphin-watching & other marine excursions. There's a decent restaurant with indoor and outdoor seating, & seafood and other dishes in the US$6–8 range. *US$ 100–250 for 4–8 bed huts & chalets; US$55 dbl hut; US$25 pp standing tent; US$15 pp camping.*

WHERE TO EAT Aside from the restaurant at Parque de Malongane, you could try the locally run **Come To See Restaurant** (*08.00–22.00 daily*), in the village outside the entrance to Tartaruga Maritima, which serves a range of seafood and other dishes, mostly in the US$6–10 range, though prawns are a lot pricier. The **Peace Bar** next door, we were told by the owner, is named after him, in which case a name change might be in order.

PONTA DO OURO

Situated in the far south of the country, just a few kilometres north of the South African village of Kosi Bay, small, isolated Ponta do Ouro (literally Cape of Gold) is something of an anomaly in Mozambique, operating almost as an annexe of South Africa, with rands more freely accepted than meticais, and English and Afrikaans heard as much as Portuguese. The main reasons for this, aside from the obvious one of border proximity, are that road links between Ponta do Ouro and the rest of Mozambique are very poor indeed, and that its waters offer perhaps the finest fishing and diving opportunities anywhere along the African coastline south of Maputo. Difficult of access without a 4x4, Ponta do Ouro is seldom visited by people travelling on public transport. Once there, however, facilities are quite good, and include several resorts and restaurants, a few basic shops and even a brand-new ATM.

Diving is the main thing here, and in addition to some excellent reef fish, lucky visitors stand a chance of seeing, among other things, Zambezi and hammerhead shark, kingfish, barracuda and potato bass. The beaches around here are also strikingly beautiful, hemmed in by tall and largely untouched forested dunes, whose lush indigenous vegetation stands in contrast to most other Mozambican resorts, whose natural ecology has been degraded by the planting of casuarinas, palms and various invasive species. The birdlife is excellent too, with the dune forests sheltering a host of colourful and eagerly sought species, including green coucal, Livingstone's turaco, yellow-rumped tinker-bird, square-tailed drongo, fan-tailed flycatcher, olive bush-shrike, starred robin and forest weaver. The walking trail at Praia do Ouro Sol is an excellent place to seek out these forest birds, while another popular walk leads to the lighthouse about 3km south of the town centre.

GETTING THERE AND AWAY Most visitors come from the South African side, crossing the border at Kosi Bay (which is accessible on a good tar road) and then driving along the 10km track to Ponta do Ouro. This is a very sandy track, crossing

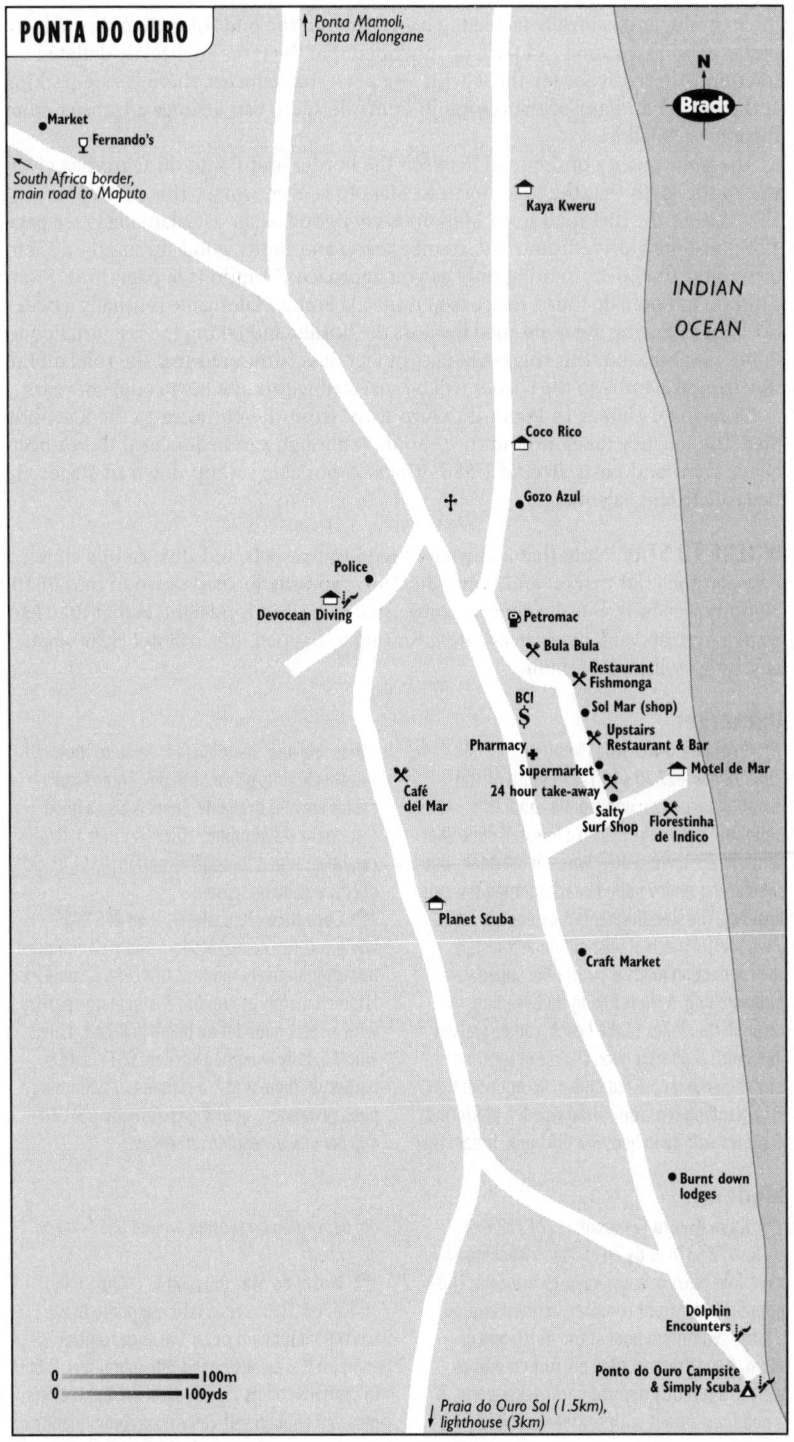
PONTA DO OURO
Ponta Mamoli,
Ponta Malongane
N
Bradt
Market
Fernando's
South Africa border,
main road to Maputo
Kaya Kweru
INDIAN
OCEAN
Coco Rico
Gozo Azul
Police
Devocean Diving
Petromac
Bula Bula
Restaurant
Fishmonga
BCI
Sol Mar (shop)
Upstairs
Restaurant & Bar
Pharmacy
Supermarket
Motel de Mar
Café
del Mar
24 hour take-away
Salty
Surf Shop
Florestinha
de Indico
Planet Scuba
Craft Market
Burnt down
lodges
Dolphin
Encounters
Ponto do Ouro Campsite
& Simply Scuba
0 100m
0 100yds
Praia do Ouro Sol (1.5km),
lighthouse (3km)

thick dunes, and is ideally tackled in a 4x4, though the odds of getting through are pretty good in a strong 2x4 pick-up, provided that the tyres are heavily deflated for traction. Alternatively, for those with less powerful vehicles, there is safe parking at the border and any of the resorts in Ponta do Ouro can arrange a transfer from there for a small fee.

The poor quality of the road between the border and Ponto do Ouro has given rise to the myth that the road north to Maputo is even worse. This isn't the case at all – indeed the dirt road from Maputo is very good as far as Salamanga (see page 132), an hour's drive from the Catembe ferry, and pretty good for another 25km or so after that, deteriorating only as you approach Zitundo (see page 135). From Zitundo to Ponta do Ouro, the coastal route via Ponta Malongane is usually a better bet than following the main road towards the border and taking the last junction to Ponta do Ouro, but this might change. In fact, it is rumoured that the road all the way from Catembe to the border will be surfaced within the next couple of years

Occasional chapas to Ponta do Ouro leave from the entrance to the Catembe pier. The journey takes around three hours (although can be longer if there's been heavy rain) and costs around US$6. It is also possible to hop down in stages via Bella Vista and Salamanga.

WHERE TO STAY Note that a cluster of reed-hut resorts and dive camps situated between the craft market and Ponto do Ouro campsite burned down in mid-2010. Nobody was hurt, but the general consensus, at least in hindsight, is that they had been a firetrap, and it was an accident waiting to happen. It is still not clear what, if anything, will replace them.

Upmarket

Praia de Ouro Sol (15 units) +27 82 786 7283 or +27 79 636 1271 (South Africa); e info@praia.co.za; www.praia.co.za. This delightful eco-lodge lies on a forested dune 3km south of the town centre, where it overlooks the spectacular undeveloped beach running towards Kosi Bay. The standing tents & cabins are set in a wonderful patch of unspoilt dune forest, & the connecting roads & paths offer superlative birdwatching. A short hiking trail, leading through the dunes to the beach, can be walked in 45mins & offers a good chance of spotting samango monkey & red duiker. Accommodation is in standing tents on stilted wooden platforms, & comes with twin beds & a dbl bunk, fridge, tea/coffee-making, standing fan, en-suite shower, private parking, private balcony. Three family cabins are also available. There is also a good restaurant & swimming . Dives & other activities can be arranged through reception. *US$170–200 dbl depending on season.*

Coco Rico (20 chalets) m 84 875 8029; www.cocorico.co.mz. Modern and well equipped, but comparatively soulless, this central complex is aimed mainly at families & other large parties, with all accommodation being in 8-bed chalets with AC, fully equipped kitchen, DSTV, safe & barbecue. There is also a communal swimming pool, restaurant, gym & games room. *US$250–400 per unit depending on season.*

Moderate

Kaya Kweru (24 rooms) 21 758403; m 82 527 6378 or 84 763 5081; e bookings@kaya-kweru.com; www.kaya-kweru.com. This popular beachfront complex, centred around a large swimming pool at the north end of town, has attractive tiled en-suite rooms as well as a recently opened backpacker dorm, & a good restaurant with sea views. *US$85–115 dbl depending on season; around US$2–00 pp dorm bed.*

Motel do Mar (60 rooms) 21 650000; m 82 764 0380 e reservations@ponta.co.za; www.pontadoouro.co.za. The large, central complex has an outmoded '60s-motel feel, & fails to capitalise on its seaside location, but it offers pleasant enough self-catering accommodation in small mini-suites with tiled floor, twin beds, fan, fridge, barbecue area & kitchenette. A restaurant is attached & the so-called museum houses a hydro-electric generator from the 1960s. *US$70–115 dbl depending on season & location.*

Planet Scuba (9 rooms) m +27 83 227 4872 (South Africa); e reservations@planetscuba.co.za; www.planetscuba.co.za. This friendly private house, set on a dune overlooking the town centre, has a shared kitchen, DSTV lounge, plunge pool & a variety of rooms, all with their own bathroom but not always en-suite. *From US$50 pp FB.*

Devocean Diving m +27 84 811 4626 or +27 83 657 4050 (South Africa); www.devoceandiving.com. This diving operation in the town centre offers accommodation in standing tents, rooms or 8-bed chalets. *Tents from US$25/35 sgl/dbl; rooms from US$35 dbl.*

Budget and camping

Café del Mar (10 rooms) 21 654008. Mainly known as a restaurant, this place also has some rooms set around a grassy courtyard on a wooden deck behind the dining area. Rooms have dbl beds with nets, & there are common showers. *US$60 dbl.*

Ponta do Ouro Campsite (24 chalets) 21 650006; info@simplyscuba.co.za. www.simplyscuba.co.za. With a perfect beachfront location at the southern end of the beach & town centre, this established & well-run campsite doubles as a dive camp for Simply Scuba & also has a selection of chalets sleeping 2–6. *US$45/105/160 2/4/6-bed unit; US$12 pp camping; rates increase by around 20% over w/ends.*

WHERE TO EAT

Upstairs Restaurant & Bar 07.00–late daily. Situated on the top floor of the town's small shopping mall, this has indoor & outdoor seating & serves a range of savoury pancakes, b/fasts, sandwiches & other light meals. There's a big-screen TV for sports enthusiasts, full bar & espresso coffee. *US$3–6.*

Florestinha do Indico lunch & dinner Tue–Sun. The speciality at this Portuguese eatery near the Motel do Mar is chicken piri-piri, but it also has a good seafood menu. *Most mains in the US$6–8 range.*

Café del Mar 21 654008; 10.00–24.00 daily except Tue. With its wide veranda offering a lovely view over the town centre to the open ocean, this is a pleasant place to stop in for a coffee or inexpensive snack, but it also has a good menu of more substantial mains – filled pancakes & French cuisine being the specialities. *US$7–12.*

Restaurant Fishmonga 21 650023; b/fast, lunch & dinner daily except Wed. Reckoned to serve the best seafood & fish in town, this place is clearly modelled on the South African Fishmonger chain, with a good wine list and likeable ambience. *Steeply priced, with mains in the US$10–20 range.*

Bula Bula lunch & dinner daily except Wed. This central restaurant has breezy balcony seating & a menu dominated by excellent Portuguese cuisine. Mains from US$7.

Fernando's 08.00–20.00. This popular drinking hole next to the market has a relaxed ambience, beer on tap, & a limited selection of typical Mozambican dishes – grilled prawns, chicken piri-piri. *Around US$12–15 per plate.*

24 Hours Take-Away 11.00–21.00 Mon–Sat, 11.00–18.00 Sun. The deceptively named ground-floor window in the main shopping mall serves burgers, sandwiches & chips. *US$2–4.*

OTHER PRACTICALITIES

Banks It should be stressed that this part of Mozambique is so economically tied to its neighbour that the South African rand is accepted everywhere and some places might actually refuse meticais. So if you are coming from South Africa, you are unlikely to need any local currency. However, there is now a BCI Bank with two ATMs in the main mall.

Diving, snorkelling and fishing There are several dive operations scattered around town, and their websites provide detailed breakdowns of the strengths of each of the the area's main dive sites, which include a full 18 offshore reefs, some of which also provide great snorkelling opportunities while others are better suited for seeking large fish such as sharks and rays. Also on offer are 'swim with dolphins' excursions and various fishing trips. Recommended operators include **Devocean** (m *+27 84 811 4626 or +27 83 657 4050 (South Africa); www.devoceandiving.com*), **Dolphin Encountours** (☏ *+27 11 462 1689 or +27 11 462 8103 (South Africa);* e *info@dolphin-encountours.co.za; www.dolphin-encountours.co.za*) and the mercifully pun-free **Gozo Azul** (m *84 339 2910 or 82 739 2910; www.gozoazul.co.za*) and **Simply Scuba** (☏ *21 650006;* e *info@simplyscuba.co.za; www.simplyscuba.co.za*). Most offer the choice of single dives, courses or full packages including accommodation at a dive camp.

Internet So far as we could ascertain, there is no public internet facility in Ponta do Ouro.

Shopping The main market, at the north end of the town centre alongside the road to the border, is reasonably well stocked with vegetables and other fresh fare. There is a small shopping mall in the heart of town with a supermarket that will seem reasonably well stocked if you are coming from elsewhere in Mozambique but somewhat less so to any freshly arrived South African. In the same mall, the Fishmonga Deli (☏ *21 650023;* ⏲ *09.00–13.00 & 14.00–18.00 daily except Wed*) doubles as butchery, fishmonger and delicatessen. There are also several surf and fishing shops in the mall. If it is handicrafts and gifts you are after, there is a good craft market along the main road between the shopping mall and Ponta do Ouro Campsite. Also worth a look is Magenta Moon, which has the vaguely hippyish feel its name projects, and sells a miscellany of soaps, beads, jewellery and other items. In the Petromac filling station, a small shop called Ponki sells hand-weaved kikois made on the premises (you can watch the weaver at work on a wooden loom).

8

The Limpopo Valley and Coast South of Inhambane

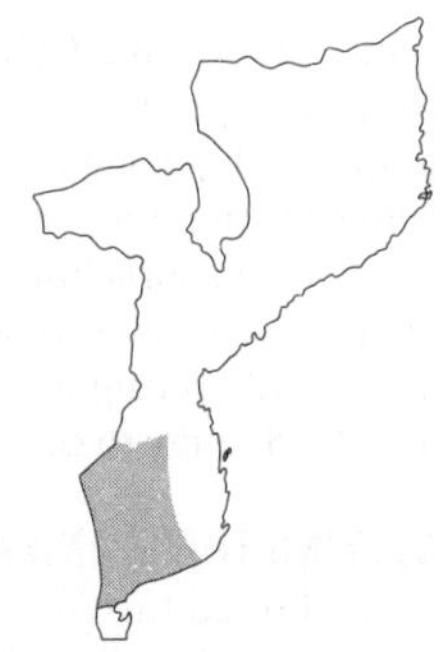

The long and heavily populated coastline between the cities of Maputo and Inhambane is one of the most developed parts of Mozambique in touristic terms, and is lined with a series of resorts that collectively offer a full range of beach and marine activities. Some resorts, for instance Marracuene and Praia do Xai-Xai, are oriented mainly towards the fishing fraternity, while others such as Závora and Bilene are more suited to snorkelling and diving. As the closest stretch of coastline to South Africa's densely populated province of Gauteng, the region looks squarely across the border for its main source of tourist custom, and facilities tend to reflect the sensibilities and requirements of self-catering South African family parties rather than those of international tourists or backpackers.

In comparison with the coastal belt, the interior of Gaza (the province that divides Maputo and Inhambane provinces) is thinly populated and visited by relatively few tourists. Its rather monotonous landscape of dry acacia and mopane woodland is run through by Kipling's 'great grey-green, greasy Limpopo', the second-largest African river (after the Zambezi) to drain into the Indian Ocean. The Limpopo reaches the ocean a short distance south of Xai-Xai, the provincial capital of Gaza, but before doing so it flows for about 200km along the northeastern border of Mozambique's largest national park, to which it also lends its name. This is the 1,000km^2 Limpopo National Park, a former hunting concession which – after long decades of only nominal protection – is currently enjoying a welcome renaissance, both as the site of several new tourist developments and as the Mozambican component in the Great Limpopo Transfrontier Park (which also includes South Africa's world-famous Kruger).

The emphasis on the South African market means that the coast between Maputo and Inhambane displays high seasonal duality dictated by the timing of school holidays across the border (see page 39). During the holidays, resorts and campsites throughout the region charge inflated prices and are often booked solid and unpleasantly crowded. At other times of the year, the same resorts can feel a little *too* abandoned for comfort (the Morrissey line about 'the coastal town that they forgot to close down' springs to mind). In all honesty, unless you are visiting Mozambique from South Africa and have strict time limitations, our firm recommendation would be to bypass this stretch of coast entirely, and head further north to the likes of Inhambane, Tofo or Vilankulo, or else to veer inland to Limpopo National Park.

MARRACUENE AND SURROUNDS

Straddling the EN1 about 35km past Maputo, Marracuene is where northbound travellers can start to relax and take a deep breath of fresh coastal air, and southbound travellers must brace themselves for the traffic bottlenecks and exhaust fumes of the capital. Situated near the Incomati River mouth, it is also the junction town for Macaneta, the closest beach resort to Maputo and a popular weekend outing with people working in the capital. The major attractions here are excellent game fishing and an attractive clean beach, but the sea here isn't particularly suitable for snorkelling, diving or swimming. For those arriving late in the day from South Africa, it's also worth knowing that a couple of very pleasant lodges provide affordable overnight accommodation on the west side of the EN1 near Bobole, about 20km north of Marracuene.

GETTING THERE AND AWAY Macaneta can only be reached by ferry, following an unsignposted turn on the east side of the EN1 just outside Marracuene, passing a mosque to the left and taking the left turn at the bottom of the road. The dock is nearby, down a small sand road. The wait for the ferry should take no more than 20 minutes but allow longer on Sundays and holidays.

WHERE TO STAY

Macaneta

Complexo Turístico da Macaneta m 82 307 0190; e macanetalodge@tdm.co.mz; www.macanetaaccommodation.com. This popular resort has 2 & 4-bed chalets for rent, as well as a campsite, & it is known for good seafood. *2-bed chalets from US$80; 4-bed chalets from US$150; camping US$12 pp.*

Jay's Beach Lodge m 84 863 0714; e reservations@jaysbeachlodge.co.za; www.jaysbeachlodge.co.za. This relaxed lodge offers inexpensive en-suite self-catering accommodation with fridges, & is also has a restaurant & campsite. *US$25 pp chalet.*

Bobole

Casa Lisa m 82 304 1990; e buckland@teledata.mz. Signposted to the left of the EN1 3km north of Bobole, this is a very pleasant place to break the drive north, with a genuine bush feel, friendly owner-managers & a good restaurant serving 3-course set menus. Accommodation is in rustic en-suite chalets scattered in the woodland. *US$25 pp or US$ pp to camp.*

Blue Anchor Inn 219 00559; m 82 325 3050; e blueanchorinn@teledata.mz; www.blueanchorinn.com. This rather misleadingly named place is actually a landlocked bush lodge situated a few hundred metres from Casa Lisa. Rates are slightly higher than Casa Lisa & it also serves good food.

BILENE

The first major resort along the coast northeast of Maputo, this quiet town of around 5,000 inhabitants overlooks the pretty Uembje Lagoon, which is separated from the Indian Ocean by a large tidal sandbar. Historically, Bilene is of significance as the headquarters and burial place of the Nguni general Soshangane, who fled northwards from present-day KwaZulu-Natal with his followers c1819 following a defeat by Shaka Zulu, then went on to overrun the Portuguese settlements at Maputo and Inhambane, and to found and give (most of) his name to the Shangane nation, prior to his death in 1856. In colonial times, Bilene was called São Martinho, a name that is still much in evidence there today, and whose feast day of 11 November is still celebrated with some vigour by locals.

Today, Bilene is known less for its tempestuous past than for the calm waters of its lagoon, which is popular with watersports enthusiasts and offers safe swimming from idyllic white beaches, but lacks the game-fishing opportunities that exist further north. The lagoon is also ideal for snorkelling, canoeing, windsurfing and,

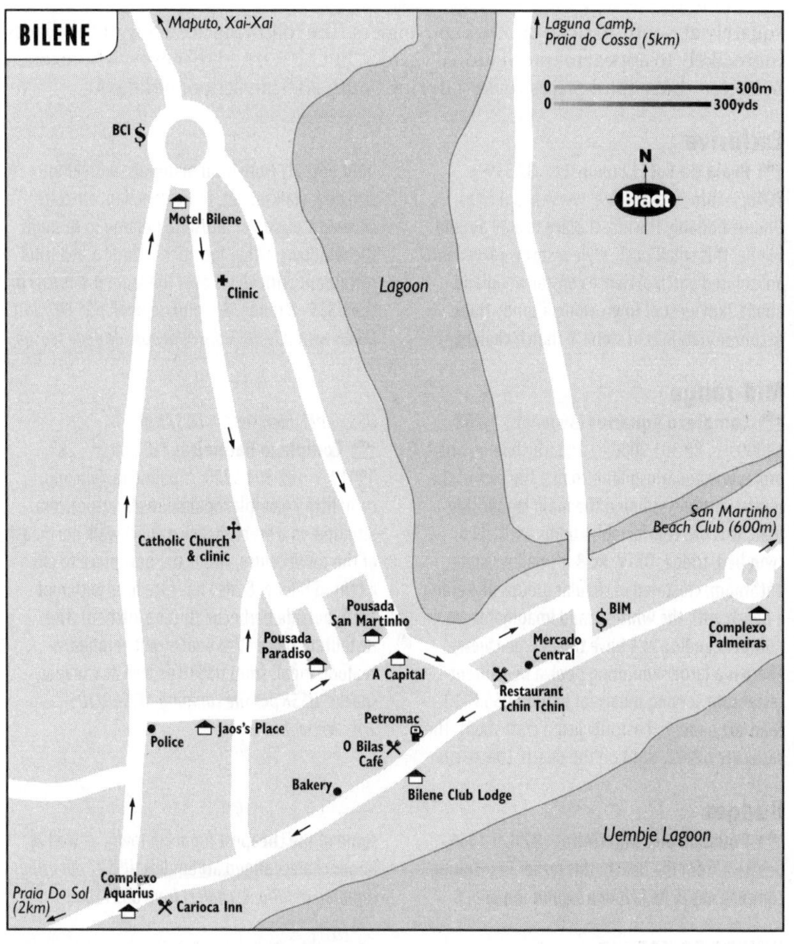

when the open sea is too rough, diving (you can see seahorses in the lagoon). Otherwise, there is 22km of reef beyond the lagoon for more serious dives. Whale watching is also possible from roughly September to the middle of November.

Bilene is the closest Mozambican resort to Johannesburg, and particularly suitable for family holidays, so it tends to be very crowded during South African school holidays, while at weekends the wealthy of Maputo descend on the resort to race their cars along the its main drag. The rest of the time it's practically deserted.

GETTING THERE AND AWAY The signposted turn-off to Bilene is at the village of Macia, about 150km from Maputo along a well-maintained surfaced stretch of the EN1. From Macia, a good 30km surfaced road leads to the main roundabout, about 1km from the beach. Using public transport, chapas between Maputo and Macia cost US$3 and take about four hours, while chapas from Macia to Bilene cost around US$0.80 and take up to 45 minutes.

WHERE TO STAY Bilene boasts one of the highest concentrations of tourist facilities in Mozambique, though the vast majority are self-catering establishments aimed squarely at South African families and anglers. The following are a few of the places more likely to appeal to international visitors, but be warned that everywhere tends to be very busy (and prices rocket) during South African school holidays.

Exclusive

Praia do Sol (12 rooms) m 82 319 3040; e info@pdsol.co.za; www.pdsol.co.za. Unquestionably the nicest place to stay around Bilene, this small bush-style resort is carved into an isolated patch of dense coastal woodland about 2km west of town along a sandy track. Accommodation is in stone & thatch chalets, built entirely from local materials, with king-size bed, walk-in net, tea/coffee, fan, en-suite shower & plenty of birdsong floating in through the windows. Other facilities include a beautiful restaurant with views over the lagoon & meals in the US$5–8 range, & a plunge pool. *US$170/250 DB&B with 20–30% discount outside peak season.*

Mid-range

Complexo Aquarius (36 rooms) 282 59000; m 82 301 9000; e aquariusbilene@mail.org; www.aquariusbilene.co.mz. The pick of the tourist complexes lining the main lagoonside road, this has comfortable rooms with dbl or twin bed, fridge, DSTV, AC & a small en-suite bathroom, clustered in circular groups of 4 along a beach with the whitest sand imaginable (room numbers ending in 4 have the best sea view). There is a large swimming pool, a beachfront restaurant serving meals for around US$8–10, & an 'art gallery' (basically just a craft shop). The casas are nice, & right on the beach. *Low season US$57 dbl, high season US$75 dbl.*

Complexo Palmeiras (10 units) 282 59019; m 82 304 3720; e palmeira@virconn.com; http://complexopalmeiras.blogspot.com. Situated on a pretty beach a short walk northeast of the town centre, this is the best place to pitch a tent in Bilene, & also has nice huts with roof fan & outside barbecue (but no kitchen). The restaurant has a TV, a beachfront veranda, & seafood meals from US$10 as well as cheaper snacks. *US$8 per site camping; US$90/105 2/4-sleeper hut.*

Budget

Pousada São Martinho 82 421 7366. Set back from the beach, this rather uninspiring complex has in its favour a swimming pool & some of the cheapest rooms in town, as well as larger chalets aimed at families. *US$27 dbl using common ablutions; chalets from US$150.*

WHERE TO EAT Of the places listed above, Praia do Sol, Complexo Aquarius and Complexo Palmeiras all have good restaurants with seafront terraces and outdoor seating. The other place that stands out is **O Bilas Café** (*285 59078; 07.00–21.00 daily except Tue*), which serves a selection of sandwiches, burgers and other snacks for US$3–4, as well as fresh coffee and bread, and a selection of imported packaged goods.

LIMPOPO NATIONAL PARK

The recently created Limpopo National Park (or more properly Parque Nacional do Limpopo) is the Mozambican counterpart to South Africa's legendary Kruger National Park, with which it shares the full length of its 200km eastern border. Something of a work in progress, it is the main Mozambican component in the proposed Greater Limpopo Transfrontier Park (GLTF), and there is every reason to hope it will emerge as one of the country's most popular tourist destinations over the next decade or so. As things stand, however, wildlife densities are very low by comparison with its western neighbour, the internal road system is negligible, and overnight facilities are limited to one luxury tented camp and a trio of more basic camps and campsites, all concentrated in the far southwest close to Massingir Dam. But while it hardly qualifies as a populist safari destination, Limpopo National Park does now offer a range of adventure activities – overnight hikes, canoeing and 4x4 trails – that make it highly alluring to active safari-goers looking for a genuinely participatory wilderness experience in Big Five terrain. A daily entrance fee equivalent to around U$S6 per person and US$6 per vehicle is levied.

HISTORY AND CONSERVATION In November 2000, the environmental ministers of Mozambique, South Africa and Zimbabwe signed a Memorandum of Understanding to initiate the creation of the Great Limpopo Transfrontier Park, the first phase of which involves linking South Africa's Kruger National Park to Gonarezhou National Park in Zimbabwe and what was then a poorly managed Mozambican hunting concession called Coutade 16, to form a contiguous unfenced 35,000km^2 cross-border conservation unit. A year later, Coutade 16 was regazetted as the 10,000km^2 Limpopo National Park, and subsequent years have seen the formal translocation there of substantial elephant and antelope herds from Kruger, along with an increased amount of natural migration between the two parks as damaged fences are left unrepaired, with a long-term view to dropping them entirely. Other developments have been the gradual resettlement of about one-third of the 20,000 people who were resident in the park at the time of its creation, and the opening of the Giriyondo Border Post, allowing tourists to travel directly between Limpopo and Kruger, in August 2006. The establishment of the GLTP is perceived as the first phase in creating a 100,000km^2 transfrontier park whose Mozambican component will stretch northwest to Banhime and Zinave national parks. Conservation considerations aside, the economic implications for Mozambique could be enormous, bearing in mind that the Kruger National Park now attracts more than one million visitors annually.

GEOGRAPHY AND VEGETATION The terrain of Limpopo National Park is mostly flat and dry, with the main relief feature being the Lebombo Mountains, which rise to about 500m above sea level along the border with South Africa. The entire park falls within the drainage basin of the Limpopo River, which runs along its northeast border for around 200km. Other important perennial waterways that flow across from South Africa include the Olifants (or Elefantes), whose confluence with the Limpopo forms the park's southeastern extremity, and the Shingwedzi, a tributary of the Olifants. The Olifants is dammed at Massinger, near the park's main entrance gate, to form a pretty dam that extends over 120km^2. The main vegetation types are mopane woodland, which dominates in the poorly drained sandy-clay soils of the north, giving way to mixed acacia–combretum woodland in the south. The rivers and waterways also support ribbons of lush riparian forest.

WILDLIFE Limpopo National Park has been poorly studied relative to the Kruger, and it probably supports a more limited habitat diversity. Furthermore, wildlife populations have been compromised by decades of hunting and encroachment, though this is improving, a trend that will most likely gather pace as fences between the two parks deteriorate further or are removed altogether. In essence, most large mammals associated with the Kruger might be seen in Limpopo, and a quick overview of this diversity makes for tantalising reading indeed. In total, 147 mammal species have been recorded in Kruger, more than any other African national park, with some of the more abundant species being African elephant (estimated 2009 population 11,600), Cape buffalo (27,000), plains zebra (18,000), giraffe (5,000), greater kudu (6,000), hippopotamus (3,000), waterbuck (5,000), blue wildebeest (10,000) and impala (90,000). The park also harbours high predator densities, including an estimated 2,000 spotted hyena, 1,500 lion, 1,000 leopard and 200 cheetah. The Kruger population of African wild dogs, estimated at 350, is probably the largest outside of the Selous-Niassa ecosystem, the black rhinoceros population of 300–400 is the second highest in the world, and the estimated 7,000–10,000 white rhinoceros represent about half the global total. In addition, around 510 bird, 115 reptile and 30 amphibian species have been recorded.

GETTING THERE AND AWAY Coming from elsewhere in Mozambique, the only entrance gate is at Massingir, about 400km from Maputo along a surfaced road that is in pretty good condition except for the last (potholed) 30km. The drive takes about five hours. As with Bilene, the junction for Massingir is about 150km northeast of Maputo, at Macia, where the park is signposted to the left. The limited unsurfaced road network within the park will require high clearance, or better still 4x4, and a speed limit of 40km/h is imposed. Estimated driving times from Massingir are 45 minutes to Campismo Aguia Pesqueira, 1½ hours to Machampane Luxury Camp and two hours to the Giriyondo border post.

Coming from South Africa, as many visitors currently do, the main point of entry is Giriyondo, which lies on the eastern border of the Kruger Park about 95km from the town of Phalaborwa (which is serviced by regular flights from Johannesburg) and 40km from Letaba Rest Camp. This road is surfaced for all but the last 25km, which are decent gravel, but allow at least three hours as game viewing can be excellent, particularly in the vicinity of Letaba. The border post at Giriyondo is open from 08.00 to 16.00 in summer and 08.00 to 15.00 in winter, and visas take a few minutes to be issued. The drive from Giriyondo border post to the Elephant Release Boma (starting point of the Palarangala Wilderness Trail, Lebombo Hiking Trail and Olifants Gorge Backpacking and Fishing Trail) or Machampane Tented Camp takes about an hour, and a high-clearance vehicle is advised. The management of Machampane can also arrange transfers from Letaba or Phalaborwa to the camp or trailheads.

It is also possible to enter Limpopo National Park at the Pafuri border post in the far north of the park, but this is only viable with a sturdy 4x4 and should ideally be done in convoy. The Shingwedzi 4x4 Eco-trail uses this route, first meeting at the Pafuri Picnic Site in the Kruger Park.

WHERE TO STAY

Exclusive

Machampane Luxury Camp (5 rooms) 21 327288; m 84 22 41 460; e mozaic.maputo@gmail.com; www.dolimpopo.com. Set on the forested banks of the Machampane River, a tributary of the Olifants, this is the only upmarket tented camp on the Mozambican side of the GLTP. It lies in the south of the national park, about halfway between Massingir Dam & the Giriyondo border post, and 2–3hrs' drive from the Kruger's Letaba Rest Camp. Accommodation is in comfortable twin tents with en-suite hot showers & private balconies facing the river. There are no roads in the area, so the main activity is guided bush walks, & the emphasis is less on the Big Five (all of which are present, but cannot be considered common) than on general ecological awareness encompassing insects, plants, birds & smaller mammals. The bush atmosphere is complemented by the cuisine, which incorporates elements of Mozambican cooking & is eaten at a communal table, whenever possible under the stars. *US$380/580 sgl/dbl including meals & activities.*

Budget and camping

Covane Community Lodge (7 units) m 82 760 7830; e helmoz@tvcabo.co.mz; www.covanelodge.com. Perched on an escarpment overlooking Massingir Dam, this rustic community-run lodge lies outside the park about 13km from Massingir township & the eponymous entrance gate. Accommodation is in twin or 5-bed chalets or 3-bed standing tents, & there is also a campsite. Simple meals are available for around US$3, & other facilities & activities include traditional Shangaan dances, guided game walks, cultural visits & boat trips on the lake. *US$25 dbl chalet; US$50 5-bed chalet; US$18 dbl tent; US$7 pp camping.*

Campismo Aguia Pesqueira +27 (0)72 447 4279 (South Africa); e limpopo@wol.co.za. One of 2 basic campsites operated by the national park authorities, this stands on a plateau about halfway between the Giriyondo & Massingir gates, & is named after the handsome fish eagles that are common along the shores of Massingir Dam, which it overlooks. Chalets are under construction. *US$3 pp camping.*

Campismo Albufeira (10 chalets) +27 (0)72 447 4279 (South Africa); e limpopo@wol.co.za. Situated immediately inside the Massingir entrance gate, this offers accommodation in well-equipped self-catering chalets, as well as space for camping. *US$50 dbl or US$5 pp camping.*

ACTIVITIES Limpopo National Park has a very limited road system and as things stand game drives are effectively limited to the main road between Massingir and Giriyondo as well as a smattering of short side roads leading out from it. For this reason, Machampane Luxury Camp concentrates mainly on game walks rather than drives, and guided walks and boat trips on Massingir Dam are also offered at Covane Community Lodge. The management of Machampane has also established a range of multi-day wilderness trails suited to reasonably fit and adventurous travellers (all described in further detail at *www.dolimpopo.com*) as follows:

Rio Elefantes Canoeing Trail This catered three-night/four-day canoe trail starts at Campismo Albufeira, from where it's a 40km drive to the trailhead at the confluence of the Shingwedzi and Olifants rivers. From there you paddle a total of 50km downstream to the Limpopo confluence, sleeping in three different rustic bush camps on the forested riverbanks. Trailists are bound to see hippos, crocs and an abundance of birds, with the chance of larger terrestrial wildlife too, and tiger fishing is possible. Group size 4–8; around US$600 per person.

Shingwedzi 4x4 Eco-Trail This is an uncatered five-night/six-day guided self-drive trail, travelling the full length of the park from Pafuri in the north to Massingir in the south. It is emphatically more about the wilderness experience and 4x4 challenge than ticking off the Big Five, but there is a fair amount of wildlife around and previous trailists have encountered species previously thought to be extinct in the park, such as wild dog, cheetah and black rhino. 3–6 vehicles; around US$850 per vehicle.

Hiking trails There are three options: the portered and catered three-night/four-day Lebombo Trail through the Lebombo Foothills, the unportered but catered three-night/four-day Palarangala Tail based out of a rustic unfenced bush-camp set in the riverine forest along the Palarangala River, and the fully self-sufficient five- day/four-night Elefantes Gorge Backpacking and Fishing Trail in the gorge of the same name. Prices start at around US$450 per person.

BANHINE AND ZINAVE NATIONAL PARKS

Remote and little visited even by the standards of Mozambique's national parks, Banhine extends over some 7,000km² of mixed woodland and open grassland to the northwest of Limpopo National Park, and is likely to be eventually co-opted into the Greater Limpopo Transfrontier Park. Gazetted as a restricted hunting area in 1969 and upgraded to national park status three years later, it was reputedly dubbed the 'Serengeti of Mozambique' in its heyday, thanks to the large herds of zebra and eland that grazed on its open plains. It is also known for the extensive seasonal pans and wetlands in the north, which are fed by the Changane and associated tributaries and host an important population of the endangered wattled crane, but cannot easily be visited in the wet season when birdlife is most prolific. Recent reports suggest that while the birdlife can be spectacular, other wildlife populations are less than impressive. Elephant, giraffe, antelope, eland and zebra are all thought to be locally extinct, though an arial survey undertaken by the African Wildlife Foundation (AWF) in 2004 reported healthy populations of ostrich, greater kudu, impala, reedbuck, duiker, oribi, steenbok, porcupine and warthog. The scenery is impressive, however, and guided walks can be undertaken with the rangers.

The only accommodation in Banhine is is the AWF Camp, which comprises six standing twin tents and a fully equipped communal self-catering kitchen, and costs US$50 per person. It is seldom full, so small parties should be safe just pitching up on the day, but bookings can be made through Mozaic Travel (see page 125). Access is by 4x4 only, and even then it is only a realistic prospect in the dry winter months, ideally travelling in expedition mode and frame of mind, with two or more vehicles in convoy. One possible approach road is from Pafuri in the northern Kruger Park, from where you can follow the southwest bank of

XAI-XAI

The capital of Gaza Province, Xai-Xai (pronounced *Shy-Shy*) is the largest town in the southern Mozambican interior, with a population of 120,000 and a convenient location along the EN1 immediately after it crosses the Limpopo 215km northeast of Maputo. Coming from the north, the South African influence here is tangible, but otherwise this is a fairly nondescript and functional town, and the majority of motorised travellers will probably take one look around before heading on to somewhere more inspiring. For backpackers, it is of interest as a potential stopover along the EN1 or to pick up public transport to the nearby beach. It is worth noting that, contrary to expectations, the local orientation of the EN1 means that people heading from Maputo and other places further south along the coast will actually enter Xai-Xai at the north end of town, and vice versa.

Should you overnight in Xai-Xai, the bustling **Limpopo Market** on the outskirts of town is definitely worth a visit, and you might also want to take a peek at the colonial **cathedral** *en route*. That the town lies on the west bank of the mighty Limpopo is not immediately obvious, but there is actually a good viewpoint over the river opposite the central Praça Municipalia, and a stroll along the lush, marshy riverbank further north might prove rewarding to birders. Of greater tourist interest than the town itself, however, are the nearby beaches of **Praia do Xai-Xai** and **Zongoene** (see page 152).

HISTORY Xai-Xai was founded on the southwest bank of the Limpopo in the early 20th century as a satellite port to Lourenço Marques (Maputo) and to the Limpopo through Limpopo National Park to Mapai. This is the best place to cross the Limpopo in the dry season, over a rickety log crossing maintained by locals, who charge around US$3 to use it. Northeast of Mapai, the well-maintained road to Machaila skirts the northern border of Banhine. Another approach is from Macia on the EN1 via Chokwe and Dindiza to Chigubo, on the southeastern boundary of the park. Either way, a usable dry-season track connects Chigubo to Domase on the road between Mapai and Machaila.

Even more remote than Banhine, but also mooted as a future element in the Greater Limpopo Transfrontier Park, the more northerly Zinave National Park protects a 4,000km^2 tract of mixed brachystegia, mopane and acacia-combretum woodland. Although not exactly prolific, the wildlife here is considerably more visible than in Banhine, with significant populations of greater kudu, sable antelope, hippo, impala, leopard and lion thought to survive. The main centre of activity here is the national park headquarters at Cavane, which has a superb location alongside a section of the Save River where hippos and crocs are resident. As things stand, self-sufficient campers can pitch a tent here, but a more upmarket concession with chalets is also under construction and should be operational by the end of 2011 (contact Mozaic Travel, page 125, for details). Coming from Banhine, it is possible to continue eastward from Machaila to Mabote, passing within about 20km of the main access road to Zinave. Mabote can also be approached from Mapinhane, on the EN1 south of Vilankulo, following an excellent unsurfaced road. Allow at least two days to drive from either Pafuri or Chigubo to Vilankulo in 'getting from A to B' mode, several days if you want to explore the region properly.

service local towns. Known as João Belo prior to independence, it was the terminus of a narrow-gauge railway that stretched 100km inland and was constructed during 1909–12. Of all the large towns in Mozambique, it was the hardest hit by the 2000 floods, thanks to its proximity to the Limpopo. Locals talk of the lower parts of town being submerged under 3m of water, and landmarks such as the BCM Building only just peeking above the rising waters. Miraculously, however, once the waters had receded and the buildings dried out, most businesses reopened and continued trading as before, and today there is no indication of the flooding.

GETTING THERE AND AWAY

By car Xai-Xai town straddles the EN1 roughly 215km north of Maputo – your arrival is heralded by the crossing of a large bridge over the impressive Limpopo River onto Avenida Samora Machel, as the EN1 is known within the town. The road between Maputo and Xai-Xai is surfaced in its entirety and there are practically no serious potholes to worry about, but traffic can be very heavy for the first 30km or so out of Maputo, so allow three hours for the drive.

By bus/chapa Regular buses and chapas do the four-hour run from Maputo to Xai-Xai, costing around US$6. Transport north to Inhambane and Maxixe runs throughout the day; the fare is US$4.50. Transport to destinations south leaves from the depot on the same block as the municipal building and to destinations north from the depot near Limpopo Market.

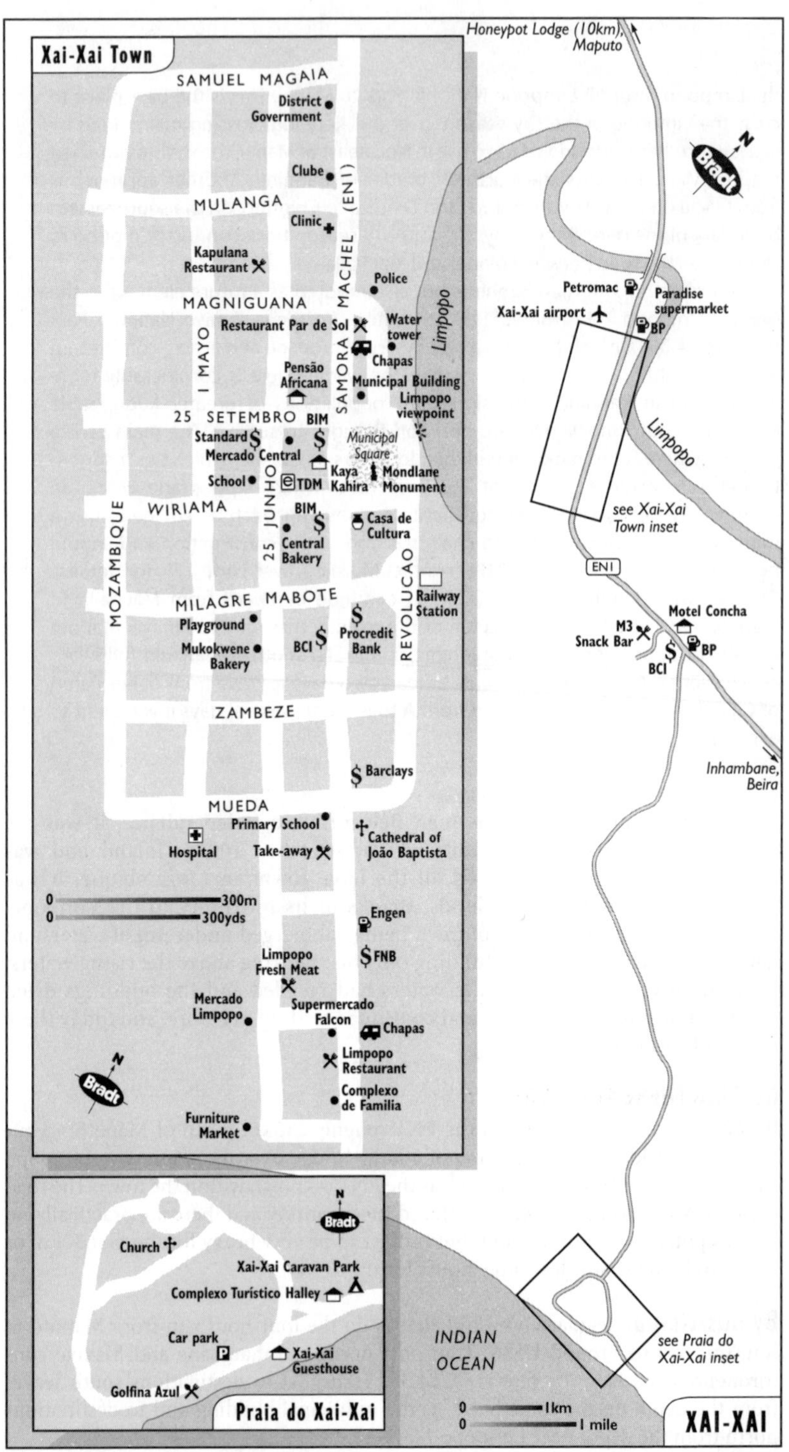
Xai-Xai Town
SAMUEL MAGAIA
District Government
Clube
MULANGA
Clinic
Kapulana Restaurant
Police
MAGNIGUANA
Restaurant Par de Sol
Water tower
Chapas
Pensão Africana
Municipal Building
Limpopo viewpoint
25 SETEMBRO
BIM
Standard
Mercado Central
Municipal Square
School
TDM
Kaya Kahira
Mondlane Monument
WIRIAMA
BIM
Casa de Cultura
Central Bakery
Railway Station
MILAGRE MABOTE
Playground
Mukokwene Bakery
BCI
Procredit Bank
ZAMBEZE
Barclays
MUEDA
Primary School
Cathedral of João Baptista
Hospital
Take-away
Engen
FNB
Limpopo Fresh Meat
Mercado Limpopo
Supermercado Falcon
Chapas
Limpopo Restaurant
Complexo de Familia
Furniture Market
MOZAMBIQUE
1 MAYO
25 JUNHO
SAMORA MACHEL (EN1)
REVOLUCAO
Limpopo
0 300m
0 300yds
Bradt
Honeypot Lodge (10km), Maputo
Petromac
Paradise supermarket
Xai-Xai airport
BP
Limpopo
see Xai-Xai Town inset
EN1
Motel Concha
M3 Snack Bar
BP
BCI
Inhambane, Beira
Church
Xai-Xai Caravan Park
Complexo Turistico Halley
Car park
Xai-Xai Guesthouse
Golfina Azul
Praia do Xai-Xai
INDIAN OCEAN
see Praia do Xai-Xai inset
0 1km
0 1 mile
XAI-XAI

WHERE TO STAY

Mid-range

Honey Pot (18 units) m 82 781 3460; e hpot@marte.co.za; www.honeypots.co.za. Situated 15km out of town alongside the EN1 towards Maputo, this friendly owner-managed complex is aimed squarely at self-drivers looking for somewhere to overnight *en route* to/from resorts further north. It is a far more attractive option than anything in Xai-Xai itself. Accommodation is in a variety of rustic wooden huts scattered in a patch of indigenous woodland, & facilities include a restaurant/bar serving meals in the US$6–8 range, a swimming pool & barbecue areas. *Small huts using common showers cost US$18 pp, while larger en-suite self-catering 3–4 sleepers cost US$70/85 per unit, & AC 8-sleeper chalets with enclosed barbecue areas cost US$180 per unit.* Camping costs US$10 pp, or US$5 for *scholars/students.*

Budget

Kaya Kahira (22 rooms) 1st Flr, 34 Av Samora Machel; 282 22391. This hotel facing the central Praça Municipalia is the smartest in town, offering a selection of reasonably priced rooms that vary in dimensions & facilities, but are uniformly clean & airy. There is also a pleasant ground-floor restaurant serving seafood & meat dishes in the US$6–10 range. *US$12/15 sgl/dbl using common ablutions; US$17 en-suite twin; US$23 large en-suite dbl with AC & TV.*

Motel Concha (25 rooms) 282 25103; m 82 560 5505. Set in large gardens on the EN1 about 3km east of the town centre (near the turn-off to Praia do Xai-Xai), this adequate but slightly run-down motel comes complete with an OK restaurant & empty swimming pool. *US$15 small twin with AC; US$21 large en-suite twin with no AC; US$27 large en-suite twin with AC.*

Pensão Africana (18 rooms) 204 R 25 Setembro; 282 59026. The most run-down option in Xai-Xai, but adequate if everywhere else is full. *US$15/18 sgl/dbl or US$21 en-suite dbl with AC.*

WHERE TO EAT

M3 Snack Bar 282 26992. Situated about 100m off the EN1 near the Motel Concha, this slick restaurant with AC, TV & terrace seating serves good pizzas for around US$5, & seafood & meat dishes. *US$4–8, with cheap daily specials.*

Limpopo Restaurant 282 22786. This unpretentious spot on Av Samora Machel, around the corner from Limpopo Market, serves everything from gullied chicken & steaks to cheese sandwiches & pizzas. *Most dishes in the US$3–7 range.*

Limpopo Fresh Meat Diagonally opposite the entrance to Limpopo Market, this serves inexpensive chicken & meat, grilled on the balcony as you wait.

OTHER PRACTICALITIES

Banks and ATMs The main banks all have branches with ATMs. Barclays, BCI, FNB and BIM Millennium are along Avenida Samora Machel. The Standard Bank is a block east on Avenida 25 de Junho. There is also a BCI with an ATM near the junction for Praia do Xai-Xai, more or less opposite the Motel Concha.

Entertainment Brightly decorated in ethnic African style, the Casa da Cultura (*Av Samora Machel*) hosts occasional live music performances and expositions.

Hospital At the south end of Avenida 1 de Maio.

Internet Phone and internet is available at the TDM behind the Hotel Kaya Kahina.

Police On Avenida Samora Machel next to the bus depot for destinations south.

Shopping Cheap meals and fruit and vegetables are available at both the **Central Market** (*Rua do 25 Setembro*) and the Limpopo Market. There are several good supermarkets along Avenida Samora Machel, the pick being the **Supermercado Falcon** (⌚ *07.00–20.00 Mon–Sat, 07.30–14.30 Sun*) and the Paradise Supermarket on the road out to the Limpopo Bridge. If you are staying at Praia do Xai-Xai and intend to self-cater then you would be advised to bring what you need from Xai-Xai itself.

BEACHES AROUND XAI-XAI

PRAIA DO XAI-XAI Situated 12km southeast of the town centre, Praia do Xai-Xai is the sort of idyllic stretch of white sand so characteristic of Mozambique, in this case with the addition of a reef about 30m out from the shore. The sea here is renowned for its excellent game fishing, and for the snorkelling and diving possibilities in the many coral reefs lying within 6km of the shore. However, it must be stressed that there are dangerous undercurrents in the area; signs on the beach indicate non-swimming places and you are highly recommended to take notice of them. There are points of interest on the shore: the ruined Motel Chonguene just next to the Golfinho Azul and the equally ruined hotel between them and the campsite. Neither motel nor hotel has been open since independence.

About 2km to the west of the main road that loops past the beach lies the Wenela tide-pool. It is linked to the sea by an underwater tunnel blow-hole, which you should not even think about trying to swim through. Lined by thick coastal scrub as opposed to the palm trees that characterise beaches further north, Praia do Xai-Xai is surprisingly rich in birdlife, with the beautiful green-and-red Livingstone's loerie being a common resident.

The range of entertainment on offer at Xai-Xai is far from vast – if you are expecting the diving schools, surfing shops and other attractions available elsewhere, you will be disappointed. Indeed, outside the South African school holidays, when it is overrun with anglers from across the border, the resort has a rather moribund boarded-up air, one that might appeal if you're after somewhere quiet to spend a few days birdwatching or fishing.

Getting there and away The turn-off to Praia do Xai-Xai is clearly signposted on the Maxixe side of town about 200m after the BP garage in front of the Motel Concha. A good surfaced 10km road leads to the main roundabout above the beach. Here, you should take the road to your left down to the beach. After a couple of hundred metres, an unsignposted dirt track to your left leads to the hotel and caravan park. Regular minibuses from Xai-Xai cost about US$0.20.

Where to stay and eat

Mid-range

Xai-Xai Guesthouse (6 rooms) m 82 682 4978. This central beachfront house has clean tiled en-suite rooms with twin beds, DSTV, fridge, AC & nets. It seems a very likeable set-up, with private gardens & self-catering facilities. *US$55–65 dbl.*

Complexo Turístico Halley (24 rooms) 282 35003; e complexohalley1@yahoo.com. This long-serving complex doesn't have much in the way of character, but the comfortable rooms seem fair value & come with AC & TV. The ground-floor restaurant serves a selection of seafood dishes for around US$8 plus cheaper sandwiches & chicken dishes. *US$43 en-suite dbl; US$50–65 suite.*

Budget

Xai-Xai Caravan Park (20 units) 282 35022; m 82 712 6520. This pleasant beachfront campismo is very spacious & surrounded by dense coastal scrub. It has adequate huts & a restaurant serving snacks for around US$2–3 & mains in the US$6–10 range (the half-chicken piri-piri is recommended), but be aware that you won't be the only diners – the mosquitoes here hunt in droves. *US$8 pp camping; US$26 dbl hut; US$80 4-bed chalet.*

Golfinho Azul This seafront eatery serves good fish dishes, as well as chicken & steaks, although the entire menu isn't always available.

ZONGOENE BEACH Beautifully located at the mouth of the Limpopo, some 20km southwest of Xai-Xai as the crow flies (but a lot further by road), Zongoene is one of the more secluded and unspoilt beaches on this part of the Mozambican coast. The most likely reason you'd be coming here is to stay at **Zongoene Lodge** (*282 42003; e zongoenelodgemoz@gmail.com; www.zongoene.com*), a highly regarded set-up that offers self-catering accommodation for US$135/225 single/double as well as camping for US$10 per person. The turn-off is signposted about 15km from Xai-Xai along the EN1 to Maputo, and it is another 35km from there to the lodge on a sandy track that may require 4x4.

NORTHEAST OF XAI-XAI

About 60km northeast of Xai-Xai, just before leaving Gaza Province, the EN1 passes within 5km of the coast at sleepy **Chidenguele**, which means 'High Place' in the local Chope language, a reference to the striking colonial church built on a hill above the town. Church aside, there is little to detain the tourist in the town itself, but the surrounding lakes are very pretty and host a varied birdlife. About 5km out of town, the **Paraiso de Chidenguele** (*m 84 390 9999; e res@thereservationsgroup.com; www.chidbeachresort.com*) is a lovely low-key resort built on a sand dune overlooking the ocean. Best known for its fishing, the resort also offers good snorkelling, walking and birding opportunities. Accommodation is in chalets sleeping two–eight people and prices vary from US$40 for a double (throughout the year) to US$230 for an eight-bed chalet in season.

Follow the EN1 northeast for another 65km and you'll arrive at the compact town of **Quissico**, set in an area notable for its deep blue freshwater lakes. One of the larger lakes lies immediately southeast of Quissico; there is a good view of it from the EN1 as you leave Quissico for Maxixe, and from the municipal building about 200m off the main road. The lake can be reached along a 10km dirt road that leaves the EN1 just outside town. You could probably get there more directly by foot – the shore can't be more than 3km from town as the crow flies, but ask for local advice regarding footpaths, as you may encounter land mines away from the established tracks. Signposted from town, the remote **Funky Coconut Backpackers** (*82 272 7530; e thefunkycoconut@gmail.com*) is a beachfront 4x4 bush camp charging around US$10 per person to pitch a tent.

Roughly 45km past Quissico, the EN1 crosses the startlingly beautiful **Lake Poelela**, reputed to be where Vasco da Gama first landed in Mozambique in January 1498. You'll get a fair view of the lake from the road, but since there are no facilities in the area and no roads leading to the rest of the lake, the risk of treading on a land mine, however slight, should be viewed as a persuasive deterrent to off-the-beaten-track exploration.

The main resort in this area, **Praia do Závora** is an outstanding spot for snorkelling and game fishing, reached along a 15km dirt road signposted a few kilometres northeast of the bridge across Lake Poelela. The wide arcing beach here is inherently very beautiful, set below tall vegetated dunes, but it suffers from a degree of unnecessary uglification in the form of the abundant concrete structures perched on the dune's rim. As compensation, a long reef 500m from the beach offers superb offshore snorkelling, and it is one of several excellent dive sites visited by the local dive company **Mozdivers** (m *82 703 0750;* e *info@mozdivers.com; www.mozdivers.com*).

The main hub of activity at Závora is **Závora Lodge** (*+27 13 750 0431 (South Africa);* m *+27 83 51 46846 (South Africa);* e *zavoralodge@mweb.co.za; www.zavoralodge.com*) an unpretentious dune-top set-up that traditionally caters to the South African fishing market, but also now doubles as a low-key backpackers, offering transfers from the nearby towns of Inhambane or Inharrime for around US$10 per person. The lodge has a varied selection of accommodation in barracas, bungalows and houses sleeping two–eight people, ranging from US$12 per person for a backpackers room throughout the year to US$250 for a four-bedroom house in high season. Camping costs US$8–16 per person, depending on season.

9

Inhambane and Surrounds

Noted for its fine beaches, seemingly endless stands of tall coconut palms and superb marine activities, the coast around Inhambane is one of the country's most important tourist hubs, studded with dozens upon dozens of homely self-catering resorts, smarter beach lodges, busy backpackers and rustic campsites, yet facilities are sufficiently spread out that it seldom feels crowded. The most popular resort in the region is Tofo, whose lovely beach is overlooked by a small village packed with lodges, restaurants, dive centres and other amenities catering to travellers. More remote and unspoilt, but difficult of access without a private 4x4, are the relatively undeveloped Barra Beach and Guinjata Bay. Whichever beach you head for, however, the diving and snorkelling around Inhambane are legendary, and there is no better place anywhere for submarine encounters manta rays and whale sharks.

The twin gateways to the region are the towns of Maxixe and Inhambane, which lie a few kilometres apart on opposite sides of Inhambane Bay, and are linked by a regular ferry service, but otherwise have little in common. Where Maxixe, straddling the EN1 some 470km north of Maputo, is large, modern, functional and unmemorable, the sleepier and smaller Inhambane is undoubtedly the most architecturally characterful town in southern Mozambique, and worth more than the fleeting visit most travellers accord it *en route* to Tofo or the other beaches.

INHAMBANE

The eponymous capital of Inhambane Province lies on the eastern shore of Inhambane Bay, an attractive natural harbour formed by a deep inlet at the mouth of the small Matumba River. It is the oldest extant settlement between Maputo and Beira, and one of the more substantial, with a population estimated at 67,000 and a distinctly Mediterranean character, thanks to its spacious layout of leafy avenues lined with eye-pleasing colonial buildings. It is also refreshingly clean and orderly, with few of the run-down buildings that exist elsewhere in Mozambique – an anomaly that may be explained by the abundance of NGOs operating out of town – and a good selection of eateries and other tourist amenities. This, in short, is an unusually pleasant town, and while most travellers treat Inhambane as nothing more than a passing stop *en route* to the nearby beaches at Tofo and Barra, it is worth an overnight stay, possibly before crossing the bay to Maxixe to catch an early morning buses north or south.

HISTORY Little is known of Inhambane's history prior to the 18th century, although it has been suggested that there was a town here by the 10th century. Vasco da Gama arrived in 1498 to resupply and liked the place so much he named it Terra de

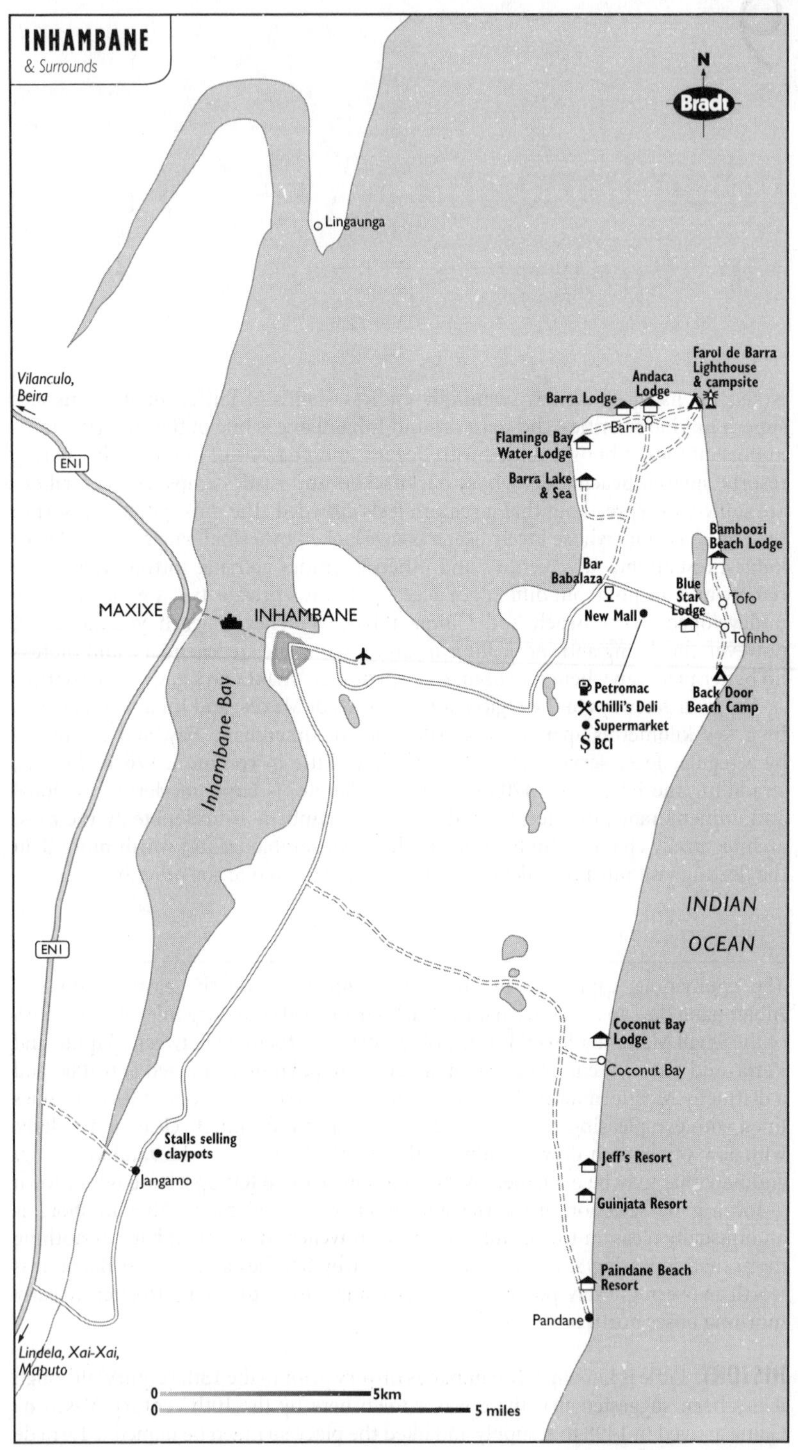
INHAMBANE
& Surrounds
N
Bradt
Lingaunga
Vilanculo,
Beira
EN1
Farol de Barra
Lighthouse
& campsite
Andaca
Lodge
Barra Lodge
Barra
Flamingo Bay
Water Lodge
Barra Lake
& Sea
Bamboozi
Beach Lodge
Bar
Babalaza
Blue
Star
Lodge
Tofo
New Mall
Tofinho
MAXIXE
INHAMBANE
Inhambane Bay
Petromac
Chilli's Deli
Supermarket
BCI
Back Door
Beach Camp
INDIAN
OCEAN
EN1
Coconut Bay
Lodge
Coconut Bay
Stalls selling
claypots
Jangamo
Jeff's Resort
Guinjata Resort
Paindane Beach
Resort
Pandane
Lindela, Xai-Xai,
Maputo
0
5km
0
5 miles

Boa Gente ('Land of the Good People'), and it was subsequently visited by several Portuguese traders in the early 16th century. In 1560, Inhambane was selected as the site of a short-lived Jesuit mission, the first in east Africa, and when the leader of the mission arrived he noted that several Portuguese traders had settled there. By the end of the 16th century it had been incorporated into the Portuguese east African monopoly and had become a regular port of call for Portuguese ivory-trading ships. During the 17th and early 18th centuries, Inhambane was, along with Delagoa Bay (Maputo), the most important trade terminus between the coast and interior of what is now southern Mozambique.

In 1727, the Portuguese commander Bernardo Soares discovered a Dutch vessel trading with the local chiefs of Inhambane. Following this, a punitive expedition led by Domingos Rebello arrived at Inhambane from Sofala, destroying several villages and killing at least two local chiefs as a punishment for trading with another European power. Commander Soares stayed on at Inhambane, where he built a fort large enough to house a garrison of 50 men. Soares's fort was hardly the most impressive defensive structure (a compatriot remarked that 'it would have been enough for [the Dutch] to have laid eyes on it to capture it'), but its presence evidently discouraged further Dutch trade, and it laid the foundation for a permanent Portuguese settlement.

Although Inhambane was officially recognised as a Portuguese town in 1763, the local ivory trade was in reality dominated by Indians rather than Portuguese. This situation dated to the early 18th century, when the port had briefly been leased to an Indian trader called Calcanagi Velabo. At the end of the 18th century, Inhambane's Christian population numbered only 200, and – remarkably – several parish priests appointed at around this time were of Indian extraction.

The town grew rapidly in prosperity during its early years (in 1770, the customs revenue raised at Inhambane was almost equal to that raised at Quelimane), not least because it was the first Mozambican port to establish a trade in slaves. Roughly 400 slaves were exported from Inhambane in 1762, a number that had quadrupled by the end of that decade while ivory export figures steadily sank. In 1834, Inhambane was practically razed by Soshangane's Gaza warriors, and most of its traders were killed, but the town soon recovered and by 1858 it had a population of roughly 4,000 (of which 75% were slaves). As recently as 1928, Inhambane was the third-largest centre of population in Mozambique, after the capital city and Beira, but today it scrapes in at the bottom of the top 20.

GETTING THERE AND AWAY Situated 470km north of Maputo and 260km past Xai-Xai, Inhambane is isolated from the rest of the Mozambican mainland by Inhambane Bay – indeed, while the town is less than 3km from Maxixe (on the opposite side of the bay) as the gull soars, the road distance between the two towns is around 60km. The only land access to Inhambane is via a well-maintained surfaced 30km feeder road that branches northeast from the EN1 at Lindela, about 30km south of Maxixe, and carries on through the town to Tofo and Barra beaches.

For this reason, public transport to/from all destinations further north leaves and arrives from Maxixe, which is connected to Inhambane by regular ferries. These run from around 05.30 to 21.00, the crossing takes an extremely pleasant 20 minutes or so, and tickets (around US$0.35 one-way) are bought on the boat itself. By contrast, direct public transport connections link Inhambane to more southerly towns such as Xai-Xai and Maputo, in the form of the plentiful minibuses that bustle around the chapa station next to the Mercado Central. There are also plenty of chapas from Inhambane to Tofo and Barra.

There are no longer rail services to Inhambane and the old station now serves as the tourism department of Eduardo Mondlane University. Inhambane Airport lies off the Tofo road about 5km east of the town centre and is serviced by one or two LAM flights from Maputo weekly.

WHERE TO STAY Inhambane is lacking in choice of accommodation in comparison with nearby Tofo, but there are a few good options:

Luxury

Hotel Casa do Capitão (25 rooms) Rua Maguiguana; t 293 21406; e info@hotelcasadocapitao.com; www.signaturehotels.co.za. Opened in June 2010, this modern hotel stands on the site of the old Captain's House on the northwest end of the town centre overlooking the bay. The architecture & decor combine clean modernistic lines with uncluttered contemporary furniture to stunning effect, while the spacious airy rooms all come with king-size bed, large flat-screen DSTV, AC, Wi-Fi, mini-bar private balcony with sea view, & en-suite bathroom with tub & shower. The stylish restaurant serves seafood & other mains in the US$15–20 range, & leads out to a large palm-lined swimming pool that juts into the harbour to dramatic effect. The existence of a hotel of this calibre & price range in sleepy Inhambane might prove a misjudgement of monumental proportions, but there is no questioning its class. *US$270/450 standard sgl/dbl DB&B, with a 20% low-season discount.*

Mid-range

Casa Jensen (2 rooms; 3 more under construction) t 293 20883; m 82 859 6150; e casajenseninhambane@gmail.com. Situated about 500m east of the town centre near Gilo Market, this small owner-managed lodge is understandably popular with businessmen. The smart tiled rooms have a king-size bed, en-suite hot shower, DSTV, tea/coffee-making, writing desk & bright ethnic decor. *Good value at US$45/60 sgl/dbl.*

Hotel Inhambane (27 rooms) Cnr Av da Vigelencia & Independência t 293 21225; m 84 389 3839; e hotelinhambane@gmail.com. Set on the first floor of a restored colonial building in the heart of town, the sparsely decorated en-suite rooms here are bright, clean & spacious, & come with writing desk, fridge, AC & DSTV. *Fair value at US$41/60/75 sgl/dbl/trpl.*

Budget

Pensão Pachiça (7 rooms) Av 3 de Fevereiro; t 293 20565; m 84 3895217; e farolturismo@teledata.mz; www.inhambane.co.za. This long-established owner-managed lodge is effectively the town's only backpackers, though it attracts a broader range of clients. Set in an old colonial house overlooking the harbour, it has a range of brightly decorated private rooms as well as dormitory accommodation, all of it clean, comfortable, with parquet floor, fan & nets (AC is coming…). The owner is a great source of local travel information; if you make advance contact, he can help with bus & other bookings from South Africa. The restaurant serves seafood, Mozambican dishes & excellent pizzas in the US$7–10 range. *US$23/40 sgl/dbl using common showers; US$45–55 en-suite dbl; US$10 pp dorm.*

Residencial Olinda (8 rooms) Av da Vigelencia; m 82 777 4781. Tucked away behind a small but brightly decorated garden bar, this central place has smart modern rooms with dbl bed, TV, AC, fridge & en-suite hot shower. It seems a good deal at the price, though best to ask for a lower-number room to create some distance between yourself and the bar. *US$33 dbl.*

Madina's Guesthouse (6 rooms) Rua Ahmed Sékou Touré; t 293 20431; m 82 489 2020. This unpretentious little guesthouse has clean en-suite dbls with TV, fridge & AC set in a small private house & the courtyard behind. *US$43 dbl.*

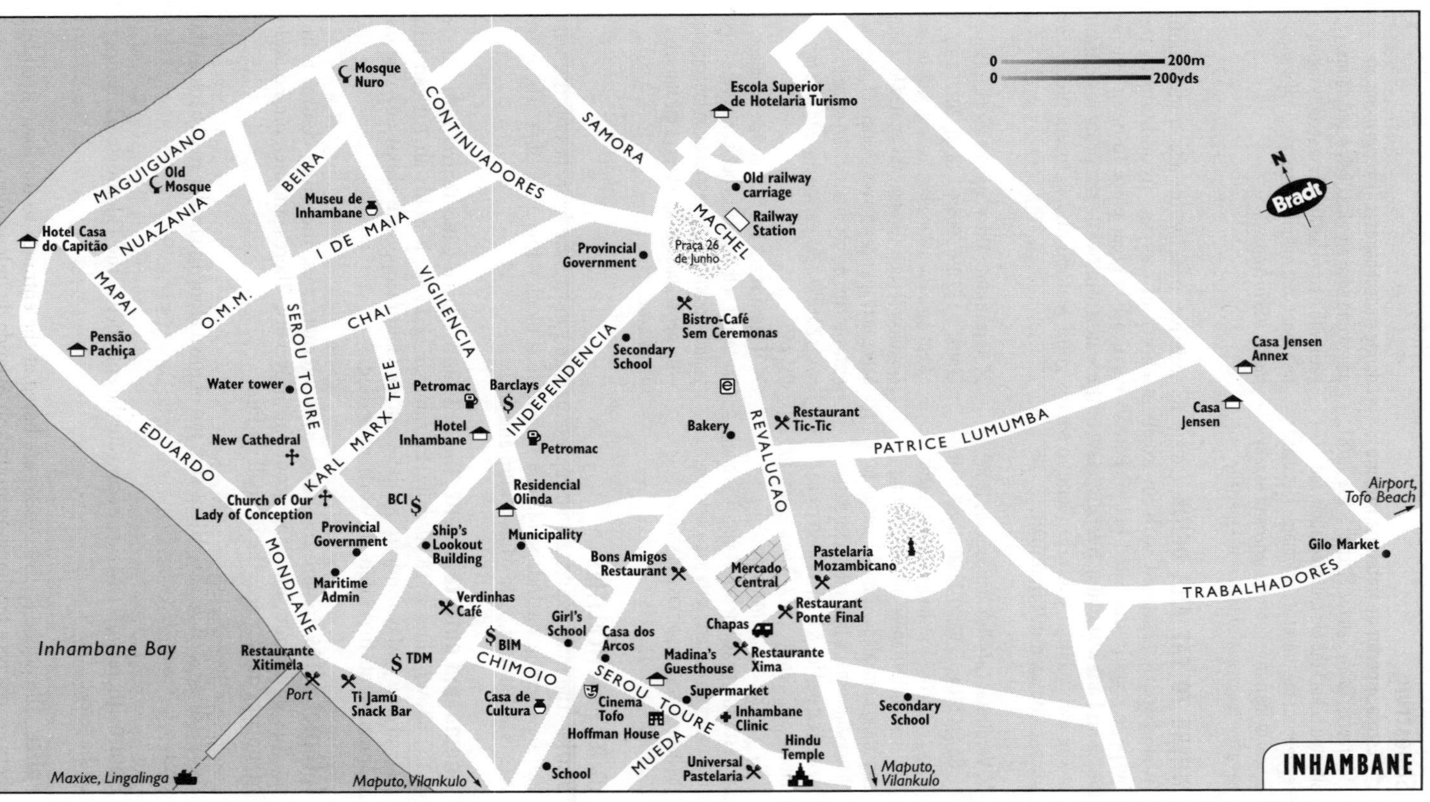
INHAMBANE
0 200m
0 200yds
Bradt
N
Mosque Nuro
Escola Superior de Hotelaria Turismo
Old Mosque
Hotel Casa do Capitão
Museu de Inhambane
Old railway carriage
Railway Station
Provincial Government
Praça 26 de Junho
Bistro-Café Sem Ceremonas
Secondary School
Pensão Pachiça
Water tower
Petromac
Barclays
Hotel Inhambane
Petromac
Bakery
Restaurant Tic-Tic
Casa Jensen Annex
Casa Jensen
New Cathedral
Church of Our Lady of Conception
BCI
Residencial Olinda
Provincial Government
Ship's Lookout Building
Municipality
Maritime Admin
Bons Amigos Restaurant
Mercado Central
Pastelaria Mozambicano
Restaurant Ponte Final
Verdinhas Café
Girl's School
Casa dos Arcos
Chapas
BIM
TDM
Madina's Guesthouse
Restaurante Xima
Restaurante Xitimela
Port
Ti Jamú Snack Bar
Casa de Cultura
Cinema Tofo
Hoffman House
Supermarket
Inhambane Clinic
Secondary School
Hindu Temple
Universal Pastelaria
School
Gilo Market
Airport, Tofo Beach
Inhambane Bay
Maxixe, Lingalinga
Maputo, Vilankulo
Maputo, Vilankulo
MAGUIGUANO
NUAZANIA
MAPAI
BEIRA
I DE MAIA
O.M.M.
CHAI
SEROU TOURE
CONTINUADORES
SAMORA
MACHEL
VIGILENCIA
INDEPENDENCIA
KARL MARX TETE
EDUARDO
MONDLANE
REVALUCAO
PATRICE LUMUMBA
TRABALHADORES
CHIMOIO
SEROU TOURE
MUEDA

Shoestring

Escola Superior de Hotelaria Turismo (100 rooms) Off Av Samora Machel; 293 20781. Situated behind the old railway station, the residence at the University of Eduardo Mondlane's School of Tourism & Hotel Management usually has a few rooms available to rent, especially during student holidays. The twin rooms are paired into what are effectively 4-bed dorms, each with its own bathroom, so security might be a slight concern unless you take 2 adjoining rooms. *US$16 twin.*

WHERE TO EAT AND DRINK Given its relative paucity of accommodation, Inhambane is scattered with an excellent choice of eateries. In addition to the bespoke restaurants listed below, Pensão Pachiça is a great place to hang out for pizza and a few sociable beers in view of the waterfront, while the pricy restaurant at the swish Hotel Casa do Capitão serves good seafood and is undoubtedly *the* place to be seen in Inhambane.

Verdinhas Café Rua Ahmed Sékou Touré; m 84 484 6104; 08.00-23.00 Mon–Sat. This funky central café has shady courtyard seating & a varied Mediterranean menu embracing everything from salads, soups & hummus to panini sandwiches & light meals. Vegetarians are well catered for, & it serves fresh coffee & most alcoholic drinks. *US$2–3 for a light snack; US$4–7 for a more substantial meal.*

Restaurante Xitimela Port Bldg. This bright little eatery on the ferry jetty has a view over the harbour & serves pizzas and seafood. *US$6–11.*

Restaurante Xima Opposite the Mercado Central; m 82 066 6006; 10.00–20.00 daily except Wed. Clean & modern looking, with indoor & outdoor seating. Conveniently located for a bite between chapa rides. Serves a variety of burgers, pizzas, b/fasts & light meals. *Mains in the US$4–8 range, & a filling plate of the day with soup for US$4.50.*

Ti Jamú Snack Bar Rua Eduardo Mondlane. The food is nothing special but it enjoys the finest seafront location of any restaurant in Inhambane – the perfect place to sip a beer as the sun sets over Maxixe.

OTHER PRACTICALITIES

Banks The main banks are all represented and most have branches on the west end of Avenida da Independência or within a block either side of it. There are ATMs at Barclays, BIM Millennium and BCI.

Cinema and entertainment The striking Art Deco **Ciné-Teatro Tofo** (*Av de OAU*) shows films at 18.00 daily. Entrance is US$1.50. It holds an African film festival every May. Enquire at the Casa de Cultura opposite about any one-off cultural events that might be worth attending.

Internet cafés Inhambane boasts two internet cafés, the more central being on Rua da Revolução, 100m from the university. There's another on Eduardo Mondlane, out towards the football stadium.

Hospital (*29 320 345*) About 1km out of town along the feeder road back to the EN1.

Phone There is a TDM office opposite the entrance to the Ti Jamú Snack Bar next to the jetty.

Police The police (*293 20830*) are based at the entrance to the town itself but there are always a few hanging around on Avenida de Independência.

Shopping The **Mercado Central** is an excellent place for craft shopping, with a good selection of basketry, woodcarvings and paintings, and tends to be cheaper than Tofo. Also on sale is an unusually varied selection of fresh and tinned produce, bootleg DVDs and music CDs, clothing and hardware. **Gilo Market** on the Tofo road is also very busy though less geared to touristic interests. There is a very good **supermarket** on Rua Ahmed Sékou Touré opposite Hoffman House. Further down the same road, the **Padaria & Pastelaria Universale** has fresh bread and pastries as well as imported confectionery on sale, while a more limited selection is available at **Pastelaria Mozambicano** opposite the Mercado Central.

Tours A company called **Terra Agua Ceu** (*293 21551; www.travel2mozambique.com*) can arrange guided historical tours of the old town, as well as providing the usual tour operator services such as transfers and hotel bookings.

WHAT TO SEE AND DO Inhambane today is anything but the bustling trade centre that it once was – it is difficult to think of a more sedate town anywhere on the east African coast – but neither has it fallen into the state of disrepair that sometimes appears to be synonymous with the term 'historical coastal town'. The seafront itself is very pretty, particularly at sunset, though swimming might not be such a great idea. Most of the older buildings are clustered around an open square at the jetty end of Avenida da Independência, and can be visited on foot within an hour or so. It's a pleasant walk just for the sake of the architecture, a peculiar mix of classic Portuguese with African and Muslim influences. The following buildings are of special note.

Church of Our Lady of Conception (*Rua Karl Marx*) Probably the most distinctive building in Inhambane, this Catholic edifice stands on the site of an earlier wooden church shown on the original 17th-century Portuguese plan of the town. The present building was constructed between 1854 and 1870, and its striking clock tower dates to the 1930s, when the clock was donated by a wealthy local family. The church fell into disuse in the late 20th century, but has recently been restored to serve as a library. It is the only building on one side of the street (which was surely named with deliberate irony), while the uglier new cathedral is the only building on the other.

Museu de Inhambane (*Cnr Av 1 de Maio & da Vigelencia; 293 20154; 09.00–17.00 Tue–Fri, 09.00–14.00 Sat & Sun; entrance free but donation expected*) Though not exactly a 'must see', this moderately diverting museum, established in 1988, probably deserves 15 minutes of your time. It houses a seemingly arbitrary selection of African musical instruments and household items, imported oddities (such as vintage radios and trunks) as well as displays relating to the history of the railway and some photographs of the town taken in the 1920s. Most explanations are in English as well as Portuguese.

Old Mosque (*Rua Maguiguana*) Situated near the corner with Rua da Mapai, this attractive small building, originally built from 1840–60 using French brick and stone quarried near Maxixe, was restored in 1928.

Ship's Lookout Building (*Av da Independência*) Situated a block up from the jetty, this was built between 1940 and 1950 in a style known as Streamline Moderne, a development from Art Deco. Its lines supposedly resemble those of a ship's prow, and it is now a supermarket. The Ciné-Teatro Tofo (see page 160) dates from the same period and is in the same style.

Hoffman House (*Rua Ahmed Sékou Touré*) With its ornate façade and railings, this two-storey building is one of the most ostentatious in Inhambane. Built in the late 19th century using stones quarried near Ilha de Moçambique, it was originally the home and shop of the merchant Oswald Hoffman, and later served as a hotel, but now stands unused.

Escola 7 de Abril (*Av da Vigelencia*) Built as a school in the late 19th century (a function is still serves today), this building is notable for its classical lines and extended front archway. The municipal office on Avenida da Independência is similar in style and vintage, as is the waterfront TDM office diagonally opposite the port.

Casa dos Arcos (*Av Acordos de Lusaka*) Built in the late 19th century, possibly as a church or hotel, the enigmatic 'House of Arches' was extended to a second floor, reached via an internal spiral staircase, in the early 20th century and boasts several interesting classical features, including arched doors and windows, crescent-shaped nooks and stone columns.

Mercado Central (*Av da Revolução*) Not as touristy as you might expect, the bustling central market sprawls around a handsome building that dates to the late 1950s when the market relocated here from the park in front of the municipal office.

MAXIXE

Situated on the western shore of Inhambane Bay, Maxixe (pronounced '*Masheesh*') represents the only point where the EN1 between Maputo and Beria actually skims the coast. It is also the largest town in Inhambane Province, with a population estimated at 110,000, but remains politically subservient to the eponymous provincial capital, a mere 3km across the bay. People driving from Maputo to places further north might want to break the journey here, while for southbound travellers using public transport, Maxixe is the gateway to Inhambane – a 20-minute ferry trip across Inhambane Bay as opposed to a circuitous 60km by road – and thus to nearby Tofo and Barra Beach.

For all its logistical significance, Maxixe is not the most inherently interesting of places. Indeed, the stark grid layout and bustling African market-town atmosphere couldn't offer a greater contrast to the seductive old-world sleepiness that envelops Inhambane. In its favour, Maxixe lies on a pretty palm-lined stretch of coast that offers a lovely view across the water to Inhambane at dusk, and it has a fair selection of lodges and eateries, along with other urban amenities such as filling stations and ATMs. Be warned, however, that the town centre has a somewhat seedy reputation at night – best to be off the streets or to walk in groups after dark, and for single women the streets are a definite no-no. It also has a reputation for car crime, so off-street parking should be considered: even if you aren't staying there, you can usually park in Campismo Maxixe for a fee, space permitting.

GETTING THERE AND AWAY Maxixe straddles the surfaced EN1 about 470km north of Maputo, 260km from Xai-Xai and 600km south of the Inchope junction

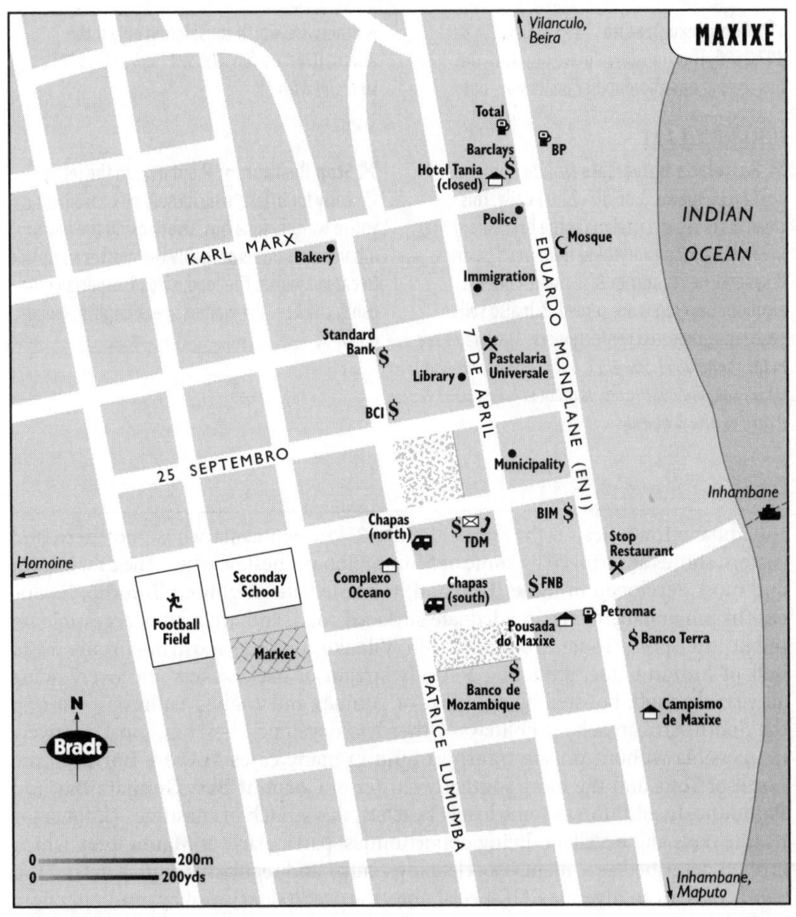

with the EN6 connecting Beira to Chimoio. It is an easy drive in all directions. Chapas to most destinations between Maputo and Beira leave the same praça as the post office and TDM, two blocks west of the ferry jetty. Chapas to Maputo cost US$12 and to Vilankulo US$9. Coming from further afield – Maputo, Beira or Chimoio – it is worth paying extra to catch the TCO bus, which is far more comfortable than a chapa. Boats between Inhambane and Maxixe run regularly from 05.30 to 21.00, a 20-minute crossing that costs US$0.35.

WHERE TO STAY

Campismo de Maxixe (7 rooms) 293 30351. This is probably the best place to stay in Maxixe, set in large leafy grounds that occupy an attractive spot on the bay, though the proximity to the EN1 might make the evenings noisy. In addition to camping, wooden huts are available & there are also a couple of caravans for hire. *US$16 en-suite dbl; US$13 twin using shared showers; US$11 twin caravan; US$3 pp camping.*

Pousada do Maxixe (15 rooms) 293 30199; m 82 780 3142. Situated right opposite the jetty, this is the pick of the town's limited guesthouse-style accommodation. The clean & pleasant en-suite dbls have hot water, AC & TV, & there are also more basic rooms using shared showers. The ground-floor restaurant serves the usual Mozambican staples. *US$30 en-suite dbl; US$17/24 sgl/dbl with common showers.*

Complexo Oceano 293 30096; m 82 307 2600. This run-down place opposite the bus station has affordability on its side, but is otherwise worth considering only if the alternatives are full. *US$9/11 sgl/dbl; US$15 en-suite dbl with TV.*

WHERE TO EAT

Pastelaria Universale Av 7 de Abril; m 82 536 1058; 06.30–22.00 daily. This clean & versatile pastelaria is the best eatery in town, serving everything from fresh pastries & sandwiches to curries & seafood. Coffee & alcoholic beverages are served, & it also sells pastries & imported confectionery. *Most items are in the range US$1.50–4.50, but pizzas are around US$7. The plate of the day is great value at US$3 & it arrives nice & quickly.*

Stop Restaurant Right next to the jetty; early for b/fast, which could be convenient if you're waiting for a bus. Overlooking the bay to Inhambane, this is probably the most scenic place to eat in Maxixe. The food is good, especially the fish & chicken, the waiters speak English. *Mains US$4–7.*

BEACHES AROUND INHAMBANE

Inhambane town lies on the west side of a 25km peninsula whose northern and eastern shores are fringed by some of Mozambique's finest beaches. The best known and most developed of these, **Tofo** and its immediate neighbour **Tofinho**, lie due east of Inhambane along an adequate surfaced road, and are readily accessible on public transport. Today, Tofo vies with Vilankulo as the most important travel hub in Mozambique, attracting a steady stream of backpackers and overlanders all year through, boosted by an influx of families and angling enthusiasts during the South African school holidays. Other less developed beaches, most relatively inaccessible without private transport (and in many cases 4x4) are **Barra**, to the north of Tofo, and the more southerly cluster of **Coconut Bay**, **Guinjata Bay** and **Paindane**. In addition to some lovely beaches, this stretch of coastline is known for its fine reefs and excellent diving opportunities, particularly at **Manta Reef**, which is often described as a 'manta ray cleaning centre' and regularly features in the 'Top 5' lists of African dive sites. Of special note, the ocean safaris run by most operators in Tofo offer a rare opportunity for non-divers to encounter and snorkel with such outsized marine creatures as manta rays, whale sharks, turtles and dolphins. Between July and the middle of November, divers and snorkelers might also see humpback whales, or hear their plaintive moans.

TOFO AND TOFINHO Probably the most developed resort in Mozambique, Tofo (often pronounced more like 'Tofu') Beach sprawls for several kilometres along the sliver of land that separates the Indian Ocean and the freshwater Lake Pembane. The hub of activity here is the small village of Tofo, a 500m triangle of sandy roads lined with an assortment of shops, lodges and eateries, leading down to a central market that overlooks the tantalising wide sandy beach known as Praia do Tofo. This south side of this beach is hemmed in by the elevated black coral rock peninsula on which lies Tofinho, a suburb of holiday homes and self-catering resorts that lies 20 minutes' walk from central Tofo by road but can be reached in a couple of minutes along the beach. By contrast, the sandy road that heads northward from the village towards Bamboozi Beach Lodge (see page 168) is flanked by the lake to the west and by tall vegetated dunes to the east, the latter forming an elongated crest above a fine white beach that is effectively an extension of Praia do Tofo.

The main attraction of Tofo is its beach, which is the sort of place people dream about, and the fishing, diving and surfing are as good as they get in the area. The small town centre boasts arguably the densest concentration of tourist facilities in Mozambique, ranging from dive and surf shops to budget lodges and seafood eateries, and the lively easy-going mood recalls such backpacker-friendly haunts

GIANTS OF TOFO

The whale shark *Rhincodon typus* is the largest living species of fish, measuring up to 12m long, weighing up to 35 tonnes, with a lifespan comparable to a human or elephant. As one of only three filter-feeding shark species, this passive, slow-swimming giant is essentially harmless to humans (or anything else much larger than a goldfish), though there is a slight danger of snorkelers or divers being swiped by its powerful tail fins. In common with whales, this gigantic shark feeds mainly on plankton and other microscopic organisms, which are imbibed together with water through its wide mouth and trapped in a specially adapted gill apparatus when the water is expelled, though it will also occasionally eat small fish. Found throughout the tropics, it is listed as Vulnerable by the IUCN, with the main threat to its survival being commercial fishing. Easily distinguished by the combination of immense bulk, wide mouth and yellow striped and spotted skin pattern, it is especially common in the waters around Tofo and Inhambane, with numbers peaking during the southern summer.

Commoner still, and present in large numbers all year through, is the manta ray. *Manta birostris* is the world's largest ray, with some specimens weighing more than two tonnes and boasting a wingspan of 7.5m. The manta is the subject of some taxonomic controversy: at one time several species were recognised, while more recent studies indicated that all mantas belong to a single species, but the latest findings (based on research undertaken at Tofo by Dr Andrea Marshall of the Manta Ray and Whale Shark Research Centre) indicate that at least two valid species exist, one being larger and migratory, the other(s) slightly smaller and non-migratory. Although mantas have a flattened shape and long tails similar to stingrays, they cannot sting and are totally harmless to divers. Indeed, like so many other marine giants, they are filter feeders whose main diet is plankton and other tiny suspended organisms. An intriguing aspect of manta behaviour is the regular gathering of several individuals at cleaning stations (such as the one at Manta Reef), where wrasse and other reef fish feed on the parasites and dead tissue accumulated in their gills. They are also capable of breaching the surface and launching into the air, a rare but spectacular sight.

The Manta Ray and Whale Shark Research Centre, which works with marine biologists, the marine tourism industry, conservation organisations and the Mozambican government to identify and solve problems faced by manta rays and whale shark, is based at Casa Barry and gives talks there at 18.00 every Monday, Wednesday and Friday. The Research Centre is affiliated to the Foundation for the Protection of Marine Megafauna (FPMM), which was created in 2009 to research and conserve Mozambique's sharks, rays, turtles, whales and dolphins. Visit their website (*www.marinemegafauna.org*) for further details.

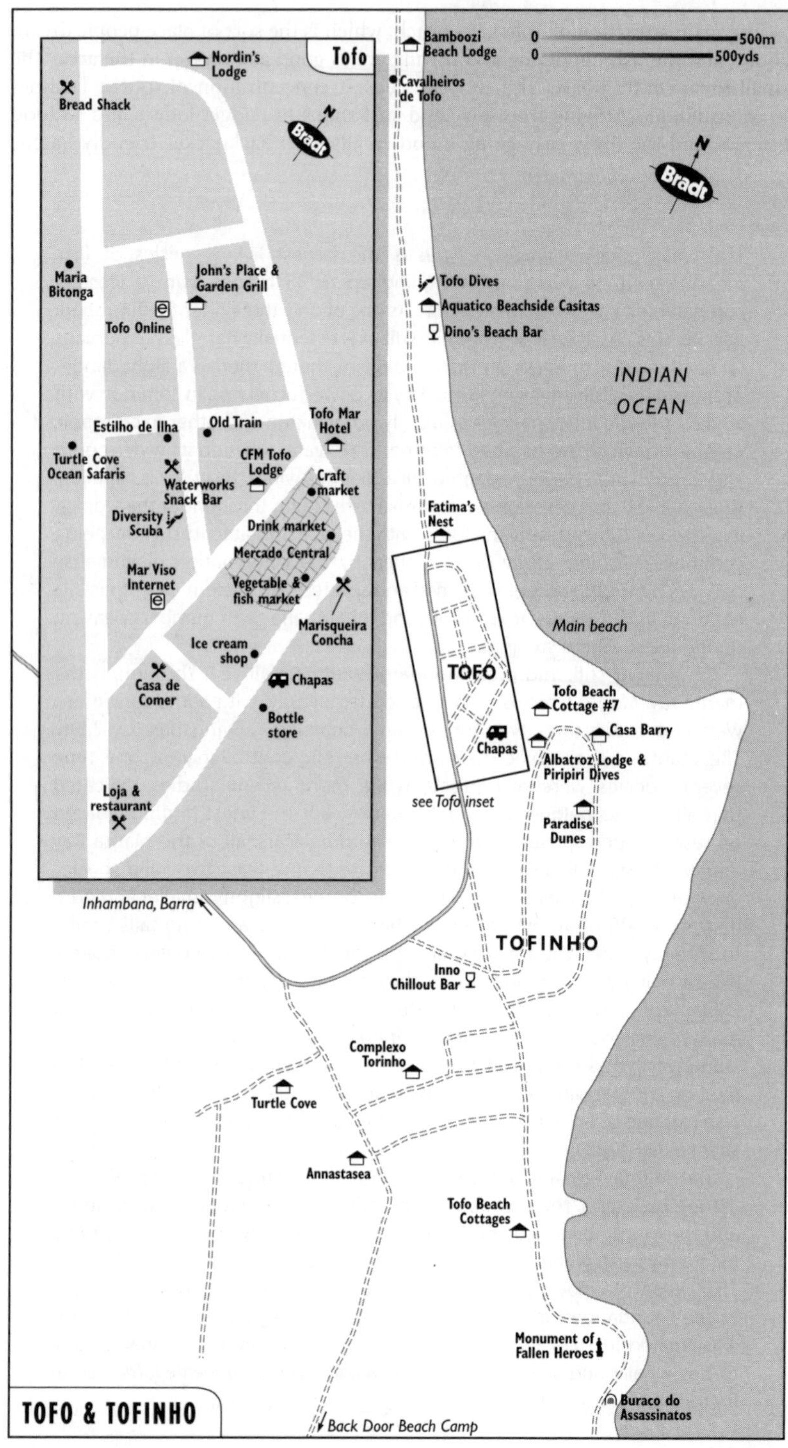

TOFO & TOFINHO
Tofo
Nordin's Lodge
Bread Shack
Maria Bitonga
John's Place & Garden Grill
Tofo Online
Estilho de Ilha
Old Train
Tofo Mar Hotel
Turtle Cove Ocean Safaris
CFM Tofo Lodge
Craft market
Waterworks Snack Bar
Diversity Scuba
Drink market
Mercado Central
Mar Viso Internet
Vegetable & fish market
Marisqueira Concha
Ice cream shop
Casa de Comer
Chapas
Bottle store
Loja & restaurant
Bamboozi Beach Lodge
Cavalheiros de Tofo
0 500m
0 500yds
Tofo Dives
Aquatico Beachside Casitas
Dino's Beach Bar
INDIAN OCEAN
Fatima's Nest
Main beach
TOFO
Tofo Beach Cottage #7
Casa Barry
Chapas
Albatroz Lodge & Piripiri Dives
see Tofo inset
Paradise Dunes
Inhambana, Barra
TOFINHO
Inno Chillout Bar
Complexo Torinho
Turtle Cove
Annastasea
Tofo Beach Cottages
Monument of Fallen Heroes
Buraco do Assassinatos
Back Door Beach Camp

as Nkhata Bay and Cape Maclear in neighbouring Malawi, frequently tantalising travellers into staying for far longer than they had planned. There is plenty of nightlife, too, and this can be as raucous or as sedate as you wish – it's all a matter of picking the right place to hang out. Note, however, that Tofo can become uncomfortably busy, and undergoes a distinct change in atmosphere, during South African school holidays.

Getting there and away Tofo lies 22km east of Inhambane along a surfaced road that can be traversed in any vehicle, though some caution is advised with low clearance, and a couple of the roads within Tofinho might be tricky without 4x4. Turn right when you reach the traffic circle about 17km out of Inhambane.

As far as public transport is concerned, there are regular chapas to Tofo from Inhambane, leaving from the station in front of the Mercado Central. Coming from Maputo, it is also possible to get a direct chapa to Tofo, but these leave less frequently and since they have to pass through Inhambane anyway, there is no real point in waiting around for one. Coming from the north, you'll need to get a chapa or bus to Maxixe, cross to Inhambane by ferry, and then pick up a chapa to Tofo. Some travellers coming from Maputo may also prefer to bus to Maxixe with TCO, which is more comfortable and faster than a chapa, and then cross to Inhambane by ferry.

Where to stay

Upmarket

Casa Barry (25 units) +27 31 767 0111 (South Africa); e peggy@dbnmail.co.za; www.casabarry.com. Situated in Tofinho right above Praia do Tofo, & only 2mins' walk from the village centre, Casa Barry has maintained an excellent reputation for several years now, and it is also the base for the Manta Ray & Whale Shark Research Centre, which gives 3 weekly talks here. Accommodation is in rustically attractive chalets with various sleeping capacities, but all have fan, nets & tiled en-suite hot shower. An excellent beachfront restaurant is attached. *US$75 reed & thatch dbl; US$92 brick dbl; US$220 4-bed chalet; US$230 6-bed chalet; US$300 12-bed chalet. Slight low-season discounts are offered.*

Hotel Tofo Mar (13 rooms) 293 562012; m 82 303 5063; e htofomar@gmail.com; www.hotel-tofomar.com. Closed for extensive renovations in 2010, this is the only central beachfront hotel in Tofo. It was looking a little moribund prior to closing, as though it had experienced one too many cyclones, but should be vastly improved when it reopens in 2011. Most rooms will have AC & a sea view. *Expect rates in the US$80–120 range.*

Mid-range

Tofo Beach Cottages (7 units) +27 72 129 4278 (South Africa); e bookings@tofo.co.za; www.tofo.co.za. This collection of 7 individualised cottages, sleeping up to 5–8 people each, is scattered all around Tofo & Tofinho. The cottages are very well equipped & cover some prime spots: Casa #7, for instance, enjoys a superb location right on Praia do Tofo, while several other units stand on the slopes leading down to sleepy Tofinho Beach (for photos & details of individual cottages, check their website). *Different cottages are rented out at US$60–100 per unit in low season, & up to US$170 in peak season, which makes them very attractive to small groups.*

Turtle Cove (20 units) m 82 719 4848 or 84 731 2027; e info@turtlecovetofo.com; www.turtlecovetofo.com. This pleasant, reasonably priced, owner-managed lodge in Tofinho offers comfortable bungalow accommodation in leafy gardens about 15mins' walk from the beach. Combining west African architectural influences with earthy decor, it is one of the few lodges in the area with any discernible character, & facilities include a swimming pool, a good restaurant & daily yoga classes in a special yoga room. All rooms are en-suite with dbl or twin beds, net & fan, & family units are available. *US$55/70 sgl/dbl with a low-season discount of around 30%. Family rooms start at US$20 pp. Camping US$8 pp.*

Annastasea (4 units) m 82 719 4848; www.annastasea.com. This attractive property in Tofinho, about 10mins' walk from the beach, consists of 4 thatched dbl chalets & a common self-catering *lapa* offering a view to a nearby dune. *Aimed mainly at groups, it is rented out in its entirety for around US$280 pn in high season, but the chalets may be rented out individually for around US$28 pp at other times of year.*

Bamboozi Beach Lodge (20 rooms) 293 29040; m 82 803 0413; e reservations@bamboozibeachlodge.com; www.bamboozibeachlodge.com. Set on a magnificent vegetated dune about 1.5km north of the village centre, this beachfront lodge is currently in something of a transitional state under new ownership, as signified by a recent name change from Bamboozi Backpackers. Formerly, it had the reputation as a more chilled & less central counterpart to Fatima's Nest (see below), but it now seems to be aiming at a higher-paying market, though camping & dormitory facilities still exist to attract backpackers. Facilities include a small swimming pool, an excellent on-site dive centre called Liquid Adventures, a great restaurant/bar perched high on the dunes, bicycle rental & free pick-ups from Tofo chapa station or Fatima's Nest. All rooms are en-suite with nets & hot water. *US$150 twin beachfront chalet; US$100 dbl sea-view chalet or A-frame; US$18 pp in 14-bed dorm; US$16 pp camping; all rates 20% lower out of season.*

Aquatico Beachside Casitas (5 rooms) m 82 857 2850 or 82 30 01 057; e aquatico.lodge@teledata.mz; www.aquaticolodge.com. Sandwiched between Tofu Diving and Dino's Bar (see opposite) about 1km north of Tofo village, these beachfront rooms each sleep3 & have a kitchenette at the rear & a bathroom at the side. The location is superb & the accommodation very comfortable. *US$75 per unit.*

CFM Tofo Lodge (11 rooms) m 82 807 8033. Situated opposite Hotel Tofo Mar just 50m from the beach, this central lodge has pleasant tiled rooms with AC, nets & en-suite hot shower. *US$50 dbl, rising by 50% in peak seasons.*

Budget

Albatroz Lodge 293 29005; m 82 255 8450; e enquiries@albatrozlodge.com; www.albatrozlodge.com. Situated in Tofinho near Casa Barry, this clifftop lodge overlooking Tofo Beach is one of the best value set-ups in the area, offering accommodation in comfortable thatched & whitewashed chalets with fan, nets & private balconies. *US$33 dbl with significant high-season hikes; US$80–210 for a 4–8 sleeper, depending on number of people & season.*

Fatima's Nest m 82 307 0870; e fatimas@tvcabo.co.mz; www.mozambiquebackpackers.com. The busiest & most central backpacker hub in Tofo, this younger sister of Fatima's in Maputo (see page 109) has an all-day party atmosphere, with music playing from early morning through to late evening. It also has an attractive beachfront setting on the edge of the village centre, just 500m from the chapa station. It offers a range of accommodation from camping to en-suite chalets, the latter often fully booked, & a lively restaurant serves decent meals, including a daily special at around US$3 & good vegetarian fare. *US$29/53 en-suite sgl/dbl; US$23/29 sgl/dbl using shared bathroom; US$23 dbl standing tent; US$12 pp dorm; US$9 pp camping. Prices rise up to 50% over Easter & Christmas school holidays.*

Nordin's Lodge (6 rooms) 293 29009/28. This has a perfect location in a beachfront casuarina grove around the corner from Fatima's, but the accommodation – a row of rather gloomy chalets with fan, fridge, en-suite shower & balcony – doesn't quite match up. Still, decent value at *US$43 twin*.

Shoestring

John's Place (4 rooms) m 84 773 3640; e johnintofo@gmail.com. The simple but clean rooms with fan, on the same central property as Garden Grill, are as good value as you'll get in Tofo, & there is also a 4-bed dorm. *US$20 twin; US$25 dbl with AC; US$9 per dorm bed.*

Back Door Beach Camp 293 20565; m 84 3895217; e farolturismo@teledata.mz; www.inhambane.co.za. Under the same management as Inhambane's Pensão Pachiça, this rustic camp lies 250m from the beach outside Tofinho, about 2km past Annastasea. Aimed mainly at campers, it also has tents for hire, 24hr electricity, self-catering facilities & a restaurant & bar. *US$3 pp camping.*

Where to eat

In addition to the places listed below, the restaurants at Fatima's Nest and Bamboozi Beach Lodge (see opposite) are both worth a try – the former for its affordable plate of the day, and the latter for its dune-top location and beach view.

Casa de Comer 09.00–22.00 daily except Tue. Probably the most stylish restaurant in Tofo, this has a contemporary feel, outdoor seating under a thatched roof, & an imaginative seafood-dominated menu that fuses French & Mozambican influences. *Most mains are in the US$6–10 range.*

Dino's Beach Bar 10.00–late daily except Wed out of season. Situated halfway between Fatima's & Bamboozi, Dino's is a long-standing favourite for sundowners, not least for its superb beachfront location. It's a reliable party spot too. *Seafood, meat dishes & pizzas are in the US$6–9 range.*

Casa Barry (see page 167) b/fast, lunch & dinner daily. The restaurant at this lodge overlooking Praia do Tofo certainly has a great location, especially for catching sunsets, & many residents rate it the best in town. *The seafood & meat dishes are relatively pricey at around US$10–20 for main course.*

Turtle Cove (see page 167) b/fast, lunch & dinner daily. Owned by a qualified chef, this lodge offers the usual Mozambican seafood dishes, along with a more innovative menu of daily specials, often with Thai or other Asian influences. Vegetarians are catered for, & it hosts regular sushi evenings. *US$5–9.*

Marisqueira Concha 10.00–22.00 daily. Directly opposite the market and main praia, this is a popular spot for sundowners, with outdoor seating positioned to catch the sea breeze, & it serves a varied selection of seafood & meat as well as cheaper snacks. *US$5–12 range.*

Waterworks Snack Bar m 84 643 6850; 08.00–17.00 Tue–Sun (from 07.00 in season). Under the same management as Estilo da Ilha surf shop, this relaxed outdoor café serves good coffee as well as all-day b/fasts, sandwiches, salads & light meals. There's a large-screen TV for crunch rugby matches & other sports fixtures. *US$3–6.*

Garden Grill 84 773 3640; 11.00–23.00 daily. The option of sitting outdoors or in the cosy bar, the best steaks in town, a good vegetarian selection, tasty curries & reasonable prices make this place well worth a visit. *US$5–8 for meat dishes; US$3 for curries.*

Chilli's Deli m 82 393 8310; e chillsdeli@gmail.com; 11.30–18.00 Mon, 09.00–17.00 Tue-Fri, 09.00–13.00 Sat & Sun. Situated in the new mall about 4km back along the road to Inhambane, this deli serves delicious sandwiches & cakes, & the best filter coffee in this part of Mozambique.

Tofo Online 09.00–18.00 daily except Sun (closes at 13.00) & Wed (closed). This internet café offers a range of snacks, smoothies & milkshakes.

Bread Shack Diagonally opposite Fatima's Nest, this is the bakery in town, & it can also rustle up sandwiches, pizzas & doughnuts, though based on our experience the advertised claim to open at 05.00 is fanciful by the order of several hours!

Shopping

Estilo do Ilha m 84 643 6850; 08.00–17.00 Tue–Sun. In the same compound as the co-managed Waterworks (see above), this sells various surfing accessories & can also rent out snorkel and fins, surfboards & body boards for US$4–5 per item per half day.

Maria Bitonga 82 780 7025; 10.00–17.00 Tue–Sun. A must for craft shoppers, this unexpectedly trendy shop stocks an interesting selection of local fabrics, jewellery & other artefacts, many made with recycled materials.

Mercado Central Opposite Praia do Tofo, this is one of the best places for craft shopping in the country, with numerous stalls selling all manner of paintings, wood & stone carvings, batiks & other handicrafts. There is also a good booze section (huge choice of wine & spirits) & plenty of fresh produce in the market right next door, where local fishermen gather to sell fresh fish, calamari, prawns & other seafood to self-caterers.

Shopping mall The mall on the south side of the Inhambane road 4km out of Tofo has several shops of interest. The anonymous supermarket here stocks a more varied selection of goods, many imported from South Africa, than anywhere else in town. Better still is Chilli's Deli (see page 169) with its tantalising selection of cheeses, cold meats, fresh bread & luxury tinned & bottled goods. There is also a boutique here called Mozkito, specialising in ethnic style clothes.

Other practicalities

Banks There is no bank in Tofo itself, but there is a BCI ATM at the same mall as Chilli's Deli, and of course plenty of banks and ATMs in Inhambane itself.

Fuel The only filling station this side of Inhambane is the Petromac in the same mall as Chilli's Deli.

Internet cafés There are two in the village. **Mar Viso Internet** (*opposite Casa de Comer; ☎ 82 711 7555; e marviso@email.de; ⏲ 10.00–13.00 & 16.00–19.30 daily*), and **Tofo Online** (*opposite John's Place; ⏲ 09.00–18.00 daily except Sun (closes 13.00) & Wed not open*).

Marine talks The researchers based at Casa Barry hold talks in the Big Screen Room there three times a week, starting at 18.00, with a cover charge of US$3. The talks cover manta rays (Monday), whale sharks (Wednesday) and general marine life (Friday).

What to see and do It wouldn't be difficult to spend a few days at Tofo and do very little that qualified as an organised activity. The beaches that run north and south from Praia do Tofo are little short of idyllic, whether you fancy swimming, sunbathing, surfing or a long seaside walk, and the village itself is a very relaxed place to hang out. For more active travellers with a bit of spare cash, however, Tofo is renowned for its diving opportunities and 'ocean safaris', while other activities include horseback trips along the beach, kayak safaris and big-game fishing.

Marine activities Compared with most other diving and snorkelling sites in Mozambique, Tofo isn't so much about masses of colourful reef-dwellers as a pair of gargantuan plankton-eaters, namely the manta ray and whale-shark (see box, *Giants of Tofo*, on page 165). These two immense but harmless fish are especially common in the waters off Tofo, and are likely to be seen on most dives, though whale-sharks are mostly summer visitors and commonest from November to April. The top diving site in the vicinity, Manta Reef (24–28m) lies a short distance offshore some 15km south of Tofo, and though reliably good for mantas, it also usually yields sightings of smaller rays and sharks, moray eels and barracudas, along with myriad smaller reef fish. Other excellent diving sites include Oasis Reef, which lies to the north of Tofo about 10km out at sea, and the relatively shallow Crocodile Rock (named for the crocodile fish, not the reptile) and Praia do Rocha (seasonally very good for whale sharks). Single dives start at around US$50 per person, with each one getting progressively cheaper, and courses are also offered by most operators.

For non-divers, the most alluring activity at Tofo, offered by at least three operators, is one of the ocean safaris that leave daily at around 10.30. These safaris run on semi-inflatable boats that launch from Praia do Tofo and scour the surrounding waters for about two hours in search of large marine creatures such as manta rays, whale sharks, dolphins and turtles. The odds of seeing at least one or two of these marine giants is excellent, and all participants are issued with snorkelling masks and fins so they can jump in alongside them – an utterly thrilling experience. From June until late October, humpback whales visit the area in large numbers, and they are frequently seen on ocean safaris, though it isn't permitted to snorkel alongside them. Most companies charge around US$40 per person for ocean safaris.

The following operators all offer ocean safaris, and most can also offer dives, game-fishing excursions and other activities:

Diversity Scuba 293 29002; m 82 468 5310; e info@diversityscuba.com; www.diversityscuba.com. Based right in the heart of Tofo, next to Waterworks.

Liquid Adventures 293 29046; m 84 545 3094; e liquidadventures@gmail.com; www.liquidadventures.co.za. Based in Bamboozi Beach Lodge, this offers the usual range of diving courses, as well as sea-kayaking trips to a nearby island, 4x4 trips in the surrounding countryside & whale watching (in season). They have surf & body boards for hire.

Peri-Peri Divers 293 56038; m 82 594 4717 or 82 550 5661; e nick@peri-peridivers.com or steve@peri-peridivers.com; www.peri-peridivers.com. Situated in Tofinho next to Albatroz Lodge.

Tofo Scuba 293 2 030; m 82 826 0140; e tofoscuba@tdm.co.mz; www.tofoscuba.co.za. Based at Casa Barry at the south end of the beach, but also have a shack next to Dino's Bar.

Horseriding Ninety-minute horseback safaris through the coconut groves and beaches are offered by **Cavalheiros do Tofo** (m *82 308 0300 or 82 391 5680*; e *gvhorst@gmx.net*) for around US$20 per person. The stables are about 1.5km from central Tofo opposite Bamboozi Beach Lodge, but they will pick up clients in the village by arrangement.

BARRA BEACH To the north of Tofo, Barra lies at the northern tip of the peninsula, where it is guarded by the prominent Farol de Barra (Barra Lighthouse). Though rather remote, the site is flanked by attractive beaches in both directions, and the

BARRACO DOS ASSASSINATOS

Situated on the Tofinho headland about 2km south of Praia do Tofo, the Barraco dos Assassinatos (House of Murders) was the site of some the most callous atrocities committed by the notorious Portuguese security police during the war for independence. The police would chain suspected dissidents and Frelimo members to the wall of this coral sea cave at low tide, and leave them to drown as the water rose, or to be battered to death by waves. Today, the site is commemorated by the Tofinho Monument, or Monument of Fallen Heroes, a large unadorned obelisk topped by a small statue of an shackled arm. The base of the monument reputedly holds several human bones recovered from the cave, which is signposted a few metres further along the coast.

area also protects some extensive areas of mangroves. Few independent travellers make it up here, however, as most of the accommodation is strongly geared towards South African self-caterers, though there are a few exceptions, notably the stalwart Barra Lodge beach resort and affiliated Flamingo Bay, which rank among the most alluring upmarket retreats in this part of Mozambique, while the campsite at Farol de Barra, though accessible by 4x4 only, is legendary among overlanders. Marine activities on offer here are very similar to Tofo, with Barra Dive at Barra Lodge being the main operator in the area.

Getting there and away Coming from Inhambane, you need to follow the road to Tofo for 17km, but instead of turning right at the traffic circle, just keep going straight. This road was once passable by 4x4 only, but today you can easily get as far as Barra Lodge or Flamingo Bay in a sturdy saloon car. Note, however, that the 2km turn-off to Farol de Barra is very sandy and 4x4 is essential.

Where to stay

Exclusive

Flamingo Bay Water Lodge (20 rooms) 293 56005; e info@barraresorts.com; www.barraresorts.com. Set on the northwest of the peninsula, this unique stilted lodge, a popular honeymoon destination, gets full marks for originality. Built almost entirely from wood, the lodge is reached via a long boardwalk through the mangroves, & a similar construction links the main building to the rooms, which stand in a stilted arc in a calm clear turquoise lagoon which usually fills with flamingos over Apr/May. The comfortable rooms all have king-size or twin beds, mini-bar, tea/coffee, AC, en-suite hot shower & private balcony facing the open sea. The main building is a fabulous wooden construction that includes a swimming pool, dining room, well-stocked gift shop & spa. Dives & other activities are operated out of the affiliated Barra Lodge, about 2km back towards Inhambane. The stuff of desert-island fantasies. *US$250/400 sgl/dbl DB&B, rising to US$300/500 in the high season, though it's worth checking the website for specials*

Upmarket

Barra Lodge (40 units) 293 20561; e info@barraresorts.com; www.barraresorts.com. Not quite so luxurious or architecturally ambitious as Flamingo Bay, this is nevertheless a very smart lodge, with a wonderful beach location on the north end of the peninsula. Geared more towards family holidays than honeymooners, accommodation is in neat tiled en-suite casitas with thatch roof & sea view, or 2-bedroom self-catering cottages. The on-site dive centre offers a host of facilities & activities including 4x4 biking, sunset cruises, horseriding, diving, fishing & sailing. *US$160/300 sgl/dbl DB&B or US$230 per unit for a 4-bed cottage. Rates rise by around 20% in season.*

Camping

Barra Lighthouse Campsite 293 20565; m 84 3895217; e farolturismo@teledata.mz; www.barralighthouse.com. Under the same management as Pensão Pachiça in Inhambane, this remote campsite is also sometimes known as Farol de Barra or Ponta Barra. It is accessible by 4x4 only, & caters mainly to self-sufficient overlanders or anglers, though facilities include a bar, ablution block with hot water, & electricity. *US$13–19 pp depending on season.*

COCONUT BAY, GUINJATA AND PAINDANE Strung along the east shore of the peninsula 15–25km south of Tofo, this trio of beaches is much more quiet and secluded out of season than Tofo or Barra, making it the place to head for if you really want to get away from it all but don't want to make the arduous slog up to the coastal areas of northern Mozambique. However, since the resorts here cater almost exclusively to the South African market, it can be pretty hectic during school holidays across the border, and prices rocket as a result. Activities and attractions are similar to those in Barra and Tofo (indeed, these are the closest mainland resorts to the legendary Manta Reef, see page 170) but access is difficult without private transport (ideally 4x4) and there is no equivalent to Tofo village's cluster of amenities when it comes to eating, drinking or chilling out.

Getting there and away These resorts all lie southeast of Inhambane and the junction to them is signposted about 10km south of the town centre along the feeder road back to the EN1. The road is unsurfaced and sandy in patches, but it should be possible to drive the 15km from the junction to Coconut Bay in a saloon car. The 12km road south of here to Guinjata and Paindane is best tackled in a 4x4. There is no public transport along this road, but most resorts can provide a transfer from Inhambane by prior arrangement.

Where to stay

Mid-range

Guinjata Resort (44 units) 293 56013 or +27 13 741 2795 (South Africa); e reservations@guinjata.com; www.guinjata.com. This large family-run resort opposite Manta Reef has been going since 1996. Accommodation is in thatched beachfront chalets with anything from 2 to 8 bedrooms & comes equipped with deep freeze, fridge, stove, bedding, hot water & fully equipped kitchen. There is a sports bar with satellite TV, a beach restaurant serving good seafood dishes & pizzas, & a dive centre offering all the usual activities. *Prices range from US$150 for a 2-bedroom chalet out of season to US$700 for an 8-bedroom chalet in season. Sheltered* baracas *for camping cost US$12 pp out of season & a minimum of US$120 for 4 people in season.*

Paindane Beach Resort (25 units) 293 56310; m +27 82 569 3436 (South Africa); e paindane.sa@mweb.co.za; www.paindane.com. Sited about 20km south of Inhambane, Paindane stands on a magnificent vegetated dune overlooking an 800m-long reef that not only provides shelter for swimmers, but also offers superb offshore snorkelling. Aiming mainly at self-caterers, accommodation is in well-equipped chalets with anything from 2 to 6 bedrooms. There is also a campsite & an on-site dive centre offering the usual activities. *From US$80 for a 2-bedroom chalet out of season to US$350 for a 6-bed chalet in season. Camping from US$10 pp.*

Jeff's Resort +27 13 932 1263 (South Africa); m +27 83 254 4865 (South Africa) or 82 71 40 220; e jeffsmoz@mweb.co.za; www.jeffsmoz.com. Sited on a palm-lined dune about 30km south of Inhambane, Jeff's offers a range of accommodation from barracas to an 8-bed villa. Fishing, diving, snorkelling & swimming are all available, plus day trips to Inhambane. *From US$120 for a 4-bed unit out of season to US$300 for an 8-bed villa in season.*

NORTH OF INHAMBANE

A sprinkling of small, low-key resorts runs along the coast between Inhambane and Vilankulo, all of them offering a similar range of activities and attractions to Tofo, but with a more isolated location and a less sociable vibe. First up is the isolated peninsula of **Ponta da Linga Linga**, site of a village that more or less faces Inhambane but lies on the northern side of the same bay. Further north, about 100km north of Maxixe, **Morrungulo** is renowned for the diving and snorkelling at Zambia Reef, with its outstanding soft and hard corals. Another 50km north of this is **Pomene**, site of the latest and most remote of the three lodges operated by Barra Resorts.

GETTING THERE AND AROUND Linga Linga is not accessible by road, but occasional ferries make the short crossing there from Inhambane, and it is also possible to catch a dhow from Morrumbene on the EN1 30km north of Maxixe. To get to Morrungulo in a private vehicle, you must follow the EN1 70km north of Maxixe to Massinga, then stick on the EN1 north for another 7km until you reach the signposted junction, from where it is 13km along a very sandy road that sometimes necessitates 4x4. The turn-off for Pomene is another 5km or so past the one for Morrungulo, and from there it is a 50km drive along a sandy track that requires 4x4.

Where to stay

Castelo do Mar (6 rooms) Ponta da Linga Linga; m 82 027 8356; e info@castelodomar.co.za; www.castelodomar.co.za. This upmarket self-catering villa comprises 6 en-suite bedrooms, sleeping a total of 12, & comes with AC, library, pool table, fully equipped kitchen with gas cookers, & blissfully isolated location. *Rented out as a unit for around US$600.*

Funky Monkeys Ponta da Linga Linga. This back-to-basics campsite can provide food. *US$3 pp.*

Ponta Morrungulo Beach Resort (15 units) Morrungulo; 293 70101; e morrungulo@iwayafrica.com; www.pontamorrungulo.co.za. Camping facilities & a few smart self-catering chalets. Facilities include organised scuba diving & deep-sea fishing excursions, & you can also rent snorkelling equipment. *Camping from US$12 pp, 4-sleeper chalets from US$140.*

Pomene Lodge Pomene; m 82 369 8580; e info@barraresorts.com; www.barraresorts.com. Part of the Barra Group, this isolated lodge is renowned for its lovely setting, & its choice of DB&B accommodation in chalets or self-catering in fishermen's cottages. Diving & other marine activities are offered in-house. Rates are similar to Barra Lodge (see page 172).

10

Vilankulo, Inhassoro and Bazaruto National Park

Vying with the Inhambane area as the most important centre of coastal tourism in Mozambique, the twin mainland towns of Vilankulo and Inhassoro are also gateways to the spectacular Bazaruto National Park. The country's only dedicated marine park, gazetted back in 1971, it protects the offshore Bazaruto Archipelago, whose unspoilt reefs rank among the most exciting diving and snorkelling sites on Africa's Indian Ocean coastline.

The three main tourist bases in the area offer access to similar sights and activities, but each targets a very different market. Within Bazaruto National Park, there are only five beach lodges, which range from the expensive and luxurious to the even-more-expensive and even-more-luxurious, and essentially attract an international fly-in safari clientele. By contrast, low-key Inhassoro is an increasingly popular base for family holidays (in particular with Zimbabweans), whereas cosmopolitan Vilankulo has pretty much cornered the backpacker and independent travel market, though it too has some genuinely upmarket options and several more family-oriented resorts. Wherever you base yourself, however, the area offers some of the best facilities anywhere in Mozambique, and the diving and snorkelling are truly unforgettable.

VILANKULO

The small but sprawling and fast-growing town of Vilankulo, supporting a population of 25,000 and site of an increasingly important international airport, vies with the more southerly resort of Tofo as the most important tourist focal point in Mozambique. It is also one of the few Mozambican coastal resorts to cater to the full spectrum of tourists, from backpackers and overlanders to fly-in holidaymakers and parties of anglers and diving enthusiasts from across the border, with the latter dominating the scene during South African school holidays. Consequently, the town has as diverse a range of accommodation, restaurants and other tourist facilities as you'll find in the country, many of which were flattened in by Hurricane Favio in 2007, though you'd scarcely notice it today.

Vilankulo is a pleasant place simply to hang out for a few days to enjoy the sunshine and beaches. Of particular interest is the beach running east of the town centre, south past Baobab Beach Backpackers, a hive of activity when the fishing boats come ashore in the early morning or late afternoon. There are lots of shorebirds here, too, particularly along the mangroves, which often harbour plentiful little egrets along with various gulls, terns, plovers and other waders. There shouldn't be a problem with theft here so long as you carry your possessions with you, but don't leave valuables on the beach while you swim.

The main local attraction, however, is the nearby Bazaruto Archipelago, whose reefs offer some of the finest snorkelling and diving anywhere in southern

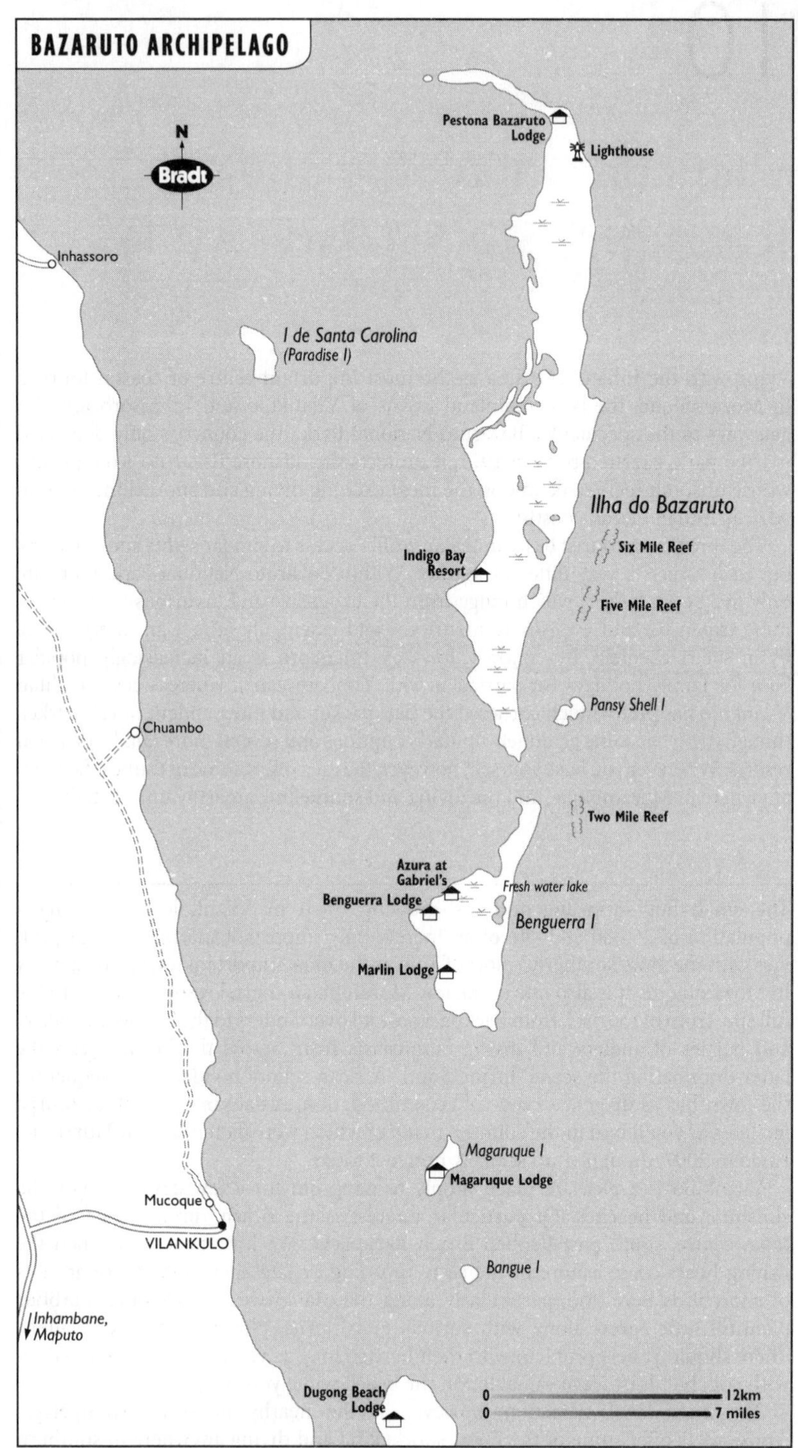
BAZARUTO ARCHIPELAGO
N
Bradt
Pestona Bazaruto Lodge
Lighthouse
Inhassoro
I de Santa Carolina
(Paradise I)
Ilha do Bazaruto
Six Mile Reef
Indigo Bay Resort
Five Mile Reef
Pansy Shell I
Chuambo
Two Mile Reef
Azura at Gabriel's
Fresh water lake
Benguerra Lodge
Benguerra I
Marlin Lodge
Magaruque I
Magaruque Lodge
Mucoque
VILANKULO
Bangue I
Inhambane, Maputo
Dugong Beach Lodge
0
12km
0
7 miles

Mozambique, and can be visited as a day trip out of Vilankulo by those who cannot afford the ultra-expensive lodges that stud the actual islands.

The town is named after the late chief Gamala Vilankulo Mukoke, whose surname is still borne by many people living in the area. During colonial times the town was known as Vilanculos – as the district of which it is capital is still called – but the traditional spelling of Vilankulo was restored shortly after independence.

GETTING THERE AND AWAY

By air LAM (*www.flylam.co.za*) flies several times weekly from Maputo to Vilankulo International Airport, about 5km from the town centre, and international flights from Johannesburg are operated by **Kulula Air** (*www.kulula.com*) and **Pelican Air** (*www.pelicanair.co.za*). In addition, **CFA Air Charters** (*www.cfa.co.za*) operates at least one daily flight connecting Vilankulo to the various islands of the Bazaruto Archipelago.

By car Coming by road from the south, as most people do, Vilankulo lies 20km east of the **EN1** along a good surfaced road. The signposted turn-off at Pambora junction is roughly 220km north of Maxixe, but watch for a BP garage to your left – shortly afterwards you'll reach a large intersection around which lies a cluster of small shops. The drive from Maxixe usually takes up to three hours, while those heading north to Beira should expect it to take around seven to eight hours.

By bus/chapa Most buses and chapas leave in the early morning (check the afternoon before for current departure times) from near the new market. These include at least one daily bus to/from Maputo, leaving at around 02.30, costing around US$16 and taking up to ten hours, and a bus to Beira leaving at around 04.30, and costing US$13. A more attractive option in terms of comfort and timing is the **TCO/ Oliveira** coach between Maputo and Beira, which passes through Pambora junction at around 10.00; check locally at Dodo's Garage for details, or ring their Beira (m *82 775 0554 or 84 601 6861*) or Maputo (*21 300634*) offices. Regular chapas to Maxixe (from where you can catch a ferry to Inhambane) cost around US$4, take four hours, and run throughout the day, as do chapas to Inhassoro (US$1.50; one hour). The walk between the chapa station and virtually all of the town's accommodation options is long, and dark in the early morning, so you might want to enquire about the taxi services listed under *Personal safety* below.

PERSONAL SAFETY Although Vilankulo is as safe as anywhere in Africa in the daytime, it does have a reputation for occasional assaults on tourists walking between the market and one of the lodges at night. Generally, it would be unwise to walk along the unlit roads or the Avenida Marginal at after dark, particularly if you are alone. Some of the restaurants will arrange free transport back to your lodging if you ask. Failing that, try the reliable 24-hour taxi services operated by **Junior** (m *82 462 4700*) or **Eusebio** (m *82 681 3383*). If you're staying at one of the upmarket hotels to the north, then ask at reception – they may have a bus running in your direction.

WHERE TO STAY

Exclusive

Casa Rex (15 rooms) 29 382048; m 82 917 7720; e casarex@teledata.mz; www.casa-rex.com. Shady well-tended gardens set around a swimming pool & a clifftop location offering a lovely view over the bay are features of this slick, spacious & stylish small lodge about

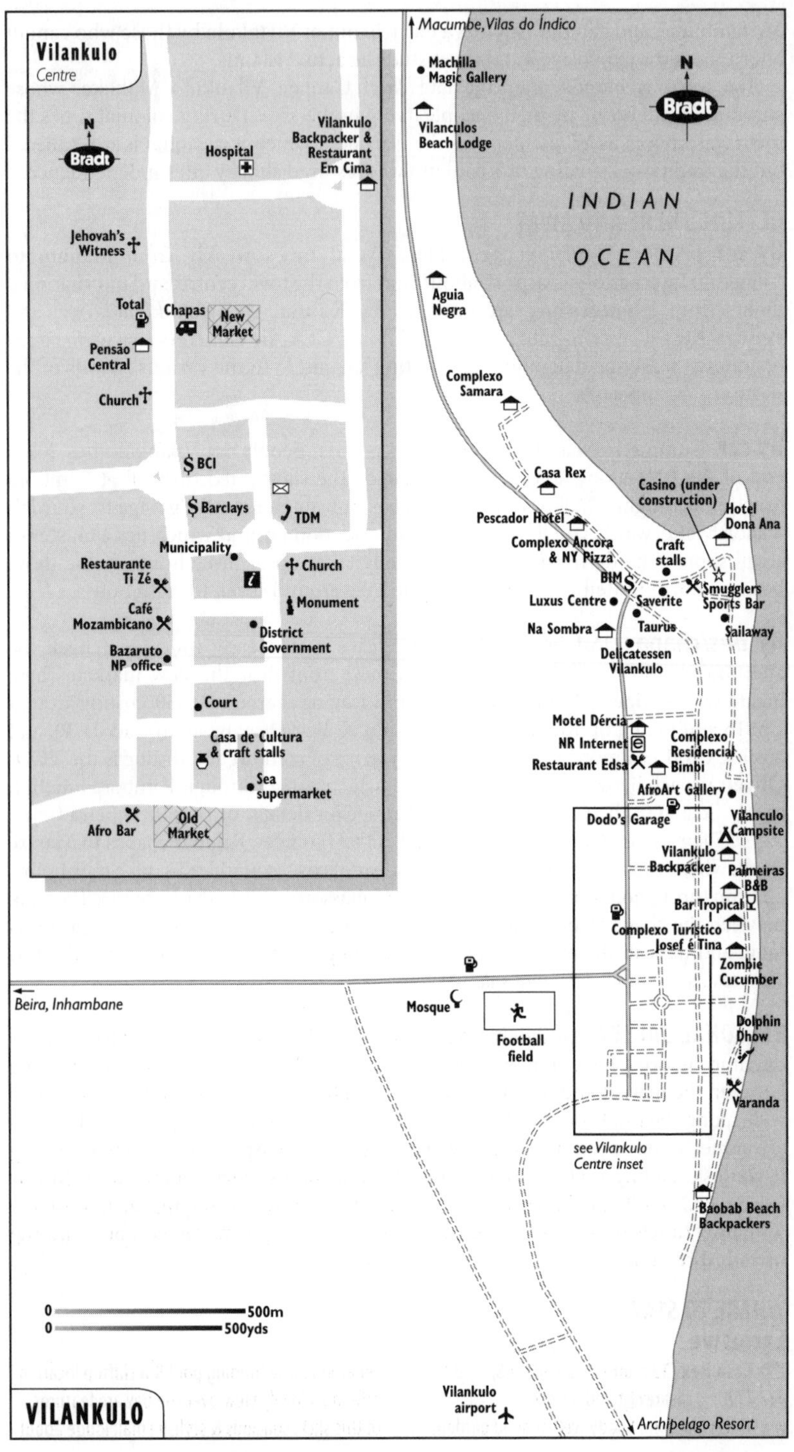

Vilankulo
Centre
Bradt
N
Hospital
Vilankulo Backpacker & Restaurant Em Cima
Jehovah's Witness
Total
Chapas
New Market
Pensão Central
Church
BCI
Barclays
TDM
Municipality
Restaurante Ti Zé
Church
Café Mozambicano
Monument
District Government
Bazaruto NP office
Court
Casa de Cultura & craft stalls
Sea supermarket
Afro Bar
Old Market
Macumbe, Vilas do Índico
Machilla Magic Gallery
Vilanculos Beach Lodge
INDIAN
OCEAN
Aguia Negra
Complexo Samara
Casa Rex
Casino (under construction)
Pescador Hotel
Hotel Dona Ana
Complexo Ancora & NY Pizza
Craft stalls
BIM
Luxus Centre
Saverite
Smugglers Sports Bar
Na Sombra
Taurus
Sailaway
Delicatessen Vilankulo
Motel Dércia
NR Internet
Complexo Residencial Bimbi
Restaurant Edsa
AfroArt Gallery
Dodo's Garage
Vilanculo Campsite
Vilankulo Backpacker
Palmeiras B&B
Bar Tropical
Complexo Turístico Josef é Tina
Zombie Cucumber
Beira, Inhambane
Mosque
Football field
Dolphin Dhow
Varanda
see Vilankulo Centre inset
Baobab Beach Backpackers
0 500m
0 500yds
VILANKULO
Vilankulo airport
Archipelago Resort

1km northwest of the town centre. There's also an appealing combination of contemporary and vintage colonial furniture, a footpath leading directly to the beach, an excellent seafood restaurant, & good amenities including WiFi. This lodge aims for the same market as its counterparts on the islands, with a comparable standard of accommodation & range of activities, but is cheaper & has the advantage (or disadvantage, depending on your point of view) of being closer to town. The premier courtyard suites come with king-size beds, walk-in nets, sofa, great sea views, en-suite bathroom with tub, AC & plenty of wood and muted pastel colours. Other rooms are similar but smaller, with twin or dbl bed. *US$140/220 standard sgl/dbl; US$180/300 in Acacia Wing; US$210/360 Courtyard Suite. All rates B&B.*

Vilanculos Beach Lodge (24 rooms) 293 82314 or +27 21 304 3442; e reservations@vilanculos.co.za; www.vilanculos.co.za. Situated at the end of the newly surfaced road stretching some 3km northwest from the town centre, this venerable lodge has been completely refurbished following hurricane damage in 2007. Accommodation is in thatched stilted chalets with a king-size bed, walk-in netting, fridge, en-suite shower, writing desk & private balcony overlooking the manicured, palm-shaded gardens & what is easily the prettiest & most private swimming beach in the immediate vicinity of town. There is also a large infinity pool, one of the top seafood restaurants in town, & a full range of marine activities. *US$195/330 sgl/dbl B&B.*

Vilas do Índico (12 rooms) m 82 874 1915 or 84 713 2018; e reservations@outdoorvilanculos.com; www.outdoorvilanculos.com. Situated on an isolated beach about 10km north of town along a 4x4-only road, this intimate lodge offers accommodation in en-suite thatched chalets with private seafront verandas offering a panoramic view of the Bazaruto Islands. The seafood has a great reputation & the usual range of activities is offered. *US$150/200 sgl/dbl B&B or US$200/300 FB.*

Dugong Beach Lodge (12 rooms) +27 11 729 6700 (South Africa); e reservations@legendlodges.co.za; www.dugonglodge.co.za. This highly exclusive lodge on the Ponta de São Sebastião south of Vilankulo is accessible only by boat or light aircraft charter from the airport. *US$545/780 sgl/dbl low season, rising to US$690/980 high season, inclusive of all meals & non-motorised activities, but excluding boat or air transfer.*

Upmarket

Pescador Hotel (14 rooms) 293 82327; m 84 891 0003; e reservations@pescadormoz.com; www.pescadormoz.com. Opened in 2007, this smart modern hotel is well equipped with a saltwater swimming pool, DSTV in the lounge, good seafood restaurant, internet access & spacious, attractively decorated rooms with tiled floor, AC, fan & en-suite bathroom with tub. It is not on the sea but has good beach access & seems like excellent value if you can live with that one drawback. *US$80 for a smaller downstairs dbl or twin; US$120–140 for an upstairs dbl; all rates B&B.*

Aguia Negra (12 rooms, 12 more under construction) 29 382387; e aguianegra@tdm.co.mz; www.aguianegra.co.za. This offers accommodation in stilted & thatched A-frame chalets, all of which have 1 large main bedroom with dbl bed, a loft with twin beds, AC & private balcony. There are spectacular sea views from the restaurant, which serves seafood in the US$5–9 range, & 2 swimming pools set within lush gardens which run down to an adequate swimming beach. *US$100/150 sgl/dbl B&B, while the new luxury rooms cost US$160/200.*

Archipelago Resort (18 rooms) 293 84022; m 84 712 8180; reservations@archipelago-resort.com; www.archipelago-resort.com. Situated about 10mins' drive south of the airport, this attractively rustic isolated resort effectively has its own private beach, overlooked by the excellent stilted Vista do Mar Restaurant, & is also the home of Dive Bazaruto, which offers the full range of marine activities. Accommodation is in large stilted thatch cottages, all of which have an en-suite master bedroom with king-size bed, walk-in nets & fan, room for 4 more people to sleep, & full self-catering facilities including fridge & freezer for those who prefer not to use the restaurant (*07.00–22.00*). *Rates are affected by group size, seasonality, & whether you take a beachfront chalet, but expect to pay around US$160 for up* *to 4 people except over the Christmas & Easter holidays, when prices double. Low-season specials of as little as US$50/80 sgl/dbl are often offered on the website & to walk-in clients.*

Complexo Ancora (5 rooms) 293 82444; m 82 389 9999; e godah2000@yahoo.com. This beachfront complex at the north end of the town used to function mainly as a restaurant, but now also provides limited accommodation in large clean tiled dbl rooms with walk-in nets, AC, DSTV, fridge, Wi-Fi & en-suite shower. Feels a little overpriced at *US$75/120*.

Mid-range

Palmeiras B&B & Backpackers (5 rooms, 1 dorm) m 82 753 8980 or 84 829 2126; e smugglers@teledata.mz; www.smugglers.co.za. Set in pretty flowering beachfront grounds with a small swimming pool, this smarter, quieter annexe of Smugglers (see below) has clean en-suite chalets, bathrooms with fans & nets, as well as a 10-bed A-frame dorm with linen & towels, kitchenette (with basic utensils), lock-up storeroom, fridge & freezer. 2 potential inconveniences for those without transport are that no meals other than b/fast are available, & check-in is at the reception of Smugglers Inn about 1km away. *US$105 dbl B&B; US$15 per dorm bed.*

Smugglers (13 rooms) m 82 753 8980 or 84 829 2126; e smugglers@teledata.mz; www.smugglers.co.za. Set in a green courtyard behind the ever popular Smugglers Sports Bar, this clean, neat & well-managed complex has the choice of twins using shared bathrooms, en-suite dbls with AC, or a self-catering chalet sleeping up to 4. *US$50 twin; US$75 en-suite dbl; US$150 4-bed chalet.*

Complexo Samara (11 rooms) m 82 380 6865; e sabira@tdm.co.mz. Set in busy gardens overlooking the beach, this place is known as one of the best-value seafood eateries in town, but also has a variety of clean en-suite rooms, some with self-catering kitchenettes. *From US$70/80 sgl/dbl (negotiable for larger groups).*

Complexo Residencial Bimbi 29 382 043; e acomo.king@enh.co.mz. This rather quirky village-like set-up comprises a couple of dozen 2- & 3-bedroom casas, all with TV, fridge, well-equipped kitchen & dining room, set along its own named roads, and a large swimming pool & restaurant. It's not exactly resort-like but it is central & close to the chapa station; the only real drawback is that it's a bit of a walk to the beach. *US$50 4-bed casa; US$70 6-bed casa.*

Budget

Zombie Cucumber (4 rooms; 1 dorm) m 82 804 9410; e info@zombiecucumber.com; www.zombiecucumber.com. This popular beachfront backpackers is owned by a British couple, & has a very friendly atmosphere & pleasant layout. Facilities include a small swimming pool, useful noticeboard, good food (lunchtime sandwiches are in the US$2–3 range & set dinners cost around US$6–7), inexpensive internet access & Wi-Fi, & hammocks hung between the trees that shade the compound. The bungalows are simple but clean with dbl bed, walk-in netting & a macuti thatch roof. The current managers also own Odyssea Dive (see page 183) & can arrange all sorts of marine excursions. *US$10 pp in the 9-bed dorm; US$28 dbl.*

Baobab Beach Backpackers (13 rooms & 3 dorms) m 82 731 5420; e baobabmoz@yahoo.com; www.baobabbeach.net. This has a pleasantly shaded location, but is quite a walk from the town centre, which may be a factor if you have an early bus to catch, although there are signs indicating that the guard will accompany you to the market if you ask. It's got a range of accommodation – camping, dorms & some lovely chalets overlooking the beach – as well as a varied menu with most meals under US$6. The staff are generally very pleasant & helpful, speaking good English. Odyssea Dive (see page 183) is based here. *US$35 en-suite dbl beach chalet; US$16 dbl chalet; US$7.50 dorm bed; US$5.50 pp camping.*

Complexo Alemanha/Vilankulo Backpacker (6 rooms; 2 dorms) 29 382051; m 82 082 2070; e kontakt@vilanculosbackpacker.com; www.vilanculosbackpacker.com. Two names for the same operation, owned & run by an energetic German, this has pleasant chalet accommodation with private balcony and fan, as well as 2 10-bed dorms. It's very close to the chapa station, sited on a rise overlooking the bay with great views. There is also the inexpensive rooftop

Restaurant Em Cima, occasional disco nights, some self-catering facilities, safe parking, a hot shower block. There are 2 dbl beds in the dorms for couples tired of being separated on bunk beds. *US$17 dbl; US$6 pp dorm.*

Pensão Central (29 rooms) m 82 938 2508 or 82 756 3998. Conveniently situated right opposite the chapa station, this recently renovated & totally non-resort-like establishment is unexceptional & unmemorable but adequate value, with a variety of clean rooms with nets, & a decent restaurant attached. *US$25 dbl; US$35 en-suite dbl; US$55–80 dbl with DSTV, walk-in net & AC.*

Shoestring

Na Sombra (7 rooms) m 82 77 0 1170; e nasombra@tdm.co.mz. Run by a Belgian family & attached to a popular restaurant (one of the finest in town), this stands out as exceptional value for money. There are small but nicely decorated rooms with nets, clean common showers, the staff speak reasonable English & they'll dig you out a fan if you ask them. *US$8/11 sgl/dbl.*

Complexo Turístico Josef é Tina m 82 311 4200. One of the more established options, this unpretentious place offers accommodation in simple reed huts using common showers. It is probably not as good value as the other places listed in this price range, nor so convenient for catching chapas, but does have the advantages of being in a large green compound right on the beachfront Av Marginal. *US$17 dbl.*

Motel Dércia (30 rooms) m 82 933 1677. This quiet little place off the main road is quite close to the bus station & well placed for eating out, if less so for the beach. Rooms are nothing to write home about, but pleasant enough & sensibly priced, though it is worth looking at a few, as the quality of rooms varies a lot more than prices. *US$15 twin without shower; US$17 en-suite dbl with net & fan.*

Camping The nicest place to camp is probably Baobab Beach Backpackers, opposite.

Vilankulo Campsite On the Av Marginal right on the seafront; t 29 382043; m 82 53 15 462. Offers a selection of camping options. Fixed tents are available if you've forgotten your own. It gets packed out at high season & the staff aren't the most welcoming in the world. *US$6 pp.*

WHERE TO EAT The upmarket hotels all have their own restaurants, which are as good as you would expect them to be, but there are also several other options in town.

Town centre

Na Sombra m 82 770 1170; e nasombra@tdm.co.mz; b/fast, lunch & dinner daily. Set in a large, airy macuti-thatch construction, this Belgian-owned restaurant serves a good selection of seafood dishes, including stews, curries & paella, as well as a popular evening barbecue. *The food is excellent & reasonably priced, with most dishes in the US$6–8 range, & service is good.*

Restaurant Em Cima t 29 382051; m 82 082 2070. This worthwhile budget eatery, part of Vilanculos Backpackers, combines a breezy rooftop setting, ocean views, a pleasant semi-outdoor ambience & an affordable menu of seafood, burgers, pasta & local vegetarian dishes. *Mostly less than US$4 per main.*

Restaurante Ti-Zé B/fast, lunch & dinner daily. Situated on the main road, just outside the market, Ti-Zé does good local food. It is a good place to try matapa, although they'll need some notice to gather the ingredients. *Mains mostly in the US$4–5 range.*

Café Mozambicano 07.00–17.00 Mon–Sat. Fresh espresso, pastries, filled rolls & a selection of imported confectionery are sold at this small pastelaria near the old market.

Afro Bar Around the corner from the market, this is a likeable, no-nonsense place, popular with locals & probably more geared to backpackers than the upmarket traveller. It has occasional live music, mostly at w/ends. Walking back to your hotel from here at night is not recommended; catch a taxi.

Seafront

Casa Rex 29 382048; m 82 917 7720; b/fast, lunch & dinner daily. This attractive, refined hotel overlooking the sea has possibly the most highly regarded restaurant in town, with seafood the main speciality alongside a varied selection of curries & salads. *Mains in the US$10–20 range.*

Samara Restaurant m 82 380 6865; b/fast, lunch & dinner daily. A short walk past Casa Rex, this good-value restaurant has nice sea views from the upper deck and serves a good selection of seafood, chicken & other grills, cooked to perfection on hot coals. *Main in the US$6–10 range.*

Smugglers Sports Bar m 82 753 8980 or 84 829 2126; 08.00–22.00 daily. This long-serving bar is very popular with expat South Africans & Zimbabweans, who gather to watch sports on the large-screen TV or sup a beer on the veranda or in the small garden. The menu reflects the South African clientele, with an emphasis on steak & other grills, & it's arguably slightly overpriced for what you get. *Snacks are in the US$4–5 range & mains US$6–15.*

New York Pizza m 82 389 9999; lunch & dinner daily. Part of Complexo Ancora, this place has long served the best pizzas in town, but also has a good selection of pasta & seafood, & a great view over the bay. Orders can be phoned in and/or collected as take-away. *Most mains & medium pizzas are around US$7.*

Varanda 29 382412; m 82 861 2540; e varanda.barka@yahoo.com; 07.30–21.00 Tue–Sun. Situated on the dunes overlooking the beach where the fishing *dhows* come to land their catches, this long-standing favourite serves great Mozambican-style seafood & superb chicken piri-piri. The only downside is that the street immediately outside is unlit, so you might want to go in a group. *Mains are in the US$7–10 range.*

Bar Tropical On the Av Marginal near Zombie Cucumber, this is a good place to have sundowners overlooking the sea. *Also serves a few local dishes for under US$6.*

WHAT TO SEE AND DO

Manyikeni Ruins Some 50km inland of Vilankulo, the overgrown ruins of Manyikeni are probably the best surviving example of a Zimbabwe-style stone enclosure in Mozambique. Occupied from the 12th to the 17th centuries, this was the site of an important outpost of the Karanga Kingdom, and the main enclosure, typical of such sites, was situation on the top of a small hill, a location believed to by symbolic of royal power. A wealth of glass beads has been unearthed at the site, along with loose globules of gold and a single iron gong, suggesting strong cultural links with what is now the Zimbabwe interior as well as trade links with the coast, probably through the abandoned port of Chibuene. Although it is not developed for tourism, Manyikeni (together with Chibuene) as placed on the tentative list of UNESCO World Heritage Sites in 1997. To get there from Vilankulo, follow the EN1 south from Pambora junction for about 30km as far as Mapinhane, then turn right onto a good dirt road and follow it inland for about 10km until you reach an unsignposted dirt road heading north. The ruins are about 5km along this road and may be difficult to locate without a guide.

Diving and snorkelling The prime reason for visiting Vilankulo is to go snorkelling or diving in the Bazaruto Archipelago, a subject dealt with in detail on pages 190–1. Boats to the islands are readily available through a number of diving operations scattered around town. Many first-timers are persuaded to join an excursion to **Magaruque**, which is the closest island to Vilankulo, and thus the cheapest to visit, but offers significantly inferior snorkelling to other reefs in the area. A far better option, emphatically worth the additional cost, is a day trip to **Two-Mile Reef**, which offers the best snorkelling and diving in the archipelago, and can easily be combined with a visit to the spectacular dunes at the southern end of **Bazaruto Island**.

The operators listed below are all recommended for diving, snorkelling and other activities.

Odyssea Dive m 82 781 7130; e info@odysseadive.com; www.odysseadive.com. This established company, situated in the grounds of Baobab Beach Backpackers, offers a range of good-value activities in & around the water, starting with a full-day island safari, taking in Bazaruto & Benguerra Island, as well as snorkelling on Two Mile Reef, for US$50 pp. Dives start at US$75, and full courses are available too.

Dive Bazaruto 29 384252; m 84 850 6507 or 82 870 6996; e info@atoz-tours.com; www.divebazaruto.com. Based at Archipelago Resort. Prices are around US$65/90 pp for a snorkelling trip to Magaruque/Two Mile Reef, & US$90/120 pp for diving trips to the same destinations.

Sailaway 29 382385; m 82 387 6350; e david@sailaway.co.za; www.sailaway.co.za. Sailaway runs *dhow* trips to the various islands, with 1-, 2- or 3-day excursions, & respectively costing US$70, US$230 and US$345 pp, including food, soft drinks, snorkelling kit & park fees – in fact everything except alcohol.

Big Blue 29 382431/5; m 82 318 0450; e bigbluelda@teledata.mz; www.bigbluevilankulo.com. Next to the Aguia Negra. Big Blue offers a range of activities, including diving, fishing, snorkelling, whale watching, island drop-offs & other watersports. Check website for full rates.

Dolphin Dhow 29 382488; m 82 462 4700; e dolphindhowvlk@yahoo.com; http://dolphindhow.ning.com. Sited on Av Marginal & run by Junior who also has a taxi service, this does full-day trips to Magaruque for US$65 pp & Benguerra for US$75.

Other tours Very popular are the horseback trips around Vilankulo and on the islands run by **Mozambique Horse Safaris** (*29 384247;* m *84 251 2910; www.mozambiquehorsesafari.com*), which charges from US$45 per person for a ride and is based south of town near the Archipelago Resort. For a glimpse into local village life, contact Faquir Nhamué of **Vilankulo Village Tours** (m *84 711 2948*). Tours cost US$10 per person. Camelback excursions on the beach are offered by the **Complexo Ancora** at the north end of town.

OTHER PRACTICALITIES

Banks Standard, Barclays, BCI and BIM Millennium all have branches in the town centre, and ATMs taking international Visa cards. BIM Millennium also takes MasterCard.

Hospital For emergencies contact the hospital (*29 330622*); for non-emergencies try the doctor at the *farmacia* (pharmacy) next to the Banco Austral at the roundabout in the centre of town.

Internet Options include the TDM office and tourist office near the main roundabout, NR Internet near the Motel Dércia, and Zombie Cucumber (though preference is given to people staying here).

Police The police station is on the main road leading into town.

Shopping Vilankulo has two excellent markets, the old one being situated at the southern end of the town centre and the new one behind the chapa station opposite the Pensão Central. The former is good for crafts and both are good for fresh groceries. The Taurus Supermarket at the north end of the town centre is outstanding, selling fresh fruit and frozen meat, and a huge selection of imported goods, but the SaveRite Supermarket around the corner is also very good. For craft shopping, there are a few stalls on the Avenida Marginal, as well as at the north end of the town centre near Complexo Ancora, and at the south end of town in front of the Casa Cultural. Also worth a mention is the Afro Art Gallery next to Vilanculos Camping, and the upmarket Papagayo Craft Shop in the Luxus Centre.

A special mention goes to **Machilla Magic** (m *82 393 3428;* e *info@machillamagic.com; www.machillamagic.com*), which sells a huge variety of crafts made by more than 50 local families at the village of Macumbe, 25km north of town, for distribution throughout southern Africa. The crafts are good quality and very varied in style, and a new gallery, under construction at the time of research, should open next to the Vilanculos Beach Lodge in 2011.

The helpful **tourist office** (m *82 525 0457;* e *ndembeka@gmail.com;* ⌚ *08.30–12.30 & 13.30–18.30 Mon–Fri, 08.30–12.00 Sat*) is set in the central municipal building and can arrange accommodation and provide you with a useful range of brochures and booklets, as well as advice on *dhow* trips. It is run as a community project, and an internet café is attached.

INHASSORO

Heading north along the EN1, Inhassoro is the final mainland coastal resort before the road veers inland for the 330km trip via the Save River to Inchope junction (on the EN6 between Beira and Chimoio). Much smaller than Vilankulo, but with a similarly sprawling layout, Inhassoro hasn't traditionally attracted much in the way of international tourism. However, as the closest beach resort to Zimbabwe, it has become a popular retreat with expats from across the border, so that high seasons tally more or less exactly with Zimbabwean school holidays. At the time of writing, there is something of a work-in-progress feel about the small town centre: banking facilities arrived in 2009 in the form of two different outlets with ATMs, as did the first filling station and a spanking new supermarket, and there is an unusually high proportion of half-constructed buildings, creating the overall impression of a small village rapidly filling out to become a fledgling resort town.

The main attraction at Inhassoro is the near-perfect beach, which stretches for several kilometres either side of the town centre. The beach here is far cleaner and quieter than its counterpart at Vilankulo, and considerably better suited to swimming and beach-oriented holidays. The resort lies opposite the northern end of the Bazaruto Archipelago, and is the closest place to pick up boats to the Santa Carolina Island and the northern end of Bazaruto Inland, though in practice it is probably less often used for that purpose than Vilankulo. In theory, Inhassoro offers similar snorkelling and diving opportunities to Vilankulo, centred on the islands rather than the town itself, but at the time of writing there is no dive operation here, nor any operator offering affordable *dhow* and snorkelling excursions to the islands (though this may well change in the near future).

GETTING THERE AND AWAY

By car Inhassoro lies 13km along a surfaced feeder road that's clearly signposted on the east side of the **EN1**, some 50km north of the turn-off to Vilankulo, and about 330km south of Inchope on the **EN6** between Beira and Chimoio. The drive from Vilankulo should take an hour at most, but you are looking at around five hours to or from Beira or Chimoio.

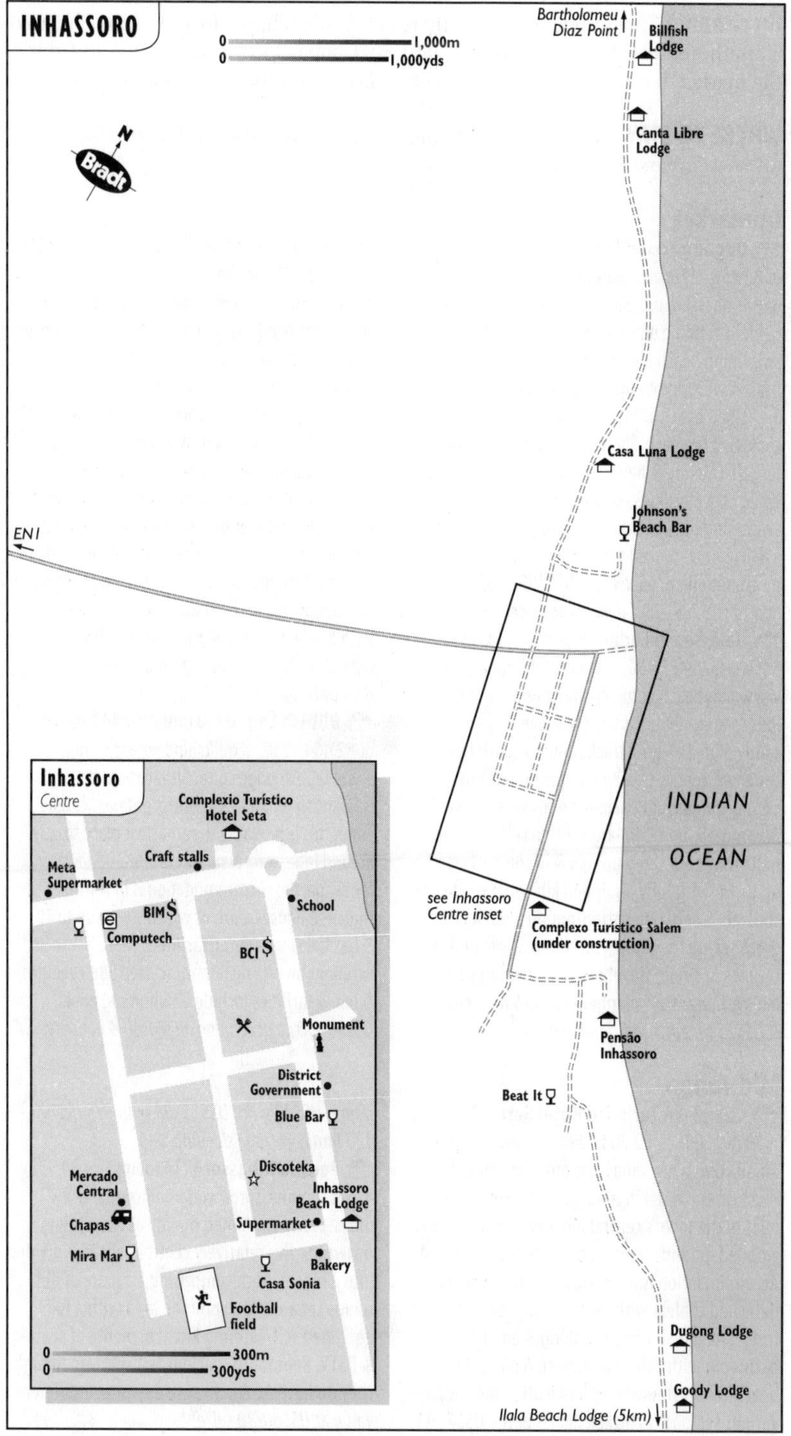
INHASSORO
0 1,000m
0 1,000yds
Bradt
N
Bartholomeu Diaz Point
Billfish Lodge
Canta Libre Lodge
Casa Luna Lodge
Johnson's Beach Bar
EN1
INDIAN OCEAN
see Inhassoro Centre inset
Complexo Turístico Salem (under construction)
Pensão Inhassoro
Beat It
Dugong Lodge
Goody Lodge
Ilala Beach Lodge (5km)
Inhassoro
Centre
Complexio Turístico Hotel Seta
Craft stalls
Meta Supermarket
BIM
School
Computech
BCI
Monument
District Government
Blue Bar
Discoteka
Mercado Central
Inhassoro Beach Lodge
Chapas
Supermarket
Mira Mar
Bakery
Casa Sonia
Football field
0 300m
0 300yds

By chapa Using public transport, there are regular chapas to and from Vilankulo, a one-hour ride that costs around US$1.50. Chapas mostly leave from in front of the market, but they can usually also be picked up on the main road into town.

WHERE TO STAY Note that most of the lodges and resorts in Inhassoro have pages on www.inhassoro.org showing up-to-date rates.

Upmarket

Dugong Lodge (10 units) m 84 389 1471 or 82 456 7170; e dugonginv@vodamail.co.mz; www.inhassoro.org. Situated in idyllic indigenous gardens running down to a postcard-perfect swimming beach about 2km south of town, this bush-style lodge comprises a cluster of immaculate 5–10-bed beach lodges, plus a few smaller dbl chalets at the back. The lodges are fully equipped for self-catering & have large private balconies, while other facilities include a beachfront infinity swimming pool, attractive bar-restaurant serving a daily home-cooked set menu, & fishing charters by arrangement. *Chalets are US$100–140 dbl & houses US$235–350, depending on season.*

Ilala Beach Lodge (9 units) m 84 343 3450 or 82 243 3450; e ilalabeach@gmail.com; www.ilalabeach.com. The most remote of the lodges around Inhassoro, set at the end of a sandy 6km 4x4-only track running south from the town centre, this 7ha property runs out onto a wonderful beach, ideal for swimming. Accommodation is in large stilted self-catering units that each sleep up to 6 & in some cases up to 14, with fully equipped kitchen, private showers & separate sitting/dining area. It is a great set-up for groups, but not really suited to couples or single travellers. A swimming pool & a bar-restaurant are planned. *US$125 for 2 people & US$25 for each additional person.*

Casa Luna Lodge (18 rooms) t 29 384259; m 82 520 3486 or 84 885 6788; e info@inhassoro.org or casalunalodge@tdm.co.mz; www.inhassoro.com. Set on a slight rise overlooking the beach north of the town centre, this attractive bush-meets-beach lodge lies in compact green gardens whose indigenous scrub is offset by a network of wooden walkways, decks & a swimming pool. There is the choice of stilted safari-style standing tents with fan & private veranda, or more conventional chalets with AC, en-suite bathroom with tub & outdoor shower. A highly rated restaurant serves seafood & other dishes in the US$8–14 range along with a selection of cheaper snacks. *US$100 dbl tent; US$120 dbl room; significant low-season discounts; all rates B&B.*

Billfish Lodge (10 units) m 84 238 7866 or 82 464 1910; e billfishlodge@lantic.net; www.billfishlodge.co.za. Situated on the low cliffs north of the town centre, out past Canta Libre, this is probably the smartest place to stay around Inhassoro, & mainly orientated towards family parties. Accommodation is in warm, earthy thatched houses, each of which sleeps up to 10 & has full self-catering facilities. There is also an excellent on-site restaurant (closed Sun evenings) & bar, & facilities include a swimming pool. *US$30–50 pp depending on season & house type.*

Mid-range

Complexo Turístico Hotel Seta (38 rooms) t 29 391000; m 82 203 0990; e egnessmoyo@gmail.com; www.inhassoro.org. The oldest & most central hotel in Inhassoro, the Seta stands next to the town's central junction, set in large wooded grounds running down to the beach. Accommodation is in spacious detached or semi-detached chalets with thatch roofs, veranda, fridge, AC, nets, terracotta tiling & en-suite bathroom with tub &/or shower. A pleasant beachfront restaurant with macuti roof serves various seafood & chicken dishes in the US$7–11 range. *US$40 twin; US$55 dbl with TV; US$100–120 family cottage sleeping 5–6.*

Pensão Inhassoro (14 rooms) m 84 331 4282; e pinhassoro@vodamail.co.mz; www.inhassoro.co.za. Aimed mainly at the angling fraternity, this relatively central pensão is divided into 2 blocks, each comprising a square of dbl rooms set around a common area with a fully equipped self-catering kitchen, plenty of seating & DSTV. Rooms are spacious but spartan, though they do have AC & some are en-suite. Indifferent value at *US$60/80 sgl/dbl.*

Budget

Inhassoro Beach Lodge (18 rooms) m 82 459 0820 or 82 525 0365; www.inhassoro.org. This sprawling locally managed complex lies in large & rather untidy grounds stretching down from the town centre to the beach. It is friendly, relatively affordable & convenient for public transport, but there is a slightly untended feel about the place. All rooms are en-suite with TV & AC. *US$35 dbl; US$45–55 chalet.*

Canta Libre (4 rooms) m 84 272 6603; e cantalibre@yahoo.com; www.cantalibre.net. This attractive stilted complex stands on a cliff overlooking the beach about 3km north of the town centre. Accommodation is in wooden self-catering en-suite twin or dbl chalets with walk-in net, standing fan, safe, & small private deck. There is a large deck, small swimming pool, & b/fast served on request. A full dive & fishing centre should be up and running by 2011; check website for details. *US$25 pp.*

WHERE TO EAT The lodges and resorts listed above mostly have good restaurants, with those at Billfish Lodge and the Complexo Turístico Hotel Seta most likely to appeal to non-residents. Otherwise, a popular spot for a beachfront drink, a short walk north of the Seta, is **Johnson's Beach Bar**, which also serves a limited selection of daily specials in the US$7–10 range. There are several small bars and unpretentious local eateries dotted around the market area. The **Blue Bar** has two pool tables.

OTHER PRACTICALITIES

Banks There are recently opened branches of the BCL and BIM Millennium in the town centre, both within a few metres of the main junction and with outside ATMs.

Internet Inhassoro Computech is an unexpectedly modern-looking internet café, and charges around US$2.50 per hour.

Marine activities Inhassoro is poorly equipped for marine activities at the time of writing, but a dive centre is likely to open at Canta Libre in 2011. This will arrange diving and snorkelling excursions to the Bazaruto Archipelago, as well as fishing charters, and it will be open to people staying at other hotels. Check the Canta Libre website (see above) for up-to-date details.

Shopping The anonymous supermarket opposite Inhassoro Beach Lodge stocks a pretty decent selection of imported and packaged goods, including wine and frozen meat, and there is a good bakery right next door. The Meta Supermarket on the road out of town is also quite well stocked. For fresh fish and greens, the Mercado Central is a couple of blocks west of the main road, while the best place to shop for crafts are the stalls outside the entrance to the Complexo Turístico Hotel Seta.

BAZARUTO NATIONAL PARK

Comprising a string of small sandy islands lying roughly 15–25km from the mainland north of Vilankulo and south of Inhassoro, the Bazaruto Archipelago was one of the few parts of Mozambique that remained safe to visit during the closing years of the civil war, when it developed as an upmarket package-based tourist destination that functioned in near isolation from the rest of the country. That much is arguably still true today, since all the archipelago's lodges slot comfortably into the upmarket or exclusive price bracket, and their fly-in clientele consists mostly of people on a multi-country itinerary who barely set foot on the Mozambican mainland. That said, Bazaruto is also the focal point of marine activities out of

Vilankulo and Inhassoro, and its islands and reefs are the target of almost all diving, snorkelling and other day excursions from these popular mainland resorts.

In 1971, the archipelago's five main islands and the surrounding ocean were gazetted as Bazaruto National Park, which extends eastward from the coastline between Vilankulo and Inhassoro to cover some 1,430km^2. The three largest islands were formerly part of a peninsula that is thought to have separated from the mainland within the last 10,000 years. The largest and most northerly island is Bazaruto itself: 30km long, on average 5km wide, and punctuated by a few substantial freshwater lakes near its southern tip. South of this, Benguerra, the second-largest island at 11km long by 5.5km wide, was known to the Portuguese as Santa Antonio, but was later renamed after an important local chief. South of this, the much smaller Magaruque lies almost directly opposite Vilankulo. The smallest island, Santa Carolina, also known as Paradise Island, is a former penal colony covering an area of about 2km^2 roughly halfway between Bazaruto and the mainland near Inhassoro. The fifth island, Bangue, is only rarely visited by tourists.

With its white, palm-lined beaches, the Bazaruto Archipelago is everything you would expect of an Indian Ocean island retreat. It is of great interest to birdwatchers, with roughly 150 species recorded, including several that are rare or localised in southern Africa, for instance: green coucal; crab, sand and Mongolian plovers; olive and blue-cheeked bee-eaters; and a variety of petrels, gulls and waders. Lesser flamingos seen on the islands come from a nearby breeding colony, the only one known in eastern Africa south of Lake Natron in Tanzania. An estimated 45 reptile and amphibian species occur on the islands, including two endemics.

The freshwater lakes on Bazaruto and Benguerra support a relic breeding population of crocodiles, while the shores of the islands are nesting sites for at least three types of turtle including the rare loggerhead. Mammals present on one or other island include the localised suni antelope, red duiker, bushbuck and samango monkey. An endemic butterfly species is found on Bazaruto Island.

However, the main attractions of the islands lie off their shores. The surrounding sea, warmed by the Mozambique Stream, is crystal clear and its reefs support a variety of brightly coloured fish, making the area one of Mozambique's finest snorkelling and diving destinations. There are well-established diving centres on the north of Bazaruto Island and on Benguerra Island. Visitors to the islands frequently see marine turtles, humpback whales, and bottlenose, spinner and humpback dolphins, as well as large game fish such as marlins and barracudas. The islands are also renowned for their game fishing (see box opposite).

The Bazaruto area supports what is probably east Africa's last viable population of the endangered dugong.

The Bazaruto Islands have a long history of human occupation. Prior to the Portuguese occupation of the coast, the islands were almost certainly the site of east Africa's most southerly Muslim trading settlements. By the middle of the 16th century, the islands were lorded over by Portuguese traders, and the surrounding sea was known for producing high-quality pearls. The first formal Portuguese settlement was established in 1855, on Santa Carolina. Initially an ivory trading post, the island was later used as a penal colony, but it was evidently abandoned by the beginning of the 20th century. Interesting historical relics include a ruined 19th-century fort on Magaruque and a fully intact but non-operational 100-year-old lighthouse on Bazaruto.

Day visitors must pay an entrance fee of around US$6 in advance at the WWF Office in Vilankulo. If you are on a package deal or staying at one of the lodges on the islands, the fee will almost certainly be included in your bill.

GETTING THERE AND AWAY Most overnight visitors to Bazaruto fly from Maputo or Johannesburg to Vilankulo (see page 177) and either fly to their lodge with **CFA Air Charters** (*www.cfa.co.za*), which operates at least one daily flight connecting Vilankulo to the various islands, or transfer there by boat. Either way, this is something that can be arranged with the company that books your accommodation (or, if you book directly, with the lodge itself). Day visitors most often come on a motorised ***dhow*** trip from Vilankulo, which can be arranged with any of the local dive operators listed on page 183.

WHERE TO STAY Accommodation options are limited to a handful of exclusive upmarket resorts, whose prices and facilities are in line with private safari lodges in South Africa, Botswana and Zambia.

Benguerra Island The three lodges on this island are all small, intimate and utterly wonderful, typifying the spirit of barefoot luxury, but they do fit firmly into the exclusive price bracket.

Marlin Lodge (17 rooms) +27 41 407 1000 (South Africa); reservations@mantiscollection.com; www.marlinlodge.co.za. Recently incorporated into the highly regarded Mantis Collection, this is arguably the finest beach lodge anywhere in Mozambique, offering the winning combination of luxurious accommodation, superb food, great activities & super-friendly & efficient staff. The spacious beachfront chalets, strung out in the coastal woodland to create a strong sense of privacy, have a king-size 4-poster bed with walk-in netting, AC, roof fan, earthen slate tile floor, macuti roof, private wooden deck, mini-bar, en-suite bathroom & outdoor shower, & are attractively furnished with plenty of leather & wood to create an organic feel. Facilities include a spa, business centre, internet access, lounge bar, library, large outdoor swimming pool area & a dive centre offering a large range of marine activities, from diving, snorkelling to kayaking & windsurfing. *US$628/1,160 sgl/dbl including all meals, most drinks, non-motorised watersports & sunset dhow cruise.*

Benguerra Lodge (13 rooms) +27 11 452 0641 (South Africa); reservations@benguerra.co.za; www.benguerra.co.za. This popular & highly rated owner-managed lodge is the oldest on the islands, founded in the early 1990s, & offers the choice of luxury

GAME FISHING AND DIVING FROM BENGUERRA

Bob de Lacy Smith

The Bazaruto area offers some of the most challenging game fishing in southern Africa. Large black and striped marlins are regularly taken between October and December. Prior to the civil war, specimens weighing in the region of 500kg were caught off the islands, and the recent record is more than 400kg. Sailfish can be caught throughout the year, with July and August being the best months for these fine fighters. The largest specimen so far is 55kg. Other game fish to be taken include tuna, all types of bonito, wahoo, king and queen mackerel, dorado, rainbow runner, prodigal son, giant barracuda and several species of kingfish including the mighty giant trevall (*Caranx ignoblis*).

Saltwater fly-fishing has also taken off in the area and regular clinics are held where experts pass on their knowledge to novices. The sport has a growing following and conditions on the islands are ideal. The much sought-after bonefish occurs in the area, and specimens of up to 8.2kg have been caught by local fishermen.

beachfront cabanas with queen-size bed, roof fan, private deck with jacuzzi/plunge pool or larger & more luxurious casitas. *US$800–1,200 dbl FB, depending on season & type of accommodation.*

Azura at Gabriel's (15 rooms) +27 76 705 0599 (South Africa); e reservations@azura-retreats.com; www.azura-retreats.com. Built on the site of what used to be the islands' only backpacker-friendly venue, this is now the most upmarket venue in the region, offering a choice of very spacious beachfront villas, all of which come with a king-size bed with walk-in netting, private plunge pool, AC, roof fans, indoor & outdoor bathroom, mini-bar & a large partly shaded deck. *US$1,100–1,980 dbl, depending on season & type of accommodation, including all meals, most drinks & some activities.*

Bazaruto Island The two lodges on this island are both larger, more conventionally resort-like, and more impersonal that their counterparts on Benguerra, but Indigo Bay in particular operates to a similar standard of service and facilities. The Pestana Bazaruto Lodge is a step down, as these things go, but still very luxurious and far more affordable than the archipelago's other resorts, especially if you take advantage of the seasonal website-only specials.

Indigo Bay Resort (44 units) 213 01618; e enquiries@raniresorts.com; www.indigobayresort.com. Run by the ever reliable Rani Resorts, this sprawling lodge lies in well-wooded grounds leading down to beautiful swimming beach. Its chalets are attractive & well equipped, with pastel-shaded contemporary decor, queen-size beds (walk-in net), AC, flat-screen DSTV, private balcony overlooking the sea, & a large en-suite bathroom with tub & shower. The restaurant is very good, the dive centre arranges all the usual marine activities, & there's an exquisite hilltop spa offering great views over the beach. *From US$465 pp including meals & non-motorised watersports.*

Pestana Bazaruto Lodge (40 rooms) 213 05000; e reservas.africa@pestana.com; www.pestana.com. Set at the northern end, this relatively affordable resort offers accommodation in en-suite A-frame thatched bungalows set amid tropical gardens with an ocean view. All rooms have queen-size or twin beds with walk-in nets, DSTV, AC, fan, safe, bathtub & private outdoor shower. *From US$450 dbl FB, though much cheaper special offers are often offered on website bookings.*

WHAT TO SEE AND DO All lodges on the islands can arrange excursions to the sites described below, and most are also routinely visited on day trips from the mainland.

Diving and snorkelling There are numerous dive sites dotted around the islands, but the undisputed champion is Two Mile Reef, a barrier reef that lies on the outer side of the archipelago between the islands of Bazaruto and Benguerra. Tides permitting, the best snorkelling spot is The Aquarium, a calm coral garden that lies on the inner reef and supports a dazzling selection of hard and soft corals, as well as reef fish of all shapes and colours, from tiny coral fish to the mighty potato bass and brindle bass. It is also a good spot to see reef sharks and marine turtles, though neither is guaranteed, while lucky divers might see manta rays and whale sharks. There are a host of dive sites on the seaward side of the same reef, with evocative names such as The Arches, Shark Point, Surgeon Rock, The Cathedral and The Gap. Any dive centre can advise on the site most suitable to your interests and current conditions, but if you are setting up a trip from Vilankulo, it is emphatically worth paying the extra to visit Two Mile Reef as opposed to taking the cheaper excursion of Magaruque, which has no proper reefs and thus offers vastly inferior diving and snorkelling.

Pansy Island Not so much an island as a tidal sandbar situated a short distance south of Bazaruto Island, this popular landmark can easily be visited as an extension of a trip to Two Mile Reef. It is named for the so-called pansy shells (also known as sea biscuits or sand dollars) that are abundant in its intertidal shallows. This pretty shell-like object, with a distinctive five-petalled floral pattern on its it flattened face, is not a shell at all, but the endoskeleton of a burrowing sea urchin of the order Clypeasteroida. The living creature is usually black or purple in colour, and covered in bristles, but after it dies the endoskeleton is bleached white by the sun and saline water. The five petals are formed by a series of perforated pores through which the podia project from the body, and reflect the fivefold radial symmetry associated with all sea urchins. There are also 2cm slits above the floral pattern, the relicts of two grooves used for feeding. Any experienced guide will be able to find you examples of the pansy shell here, as well – with luck – of the living urchin.

Bazaruto Island A striking feature of the archipelago's largest island is the immense dunes that rise from its southern shore, and these too can easily be visited in conjunction with Two Mile Reef and Pansy Island. Reputedly the highest point on the islands, rising around 100m above the surrounding water, the steep dunes can be climbed, albeit in something of a two-steps forward, one-step back mode, and with some serious sandblasting in windy weather. Once at the top, the view in all directions is utterly exhilarating, with the open ocean and other islands stretching away to the south, and a landscape of lakes and dunes running to the north. If you are staying at one of the lodges on Bazaruto, island tours can be arranged to visit some of the lakes and other dune fields, some of which are spectacular, and to meet local communities.

Benguerra Island Like its larger and more northerly neighbour, Benguerra supports and attractive and varied landscape of marshes, lakes and tall climbable dunes, well worth exploring on a guided drive if you are staying at one of the lodges. Wildlife includes plentiful monkeys, small antelope such as red duiker and suni, some impressive crocodiles on the lakes, and a superb mix of birds, with brown-headed parrot, African hoopoe, green pigeon, crowned hornbill and various bee-eaters conspicuous, while flamingos and other waterbirds frequent the lakes. Community visits can also be arranged.

Untouched, unspoilt
and unbelievably beautiful
raniresorts.com
Take the time to discover Rani Resorts
in Mozambique and Victoria Falls.
+ 27 11 658 0633 • info@raniresorts.com
www.raniresorts.com

Shipwreck on Beira beach
(AVZ)

left **Traditional silversmith, Ibo Island** (AVZ)

below **Fortaleza de São João Baptista, Ibo Island** (AVZ) page 332

above Capela da Nossa Senhora do Baluarte inside the Fortaleza de São Sebastião compound, Ilha de Moçambique (AVZ) page 293

below 17th-century Ilha-Fortim de São Lourenço (AVZ) page 298

above **Elephant bathing in Gorongosa National Park** (AVZ) page 227

below **Young male lion, Gorongosa National Park** (AVZ) page 227

above **Nyala in the scrub, Gorongosa National Park**
(AVZ) page 28

right **Red-necked spurfowl, Gorongosa National Park**
(AVZ)

below **Morumbodzi Falls on Mount Gorongosa**
(AVZ) page 232

above Mozambique is one of the best places in the world to swim with manta rays (WF) page 36

left Despite their daunting size whale sharks are harmless filter feeders (WF) page 165

below Humpback whale sightings are virtually guaranteed between September and mid November (FN/MP/FLPA) page 34

Potato grouper guarding its territory (WF)

Part Three

CENTRAL MOZAMBIQUE

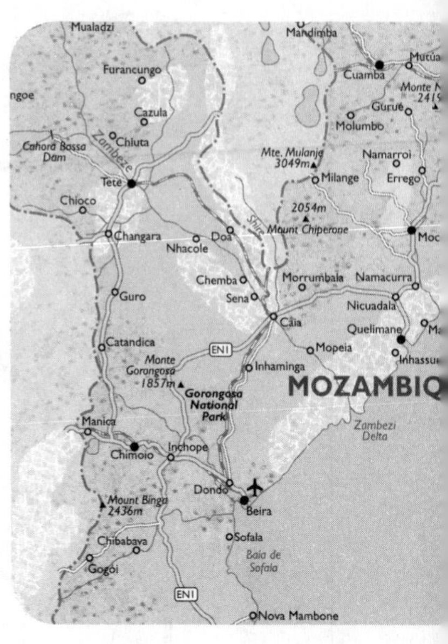

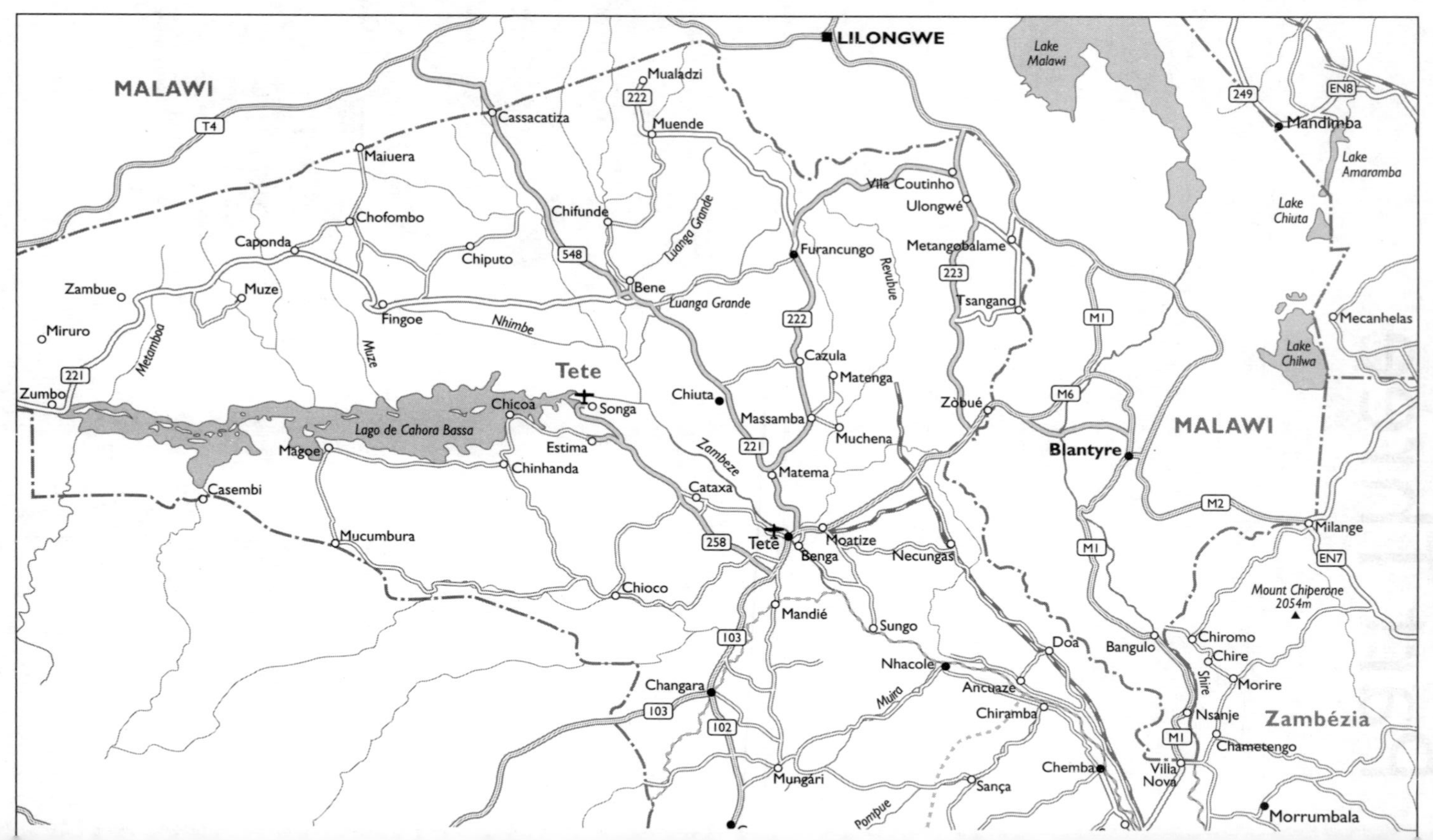

MALAWI
LILONGWE
Lake Malawi
Lake Amaramba
Lake Chiuta
Lake Chilwa
Mandimba
Mecanhelas
Milange
Mount Chiperone 2054m
Zambézia
Morrumbala
Chiromo
Chire
Morire
Shire
Nsanje
Chametengo
Villa Nova
Bangulo
Blantyre
Doa
Chemba
Chiramba
Ancuaze
Nhacole
Sança
Sungo
Necungas
Zóbuè
Tsangano
Metangobalame
Ulongwé
Vila Coutinho
Revubue
Furancungo
Matenga
Cazula
Muchena
Massamba
Matema
Moatize
Benga
Tete
Mandié
Mungári
Changara
Zambeze
Chiuta
Cataxa
Chioco
Songa
Estima
Chinhanda
Chicoa
Lago de Cahora Bassa
Mucumbura
Magoe
Casembi
Mualadzi
Muende
Luanga Grande
Bene
Chifunde
Cassacatiza
Chiputo
Nhimbe
Fingoe
Muze
Maiuera
Chofombo
Caponda
Metamboa
Zambue
Miruro
Zumbo
Muira
Pompue
EN8
249
EN7
M2
M1
M6
223
222
221
548
258
103
102
T4

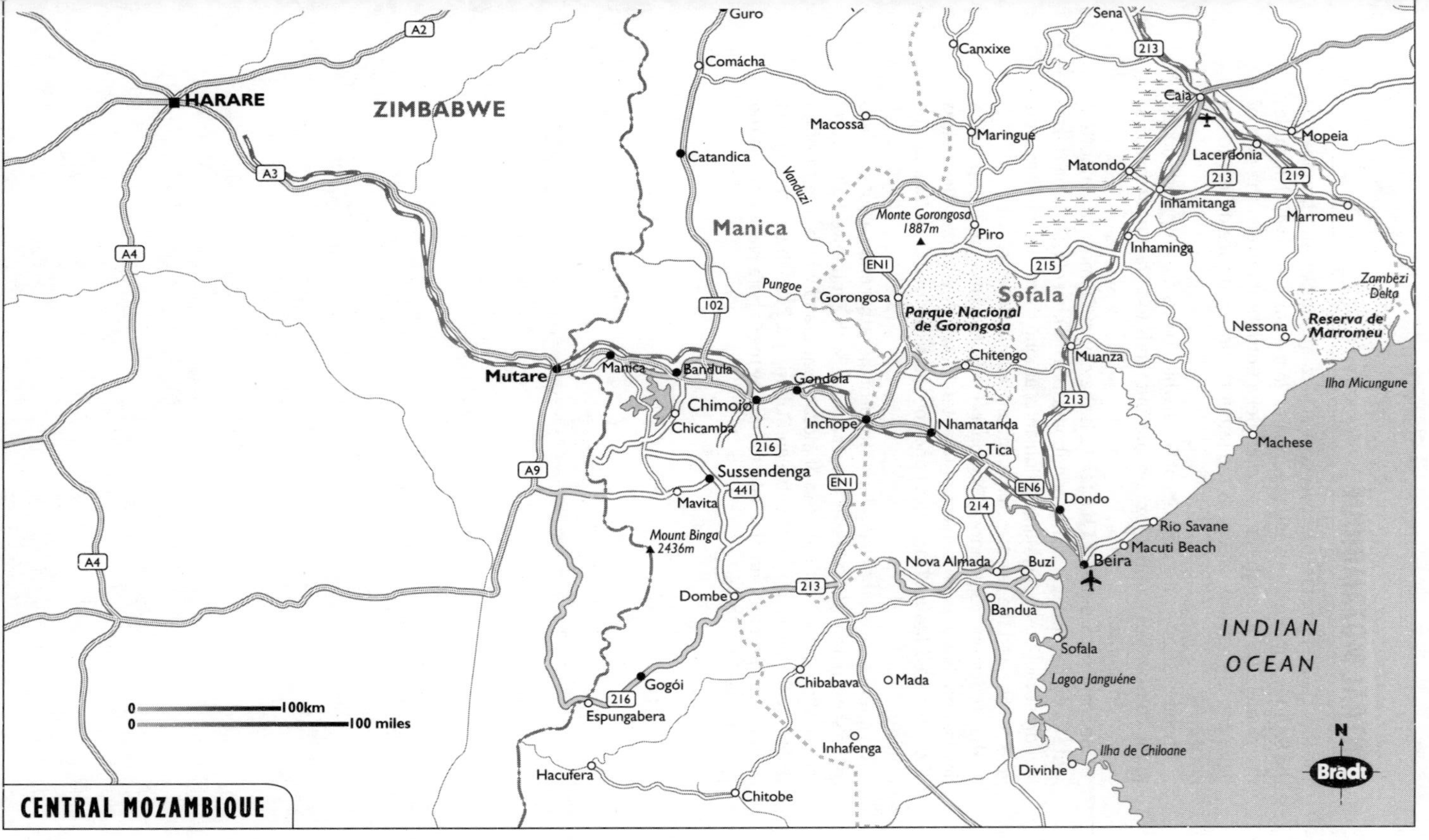

CENTRAL MOZAMBIQUE
ZIMBABWE
HARARE
Mutare
INDIAN
OCEAN
Manica
Sofala
Parque Nacional de Gorongosa
Reserva de Marromeu
Zambezi Delta
Ilha Micungune
Ilha de Chiloane
Lagoa Janguéne
Monte Gorongosa 1887m
Mount Binga 2436m
Pungoe
Vanduzi
Guro
Comácha
Catandica
Macossa
Canxixe
Maringue
Sena
Caia
Mopeia
Lacerdonia
Matondo
Inhamitanga
Marromeu
Inhaminga
Piro
Gorongosa
Nessona
Chitengo
Muanza
Manica
Bandula
Gondola
Chimoio
Chicamba
Inchope
Nhamatanda
Tica
Machese
Sussendenga
Mavita
Dondo
Rio Savane
Macuti Beach
Beira
Nova Almada
Buzi
Bandua
Dombe
Sofala
Chibabava
Mada
Gogói
Espungabera
Inhafenga
Hacufera
Chitobe
Divinhe
A2
A3
A4
A9
102
213
215
219
216
441
214
EN1
EN6
0
100km
100 miles
N
Bradt

CENTRAL MOZAMBIQUE

The four chapters that follow cover central Mozambique, an area bounded by the Save River in the south and the Zambezi in the north, and which includes the pivotal EN6 through the so-called Beira Corridor (between the port of Beira and Zimbabwe), as well as the rather disjunct province of Tete to the northwest.

Chapter 11 covers the port city of Beira, which offers the only ready access to the coast in this part of Mozambique, but tends to attract more business travel than tourism.

The main focal point of Chapter 12 is the city of Chimoio, an important route focus that also acts as the springboard for a number of worthwhile hiker-friendly attractions in the Manica Highlands, among them the Chinhamapere Rock Art Site and the remote Chimanimani National Reserve,

The renascent Gorongosa National Park, Mozambique's top safari destination, is the main subject of Chapter 13, which also provides details of the forested Mount Gorongosa and the main road north to Caia on the Zambezi River.

Chapter 14 covers the city of Tete, capital of the rather anomalous province of the same name, which shares longer borders with Zimbabwe, Zambia and Malawi than it does with the rest of Mozambique, and which is most often visited by travellers in transit between Malawi and Zimbabwe. The region's main attraction is the immense lake formed by the Cahora Bassa Dam on the Zambezi upriver of Tete.

11

Beira

Mozambique's busiest port and third-largest city, Beira enjoys a mixed reputation among travellers. In the immediate post-war era, it was notorious as a crime hotspot, but that no longer seems to be a problem today. Even so, the city boasts no compelling tourist attractions, and not a great deal more in the way of traveller-oriented accommodation. Furthermore, it is something of a cul-de-sac, lying at the eastern terminus of the EN6, 135 potholed kilometres from the pivotal junction with the EN1, so there is unlikely to be a strong logistical reason for including Beira in your travel plans. Chimoio, 200km inland, is a more convenient travel pivot for crossing between almost anywhere south and north of the EN6.

Then again, approached in a spirit of 'because it's there', Beira can be a very enjoyable place to explore. The main business centre, laid out with an attention to detail rare in African cities, has plenty of architectural character, particularly in the vicinity of the two main squares. The old residential area to the southwest is also oddly appealing, lined with block after block of Portuguese villas in varying states of repair and disrepair. The area around the bus terminus and the docks is seedier, but has a definite sense of bustle and energetic commerce. And the long miles of seafront, though not exactly comparable to the likes of Tofo or Vilankulo, do much to enhance the city's rather agreeable atmosphere. So, yes, Beira lacks the overt charms of the popular resort towns to its south, but therein lies its potential interest – after a couple of weeks of beach-oriented travel, spending a day or two in this totally non-touristic port city can be a gratifyingly real and rewarding experience.

HISTORY

Sofala, a short distance south of Beira, was the medieval gateway to the south-central African interior, and an active trade centre from 900AD to the 19th century (see box on page 208). By comparison, Beira itself is a modern entity, founded in 1884 on the sandy, marshy shore near the mouth of the Pungue River, as a base of operations for the rich *prazero* Joaquim Carlos Paiva de Andrada. In the late 1880s, the British imperialist and founder of Rhodesia, Cecil John Rhodes, attempted to annex the Beira area, but his attempts at warmongering garnered no support from the British government and in 1891 the area was formally incorporated into Mozambique. The town centre was laid out in 1887, and at the same time a permanent garrison was installed. Beira was granted city status in 1894. Serious development of the port started in 1891, when it was leased to Andrada's Mozambique Company, and it accelerated after 1898 following the completion of Rhodes's railway line to Rhodesia.

In its early days, Beira was a scruffy shanty town with a reputation as the most drunken, lawless settlement in Africa. At the start of the 20th century, the city boasted some 80 bars serving a population of only 4,000, roughly a quarter of which consisted of Europeans, mostly of Portuguese or British origin. The town did not have the most amenable of settings: the company that built the railway line to Rhodesia lost 60% of its European staff to malaria in two years, and the surrounding area was so untamed that lions were frequently seen walking through the main street. The sand on which the town was built was so deep that 40km of trolley lines had to be laid to allow residents to transport goods to their homes. The trolley lines later served as public transport, before they were torn up in 1930.

Beira's rapid expansion was curbed after rail links were completed between Rhodesia and South Africa in 1903. Nevertheless, the figures produced by the 1928 census show that by this time Beira was well established as the country's second city, with a population of almost 23,694 – more than half that of Lourenço Marques, and well over double that of the next-largest town in Mozambique. By 1970, the city had a population of 114,000, and it was entrenched as a popular holiday destination for residents of landlocked Rhodesia. Beira remained the country's second-largest city in 1997, according to a census taken that year, but it was overtaken sometime before the 2007 census by faster-growing Nampula, and its 2010 population is estimated at 450,000.

GETTING THERE AND AWAY

BY AIR Beira's airport [199 B1] is about 10km from the centre of town, and there are daily LAM flights to Maputo. The LAM office [204–5 E5] (*23 324 142*) is on Rua Major Serpa Pinto.

BY CAR Beira is the eastern terminus of the EN6, situated 135km from Inchope (the junction with the EN1), 200km from Chimoio, and almost 300km from the Machipanda border with Zimbabwe. The EN6 is surfaced in its entirety but the part between Inchope and Beira has some heavily potholed stretches, and also carries heavy truck and and chapa traffic, which makes for a relatively stressful drive. If you are driving yourself, take it easy, and bank on two hours to/from Inchope. Further afield, bank on a total driving time of three hours from Beira to Chimoio, four hours to Machipanda, at least three hours to to Gorongosa National Park, and around six to seven hours to Vilankulo or seven to eight hours to Quelimane.

BY BUS AND CHAPA Of the public transport options, most chapas and buses start or end their journey on Avenida Daniel Napatima [204–5 E4], although it's just possible that you'll be dropped at the roundabout Praça 11 de Outubro [204–5 F1], which lies on the junction of Avenida Samora Machel and Avenida Armando Tivane (near the Shoprite Supermarket). Sticking with relatively local destinations, there are plenty of chapas along the EN6 between Beira and Inchope (US$3), Chimoio (US$4.50) and Manica (US$6). In either case you're not far from the Central Business District (CBD), and the two best hotels in this part of the city stand at the western end of Avenida Daniel Napatima. Crime is no longer the issue it was a few years back, but it is still wise to be on guard should you arrive at the chapa terminus late in the afternoon or evening.

Chapas also cover longer-haul routes, but most people prefer to use the more comfortable air-conditioned **TCO/Oliveira** coach service to/from Maputo and Nampula, which leaves from a special terminal on Rua dos Irmãos Roby (m *82 775 0554 or 84 601 6861*). The TCO coach to Maputo leaves at 04.00 in either direction daily except Sunday and takes about 16 hours, with stops at Vilankulo, Maxixe (for

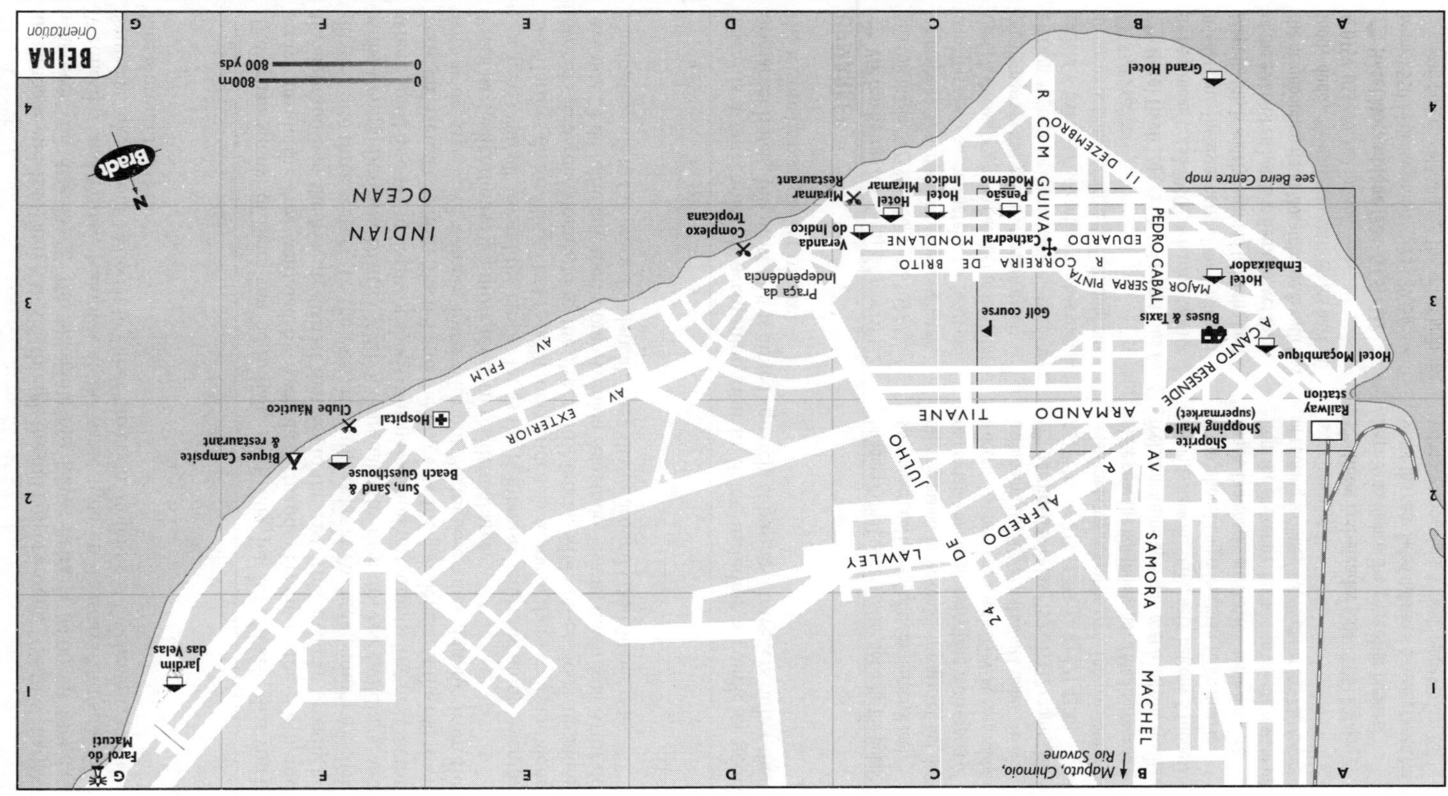
BEIRA
Orientation
INDIAN
OCEAN
0 800m
0 800 yds
Maputo, Chimoio, Rio Savane
Farol do Macuti
Jardim das Velas
Biques Campsite & restaurant
Clube Náutico
Sun, Sand & Beach Guesthouse
Hospital
Complexo Tropicana
Praça da Independência
Veranda do Indico
Miramar Restaurant
Hotel Miramar
Hotel Indico
Pensão Moderno
Cathedral
Golf course
Buses & Taxis
Hotel Embaixador
Hotel Moçambique
Railway station
Shoprite Shopping Mall (supermarket)
Grand Hotel
see Beira Centre map
AV SAMORA MACHEL
AV 24 DE JULHO
R ALFREDO DE LAWLEY
AV ARMANDO TIVANE
AV EXTERIOR
AV FPLM
R CORREIRA DE BRITO
EDUARDO MONDLANE
MAJOR SERPA PINTA
PEDRO CABAL
GUIVA
R COM 11 DEZEMBRO
A CANTO RESENDE

Inhambane and Tofo) and Xai-Xai, though the full fare of around US$40 is charged wherever you disembark. The Nampula bus leaves Beira at 04.00 on Monday, Wednesday and Friday, Nampula at the same time on Tuesday, Thursday and Saturday, takes about 14 hours in either direction, stopping at Quelimane, and the fare is around US$45.

ORIENTATION AND GETTING AROUND

The urban sprawl of Beira can be initially confusing, but it's unlikely that you'll stray outside the area bounded by Avenida Armando Tivane to the north and the lighthouse in the Macuti district that lies to the east. This area can broadly be divided into three sectors. To the west, running as far as Avenida Samora Machel, is the Central Business District (CBD), dominated by medium-rise buildings, and where you'll find the majority of shops, businesses and restaurants. The next sector, between Avenida Samora Machel and the Praça da Independência, is the old town with wide, tree-lined avenues lined with old Portuguese villas. Finally, from the Praça to the lighthouse is a more modern residential area.

Chapas run all around the city as far as the lighthouse, returning along Avenida dos Mártires da Revolução to Praça da Independência. Some of them continue along Avenida Eduardo Mondlane to the Praça do Metical, while others loop up along Avenida 24 de Julho and then along Avenida Armando Tivane, down Rua Artur do Canto Resende to the Praça do Metical. They charge around US$0.30 per ride.

WHERE TO STAY

There is a fair choice of accommodation in Beira, including a couple of good upmarket hotels, but most of it is aimed squarely at business travellers rather than the leisure or backpacker market.

UPMARKET

VIP Inn Beira [204–5 A3] (54 rooms) 172 Rua Luis Inácio; 233 40100; m 82 305 473; e hotelbeira@viphotels.com; www.viphotels.com. This newly opened hotel in the heart of the CBD throws down the gauntlet to its stuffier counterparts below, with its modern decor, efficient atmosphere, comfortable en-suite rooms with AC & DSTV, & 21st-century touches such as an online booking service & Wi-Fi throughout. *US$81/93 sgl/dbl.*

Hotel Tivoli [204–5 C3] (74 rooms) 363 Av de Bagamoio; 233 20300; e h.tivoli-beira@teledata.mz. The sister hotel of the Tivoli in Maputo, this is widely regarded to be the best of the established hotels in Beira, newer than the neighbouring Hotel Moçambique & with less fuddy-duddy décor. The en-suite rooms have AC & DTSV. *US$110/142 sgl/dbl.*

Hotel Moçambique [204–5 C3] (132 rooms) 550 Av de Bagamoio; 233 29354; e mozambhotel@teledata.mz. This smart high-rise building in the business sector opposite the public swimming pool has a slightly institutional feel, catering mainly to the conference market, but the comfortable rooms are everything you'd expect of a decent business hotel, with DSTV, AC & en-suite bathrooms. *US$60/78/100 sgl/dbl/suite.*

Jardim das Velas [199 G1] (12 rooms) 282 Av FPLM; /f 233 12209; m 82 421 4300; e jardimdasvelas@yahoo.com. This pleasant place near the lighthouse has a Mediterranean feel, comprising apts split over 6 dbl-storey villas. All units have AC, DSTV, nets, balcony & fridges, & the whole thing is less than 100m from the beach. Drawbacks are that it is some distance from the city centre, but has no on-site restaurant or cooking facilities. *US$95 dbl or US$110 family room (sleeping 4).*

Hotel Embaixador [204–5 D5] R Major Serpa Pinto. Right in the centre of the business sector, this once-faded stalwart is currently closed for extensive renovations, & should reopen in late 2011.

MID-RANGE

Beira Guesthouse [204–5 H7] (6 rooms) 1311 Av Eduardo Mondlane; 233 24030; m 82 315 0460. This low-key gem really is a very pleasant place to stay, with an ambience all its upmarket competitors lack. It lies in the lovely old residential area verging the CBD, & though newly constructed, is very similar in design to the surrounding old villas. The rooms are tiled & come with AC, net, writing desk DSTV & a large en-suite bathroom with tub & shower. Facilities include an internet area, Wi-Fi access throughout the building, & a swimming pool in the back garden. Highly recommended. *US$66 dbl B&B.*

Aulio's Residencial [204–5 H7] (9 rooms) R Mouzinho de Alburquerque; 233 27549; m 82 269 1829; e reservas@auliosresidencial.com; www.auliosresidencial.com. This beautifully restored old house near the cathedral has safe parking, free internet & clean stylish rooms with tiled floor, twin beds, net, DTSV, fridge & large en-suite bathroom with combination tub/shower. Good value at *US$52/57 sgl/dbl, or US$70 for suite with balcony & AC.*

Pensão Residencial Beirasol [204–5 C3] (6 rooms) 168 Rua da Madeira; 233 27202. This restored colonial villa opposite the Tivoli has a useful central location & plenty of character. The rooms are on the small side, but very comfortable, and come with DSTV, AC, Wi-Fi & fridge. The ground-floor restaurant, temporarily closed when the research for this edition was undertaken, has been warmly recommended. *US$70 dbl.*

Sun, Sand & Beach Guesthouse [199 F2] (6 rooms) 2196 Av FPLM; m 84 519 0243 or 82 848 6880; e admin@ssbguest.com; www.ssbguest.com. On the beachfront near Club Nautico, 2.5km east of Praça da Independência, this newish guesthouse has a great location and is a pretty good bet overall, assuming you can get over the bombastic colour scheme. The large clean rooms have DSTV, AC, fridge, dressing area & en-suite hot shower, & facilities include a small swimming pool & Wi-Fi. *US$70 dbl or US$118 suite.*

Hotel Indico [199 C3] (20 rooms) Rua Frei João; 233 29944; m 82 329 9444; e hotelindico@teledata.mz. Set a block back from the beach near the Hotel Miramar, this smart modern hotel has clean rooms with AC, DSTV & en-suite hot showers. Arguably a bit overpriced at *US$$43/73/85 sgl/twin/dbl.*

BUDGET

Pensão Moderno [204–5 G7] (42 rooms) R Mouzinho de Alburquerque; 233 24537. Our pick in this the range is this pleasant new guesthouse in the leafy suburbs a short walk south of the CBD. The rooms are very clean & comfortable, some are en-suite & some also come with a balcony. There is no restaurant, but the outdoor bar in the park opposite serves a selection of affordable meals. *US$21 twin; US$28 ensuite twin.*

Hotel Miramar [199 C3] (24 rooms) R Vilas Boas Truão; 233 22283; e travassos_gm@hotmail.com; miramar.no.sapo.pt. This has been a strong contender for Beira's best-value accommodation for some years, & it remains a great choice, albeit not all that central. The rooms are pleasant enough, & some have a view over the bay to the south. *US$11 sgl; US$17 dbl with AC; US$20 en-suite dbl.*

Hotel Infante Residencial [204–5 D6] (35 rooms) R Jaime Ferreira; 233 26603. Boasting a prime location in the heart of the CDB, a few paces from Praça de Municipalia, this sober multi-storey hotel has also been a reliable & reasonably affordable bet for some years. The comfortable & rather busily furnished en-suite rooms have parquet floor, TV, fan & in some cases AC. There's an adequate ground-floor bar & restaurant. Unusually in this range, Visa is accepted. *US$34 dbl; US$26/37 sgl/dbl with AC.*

Rio Savane [119 B1] 233 23555; m 82 385 7660. With its idyllic river-mouth location about 35km north of town, this is an excellent place to chill out for a few days enjoying the excellent restaurant, deserted beach & unspoilt bush, which supports a rich birdlife. It'a accessible in any saloon car: follow the EN6 towards Inchope until 300m before the main flyover to Beira Airport, then turn left onto a secondary road & follow for 34km to a safe guarded car park. From here, you cross to the resort by boat (the last leaves 17.00*). From US$23/31 sgl/dbl; US$10 pp camping.*

SHOESTRING

Hotel Savoy [204–5 F5] (9 rooms) 1299 R Pedro Alvares Cabral; m 82 546 4467. Unlikely to pose too many difficulties in a 'spot the difference' contest with its London namesake, this improbably timeworn hotel has what might diplomatically be called an excess of character, but it's a useful option for budget travellers taking early morning chapas, only 5mins' walk from Av Daniel Napatima. *US$12/15 sgl/dbl using common shower; US$26 en-suite dbl; US$30 en-suite dbl with AC; US$30/40/40 per unit for a 3/4/5 bed dorm.*

Pensão Sofala [204–5 E3] Off Rua de Bagamoio. The main virtue of this place is its proximity to the bus station on Av Daniel Napatima, but it is also pretty well priced, & looks habitable enough following a recent facelift. Rooms are spacious & en-suite, with parquet floor & fan. *US$20 dbl.*

Camping The only campsite in town is Biques, described below, but camping is also permitted at Rio Savane, 35km further north (see page 201).

Biques Campsite [199 F2] Av FPLM; 233 13051. The only campsite in the city is attached to this South African-style sports bar. It has a great beachfront location, but is a long way from the chapa terminal, so it isn't an option for early morning starts. *Camping US$2.50 pp.*

WHERE TO EAT AND DRINK

There is a great choice of eateries in Beira, with seafood inevitably being the main local speciality. There are also a couple of Chinese restaurants, which come as a welcome change if you've been in Mozambique a while. On the whole, eating out in Beira is cheaper than in more touristy parts of the coast. For nightlife, the most popular spots in the CDB include the Baixa Ba, Acuario Club and Imperial, while the larger Monte Verde Club lies along the road running north from Macuti towards the airport.

CBD

Restaurante Pique-Nique [204–5 A3] R Costa Serrão; 19.00–24.00 daily. Bizarrely tucked away on an unpleasant street near the docks, this Beira institution might have come out of a film noir set, with its unobtrusively attentive tuxedoed waiters & no-nonsense maître d'. The food is equally memorable, not straying hugely from the traditional seafood & *prego no prato*, but produced with a flair that's so often missing, & not as expensive as you might fear. To summarise: if you're in Beira a while & don't eat here, then you've missed a trick. *Most mains are in the US$5–10 range, though prawns are steeper.*

Restaurante Kanimambo [204–5 E5] R Pêro de Alenquer; 233 23132; m 82 888 8560; 10.00–15.00 & 18.00–22.00 daily except Sat. This long-serving Chinese restaurant contrives to look closed from the outside even when open, & the canteen ambience only furthers indifferent first impressions. That said, it's centrally located, the menu is refreshingly varied, vegetarians are well catered for, the food is very good, there's a helpful English-speaking owner-manager, & it would undoubtedly be our first culinary port of call in Beira. *Bank on around US$7 for a main with steamed rice.*

Muca's Place [204–5 C4] R Major Serpa Pinto; m 82 601 5803; 09.00–23.00 daily. The hippest night venue in the CBD is this idiosyncratic little bar tucked away at the rear left side of the Novaciné. The decor has the feel of 1950s bohemia transported to modern Africa, & there is usually live music at w/ends. More of a drinking hole than a restaurant proper. *But serves a decent selection of meals for around US$6 apiece.*

Café Riviera [204–5 C5] Praça do Município; 06.30–21.00. Overlooking the main square, this is a popular b/fast spot, & rightly so, but it would do for a snack, a boost of caffeine, or a bout of people-watching at any time of day. *Inexpensive croissants, pastries & fresh espresso are the prime attractions, but it also serves a good range of sandwiches & snacks for around US$1.50.*

Café des Artes [204–5 C4] R Major Serpa Pinto. This unsignposted café alongside the Novaciné Cinema is one of the most appealing in Beira, boasting funky décor, music videos projected onto a screen, good espresso & pastries, a limited range of other food, & a full bar.

Restaurante Chin Wan [204–5 D5] R Pêro de Alenquer; 09.00–20.00 Mon–Sat. Despite the name, this new place opposite the Kanimambo doesn't serve Chinese dishes but a combination of pizzas, Mozambican grills & lighter snacks. There's comfortable outdoor seating. *Most mains clock in at around US$6.*

Restaurante Mozambique [204–5 A4] Largo Luis de Camões; 12.00–late daily. The former Cabine do Capitão looks a little timeworn on the inside, but the shady veranda is a great spot for a relaxed drink & it retains a good reputation for seafood. *Prawns, the speciality, cost US$6–8, while other mains are in the US$4–5 range.*

Sunlight Food Court [204–5 C4] R Daniel Napatima. Keeping long hours & conveniently situated on the same road that effectively serves as the long-haul chapa station, this self-service set-up in the middle of a traffic circle sells a varied selection of Mozambican grills, Chinese noodle & rice dishes & fast foods. It's very cheap, with plenty of seating, & beer is served too.

Restaurante dos CFMC [204–5 B1] Tucked away underneath the railway station (head down the steps to the right), the place is clearly popular with locals, possibly due to the cheap buffet & pool tables on offer.

SEAFRONT

Complexo Tropicana [199 D3] R Brito Capelo; 12.00–late daily. Overlooking the beach about 300m east of Praça da Independência, this complex is centred around a large swimming pool & it has a shaded deck positioned perfectly to hear the waves crash & catch a sea breeze over dinner. *Tasty seafood dishes are in the US$7–11 range while pizzas & other mains cost US$46.*

Biques [199 F2] Av FPLM; 233 13051; 10.00–22.00 daily. This perennially popular sports bar 3.3km west of Praça da Independência has a very South Africa feel, with its pub-like decor, thatched roof & large-screen TV, & it serves good steaks as well as seafood. Most mains are in the US5–9 range.

Miramar Bar & Restaurant [199 C4] Av Mateus Sansão Muthemba; 233 22283; e travassos_gm@hotmail.com; www.miramar.no.sapo.pt; 10.00–late daily. Situated a short walk west of Praça da Independência, this beachfront spot with outdoor & indoor eating is a good place for a sundowner & serves decent meals. There is occasional live music, usually at weekends, & a large screen for major sporting events. *US$4–8.*

Clube Náutico [199 F2] Av FPLM. This venerable beachfront complex 2.5km west of Praça da Independência has a well-maintained swimming pool & a bar-restaurant serving decent *seafood & other mains in the US$6–8 range.*

OTHER PRACTICALITIES

BANKING AND FOREIGN EXCHANGE The usual banks are all represented, including Barclays, Standard, BCI and BIM Millennium. Most have branches with 24-hour ATMs dotted within a block of Praça do Município and Praça Metical. There is also an ATM at the Shoprite Centre on Avenida Samora Machel. Forex bureaux include Safari Bureau des Change [204–5 C3] on Rua da Madeira and Multi Combo [204–5 C2] off Avenida Armando Tivane.

CINEMA The Novaciné [204–5 C4] on Rua Major Serpa Pinto shows Hollywood films and sells popcorn.

GOLF Unbelievably a golf course [204–5 H4] has been built on one of the swamps in the middle of the city. To go around it will cost you US$3.20 and they have kit for hire for US$3.70 if for some peculiar reason you neglected to include your clubs in your 20kg of luggage (m *82 702 5330*).

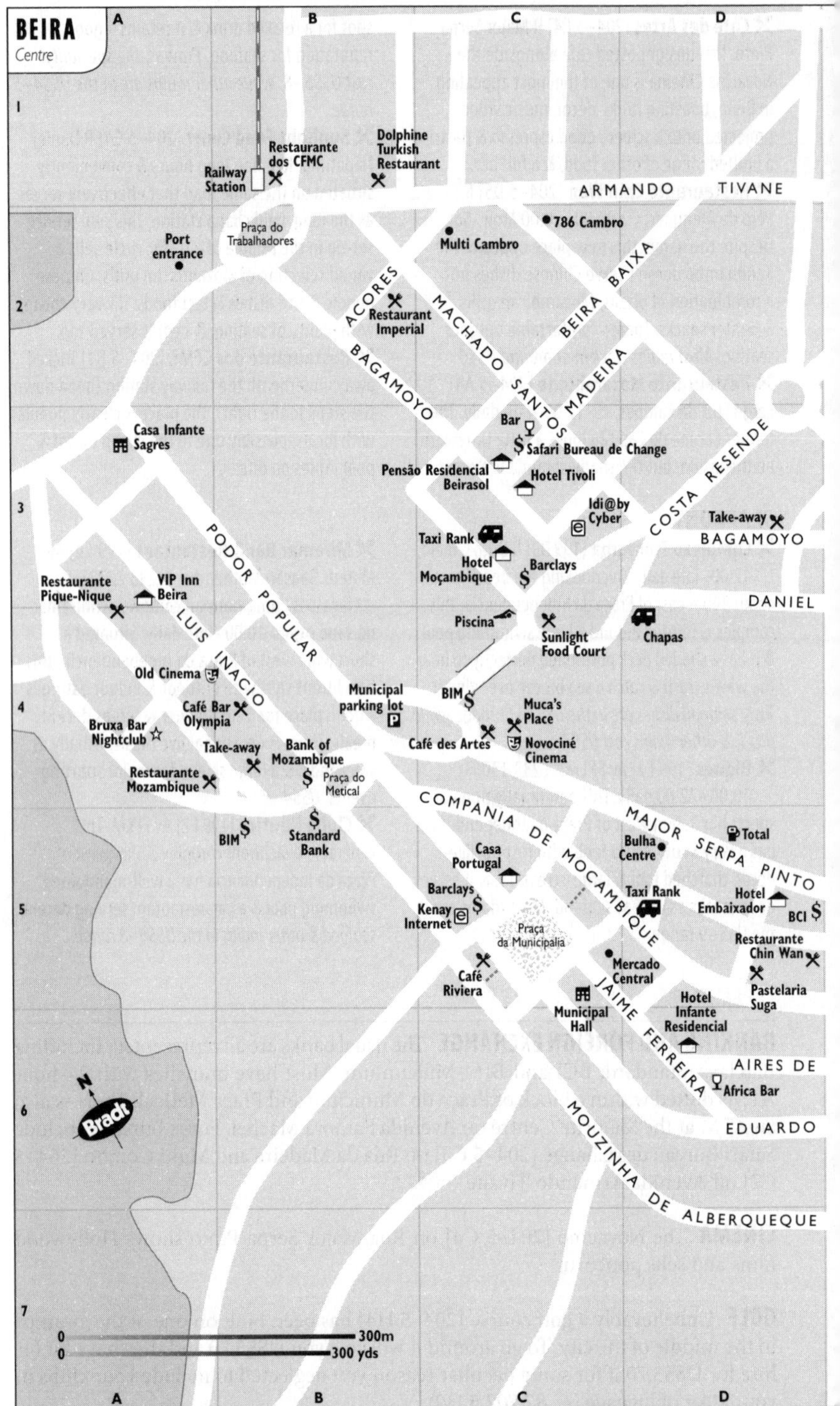
BEIRA
Centre
Railway Station
Restaurante dos CFMC
Dolphine Turkish Restaurant
ARMANDO TIVANE
Praça do Trabalhadores
Port entrance
Multi Cambro
786 Cambro
ACORES
Restaurant Imperial
MACHADO SANTOS
BEIRA BAIXA
MADEIRA
BAGAMOYO
Casa Infante Sagres
Bar
Safari Bureau de Change
Pensão Residencial Beirasol
Hotel Tivoli
Idi@by Cyber
COSTA RESENDE
Take-away
BAGAMOYO
Taxi Rank
Hotel Moçambique
Barclays
PODOR POPULAR
Restaurante Pique-Nique
VIP Inn Beira
LUIS INACIO
DANIEL
Piscina
Sunlight Food Court
Chapas
Old Cinema
Municipal parking lot
BIM
Café Bar Olympia
Bruxa Bar Nightclub
Muca's Place
Café des Artes
Novociné Cinema
Take-away
Bank of Mozambique
Restaurante Mozambique
Praça do Metical
COMPANIA DE MOCAMBIQUE
MAJOR SERPA PINTO
BIM
Standard Bank
Total
Bulha Centre
Casa Portugal
Barclays
Kenay Internet
Taxi Rank
Hotel Embaixador
BCI
Praça da Municipalia
Restaurante Chin Wan
Café Riviera
Mercado Central
Pastelaria Suga
Municipal Hall
JAIME FERREIRA
Hotel Infante Residencial
AIRES DE
Africa Bar
EDUARDO
MOUZINHA DE ALBERQUEQUE
Bradt
0
300m
0
300 yds
A B C D
1 2 3 4 5 6 7

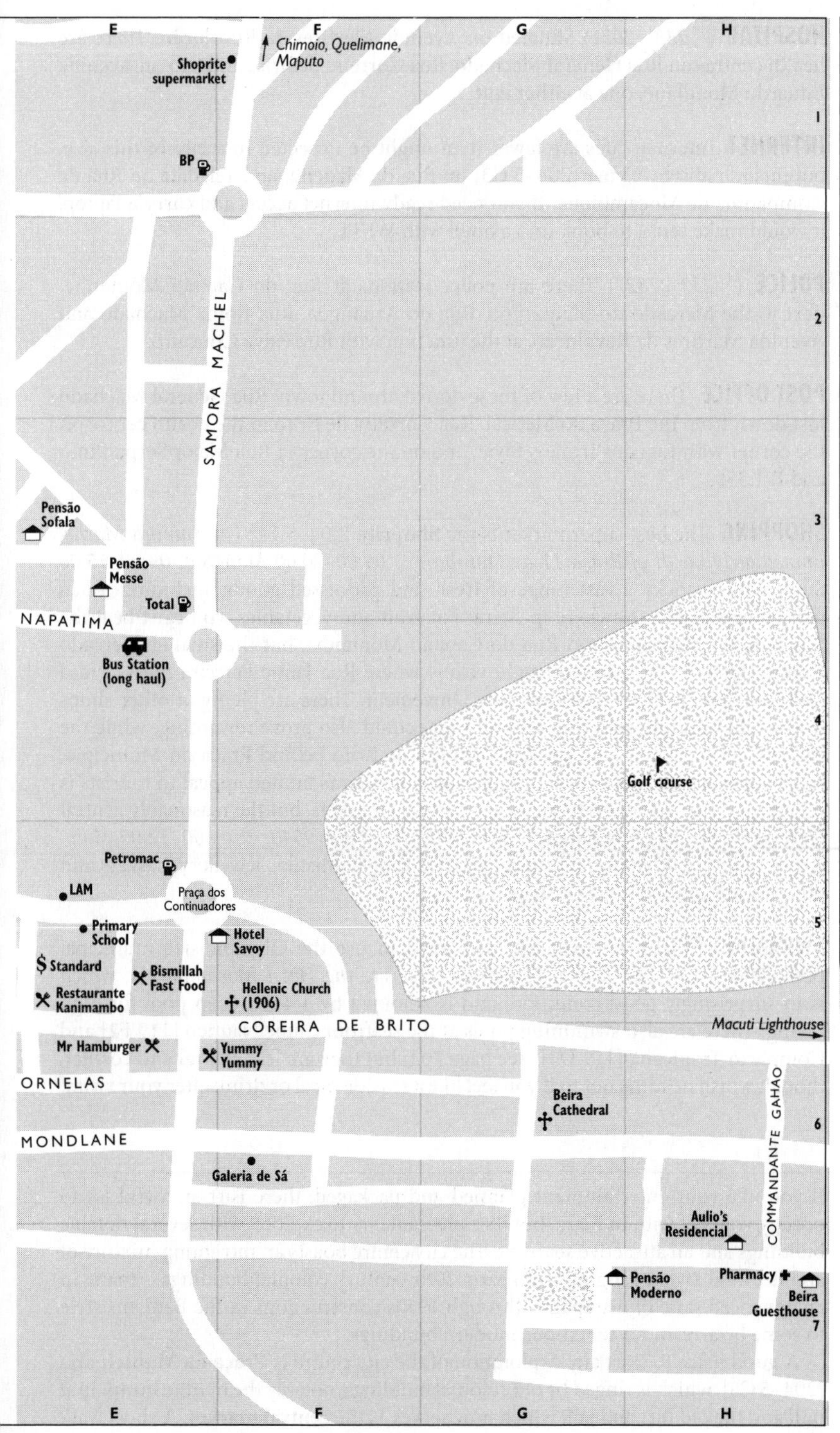

E
F
G
H
Chimoio, Quelimane, Maputo
Shoprite supermarket
BP
1
2
SAMORA MACHEL
3
Pensão Sofala
Pensão Messe
Total
NAPATIMA
Bus Station (long haul)
4
Golf course
Petromac
LAM
Praça dos Continuadores
5
Primary School
Hotel Savoy
Standard
Bismillah Fast Food
Hellenic Church (1906)
Restaurante Kanimambo
COREIRA DE BRITO
Macuti Lighthouse
Mr Hamburger
Yummy Yummy
ORNELAS
Beira Cathedral
COMMANDANTE GAHAO
6
MONDLANE
Galeria de Sá
Aulio's Residencial
Pensão Moderno
Pharmacy
Beira Guesthouse
7

HOSPITAL (*233 12071*) Situated on Avenida Mártires da Revolução. There are health centres on Rua General Machado, Rua Correira de Brito and two on Avenida Eduardo Mondlane, one at either end.

INTERNET Internet cafés are fewer than might be expected in a city of this size, but include Idi@by Cyber [204–5 C3] on Rua da Madeira, and Teledata on Rua da Companhia de Moçambique. If you need ready internet access and carry a laptop, it would make sense to book into a hotel with Wi-Fi.

POLICE (*233 27827*) There are police stations at Rua do Capitão Montanha, next to the Mercado do Maquinino, Rua do Aruângua, Rua Roma Machado and Avenida Mártires da Revolução, at the junction with Rua Paiva Couceiro.

POST OFFICE There are a few of these dotted around town: Rua General Machado just down from the Praça do Metical, Rua Correira de Brito in the health centre on the corner with Rua dos Irmãos Bivar, and on the corner of Rua Major Serpa Pinto and R 1.350.

SHOPPING The best supermarket is the **Shoprite** [204–5 F1] (*Av Samora Machel immediately north of Praça 11 de Outubro; 09.00–20.00 Mon–Sat, 09.00–15.00 Sun*), which stocks a vast range of fresh and processed goods, including much that is unavailable elsewhere in Beira. For fruit and vegetables, you can't beat the Mercado do Maquinino on Rua do Capitão Montanha, but the smaller Mercado Central [204–5 C5], painted bright yellow where Rua Jaime Ferreira meets Praça do Município, is likely to prove more convenient. There are plenty of other shops in the CBD, and meandering around them could also prove rewarding, while the Bulha Centre [204–5 D5], on Rua Correira de Brito behind Praça do Município, has a supermarket, pastelaria and internet café. Beira's limited appeal to tourists is reflected in the lack of craft and other touristic markets, but the reasonably central **Galeria de Sá** (*1839 Av Eduardo Mondlane; m 82 509 9540; 09.00–12.00 Mon–Sat & 14.00–18.00 Mon–Fri*) stocks a varied range of batiks, jewellery, baskets and other locally crafted knick-knacks.

SWIMMING POOLS A small fee is charged to use the Olympic-size municipal pool [204–5 C4] (*Av Daniel Napatima, opposite the Hotel Moçambique*), which is in surprisingly good condition, and is adjoined by a 4.5m-deep pool for high diving. There are also swimming pools at the seafront Clube Nautico [119 F2] and Complexo Tropicana [119 D3] (see page 203) but they are less central and costlier, though worth heading out to if you feel like a seaside meal or drink after your swim.

WHAT TO SEE AND DO

If you like your entertainment planned and packaged, there isn't an awful lot to occupy yourself with in Beira, but it's a pleasant city to explore, with several notable buildings and an attractive seafront. The city centre boasts an intriguing mixture of architectural styles, ranging from early 20th-century colonial buildings – many in an advanced state of disrepair – through 1950s constructions in the Bauhaus style to some bizarre and ostentatious modern buildings.

A good place to start any exploration of the city centre is **Praça da Municipalia** [204–5 C5], which is ringed by old colonial buildings, notably the marble **municipal hall** and the old fort and jail, which now serves as the **central market**. A short walk away, on Rua Luis Inácio at the corner of Praça do Metical, the restored red-brick **Casa Portugal** [204–5 C5] is one of the best surviving examples of a turn-of-the-century Portuguese dwelling.

Praça do Metical [204–5 B4], named after the country's currency, is appropriately ringed by banks housed in buildings of various vintages. From Praça do Metical, walk up Avenida Poder Popular to the recently restored **Casa Infante Sagres** [204–5 A3], an old colonial building. Apparently it used to be covered in mosaics; if that's the case, some bright spark has ruined it by painting it brown and white. It's still fairly impressive, although from the wrong angle it looks a little like a Black Forest gateau.

Just behind the Casa Infante Sagres is the entrance to the **fishing port**, where you can poke around the docks. If you do decide to visit (for whatever reason), it's crucial that you introduce yourself to the policemen on duty at the gate – they are very amicable but might start asking awkward questions if you fail to talk to them first.

To the right of the Casa Infante Sagres, a short and bumpy dirt road runs beside an old railway bridge to open out on **Praça dos Trabalhadores** (Workers' Square) [204–5 B2], the **freight port**, and the adjacent **railway station** [204–5 B1]. Completed in 1966, the railway station has been described in the tourist literature as 'one of the most beautiful modern buildings in Africa' and by a correspondent to the previous edition as 'a hideous example of imperial overlord modern school architecture'. The latter description rings more true.

Return to Praça da Municipalia and follow Avenida República into Avenida Eduardo Mondlane. A short distance along the road, is the striking **Beira Cathedral** [204–5 G6], which was erected between 1907 and 1925 using stones taken from the Portuguese fort at Sofala. It has a children's playground in its grounds. There is a pretty chapel a block further along the same road, as well as one a block up on Rua Correia de Brito. In addition to housing Beira's main cluster of old ecclesiastical buildings, this part of town was formerly the most upmarket residential area, and there are several pleasing old houses, some beautifully maintained, others utterly derelict – you could happily pass an afternoon or two exploring this area.

A brisk 30-minute walk along Avenida Eduardo Mondlane, under a canopy of overhanging trees and over a rather rough pavement with flagstones that have been pushed up by the roots of those trees, brings you out at **Praça da Independência** [119 D3], a large open circle on the seafront. From here, you could continue 5km west, walking or catching a chapa along Avenida FPLM, to the **Farol do Macuti** (Macuti Lighthouse) [119 G1], where there is a pretty beach and a cluster of cheap eateries and bars. The lighthouse was built in 1904, stands 28m tall, and has a conical top with two red stripes. Whether the two rusting ship hulks that lie on the nearby beach are testament to the lighthouse's efficacy is unclear.

Alternatively, if you feel like heading back from the city centre from Praça da Independência, then follow the seafront Avenida Mateus Sansão Muthemba back east, with the crumbling seafront wall to your left – possibly taking a break at the Miramar Restaurant [119 D4]. A short diversion leads down to the **Grand Hotel** [199 B4]. The Grand has clearly not been a hotel since independence and is now a thriving high-rise slum. Entering the building today would be both dangerous and a little insensitive, but it's worth taking five minutes to observe from the outside – not because of the poverty and poor condition of the building, but more to see the people. You'll see children playing in the grounds, women doing their washing in the pool, men sitting chatting together on the entrance steps. It is, in a slightly

SOFALA

For centuries prior to the Portuguese occupation, the most important trading centre in what is now Mozambique was Sofala, which lay amid the shallow waterways and impermanent sandbars of the Buzi River mouth, about 50km south of present-day Beira. Founded in 900AD and described in a contemporary document by the Arab writer al-Masudi, Sofala formed the main medieval link between the inland trade route to the gold mines of present-day Zimbabwe and Manioc, and the prosperous Swahili city of Kilwa (in southern Tanzania), as well as being an important trading centre in its own right. By the 15th century it probably had a population of around 10,000.

The first European visitor to Sofala was the Portuguese explorer and spy Pêro de Covilhã, who travelled there overland disguised as an Arab merchant in 1489. In 1500, Sofala was visited by Sancho de Toar, who recognised its pivotal role in the gold trade. Five years later, Portugal erected a small fort and trading factory at Sofala. Although this was done with the permission of the local sheikh, Portugal rapidly set about establishing its own local trade network, bypassing the Muslim traders. Within a year of its foundation, the Portuguese fort was attacked without any marked success by the sheikh and his allies. Portugal responded by killing the sheikh in a punitive attack, and installing a puppet ruler in his place.

The Portuguese occupation of Sofala evidently coincided with a northward migration of the main chieftaincies of Karangaland and a corresponding shift in the main inland trade routes. Combined with the increasing dominance of ivory over gold as a trading commodity, this shift in trade routes caused Sofala to diminish in importance. As early as 1530, the main captaincy of the coast moved from Sofala to Mozambique Island. By the 17th century, Sofala was a neglected backwater, with the token Portuguese occupancy largely to prevent the fort from falling to a rival European power. By the 1750s, the stone buildings of the Portuguese quarter were partially submerged, and Sofala was more or less left in the hands of a few Muslim traders. By the time that modern Mozambique came into being, Sofala's permanent buildings had mostly disappeared beneath the sea, and the ancient port was passed over in favour of Chiluane as the local administrative centre. The stone fort at Sofala was dismantled and its bricks were used to build Beira Cathedral.

Sofala still exists today, though as little more than an overgrown fishing village. It is possible to visit the site (there is reputedly even a pensão in the town), but you'll need a couple of days as it will be more than a day trip. There are two routes to Sofala. The road route is in poor condition, and entails following the EN6 northwest for 65km to Tica, then turning south along the EN214 and following it for about 60km to Nova Almada, then crossing the Buzi River by motor ferry, and continuing another 50km southeast to Sofala.

The second option, which is rather more in keeping with the spirit of old Sofala, is to go by boat. A daily ferry heads in this direction from Beira, leaving the Praia Nova at 07.00 and costing around US$5. To get to Praia Nova you need to walk through the Mercado Praia Nova – the best entrance to use is the one opposite the police barracks on Rua do Aruângua. Just walk straight down the main path through the Mercado (if you come to any forks, stay on the left) and once you reach the crossroad, carry straight on over onto the bottom end of the beach.

bizarre way, a tribute to the resilience of the Mozambicans and their ability to take the little that is available to them and make the best of it.

Continuing along from the Grand Hotel, the avenue bends to the right and stops in the Largo Artur Brandão. Head directly over it onto the Rua 1 de Dezembro. This will take you through some of the swampland that the city was built on to the crossroads with Rua do Governador Augusto Castilho. Turn left and walk up past the **Mercado Praia Nova** back to the Praça do Município.

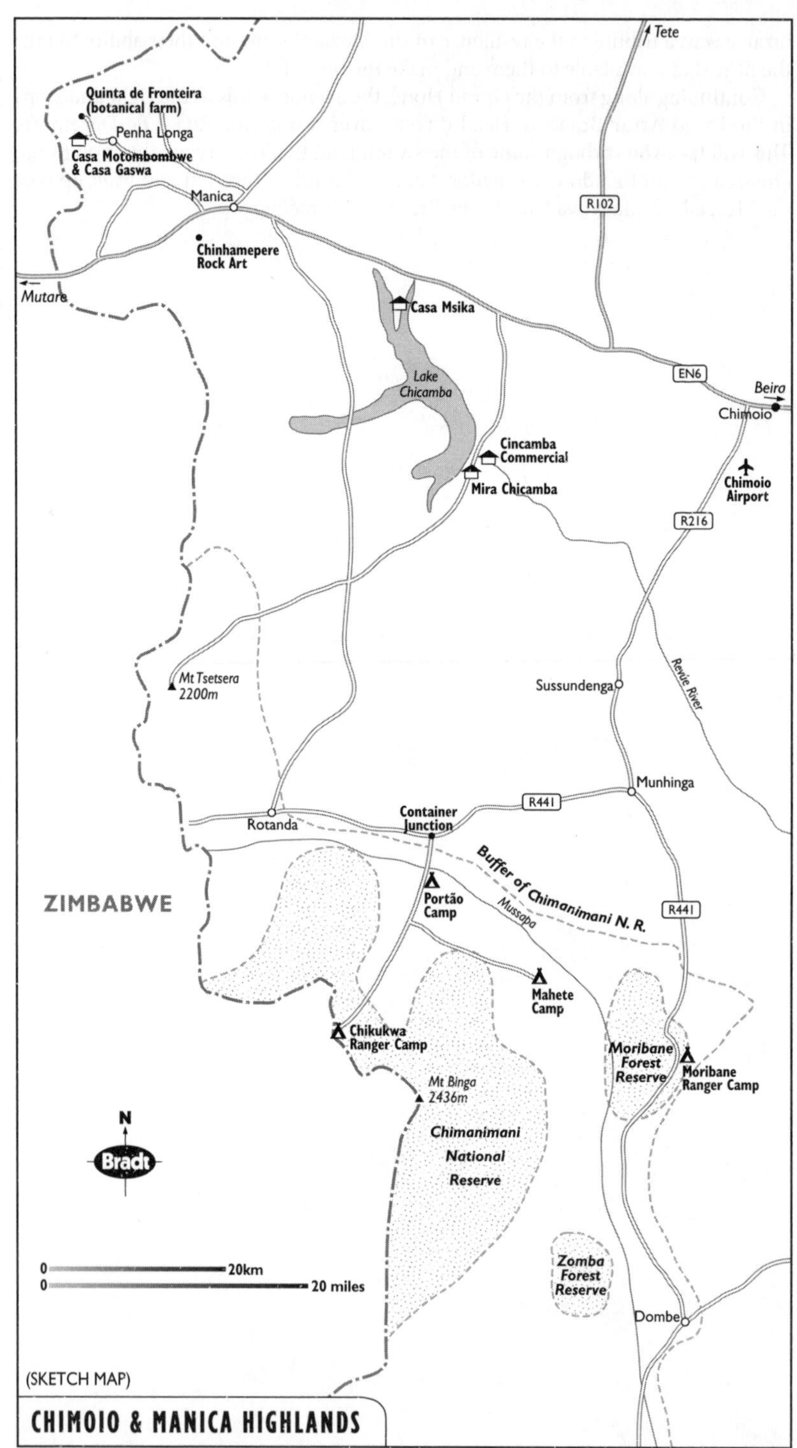
Tete
Quinta de Fronteira
(botanical farm)
Penha Longa
Casa Motombombwe
& Casa Gaswa
Manica
R102
Chinhamepere
Rock Art
Mutare
Casa Msika
EN6
Lake
Chicamba
Beira
Chimoio
Cincamba
Commercial
Mira Chicamba
Chimoio
Airport
R216
Revúe River
Mt Tsetsera
2200m
Sussundenga
Munhinga
R441
Container
Junction
Rotanda
Buffer of Chimanimani N. R.
Mussapa
ZIMBABWE
Portão
Camp
R441
Mahete
Camp
Chikukwa
Ranger Camp
Moribane
Forest
Reserve
Moribane
Ranger Camp
Mt Binga
2436m
N
Bradt
Chimanimani
National
Reserve
Zomba
Forest
Reserve
0
20km
0
20 miles
Dombe
(SKETCH MAP)
CHIMOIO & MANICA HIGHLANDS

12

Chimoio and the Manica Highlands

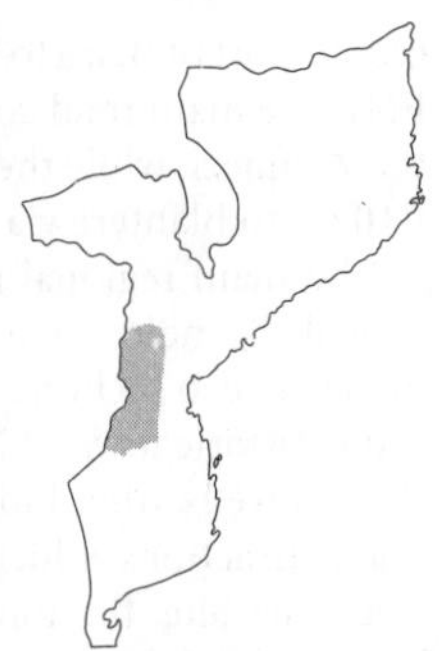

The landlocked province of Manica is bordered by the Save and Zambezi rivers to the south and northeast, the province of Tete and Sofala to the northwest and east, and Zimbabwe to the west. The gold deposits associated with the so-called Manica Greenstone Belt along the Zimbabwe border have been exploited since medieval times, when the Monomotapa Kingdom exported gold via the Zambezi Valley to the coastal port of Sofala. The province formed the centre of the Manica Kingdom, which was most likely established in medieval times and survived into the 19th century, and several of its larger towns, including Manica itself, were founded in the pre-Portuguese era.

Few travellers spend much time in Manica, at least by comparison with coastal provinces such as Inhambane and Sofala. The province does, however, see quite a bit of passing tourist traffic, bisected as it is by several pivotal trunk roads. Most important of these is the EN6 through the Beira Corridor, which links the Indian

THE BEIRA CORRIDOR

The strategic importance of the Beira Corridor, which consists of the 300km-long EN6 and a parallel oil pipeline and railway (which now operates for freight only), grew after Zimbabwe achieved full independence in 1980, leaving South Africa and Namibia as the last bastions of white rule in southern Africa. Zimbabwe and the various other states neighbouring South Africa formed the SADCC (Southern Africa Development Co-ordination Conference), with the declared aim of reducing the region's economic dependence on the apartheid regime. For landlocked countries such as Zimbabwe, Zambia and Botswana, a crucial factor in achieving this goal was to have access to a sea port that was not under South African control.

Beira was the obvious choice on account of its proximity to the Zimbabwean border. However, by the mid-1980s, years of neglect had caused Beira's harbour to silt up to the point where it was practically unnavigable, while the rail link to Zimbabwe had become a regular target for terrorist attacks by Renamo. The Mozambican national army was too weak to protect it against these attacks, and so Zimbabwe's defence forces took responsibility for defending the Beira Corridor. After large amounts of foreign aid were used to make Beira harbour operational, Zimbabwe and Zambia steadily increased their imports via Beira during the late 1980s – although neither country ever came close to being independent of the South African transport system. See the box *Corridors of power* on page 57 for more about Mozambique's transportation corridors.

Ocean port of Beira to Mutare (Zimbabwe). At Inchope, the EN6 intersects with the EN1, the main road connecting all coastal ports south of Beira to regions north of the Zambezi, while the only surfaced road connecting Mozambique to Malawi, the R102/3 to Blantyre via Tete, runs north from the EN6 at Bandula.

The main regional route focus, about 200km inland of Beira, is the provincial capital Chimoio, an affably unremarkable town that lies immediately north of the EN6 between Inchope and Bandula. The other main population centre in the region is the historic town of Manica, which is bisected by the EN6 about 30km east of the Zimbabwe border. Either town can be used as a base for exploring the province's main attractions, which include the little-known but very accessible Chinhamapere Rock Art Site, the mountains around Penhalonga, the attractive Chicamba Real Dam and the remote Chimanimani National Park.

CHIMOIO

The capital of landlocked Manica Province, Chimoio (pronounced 'Shimoio') is the fourth-largest city in Mozambique, with a population estimated at 260,000, and the most important town along the EN6 between Beira and the Zimbabwean border. At 750m above sea level, Chimoio has a refreshing mid-altitude climate and a compact and well-equipped town centre, comprising a neat oval grid of roads, lined with leafy trees and two- to three-storey buildings, a few hundred metres northeast of the EN6. It's not the sort of town you'd make a special effort to visit, but it is a pleasant enough place and its significance as a route focus means that a fair number of travellers pass through. The most significant local attraction is the striking outcrop known as Cabeça de Velho, but Chimoio also forms an increasingly popular base for visits to other sites of interest covered in this chapter.

HISTORY Oral tradition has it that Chimoio is the name of a prince who was executed by a local clan chief as punishment for hunting in his territory, and buried in the area. The modern town dates to 1893, when the Mozambique Company established their district headquarters at a nearby site known as Vila Barreto, relocating to the present-day site in 1899 following the completion of the railway connecting Beira to Zimbabwe. Initially known as Mandigos, the town prospered as a transportation and agricultural centre in the early 20th century, thanks partly to the implementation of a cotton scheme in 1902.

Mandigos was renamed Vila Pery in 1916 (after the Governor of Manica, João Pery de Lind), accorded city status in 1969, and given the name Chimoio at a post-independence rally held there by President Samora Machel in 1975. A mortar strike on the town in 1974 was the only instance in which Frelimo attacked a major settlement during the war for liberation from Portugal. In November 1977, the Rhodesian Security Forces launched an aerial attack on Robert Mugabe's ZANLA (Zimbabwe African National Liberation Army) headquarters at Chimoio, killing an estimated 3,000 ZANLA soldiers.

GETTING THERE AND AWAY Chimoio is one of Mozambique's most important public transport hubs. It is the closest substantial town to the crossroads of the **EN6** between Beira and Mutare (Zimbabwe) and the **EN1** from Maputo and Vilankulo to Quelimane, as well as lying only 20km east of where the **R102/3** branches north from the EN6 to Tete and Blantyre (Malawi). As such, Chimoio is passed through by many people travelling between southern and northern Mozambique, or crossing into or out from Malawi or Zimbabwe.

By car For self-drivers, trunk roads in all directions are in fair to good condition, and typical driving times would be around 45 minutes to Inchope junction, three hours to Beira, four hours to Tete, one hour to Mutare (excluding border formalities) and six hours to Vilankulo.

By bus and chapa Almost all public transport out of Chimoio leaves from the bus station between the Mercado Central and the disused railway station. **Chapas** to destinations along the Beira Corridor leave regularly throughout the day, as do vehicles heading for Sussundenga (for Chimanimani National Park) and other local destinations. Sample fares are US$4.50 to Beira, US$1.50 to Manica and US$1 to Sussundenga.

All **long-haul buses** out of Chimoio leave in the wee hours. At least one bus runs daily to Tete, costing US$8.50, leaving at around 04.00 and arriving at 11.00. The daily bus to Quelimane costs US$12, departs at 04.30 and arrives 10–12 hours later. One or two buses leave for Maputo daily, setting off at 03.00, taking six hours to Vilankulo, ten hours to Maxixe (for Inhambane) and 19–20 hours to Maputo. The full US$27 fare to Maputo is charged, irrespective of where you disembark. Long-haul tickets should be bought directly from the bus conductor on the afternoon before departure. Different companies cover the various routes on different days, so ask around at the bus station to locate the correct vehicle. If you stay at Pink Papaya, the management is a good source of current information about bus schedules (and they will also arrange an escort to the bus station for early morning starts).

By air Roads aside, the only other way in and out of Chimoio is by air, with one of LAM's thrice-weekly flights to/from Maputo. The **airport** lies just outside the city off the EN6 heading towards Zimbabwe. The LAM office is on Avenida 25 de Setembro between Rua dos Oprimidos and Rua Patrice Lumumba.

WHERE TO STAY Chimoio boasts a decent choice of accommodation, and prices are generally quite reasonable by Mozambican standards.

Upmarket

Hotel Inter-Chimoio (42 rooms) 18B Av 25 de Setembro; 251 24200/1; e interchimoio@gmail.com; www.interhotels.co.mz. Opened in 2009, this centrally located business hotel is easily the smartest option in town, even if the décor in some public areas feels a touch overbearing. The large carpeted rooms come with king-size or dbl bed, flat-screen DSTV, Wi-Fi, AC, safe, mini-bar & wooden furnishings. Larger suites are available. Facilities include a terrace swimming pool, 2 restaurants, business centre & airport transfers to tie in with all LAM flights. *US$82 dbl; US$105–170 suites; all rates B&B.*

Hotel Residencial Castelo Branco (40 rooms) Rua Sussundenga; 251 23934; m 82 522 5960; e hrcastelobranco@tdm.co.mz. Situated at the western end of the town centre just off Praça dos Heróis, this clean, bright & modern family-run place has been offering quality accommodation at decent prices for some years now. Spacious en-suite standard rooms come with queen-size or twin beds, flat-screen DSTV, Wi-Fi, AC, fridge & muted but appealing décor. Suites also have a small sitting area & bathroom with tub and shower. A new block containing swish apts (aimed at longer stay visitors) & a restaurant will be open by the time you read this. Other facilities include a new swimming pool & secure parking. *US$66/71 sgl/dbl; suites & apts US$92–162; all rates B&B.*

Mid-range

Complexo Hoteleiro Vila Pery (26 rooms) Rua Pigivide; 251 24391; m 82 501 4570; e ch.vilapery@tdm.co.mz. This central 3-storey hotel, built around a small central courtyard,

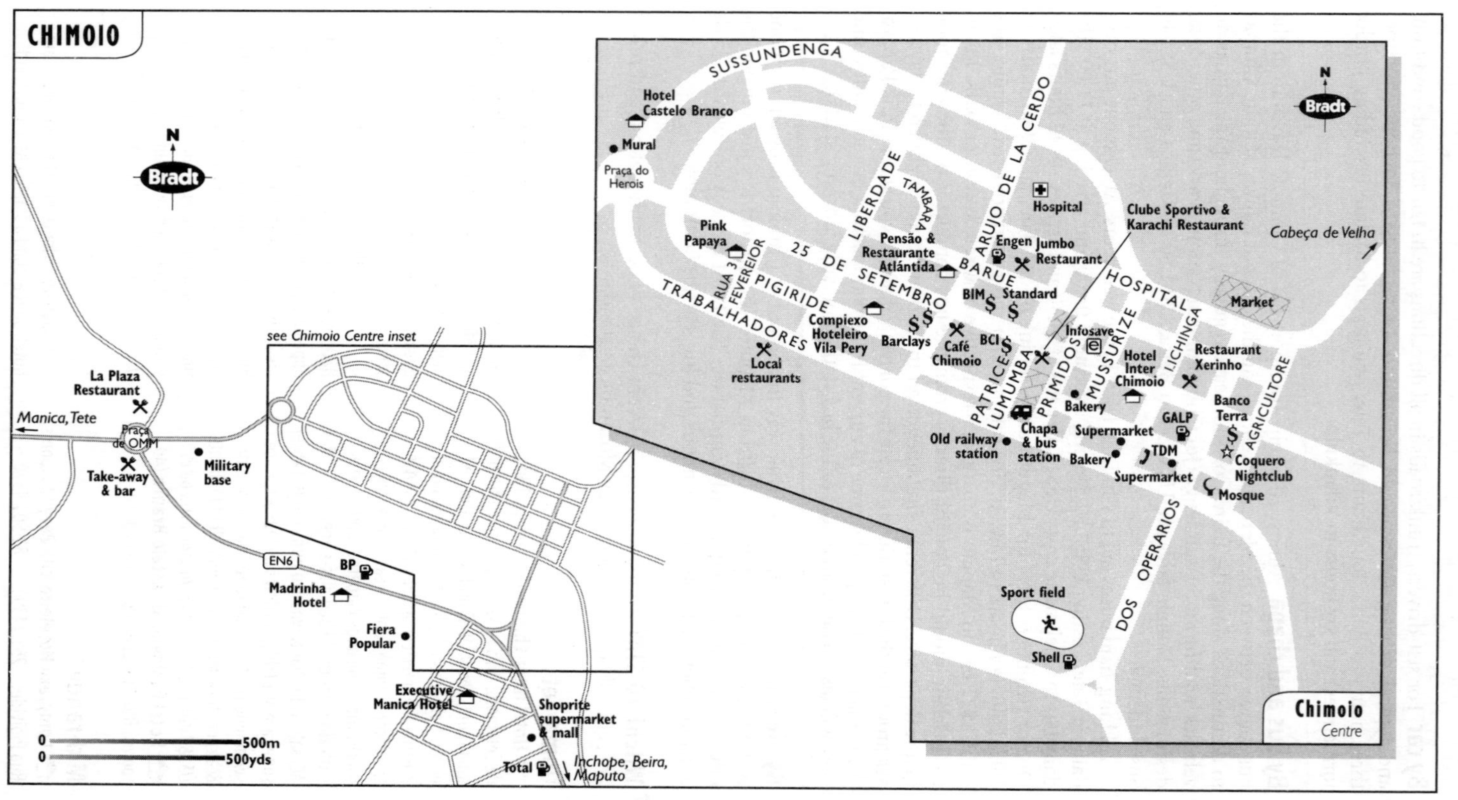
CHIMOIO
N
Bradt
La Plaza Restaurant
Manica, Tete
Praça de OMM
Take-away & bar
Military base
see Chimoio Centre inset
EN6
BP
Madrinha Hotel
Fiera Popular
Executive Manica Hotel
Shoprite supermarket & mall
Total
Inchope, Beira, Maputo
0 500m
0 500yds
SUSSUNDENGA
Hotel Castelo Branco
Mural
Praça do Herois
LIBERDADE
TAMBARA
ARUJO DE LA CERDO
Hospital
Pink Papaya
RUA 3 FEVEREIOR
25 DE SETEMBRO
Pensão & Restaurante Atlântida
Engen
Jumbo Restaurant
BARUE
Clube Sportivo & Karachi Restaurant
Cabeça de Velha
PIGIRIDE
TRABALHADORES
BIM
Standard
HOSPITAL
Market
Complexo Hoteleiro Vila Pery
Barclays
Café Chimoio
BCI
Infosave
Local restaurants
PATRICE LUMUMBA
PRIMIDOS
MUSSURIZE
Hotel Inter Chimoio
LICHINGA
Restaurant Xerinho
Bakery
AGRICULTORE
Banco Terra
GALP
Old railway station
Chapa & bus station
Supermarket
Bakery
TDM
Supermarket
Coquero Nightclub
Mosque
DOS OPERARIOS
Sport field
Shell
Chimoio
Centre

has clean but rather dark tiled rooms with DSTV, writing desk, AC & en-suite shower. *US$57/60 sgl/dbl B&B.*

Executive Manica Hotel Barrio 4 Zona Residencial; 251 23135. Formerly the priciest & most luxurious option in Manica, this suburban hotel, a short walk from the Shoprite Centre, has gone downhill of late. The en-suite rooms remain light & airy, with AC & TV, but the small compound has an aura of neglect epitomised by the empty swimming pool at its centre. Still, there's secure parking & it's a lot quieter than its more central competitors. *US$57/62 sgl/dbl; US$85 suite.*

Budget

Pink Papaya (2 rooms; 1 dorm) Casa 795, Rua Pigivide; m 082 555 7310; e anjamann@gmx.de; http://pinkpapaya.atspace.com. Chimoio's only backpacker hostel, situated a short walk from the bus station, is the obvious first port of call for budget travellers, not only for the clean & comfortable accommodation, but also for the relaxed vibe created by the German owner-managers, who are an excellent source of travel advice for Chimoio & can help with public transport information further afield & visa extensions. Facilities include hot bucket showers, honesty bar, tent & camping gear rental, left luggage, fully equipped self-catering kitchen, comfortable veranda with DSTV & a visitors' book filled with useful trip accounts from other travellers. The dbl rooms have walk-in nets & cane furniture. Beds in the 10 bed dorm also have nets. *US$20/25 sgl/dbl; US$11.50 dorm bed.*

Pensão Atlántida (16 rooms) Av Dr A de Lacerda; 251 22027/169. Situated above the eponymous restaurant, this is a clean & pleasant *pensão* offering good value rooms, some en-suite, and all with fan & writing desk. *US$15/23 sgl/twin with common shower; US$28 en-suite twin with balcony, or US$43 with AC & TV.*

WHERE TO EAT AND DRINK There's no shortage of decent places to eat in Chimoio. For cheap local dishes, try one of the no-frills eateries marked on the map around the corner from Pink Papaya. Other acceptable and affordable options serving typical Mozambican fare include Restaurant Xerinho, Restaurante Jumbo and the Clube Sportivo (as shown on the map), all of which double as bars. Otherwise, the following stand out:

La Plaza Restaurant & Pizzeria Praça OMM; 251 23716; m 82 601 4980; 06.00–22.30 Tue–Fri, 06.00–13.30 Sat. This slick new complex comprises a bakery (fresh bread & croissants throughout the day), bottle store, café (good coffee), bar (with large-screen DSTV) & restaurant in a cavernous open-plan building reminiscent of a warehouse. *The pizzas, starting at US$4, are the best in town, & there is also a good selection of seafood & meat dishes in the US$4–11 range, while snacks & sandwiches are mostly under US$2.*

Restaurante Atlántida Av Dr A de Lacerda; 251 22027/169; lunch & dinner daily. On the ground floor of Pensão Atlántida (see above), this place has plenty of old-fashioned charm, with its tall ceiling, wood-panelled walls & red checkered tablecloths. The daily special is usually good value, or you can choose from the extensive menu of seafood & meat dishes. There's a good wine list, too. *Mains US$4–6.*

Karachi Restaurant Av 25 de Setembro; m 82 799 8366; lunch & dinner daily. This Pakistani restaurant isn't easy to find (follow the alley immediately left of Clube Sportivo & enter the only door to the left) & has zero ambience, overlooking an indoor sports field, but the food is very well priced & makes a refreshing change from the usual Mozambican fare. It's best to choose the daily special or phone ahead if you don't want a long wait. No alcohol served. *Mains cost around US$3.50.*

Cafe Chimoio Av 25 de Setembro. This pleasant central eatery keeps long hours & serves a selection of sandwiches, burgers, torrados & light meals. Also has pastries & espresso coffee. *Mostly under US$3.*

Feira Popular Immediately south of the EN6, more or less opposite the railway station, this cluster of drinking holes & low-cost eateries is the place to head for a cheap night out.

OTHER PRACTICALITIES

Banks and foreign exchange There are several banks, mostly clustered around the junction of avenidas 25 de Setembro and Dr A de Lacerda. The Standard, Barclays, BIM Millennium and BCI all have 24-hour ATMs. There is also a BIM Millennium ATM at the Shoprite Centre on the EN6 to Beira. Note, too, that many private moneychangers hang around the park at the corner opposite the Standard Bank, but they are very sharp operators, and attempted robberies aren't unknown, so be careful.

Hospital Rua do Hospital, opposite the junction with Rua Patrice Lumumba (☏ *251 22415*). There's a medical centre on the corner between Avenidas 25 de Setembro and Dr A de Lacerda, and a pharmacy on Rua Dr A Boavida between Rua Cidade de Lichinga and Rua dos Operários.

Internet There are two TDM offices, one at the Shoprite Centre and the other on Avenida 25 de Setembro behind the stadium.

Immigration The Immigration office in Chimoio, on Avenida 25 de Setembro between the BIM Millennium and Standard banks, has the reputation of being one of the best places in Mozambique to try for an extension on a 30-day visa. If you are staying at Pink Papaya, ask the managers for details before you head out to the immigration office.

Police Rua dos Operários, just up from the junction with Rua do Bárue (☏ *251 22213*).

Shopping The **Shoprite** (🕘 *09.00–20.00 Mon–Sat, 09.00–15.00 Sun*) in the eponymous centre (on the EN6 to Beira) is very well stocked – coming from the north, it'll be the best supermarket you'll have seen in a long time. The centre also has a fast-food outlet, BIM Millennium with ATM and internet café. More centrally, there are several good supermarkets dotted around the market area, and there's a decent enough bakery on Rua Cidade de Lichinga (though it's not as good as La Plaza).

WHAT TO SEE AND DO It has to be said that, while pleasant enough and having some startlingly pretty sunsets, Chimoio is not in itself the most interesting of towns. Within the town itself, the only real point of interest is the colourful mural of the revolution that runs around the wall of the Praça dos Heróis at the western end of Avenida 25 de Setembro. Further afield, the town makes a good base for day or overnight trips to most other sites of interest covered in this chapter, and Pink Papaya is an excellent place to catch the latest news about tourist developments in the region.

It is definitely worth heading a short way along the 3km road towards **Cabeça do Velho**, a vast granite outcrop that resembles an old man's face in repose. It is also possible to walk to the top of the formation's three peaks, though recent reports of theft suggest it would be inadvisable to do it alone or carrying valuables. To get there, walk along Rua do Bárue until it becomes dirt road and then follow it past the Restaurant os Bambus and through the market stalls. This road eventually meanders off around the mud huts, but you won't get lost – the rocks are right in front of you. Unless you really dawdle you'll be able to do all three peaks in a morning or afternoon, but (as ever) take water and a hat – there's little shelter from the sun on the route. Once at the top, the view of the surrounding countryside is impressive.

LAKE CHICAMBA

Also known as Chicamba Real, this scenic lake was created in 1968, when the colonial government constructed a new hydro-electric dam on the Revué River about 40km downstream of Manica town and a similar distance from Chimoio. Set in a distinctively African landscape of rocky hills swathed in dense brachystegia woodland, the lake extends over 160km² northwest from the dam wall, and numerous inlets and coves follow the surrounding contours, with the Chimanimani and Vumba mountains providing a backdrop on the Zimbabwe border. Lake Chicamba is popular with fishermen from neighbouring Zimbabwe, with Florida-strain largemouth bass being their main quarry, and accommodation tends to fill up over weekends and during Zimbabwean school holidays. At other times it is generally very quiet, and the surrounding wooded hills would be of great interest to birdwatchers, while the attractive scenery, pleasant climate and sense of isolation add up to a potentially alluring stopover for backpackers seeking a change of scene after a period on the coast.

GETTING THERE AND AWAY Casa Msika, the main tourist focus, stands on a northwestern arm of the lake, 5km – and clearly signposted – from the south side of the **EN6** some 30km east of Manica town and 40km west of Chimoio. Alternatively, a scenic and very good unsurfaced road runs all around the east side of the lake, leading south from the EN6 about 5km closer to Chimoio. After 15km, this road reaches the tiny village of Chicamba, from where it is another 1km to the bridge that spans the Revué immediately below the hydro-electric dam, then another few hundred metres to Mira Chicamba Lodge. From here, it continues southwards to Rotanda and Tsetsera (see *Chimanimani National Reserve*, page 221).

Using public transport, **chapas** from Chimoio to Manica can drop you at the junction for Casa Msika (an hour's walk further) while chapas from Chimoio to Nyamakamba (less than US$1) can drop you right at Mira Chicamba Lodge.

WHERE TO STAY AND EAT

Casa Msika (30 rooms) m 82 440 4304 or 82 960 9418; e casamsika@gmail.com; www.casamsika.com. This long-serving lodge is aimed mainly at the Zimbabwe w/ender crowd, so the focus is firmly on fishing, though it also has a lovely location for rambling & an animal-rehabilitation project on site. A varied selection of thatched family chalets, dbl rooms & self-catering units is offered, while the campsite has a new ablution block (hot showers) & barbecue areas. *US$63–73 chalet (sleeping 3 or 4); US$40 dbl or twin room; US$44 self-catering dbl; US$3 pp camping.*

Mira Chicamba (6 rooms) 239 10076. Set on the east side of the lake about 1km south of the dam wall, this pleasant new resort offers clean no-frills accommodation in semi-detached cottages, all of which have a dbl bed, en-suite hot shower, writing desk & small private balcony. The open thatched bar/restaurant has DSTV & a selection of meat & fish dishes in the US$4–6 range. *US$14 dbl; US$10 per tent camping.*

Cincamba Commercial (10 rooms) Situated between Mira Chicamba & the dam wall, this place is primarily a bar, but also serves basic meals for around US$3, offers good sunset views over the lake. *Has a few very basic rooms at the back for around US$10.*

MANICA

Flanking the EN6 about 30km east of the Zimbabwe border, this agreeable small town (population 33,000) is today overshadowed by the provincial capital Chimoio some 70km to its west. In times past, however, it was one of the most important settlements in the Mozambican interior, serving as capital of the Manica Kingdom, and the site of a gold fair that operated intermittently from medieval times into the early 19th century. Tourist attractions fittingly include a venerable geological museum, which is unlikely to be of more than passing interest to most visitors, and the altogether more compelling Chinhamapere Rock Art Site, 5km out of town. Manica is also the springboard for visits to the mountainous Penhalonga region on the Zimbabwe border northwest of town.

HISTORY Manica's fortunes have traditionally risen and slumped with that of the regional gold trade. Chipangura, the pre-Portuguese capital of the Manica Kingdom, stood on the same site as the present-day township, and served as one of the most important regional centres of medieval gold extraction for trade with the coastal Arabs. Chipangura was a major objective of Francisco Barreto's failed expedition to Monomotapa in the early 1570s, but Barreto's successor Vasco Homem reached it in 1575 and established good trade relations with the ruling Chicanga dynasty. From then onwards, Portuguese traders regularly visited the gold fair at Chipangura, and some even settled in Manica, an amicable arrangement that endured until 1695, when the Rozvi crossed from modern-day Zimbabwe to sack the town.

In 1720, a trade fair was re-established at the site, by then known as Macequece (aka Masekesa). It soon gained official Portuguese status, and fell under the joint rule of a traditional Chicanga and a foreign captain appointed by the Portuguese administration. Gold extraction remained the exclusive preserve of the Chicanga, but many other valuable items were traded at Macequece, among them ivory, crystals, gemstones, copper, iron and livestock. From the 1790s onwards, however, Macequece fell into decline: a series of Chicanga secession disputes that created political instability in Manica and led to a decreased Portuguese presence was followed by an extended drought c1830 and then by the arrival of militant Nguni refugees from Zululand. In 1835, following an Nguni raid led by a chief called Nxaba, Macequece was abandoned.

The Portuguese attempted to re-establish a gold fair in Manica in the 1850s, but by this time ivory had replaced gold as the most important item of regional trade. Renewed interest in the region's mining potential led the Portuguese to name Manica as an administrative district in March 1884, and Macequece was established as its capital. In 1890, Fortaleza Macequece was built in the hills outside town in response to territorial tensions with Rhodes's British South Africa Company, then in the process of staking out Southern Rhodesia (Zimbabwe), and the two rival powers clashed at the fort in 1891. A year later, Manica became the inland headquarters of the Mozambique Company, a Beira-based mining company, though this role was later usurped by Chimoio. The village was chartered as a town in 1956 and upgraded to city status in 1972.

Aside from agriculture, the biggest local industry today is the Vumba Bottling Plant, which extracts mineral water from the Vumba Mountains outside town. However, Pan African Resources' successful 2009 pre-feasibility study of the mooted Manica Gold Project, 4km out of town, suggests that gold may once again play a significant role in Manica's economic fortunes.

GETTING THERE AND AWAY Manica town is bisected by the surfaced **EN6**. In a private vehicle, the drive from Chimoio takes about 45 minutes and from the Zimbabwean border about 20. There is also plenty of **chapa** transport along this road; the fare from Chimoio is US$1.50. The chapa station, two blocks north of the EN6 behind the market, is also the place to pick up transport to Chinhamapere and Penhalonga.

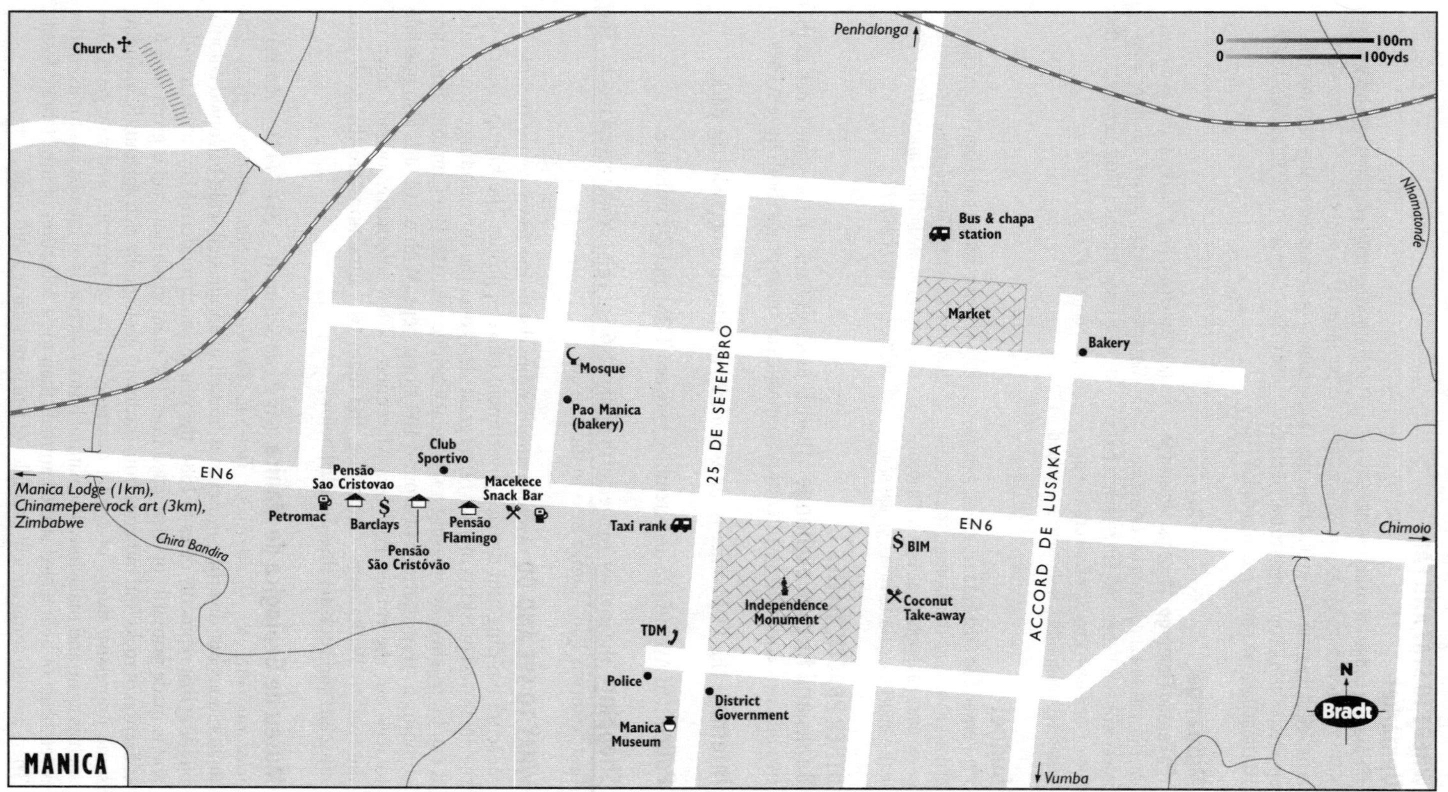
Church
Penhalonga
0 100m
0 100yds
Nhamatonde
Bus & chapa station
Market
Bakery
Mosque
Pao Manica (bakery)
25 DE SETEMBRO
Club Sportivo
Pensão Sao Cristovao
EN6
Manica Lodge (1km), Chinamepere rock art (3km), Zimbabwe
Petromac
Barclays
Pensão São Cristóvão
Pensão Flamingo
Macekece Snack Bar
Taxi rank
EN6
ACCORD DE LUSAKA
Chimoio
BIM
Chira Bandira
Independence Monument
Coconut Take-away
TDM
Police
District Government
Manica Museum
N
Bradt
Vumba
MANICA

WHERE TO STAY AND EAT

Upmarket

Manica Lodge (18 rooms) m 082 501 5790; e anabelaching@gmail.com. Signposted to the left of the main road to Zimbabwe, this unexpected gem lies in manicured leafy grounds 1km from the town centre. Accommodation is in attractive thatched chalets with DSTV, hot shower & (in most cases) AC. An excellent outdoor restaurant serves large tasty mains in the US$7–10 range. *US$35/50/85 sgl/dbl/suite.*

Mid-range

Pensão Flamingo (10 rooms) Situated on the EN6, this pleasant *pensão* has clean twin rooms with two 3/4 beds, AC, fan & parquet floors. Some rooms have a balcony & all use a clean shared bathroom with hot showers. The ground floor bar serves cheap snacks, as well as the usual Mozambican chicken, meat & fish mains in the US$4–8 range. There is a small garden bar at the back. Poor value at *US$32 twin.*

Budget

Pensão São Cristóvão (16 rooms) A couple of doors down from the Flamingo, this sensibly priced place has bright clean twin & dbl rooms with parquet floor, clustered in 4 groups of 4, each of which shares a bathroom. The ground-floor snack bar has a limited menu of chicken & meat dishes for around US$4 apiece. *US$17/20 dbl/twin, or US$23 with TV.*

OTHER PRACTICALITIES

Banks and foreign exchange There is Barclays Bank on the same block as the two *pensões*, and a BIM Millennium opposite the main praça. Both have ATMs.

Internet The TDM office is on Avenida 25 de Setembro opposite the park.

Police Off Avenida 25 de Setembro, between TDM and the museum.

Shopping The market, to the north of the EN6, sprawls across several blocks. The best bakery is Pão Manica next to the mosque.

WHAT TO SEE AND DO Architectural landmarks in the town centre include the museum building and district government office opposite. The hilltop church on the northwest outskirts of town offers great views over the surrounding countryside; it can be reached by crossing a secondary bridge over the Rio Chirabandina, then climbing a steep staircase of around 100 stone steps. With a 4x4, it is also possible to seek out the ruined Fortaleza Macequece, a few kilometres outside town off the road to Penhalonga. Otherwise, the main two attractions are the geological museum and rock art sites detailed below.

Museu de Geologica de Manica (*Av 25 de Setembro; 251 24433; e dprmem@teledata.co.mz; 07.30–15.30 Tue–Sat, 09.00–15.00 Sun; entrance free*) This unambitious but diverting museum is housed in an unusual wide-balconied colonial building that reputedly dates to 1884, the year in which modern Manica was founded, and is made primarily of corrugated iron. The main exhibition hall is given over to a collection of rocks and minerals from the town's geologically rich surrounds, including some impressive hunks of crystal quartzite, lumps of graphite, and raw gemstones such as agate and malachite. The natural history section is of interest less for its motley assemblage of bedraggled stuffed animals than for a collection of invertebrate fossils. There are also some ancient examples of *bao* games carved into rock.

Chinhamapere Rock Art Site Essentially the Mozambican extension of Zimbabwe's misty Vumba Mountains, Chinhamapere Hill, situated to the south of the EN6 about 5km from central Manica, is the site of one of the country's most important and sacred rock art shelters, submitted for consideration as a UNESCO World Heritage Site in 2008. The main shelter, a 20m-high panel, is thought to comprise paintings from three distinct eras, ranging from 6,000 to a few hundred years old. The most impressive is a well-preserved brown frieze depicting six hunters carrying bows, arrows and spears; dozens of other less distinct human, antelope and other animal figures can also be discerned. As with other rock art in southern Africa, the Chinhamapere paintings are the work of the hunter-gatherer peoples (sometimes referred to as Bushmen or San) that inhabited the entire region prior the arrival of the first pastoralists about 2,000 years ago, and they are thought to be associated with shamanic trance states and rainmaking rituals, though some pictures also appear to depict battle scenes. Unusually, however, the paintings here are considered sacred by the region's modern inhabitants, who still hold rainmaking and other rituals at the site.

Practicalities Getting to Chinhamapere is very straightforward. The unsignposted junction to the base of the mountain lies on the left side of the EN6 precisely 3.4km west of the bridge across the Rio Chirabandina on the west side of Manica town centre. Those without a vehicle could walk there in around 45 minutes, or catch a chapa from the station behind the market (around US$0.30). If in doubt, ask for Escola Chinhamapere (or *pinturas respestres*). At the junction, turn left along a dirt road for about 1km until the track peters out, then enter the compound on the left (known locally as Casa Ganda) where you will find the caretaker Veronica, an official spiritual healer (with a certificate issued in Zimbabwe to prove it). Because the site is so sacred, it is unacceptable to visit it without Veronica (or, possibly, a similarly qualified local). The short but steep walk up takes about 30 minutes at the guide's leisurely pace, and includes at least two stops at other ceremonial sites to communicate with the spirits associated with the paintings. The paintings are well worth the effort, and the views from the shelter are also pretty special.

There is no official fee for visiting the site, but budget on around US$3–5 per person in fees and tips for the expedition – up to US$1 per person when you set out, a similar figure when you arrive at the paintings, and a tip on the way down. Best to carry plenty of small denomination notes and coins, or you might find you have no choice but to hand over a few larger notes as things progress!

PENHALONGA

The Penhalonga region, which straddles the Zimbabwe border some 20km northwest of Manica town, is characterised by fertile rolling hills covered in Shona smallholdings with neatly painted huts and extensive eucalyptus plantations scattered with a few relict patches of indigenous forest. An important source of alluvial gold in pre-colonial times, this is a pleasant area for rambling, birdwatching, unforced interaction with rural Mozambicans (a fair bit of English is spoken this close to the border) or simply escaping the tropical summer heat after a period on the sticky coast. The Shona people living on either side of the border retain a strong shared identity, despite having their territory cut in half by the Anglo-Portuguese treaty of 1891. As a result, the name Penhalonga (Portuguese for 'Long Rock') evidently applies to the entire cross-border region and to the largest village on the Mozambican side, but (especially when looking at maps) do be aware that it is also the name of a larger mining town established on the Zimbabwean side of the border in 1895.

The main tourist focus, set at around 1,050m above sea level, is the Quinta de Fronteira (literally 'Border Farm'), a botanical garden (🕘 *08.00–18.00 daily; entrance US$0.60 pp & US$1 per vehicle*) that was seemingly founded in colonial times and now houses the slightly decrepit Penhalonga Inn. Planted mainly with non-indigenous trees, the botanical garden is a peaceful retreat, and there are still a few stands of bamboo, forest and other naturally occurring vegetation, especially along the gullies and streams that run between the slopes. The only mammals likely to be seen are vervet and possibly samango monkey, but there is a fair amount of birdlife around, and plenty of footpaths to explore the surrounding hills. There's a small waterfall in the gardens about ten minutes' walk from reception, and a larger one about 30 minutes' walk from Casa Motombombwe (see *Where to stay*, below) *en route* to Quinta de Fronteira.

GETTING THERE AND AWAY

By car The main village of Penhalonga lies about 20km from Manica along a good dirt road. To get there in a private vehicle, drive northward out of Manica, passing the market and bus station to your right before you cross a bridge leading out of town. Turn left at the junction about 2km out of town and then left again at a second junction halfway to Penhalonga. When you reach Penhalonga, follow the signpost left for Quinta de Fronteira/Penhalonga Inn, and branch to the right when you reach a fork in the road about 1km later. After another 1.2km, there's another sign-posted fork in the road: the right fork takes you to Quinta de Fronteira/Penhalonga Inn after 3km, while the left fork leads to Casa Motombombwe and Casa Gaswa after about 500m.

By chapa Regular chapas connect Manica to Penhalonga village, but you will need to walk the last stretch. Note that a 4x4 is not normally required to get to Quinta de Fronteira, but is absolutely necessary for the last 500m stretch to the two Casas.

WHERE TO STAY AND EAT

Penhalonga Inn (6 rooms) m 82 309 0190; e penhalongainn@gmail.com. Set in the Quinta de Fronteira botanical garden, this doesn't come across as an inn as much as a rest camp. The 6 basic twin brick-and-thatch huts have en-suite cold showers & are scattered through the forest clearings, & there is also a campsite. No food is available, but a limited selection of drinks is sold at reception when somebody has bothered to stock up. Self-caterers are provided with a fireplace but no cooking utensils. It's a lovely spot, with plenty of unrealised potential, but feels overpriced given the lack of facilities & aura of neglect. *Huts US$18 pp; camping US$7.50.*

Casa Motombombwe & Casa Gaswa t 239 15017; m 82 659 0358 or 84 648 2566; e giftmashiri@yahoo.com.br. These 2 comfortable & attractively located private houses lie about 3km from Penhalonga village & 500m from the road towards Quinta de Fronteira. Either house sleeps up to 4 people in 2 rooms & also has a self-catering kitchen & lounge. If you have exacting requirements then best bring all the food you need from Manica or Chimoio, but simple meals like chicken & potatoes can be provided with a bit of warning. Each house is rented out as a unit, & it is strongly recommended you book in advance through the helpful English-speaking caretaker Gift Mashiri (contact details as opposite). Gift can also arrange for somebody to meet you in Manica if required, & for local guides to take you to visit nearby waterfalls and other sites of interest. *US$35 per night for either house, plus US6.50 per day for the services of a cook & cleaner.*

CHIMANIMANI NATIONAL RESERVE

The 640km² Reserva Nacional de Chimanimani is Mozambique's newest protected area, created in 2003 as part of the Chimanimani Transfrontier Park, two-thirds of which lies in Zimbabwe. It protects the eastern slopes of the Chimanimani range above an altitude of around 1,000m, rising to the 2,436m Mount Binga, the highest point in Mozambique. Dominated by brachystegia woodland and montane grassland, the reserve also harbours some impressive stands of Afro-montane forest and is cut through by numerous mountain streams and waterfalls. At least 45 of the 1,000 plant species recorded are endemic, among them five types of aloe, two proteas and a dwarf palm, and the reserve is listed as an Important Bird Area, home to a long list of specials that includes chestnut-fronted helmet-shrike, briar warbler, Chirinda apalis, boulder chat, Swynnerton's robin and Gurney's sugarbird. A significant elephant population still survives in the forests of Chimanimani, with regular sightings being had by hikers in the vicinity of Moribane Rangers Camp, and other mammals include rock hyrax, bushbuck, red duiker, samango monkey, bushpig and various small predators.

Few travellers make it to Chimanimani as things stand, but the reserve is readily accessible to self-drive visitors with a 4x4 or other high-clearance vehicle, while it also makes a worthwhile goal for adventurous backpackers using public transport. At the time of writing, accommodation is limited to a handful of basic ranger camps, and all visitors need to be self-sufficient in terms of food. However, this situation should improve following the planned opening of two new community-owned camps (currently being constructed by Mozambique Eco-Tours), which are likely to help the reserve realise its potential to be Mozambique's premier hiking and rambling destination.

Charges are as follows: US$6 per person entrance; US$3 per person per night camping and US$15 per party per day for guided walks. Further information about new developments can be obtained from **Mozambique Eco-Tours** (*www.mozecotours.com*), the **ACTF-Chimanimani Office** (☎ *251 24056*) or from Pink Papaya in Chimoio, which also rents out tents and camping gear, and can hold onto hikers' excess luggage.

Three main sectors of the reserve are open to tourists, and since each functions more or less as a self-contained unit in terms of travel logistics, they are discussed separately below.

MORIBANE FOREST RESERVE Proclaimed back in 1957, this 120km² forest reserve doesn't actually lie within the national reserve, but rather forms part of an extensive buffer zone to its east. Nevertheless, it is currently the most popular goal for visitors to Chimanimani, protecting an area of largely unspoilt lowland forest that harbours a substantial and regularly observed population of elephants, as well as a good selection of birds associated with forest and brachystegia habitats. At the time of writing, the main centre for exploring the forest here is Moribane Rangers Camp, which caters only to those with their own tents and camping gear. However, Ndzou Eco-Camp, currently under construction 3km from the ranger camp, should be open by the time you read this, and it is expected to offer accommodation in standing tents, basic rondawels and smarter lodges, along with camping, and it will also be able to provide meals.

At present, the only formal activity in this sector is the seven-hour round hike from the ranger camp to the rainforest where elephant are resident – most people see plenty of spoor, though the actual beasts are more elusive – but it is likely that a network of new themed nature trails will be created around Ndzou once the camp is ready.

Practicalities The springboard for Moribane is the modest district capital Sussundenga, which lies about 40km south of Chimoio. To get to Sussundenga in a private vehicle, follow the EN6 west out of Chimoio for about 5km, then turn left at the signpost for the airport onto the R216, which is surfaced for the first 7km or so, then well-maintained dirt. From Sussundenga, head south for 15km to the village of Munhinga, from where you need to follow to R441 southeast towards Dombe. Moribane Camp is clearly signposted on the west side of the Dombe road about 30km past Munhinga, and the new Ndzou Camp will be about 3km past it.

Using public transport, regular chapas run from Chimoio to Sussundenga, charging US$1, and the trip shouldn't take longer than a hour. From Sussundenga, chapas to Dombe leave every hour or so (less frequently on Sunday), charge US$2, and will drop you at the signposted turn-off for Moribane, from where it is 100m to the camp.

MOUNT BINGA Mozambique's highest mountain is an obvious draw for keen hikers, and the surrounding area also protects plenty of wildlife, while some of the country's finest prehistoric rock art can be seen in a gorge near Chikukwa Rangers Camp. The closest camp to the mountain base is Chikukwa, which can be reached from Chimoio in a day in a private 4x4, but otherwise takes two days to reach (with an overnight stop at Portão Camp) on a combination of public transport and foot. As with Moribane, culinary self-sufficiency is required to explore the area at the time of writing, but this is likely to change when the new Binga Eco-Camp opens 5km from Chikukwa, offering accommodation in fixed safari tents as well as a campsite and simple meals. In the longer term, it is hoped that an activity centre will offer kayaking, climbing, orienteering and horseriding among other activities. About 20km further east, the little-visited Mahete Camp, with four simple thatched huts and bamboo platforms for campers, is the best base for exploring the bamboo forest and some of the sacred sites associated with the mountains.

Practicalities As with Moribane, the first point of call *en route* to Binga is Sussundenga, and self-drivers will need to head south for 15km from here to Munhinga. Here, instead of heading southeast along the R441, however, you need to fork west for 25km to a signposted junction known locally as 'Container' (though the container for which it is named disappeared a couple of years back). After heavy rains, 4x4 may be required to cross a river along the 4km road between the junction and Portão Camp. From here, you can drive to either Mahete or Chikukwa in about one hour, ideally with a guide to show you the way. Using public transport, chapas from Sussundenga to Rotunda can drop you at Container, from where it takes the best part of an hour to reach Portão Camp. If you plan to head on to Chikukwa, it is a ten-hour walk, so you'll need to overnight at Portão, where a few military-style tents are available for rent, and an ablution block is under construction.

MOUNT TSETSERA Situated along the Zimbabwe border at the very north of the national reserve, the 2,200m Mount Tsetsera is noted for the pristine condition of its forested slopes, which run the span from lowland brachystegia woodland at the base to Afro-montane rainforest at higher altitudes. It is a particularly popular spot with birdwatchers, as the forest hosts such regional specials as Chirinda apalis, briar warbler, red-faced crimsonwing, lemon dove and rufous-bellied tit.

Practicalities Reaching Tsetsera is only realistic with a private 4x4. The best approach is to following the dirt road around the east side of Lake Chicamba, passing Mira Chicamba Lodge to your right (see page 217), and continuing for about 55km to the base of the mountain. The final ascent requires 4x4 and takes at least one hour. There is no formal development here, but it is permitted to camp in the grounds of the ruined mansion at the top of the mountain.

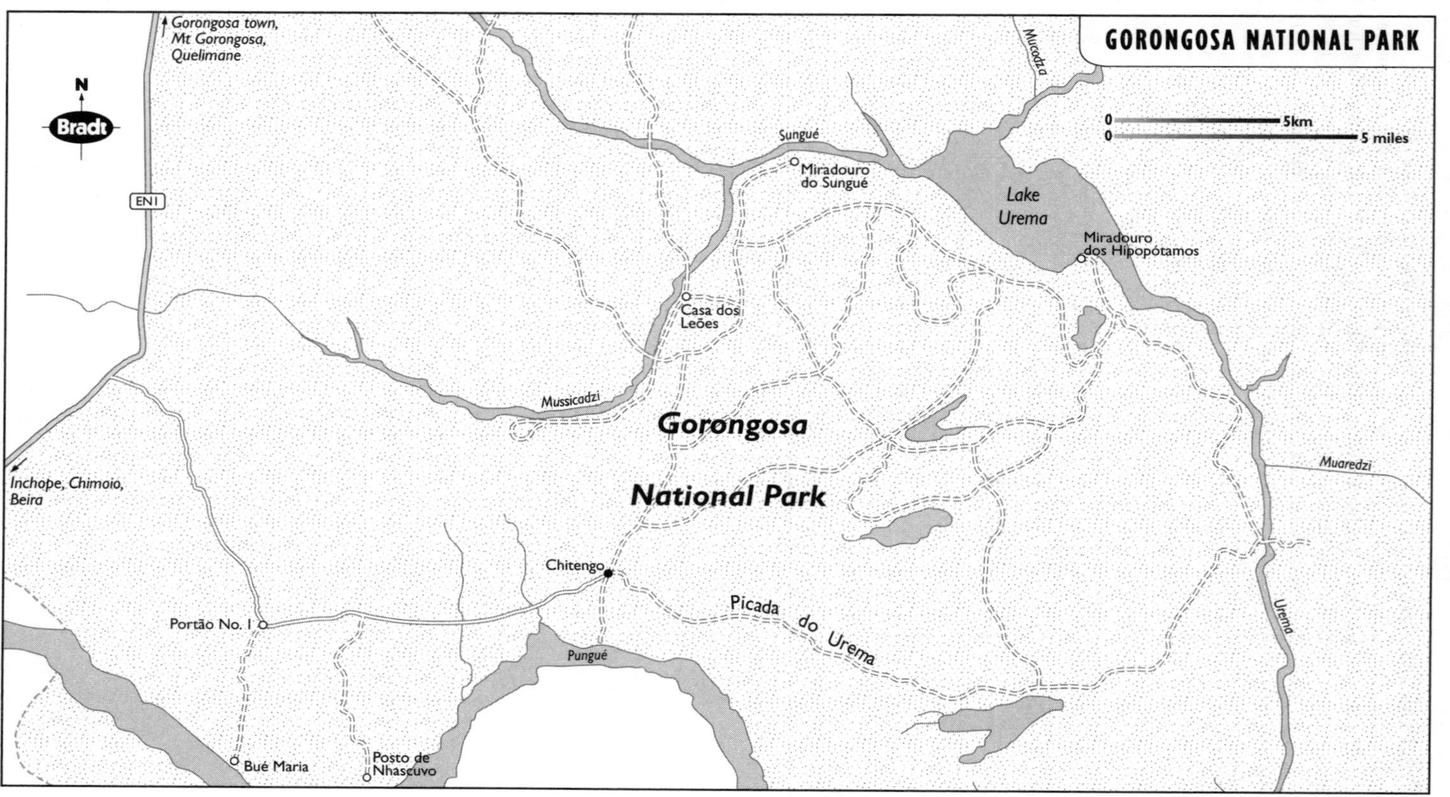
GORONGOSA NATIONAL PARK
0 5km
0 5 miles
Gorongosa town, Mt Gorongosa, Quelimane
N
Bradt
EN1
Mucodza
Sungué
Miradouro do Sungué
Lake Urema
Miradouro dos Hipopótamos
Casa dos Leões
Mussicadzi
Gorongosa National Park
Muaredzi
Inchope, Chimoio, Beira
Chitengo
Picada do Urema
Urema
Portão No. 1
Pungué
Bué Maria
Posto de Nhascuvo

13

Gorongosa and the Caia Road

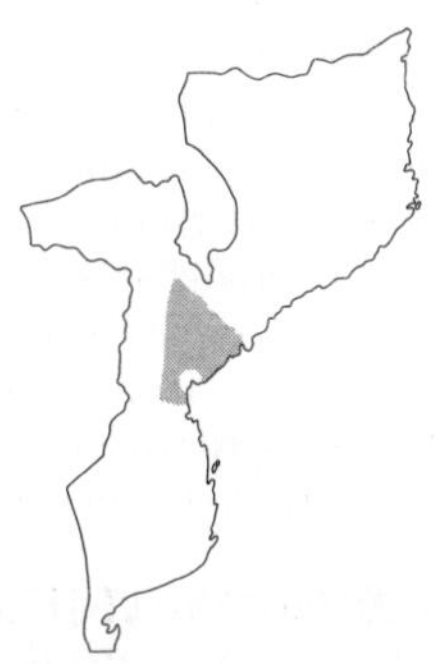

North of the EN6 through the Beira Corridor, the EN1 continues from the junction town of Inchope to the sleepy port of Quelimane, crossing the Zambezi at Caia. The 550km drive can easily be covered in a day – the road is surfaced all the way, and the Caia is now the site of a nippy bridge rather than a ponderous ferry – but it also offers access to some of Mozambique's most worthwhile inland landmarks, and the areas could as easily keep nature lovers (and birders in particular) busy for a week. Foremost among these attractions, only an hour's drive north of the EN6, is the vast Gorongosa National Park, which is gradually re-emerging from a long period of neglect to reclaim its slumbering reputation as the country's most alluring safari destination. Further north, Mount Gorongosa protects the largest extant Afro-montane forest in southern Africa, making it a green haven for hikers and birders. Also of interest as you approach Caia is the dense and bird-rich miombo woodland of the roadside Catapu Forestry Concession, and the relatively inaccessible but inestimably lush Zambezi Delta, part of which is protected within Marromeu National Park.

GORONGOSA NATIONAL PARK

Extending over 5,250km^2 at the southern end of the Rift Valley, Gorongosa National Park was Mozambique's flagship conservation area in the last years of the Portuguese colonial era, when it was widely regarded as one of the finest safari destinations anywhere in Africa, rivalling the Serengeti for its prodigious concentration of wildlife. Gorongosa has been through some lean times since then, particularly during the post-independence civil war, but it is now well on the road to recovery, and following the welcome intervention of the Carr Foundation in 2004, there is some cause for optimism that it might yet reclaim its place as one of the region's finest wildlife destinations.

Realistically, Gorongosa has some way to go in attaining this goal. For aficionados of the Big Five, there is a sporting chance of encountering lion and elephant, which are both increasing in number and reasonably habituated to vehicles, but buffalos are scarce, leopards are predictably furtive and rhinos are – no less predictably – extinct. Still, even as things stand, Gorongosa is unquestionably the best non-marine wildlife-viewing destination in Mozambique, with the floodplains around Chitengo in particular supporting large and rapidly increasing herds of waterbuck, reedbuck, impala and other antelope. And if most safari-goers might need a little persuasion to give Gorongosa a try, birdwatchers should have no such qualms: the park's tangled bush and mesmerising waterways are literally teeming with avian activity, and there is the added bonus of potential day visits to nearby Mount Gorongosa and its eagerly sought endemic race of green-headed oriole.

For independent travellers, especially self-sufficient campers with their own wheels, Gorongosa also has in its favour its relative affordability and accessibility, with the main camp situated perhaps an hour's drive north of the pivotal junction of the EN1 and EN6. For bigger-spending Africa addicts, the park already boasts one utterly charming exclusive tented camp run by Explore Gorongosa, whose knowledgeable owner-managers are all but guaranteed to infuse guests with their sense of excitement and wonder at witnessing the re-emergence of this formerly war-ravaged wilderness. And if all goes to plan, several more upmarket concessions will open in Gorongosa during the lifespan of this edition.

ECOLOGY AND VEGETATION Bounded by the Pungué River in the south and the Mucombeze in the north, the park is set within the Zambezi Basin and much of the terrain is low-lying, typically below 50m. It is traversed by a series of east-flowing waterways and associated floodplains that empty into a large seasonally fluctuating sump called Lake Urema, which lies at the heart of a 7,850km^2 catchment area on the park's eastern border. Several of these rivers rise on Mount Gorongosa, whose forested peak is prominent on the park's northern horizon, while others cross into the country from the highlands of eastern Zimbabwe. As with so many African parks, the ecology of Gorongosa is highly seasonal. During the rainy summer months of November to March, the park essentially comprises a vast partial wetland of which up to 200km^2 is completely submerged and much of the rest is waterlogged and all-but inaccessible to landlubbers. The floodwaters usually retreat over April and May, and by the end of the dry season, over August to October, the park has a more parched appearance, comprising large tracts of dry grassland and savanna interspersed with a few precious perennial water sources. The main vegetation type is mixed savanna, dominated by typical miombo species of the *Brachystegia* genus, but there are also large tracts of grassland, particularly along the floodplains, and some 14% of the park supports a cover of closed-canopy miombo or riparian woodland.

HISTORY Gorongosa National Park has its roots in a 1,000km^2 hunting reserve set aside in 1920 for the amusement of management and guests of the Mozambique Company, which controlled this part of the country by charter until 1940. In 1935, the reserve was enlarged by another 2,000km^2, partly to preserve its dwindling trophy herds of black rhinoceros and nyala antelope. The first tourist facility (the so-called Casa dos Leões or Lion House) was built on the Mussicadzi floodplain in 1940 but abandoned a year later after heavy flooding, leading to the construction of Chitengo Camp at its present-day site in 1941. In July 1960, the former hunting reserve was gazetted as a national park and expanded to cover its present-day area. By this time, Gorongosa was one of the most popular safari destinations in southern Africa, attracting more than 50,000 guests annually, and in the mid-1960s Chitengo was expanded to sleep more than 100 overnight guests.

The first aerial survey of the park, undertaken by Kenneth Tinley in 1972, counted 13,300 buffalo, 6,500 wildebeest, 3,500 hippo, 3,500 waterbuck, 3,300 zebra, 2,000 impala, 1,000 greater kudu, 800 hartebeest, 700 sable antelope, 500 eland, 200 lions and 100 spotted hyena. Then came the civil war, and following a Renamo attack on Chitengo in 1983, the park effectively ceased to function as a protected area, and instead became the site of frequent battles between the two opposing forces. Elephants were shot for their valuable ivory, antelopes and other ungulates were harvested as a source of meat, and although large predators such as lions and leopards were probably not directly targeted by the combatants, their numbers dwindled dramatically with this loss of suitable prey. Two years after the war ended, a 1994 survey indicated that the number of hippo, wildebeest and buffalo stood at fewer than 50 each, the elephant population at around 100 and waterbuck at 130.

Since then, rehabilitation of Gorongosa has been a gradual but steady process. In 1994, a joint initiative by the IUCN and African Development Bank attempted to re-establish the park by reopening some 100km of internal roads, clearing land mines, and appointing a team of former soldiers to help curb illegal hunting. This, however, was a relatively low-key initiative by comparison with the three-year agreement signed between the Mozambican government and the American entrepreneur and philanthropist Greg Carr in 2004, which led to the Carr Foundation's investment of more than US$10 million into the restoration of the park's battered infrastructure and diminished wildlife populations. By now, animal populations were visibly on the road to recovery, and a 2007 aerial survey counted 4,930 waterbuck, 3,830 warthog, 300 elephant, 300 sable antelope and 150 hippo, while buffalo and wildebeest numbers, partially boosted by a programme of reintroductions, both stood at around 200 head.

The Carr Foundation recommitted to Gorongosa in 2008 when it signed a fresh agreement undertaking to manage development of the park on behalf of the Mozambican government before handing it back to them at the end of 20-year period. Since then, Chitengo Safari Camp has been thoroughly revamped, and the pioneering private ecotourism operator Explore Gorongosa has opened an exclusive tented camp along the lines of the private reserves and concessions found in many other African countries. Wildlife is doing well too, with counts in 2009 suggesting that the elephant population has topped the 500 mark, while lion numbers have recovered to more than 50 and the sheer volume of ungulates on the floodplains starts to recall the park's pre-war heyday. Overall, Gorongosa had much to celebrate when it reached its 50th anniversary as a national park in July 2010, just months after *Africa's Lost Eden,* an acclaimed documentary about the park, debuted on the National Geographic to gave it the publicity boost of its lifetime.

The future looks exciting too. The latest move in ecotourism development has been to carve the park into eight sectors, one of which (essentially the existing game-viewing circuit) will continue to be utilised as a public sector, catering mainly to visitors to Chitengo, while the others will be leased to private concessionaires for the development of around 200 beds in total. These concession should start to open in 2011, an encouraging development in the broader context of a national tourist industry that is currently found wanting when it comes to the first component in the sort of world-class bush 'n' beach circuit that might encourage more international visitors to take an extended holiday in Mozambique (rather than tagging a Bazaruto Beach stay on to a safari elsewhere in southern Africa). Just before going to print, the Mozambican government announced that all of Mount Gorongosa above the 700m contour would be incorporated into the national park, and future plans include the creation of a buffer zone to extend the greater protected ecosystem by 3,500km^2, in line with a proposal first mooted by Tinley in 1972. In keeping with the Carr Foundation's broader philanthropic outlook, there are also solid plans in place to involve local communities as stakeholders in the park's development.

FEES Gorongosa National Park is shut during the rainy season, closing in December and reopening in April when the tracks have been repaired. The one-off park entrance fee works out at US$15 per person and US$15 per vehicle. An additional 'game drive fee' of US$25 per vehicle per day is charged to self-drivers who want to explore beyond Chitengo Camp. Guided three-hour game drives in open 4x4s are also offered out of Chitengo for US$25 per person. It is possible fees will rise significantly as tourism is re-established, so check the park website (*www.gorongosa.net*) for the latest details.

GETTING THERE AND AWAY

By car Gorongosa National Park lies to the north of the **EN6** and the main entrance gate can be accessed by heading along the **EN1** north from Inchope for 40km until you reach the clearly signposted turn-off to the right. From here it is another 10km to the entrance gate, where you need to stop and pick up a gate pass before driving another 18km to Chitengo Safari Camp, where the gate pass must be shown and entrance fees paid at reception. Except after heavy rain, Chitengo can be reached in most vehicles, but take it easy on the bends – there are some very corrugated stretches. A high clearance or better 4x4 maybe required to explore deeper in the park for a couple of months after the park reopens at the end of the rainy season. Note that while fuel may sometimes be sold to guests at Chitengo, this is not a formal service and it is best to arrive with a full tank (last fill-up points coming from north and south respectively are Vila Gorongosa and Inchope).

By transfer For those without private transport, road transfers can usually be arranged through the reception desk at Chitengo Safari Camp (see below), ideally with a few days' notice, but this will depend on vehicle availability. Transfers cost the equivalent of US$11 from the main junction on the EN1 (accessible by chapa from Inchope or from Vila Gorongosa), US$23 from Inchope; US$57 from Chimoio or US$63 from Beira. Alternatively, Explore Gorongosa, which runs Explorers Camp, can arrange full packages inclusive of air charters and/or road transfers from Beira, Vilankulo, Chimoio and pretty much anywhere else in Mozambique.

WHERE TO STAY

Exclusive

Explorers Camp (4 units) +263 4 291 7173 (Zimbabwe); m 82 862 4975; e info@oneafrica.co.za; www.exploregorongosa.com. The 1st, & thus far, only upmarket camp in the national park is a small relaxed owner-managed affair operated by Explore Gorongosa about 7km from the park headquarters at Chitengo. It currently comprises 4 spacious standing tents set along a seasonal watercourse lined with tall trees, each with king-size or twin sgl beds & an alfresco eco-friendly bathroom. It will eventually expand to 7 units including 2 treehouses. The camp has an intimate bush feel, with plenty of birdlife around, & a flexible roster of activities includes game drives & guided walks within the park, as well as day or overnight hikes to Mount Gorongosa, & fly-camping deeper in the park by special arrangement. The guides here are very knowledgeable about birds. *From US$475/800 sgl/dbl including all meals, drinks, activities & park fees.*

Mid-range and camping

Chitengo Safari Camp (18 rooms) 235 35010; m 82 302 0604; e reception@gorongosa.net; www.gorongosa.net. Situated 18km past the main entrance gate, this venerable rest camp opened back in 1941, was destroyed & closed in 1981, but reopened in 1995, since when it has seen immense developments funded partially by the Carr Foundation. Accommodation is in comfortable semi-detached bungalows with thatched roofs, twin or king-size beds, AC, netting & en-suite hot shower. There are also backpacker rooms & serviced platform tents using common ablutions, as well as a large campsite. Facilities include 2 swimming pools, a small gift shop selling T-shirts, lip balm & not much else, free Wi-Fi in the common areas,

& a selection of activities aimed at travellers without their own 4x4. The on-site Restaurant Chikalango has comfortable indoor & outdoor seating, a good selection of drinks, & à la carte meals in the US$4–8 range. Surprisingly, Visa cards are accepted. *US$96/126 sgl/dbl cabana B&B; US$39/60 sgl/twin backpacker room B&B; US$48/65 sgl/twin serviced platform tent B&B; US$9 pp camping.*

EXPLORING GORONGOSA Visitors to Explorers Camp (and doubtless any other concessions that open during the lifespan of this edition) will be offered a range of guided activities included in the room rate, while Chitengo Safari Camp also offers reasonably priced guided game drives every morning and afternoon. With your own 4x4, however, it is perfectly possible to explore the public part of the park – bounded by the Sungué River to the north and Pungué to the south – along a network of roads that are clearly numbered for use in conjunction with a map available at Chitengo's reception. Some of these roads may be closed after the rainy season, especially the approaches to Lake Urema, in the northeast of the public area, but they usually reopen as the floodwaters recede and the dry season takes grip.

GORONGOSA'S BIRDS

with Keith Barnes & Josh Engel (www.tropicalbirding.com)

Gorongosa National Park is one of the most rewarding destinations in Mozambique, with more than 500 species recorded, and what it lacks in terms of the sort of forest specials associated with Mount Gorongosa, it compensates for in terms of variety, with waterbirds in particular being very well represented. The open woodlands, grassland and huge wetlands of this national park make for easy and highly rewarding birding.

The road into Chitengo passes through many grassy areas (keep an eye out for moustached grass warbler and a wide variety of finches) as well as extensive miombo woodlands, with thick-billed and barred long-tailed cuckoos, racket-tailed roller, Arnot's chat, southern hyliota, purple-banded sunbird, broad-tailed paradise whydah and Cabanis's bunting heading a list of local specialities. The localised sooty falcon is among the many raptors that can be seen along the road, and bronze-winged coursers are present, but probably seasonal.

The area around the campground has quite good birding. Collared palm-thrush is fairly common, but black-and-white flycatcher is more difficult to find, though it is often seen calling from the tall trees around the cabanas. Dickinson's kestrel, red-necked falcon and racket-tailed roller all occur here too.

The most important seasonal wetlands accessible from Chitengo are the Mussicadzi and Urema floodplains. There's always a fair amount of avian activity at these floodplains, and sometimes they host fantastic numbers of pelicans, storks and other large waterbirds, alongside such sought-after species as Baillon's crake, long-toed lapwing, wattled crane and greater painted snipe.

A useful checklist of birds recorded in the park can be downloaded at http://files.gorongosa.net/Gorongosa%20Bird%20Checklist.pdf. Also worth noting is that Chitengo Camp offers 90-minute early morning guided bird walks along the Pungué River for US$10 per person -- a great opportunity to seek out species that aren't easily picked up from a vehicle.

An excellent short drive from Chitengo follows Road 1 north to the Mussicadzi floodplain, from where you can follow Road 4 up the east side of the plain or Road 9 up the west side. While you are heading out this way, be aware that the pan alongside Road 1 between the junction with roads 2 and 3 is a favoured drinking hole for the shy but beautiful nyala and sable antelope. On the floodplain, you'll see plenty of waterbuck, reedbuck, impala, oribi and warthog in this area, as well as a dazzling selection of waterbirds, and most likely a few troops of baboon (officially listed as yellow baboon, but some experts believe that the population here is intermediate with the Chacma baboon and may warrant a unique subspecific status). You'll also pass the legendary Casa dos Leões, the ruins of the original tourist accommodation built here in 1949, and so named because its roof was a favoured resting place for lions in the 1970s. You could return via Road 6 and Roads 2 or 3; there is generally less wildlife in this area, but the thickets are good for greater kudu, nyala, bushbuck and the pretty samango monkey. For a longer game drive, return along road 4 via Lake Urema, which is known for its waterbird concentrations and forms the main foraging ground for the park's 500-odd elephants. A short diversion up Road 11 leads to a hippo pool at the southeast end of the lake. From here you can return to Chitengo via Roads 8 and 2.

MOUNT GORONGOSA

Towering above the northwest horizon of the namesake national park, the Serra de Gorongosa is a wide isolated massif that rises almost 1.5km above the surrounding plains to a 1,862m peak called Gogogo. The mountain has long been legendary among birders as the only southern African location for the green-headed oriole, a spectacular and vociferous forest dweller whose main range is centred upon the Eastern Arc Mountains of Tanzania. However, this eagerly sought bird might be most significant as a flagship species for what is probably the largest continuous area of Afro-montane south of the Zambezi, a magnificent stand of tall evergreen trees and tangled undergrowth alive with birdsong and the chattering of monkeys. Threatened by encroaching cultivation and charcoal production, these forests swathe the upper slopes of the mountain, a major regional watershed that feeds five rivers, including three that drain into Lake Urema and two that empty into the Pungué River on its southern boundary.

Mount Gorongosa was not accorded any official protection until recently, but the boundaries of the nearby national park are in the process of being redefined to incorporate the dwindling forests above the 700m contour. There are also plans to establish a formal ecotourism programme to help benefit the estimated 2,000 people who inhabit the lower slopes and depend on the mountain for their livelihood. The long-term goal is that community members will train as guides and that a fee structure will be put in place to help boost community coffers. As things stand, however, the situation with visiting Mount Gorongosa is rather fluid and flexible: day or overnight hikes out of the national park can be arranged through Explore Gorongosa or Chitengo Camp (see page 230), but it is also possible to visit independently from Vila Gorongosa (see page 235) or from the new Nyankuku campsite at the base of the mountain, though the last is difficult without a private 4x4. It is more than likely that further tourist development will take during the lifespan of this edition.

Several hiking options are possible, all starting at Nyankuku, which doubles as the site of a community-based reforestation project. An attractive short walk, about one hour in either direction, and without too many steep gradients, leads to the

BIRDING MOUNT GORONGOSA

with Keith Barnes & Josh Engel (www.tropicalbirding.com)

More than 250 species have been recorded on the mountain and in its immediate vicinity, including several specials. The best known of these is the green-headed oriole, an isolated population regarded as a distinct endemic subspecies. Another subspecies confined to the mountain is an isolated sunbird population that was originally listed as Miombo double-collared and is now officially listed as greater double-collared, but may in fact be an endemic species. The forests of Gorongosa are also thought to harbour the world's largest single population of the localised and very attractive Swynnerton's robin.

Experienced birders have recorded a total of 100 species on the mountain in one day, not all of them associated with forests. The trail from Nyankuku passes first through agricultural areas, then a patchwork of thickets and farmland. These open areas are excellent for finches, and as well as the bronze and red-backed mannikins, Jameson's fire-finches, red bishops and other common species, keep an eye out for magpie mannikin, orange-winged pytilia, and grey- and yellow-bellied waxbills. This is also the favoured habitat of the mystery double-collared sunbird and the localised moustached warbler, while thickets and forest patches can be rewarding for birds like blue-spotted wood-dove, Anchieta's tchagra, pale batis, Vanga flycatcher and red-throated twinspot.

The endemic race of green-headed oriole is occasionally seen in the forested ravine below Morrumbodze Falls, but this is a long shot and anybody who is serious about seeing this bird will need to hike into the forest proper. Fortunately, it is not uncommon, and its presence is often betrayed by a typically fluid oriole call, but the odds of seeing it are highest if you get to the forest edge before 08.30 or so. Other notable forest species here include silvery-cheeked hornbill, trumpeter hornbill, Livingstone's turaco, eastern bronze-naped pigeon, Narina trogon, pallid honeyguide, white-tailed blue flycatcher, Chirinda apalis, Swynnerton's robin, thrush-nightingale, white-starred robins, black-fronted bush-shrike. If you hike to the peak, you might well see the endangered blue swallow, and at all altitudes, keep an eye out for raptors, which include Ayres's hawk-eagle, African cuckoo-hawk, lizard buzzard, African goshawk and African crowned eagle.

Morrumbodze Falls, a spectacular sight as it crashes over a series of ledges into the base of a ravine about 100m below. For dedicated birders, the most popular option is to head to the forest edge about two hours' walk from Nyankuku, a steepish hike that requires the earliest possible start to boost your chances of seeing green-headed oriole, and then to return via the waterfall, which takes about two hours. It is also possible to hike through the forest all the way to the summit, which lies on a plateau of heath-like vegetation dotted with proteas, strelitzias and other species reminiscent of Cape fynbos. The summit can be reached on a very long day trip (bank on at least six hours up, and two hours down) or as an overnight hike, carrying all camping gear, food, etc.

GETTING THERE AND AWAY The normal trailhead for hikes is a campsite called Nyankuku (literally 'Place of the Chicken'), where facilities amount to a patch of cleared lawn surrounded by invasive eucalyptus trees, and a drop toilet. To get there, follow the EN1 north from Vila Gorongosa for about 10km, then turn right onto an unsignposted dirt road surrounded by huts near the top of a rise, a short distance before a bridge across the Morrumbodze River. It's about 12km from this junction to the campsite along a rough intersecting track (if in doubt, stick to the right), so it requires high clearance (possibly 4x4 after rain) and most of an hour to get there. There is safe parking at the campsite for day or overnight visitors; pitching a tent costs US$5 per person, and guide fees are US$10 per half-day per party.

For travellers without a vehicle, the easiest option is to arrange a formal day trip from Chitengo, which costs US$42 per person including transport to and from the base camp, and guides. Alternatively, it might be possible to rent a car or bicycle in Vila Gorongosa, or you could walk in with all the gear you require and camp overnight at the Nyankuku. Trips can also be arranged through a local organisation called Mangwana (e *info@ecomangwana.com; www.ecomangwana.com*) but best contact a while in advance. For people without private transport, Mangwana can arrange to have a guide waiting at the village of Canda, which lies on the EN1 some 25km north of Vila Gorongosa, and is the closest trailhead accessible by chapa.

So far as we can ascertain, it is easy enough to arrange a day hike into the forest informally and to find a guide locally. However, it is not technically clear whether this is permitted or you are obliged to make all arrangements through Chitengo or Mangwana. Either way, a more structured approach to hikes and ecotourism seems likely now that the upper slopes of the mountain fall within Gorongosa National Park. The local Chigorongosa people hold the mountain sacred and it is our understanding that summit hikes may be undertaken only with the ceremonial blessing of the local chief (known as the *regulo*). You don't need to attend this ceremony yourself, unless of course you want to, but some advance warning may be required and you will need to provide a bouquet of tobacco, alcohol and other goodies to ensure all goes well.

THE EN1 FROM INCHOPE TO CAIA

The surfaced 550km road running northeast from Inchope on the EN6 to the port of Quelimane, crossing the Zambezi using the new motor bridge at Caia, is the most important through-route connecting northern and southern Mozambique, and it will be used by almost all travellers heading between these two halves of the country. The drive, though long, is not too demanding, as the road is in good condition for most of its length, and traffic volumes are quite low. For those using public transport, chapas cover the route in stages, with the most likely places you'll need to change vehicle being Vila Gorongosa (60km from Inchope), Caia (320km from Inchope) and Nicoadala (about 40km before Quelimane). The TCO coach between Beira and Nampula (a 14-hour trip stopping in Quelimane), also follows this road, leaving Beira at 04.00 on Mondays, Wednesdays and Fridays, and Nampula at the same time on Tuesdays, Thursdays and Saturdays.

The southern part of this road offers access to Gorongosa National Park and Mount Gorongosa, the turn-offs to which respectively lie about 40km and 70km north of Inchope. The drive can also be broken up at the Catapu Forestry Concession, a favourite with birdwatchers, or at the riverside town of Caia, which provides a useful base for several motorised excursions upstream or downstream along the Zambezi.

INCHOPE Situated at the junction of the EN1 and the EN6 between Chimoio and Beira, Inchope is arguably the single most important road pivot anywhere in Mozambique, though that's about as far as it goes in the superlative stakes. Spreading for a couple of hundred metres along the EN6 east of the main intersection, it has a bustling little market – cashews and pineapples are the local specialities – and a few shops and local restaurants, and there is plenty of chapa transport available in all directions. There's no accommodation here, or any bank or ATM, and private moneychangers tend to offer a lousy rate. Otherwise, facilities are limited to a solitary BP filling station about 100m along the EN1 north of the junction.

VILA GORONGOSA Straddling the EN1 about 60km north of Inchope, Vila Gorongosa is a substantial town of around 15,000 people set at an altitude of 380m in the shadow of the eponymous mountain. Prior to independence, the town was known as Vila Paiva de Andrade (after a 16th-century Portuguese philosopher) and it had a reputation as being rather pretty, an adjective that doesn't really seem apt today. It is potentially a useful springboard for visits to Gorongosa National Park and even more so to Mount Gorongosa; the turn-off to the former lies 20km south along the EN1 towards Inchope, while the latter can be reached along a dirt road that branches eastward from the EN1 about 11km north of town. The town is notable for its busy agricultural market, at the main intersection, which sells fresh produce from the nearby mountain slopes. The chapa station opposite this is the place to pick up chapas to Inchope, Beira or Caia. Other facilities include a BIM Millennium bank with two ATMs about 500m back along the Inchope road, and a rather inconspicuous filling station alongside the EN1 north, immediately after the turn-off to Inhaminga.

If you need a room or bite to eat, the place to head for is the **Pousada Azul**, which lies about 200m from the main intersection along the side road running northeast past the market. Here you'll find a selection of neat rooms ranging from US$11 for a single using common showers to US$27 for the best en-suite double, safe parking, and a pleasant balcony where you can enjoy a cold beer or meal – typical Mozambican fare ranging from US$2 for a sandwich to US$4–6 for a full meal.

CATAPU FORESTRY CONCESSION This 250km^2 private concession, bisected by the EN1 some 30km south of Caia, is managed by TCT Dalmann, an advocate of sustainable forestry of indigenous tress, in particular the African blackwood (*Dalbergia melanoxylon*). The trees here are harvested using a traditional method of woodland management called coppicing, which entails the cyclic felling of trees in a manner that allows them to regrow from the original stumps to attain maturity about four times faster than they would from seedlings. As a result, the miombo woodland here feels more like wild bush than artificial plantation, and supports a varied fauna, including various medium–small mammals (red duiker, warthog, vervet monkey) as well as offering some of the finest miombo birding in Mozambique along a great network of walking trails. This is perhaps the best place in Mozambique to see the localised chestnut-fronted helmetshrike, alongside the likes of Narina trogon, Angola pitta, Livingstone's flycatcher, Vanga flycatcher, Woodward's batis and Arnot's chat, while patches of riparian woodland host silvery-cheeked hornbill, crested guineafowl and African broadbill. Catapu is also a popular base with dedicated birdwatching tours wanting to explore the bird-rich Zambezi floodplain 20 minutes' drive north, and it can be used as a base to visit Mary Livingstone's grave at Chupanga.

Where to stay and eat

Mphingwe Camp (11 rooms) 23 302161; m 82 301 6436; e tctcatupu@gmail.com; www.dalmann.com. Mhpingwe is the Sena name for the African blackwood, one of many varieties of tree that grow wild around this lovely bush camp, which opened on the Catapu Forestry Concession in 2007. A couple of hundred metres from the EN1 & clearly signposted, it is staffed by English speakers & offers accommodation in neat wood cabins, some en suite, & a shady outdoor restaurant-bar serves meals in the US$5–10 range. *Great value at US$15/20 sgl/dbl with shared bathroom, or US$18/28 sgl/dbl ensuite.*

CAIA Situated 320km past Inchope, Caia is an inherently unremarkable town, though it does have a rather attractive setting on the banks of the Zambezi, and it seems set for some economic expansion following the long-awaited opening of the 2,376m-long Armando Guebuza Bridge to replace a tired old ferry service in August 2009. Built at a cost of around US$80 million, this is the longest road bridge anywhere along the Zambezi's length (though it is shorter than the rail bridge at Sena) and it is also the only place downriver of where drivers can cross between northern and southern Mozambique. The biggest focal point for passing traffic seems to be the Petromac filling station alongside the main road, which is attached to a good supermarket, clean toilets and a Standard Bank with ATM. A couple of interesting days out from Caia can be had (see *Excursions from Caia* below), although you'll need your own wheels.

Where to stay Arguably the nicest place to stay in the Caia region, and certainly the best value, is Mphingwe Camp, 30km south along the EN1 (see above), but there are a few other options closer to town.

Cuácua Lodge (9 units) m 82 312 0528 or 960 1198; e cuacualodge@gmail.com. Situated on a rocky wooded hill overlooking the Zambezi about 1km north of the Caia Bridge, this attractive new lodge offers good birding & fishing, free bicycle usage, a decent restaurant specialising in meat dishes (beef & lamb from an associated ranch) & a newly built swimming pool. There is the choice of 1- or 2-bedroom houses, the latter sleeping up to 5, spaced out along the thickly wooded slopes, with AC, en-suite hot shower & veranda. *From US$50/60 sgl/dbl. US$4 pp camping.*

Hotel Caia (20 rooms) 237 10026. Situated about 1.5km from the town centre (turn left immediately after the Petrocom) where it overlooks a seasonal inlet of the Zambezi, this adequate but characterless hotel is housed in a large pink building with rooms arranged around a courtyard. Clean en-suite rooms come with TV, AC & en-suite hot shower, & a restaurant is attached. *Not the greatest value at US$35/42/53 sgl/dbl/twin.*

Caia Lodge m 82 77 38 770; e caialodge@yahoo.co.uk. Sited about 2.5km down the road between Caia & Sombreiro, the accommodation is either camping or in casas. There is a restaurant & bar on site, & they also allow self-catering. *Camping US$15.50, casas from US$20.*

Excursions from Caia

Mary Livingstone's grave Mary Moffat was the daughter of Robert Moffat, a Scottish missionary also known for his prowess as a gardener. Moffat worked at Kuruman in South Africa for most of his life and during his infrequent visits back to Britain gave lectures on the work that the Missionary Society was doing in Africa. In was at one such lecture that the young Dr Livingstone, then on the verge of leaving for China, changed his mind and decided to work in Africa. In 1844, Livingstone married Moffat's daughter Mary, who accompanied him on several of his journeys (much to the disapproval of her parents) and died in 1862 at Chupanga.

BIRDING CHINIZUIA FOREST AND THE ZAMBEZI DELTA

Keith Barnes & Josh Engel (www.tropicalbirding.com)

The Chinizuia Forest, which lies along the old 4x4-only route from Dondo to Caia (passing along the east side of Gorongosa National Park), is famous among birdwatchers as the site to see a slew of local specialities while offering some of the best miombo and forest birding in all of southern Africa. The area remains unprotected and under severe logging pressure, but there is still excellent forest, both along the road from Dondo to Muanza, and from the turn-off (11km north of Muanza, towards Chenapamima) to the Chinizuia River. Take the turn-off on the left about 35km after leaving the main road to find a camping area and a forested stream.

The birding is outstanding, and a wide variety of uncommon and local species are regularly seen. Among the numerous common miombo species are the localised southern banded snake-eagle, Ayres's hawk-eagle, racket-tailed roller, black-and-white flycatcher, chestnut-fronted helmet-shrike (alongside Retz's and white helmet-shrikes), yellow-bellied hyliota, red-throated twinspot and lesser seed-cracker. Near the camping area and stream, East Coast akalat, white-breasted alethe and barred long-tailed cuckoo are common but very difficult to see, and African pitta is uncommon and also difficult to see. Also in this area are eastern bronze-naped pigeon, silvery-cheeked hornbill, African broadbill, Narina trogon, speckle-throated woodpecker, tiny greenbul, black-headed apalis, and plain-backed and western violet-backed sunbirds. Camping will be anything but quiet, as African wood-owl, barred owlet, Verreaux's eagle-owl and fiery-necked nightjar create a night-time chorus.

Perhaps even better than Chinizuia, because of its better roads and easier accessibility, the Zambezi Coutadas (hunting concessions) offer a very similar birdlife to Chinizuia but with the added excitement of abundant big game. The area is best accessed from Mphingwe Camp in the Catapu Forestry Concession (see pages 235–6), where up-to-date access and road-condition information should be sought. It contains an exceptional diversity of habitats, including outstanding coastal forest, savanna and wetlands. The forest birding, including such gems as white-chested alethe and East Coast akalat, is very similar to Chinizuia. However, it also contains grasslands and wetlands with birds like wattled crane, lesser jacana and huge flocks of African openbill and other waterbirds.

Her grave can still be seen in the Catholic Mission grounds at Chupanga, which lies about 25km downriver of Caia along a dirt road that may require 4x4, especially during the rainy season.

Marromeu Buffalo Reserve Nominally protecting a 1500km² area of grassland and seasonal swamps on the southern side of the Zambezi Delta, this special reserve was set aside during the colonial era to protect one of the world's densest populations of buffalo, estimated to stand at 30,000–60,000 at its peak. Unfortunately, however, the ecology of this seasonally inundated delta has changed greatly in recent decades as the result of the multiple dams built along the Zambezi, which have collectively controlled and contained the river's flow to reduce the natural flooding that occurs during the rains and open the area up to hunters. The area also suffered badly during the civil war, and by 1994 it was estimated that around 1,000 buffalo remained, while waterbuck numbers were reduced from around 50,000 in the 1970s to fewer than 200, and the hippo population crashed from almost 3,000 to about 250.

Wildlife numbers have reputedly increased since the end of the war, and the delta still holds significant numbers of elephant, Lichtenstein's hartebeest, sable antelope and predators such as lion and leopard. The reserve also still supports the country's densest waterbird populations, including 100 breeding pairs of the endangered wattled crane. Marromeu is currently undeveloped for tourism but it is possible to drive there from Caia, following a 100km track that runs southeast from Chupanga. About 34km along this road, you reach Vila Marromeu, the site of Mozambique's largest sugar refinery, and a couple of adequate small hotels. The road is good as far as Vila Marromeu, but 4x4 will almost certainly be necessary as you approach the reserve itself

Sena Railway Bridge Heading west from Caia for around 60km brings you to Vila de Sena, which was one of the most important outposts on the Zambezi throughout the Portuguese colonial era, and may well stand on the site of the Swahili trading post of Seyouna mentioned in a 12th-century Arab document by Abu al-Fida. It is also the site of the 3,670m Dona Ana Bridge, built by the Portuguese in 1934, and the longest railway bridge in the world at the time of its construction. The bridge was blown up and rendered unusable by Renamo in the 1980s, but it reopened as a single-lane car bridge following repairs in 1995. It closed again in 2006, and might possibly reopen as a railway bridge during the lifespan of this edition. With a decent 4x4, it is possible to continue along the Zambezi all the way to Tete, a little-used route that's best explored in the dry season.

14

Tete

Seen from a bus window, Tete is not the most inviting province of Mozambique: the dry, dusty badlands are covered in puny acacia scrub punctuated by the occasional thatched village whose inhabitants do well simply to subsist in this harsh, arid climate. The main tourist focus, if you can call it that, is the city of Tete, which lies at a low altitude on the south bank of the Zambezi, in a climate that contrives to be both dusty and almost intolerably humid. In the harsh light of the day, the town has little to no aesthetic appeal, though in the softer light of dusk its riverbank takes on an altogether more pleasing hue. And a recent influx of mining investment has clearly given its restaurants and hotels a facelift, so that the town appears far less run-down than it did a few years back.

Mozambique's most westerly province, Tete ranks among the most peculiar relics of the colonial carve-up of Africa. Following four centuries of intermittent Portuguese settlement, Cecil Rhodes tried to append the region to Britain's so-called 'red corridor' between Cape Town and Egypt in the 1870s. This claim was thwarted when the French politician Patrice Mac-Mahon formally awarded Tete to Portugal (earning himself bar-room posterity in the name of the Mozambican beer 2M), even though most bordering territories went to Britain. As a result, the wedge-shaped province, which juts northwest from Manica into what was formerly the British Central African Protectorate, shares longer borders with three other countries (Zimbabwe to the west, Zambia to the north and Malawi to the east) than it does with the rest of Mozambique.

Looking at a map, one would most likely classify Tete as part of northern Mozambique. In reality, however, it has long been isolated from the other four provinces of the north by Malawi and the Shire River, and both the province and its capital enjoy far closer economic links to south-central Mozambique. Indeed, the only surfaced road that connects Tete to the rest of Mozambique, the EN102 from Chimoio, is far less busy than the EN103 (or Tete Corridor) that links Blantyre (Malawi) to Harare (Zimbabwe) via the city of Tete.

The province has a population of around 1.7 million, and the main ethnic groups are the Nyanja, the Nyungue and the Sena. Its virtual separation from the rest of Mozambique and its importance as the most straightforward route between Zimbabwe and Malawi have resulted in several mild anomalies; for instance, that considerably more English is understood in Tete than in most other parts of the country.

In the 1990s, when Zimbabwe was enjoying its heyday as a backpacker hub and Mozambique was still emerging from decades of turmoil, the Tete Corridor (known as the 'Gun Run' during the civil war) probably saw more traveller through-traffic than the rest of Mozambique's provinces combined, even if few spent longer in the country than the few hours required to drive between Blantyre and Harare. This

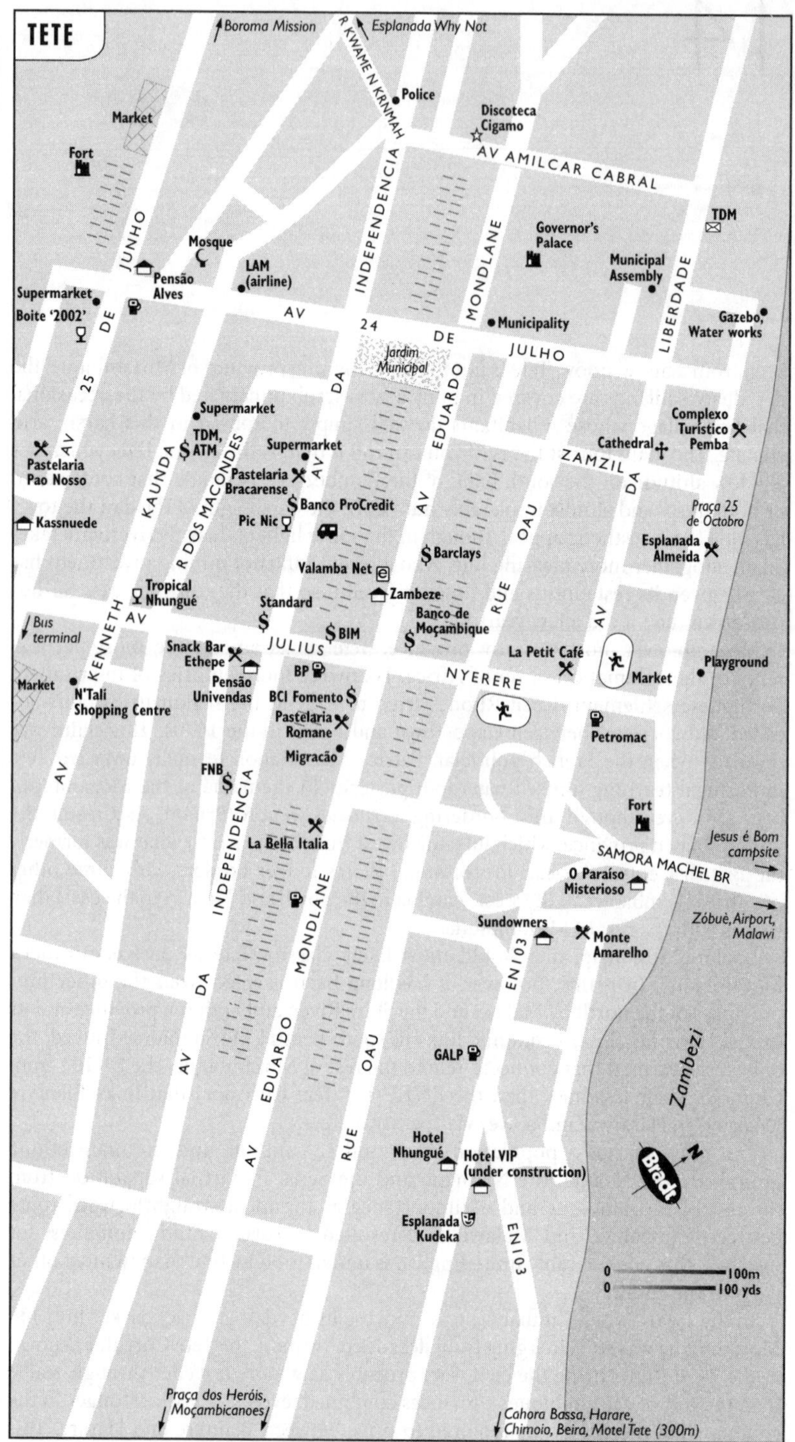

TETE
Boroma Mission
Esplanada Why Not
R KWAME N KRNMAH
Police
Discoteca Cigamo
AV AMILCAR CABRAL
Market
Fort
TDM
Governor's Palace
Municipal Assembly
Mosque
LAM (airline)
Pensão Alves
Supermarket
Boite '2002'
AV 24 DE JULHO
Municipality
Gazebo, Water works
Jardim Municipal
AV 25 DE JUNHO
AV DA INDEPENDENCIA
AV EDUARDO MONDLANE
AV DA LIBERDADE
Supermarket
TDM, ATM
Supermarket
Complexo Turistico Pemba
Cathedral
ZAMZIL
Pastelaria Pao Nosso
AV KAUNDA
R DOS MACONDES
Pastelaria Bracarense
Banco ProCredit
Pic Nic
Kassnuede
Praça 25 de Octobro
RUE OAU
Barclays
Esplanada Almeida
Valamba Net
Tropical Nhungué
Zambeze
Standard
Banco de Moçambique
Bus terminal
AV KENNETH
BIM
AV JULIUS NYERERE
Snack Bar Ethepe
La Petit Café
Market
Playground
Market
N'Tali Shopping Centre
Pensão Univendas
BP
BCI Fomento
Pastelaria Romane
Petromac
Migracão
FNB
Fort
La Bella Italia
Jesus é Bom campsite
SAMORA MACHEL BR
O Paraíso Misterioso
Zóbuè, Airport, Malawi
Sundowners
Monte Amarelho
EN103
GALP
Zambezi
Hotel Nhungué
Hotel VIP (under construction)
Esplanada Kudeka
0 100m
0 100 yds
Praça dos Heróis, Moçambicanoes
Cahora Bassa, Harare, Chimoio, Beira, Motel Tete (300m)

backpacker traffic has of course diminished greatly over the past decade, though the route through Chimoio and Tete is still the quickest and easiest option between southern Mozambique and Malawi. But while it has fallen off the travel map, Tete is experiencing a local economic boom thanks to the discovery of several rich coal seams in the province and a spate of multi-national investment.

Away from the main road, Tete Province offers at least one worthwhile and straightforward excursion in the form of the vast Cahora Bassa Dam and the nearby town of Songo – the latter with a remarkably fresh highland climate after the claustrophobic humidity of Tete. Further off the beaten track, but also of interest, is the attractive mission at Boroma, which lies on the west bank of the Zambezi some 60km upriver from Tete.

TETE

The eponymous capital of Tete Province, often and with some justification claimed to be the hottest town in Mozambique, is situated on the southwest bank of the Zambezi roughly 650km upriver from its mouth, at an altitude of only 175m above sea level. It is an important transport hub, thanks to its position on the Tete Corridor between Malawi and Zimbabwe. The city expanded greatly during the construction of the Cahora Bassa Dam, and it is now the third-largest town in the Mozambican interior after Nampula and Chimoio, with a population estimated at 170,000.

Tete became very run-down during the civil war, and plenty of ruinous old buildings still evoke the city's moribund aura at the start of the millennium, but today the overall impression (at least by comparison with ten years ago) is of rejuvenation and rehabilitation. For this writer, the definitive moment was walking into the renovated Hotel Zambeze and trying to absorb the fact that this plush establishment was the same dump that had reduced several of my tour clients to tears back in 2001. But everywhere in town there are freshly painted façades, newly tarred roads and other encouraging signs of urban renewal, much of it associated with the region's emergent coal-mining industry, which is set to boom over the next decade.

HISTORY Tete is a settlement of some antiquity. Even before the Portuguese arrived in east Africa, it lay at the junction of the Zambezi and three of the four main trading routes from the Sofala area into the African interior. The site of the modern town was probably occupied by Muslim traders in the 15th century, when it formed the main link between the coast and the gold fairs of Karangaland. Tete was settled by a few Portuguese adventurers in 1531, and by 1630 it supported around 20 *mazungo* households.

Contemporary reports suggest that Tete was rather makeshift in appearance until around 1767, when it was made the seat of administration for the Zambezi Valley and a permanent garrison of 100 soldiers was posted there. By the end of the 18th century, Tete's city centre consisted of roughly 30 stone houses enclosed by a 3m-high wall, as well as a hospital, trade factory, governor's residence and council building.

Today the concrete part of Tete is on the southern side of the river, linked to the northern side by the Samora Machel Bridge. As with the other provincial capitals, there are very few buildings remaining that pre-date World War II.

GETTING THERE AND AWAY

By air The **airport** is 5km out of town towards Zóbuè and any bus travelling between Tete and Moatize, a small town 20km to the east, can drop you at the entrance. **LAM** flies between Maputo and Tete and has an office office on Avenida 24 de Julho (*25 222056*).

By car Tete lies about halfway along the **EN103** (Tete Corridor), a 280km road that connects the Zimbabwean border at Nyamapanda to Zóbuè on the Malawian border. This road is surfaced and in good condition all the way, although due to the amount of heavy traffic you may come across the odd pot-holed section. The drive to Tete from Blantyre (Malawi) usually takes about three to four hours, not allowing for border crossings, and the drive from Harare (Zimbabwe) about an hour longer. About 16km before Zóbuè, the **EN223** heads north from the EN103 heading for the other major border with Malawi at Dedza, which is a little closer to Lilongwe. The road is of a similar quality to the EN103, but it adds another 150km or so to the journey. The EN221/548 from Tete via Bene to the Zambian border at Cassacatiza is seldom used by travellers, and we have no recent reports about its condition. The main access road to Tete from within Mozambique is the EN102 from Chimoio, a 430km stretch of well-maintained asphalt that shouldn't require more than five hours' driving time.

By bus and chapa The long distance **bus terminal** is on Avenida da Independência, just up from the junction with Avenida Julius Nyerere. At least one bus daily travels between Chimoio and Tete, costing US$8.50, and leaving at around 04.00 and arriving at 11.00 in either direction. This gives Malawi-bound travellers from Chimoio plenty of time to head on to Blantyre: **chapas** to Zóbuè usually wait outside the bus terminus (failing that, you may have to walk a few hundred metres to the larger of the two markets along Avenida 25 de Junho), and once across the border there is lots of transport from Mwanza to Blantyre.

Most other chapas park below Samora Machel Bridge at the junction of Avenida Julius Nyerere and Rua Unidade Africana. If you are heading to Songo or Estima (also known as Chitima) then chapas can also be found outside the post office on Avenida da Liberdade. Another good place to wait is outside the smaller of the two markets on Avenida 25 de Junho, just up from Avenida Julius Nyerere, as many chapas will run by here looking for extra passengers. If you are heading to Boroma, then you'll need to wait just beyond the junction out on Avenida 25 de Junho (for more details, see pages 247–8).

WHERE TO STAY Tete has a fair range of accommodation, although it is rather short on budget options. If you're camping, then the only dedicated campsite is the rather grim Jesus é Bom – there are other places that will let you camp, but it's clearly a matter of their just using whatever space they happen to have available rather than actually setting up a campsite.

Upmarket

Hotel Zambeze (81 rooms) Av Eduardo Mondlane; 252 23100; e f.pinto@tvcbo.co.mz. This 5-storey colonial-era landmark in the heart of the city had become seriously seedy & run-down prior to a 2007 makeover that re-established it as Tete's most prestigious address. The spacious, tastefully refurbished rooms have tiled floors, DSTV, AC, Wi-Fi & en-suite hot shower, & suites are available. There's also a chic 5th-floor bar & restaurant offering fabulous views over the city to the river. *US$77/105 budget sgl/dbl; US$100/128 standard sgl/dbl; suites from US$135; all rates B&B.*

Hotel Nhungué (31 rooms) Rua Agostinho Neto; m 82 522 4071 or 84 749 3547; e hotelnunghue@gmail.com. Set around a green central courtyard about 200m south of the bridge, this smart business hotel opened in 2009 & is already attracting plenty of repeat business. The spacious rooms are tiled, with AC, DSTV & en-suite hot shower. There's Wi-Fi, a good bar & restaurant, & the staff seem very switched on. *US$67/80/90 sgl/dbl/suite B&B.*

Mid-range

Motel Tete (35 rooms) EN103; 252 22345; m 82 588 2040. The pleasant & fairly big rooms at this popular waterfront motel have AC fridges, DSTV & Wi-Fi. There's a restaurant on site, tables & chairs overlooking the river itself, & secure parking. *US$57 dbl.*

Pensão Univendas (20 rooms) Av da Independência. Set above the Univendas store on the junction with Av Julius Nyerere, this can be identified by a set of stairs with 'Flats, Suites, Quartos' on the window above the entrance. The twin rooms are quite nice, & have AC & TV, but steeply priced given that they all use common bathrooms. *US$46/80 sgl/dbl.*

Budget

O Paraíso Misterioso (20 rooms) Off the EN3 past Sundowners; m 82 431 9560. Though it's not quite as enigmatic or heavenly as the name suggests, this is definitely the most pleasant option in this price range, with a great waterfront position in view of the bridge, & large green grounds centred around a well-chlorinated swimming pool. Currently under renovation, it still feels like a work in progress, but the comfortable dbl rooms have AC, nets, flat-screen DSTV & en-suite hot shower. A good restaurant is attached. *US$43 dbl.*

Sundowners (10 rooms) EN103 about 200m from Samora Machel Bridge; m 82 568 1568 or 82 960 5343. Set at the back of a large thatched sports bar, the rooms here are potentially noisy but otherwise seem pretty decent, & come with en-suite hot shower, DSTV & AC. *US$43 dbl.*

Pensão Alves (10 rooms) Av 24 de Julho; 252 22523. Basic but comfortable, this family-run place has a brightly painted exterior reflecting the friendly mood you'll encounter inside. There is a decent restaurant/bar downstairs that normally closes very early, but hosts a disco at w/ends, when it may get rather noisy. The clean rooms have 2 3/4 beds, AC, TV & a writing desk. *US$29 twin using common showers, or US$34 en suite.*

Shoestring

Hotel Kassuende (30 rooms) Av 25 de Junho; 252 22374. This place isn't the smartest, but it's about the cheapest option in Tete, & the better rooms come with balcony, TV & fan. *US$18/23 sgl/dbl using common showers, or US$27–45 en suite.*

Jesus é Bom m 82 525 0300. The only official campsite in Tete, but it's a bit of a dump, and set on the opposite side of the bridge to the town centre. The kitchen & toilets are both somewhat tumbledown. *Camping US$3 pp.*

WHERE TO EAT AND DRINK Tete has a wide selection of restaurants and bars, and the influx of mining capital means that new places are opening all the time.

Hotel Zambeze Av Eduardo Mondlane; 252 23100; 07.00–10.30, 12.00–13.30 & 17.00–22.00. The 5th-floor restaurant here is the finest in town, & priced accordingly, with a tempting selection of seafood & steaks. The view over town is immense, especially after dark. *US$12–15.*

La Bella Italia Av Eduardo Mondlane; 252 22821; m 84 736 9264; 19.00–23.00 daily. This highly rated restaurant/pub serves good pizzas, pasta & seafood. Indoor & outdoor seating available. *US$8–15.*

La Petit Café Av Julius Nyerere; m 82 502 1211; e lapetitcafe@valzamb.net; 06.30–22.00 daily. This welcome addition to Tete's culinary scene serves some of the best pastries, croissants & sandwiches outside Maputo, as well as ice-cream pizzas, full meals & great espresso. Indoor & outdoor seating available. No alcohol served. *Pastries are less than US$1, & snacks around US$2, while mains start at US$3.50.*

Snack Bar Ethepe Av Julius Nyerere; 10.00–23.00 Tue–Sun. This smart new place serves a typical selection of *seafood & meat dishes for US$8–12, as well as a recommended plate of the day for around US$4.50.*

✕ **Complexo Turístico Pemba** Rua Poder Popular; m 82 710 2762; ◷ 12.00–23.00 Tue–Sun. This has a great riverside setting, shady seating & an attractive flowering garden, making it a good place to sip a beer as the sun goes down. *Large helpings of typical Mozambican fare are mostly in the US$6–10 range, though 1/4 chicken is just US$3.*

✕ **Esplanada Almeida** Rua Poder Popular. Situated next door to the above & with a similarly pretty setting, this is more drinking hole than restaurant, and is pleasant enough for a beer, though it does serve *a small daily selection of mains in the US$3.50–6.50 range.*

✕ **Pastelaria Bracarense** Av de Independência. Situated directly opposite the bus station, this modern café serves good pastries & espresso, pizzas, sandwiches, burgers, curries & other meals. *From around US$1.50 for a snack to US$2.50–4.50 for a full meal.*

🍸 **PicNic** Av de Independência. Also opposite the bus terminal, this is more a bar than an eatery, & has a slightly seedy air, but it's a good place to sit & people-watch & light meals are served.

🍸 **Sundowners** EN103. The thatched sports bar here is one of the liveliest in town, especially when big matches are shown on the flat screen. *Serves decent steaks and seafood in the US$8–12 range.*

🍸 **Tropical Nhungué** Av de Independência. Thatched bar with large-screen DSTV for big sporting events, occasional live music, & a lively atmosphere at w/ends.

☆ **Esplanada Why Not** Av 3 Fevereiro. The hottest nightspot in town.

OTHER PRACTICALITIES

Banks and foreign exchange The usual banks are all represented in Tete. There are ATMs at Barclays, Standard, BIM Millennium and BCI. There are no dedicated forex bureaux, other than the banks, but it is easy enough to change US dollars with private moneychangers at the borders with Zimbabwe or Malawi, or excess Malawi kwacha at that country's border.

Further information The website www.info-tete.co.mz has some useful information.

Hospital Situated on Rua Kwame Nkrumah (☎ *252 22152*).

Internet There only internet café is ValambaNet on Avenida Eduardo Mondlane next to the entrance of the Hotel Zambeze.

Police On the corner of Avenida da Independência and Rua Kwame Nkrumah.

Post office On the corner of Avenida da Liberdade and Avenida 24 de Julho.

Shopping Tete has plenty of supermarkets, most of them along Avenida 25 de Junho, Avenida Kenneth Kaunda and Avenida da Independência. There are two markets selling food, both on Avenida 25 de Junho. One is on the road towards Boroma, and the other in the opposite direction just past the junction with Avenida Julius Nyerere.

Swimming pool The Paraiso Zambeze Misterioso charges a day fee equivalent to around US$3 to swim in its pool.

WHAT TO SEE AND DO Tete is a town of limited interest to tourists, and for many its few attractive qualities will be outweighed by the oppressive humidity of the Zambezi Valley. The old part of town is not without a certain decrepit charm: there are some beautiful old houses here, though most are in urgent need of restoration.

The oldest building is the disused **cathedral**, which reportedly dates back to 1563. The most unlikely is a **domed gazebo** on the riverfront. It's been suggested that it was a bar where the Portuguese used to drink sundowners, but the inside is dominated by some form of water pump with associated pipes, so it appears that it's actually part of the water system. Either way, it is now fenced off and can only be admired from a distance.

Also worth a look is the old **slaving fort** near the municipal market, though it now protects a couple of water tanks so it may be difficult to get inside. A second fort, situated on the riverfront below the bridge, is now used as a football training ground.

Tete's best-known landmark is the **Samora Machel Bridge**, the kilometre-long multi-span suspension bridge that spans the Zambezi immediately northwest of the town centre. Built in the 1960s, this was the only permanent crossing of the Zambezi anywhere in Mozambique prior to the opening of the Caia Bridge in August 2009. A new toll bridge is scheduled to open at the mining settlement of Benga, 6km downstream of Tete, in 2014.

An attractive feature of Tete is the row of bars and restaurants that lines the riverfront – this is, after all, the one place in Mozambique where the Zambezi is readily accessible to casual visitors, and even if the riverbank around Tete itself is somewhat denuded of natural vegetation, it would be a shame to visit Mozambique and not spend at least one evening drinking in sight of Africa's fourth-largest river. More adventurously, you could ask around to find a fisherman to paddle you along the river in a dugout: the papyrus beds near the town support a good variety of birds, and you wouldn't need to go more than 1km or so upriver to stand a chance of seeing hippos and crocs.

AROUND TETE

Sightseeing opportunities in Tete Province are rather sparsely distributed and, for the most part, time-consuming to reach without private transport. The main attraction in the region is the **Cahora Bassa Dam**, but **Boroma** and **Zumbo** are both of some historical interest.

CAHORA BASSA DAM Situated on the Zambezi in the north of Tete Province, Cahora Bassa is the fifth-largest dam in the world, and it confines one of Africa's ten largest bodies of water, covering an area of 2,660km^2. Construction of the 300m-wide and 160m-high concrete wall started in 1969 and, despite Frelimo's attempts at sabotage, it was completed in 1974.

Cahora Bassa is potentially Africa's largest supplier of hydro-electric power and a vital source of foreign revenue for Mozambique. The five turbines, housed in a rock-hewn cavern of cathedralesque dimensions, have a total capacity of 2,075MW, roughly ten times the power requirement for the whole of Mozambique. When the dam was built, the idea was that it would supply large amounts of hydro-electric power to South Africa. Sadly, by the end of the civil war only two of the dam's turbines were still functional, and no electricity from Cahora Bassa had reached South Africa since part of the power line was destroyed by Renamo in 1986. Nowadays, since the rehabilitation of the dam in 1997 and the beginning of construction of a new plant some 70km downstream of Cahora Bassa, Mozambique can expect to earn a considerable amount of its foreign exchange from the export of electricity to South Africa and other neighbouring countries.

The closest town to the dam, **Songo**, was purpose-built in the style of a Portuguese village while the dam was under construction. By 1974 it had a population of almost 15,000. Located in the cool, breezy highlands immediately south of the dam, Songo is well worth visiting in its own right, with a spacious layout and green, flowering gardens that blend attractively into the surrounding woodland. It's unique in Mozambique in that it doesn't really have an identifiable centre – it's more a series of *barrios* (neighbourhoods) connected by roads. It's also the only town in Mozambique where it's safe to drink the water straight from the

CAHORA BASSA RAPIDS

Now partially submerged by a namesake dam, the Cahora Bassa Rapids were the obstacle that prevented Livingstone's Zambezi expedition from opening up the Zambezi as 'God's Highway' into the African interior, and which led to the explorer turning his attention to the Shire River in what would eventually become the British enclave now known as Malawi. Covering a distance of roughly 80km, and marked by two near-vertical drops of 200m, the rapids had been known to the Portuguese and other traders for several centuries before Livingstone arrived at the Zambezi – the phrase 'Cahora Bassa' means 'where the work ends' in the local dialect, a reference to the fact that the rapids were an impassable obstacle for boatsmen sailing up the Zambezi.

Livingstone had used a path that arched around the rapids in the course of his epic trans-African hike, the journey that preceded and inspired the Zambezi Expedition, so it is something of a mystery why he never thought to look at the rapids for himself, and steadfastly dismissed local advice that they would be impassable. Even when his boat, the *Ma-Robert*, was confronted by the rapids on 9 November 1858, Livingstone refused to believe they couldn't eventually be surmounted, though he was finally persuaded of this in November 1860, when he attempted to ascend the rapids with five dugout canoes, a number of which overturned, taking many of the expedition's notes and drawings with them.

Probably the first person to navigate the rapids was a rather enigmatic and obscure figure remembered in the annals of the Royal Geographical Society by the name of Mr F Monks (though his real surname was evidently Foster). In 1880, Monks made a solo canoe trip between the confluence of the Gawayi and Zambezi rivers and the port of Quelimane. Although he left no substantial journal of this trip, he did leave behind an impressively accurate topographical map of the Zambezi and several of its tributaries as far downriver as Tete. Monks disappeared into the African interior a few years after this, never to be heard of again. As a footnote, the first people known to have kayaked the full length of the Zambezi from its source near the borders of Zambia, the Democratic Republic of the Congo and Angola are two young British travellers, Rupert FitzMaurice and Justin Matterson, who did the trip to raise money for charity towards the end of 1996.

An interesting story associated with the rapids is that of the legendary silver mines of Chicova, which were shown to Portuguese explorers in the early years of the 17th century. In 1617 and 1618, the period when Madeira occupied the fort at Sena, an estimated 450kg of silver was brought there, allegedly from Chicova. The odd thing is that the mines were 'lost' shortly after Madeira left Sena, and despite the subsequent attempts of several fortune hunters, they have yet to be relocated. If the mines ever did exist, they are probably now submerged by Cahora Bassa, or close to its southern shore.

taps as it comes direct from the company's processing plant on the lake – the pipes run alongside the road between Songo and the dam.

The approach road to Songo is one of the most spectacular in Mozambique, and the well-wooded, boulder-strewn hills that surround the town offer a refreshing contrast to the humid air and stark landscape of Tete. The Songo area also promises excellent birdwatching, and there are plenty of roads along which you can explore it.

Also of interest is the remains of a Zimbabwe-style stone enclosure, dating from the 18th or 19th century, right in the heart of Songo, in an open field about 200m south of the BIM Millennium Bank.

You no longer need to get specific authorisation in Tete before visiting Songo and Cahora Bassa, but the dam and its turbine rooms can only be visited on a (free) tour arranged through the Songo office of the Hidroeléctrica de Cahora Bassa (HCB). Anybody in Songo can point you there, or else you can ring in advance (*252 82157 or 82221*).

Getting there and away

By car Songo lies 150km from Tete along an excellent surfaced road. The junction for the scenic **EN258** to Songo is roughly 25km from Tete along the **EN103** towards the Zimbabwean border. It isn't signposted, but it's the only major junction along this stretch of road. The drive from Tete to Songo can comfortably be done in two hours in a private vehicle.

By chapa Chapas run to Songo daily, leaving from outside the post office on Avenida da Liberdade in Tete. You could also take a chapa to Estima (also known as Chitima), a small town at the base of the mountains about 15km from Songo, and pick up a lift to Songo from there. They cost US$3.70 and the journey takes up to four hours. Given the lack of a town centre at Songo, getting back to Tete requires some organisation, but the best method is to talk to the driver of the chapa that brought you here.

Where to stay and eat

Ugezi Tiger Lodge (16 units) +27 82 539 6411 (South Africa); e info@ugezitigerlodge.com; www.ugezitigerlodge.com. Aimed mainly at keen anglers, this pleasant lodge lies on the lakeshore about 3km south of the dam wall, an area rich in birdlife & fishing opportunities. Accommodation is in comfortable en-suite chalets with AC, & there is a nice campsite. *US$35/50 sgl/dbl or US$8 pp camping.*

Centro Social do Songo 252 82508; m 82 49 56 690. Also known as The Club, this HCB institution offers the only formal accommodation in Songo, & is very good value, with well-equipped en-suite rooms that are more like suites. The place has a swimming pool, which is a very pleasant way of passing an afternoon, & a good restaurant serves mains in the US$6–8 range. *Rooms US$29, suites US$34.*

O Sitio m 82 54 55 110 or 82 30 62 640. About 15mins' walk from 'The Club', with startlingly good food, in particular the *steak o sitio*. It's also the local disco & open all night on Fri/Sat nights.

BOROMA MISSION Situated along the Zambezi about 25km upriver of Tete, the Missão de São José de Boroma, founded in 1891, is one of the country's most attractive missions. Its centrepiece is a large and beautiful church on a hill overlooking the river. This building was abandoned by the missionaries shortly after independence, and the complex now seems to house a school. The site was reputedly an important source of alluvial gold even before Portuguese times, but this resource had been exhausted long before the mission was founded. The Boroma area is also a good place to see hippos and crocs, and offers good birdwatching.

Getting there and away

By car Although Boroma is only 25km northwest of Tete, the road there is in variable condition, crossing several seasonal watercourses, and certain sections may require a 4x4, especially after rain. To get there, follow Avenida 25 de Junho out of town northwest for about 1.5km past the old slave fort until you see a large blue signpost pointing left to Boroma. From here the road follows the Zambezi closely, passing through the villages of Dege and Mufa, and it offers some excellent views over the water, as well as a good chance of encountering monkeys, hippos and crocodiles.

By chapa A few chapas run between Tete and Boroma daily. They start and end in the huge local market to the south of Avenida 25 de Junho, but it's a very confusing walk through the huts and you'd be ill-advised to try it without a guide. Better perhaps to walk out along Avenida 25 de Junho to the signpost mentioned above; the chapas reach this junction about five minutes after they leave the market. The journey will cost less than US$1 and it takes around 90 minutes. Every now and again someone coming in the opposite direction will give a little signal to the driver, and he'll drop a few people off who vanish into the bush. The signal means that there is a police roadblock a little further on; the people being dropped off will not have their identity papers so will be skirting around it, to be picked up later on.

Where to stay There is no formal accommodation at Boroma, and it's easy enough to visit the mission as a day trip out of Tete. You may be able to camp near the mission, and there are several bars in Boroma where you'll be able to get food and drink.

ZUMBO The most westerly town in Mozambique is Zumbo, which lies on the Zambian border at the confluence of the Zambezi and Luangwa rivers near the western end of Lake Cahora Bassa, 240km west of Songo. Well off any beaten track today, Zumbo was once the site of an important gold fair, reputedly founded in 1715 by Francisco Pereira, a Goan trader and refugee from the Rozvi attack on Dambarare. By 1750, a lively trade in gold with the Rozvim, supported by ivory potted in the Bangweulu Basin (in what is now northern Zambia), had made Zumbo the largest Portuguese town on the Zambezi, with a Christian population of almost 500 including 80 Europeans. By 1764, when it was granted municipal status, Zumbo was possibly the most prosperous settlement in Portuguese Africa.

Zumbo's decline can be linked to the political tensions that gripped the upper Zambezi in the late 18th century, combined with the great drought that started in 1832. After being attacked several times, Zumbo was fortified in 1801, and at the same time a Portuguese garrison moved in. This was not enough to prevent further attacks, so the town was evacuated in 1813. The fair was reoccupied in 1820, but following the resurgence of drought conditions and the looming threat of the Nguni after they deposed the Rozvi dynasty in 1836, Zumbo was permanently abandoned by Portugal.

In 1859, the British explorer Richard Thornton passed through the ghost town that had once been described as the metropolis of the whole trade of the rivers. Thornton recorded seeing the ruins of some 200 stone houses lining the riverbank over a distance of 3km. A more recent report confirms that a fort of unknown antiquity, built around a 500-year-old fig tree, was still in use at Zumbo during World War II. It is still a reasonably sizeable town, serving as district capital and supporting a population of around 35,000, but it remains very isolated from the rest of the country.

Getting there and away

By road Getting to Zumbo requires a bit of determination. By road, you need to follow the EN221 north for about 135km to Bene, where the 325km dirt road to Zumbo, via Fingoe and Caponda, branches to the right. This has never been a very good road and it suffered considerable flood damage in 2001. We have no recent reports regarding its condition, but there is certainly no public transport along it, and self-drivers should only consider trying it if they have a solid 4x4 and feel up for a genuine adventure.

By ferry Another option is a pontoon ferry called the *Kuza*, which theoretically makes a return passage along the length of Cahora Bassa from Songo to Zumbo every ten to14 days. By all accounts, however, this boat is old, unreliable and in less than shipshape condition, so delays are frequent and it might be a risky trip, especially in the rainy season. If you decide to risk it, be prepared for a journey of some days and carry all your own food.

Where to stay There is at least one basic lodging in Zumbo. The only other option is **Chawalo Safari Camp** (*www.southernsafaris.co.za*), a hunting and fishing camp set in a private concession on the Mozambican bank of the Zambezi 15km northeast (downstream) from Zumbo.

Part Four

NORTHERN MOZAMBIQUE

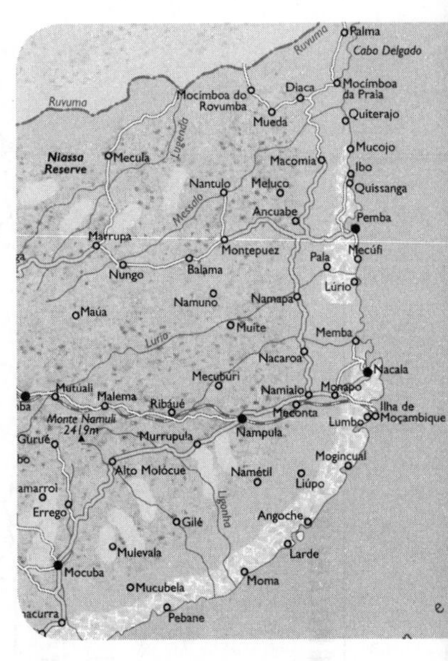

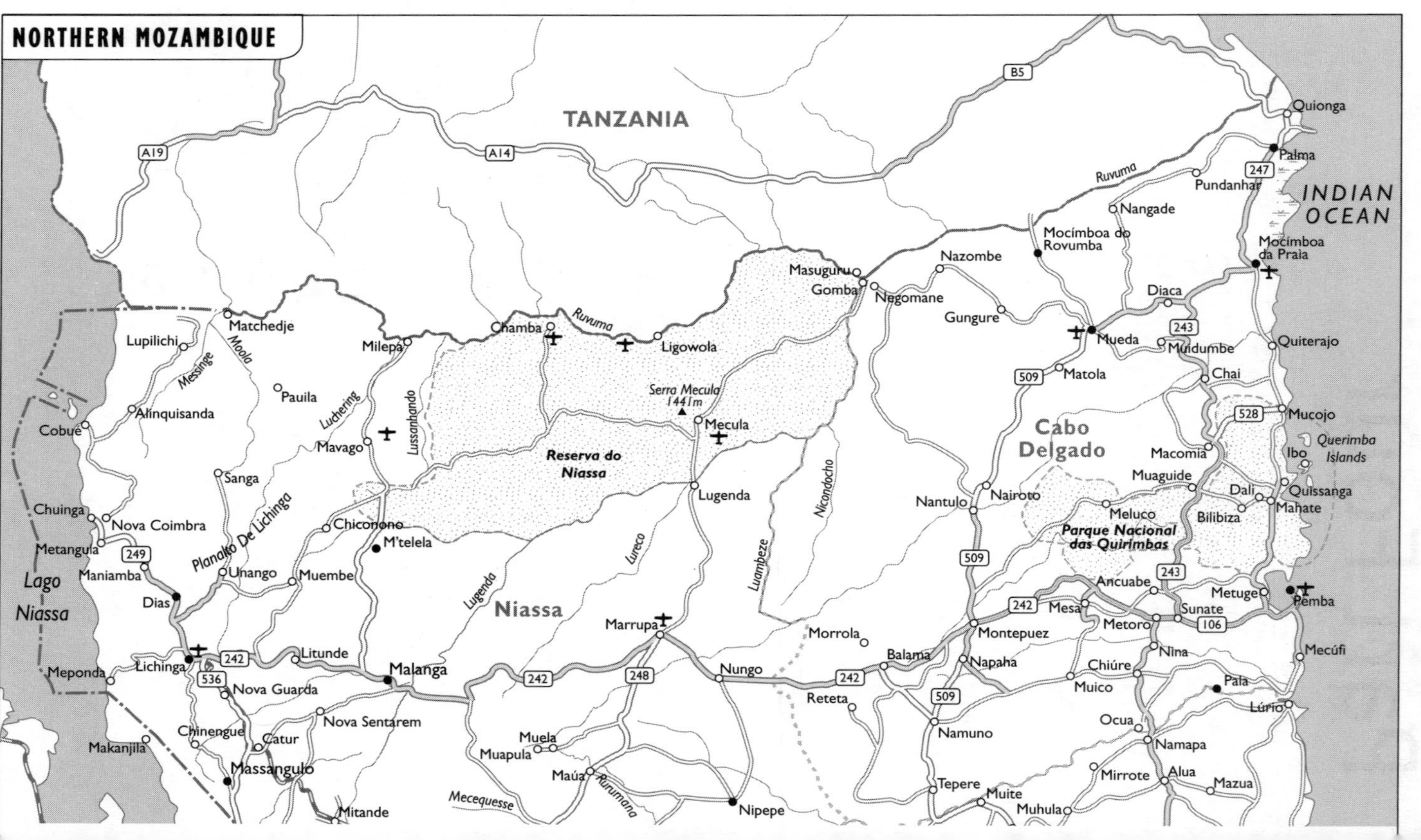
NORTHERN MOZAMBIQUE
TANZANIA
INDIAN OCEAN
B5
A19
A14
Ruvuma
Quionga
Palma
247
Pundanhar
Nangade
Mocímboa do Rovumba
Mocímboa da Praia
Nazombe
Masuguru
Gomba
Negomane
Gungure
Diaca
243
Mueda
Muidumbe
Quiterajo
Chai
509
Matola
528
Mucojo
Querimba Islands
Ibo
Cabo Delgado
Macomia
Muaguide
Quissanga
Dali
Mahate
Bilibiza
Nantulo
Nairoto
Meluco
Parque Nacional das Quirimbas
Ancuabe
Metuge
Pemba
Mesa
Sunate
106
Metoro
Montepuez
Nina
Mecúfi
Napaha
Chiúre
Muico
Pala
Lúrio
Namuno
Ocua
Namapa
Mirrote
Alua
Mazua
Tepere
Muite
Muhula
Matchedje
Lupilichi
Moola
Messinge
Pauila
Alinquisanda
Cobue
Luchering
Milepa
Chamba
Ligowola
Serra Mecula 1441m
Mecula
Lussanhando
Mavago
Reserva do Niassa
Sanga
Lugenda
Nicondocho
Chuinga
Nova Coimbra
Planalto De Lichinga
Chiconono
M'telela
Metangula
249
Lureco
Luambeze
Lago Niassa
Maniamba
Unango
Muembe
Lugenda
Niassa
Dias
Marrupa
Morrola
Balama
Lichinga
242
Litunde
Malanga
Nungo
248
Meponda
536
Nova Guarda
Reteta
Nova Sentarem
Makanjila
Chinengue
Catur
Muela
Muapula
Massangulo
Maúa
Rurumana
Mecequesse
Nipepe
Mitande

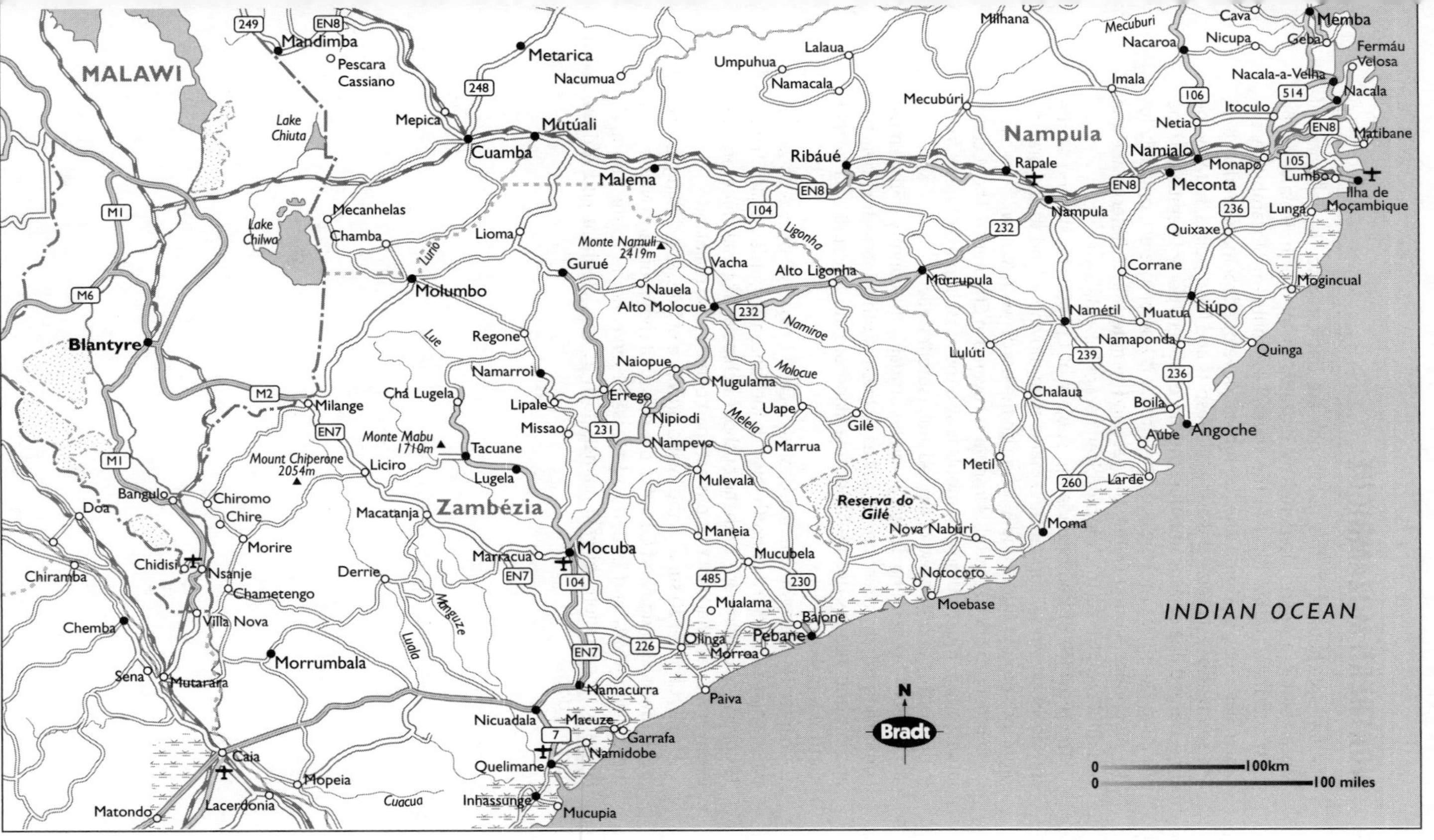

MALAWI
Nampula
Zambézia
Reserva do Gilé
INDIAN OCEAN
N
Bradt
0 100km
0 100 miles
Mandimba
Pescara
Cassiano
Metarica
Nacumua
Umpuhua
Lalaua
Namacala
Milhana
Mecuburi
Nacaroa
Cava
Nicupa
Memba
Geba
Fermáu
Velosa
Nacala-a-Velha
Nacala
Imala
Mecubúri
Itoculo
Netia
Matibane
Lake Chiuta
Mepica
Mutúali
Cuamba
Malema
Ribáuè
Rapale
Namialo
Monapo
Meconta
Lumbo
Ilha de Moçambique
Nampula
Lunga
Quixaxe
Mecanhelas
Lake Chilwa
Chamba
Lioma
Monte Namuli 2419m
Ligonha
Lurio
Gurué
Vacha
Alto Ligonha
Murrupula
Corrane
Mogincual
Molumbo
Nauela
Alto Molocue
Nametil
Muatua
Liúpo
Namiroe
Namaponda
Quinga
Blantyre
Lue
Regone
Lulúti
Naiopue
Molocue
Namarroi
Mugulama
Errego
Chalaua
Boila
Cha Lugela
Lipale
Uape
Milange
Nipiodi
Melela
Gilé
Angoche
Missao
Aúbe
Monte Mabu 1710m
Nampevo
Marrua
Tacuane
Mount Chiperone 2054m
Liciro
Metil
Lugela
Mulevala
Larde
Bangulo
Chiromo
Doa
Chire
Macatanja
Nova Nabúri
Moma
Maneia
Morire
Marracua
Mocuba
Chidisi
Nsanje
Mucubela
Chiramba
Derrie
Notocoto
Chametengo
Manguze
Moebase
Mualama
Bajone
Villa Nova
Chemba
Luala
Olinga
Pebane
Morroa
Morrumbala
Sena
Mutarara
Namacurra
Paiva
Nicuadala
Macuze
Garrafa
Caia
Namidobe
Quelimane
Mopeia
Matondo
Lacerdonia
Cuacua
Inhassunge
Mucupia
249
EN8
248
106
514
105
M1
104
236
232
M6
239
M2
231
EN7
260
485
230
104
226
7

NORTHERN MOZAMBIQUE

The last six chapters in this guidebook are dedicated to the far north of Mozambique, a region bordered by Tanzania to the north, Malawi to the west and the Zambezi River to the south. Like southern Mozambique, the region has a long coastline, and though less developed for mass tourism than the south, it boasts several worthwhile resorts and focal points, notably the time-warped Ilha de Moçambique, the more modern port of Pemba and the stunning Querimba Archipelago. The interior is also of interest, primarily for the mountains around Gurué, the vast and remote Niassa Reserve and the beautiful Lago Niassa (the Mozambican part of Lake Malawi).

The province of Zambézia is the subject of Chapter 15, starting at the run-down provincial capital Quelimane, then moving inland to the bracing highlands around Gurué and Milange on the border with Malawi.

Another provincial capital, Nampula, is covered in Chapter 16. The second-largest city in Mozambique, Nampula is also the most important route focus in the north, but otherwise of limited interest to travellers.

Chapter 17 covers Ilha de Moçambique, arguably the country's single most compelling urban attraction, as well as a clutch of other interesting beaches and historic villages on the facing mainland around Mossuril and further north at Nacala.

Chapter 18 deals with Pemba, capital of Cabo Delgado Province, as well as the mainland coast further north towards the Tanzanian border, while Chapter 19 covers the Quirimbas – both the offshore archipelago of that name, and the eponymous national park that protects part of the facing mainland.

Finally, Chapter 20 surveys the inland province of Niassa, including its two major towns Lichinga and Cuamba, the beautiful shores of Lago Niassa, and the thrillingly vast and underrated Niassa Reserve, home to the country's largest concentrations of wild animals such as lion, elephant and African hunting dog.

15

Zambézia

Flowing southeast along the boundary of Sofala and Zambézia provinces, the final seaborne stretch of the mighty Zambezi forms the closest thing there is to a tangible border between southern and northern Mozambique. True, the transition from south to north is less emphatic now that the time-consuming ferry crossing at Caia has been rendered redundant by the nippy 2.4km Armando Emilio Guebuza Bridge, which opened in August 2009. Nevertheless, crossing into Zambézia at Caia feels almost like journeying into another country. The goods sold at the roadside change, with fresh fruit and vegetables taking the place of the more processed and packaged foods available in the south. The quality of the vehicles falls, the chapas being more battered. The road network is worse too, with a higher proportion of dirt roads than you'll find in the south and a greater likelihood of damage during the rainy season. And Zambézia is the province where the eternal problem of getting change ceases to be a slightly charming affectation and becomes a serious annoyance.

Extending inland from the Indian Ocean to the Malawian border, Zambézia is the country's second-largest province at 105,008km^2, and the second most populous, with an estimated four million inhabitants, the main ethnic groups being the Macua, the Chuabo and the Lomwè. It is also the most topographically varied and agriculturally rich, with habitats ranging from coastal mangroves and savanna to the cultivated Rift Valley foothills, where extensive tea and cotton plantations flank isolated islands of evergreen forest on the slopes of mounts Namuli, Mabu and Chiperone. The coastline has more in common with the swathes of mangroves around Beira than the extended beaches in the south of the country, and a glance at any decent map will show a far higher number of rivers running into the Indian Ocean.

Zambézia's delights aren't immediately apparent. The province lacks the beach culture of the south, the extensive wilds of the north, or any settlement as captivating as Ilha de Moçambique or Inhambane, and most travellers simply treat it as a corridor between north and south (or to a lesser extent between Mozambique and Malawi). But there are bright points that deserve some attention. The provincial capital Quelimane is a quirky, timeworn riverside town whose history in some ways mirrors that of Mozambique itself. And the highland town of Gurué is extremely pleasant, with good walking opportunities in the surrounding hills including the possibility of walking up the country's second-highest peak, the 2,419m-high Mount Namuli.

QUELIMANE

The capital of Zambézia and most important settlement along the 1,000km road between Beira/Chimoio and Nampula, the riverport of Quelimane is Mozambique's seventh-largest town, with a population estimated at 200,000 in 2010. It is also one of the oldest towns in Mozambique, founded near the Cuácua River mouth in medieval times, probably by Swahili traders from Kilwa (in southern Tanzania), and it has remained a settlement of some significance throughout the Portuguese era to the present day.

Oddly, perhaps, the modern city centre, a curious mishmash of outmoded 20th-century architectural styles, is almost totally lacking in relicts of its early days, the nearest contender being a disused 18th-century cathedral on the waterfront. Quelimane today is also strikingly run-down, evoking the state of so many Mozambican and east African towns in their 1980s nadir: flowing sewers, broken pipes and unkempt piles of rubbish line erratically surfaced roads pocked by potholes of such a magnitude they could hide a family of wallowing buffalos in the rainy season. Baste this general aura of unkemptness in the sweltering coastal heat, unrelieved by the oceanic breeze associated with ports on the open sea, and it seems fair to say that while Quelimane is the obvious place to break up the long overland trek between northern and southern Mozambique, somewhere like Mocuba might be a more agreeable option.

HISTORY The settlement that eventually became Quelimane was almost certainly founded by Muslim traders, probably at around the same time as Tete and Sena. The site on the north bank of the Cuácua, about 25km upstream of its mouth, was chosen after it was discovered that this relatively small waterway formed part of a navigable channel that opened into the Zambezi merged near modern-day Mopeia (a far more manageable and safe prospect than entering the vast and labyrinthine Zambezi delta to the south). It is assumed that this waterway formed an important link on one of the various transport networks that connected the goldfields of the interior to the ports of the Swahili coast.

Vasco da Gama stopped at Quelimane on his pioneering 1498 voyage to east Africa. When he saw that some locals were dressed in Arab-style robes, he realised he was almost certainly on track to his ultimate goal of India, and gave the Cuácua its Portuguese name Rio dos Bons Sinais ('River of Good Signs'). One local tradition has it that the name Quelimane was inadvertently coined by da Gama, based on the response of local labourers who misunderstood his query and replied '*kuliamani*' (we are cultivating). An even more improbable (and anomalously Anglocentric) explanation is that Quelimane derives from the phrase 'Killer of Men', in reference to the high incidence of malarial deaths in the area. Far more likely is that the name pre-dates any European influence and is simply a variant spelling of the KiSwahili 'Kilimani', which means 'On High Ground'.

A Portuguese trading factory was established at Quelimane in 1530, and the town appears on Portuguese maps dating from 1560. Quelimane grew in importance as the ivory trading routes up the Zambezi replaced the older gold-trade routes out of Sofala. Reports dating to the 1590s depict it as an attractive small town, surrounded by plantations and protected by a wooden fort. In common with many other coastal settlements, Quelimane benefited from the growth in the slave trade from the interior during the latter part of the 18th century. It also became a major supplier of food to Mozambique Island during this period. Quelimane's oldest stone buildings date to the 1780s, and in 1812 the town was made a separate captaincy with its own customs house.

By the 1820s, Quelimane was the most important slaving port in east Africa, but lost its municipal status in 1826 on account of the lack of government control over the trade in slaves. The main results were that the local slave trade was driven underground, and that many visiting ships avoided Portuguese settlements altogether, preferring to enter into clandestine trade with Muslim settlements elsewhere on the coast. The town's strategic importance also declined after the late

1820s, when the channel connecting the Cuácua to the Zambezi silted up as a result of drought, never to reopen.

Quelimane nevertheless remained a prosperous settlement throughout the 19th century, mainly as a supplier of agricultural produce to other Portuguese ports. The town was the end point of David Livingstone's pioneering 1856 crossing of south-central Africa from west to east. Livingstone was officially appointed the British Honorary Consul to Quelimane in 1858, though his main interest in the town was as a base to explore the Zambezi.

GETTING THERE AND AWAY

By air Quelimane Airport lies about 3km from the town centre at the northwest end of Avenida 25 de Junho, and a cab from the city centre should cost around US$3. LAM flies to Quelimane a few times weekly from Maputo, Beira and Nampula, and has an office on Avenida 1 de Julho (*242 12800*).

By car Quelimane lies about 40km southeast of the EN1 and can be reached along the surfaced EN470, which branches from it at the small but expanding junction town of Nicoadala. Coming from the south, it is about 660km to Quelimane from Beira and 600km from Chimoio via the junction town of Inchope and the Caia Bridge. The surfaced road is in fair to good condition all the way and either drive can be completed in a day, ideally with an early start, though that is not quite so important now the old ferry at Caia has been replaced by a bridge.

For those with no particular interest in diverting to Quelimane from Nicoadala, it is possible to continue 115km north to Mocuba, the springboard for more northerly destinations such as Milange (on the Malawi border), Gurué or Alto Molócuè (all covered in greater detail later in the chapter) as well as Nampula.

By bus and chapa Chapas to Zalala Beach (*45 mins; US$0.75*) and other more local destinations leave from outside the market on Avenida Heróis de Liberdade. For chapas to Nicoadala (*45mins, US$0.85*), Mocuba (*2–3hrs; US$3*) and all other destinations reached via the EN1/EN7, you need the Romoza Terminal next to the BP on Avenida Eduardo Mondlane. This terminal is unusually well organised, with signs indicating the queues for the various destinations, but it is about 30 minutes' walk from the waterfront and several sections are unlit at night, so you might want to catch a taxi.

Heading to Milange, best get yourself to Mocuba and pick up onward transport there. You could do the same thing if your goal is Alto Molocue or Gurué, though there is also one direct daily **bus** to the latter, leaving at 04.30, taking six hours, and charging US$8.50. The Grupo Mecula bus to Nampula leaves at 04.30, costs US$10 and takes up to ten hours. A few buses leave daily for Beira, the best being the thrice-weekly air-conditioned **TCO** service, though this does cost double the price of an ordinary bus.

WHERE TO STAY

Upmarket

Hotel Chuabo (64 rooms) Av Samora Machel; 242 13181; e hotelchuabo@sdm.co.mz. Given the limited attractions on offer in Quelimane, it seems somewhat bizarre that the city centre is graced with a relatively plush hotel of sky-scraping dimensions. Nevertheless the Chuabo is exactly that, with comfortable rooms with DSTV & AC, reasonably well maintained, but rather impersonal. The view from the top-floor restaurant is impressive. *US$68/85 standard sgl/dbl; US$73/90 executive sgl/dbl; suites from US$100; all rates B&B.*

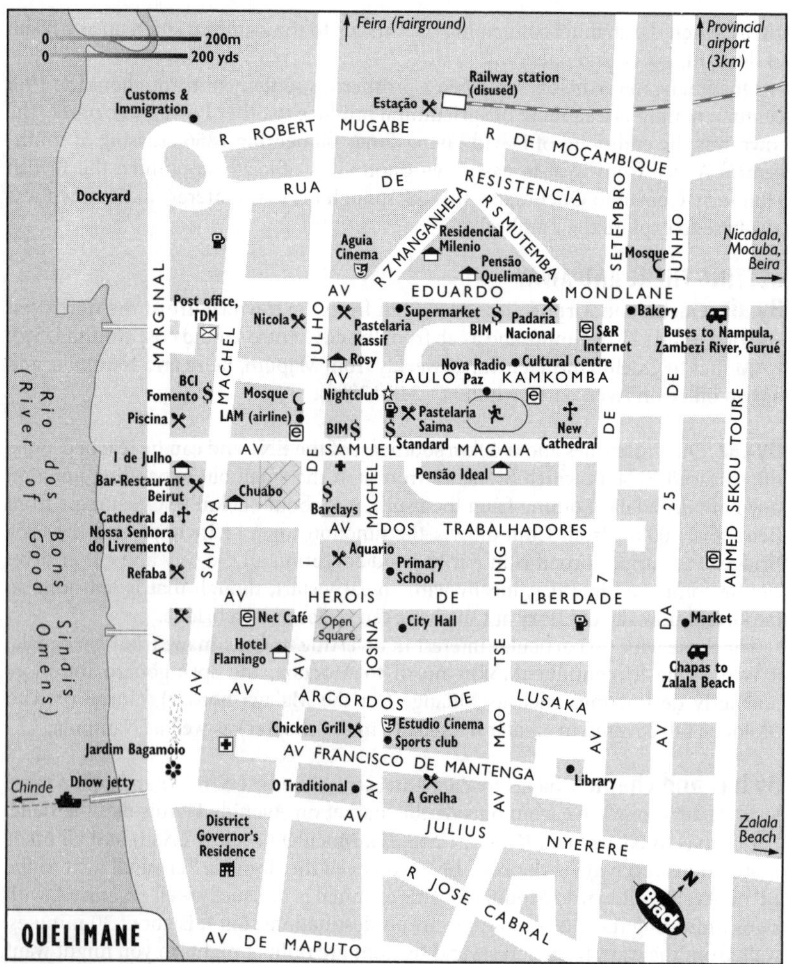

Mid-range

Hotel Flamingo (24 rooms) Av 1 de Julho; 242 15602; m 82 552 7810; e holtelflamingo.qlm@tdm.co.mz; www.hotelflamingoquelimane.com. Something of a focal point for volunteers & expats based in Zambézia, this well-run hotel is set around a private courtyard with parking, swimming pool & a very good bar/restaurant. The rooms are all well appointed, with DSTV, AC, private bathrooms & fridges, & Wi-Fi throughout. Very good value at *US$48/59 sgl/dbl or US$53/65 executive sgl/dbl; all rates B&B.*

Residencial Milenio (21 rooms) 84 Av Zedequias Manganhela; 242 13314. Another pleasant option aimed at business travellers, this is a converted old Portuguese house with a range of en-suite rooms with AC, DSTV, tea-coffee, twin beds & large bathroom with hot shower. The well-maintained buildings & neat grounds stand in sharp contrast to the general aura of decay that infests Quelimane. *US$55/75 sgl/dbl.*

Budget

Hotel 1 de Julho (21 rooms) Av Filipe Samuel Magaia; 242 13067. This likeable multi-storey hotel, half a block back from the waterfront, has distinctive if idiosyncratic décor,

& brightly painted clean twin rooms with TV, AC, fan & balcony. The only drawback is that rooms are not en-suite. *US$20 twin.*

Hotel Rosy (15 rooms) Av 1 de Julho; 242 14969. This small hotel has en-suite rooms with AC & TV, but don't let the flattering exterior fool you – the interior is shabbier, & the grotty bathrooms (swarming mosquitoes & pneumatic-drill plumbing) all but preclude a peaceful night's sleep. Poor value at *US$30 for a ground-floor twin or US$32 for a 1st-floor dbl.*

Shoestring

Pensão Ideal (20 rooms) Av Filipe Samuel Magaia; 24 212731. A long-standing backpacker's fallback, this large pink building just down from the cathedral is the best-value cheapie in town, especially following the recent addition of a new wing. It has a quiet location, rooms are clean & all come with a fan, & a restaurant in attached. *US$12/16 sgl/dbl using common shower; US$18 dbl with AC; US$23 en-suite sgl/dbl with AC & TV in new wing.*

Pensão Quelimane (24 rooms) 433 Av Eduardo Mondlane; m 82 592 9510. This faded old hotel on the periphery of the town centre looks nice enough from the outside but the interior is gloomy & some rooms have a pervasive toilet smell. A real step down from the Pensão Ideal (see opposite) & not much cheaper. *US$12/15 sgl/dbl using common shower or US$15/18 en-suite sgl/dbl with AC & TV.*

WHERE TO EAT

A Grelha Av Julius Nyerere; m 82 392 4240 or 84 271 5859; 08.00–22.00 Mon–Sat. The best restaurant in town is this owner-managed place with indoor & outdoor seating & bright African décor. *Good selection of Portuguese/Mozambican seafood & meat dishes in the US$5–10 range, along with cheaper snacks.*

Hotel Flamingo Av 1 de Julho; 242 15602; 07.00–22.00 daily. The courtyard restaurant at the Flamingo has a relaxed atmosphere & a varied menu with soups, pizza & pasta alongside more typical Mozambican meat and seafood dishes. An added bonus is free Wi-Fi for diners. *Mains US$5–8.*

Piscina Av Marginal; 08.00–22.00 Tue–Sun. With its thatched roof & cheerful outdoor feel, this waterfront swimming-pool complex is well worth a try. Swimming costs US$1.50. *Omelettes & light meals in the US$3–5 range, & more substantial mains for US$6–10.*

Restaurante Grill Chuabo Av Samora Machel; 242 13181; lunch & dinner daily. Situated on the 8th floor of the Hotel Chuabo (see page 257), this place is more notable perhaps for the spectacular views than the food, which is still among the best in town. *Most dishes in the US$6–8 range. There's a cheaper snack bar on the ground floor.*

Bar-Restaurant Beirut Av Filipe Samuel Magaia; 08.00–19.00 Mon–Sat. The former Café Riviera, set in a building with reflective glass windows & a distinct 1930s air, now serves a decent range of greasy Lebanese & Mozambican fare, ranging from *shawarmas* to *prego* rolls. *Mostly in the US$3–5 range.*

Restaurante Refaba Av Marginal; 11.00–late daily. Situated just down from the old cathedral, this cheap & cheerful old favourite has a great waterfront location, defiantly timeworn décor, indoor & outdoor seating, & a freezer packed with cold beers. *The usual range of Portuguese-influenced dishes mostly for under US$5.*

OTHER PRACTICALITIES

Banks and ATMs Barclays, Standard, BIM Millennium and BCI are all present and correct, with 24 hour ATMs attached.

Hospital On Avenida Accordos de Lusaka, between Avenidas 1 de Junho and Avenida Samora Machel (*24 213000*).

Internet Quelimane is the worst of the major towns in Mozambique for internet connections. None of the internet cafés have a reliable connection, and the only

Wi-Fi (free to diners) is at the Hotel Flamingo, though even this is rather spotty. Try the anonymous internet café on the second floor of the primary school next to the cathedral on Avenida Paulo Kankomba, or S&R Net off Avenida Eduardo Mondlane. Or if it can wait until you get to the next town, maybe don't!

Police The police station is on Avenida Heróis de Liberdade, next to City Hall (*24 213453*).

Post office On Avenida Samora Machel opposite Avenida Paulo Kankomba.

Shopping The market on Avenida Heróis de Liberdade is good for fruit and vegetables, and there are supermarkets on Avenida 1 de Junho and Avenida Eduardo Mondlane. The best bakery in town is the Pastelaria Nacional on Avenida Eduardo Mondlane, but the Pastelaria Saima and Pastelaria Kassif also look good. Otherwise, shops in Quelimane are rather poorly stocked by comparison with other similarly sized towns, and opportunities for craft shopping are very limited indeed.

Swimming pool The Piscina on Avenida Marginal (see *Where to eat,* page 257) charges US$1.50 per person to swim. The swimming pool at the Hotel Flamingo is open to non-guests, but it's a lot more expensive.

Taxis Taxis in Quelimane are all bicycles and you'll have to perch yourself on the parcel shelf. If you're lucky then you'll get a bit of cardboard as a seat. Trips around town should cost you no more than a couple of dollars and the taxis can be most easily found at the market, the bus terminal and outside the city hall.

WHAT TO SEE AND DO The entertainment options open to you in Quelimane are truly limited. There is little left of the city from before the 20th century, and the old port buildings have long disappeared. The twin-towered **Cathedral da Nossa Senhora do Livramento**, built in 1776 and situated on the Avenida Marginal around the corner from the Hotel 1 de Julho, is worth a look. From the outside it looks in reasonable condition, but peek through the doors (which will almost certainly be open) and it's a very different situation. The building is empty, the only furniture being the remains of the wooden altar, in front of which are the memorial stones of some of the old priests. At the back of the church is a gallery which you can climb up to, although you'd have to be brave or lightly built (preferably both) to try to cross it.

The **new cathedral** on Avenida 7 de Setembro is far less attractive – it looks more like a nuclear plant than a religious building. The old **District Governor's Residence** near the jetty dates to 1895, but otherwise most of the town centre's older buildings date to the early 20th century, with plenty of Art Deco on show, while the most attractive building anywhere in town is probably the well-maintained 1936 primary school on Avenida Josina Machel a block down from the city hall.

The walk along the Avenida Marginal is pleasant enough, particularly as the sun goes down. There is a variety of abandoned boats next to the jetties. Once night has fallen the only real options are the bars, although the **Aguia Cinema** on the corner of Avenidas Eduardo Mondlane and Zedequias Manganhela may show occasional martial arts films or Bollywood epics. There are also occasional events, including live **music**, at the Casa de Cultura on Avenida Paulo Kankomba; the easiest way to find out what (if anything) is on is to pop in and ask. Alternatively you could head for the **basketball** courts – there's one on the corner of Avenidas Josina Machel and

Francisco de Mantenga and another on Avenida Samora Machel between Avenida Heróis de Liberdade and Avenida Accordos de Lusaka.

THE COAST NORTH OF QUELIMANE

Zalala Beach Situated about 40km northeast of town along a road that passes through a vast coconut plantation, Zalala is the closest swimming beach to Quelimane, and while it doesn't compare to the finest beaches in the south of the country, it is a pretty enough spot, fringed with casuarina trees that separate it from the small village of Suphino. The road there is good fast tarmac, but very narrow – only big enough for one vehicle at a time, so expect to have to pull off to let something bigger past. It's also littered with bicycles, some of whose riders seem to have a death wish. Regular chapas from Quelimane leave from outside the market on Avenida Heróis de Liberdade, take 45 minutes, and cost less than US$1.

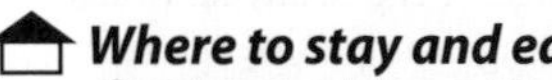

Where to stay and eat

Zalala Beach House (10 rooms) 242 17055; m 82 986 2000; e alculete@yahoo.com; www.zalalabeach.com. Opened in mid-2010 & offers accommodation in smart beachfront bungalows. Still something of a work in progress, it should soon also have a restaurant & swimming pool, & part of the proceeds will go towards local community development. *Prices start at US$70 pp.*

Pebane Situated on the east bank of the Moniga Estuary, about 150km northeast of Quelimane as the crow flies, the historic riverport of Pebane was a popular resort area in the colonial era but these days it sees few visitors and has an appealingly isolated character. The main attraction, aside from the sense of just getting away from it all, is the idyllic palm-lined beaches, which can be a little murkier than their more southerly counterparts (as a result of silt washed down by the Rio Moniga and other rivers), but offer good swimming and fishing, and some of the best surfing in the country. Of historical interest is the Ponta Matirre Lighthouse, which dates to 1913 and was recently restored, as well as the old Catholic cathedral and a colonial Portuguese cemetery.

The shortest reliable route to Pebane from Quelimane is about 300km and entails following the EN7 northeast of Nicoadala for 35km, then turning left at Namacurra and following dirt roads through Olinga and Mucubela. Patient travellers could follow this route using chapas to hop between towns, but be prepared for a long day. Another possible approach road leads southeast from the EN232, about 40km north of Mocuba, to Mucubela. A more northerly route entails driving through the Gilé National Reserve to/from Alto Ligonha on the EN232 between Alto Molócuè and Nampula.

Where to stay and eat There are a couple of inexpensive places to stay (Pensão Jemayma and Complex Miramar have been recommended), but the main focal point of tourist activities is:

Pebane Fishing Lodge (10 units) m 82 950 2605; e pebanefishing@gmail.com; www.pebane.com. Has beachfront chalets, a small restaurant & boats for fishing charters. *US$250 for a dbl.*

THE QUELIMANE-NAMPULA ROAD

The most important trunk route though Zambézia is the 525km road connecting Quelimane to Nampula via Nicoadala, Mocuba and Alto Molócuè. Although it is clearly the main road through the region, it has no clear name. Connected to

Quelimane by a feeder road called the EN470, Nicoadala is officially the most northerly point on the EN1, which runs south from here all the way to Maputo. North of Nicoadala, the EN1 becomes the EN7 for 65km, as far as the junction town of Malei, where the EN7 veers westward to Milange and the road towards Nampula becomes the EN104 for another 45km. At Mocuba, it changes to the EN232, the name by which it is known all the way to Nampula. For most of its length, the road is in good condition, but there are some abysmal stretches, particularly the 70km immediately north of Mocuba. With an early start, the trip from Quelimane to Nampula can be done in a day, but it is possible to break it at two points, Mocuba and Alto Molócuè.

MOCUBA Set on the southwest bank of the wide and muddy Licungo River, Mocuba is one of the largest towns in the Mozambican interior, with an estimated population of 70,000, and a strategic location on the main north–south road through Zambézia, immediately south of the 300m road bridge over the Licungo. It is a neatly laid-out town, and pleasant enough, with a few moderately interesting examples of colonial architecture, a fabulously busy market, and a relatively fresh and airy climate by comparison with a sweltering summer day in Quelimane. Mocuba is of interest mainly as an inland alternative to Quelimane for breaking up the long trip between Beira/Chimoio and Nampula, or as a springboard for visits to Gurué or the border town of Milange. Sightseeing options in the immediate vicinity are practically non-existent, though the river itself is quite a hive of human activity, and it can be interesting to sit on the banks or the bridge and watch the day's business unfold.

Getting there and away Mocuba is something of a route focus, situated at the junction of the main north–south road through Mozambique and the **EN7** west to Milange (the main border crossing between Zambézia and Malawi). The surfaced 85km EN7/EN104 between Nicoadala and Mocuba can be covered in under an hour, and there are loads of **chapas** between Quelimane, Nicoadala and Mocuba. By contrast, bank on three to five hours' driving along the 200km EN7 to Milange, which is unsurfaced and may be rough in parts, especially after rain, and aim for the earliest possible start if you are covering this road by chapa, as these tend to leave before 05.00 and might take up to eight hours in bad weather.

Where to stay and eat Mocuba turns out to have some of the best-value accommodation in the north of Mozambique, reason enough perhaps to choose it over Quelimane as a place to break up the trip from south to north. The restaurants at the two pensões listed below are about the best in town, but for cheaper eats you could try the Refaba Café or Café Fayez, both on Avenida Eduardo Mondlane.

Pensão Cruzeiro (14 rooms) Av Eduardo Mondlane; 248 10184. The pick of several good budget options in Mocuba, this family-run first-floor guesthouse is reached via a stairwell littered with pot plants. The pleasant ground-floor café has indoor & outdoor seating, & serves fresh bread & pastries, along with a typical selection of Mozambican mains from US$5. The big airy rooms have en-suite bathrooms, fans, twin beds & parquet floors that are clearly polished on a regular basis. *US$20 twin.*

Pensão São Cristovão (10 rooms) Av Eduardo Mondlane; 248 10607; e agemamocuba@agema.co.mz. This is another clean & reasonably priced lodging, with a restaurant serving meat & seafood dishes in the US$5–6 range, & comfortable en-suite rooms with AC & TV. *US$22/27 dbl/twin.*

Alojamento Rosa (14 rooms) R 1 de Maio; m 82 561 3000. Not as clean as either of the above, but cheaper & closer to the bus station, this place has small tiled rooms with dbl bed using shared ablutions. *US$16 dbl.*

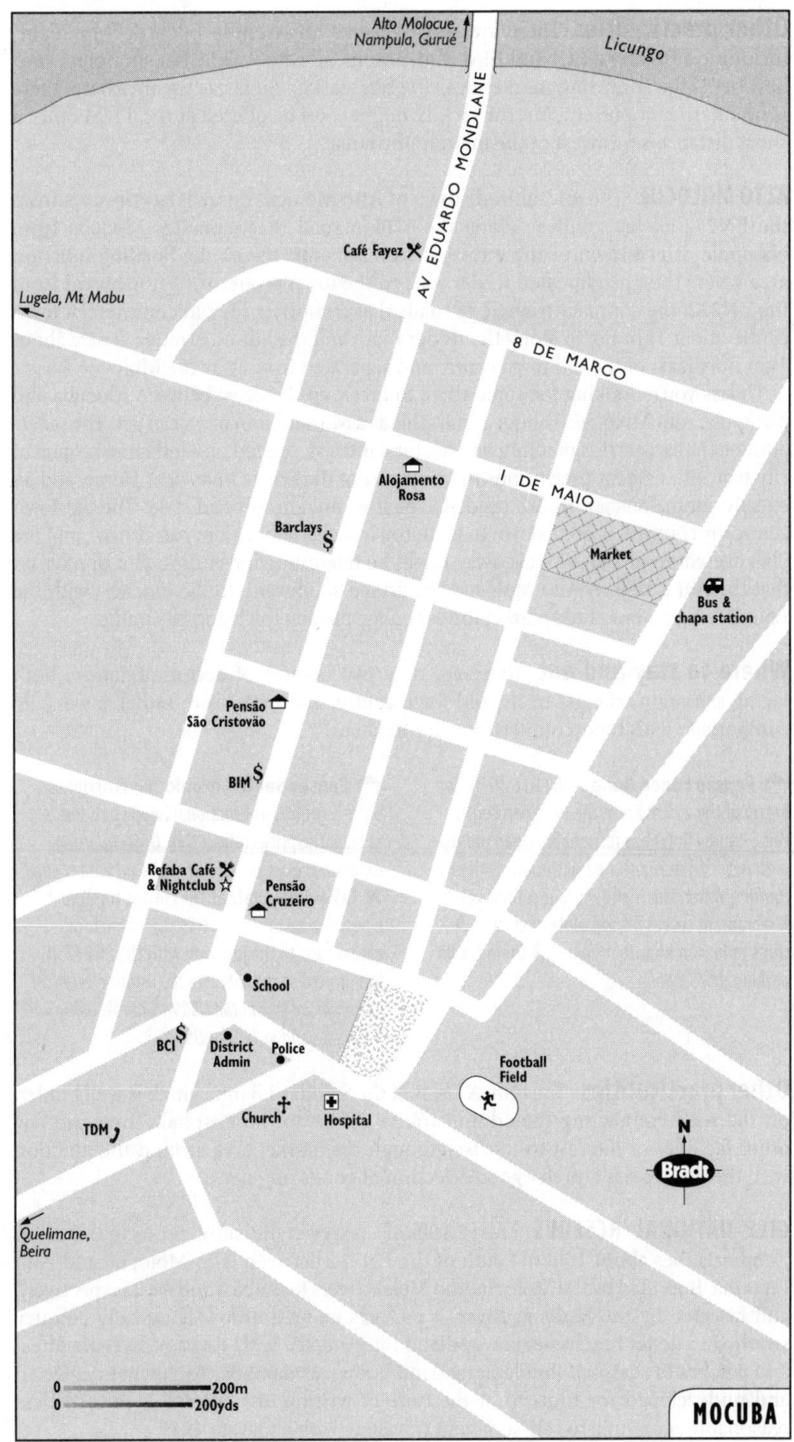
Alto Molocue,
Nampula, Gurué
Licungo
AV EDUARDO MONDLANE
Café Fayez
Lugela, Mt Mabu
8 DE MARCO
Alojamento
Rosa
I DE MAIO
Barclays
Market
Bus &
chapa station
Pensão
São Cristovão
BIM
Refaba Café
& Nightclub
Pensão
Cruzeiro
School
BCI
District
Admin
Police
Football
Field
Church
Hospital
TDM
N
Bradt
Quelimane,
Beira
0
200m
0
200yds
MOCUBA

Other practicalities There are several banks on Avenida Eduardo Mondlane, including a Barclays, BCI and BIM Millennium, all with ATMs. For shopping, your best bet is the sprawling market near the bus station. So far as we are aware, there is no internet at present, but the facility might soon be offered at the TDM office a short distance southwest of the main traffic circle.

ALTO MOLÓCUÈ The mid-altitude town of Alto Molócuè sprawls northwards from the EN232 all but midway along the 370km road that separates Mocuba from Nampula. It is a town of three distinct components: there's the bustling junction area where the unsignposted feeder road to the town proper runs northward from the EN232; the compact triangle of roads that comprises the old commercial town centre about 1km north along the feeder road; and the administrative centre about 1km northeast of the old town centre and separated from it by the Molócuè River.

Unless you're looking for somewhere to break up the drive between Mocuba and Nampula, Alto Molócuè is about as missable as a Mozambican town can get. The sedate administrative centre is of minor architectural interest, centred on a ludicrously opulent city hall with evident pretensions to being part of the senate in ancient Rome, and an equally anomalous governor's residence built in pseudo-fortified style. The old town centre, by contrast, is quite down to earth (or, less charitably, plain run-down), and the lily-covered pond a short walk away might be interesting for birding. But one senses that the real action in Alto Molócuè has drifted southward, to the junction with the EN232, where a busy little market thrives on the passing truck and bus traffic.

Where to stay and eat There are only two choices of accommodation, both facing the main triangle in the old town centre, and both seem rather tawdry by comparison with their counterparts in Mocuba.

Pensão Fundo Uone m 82 826 3010. The better of the 2 *pensões* in the old town centre, this 2-storey hotel has reasonably clean rooms with net, TV, fan & a shared bathroom with no running water. The friendly ground-floor bar & restaurant serves a good plate of chicken & chips (allow an hour to prepare), & there is safe parking. *US$18 dbl.*

Pensão Santo António This is about as basic & grubby as functional hotels get, but at least the prices reflect this. *US$6 sgl using common shower or US$9 en-suite sgl with 3/4 bed.*

Take-Away Halaal The closest thing to a bespoke restaurant is this agreeable local eatery next to the junction with the EN232. It has limited seating. *Serves the usual selection of Mozambican fare in the US$5–6 range, along with snacks & sandwiches for US$2–3.*

Other practicalities The only ATM is at the Standard Bank, which is well hidden on the road connecting the administrative centre to the hospital. There are few other facilities of interest to tourists, though the market area around the junction with the EN232 has a pretty good selection of goods on offer.

GILÉ NATIONAL RESERVE This 2,100km^2 reserve, the only protected area in Zambézia, lies about 100km south of the EN232 between Alto Molócuè and Alto Ligonha. Bounded by the Molócuè and Melela rivers to the east and west respectively, and bisected by the Malema River, it protects an area of low-lying hilly country swathed in dense brachystegia woodland interspersed with strips of riverine forest and patches of seasonal flooded grassland known as dambos. Somewhat neglected and undeveloped for tourism at the time of writing, the reserve is nevertheless reasonably accessible to self-sufficient travellers with a private 4x4.

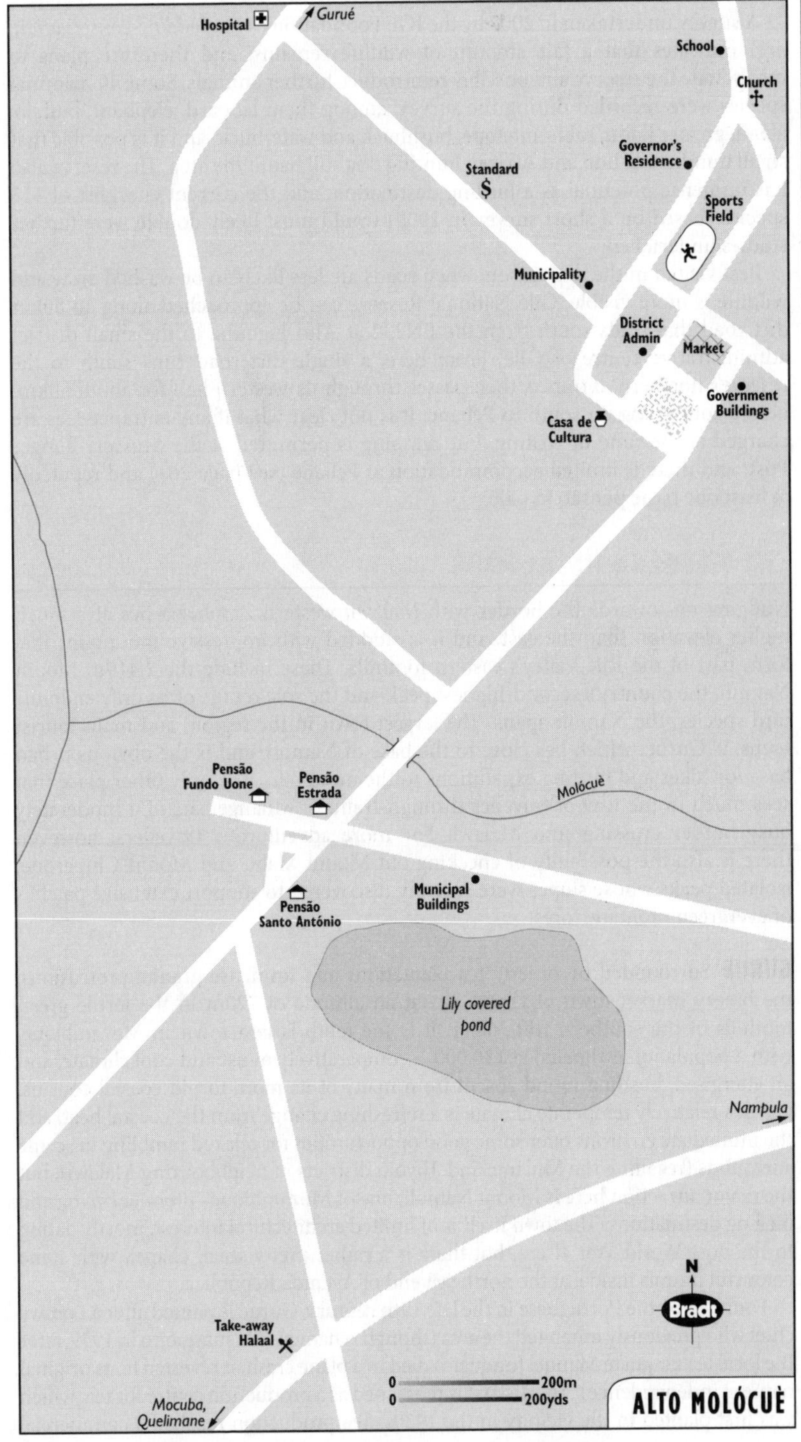
Hospital
Gurué
School
Church
Governor's Residence
Standard
Sports Field
Municipality
District Admin
Market
Government Buildings
Casa de Cultura
Pensão Fundo Uone
Pensão Estrada
Molócuè
Pensão Santo António
Municipal Buildings
Lily covered pond
Nampula
N
Bradt
Take-away Halaal
0 200m
0 200yds
Mocuba, Quelimane
ALTO MOLÓCUÈ

A survey undertaken in 2007 by the IGF Foundation (*www.wildlife-conservation.org*) indicates that a fair amount of wildlife remains, and there are plans to rehabilitate the reserve and possibly reintroduce further animals. Some 40 mammal species were recorded during the survey, among them leopard, elephant, buffalo, eland, greater kudu, sable antelope, bushbuck and waterbuck, and it is possible that small numbers of lion and African hunting dog still haunt the area. The reserve also has immense potential as a birding destination, and the current checklist of 113 species (based on a short survey in 2000) would most likely double were further studies undertaken.

Best visited in the dry season, when roads are less likely to be washed away and wildlife is more visible, Gilé National Reserve can be approached along an 80km dirt road that leads south from the EN232 at Alto Ligonha to the small district administrative centre of Gilé. From here, a single dirt road runs south to the reserve's northern entrance, then passes through its western half for about 50km, before continuing on south to Pebane. It is not clear what if any entrance fees are charged at the time of writing, but camping is permitted at the Musseia Ranger Post, and there is limited accommodation at Pebane (see page 261) and reputedly at least one basic pensão in Gilé.

THE WESTERN HIGHLANDS

Nudging up towards the border with Malawi, western Zambézia lies at a much higher elevation than the east, and it is studded with impressive mountains that form part of the Rift Valley's eastern foothills. These include the 2,419m Mount Namuli, the country's second-highest peak and the sole refuge of its only endemic bird species, the Namuli apalis. The largest town in the region, and main tourist focus, is Gurué, which lies close to the base of Namuli, and is the obvious urban base for hikes and birding expeditions to the mountain. The only other place that sees much in the way of traveller through-traffic is Milange, site of a moderately busy border crossing into Malawi. For more adventurous travellers, however, there is also the possibility of checking out Mount Mabu and Mount Chiperone, isolated peaks whose slopes were recently discovered to support extensive patches of evergreen montane forest.

GURUÉ Surrounded by orderly tea plantations and immense granite protrusions, the breezy market town of Gurué sits at an altitude of 720m in the fertile green foothills of the southern Rift Valley. It is the tenth-largest town in Mozambique, with a population estimated at 130,000, a comparatively moist and cool climate, and an energised, bustling mood absent from many of its more torpid coastal cousins. Gurué's relatively temperate climate is a refreshing change from the coastal heat, and the immediate environs offer some good opportunities for relaxed rambling in scenic surrounds (recalling the Mulanje and Thyolo districts of neighbouring Malawi), but the major attraction here is Mount Namuli, one of Mozambique's premier hiking and birding destinations. The town itself is of limited architectural interest, mostly dating to the post-World War II era, but there is a rather pretty small chapel, with some colourful murals inside, at the northeast end of Avenida República.

Founded by the Portuguese in the late 19th century, Gurué is named after a Lomwe chief who previously inhabited the area (though renamed Vila Junqueiro in 1959, after the local tea magnate Manuel Junqueiro died in a plane crash, it reverted to its original name at independence). The district is renowned as a production centre for tea, which was first planted in the vicinity in the 1920s. Tea production reached a commercial

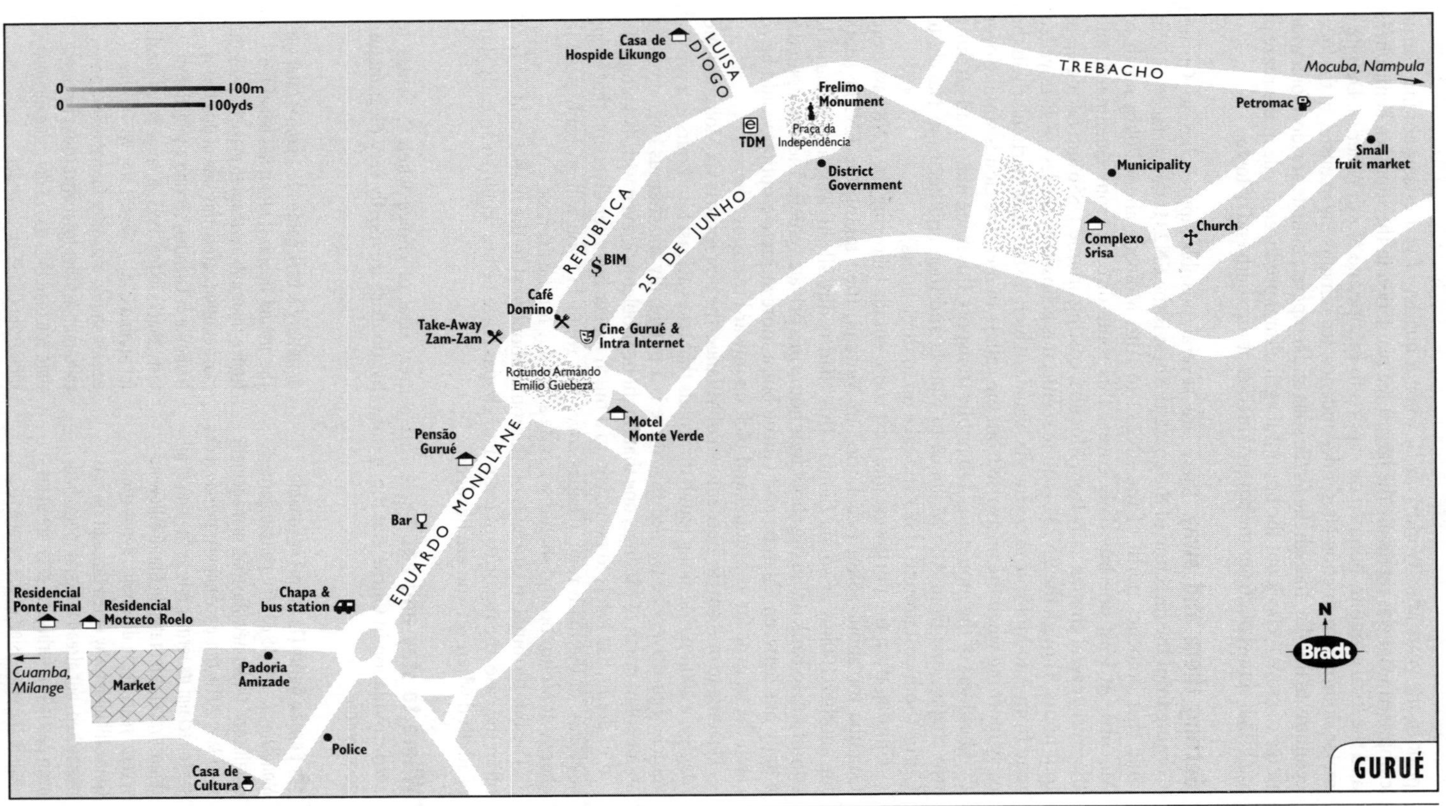
GURUÉ
0 100m
0 100yds
Casa de Hospide Likungo
LUISA DIOGO
TREBACHO
Mocuba, Nampula
Frelimo Monument
Praça da Independência
TDM
Petromac
Small fruit market
Municipality
District Government
REPUBLICA
25 DE JUNHO
BIM
Complexo Srisa
Church
Café Domino
Take-Away Zam-Zam
Cine Gurué & Intra Internet
Rotundo Armando Emilio Guebeza
Motel Monte Verde
Pensão Gurué
EDUARDO MONDLANE
Bar
Chapa & bus station
Residencial Ponte Final
Residencial Motxeto Roelo
Cuamba, Milange
Market
Padoria Amizade
Police
Casa de Cultura
N
Bradt

peak in the years after World War II, when a quartet of vast estates around Gurué comprised what was reputedly the largest tea plantation in the southern hemisphere and the local economy boomed on exports to Europe and North America. Despite a major slump in production after independence, tea remains the mainstay of the local economy to this day, though the fertile soils and temperate climate are ideal for a wide range of crops – check out the bountiful agricultural produce on sale in the maze of stalls that sprawl out from the covered market at the south end of town.

Getting there and away There are several possible approaches to Gurué. Coming from the direction of the coast, the best is the **EN231**, the surfaced 135km road that branches north of the EN232 to Alto Molócuè about 70km north of Mocuba. At least one **bus** daily covers this route directly from Quelimane, and there are several **chapas** daily from Mocuba, costing around US$6 and taking up to four hours. Though the EN231 is quite scenic, it is eclipsed by the less well-travelled road from Alto Molócuè to Gurué via Nauela, which is stunning, particularly in the early morning when the mists rise from the valleys to meet the clouds sinking over the shoulders of the mountains. On public transport, this route may entail catching two chapas, one from Alto Molócuè to Nauela and then another from Nauela to Gurué (both cost around US$3 and take up to three hours).

Coming from the northwest, the best route entails following the **EN8** east from Cuamba for about 65km (via Lurio) to Mutuali, then taking the **EN231** south for another 100km or so via Lioma. This road is dirt all the way, and in variable condition, so bank on taking about four hours in a private vehicle. There is reputedly a daily bus between Cuamba and Gurué but a more attractive option would be to catch the train as far as Mutuali and pick up onward transport there.

Heading to or from the border town of Milange, the best route is via Molumbo and Magige, a 200km ride along rough dirt roads that takes at least four hours in a private vehicle. Self-drivers be warned that there is a potentially treacherous river crossing about 30km north of Milange, one that might be problematic even with 4x4 after rain – if in doubt, ask locals to point you to a much longer but safer diversion that loops southeast of the main road. Chapas cover this route, but you will probably need to change at Molumbo and should set aside a full day for the exercise.

The bus terminal in Gurué is off the roundabout next to the market and, as is so often the case, the majority of long-haul chapas leave before 05.00, so an early start is advised wherever you are headed.

Where to stay and eat There isn't a great deal of choice when it comes to accommodation in Gurué, but the options that do exist are mostly very pleasant and good value.

Pensão Gurué (15 rooms) Av Eduardo Mondlane; m 84 305 8393; e pensao.gurue@gmail.com. Under new Austrian management as of May 2010, this once popular *pensão* looks set to reclaim its former role as the hub of all things travel-orientated in Gurué following several years in the doldrums. Renovations were still under way when this edition was researched, but already several rooms had been partially refurbished, & future plans include the conversion of the garage to a dormitory & back garden to a proper campsite. The ground-floor restaurant has benefited from a thorough overhaul to make it easily the most alluring eatery this side of Quelimane, Nampula or Cuamba, serving a selection of tasty snacks in the US$3–4 range & full meals for around US6–7. There's free Wi-Fi & the *pensão* should also offer formal excursions to Namuli & other local attractions by the time you read this. *US$25 dbl using common showers or US$35 en-suite dbl.*

Casa de Hospide Likungo (4 rooms) 24 R 25 de Setembro; 249 10441; m 82 751 3161. This small family-run guesthouse, set in a restored colonial house with parquet floors, has clean rooms with TV & fan, & a very pleasant feel about it. It's very good value, too, at *US$17 dbl using common bathroom.*

Motel Monte Verde (20 rooms) Rotunda Armando Emilio Guebuza; 249 10245. Not quite so nice as Casa de Hospide and Pensão Gurué, this central motel is still a pretty attractive set-up, offering accommodation in spacious clean rooms with 1 sgl & 1 dbl bed, TV, fan & tiled floor. The veranda bar is often busy in the evening, & serves decent Mozambican fare, ideally with a couple of hours' notice. *US$13/16 sgl/dbl using common shower, or US$16/23 en-suite sgl/dbl.*

Take-Away Zam-Zam On the main square opposite the Motel Monte Verde, this is probably the best of the town's bespoke eateries. The menu doesn't differ radically from the norm, but what there is seems to be executed with a touch of flair. *Mains cost around US$6 & snacks under US$2.*

Other practicalities

Banks and ATM BIM Millennium, on Avenida República just around the corner from the cinema, has the only ATM in town, and often huge queues.

Entertainment Gurué has a cultural centre that holds occasional events, although the only real way of finding out what's happening is to go and read the posters there. Just behind it is a very dilapidated tennis court and just behind that a swimming pool whose murky green water is evidently used as a local laundry. The Cine Gurué on Rotunda Armando Emilio Guebuza (e *cinegurue007@hotmail.com*) shows an eclectic selection of martial arts films and/or Hollywood/Bollywood epics, with two screenings daily from Wednesday–Saturday. Tickets cost around US$0.50.

Hospital At the top end of town on the road leading to Mocuba.

Internet Intra Broadband in the Cine Gurué has broadband for around US$1 per 30 minutes. The TDM on Praça do Independência is the only other option but has a typically slow connection.

Police The police station is just off the roundabout next to the market.

Shopping Though it doesn't cater specifically to tourists, the market at the south end of town is one of the largest in the country, and particularly good for fresh agricultural produce.

AROUND GURUÉ Gurué's biggest attraction is the surrounding countryside, which offers probably the best walking you'll find in Mozambique. A nice easy walk is to tour the tea plantations that surround the town. Head out to the hospital and then take the road off to the left and within five minutes you'll be surrounded by tea bushes. It's an extremely pleasant walk and very photogenic. A more serious walk is the hike up Mount Namuli, which requires three days/two nights on foot from Gurué, as well as a good head for heights for the final ascent, though theoretically it could be done in a (very rushed) day with a private 4x4 to get you to the base camp. While Namuli is not a peak along the lines of Kilimanjaro or K2, it shouldn't be undertaken lightly and you'd be well recommended to check conditions locally before you head out. The Pensão Gurué has been good at providing that sort of information in the past, and can also arrange guides.

Mount Namuli Mozambique's second-highest peak at 2,419m, Namuli is a massive granite dome that protrudes a full kilometre above a grassy rolling plateau

'LOST EDENS' OF ZAMBÉZIA

The EN7 between Mocuba and Milange flanks a pair of isolated granite inselbergs that, until recently, ranked among the least studied wilderness areas anywhere in south-central Africa. These are mounts Chiperone and Mabu, respectively situated about 10km northeast of the EN7 near Tacuane and 30km southwest of the same road near Liciro, and home to extensive tracts of moist evergreen forest.

Rising to 2,054m, Chiperone lends its name to the misty *chiperone* weather conditions that are said to form around its slopes before drifting to Malawi's Mount Mulanje, 60km further north. Jack Vincent, whose 1932 expedition to Namuli collected several previously unknown species there, trekked past Chiperone during the course of the same trip and noted that it 'should hold much interest to the naturalist', but left it at that. Indeed, the only known scientific exploration of the mountain in the 20th century was Jali Makawa's 1950 ornithological expedition, which produced eight new bird records for Mozambique.

In December 2005, Claire Spottiswoode, Hassam Patel, Eric Herrmann and Julian Bayliss undertook the most comprehensive survey of Chiperone to date, and discovered that it still supported around 15km^2 of montane forest, and a rich avian diversity comprising two globally threatened species, Thyolo alethe and white-winged apalis, alongside green-headed oriole, olive-headed weaver and Bertram's weaver. Other wildlife recorded in the forests included leopard, buffalo, samango monkey, an unidentified duiker, and one lizard and one butterfly species previously thought to be endemic to Mulanje.

Possibly the most remarkable recent biological discovery in Africa is the existence of a full 70km^2 of moist evergreen forest on the slopes of the 1,710m Mount Mabu. So far as can be ascertained, this is the largest tract of rainforest in southern Africa, yet it went completely undocumented until 2005, when Julian

incised with numerous streams and gorges. The main peak of Namuli lies only 12km northeast of Gurué, but is not visible from the town itself. Several other tall domes stand on the same plateau, and the entire massif comprises almost 200km^2 of land above the 1,200m contour. Popular with hikers for its lovely green upland scenery, Namuli is also a mountain of great biological significance, supporting a variety of montane habitats including some 12km^2 of moist evergreen forest that shows some affiliations to the Eastern Arc mountains of Tanzania. Two main patches of forest remain: the larger but relatively inaccessible Manho Forest, which borders the Muretha Plateau about halfway between Gurué and Namuli Peak, and the more accessible Ukalini Forest at the southwest base of the granite cliffs below Namuli Peak. Vincent's bush squirrel, listed as Critically Endangered by the IUCN, is endemic to these forests, which also support samango and vervet monkey, red and blue duiker, various small carnivores and at least one endemic but as yet undescribed species of pygmy chameleon.

The forests of Namuli are of particular interest to ornithologists for the presence of one endemic and several very localised species. The mountain is only known location for the Namuli apalis (*Apalis lynesi*), a pretty green, yellow, black and grey warbler that was first described on the basis of a specimen collected by Jack Vincent in 1932 and went unrecorded for more than 60 years thereafter, largely because no other ornithological party visited the area until 1998. Namuli also supports what is probably the largest extant population of two other range-restricted species: the enigmatic and little-known dapple-throat (first collected at Namuli in 1932, also by

Bayliss picked up a vast swathe of undulating green vegetation at Mabu using Google Earth, and joined the aforementioned Chiperone expedition on a five-day visit. In this short time, the team discovered Mabu to harbour what is almost certainly the largest single population of the endangered Thyolo alethe, along with the globally threatened east coast akalat.

Since then, the scientific press has labelled Mabu a 'Lost Eden' as subsequent expeditions, covering little more than 10% of the forest's area, have already collected three butterfly, two chameleon, one adder and three other reptile species new to science, and confirmed the presence of half a dozen globally threatened bird species, including Swynnerton's robin and the first record of a Namuli apalis away from Mount Namuli, along with mammals such as samango monkey, blue duiker and a species of elephant-shrew.

The combination of steep slopes, local taboos and extensive brachystegia buffer zones has discouraged large-scale local exploitation of the forests on Mabu and Chiperone, with the former in particular being in near-pristine condition. All the same, like their counterparts on Namuli, these forests are not officially protected, though the Mozambican government agreed to bar logging in Mabu in 2009, and it is to be hoped that eventually both sites will be accorded fuller protection.

For further details of the 2005 expeditions to Chiperone and Mabu, download the reports *Threatened Bird Species on Two Little-known Mountains (Chiperone and Mabu) in northern Mozambique* (*www.zoo.cam.ac.uk/zoostaff/bbe/Spottiswoode/Papers/Ostrich_Spottiswoode2008.pdf*) and *The Biodiversity and Conservation of Mount Chiperone* (*www.kew.org/science/directory/projects/annex/ChiperoneTechReport.pdf*).

Jack Vincent, and otherwise restricted to a handful of Tanzanian forests) and the Thyolo alethe (otherwise known only from southern Malawi). Though they have been seen by very few African birders, all three of these key species are common in the Ukalini Forest, along with the likes of bar-tailed trogon, green barbet, white-starred robin, olive-flanked robin-chat and many more.

Whether you are there for the scenery or the fauna, the normal springboard for exploring Namuli is the village of Mukunha (also known as Muguna Sede), which lies on the southeast footslopes about 30km from Gurué. A rough road leads from Gurué to Mukunha, heading north from the Mocuba road just past the hospital, but there is no public transport, so unless you have a private 4x4, the only option is to hike, a beautiful but long trek that takes eight to ten hours and requires a guide (a local student nicknamed Rambo has been recommended by local PCVs, and he or another guide can be arranged through Pensão Gurué).

At Mukunha is a rather rudimentary base camp operated by a female spiritual leader (also known as the *régulo* or queen), whose permission is required to climb the mountain, which is still held sacred by the local Lomwe people. It is conventional to offer the queen a few gifts (a bottle of gin, and some sugar and *ncima*), to pay her a fee equivalent to around US$12, and to take a member of her family along as a guide (another US$6). In return, the queen will hold a ceremony to bless the climb, prepare a basic evening meal, and allow you to sleep in a small hut set aside for climbers (no bedding provided, so bring plenty of warmth clothing in winter). From the base camp, the ascent to Namuli Peak is a six-to-eight-hour round trip, so you will need to spend a second night at camp after you descend. The base camp is also a pretty useful base for exploring Ukalini Forest.

For more information on Namuli's birdlife (and other fauna), check out the online report of the 1998 expedition (*www.africanbirdclub.org/feature/namuli.html*). Better still are the downloadable PDFs of Françoise Dowsett-Lemaire's 2007 bird survey of Namuli (*www.kew.org/science/directory/projects/annex/namuli-birds-Dowsett.pdf*) and the broader-ranging 115-page survey *Mt Namuli, Mozambique: Biodiversity and Conservation* compiled by 11 biologists (*www.kew.org/science/directory/projects/annex/Namuli_report_FINAL.pdf*).

Cascata de Namuli The best-known of several spectacular waterfalls on the western side of the massif, the Cascata de Namuli is formed by the Licungo River as it cascades about 100m down a sloping rock face north of Gurué. It is an excellent goal for a day walk, a five–six-hour round hike out of Gurué that passes through a variety of habitats, including the tea plantations of the Chá Zambezi Estate, stands of bamboo and small patches of indigenous forest, and you can swim in a pool above the waterfall. The riverine forest above the waterfall reputedly shelters the Namuli apalis and other rare birds, but it is unclear whether these range as far down as the waterfall itself.

To get there, follow the road past the Casa de Hospide Licungo out of town and keep going – you can't really go wrong, and if in doubt anybody will point you in the right direction (just ask for '*cascata*'). The road to the waterfall passes through the tea estate and although no charge is levied to walk to the waterfall, nor is any prior permission required, people driving may be required to park at the estate entrance gate and to do the last stretch on foot (about one hour each way).

Casa dos Noivos Situated in the hilly countryside north of Gurué, the Casa dos Noivos is an abandoned hilltop dwelling that must have been very beautiful in its prime, and that still offers one of the most spectacular views in the region, over a rolling series of verdant valleys below Mount Namuli. The origin of its name (literally 'House of the Grooms') is unclear: it maybe that the house was built for a newly-wed couple or simply that it is known locally as a place for romantic assignations. On foot, the casa can be reached by following the Mocuba road out of

THE DAPPLE-THROAT

Keith Barnes & Josh Engel (www.tropicalbirding.com)

The dapple-throat is a taxonomic enigma. It was first described from Namuli back in the 1930s, when the collector Jack Vincent thought it was a typical skulking *Phyllastrephus* greenbul. However, it would appear that he never saw the bird alive, only shooting at a shape in the undergrowth and emerging with a skin of a species new to science. But the species was found to occur locally in many forests in southern Tanzania, along with the similar spot-throat. For some time these two species were thought to represent an aberrant group of babblers, and were therefore considered part of the babbler family. However, along with the many other leaps and bounds that genetic analysis has brought us in the past ten years, these two species emerge as having deep lineages connecting them to the African passerines, and seem more closely related to the rockjumpers, rockfowl and sugarbirds. As such, they probably warrant separation in their own mono-specific families.

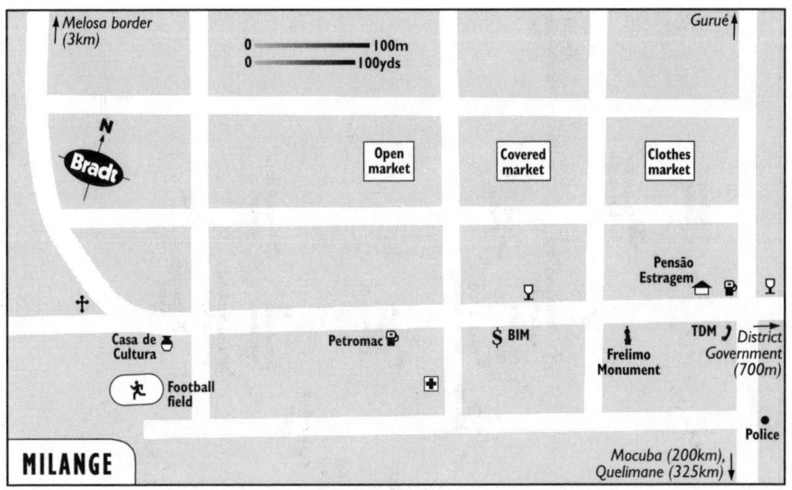

town past the hospital, then taking the second road to the left and heading more or less north for about 90 minutes, passing through scenic tea estates *en route*. If you are thinking of driving, the road is very winding, with some vertical drop-offs, so 4x4 may be necessary, especially after rain.

MILANGE This small town on the Malawi border west of Mocuba is of little interest except as a crossing point to or from the Malawian towns of Mulanje and Blantyre. Architecturally, it is notable for the district government building, an anomalously overblown edifice perched on a hilltop at the east end of town and offering good views towards the 3,001m Mount Mulanje, which is the tallest point in central Africa, but set entirely within Malawi. There is a busy market in the commercial centre, stocked with plenty of goods that have presumably slipped across the border, and, if you are trying to dispose of spare meticais or Malawi kwacha, more moneychangers per square metre than any other town in Mozambique. Other facilities include a BIM Millennium with ATM.

Getting there and away Milange lies 200km west of Mocuba along the **EN7**, a decent dirt road. A few **chapas** run there from Mocuba daily, mostly leaving in the morning, taking about four hours, and charging around US$6. The only other viable Mozambican approach road, from Gurué via Molumbo, is covered under Gurué (see page 266). The **border crossing** is at Melosa, 3km from town along a good asphalt road, and plenty of bicycle-taxis can be found waiting at either end. The border is open from 08.00–18.00 daily.

Where to stay Unless you absolutely have to stay on this side of the border, it is worth knowing that a far better range of accommodation can be found at the Malawian town of Mulanje, which is only 30km from the border by a good surfaced road, and connected to it by a steady stream of minibus taxis at all hours.

Pensão Estragem (8 rooms) m 84 389 0423. The best place to stay in Milange, this place has a selection of quite clean rooms & a decent restaurant. *US$13/15 sgl/twin with common showers; US$18 small en-suite dbl; US$27 large en-suite dbl with TV.*

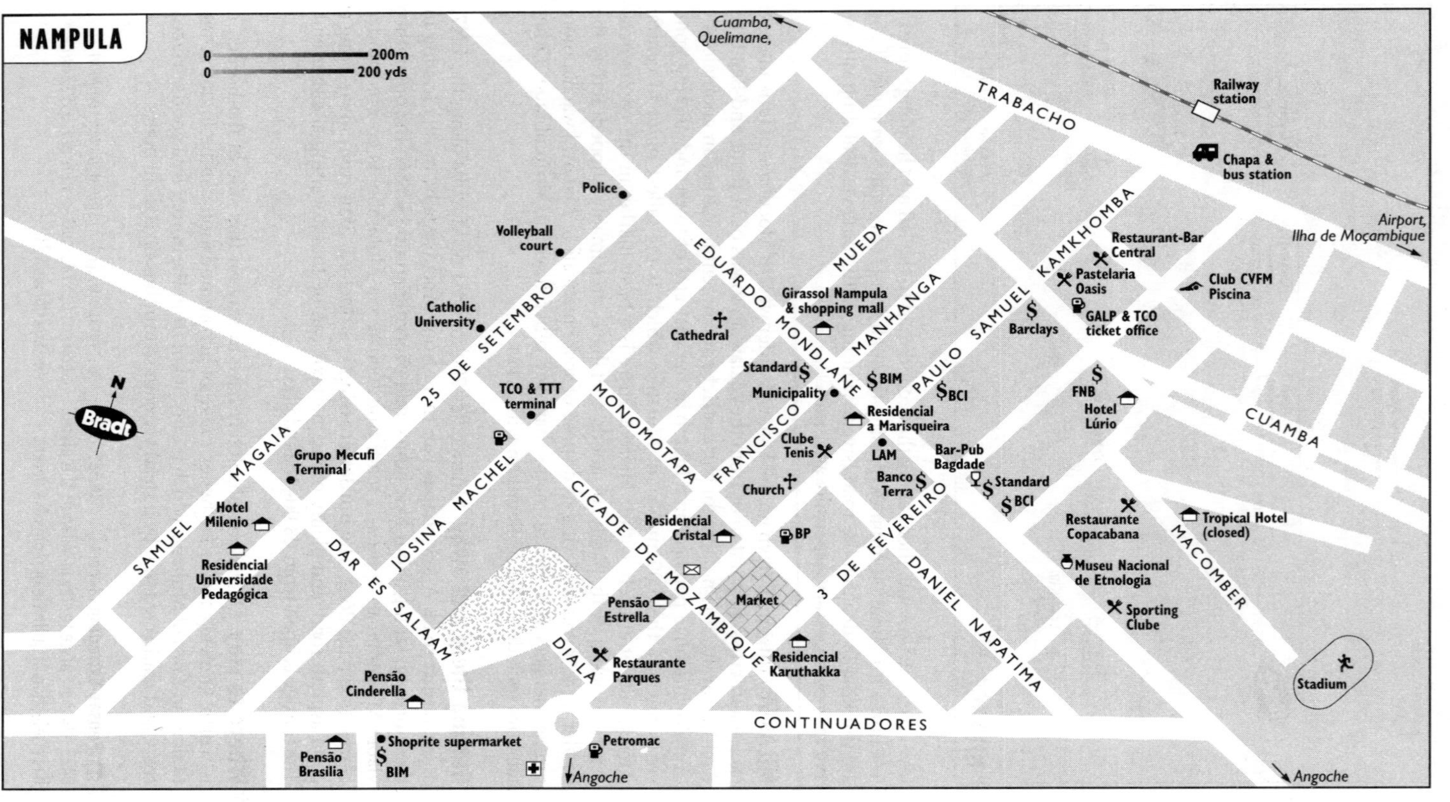
NAMPULA
0 200m
0 200 yds
Bradt
N
Cuamba, Quelimane,
TRABACHO
Railway station
Chapa & bus station
Airport, Ilha de Moçambique
Police
Volleyball court
Catholic University
25 DE SETEMBRO
EDUARDO MONDLANE
MUEDA
MANHANGA
PAULO SAMUEL
KAMKHOMBA
Restaurant-Bar Central
Pastelaria Oasis
Club CVFM Piscina
GALP & TCO ticket office
Barclays
Girassol Nampula & shopping mall
Cathedral
Standard
BIM
BCI
Municipality
FNB
Hotel Lúrio
CUAMBA
Residencial a Marisqueira
TCO & TTT terminal
MONOMOTAPA
FRANCISCO
Clube Tenis
LAM
Bar-Pub Bagdade
Standard
BCI
Banco Terra
Church
MAGAIA
Grupo Mecufi Terminal
JOSINA MACHEL
CICADE DE MOZAMBIQUE
3 DE FEVEREIRO
DANIEL NAPATIMA
Restaurante Copacabana
Tropical Hotel (closed)
MACOMBER
Museu Nacional de Etnologia
Sporting Clube
Stadium
Hotel Milenio
SAMUEL
Residencial Universidade Pedagógica
DAR ES SALAAM
Residencial Cristal
BP
Pensão Estrella
Market
DIALA
Restaurante Parques
Residencial Karuthakka
Pensão Cinderella
CONTINUADORES
Pensão Brasilia
Shoprite supermarket
BIM
Petromac
Angoche
Angoche

Nampula

The eponymous capital of Nampula Province is the commercial hub of northern Mozambique, and the main regional route focus, situated at the junction of the EN8 between Mandimba (on the Malawi border) and the port of Nacala, and the main trunk road running south to Maputo. One of the country's fastest-growing towns, Nampula recently overtook Beira as Mozambique's second-largest city, with a population currently estimated at 550,000. For all that, by comparison with Beira or even Quelimane, Nampula feels more like a large modern town than a city proper, and there is little, aside from the linguistic dominance of Portuguese, to distinguish its spacious, low-rise centre from those of a dozen other moderately sized towns in Zimbabwe or Malawi.

It would be practically impossible to travel through northern Mozambique without stopping over in Nampula at some point, and while the city boasts few tourist attractions, it has a lively and prosperous feel, and there are plenty of good shops and other facilities for visitors. It is also an agreeably compact city for travellers, with everything that matters happening in a few streets either side of Avenida Paulo Samuel Kankhomba, the main road that connects the railway station to Praça da Liberdade. If you have an afternoon spare here, the early 20th-century cathedral is interesting in a vaguely bland way, and it is definitely worth popping into the Museu Nacional de Etnologia and associated Makonde Collective on Avenida Eduardo Mondlane.

Whether one arrives by train from the west or by road from the south, Nampula is the best base for exploring the country's most populous province (estimated population around four million in 2010). Bounded by the rivers Lúrio to the north and Ligonha to the south, the interior of Nampula comprises largely open savanna broken up by any number of isolated and imposing rocky outcrops, mesas and plateaux (these reputedly offer some of the best free-face rock climbing in southern Africa, but pending further tourist development, this is of interest only to experienced and fully equipped rock climbers). One such basalt outcrop just outside Nampula town resembles a profile of a face looking at the sky. Known as 'the old man', local legend has it that this outcrop materialised upon the death of an old king of Monomotapa in 1570.

GETTING THERE AND AWAY

SOUTH

By air There are daily **LAM** flights to Nampula from Maputo and Beira. The **airport** is out on the road towards Nacala. The LAM office is on Avenida Francisco Manyanga (☎ *262 13322*).

By road The **EN232** connects Nampula to Alto Molócuè, Mocuba and Quelimane in Zambézia. The road south to Quelimane is mostly good-condition tarmac, though the stretch immediately north of Mocuba is in poor condition at the time of writing. Still, it is easy enough to drive through from Quelimane in a day. **Chapas** cover all stretches of this road, leaving from the terminus on Avenida de Trabalho five minutes away from the railway station.

For destinations further south, recommended operators are **TTT** (m *82 473 5160; US$70 to Maputo*), which runs a direct bus to Maputo leaving at 04.00 every Friday and overnighting at Muchungwe near the Rio Save, and **TCO** (m *84 601 6861; US$45 to Beira*), which operates a very comfortable bus service to Beira leaving at 04.00 on Wednesdays, Fridays and Sundays, and arriving at around 18.00 the same day. In both cases you need to pay full fare wherever you get off and buses depart from a terminal on the junction of Avenida Josina Machel and Cidade do Moçambique. Tickets are best bought a day in advance from the GALP filling station opposite the Hotel Lúrio.

WEST

By car The main trunk road west is the **EN8**, which connects to the Mandimba border post with Malawi (about 500km) via Cuamba (360km). This road is unsurfaced almost in its entirety and some stretches require 4x4, or may be impassable during the rains.

By train Here, for once, people using public transport have the upper hand, as Cuamba and Nampula are connected by the country's only long-distance passenger train, a service that may fall short of attracting superlatives, but is a whole lot more comfortable than the corresponding road. Trains run in either direction daily except Mondays, leaving at 05.00 sharp, and ten to 12 hours later. Tickets should be bought from the train itself on the evening before departure. First class costs US$15 and second class US$7.50; either way you will be in a six-berth compartment with fold-out beds and you may want to carry some provisions to supplement the simple fare produced by the restaurant carriage. Needless to say, the usual rules about not leaving your luggage unguarded apply. When the train arrives at Cuamba, it is met by buses on to Mandimba, Entrélagos and Lichinga.

NORTH AND EAST The 440km road to Pemba via Namialo is surfaced in its entirety and can be covered in around five hours. Regular **chapas** there cost around US$10. Grupo Mecufi (*Rua de Moma, just off Avenida 25 de Setembro*) also runs a daily bus to Pemba leaving at 05.00; the ticket office is a hole in the depot wall and is open 12.30–17.00 and 04.00–05.00. Regular chapas to Nacala and Ilha de Moçambique cost US$4.50 and take about four hours.

WHERE TO STAY

UPMARKET

Girassol Nampula (28 rooms) Av Eduardo Mondlane; 262 16000; e girassolnampulahotel@visabeira.co.mz; www.girassolhoteis.co.mz. This 4-star hotel, housed in the Centro Comercial Nampula, is the classiest option in town, with professional staff who speak fluent English, a small guest lounge, free internet access & modern tiled rooms with en-suite tub/shower, DSTV, AC & minibar. Aside from being on the bland side, it's everything you could ask of an international hotel in a major business centre. *US$75/90/110 B&B sgl/dbl/suite.*

MID-RANGE

Hotel Lúrio (80 rooms) Av da Independência; 262 18631; e hotel.lurio@gmail.com. Following extensive renovations in 2009, this modern 5-storey hotel comes close to giving the Girassol a run for its money. Clean international-style rooms come with dbl bed, DSTV, AC, fridge & en-suite hot shower. A good restaurant is attached. *US$60 B&B dbl or US$80 suite.*

Hotel Milenio (40 rooms) Av 25 de Setembro; 262 18877; e hotelmilenio@tdm.co.mz. This smart new hotel is already a favourite with business travellers, thanks to the efficient English-speaking staff, good restaurant, free Wi-Fi & comfortable en-suite rooms, which come with twin or king-size bed, balcony, AC, DSTV, combination bath/shower & decor that is maybe a touch old-fashioned but easy enough on the eye. *US$65/68 dbl/twin B&B.*

BUDGET

Residencial Universidade Pedagógica (22 rooms) Av 25 de Setembro; m 82 833 7434. Much the nicest option in this range, this has safe parking, free Wi-Fi & large, clean, secure en-suite rooms with fan, AC & hot water. *US$36/40 dbl/twin.*

Residencial a Marisqueira (20 rooms) Av Paulo Samuel Kankhomba; 262 13611; m 82 684 7300. One of the better-value options in town, this centrally located lodge has spacious airy rooms with 1 sgl & 1 dbl bed, fridge, TV, AC & hot showers. *US$24 used as a dbl; US$30 as a twin.*

Pensão Brasilia (23 rooms) R dos Continuadores; 262 17531. This multi-storey hotel a few doors up from the Shoprite Supermarket has decent (albeit slightly run-down) en-suite rooms with AC, TV, hot shower & in some cases a balcony. It's rather a long way from the railway & chapa station should you have an early morning departure. *US$26 dbl.*

Pensão Estrella Av Paulo Samuel Kankhomba; 262 14902. This is a likeable lodge with a range of rooms that are reasonable value, with fans or AC, TV & fridges. *US$35–40 dbl.*

Residencial Karuthakka (12 rooms) R 3 de Fevereiro; 262 16730; m 82 67 07 320; e residencialkaruthakka@hotmail.com. If you can get past the disastrous furniture, this isn't a bad place, & the large en-suite rooms come with TV & combined tub/shower. Maybe a touch overpriced at *US$40 dbl.*

CAMPING

Complexo Turístico Montes Nairucu (4 rooms) Off the EN8 towards Cuamba, 15 km out of town; 262 15297; m 82 669 3680; e idalecio@teledata.mz. Situated on a scenic farm, overlooking a small dam & surrounded by granite outcrops, this friendly owner-managed excellent camp is justifiably popular with self-drivers. It comprises a good restaurant, a campsite with a clean ablution block, barbecue facilities, & 4 en-suite rooms. *UD$50 en-suite dbl; US$3 pp camping.*

WHERE TO EAT AND DRINK

Sporting Clube Av Eduardo Mondlane; m 83 075 3950. This brightly painted outdoor venue next to the museum is about as funky as it gets in Nampula, making it a popular evening rendezvous with expats & volunteers. The menu comprises a standard selection of Mozambican seafood & meat dishes, but it is all very tasty & good value. The club itself has been turned into a school, just in case you were wondering what all the children are doing there. *Mains in the US$4–7 range, & cheaper sandwiches & snacks.*

Restaurante Parques Av Paulo Samuel Kankhomba. Far more inviting than the run-down *pensão* of which it forms part, this covered terrace restaurant serves a varied selection of Chinese & Mozambican dishes, including a fair choice of vegetarian fare. *Most mains are in the US$5–7 range.*

Restaurante Copacabana R 1.024, opposite the Hotel Tropical. A big favourite among the expat community, this large thatched restaurant concentrates on buffets, & though it seems reasonably priced, the food can start to look a little tired by late afternoon. *Around US$7.*

Restaurante a Marisqueira Av Eduardo Mondlane. Indoor & outdoor seating, a varied selection of pizzas, meat & seafood meals, & a tempting array of selection of pastries & sandwiches, to be washed down with fresh espresso, make this an excellent place to stop for b/fast, lunch or dinner. *Around US$7.*

Café Atlântico Av Eduardo Mondlane. This modern AC café on the ground floor of the Centro Comercial Nampula dishes up the best coffee, fruit juice, croissants & pastries in town.

Clube Tenis Av Paulo Samuel Kankhomba. A smart, pleasant outdoor restaurant serving everything from steak & chicken to prawns at reasonable prices, although not everything will be available. An attraction for some will be the w/end discotheque.

Bar-Pub Bagdade Av Eduardo Mondlane. Probably the nicest drinking hole in the city centre after the Sporting Clube.

OTHER PRACTICALITIES

BANKS AND ATMS The main banks are all represented by at least one branch with an ATM in the city centre. Most are within a block or two of the junction of avenidas Paulo Samuel Kankhomba and Eduardo Mondlane, but there is also a BIM millennium ATM in the Shoprite Centre on Rua dos Continuadores.

HOSPITAL On Avenida Samora Machel just down from the Praça da Liberdade (*800 198 198*).

INTERNET The fastest and most reliable option is the Teledata Internet Café in the Centro Comercial Nampula. Several of the better hotels offer free internet or Wi-Fi to guests.

PHARMACY There is a pharmacy on Avenida Eduardo Mondlane just up from the Museum of Ethnology.

POLICE The police station is on Avenida 25 de Setembro, opposite the junction with Avenida Eduardo Mondlane (*1219*). Be aware that the police in Nampula have a reputation for enforcing the ruling that travellers must carry ID on them at all times (or, more accurately, for abusing this law to intimidate travellers into offering them a bribe). So carry your passport, or better still a certified copy of it, at all times.

POST OFFICE On Avenida Paulo Samuel Kankhomba, on the corner with Rua Cidade do Mozambique.

SHOPPING The market on Avenida Paulo Samuel Kankhomba is good for fruit and vegetables, although you might find the children selling plastic bags irritating after a while. By far the best supermarket is the Shoprite on Rua dos Continuadores, just along from the Praça da Liberdade. Also good is the Supermercado Ideal in the Centre Commercial Nampula, a mall that also houses a good gift and book shop called Mabuko. For craft shopping, head to the Makonde collective behind the museum.

SWIMMING The Club CVFM Piscina on Rua 3 de Fevereiro has a large pool with diving boards set in pleasant green gardens. Swimming costs US$2.50 for adults or US$1.50 for children, and a decent restaurant-bar is attached.

WHAT TO SEE AND DO

MUSEU NACIONAL DE ETNOLOGIA (*Av Eduardo Mondlane; 09.00–17.00 Tue–Fri, 14.00–17.00 Sat/Sun; entrance US$3; photography forbidden*) This ethnological museum is well worth a visit. The ground floor houses a collection of traditional ethnic artefacts, mostly from the northern provinces of Nampula and Cabo Delgado, including copper and bead bracelets, earplugs, metre-high drums and other musical instruments, *bao* games, basketwork, and a couple of dozen garish Makonde masks (one of which bears a striking but presumably unintentional resemblance to former US president Ronald Reagan). There's more of the same upstairs, notably some wonderfully grotesque Makonde sculptures, a few sculpted metal penises that look like (but surely aren't) Iron Age dildos, and more contemporary artefacts including some excellent examples of the toy cars and bicycles you sometimes see sold on the roadside.

In the same compound as the museum is a **Makonde Collective** where you can watch the carvers at work and buy some of their output. Haggling here will be of limited value, as many of the pieces have price tags on them. Similarly if you just want to take photos without buying anything, you'll probably be expected to pay. If you want to visit the collective but not the museum itself, you need to pass through the museum's entrance hall, but won't be asked to pay the entrance fee.

AROUND NAMPULA

The main attraction in the vicinity of Nampula, set on the coast 170km to the east (and covered in the next chapter, page 283), is the historic town of Ilha de Moçambique (Mozambique Island), an absorbing and atmospheric warren of dense alleys and colonial buildings dating to the earliest years of the Portuguese occupation. Also of interest is the ancient Muslim port of Angoche, the offshore Primeiras and Segundas archipelagos, and the junction town of Namialo, all described below.

ANGOCHE Set on the Mluli River mouth, 120km southeast of Nampula as the crow flies, and a similar distance southwest of Ilha de Moçambique, the port of Angoche is one of the country's most venerable towns, having first established trade links to the Arabian peninsula in medieval times and retained these until its sultan was deposed by Portugal in 1910. Oddly, however, it seems there are no pre-20th-century buildings in the modern town, which has a very peculiar character – the long wide main avenue is lined by abandoned office blocks, warehouses and shops that hint at its former prosperity, while the residential area to its southeast is studded with attractive colonial villas fallen into disuse. An estimated population of 85,000 ensures that Angoche isn't quite a ghost town, but as you wander around the surreally sleepy old town centre, you keep thinking it must be a Sunday or public holiday.

Angoche sees few visitors, but it is a worthwhile diversion for travellers with enough time, and it does have two key draws – a long wide sandy beach fringed with mangroves to the east of the town centre, and a busy little dhow harbour and fishing market to the west – as well as being the best port to get to the Ilhas Primeiras and Segundas, a chain of islands similar to the Quirimbas but with virtually no tourist development.

History Angoche is thought to have formed a minor stop along the medieval gold-trade route that connected Sofala to Kilwa (the most important medieval trading port along the Swahili coast, in what is now southern Tanzania). However, it first came to prominence after 1485, following the foundation of the Sultanate of Angoche (covering the cities of Angoche and Moma) by an offshoot of the ruling family of Kilwa. This event coincided with the reorientation of the gold-mining industry in the southern interior, and as a result Angoche became the terminus of a new trade route from Sena on the Zambezi.

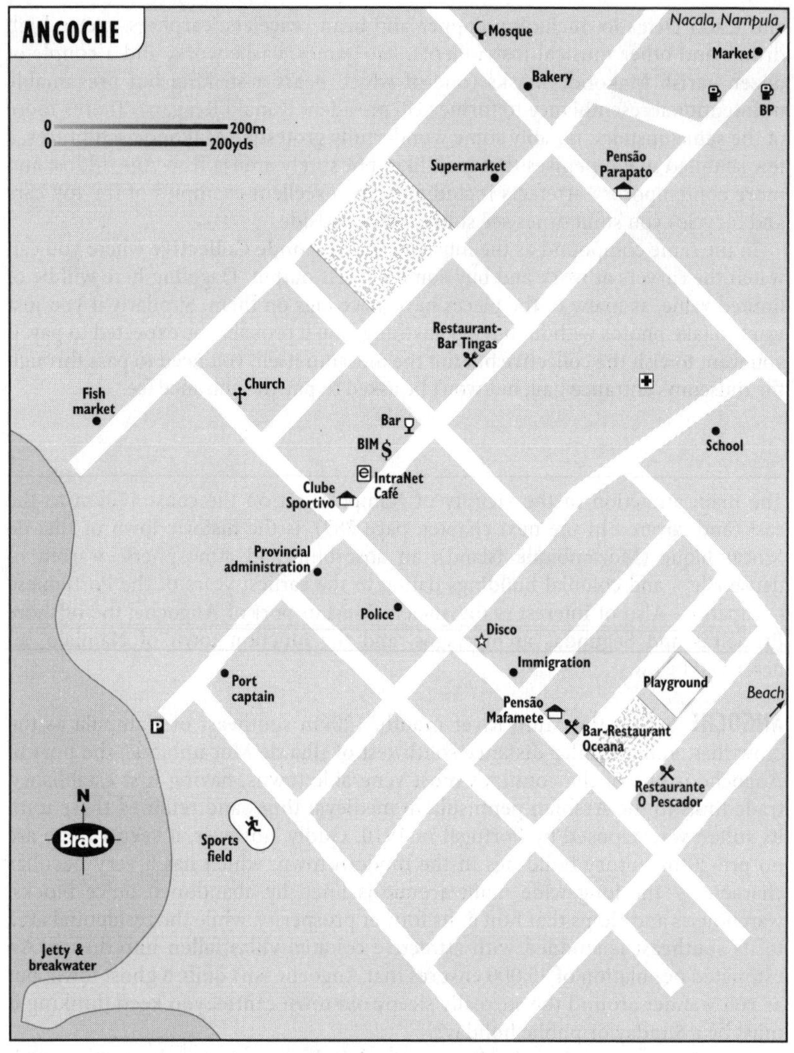

Like the Querimba Islands, Angoche became an important refuge for Islamic traders in the early years of the Portuguese occupation. The town enjoyed an economic boom between 1505 and 1511, when the route from Sena was favoured as a clandestine way of getting gold to the coast without Portuguese knowledge, and its population may have stood at around 10,000. In 1511, however, Angoche was bombarded by Portuguese ships and burned to the ground, and the sultan was taken into captivity. The town slid into relative obscurity after the 1530s, when ivory replaced gold as the major trading commodity along the coast, and Portugal established a greater presence along the Zambezi. It was dealt a further death blow when Barreto's army massacred the Islamic traders at Sena in 1572.

Angoche enjoyed a major revival in the early 19th century, largely due to the emergence of the slave trade off the Swahili coast, which led to its re-emergence as a thriving trade centre by 1830. Angoche assumed a greater importance after

Portugal abolished the slave trade, as its inaccessibility to large ships made it a good place for Islamic merchants to operate an illegal trade, undetected by the British boats that starting policing the coast in 1842. In early 1847, a Portuguese warship attempted to impose an anti-slaving treaty on the Sultanate of Angoche, but it was driven away. Later in the same year, Britain and Portugal bombarded the town from the sea, causing great damage to its buildings, but were unable to occupy it.

Angoche fell briefly to Portugal in 1862, following a bloody battle which caused its sultan to flee inland, but ultimately this led to the strengthening of its links with the interior and increased control over the slave trade at its source. The clandestine slave trade out of Angoche continued into the early 20th century, and the sultanate effectively retained independence from the rest of Mozambique until 1910, when the Portuguese overthrew the sultan and renamed the town António Enes (in remembrance of a former Commissioner of Mozambique who died in Brazil in 1901).

The town has since sunk into relative obscurity again, although it enjoyed a brief resurgence in the late 20th century as a major processing and export centre for cashew nuts, prior to the closure of its two main processing factories in 1999. The channel that was dug in its cashew-exporting heyday has since silted up though Angoche may be due another resurgence thanks to a multi-million dollar project to mine and process heavy sand (a mixture of titanium and zircon ores) in the area.

Getting there and away From Nampula, the best road to Angoche is the well-maintained dirt **EN239** via Namétil and Biola, a drive of around 160km that should take under three hours. A few **chapas** and **buses** run between Angoche and Nampula daily, costing around US$3.70. They leave Nampula from two locations: the market on Avenida FPLM, which is a good 40-minute hike from Praça da Liberdade (look for a dirt track called R 2.307 off to the left) and on Avenida Eduardo Mondlane, past the museum near the Pastelaria Expresso. The journey takes around four hours, so you should assume that you will be staying overnight.

A 170km dirt road called the **EN236** connects Angoche to Liúpo and on to Monapo, on the EN8 about 45km west of Ilha de Moçambique. This is also in pretty good condition, though rough in patches, so best allow four hours. There is not much chapa transport between Angoche and Liúpo, but it may be possible to get there by **boat** from Mossuril, on the mainland opposite Ilha de Moçambique. The best way to find out about this option in Angoche is from the port captain, who will have a good idea of what boats are in port and where they heading.

Where to stay and eat

Pensão Mafamete Set in an old colonial building overlooking the market square, this is pleasant enough in a no-frills way, & the clean (mostly en-suite) rooms have parquet floors. There's cold water only & the electrics are a bit iffy. Still, good value at *US$6/10/14 sgl/dbl/twin.*

Pensão Parapato On the main avenue into town, this place is somewhat down at heel & definitely 2nd choice to the Mafamete. *US$6–10.*

Clube Sportivo On the main avenue, this hosts occasional concerts & serves decent food & beers in the evening. The basketball court looks deserted, which is unusual for Mozambique.

Restaurante o Pescador This has a nice position on the town square & the widest menu, serving the usual seafood & meat dishes. The food's good quality & good value, even if the service is somewhat lacking. *US$4–8.*

Other practicalities

Bank There's a BIM Millennium with an ATM on the main road.

Internet The IntraNet Cafe (⌚ *08.30–12.30 & 14.00–17.30 Mon–Sat, 09.00–15.00 Sun*) on the main street has a few computers.

Hospital On the road that runs along the top of the ridge separating the main avenue from the town centre.

PRIMEIRAS AND SEGUNDAS ARCHIPELAGOS The ecologically important Primeiras and Segundas (literally First and Second) archipelagos off Angoche consist of two groups of five large islands and numerous smaller islets. The area contains the most abundant and diverse coral communities in Mozambique, possibly anywhere in Africa, along with seagrass beds of the type classically associated with dugong, that also form the nesting grounds for green, loggerhead and hawksbill turtles. The island of **Puga-Puga** is a nesting site for the sooty tern, and the area as a whole is known for the quality of its shrimp fishery. The islands are currently unprotected, but plans exist to create a marine reserve centred upon the two archipelagos. At 17,000km^2, this will be the largest protected marine area anywhere in Africa or the Indian Ocean region. This transformation is being overseen by the Primeiras & Segundas Project, which was established in 2008 by the World Wildlife Fund and Care, and it is worth visiting their blog (*http://primeirasesegundas.net*) for information on progress.

Tourist development on the islands is limited to **Fogo Island Resort** (*+27 21 863 4488 (South Africa); e bookings@fogoisland.co.za; www.fogoisland.co.za*), which opened on the 44ha Ilha do Fogo (Island of Fire) in early 2010. Surrounded by coral reefs, hemmed in by a lovely white beaches and accessible only by boat or air charter, this is a classic 'barefoot luxury' set-up offering some of the finest snorkelling and diving in the region, as well as being a breeding site for leatherback turtles. Accommodation is in thatched A-frame bungalows leading onto a beachfront balcony area. Rates are around US$585/850 single/double, with discounts to residents of SADC countries.

Otherwise, the islands have little or no tourist infrastructure, although there are thriving communities on a couple of the northern ones and it is possible to visit providing you are prepared to rough it. For now, the best source of information on getting to the islands is the port captain in Angoche. He speaks reasonable English and is a veritable mine of information. If you want to visit the islands, he should be able to point you in the direction of a suitable boat. It might also be of value to visit the governor's office. For obvious reasons the price of boats to the islands isn't fixed – it'll be down to your haggling ability – but the 12-nautical-mile journey from Angoche to Queleleli should cost around US$240, while the 18-nautical-mile journey from Angoche to Mafamedi should be around US$300.

NAMIALO The small town of Namialo lies at the junction of the EN8 between Nampula and Nacala and the EN106 north to Pemba. As you'd expect it's an unpretentious little place, and surprisingly lively – one side of the road is made up of almost continuous market. The Grupo Mecufi buses heading up to Pemba stop here around 07.00, so if you are heading from Ilha to Pemba and can't bear the idea of going to Nampula *again*, you could overnight at Namialo and meet them here. If you do decide to take this option, don't expect to get a seat. The TDM office has internet access.

There are two inexpensive lodges, of which the **Pousada Hotel** is the better, charging around US$15 for clean, comfortable rooms with bedding. It does food, but the **Restaurante Tropical** also looks good and has been recommended. Given

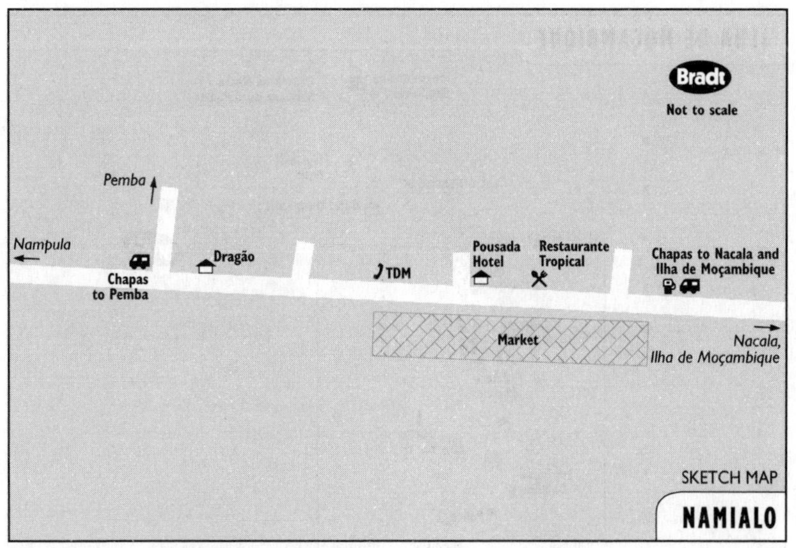

that one half of the town has been given over to market stalls, you shouldn't have too much trouble finding fruit and vegetables. You could also stop at Monapo, 38km east of Namialo, 3km before the roads to Nacala and Ilha de Moçambique diverge, and noted for its cashew factory.

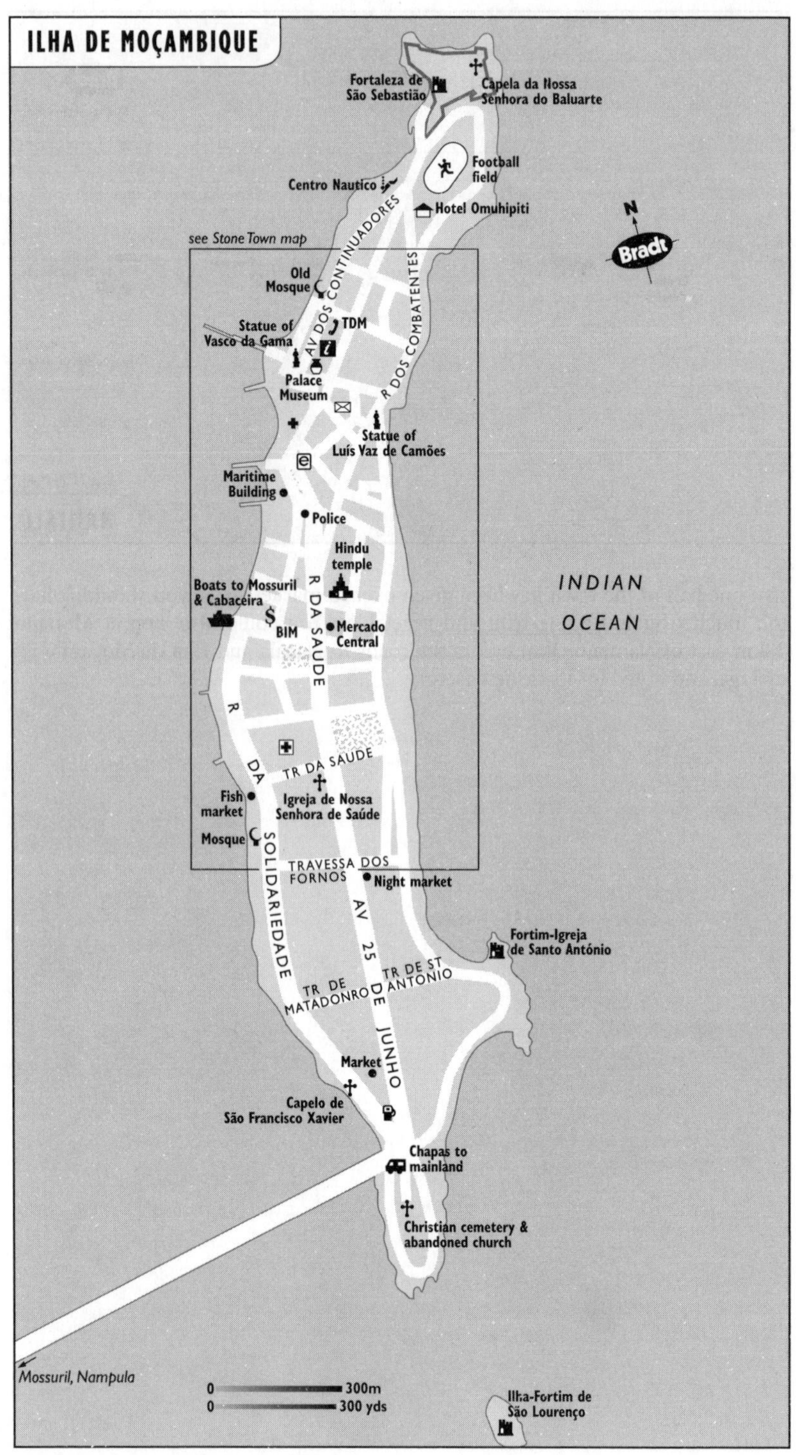
ILHA DE MOÇAMBIQUE
Fortaleza de São Sebastião
Capela da Nossa Senhora do Baluarte
Football field
Centro Nautico
Hotel Omuhipiti
see Stone Town map
Old Mosque
AV DOS CONTINUADORES
R DOS COMBATENTES
Statue of Vasco da Gama
TDM
Palace Museum
Statue of Luís Vaz de Camões
Maritime Building
Police
Hindu temple
Boats to Mossuril & Cabaceira
BIM
Mercado Central
R DA SAUDE
TR DA SAUDE
Igreja de Nossa Senhora de Saúde
Fish market
Mosque
R DA SOLIDARIEDADE
TRAVESSA DOS FORNOS
Night market
AV 25 DE JUNHO
INDIAN OCEAN
Fortim-Igreja de Santo António
TR DE MATADONRO
TR DE ST ANTÓNIO
Market
Capelo de São Francisco Xavier
Chapas to mainland
Christian cemetery & abandoned church
Mossuril, Nampula
0 300m
0 300 yds
Ilha-Fortim de São Lourenço
N
Bradt

Ilha de Moçambique and Surrounds

The town of Moçambique, which occupies the small offshore coral island of the same name in Mossuril Bay, is the oldest European settlement on the east coast of Africa, and also perhaps the most intriguing and bizarre. Measuring about 3km from north to south and at no point more than 600m wide, crescent-shaped Ilha de Moçambique (Mozambique Island) was the effective capital of Portuguese East Africa and the most important Indian Ocean port south of Mombasa for almost four centuries prior to the emergence of Maputo, peaking in prosperity during the 18th century, when it handled some 70% of the ivory exported from the Mozambican coast. It houses several of the southern hemisphere's oldest extant buildings, including the Fortaleza de São Sebastião, the former Convent of São Paulo and a trio of handsome churches. In 1991, the entire island was inscribed as Mozambique's first (and thus far only) UNESCO World Heritage Site, in recognition of its numerous old buildings and singular architectural cohesion; for the very same reasons, it surely ranks as the country's most alluring urban destination to travellers.

Often referred to locally as Ilha (pronounced *Ilya*), Moçambique drifted towards backwater status over the course of the 20th century, a trend that goes a long way towards explaining why the town centre, a maze of narrow alleys lined with old colonial buildings, has barely changed shape in centuries. But while the architectural landscape is overtly Portuguese, the overall mood of the island has greater affiliations to old Swahili ports such as Lamu or Zanzibar, a kinship underscored by the predominantly African/Muslim human presence.

In the early 16th century, when Ilha de Moçambique became the Portuguese regional capital, the original Muslim population was forced to relocate to the mainland. And there they stayed for four centuries, only starting to drift back across the water after the capital relocated to Lourenço Marques (now Maputo) in 1898, and again, in greater numbers, in the wake of the Portuguese evacuation of 1975, to give Ilha de Moçambique a strong but deceptive sense of historical continuity, one that has the odd effect of reducing 400 years of Portuguese rule to something of a passing episode.

By comparison with its lamentably run-down state when the first edition of this guidebook was researched, Ilha de Moçambique is currently enjoying a fresh lease of life as a low-key tourist destination. Several derelict houses have been rehabilitated to serve as hotels, backpackers or restaurants, while the Fortaleza de São Sebastião and other key public buildings have been renovated by UNESCO or affiliated organisations. And where in 1996 there was only one hotel and two restaurants on the entire island, today there are enough cafés, restaurants, boutique shops and lodgings to make the old town a genuinely pleasant place to hang out for a few days.

And yet the overall feel of Moçambique remains isolated, old-world and not at all touristy. Indeed, from that perspective, there may never be a better time to visit

Ilha de Moçambique, poised as it is at a most appealing point along the trajectory between the half-forgotten and rather moribund backwater it had become at the end of the long years of civil war, and the fully developed tourist hub – a kind of southern African counterpart to Zanzibar or Gorée – one senses it will be in the not-too-distant future.

HISTORY

Ilha de Moçambique, like Sofala and Angoche, was an important Muslim trading centre even before the Portuguese arrived on the east coast of Africa. When Vasco da Gama first landed on the facing mainland in 1499, he noted that the island supported a 'collection of dark huts dominated by white verandas of the sheikh's residence and mosque'. The name Moçambique probably derives from that of a local sultan Moussa Ben Mbiki, said by some to have been incumbent when da Gama reached the area, and by others to have been the founding father of the island's Muslim settlement. Back then, the island was a renowned centre of shipbuilding; indeed, the records show that the Portuguese navigator Vincente Soares had a boat assembled there in 1512.

In 1507, two years after Portugal had occupied Kilwa and Sofala, it added Ilha de Moçambique to its list of east African conquests, and built a hospital, church and small fort there. Easily defensible and positioned at the junction of the all-important trade route from Africa to Goa, the island soon replaced Kilwa as the favoured base for India-bound ships awaiting the monsoon winds, and as the main regional focus of Portuguese naval activities. As a result, Portugal abolished the Captaincy of Kilwa in 1513, then in 1530 it renamed the Captaincy of Sofala the Captaincy of Moçambique and Sofala, and the 'Praça de Moçambique' island became the *ipso facto* capital of Portuguese East Africa, a status it would retain for close on four centuries.

In 1562, the first Dominican monks settled on Ilha de Moçambique. By this time, more than 70 Portuguese officials, ranging from a judge and doctor to priests and soldiers, were listed on the island's official payroll. Depending on how many ships were docked at the island, it supported up to a thousand Portuguese inhabitants at any one time. The main activity at this time was commerce: gold, silver and ivory carried to the coast from the Zambezi Valley and elsewhere in the interior were traded for exotic spices, cloths, spirits and other items shipped from India and Arabia. Food was in short supply, and some provisions were sourced from the Muslim traders who had abandoned the island for Sancul on the facing mainland following the Portuguese occupation, while others were imported from the Comoros Islands and Madagascar. High taxes were imposed on all commercial activity following the establishment of an excise office in 1593, and most of the wealth generated on the island was diverted elsewhere: either into the overflowing coffers of the Portuguese crown, or to support the high lifestyle of the administration at Goa.

Ilha de Moçambique was the site of the earliest battle between European powers to take place in Africa, when the Netherlands attempted to seize it as an east African base for the Dutch East India Company in 1607/8 (see box on page 293). In 1671, the island was attacked by Omani Arabs, again without success. During the early 18th century, the Portuguese economic hegemony was curtailed by an influx of Indian traders, known as Baneanes, who soon came to dominate commercial activity and own a significant proportion of property on Ilha de Moçambique. The Portuguese traders based on the island resented this economic intrusion, and attempted to force out the interlopers, sometimes violently, but ultimately without success.

MOÇAMBIQUE AND THE SLAVE TRADE

Over the latter half the 18th century, commerce along the Indian Ocean coast of Africa focused increasingly on the slave trade. Ilha de Moçambique was no exception, though the main local slave markets were actually centred around Mossuril on the facing mainland, which lost ground to the emergent slave ports of Ibo and Quelimane, especially after 1787, when the Portuguese legalised the sale of firearms to indigenous Africans. Caravan routes via the southern shores of Lake Niassa were established to link ports such as Moçambique, Kilwa and Ibo with the interior of present-day Malawi and Tanzania, whose inhabitants were terrorised by murderous Yao and Arab slave raiders.

By the 1790s, around 5,000 captives passed through the warehouses of Mossuril or Ilha de Moçambique every year, with numbers peaking above 30,000 annually in the late 1820s. Some of these captives were sold into bondage to local merchants, others to Portuguese landowners in Brazil, but the vast majority ended up on the sugar plantations of Mauritius, Réunion and the other islands of the Mascarenes. The few available records indicate that only half the Africans captured in the interior ever arrived alive at their intended destination; the other half died along the inland caravan route, while held captive on the coast or in transit to Brazil or to the Mascarenes, a reflection of the harsh and insanitary conditions in which they were kept.

After Portugal abolished the transatlantic slave trade in 1836, traffic out of Mozambique declined somewhat, or was at least conducted more discreetly, with labourers exported to the Mascarenes given the nominal title of contract workers or recruits. It was only in 1869 that slavery was properly outlawed in Portugal's African colonies. This effectively terminated the slave trade out of Ilha de Moçambique, but a clandestine trade continued to operate out of nearby Angoche, which remained an independent sultanate until 1910.

It was largely in order to curb Indian activity on Moçambique that the island was declared an independent entity from Goa in 1761, with its own captain-general and town council. In 1810, it was granted the status of a city. The earliest known census, taken in 1882, shows that the island and associated mainland settlements of Mossuril and Cabaceira then supported a population of 8,500, of which 125 were classified as Portuguese or 'white', 650 as *mestizos* (mixed race), 380 as Canarins (Goans) or Baneanes, 500 as Arab, and 800 as *cafres forros* (free Africans). The remaining 6,000 were slaves.

Ilha de Moçambique slid into economic decline during the late 19th century. This phenomenon was rooted in two causes: the general southward drift of the economy towards Lourenço Marques and the Portuguese discovery of the superior natural harbour at nearby Nacala. The declining importance of the island was acknowledged as early as 1898, when it was superseded as national capital by Lourenço Marques, even though it was still handling roughly 20% of the total goods shipped out of Mozambique. The former capital was granted a lifeline in 1913, when it was agreed that a proposed railway line to the interior would terminate at Lumbo, on the mainland directly opposite Ilha de Moçambique, but the intervention of World War I delayed construction until the late 1920s, with the line reaching as far inland as Nampula in 1930.

As that time, Ilha de Moçambique was still one of the five largest urban centres in the country, supporting a population of 7,000. However, its significance dwindled further following the completion of the more modern port at Nacala. In 1935, the reins of local government were moved from the island to the new provincial capital of Nampula, while the railway connection to Lumbo was superseded by a new line to Nacala in 1947. Today, Ilha de Moçambique probably ranks outside the country's 50 largest towns, supporting a population estimated at 14,000.

GETTING THERE AND AWAY

BY AIR The closest airport with scheduled LAM flights is at Nampula. However, a major new international airport is currently under construction at Nacala, and should start receiving scheduled flights by 2012.

BY CAR Ilha de Moçambique lies in Mossuril Bay about 170km east of Nampula. It can be reached by following the **EN8** east towards Nacala as far as Monapo, then turning right onto the **EN105** and following it for 45km to its mainland terminus at Lumbo. From here, you can cross to the southern end of the island along a 3.5km-long concrete bridge built by the Portuguese in 1969 and undergoing major renovation at the time of writing. The bridge is single-lane for most of its length, but it has been widened in about half a dozen places to allow oncoming traffic to pass. A pick-up or similarly sized vehicle won't have any problems crossing, but anything wider than a minibus may not make it. The charge for the bridge is US$0.30 per vehicle, but there's no charge for foot passengers.

BY BUS AND CHAPA If you're planning to use public transport, the 36-seater 'Tanzanianosh' **chapas** that run between Nampula and Ilha de Moçambique are recommended. These leave Ilha de Moçambique from next to the bridge between 03.00 and 05.00 and from Nampula between 09.00 and 12.00. Tickets cost US$4 and the run takes about four hours in either direction. Leaving Ilha de Moçambique after 05.00, you may need to catch a chapa to Monapo, on the junction with the EN8, and to change vehicle there. In either direction, transport tends to peter out after 12.00. Heading northwards to Pemba, you will need to change vehicles at Namialo and should aim for the earliest possible start to connect with the Grupo Macula bus from Nampula.

BY BOAT The only real option for arriving on Ilha by boat is to head to Mossuril on the mainland and catch a boat from there. It'll cost around US$0.20. There are also occasional boats from Ilha to Cabaceira Pequina and Cabaceira Grande.

WHERE TO STAY

Ilha de Moçambique is now serviced by a good selection of lodges catering to most tastes and budgets, much of it very good value compared with more resort-like parts of the country, though it's worth noting that the most upmarket beach resort in the vicinity is situated on the facing mainland at Cabaceira Piquina.

EXCLUSIVE

Terraço dos Quitandas (6 rooms) Av de República; 266 10115; m 84 613 1243; e terraco.das.quitandas@gmail.com; www.terracodasquitandas.com. This restored waterfront mansion next to the Restaurante Reliquias is Ilha's closest answer to a boutique guesthouse, comprising 6 spacious suites with king-size or twin beds & AC, as well as a large internal courtyard overlooked by 2 balconies & 3 recreation rooms. *US$100 pp B&B.*

UPMARKET

Hotel Omuhipiti (22 rooms) R dos Combatentes; 266 10101–3; m 82 601 3170; e hotel.omuhipiti@gmail.com. This architecturally misplaced Art Deco relic on the northeast end of the island is the oldest & smartest hotel in town, but doesn't remotely live up to its supposed 4-star billing. The en-suite rooms, though a little frayed at the edges, are light & airy, & come with a sea view, AC, DSTV & hot shower. It has a classy restaurant too. Good value *at US$55/65 sgl/dbl; with suites starting at US$75.*

MID-RANGE

O Escondidinho (11 rooms) Av dos Heróis; 266 10078; e ilhatur@teledata.mz; www.escondidinho.net. This converted old Portuguese mansion has a range of spacious cool rooms, set around a private courtyard with swimming pool. It's probably the best-value accommodation in this range. There is an excellent restaurant on the ground floor, & reception can arrange a variety of excursions. *From US$35/40 to US$55/60 sgl/dbl, depending on whether the room is en-suite & has fan or AC.*

Patio dos Quintalinhos (6 rooms) R dos Trabalhadores; 266 10090; m 82 419 7610; e gabrielemelazzi@hotmail.com; www.mozambiqueguesthouse.com. Also known as Casa do Gabriel after its Italian owner, this lovingly restored house lies on the boundary of the stone town & the reed town, immediately opposite the island's main mosque. The rooms are simply but tastefully furnished, & very cool & comfortable. A swimming pool is under construction, the lovely rooftop b/fast area overlooks the beach, & you can arrange boat trips, bicycles & canoe rental & fishing. One drawback for those fond of a lie-in is the morning mosque call, which is so loud you could be forgiven for thinking the muezzin is lurking in your bathroom. *US$17/22 sgl/dbl using shared ablutions; US$27/33 en-suite sgl/dbl; US$ 37/43 large dbl with private courtyard & roof terrace; all rates B&B.*

Casa Azul (4 rooms) m 82 794 2540 or 84 794 2541; e imf_zico@gmail.com or casa.azul.ilha@gmail.com. Lovingly restored over 4 years, this unsignposted casa next to Ruby Backpackers has spacious en-suite rooms with timber floors, wooden beam ceilings, AC & hot shower. There is an attractively decorated living & dining room with DSTV, & a roof terrace with view over the island. *US$50 dbl.*

Alojamento Moxeleliya (7 rooms) 266 10076; m 82 454 3290; e ia.peterson@hotmail.com. The central & attractively restored old homestead has plenty of character, enhanced by antique furniture, & all rooms come with TV, standby light for power cuts, 4-poster bed with netting, & writing desk. Good value at *US$23/45 dbl with fan/AC.*

Casa Branca (3 rooms) R João Deus; 266 10076; e pmaga@hotmail.com. Set around a private courtyard & living room, this restored old casa has large en-suite rooms only 20m from the sea at high tide. *US$22 sgl with 3/4 bed & fan; US$45 dbl with 4-poster bed, fridge, TV & AC.*

BUDGET

Ruby Backpackers (2 rooms, 2 dorms) m 84 398 5862 or 82 717 9923; e ruby@themozambiqueisland.com; www.themozambiqueisland.com. This superlative new backpackers, owned & managed by a helpful multi-lingual German–Portuguese couple, is housed in a beautifully restored homestead, parts of which date back 400 years. Facilities include a fully stocked bar, well-equipped kitchen with fridge, & rooftop & courtyard seating, & it should soon offer b/fast as well as a selection of day tours on the island & further afield on Mossuril Bay. Showers & toilets are not en-suite but clean & plentiful. Rooms are simply but tastefully furnished with nets & fans. *US$23 twin; US$26 dbl; US$10 pp in 4-bed dorm.*

Casa dos Andos (2 rooms) m 82 438 6400. This waterfront homestead on the north end of the island has a quiet location & the clean rooms have nets and fans. *US$22 dbl or twin.*

Casa Kero (3 rooms) m 82 675 5890. Signposted *Hospedagem* & owned by a friendly Mozambican family, this casa on the eastern waterfront feels more like a homestay than a guesthouse, & the rooms seem very comfortable. *US$20 dbl or twin with fan & shared ablutions.*

SHOESTRING

Amakthini Guesthouse (3 rooms, 1 dorm) Barrio do Esteu, off Travessa dos Fornos; m 82 436 7570. Also known as Casa Luis, this family-run place has long been a favourite with budget-conscious backpackers. The dbl or twin rooms are small but clean & come with nets & fan, as do the bunks in the 8-bed dorm, & there is a pleasant garden area & a lounge with DSTV & a library. *US$9/18 sgl/dbl or US$7 per dorm bed.*

CAMPING

Camping Casuarinas At the other end of the causeway in the town of Lumbo; m 82 44 69 900. You'll have noticed a lack of camping on the island itself & this is currently the only site. There's a restaurant & bar & a well-equipped kitchen if you're self-catering. There are also a couple of rooms. *US$16 dbl; US$4 pp camping.*

WHERE TO EAT

The choice of restaurants has improved greatly in recent years, and you could now spend several days on the island without eating at the same place twice.

Restaurante Reliquias Av de República; 09.00–23.00 Tue–Sun. This popular eatery is set in an attractively restored old house adorned with assorted flotsam & monochrome photos from the early 20th century. You can eat indoors or in the small green garden, which offers views over the water & is very pleasant at lunch. *A varied selection of local dishes, seafood & poultry is served in the US$6–9 range.*

Café-Bar Âncora d'Ouro 266 10006; m 82 692 3930; 08.00–22.00 daily. A restaurant of this name has stood here since the first edition of this guide was researched, but the similarities between this airy European café & its dank & uninviting 1996 incarnation end there. The menu includes fresh coffee, juices, fruit salad, pizzas & a fair choice of b/fasts, while the rotating lunch & dinner menu, chalked up on a board, usually includes a filling soup of the day with bread & imaginative seafood mains for US$6–7. There's indoor & outdoor seating, a full bar, & it will usually stay open late if there's sufficient custom. *US$2.50–7.*

Flor de Rosa 17.00–24.00 Mon–Sat. This Italian restaurant diagonally opposite the hospital serves great pasta dishes & seafood grills. Eat downstairs & enjoy the simply but stylish decor, or better still grab a rooftop table & soak up the sea breeze, mosque chants & nocturnal gossip drifting up from the streets. *US$6–10.*

Hotel Omuhipiti (see page 289) 12.00–21.00 daily. The ground-floor restaurant at this stalwart hotel is as formal as it gets on Ilha, & as green (not as in 'eco-friendly', but as in 'somebody *really* likes the colour green'). *It serves tasty seafood dishes & curries in the US$6–8 range.*

O Escondidinho (see page 289) 07.00–22.00 daily. On the ground floor of the namesake hotel, this has an excellent terrace-like restaurant facing the swimming pool. *Salads, steaks & prawns are particularly recommended – the former cost around US$3 while other mains are in the US$8–10 range.*

O Palador m 82 455 9850; 08.00–19.00 daily. Situated at the back of the covered market, this likeable local place is among the cheapest eateries in town, & the freshly prepared food – a varied selection of seafood & chicken dishes – is excellent. Best, however, to order an hour or 2 in advance, or settle in for a bit of a wait. *Mains up to US$5.*

Saquina Take-Away Av dos Heróis; m 82 744 7933. This cheap & cheerful hole-in-the-wall diagonally opposite O Escondidinho serves sandwiches & also chicken & seafood mains. Service can be slow but the food is fine. *US$2–6.*

Centro Nautico Av dos Continuadores; m 82 454 2250; 10.00–late. This outdoor bar overlooks the beach at the north end of the island, close to São Sebastião. Mainly a drinking hole, it usually stays open so long as there is somebody to serve, & seafood meals can be arranged by request.

SHOPPING

The covered central market opposite the hospital is a good place to buy fruit and vegetables, while fish and fresh bread are usually on sale at the smaller beachfront market on Rua das Trabalhadores next to the main mosque. It does have to be said that the range here is limited, so serious self-caterers might want to do their shopping in the market in Nampula before they arrive. Shops catering largely to tourists include the following:

Books & Bottles Av da República; ⌚ 10.00–12.00 & 14.00–17.00 daily except Tue. This is the place to head for should you run short of reading material or fancy a bottle of wine on your balcony: it has a surprisingly good & current selection of secondhand paperbacks, mostly for around US$7 & a range of South African reds & whites for US$7–10 per 750ml bottle.

Missanga Craft Shop Av da República; ⌚ 08.00–12.00 & 14.00–18.00 Mon–Sat, 08.30–13.30 Sun. This well-stocked craft shop, a couple of doors down from Books & Bottles, has a nice selection of above-average-quality Makonde carvings, basketwork, fabrics, wooden chests & other locally crafted goods.

Orera Orera Av dos Heróis; m 82 601 3440; e info@cedarte.org.mz; www.cedarte.org.mz. Affiliated to Maputo's Centro de Estudos e Desenvolvimento de Artesanato (CEDARTE), this small shop sells a range of brightly coloured African-style clothes & fabrics.

OTHER PRACTICALITIES

BANKS AND ATMS There is a BIM Millennium branch with an ATM on the corner of Travessa da Saudade and Avenida Amilcar Cabral

BOAT TRIPS **Aqua International** (m *84 398 1401*; e *yoyomeier@gmx.net*) arranges boat trips to the mainland and other islands, as well as fishing trips, at a cost of around US$60–100 for up to six people, depending on the destination and duration of the excursion. Ruby Backpackers also soon expects to offer a range of excursions off the island soon. For cheaper transfers in local boats, a useful contact is the owner of Genito's Campsite near Chocas Mar (see page 301)

DIVING AND SNORKELLING There is no dive operation on Ilha following the folding of the long-established Dugong Dive Centre, but it is still possible to go snorkelling on the offshore shipwreck with gear and boats rented from a former employee **Jackson Mani** (m *84 481 9569*, or ask for him at the Palace Museum) or from Aqua International for around US$8 per person (see above). Diving will soon be offered by Coral Lodge at Cabaceira Piquina, a short distance by boat from Ilha (see page 299).

HAIR AND BEAUTY Try Cabeleireira Hair Salon on Avenida dos Heróis next to Saquina Take-Away (m *82 742 8783*).

HOSPITAL Situated in the magnificent old colonial administration building on Rua da Saúde (☎ *26 610173*).

INTERNET There is a TDM office with internet access on Avenida dos Continuadores just along from the Palace Museum.

POLICE The police station is in the colonnaded building at the top of Praça João Belo.

POST OFFICE On the corner of Travessa do Teatro and Rua Pedro Alvares Cabral.

EXPLORING ILHA DE MOÇAMBIQUE

The island can be divided into two parts: the **Stone Town** to the northeast and the macuti (reed-hut) zone to the southwest. Most of the historical buildings lie in the old town, which can be divided into several sectors, of which the oldest lies in the

CONTEMPORARY DESCRIPTIONS OF ILHA DE MOÇAMBIQUE

A very good port, which all the ships of the Moors that sail to Sofala and Cuama made the station for repair ... there was a sharif who governed them and carried out the laws. These Moors are of the same language and customs as those of Angoche.

Duarte Barbosa, 1517

It has an ancient fortress, but a very fine new one is now being built, on which large artillery which we brought from [Portugal] will be mounted. There is a ruined Moorish village. The Portuguese village has about 100 inhabitants, and of people of that country ... there are about 200. Different refreshments are sent from gardens on the [mainland] and a certain quantity of orange and lemons. Many deaths take place from the ships that arrive from [Portugal].

Father Monclaro, 1576

I saw lemon, orange and fig trees like those of Portugal ... a very good fortress with four bastions against the sea ... a customs house that yields 50,000 cruzados a year by the sale of ivory, with which I saw the shores covered, and ambergris and gold. It also has a royal hospital, served by the religious of São João do Deus ... to whom the king gives 250 reis a day and clothes and 500 cruzados for expenses ... It has a Misericordia, a collegiate church which they call a cathedral ... a parish church of São Sebastião within the fortress, a beautiful chapel of our Lady of Health, and another of São Antonio who protects the health and safety of the Indian ships.

Anonymous Jesuit priest, 1688

There is neither the noise nor bustle of [economic] life ... no specific diseases ... except ennui. Were I to remain here, I should die of it in three months ... There are narrow streets and high houses, the former not remarkable for cleanliness, the latter partly of a dirty yellow colour impaired by neglect and decay. The windows are barred with lattices as if the town abounded in thieves .... The exterior [of the Governor's Palace] appears more like an old warehouse than the mansion of the first personage... We were led to it by the clashing of billiard balls and the confused clamour of contending voices, so that we first took it to be a tavern or gambling house. [The macuti town] consists of a line of huts, formed of hurdles or bamboos, fixed in the ground and connected by wicker work, with sod or dry grass for the roofs ... It is filled with strong, healthy, active inhabitants whose numerous children ... displayed ample proof of health and vivacity.

James Prior, 1812

A beautiful city [of] noble houses, some of them so vast and well constructed they could rival the palaces of large cities.

Bartolomeo dos Mártires, 1822

extreme northeast, under the protective cast of the Fortaleza de São Sebastião, the only survivor of the Dutch sieges of 1607/8. A map dating to 1754 shows that, by then, the developed part of the town comprised a cluster of perhaps 50 buildings, including the former Jesuit Convent of São Paulo, the neighbouring Church of the Misericordia and São Domingo's Convent (now the courthouse), on the northwest shore between the present-day TDM Building and the police station.

The road layout of the 1752 map is still clearly recognisable, with the open space in front of the present-day Restaurante Reliquias being the former Largo do Pelourinho (Pillory Square), where a whipping post then stood. By 1800, the northwest shore as far south as the present-day hospital had also been developed: the area around the shipping market was lined with granaries and warehouses, and the Largo do Pelourinho and market were relocated to the square where the covered market stands today. The macuti town started to take shape in the early 19th century as a disease-ridden slum inhabited by several thousand slaves.

FORTALEZA DE SÃO SEBASTIÃO (*🕘 08.00–16.30 daily; entrance fee of US$6.50 foreign tourist (with discounts for residents) to be paid at the Palace Museum; photography permitted*) Dominating the northern tip of the island, the Fortaleza de São Sebastião (Fortress of Saint Sebastian) is arguably the most formidable edifice of its type in Africa. Measuring up to 20m high, it was built with dressed limestone shipped from Lisbon between 1546 and 1583 as a response to the Turkish threat of 1538–53. The shape of the fort has changed little over the intervening centuries, though all but one of the three original entrances, the impressive extant gate beneath the buttress of Santa Barbara, were walled up before 1607. Overall, its condition is remarkably similar to that were by the English sailor Henry Salt in the 1800s. The fortress was in active use as recently as the liberation war, when it served as a Portuguese barracks.

Aside from the Dutch siege of 1607 (see box on page 293), São Sebastião has witnessed several important events in Mozambican history. In February 1618, the acting captain of Moçambique and Sofala was stabbed fatally on the steps of the fort by his eventual successor, a culmination of the ongoing intrigues that surrounded the three-yearly appointment to this most profitable of the various postings available in Portugal's Indian Ocean empire. In 1671, an Omani naval attack on Ilha de Moçambique followed a similar course to the earlier Dutch attacks, as the Omanis occupied the island for several weeks but were unable to drive the Portuguese out of the fort – an outcome that had a strong influence on the modern-day boundary between Mozambique and Tanzania.

The fort remains in remarkably good condition, and its wells are still the only source of fresh water on the island. However, it has to be said that recent renovations, undertaken prior to the fortress reopening in mid-2010, seem have been executed with remarkable architectural insensitivity. Possibly they were required for structural reasons, but the concrete slabs that now form large parts of the roof possess little aesthetic merit. Furthermore, the renovations appear to have been halted without ever being completed (the story we heard locally is that a large portion of the foreign funding was diverted into various officials' pockets), and parts of the fortress compound now look more like a construction site than a historic monument. The effect is exacerbated by the two satellite towers that have been erected right outside the fortress and now dominate its skyline.

Protected within the fortress, the **Capela da Nossa Senhora do Baluarte** (Chapel of Our Lady of the Ramparts) is the island's only other 16th-century building to have survived to the present day. Built in 1522, this small church is the oldest standing European building in the southern hemisphere. The main body of the church has

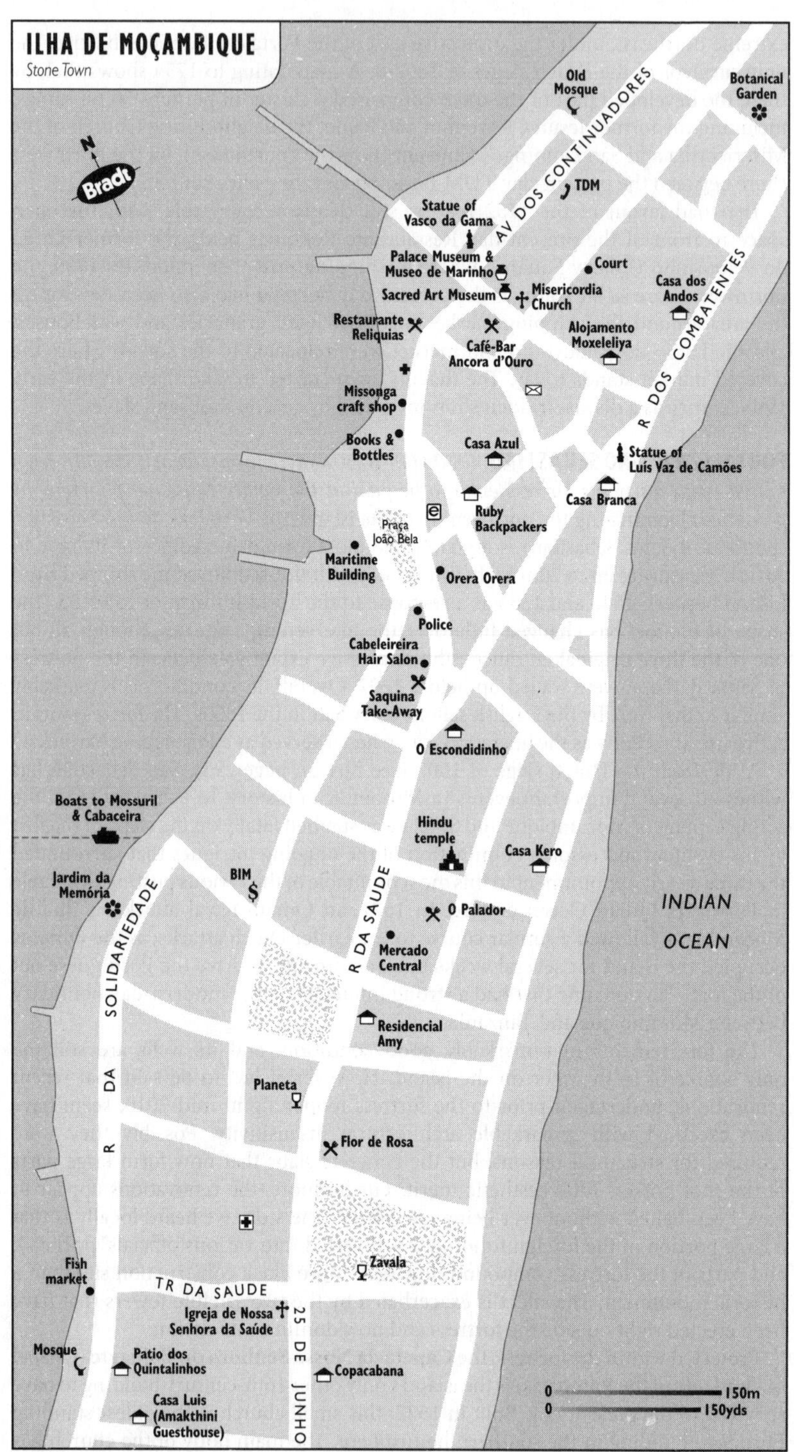

ILHA DE MOÇAMBIQUE
Stone Town
N
Bradt
Old Mosque
Botanical Garden
AV DOS CONTINUADORES
TDM
Statue of Vasco da Gama
Palace Museum & Museo de Marinho
Court
Casa dos Andos
Sacred Art Museum
Misericordia Church
R DOS COMBATENTES
Restaurante Reliquias
Café-Bar Ancora d'Ouro
Alojamento Moxeleliya
Missonga craft shop
Books & Bottles
Casa Azul
Statue of Luís Vaz de Camões
Casa Branca
Ruby Backpackers
Praça João Bela
Maritime Building
Orera Orera
Police
Cabeleireira Hair Salon
Saquina Take-Away
O Escondidinho
Boats to Mossuril & Cabaceira
Hindu temple
Casa Kero
BIM
Jardim da Memória
R DA SOLIDARIEDADE
R DA SAUDE
O Palador
INDIAN OCEAN
Mercado Central
Residencial Amy
Planeta
Flor de Rosa
Zavala
Fish market
TR DA SAUDE
Igreja de Nossa Senhora da Saúde
25 DE JUNHO
Mosque
Patio dos Quintalinhos
Copacabana
Casa Luis (Amakthini Guesthouse)
0
150m
0
150yds

THE DUTCH SIEGES OF SÃO SEBASTIÃO

Few other buildings have played such a decisive role in shaping the course of a subcontinent's history as the Fortaleza de São Sebastião. On 29 March 1607, nine Dutch ships appeared off the shore of Ilha de Moçambique, causing the Portuguese inhabitants to withdraw to the fort. The Dutch navy landed on the island and occupied it for about a month, but were unable to capture the fort, and eventually withdrew on 13 May. Meanwhile, the Portuguese, cloistered within their fortress, survived thanks to the presence of a good well within its walls, and the assistance of their African allies on the mainland, who canoed across to the island at night to drop food and other essential supplies at a point that could not be reached by the larger Dutch boats. A year later, the Dutch returned to Ilha de Moçambique with a formidable fleet of 13 ships carrying 377 guns and 1,840 men. Again, the Dutch seized the island, and again, three months after landing, they were forced to withdraw, incapable of capturing the fort.

One can only speculate, but had São Sebastião been a less imposing building, Ilha de Moçambique would almost certainly have fallen into Dutch hands in 1607/8, a power shift that would have had incalculable ramifications on the eventual course of southern African history. By the early 17th century, Portugal was a waning naval power, and it seems improbable that it would have retained a significant influence in the region had it been evacuated from its headquarters at Ilha de Moçambique. Furthermore, had the Dutch East India Company decided to adopt Ilha de Moçambique as a regional base c1607, then it seems unlikely that it would have established the outpost on Table Bay that eventually became Cape Town … in a very real sense, the 'Mother City' of South Africa as we know it today.

changed little since the 16th century, though the covered porch and pulpit both date to the 18th century. The eminent archaeologist James Kirkman, writing in the 1960s, remarked that Senhora do Baluarte is notable for its several gargoyles as well as a Manueline frieze around the roof and the royal arms of Portugal situated above the entrance. The first two are still clearly visible, but the coat of arms, while still there, has been very badly damaged by the passage of time. On the floor of the church, a stone plaque marks the tomb of the Portuguese Bishop of Japan, who was buried there in 1588. There are several other graves of bishops outside the main building, dating from between 1592 and 1969. Several human bones of unknown origin are stored in a box in the church.

PALACE OF SÃO PAULO (PALACE MUSEUM) (*☎ 267 10047; ⌚ 08.00–16.30 daily; entrance US$3 non-residents; knowledgeable guides available; photography restricted*) When the Dutch evacuated Ilha de Moçambique in 1607, they burned the old town to the ground, destroying the Muslim quarter as well as two churches and the hospital, and sparing only the Portuguese-held fortress of São Sebastião and the church that is protected within its walls. In 1671, the Omani Arabs again razed much of the old town following their short-lived occupation of the island, for which reason the only extant 17th-century building in the old town is the former Jesuit College of São Paulo.

Situated near the jetty, the college was built in 1619 on the site of the small Fortress of São Gabriel built to protect the first Portuguese trading post established here in

1507. A large red building with an impressive spire, it served as a college until 1759, when the Jesuits were banned from Portugal and its overseas territories. Two years later, following the decision to make the viceroy of Moçambique independent of the Goa, the building was converted to a governor's palace. It retained that role until the relocation of the capital to Lourenço Marques in 1898, after which it served as the official residence of the District Governor right up until 1975. The first indigenous African to sleep in the palace as a guest was reputedly President Hastings Banda of Malawi, back in 1971. The second and last was Samora Machel, who stayed here four years later on his first presidential tour of newly independent Mozambique, and decided it should be reinvented as a museum.

Still a museum today, the former palace is a fascinating place to explore. The original church, which was formally opened in 1640, is worth looking at for its garish pulpit, a cylindrical wooden protrusion decorated with some beautiful carvings of the Apostles, below which is a chaotic assemblage of rather less loveable but arguably more compelling creatures, a mixture of gargoyles, angels and dragons. Also notable are the copper-plate altar and the dozen or so religious paintings that decorate the otherwise bare walls. The courtyard separating the church and the palace also has several large statues, for some reason painted in a rather fetching shade of green.

The interior of the palace is a revelation. The 20-odd rooms are all decorated in period style, allegedly with furniture left behind when the governor moved to Lourenço Marques, though it's perfectly possible that some of it was accumulated more recently (witness the Kenwood Magimix and other state-of-the-art 1970s gadgetry gathering dust in the kitchen). In addition to any number of four-poster beds and antique chairs and tables, most of which are Goan in origin, the rooms are liberally decorated with vases and other porcelain artefacts from China. There is something strange and disorientating about walking from the ostentatious riches of the palace back out into the dusty, run-down alleys of the old town.

MUSEO DE MARINHO (🕘 *08.00–16.30 daily; entrance included in the ticket for the Palace Museum*, see page 295) Formerly the Naval Museum but reopened under a new name in August 2009, the Maritime Museum, reached through a door to the right as you leave the Palace Museum, now focuses on a fascinating collection of artefacts recovered from the *Espadarte* and *Nossa Senhora da Consolação*, shipwrecked in the waters off Fortaleza de São Sebastião in 1558 and 1608 respectively, and rediscovered in 2001. The displays includes the richest stash of Ming porcelain ever salvaged in Africa, comprising more than 1,500 pieces, many still in mint condition, whose motifs have been dated to the reign of the Chinese emperor Jiajing (1521–66). Also on display is a hoard of 16th-century gold and silver coins and other material from the two wrecks.

SACRED ART MUSEUM (🕘 *08.00–16.30 daily; entrance included in the ticket for the Palace Museum*, see page 295) Situated in the same block as the Palace Museum but entered from around the corner (opposite Café-Bar Âncora d'Ouro), this small museum is housed in a wing of the Church of the Misericordia, which still opens for Mass on Sunday mornings. The Misericordia (House of Mercy) was a religious organisation with nominally charitable aims and a gift for raising revenue through bequests and later from a large *prazo* in Zambézia. The church that houses the Sacred Art Museum served as the island headquarters of the Misericordia from when it was built in 1700 until the organisation was disbanded in 1915, and the majority of artefacts it contains are the former property of the Church. It might be difficult to get excited about the dozens of statues of saints displayed in the museum, especially after having spent time in the palace next door. The most unusual artefact is a Makonde carving of Jesus. It would be interesting to know when and how this statue was acquired, since it is very different in style and subject from most other Makonde carvings.

OTHER LANDMARKS Aside from the fortress and museums, the old town contains several buildings of considerable antiquity and/or architectural merit – indeed, most houses in this part of town are several hundreds of years old, and many have been restored to something approaching their former glory since the turn of the millennium. A feature of these houses is their homogeneity: over a 400-year period, generation after generation of builders have used the same materials (limestone and wood with lime-treated façades) and very similar construction methods and floor plans, to create a distinct architectural style rooted in the Algarve region of southern Portugal, but with Arabian and Indian flourishes.

The **old customs house** on the Praça João Belo has an impressive entrance complete with a couple of anchors and a cannon. There's a rather stylised **statue** of the 15th-century Portuguese navigator **Vasco da Gama** in the Praça da República outside the Palace Museum, while on the east side of the island, about 300m further south, is a similar statue of his approximate contemporary, the poet **Luís Vaz de Camões**, who is regarded as the Portuguese equivalent of Shakespeare (but had no direct links with Mozambique).

A recent addition to the northern waterfront, inaugurated in August 2007, the **Jardim da Memória** (Garden of Remembrance; no entrance fee) stands next to the old dhow jetty about 800m southwest of the Palace Museum. This small UNESCO-funded garden is the one site on Ilha de Moçambique to pay tribute to the hundreds

A TELLING TABLEAU

One of the most remarkable artefacts in the Palace Museum is the large tableau that hangs in the banquet hall, a depiction of one of the shipwrecks which, in the 16th century alone, stranded or killed many thousands of Portuguese along the east coast of Africa. The right-hand side of the tableau depicts a ship swirling upward through the clouds, while on the beach below a solitary grey-bearded mariner, the picture of thirst and exhaustion, is desperately dragging his tired limbs towards shade. In the left half of the tableau, a group of semi-naked Portuguese maidens sits in a huddle below the trees, subjected to the surreptitious scrutiny of two Africans whose expression is open to interpretation: does it signify innocent curiosity, recognition of an easy meal or wide-eyed lust?

Assuming this tableau is of some antiquity, it pays resonant testament to the fears, prejudices and bravery of these first Europeans to settle in east Africa, one that is somehow made more vivid by its touches of the fantastic: the line of wooden crosses erected on the beach below the airborne ship, or the manner in which the maidens' breasts are spared the immodest realism of nipples and dangle unnaturally from below their armpits. For all the architectural prowess of Ilha de Moçambique's old buildings, it is this solitary tableau that offers the one real glimpse into the psyche of their constructors: pale, God-fearing immigrants who, for all their cruelty, greed and arrogance, had more than enough demons to feed their nightmares.

of thousands of African slaves interred here *en route* to a life of bondage of the sugar plantations of the Mascarenes. The garden hosts a few information boards discussing the slave trade, and a dozen or so statues of human figures in ethnic style. Echoing the notorious Gates of No Return that stare out to sea from Cape Coast Castle and Gorée Island (west African sites that had strong links with the trans-Atlantic slave trade), a stark gateway opens out at the seaward end of the garden.

The **macuti (reed) town** that occupies the southwestern part if the island is inherently less interesting than the grandiose old town in architectural terms, though it does possess more of a bustling lived-in quality. Predominantly Muslim today, this part of town is scattered with several **mosques**, the most important of which lies on the border of the old town opposite the Patio de Quintalinhos. Next to the mosque is the main **fishing beach**: here you can watch dhows launch and return from fishing expeditions, or buy a fresh catch in the market.

A block inland of this beach, arguably the single most imposing building on the island is the **hospital**, housed in a large and very grand whitewashed 18th-century building that once served as the administrative headquarters of the colonial government. Opposite this, the **Igreja de Nossa Senhora da Saúde** (Church of Our Lady of Health) is the third-oldest building in Mozambique, built in 1633 as part of the then rather isolated Convento-Hospital de João do Deus, but extensively renovated in 1801, which makes it difficult to say how much of the original church is intact.

One important historical landmark in this part of town is the whitewashed **Fortim-Igreja de Santo António**, which has stood on a palm-covered peninsula on the widest part of the island since before 1754. On the beach in front of this church, shipbuilders still practised the craft for which Ilha de Moçambique was famous even before the Portuguese arrived as recently as the late 1990s, but this no longer seems to be the case – though the open area in front of the church is a popular spot for informal football matches.

On the southern tip of the island, past the bridge to the mainland, the island's **Christian cemetery** is scattered with dozens of elaborate tombstones. The disused church here has a haunting atmosphere, created as much as anything by the psychedelic array of mosses that colour the wall behind the pulpit. Behind it lies the old Hindu crematorium, while the original Muslim cemetery lies a couple of hundred metres to the northeast. Other landmarks in the southwest include the small **Capelo de São Francisco Xavier** and the venerable **Ponta da Ilha Well**.

Facing the old cemetery, the **Ilha-Fortim de São Lourenço** consists of a tiny, mushroom-shaped coral outcrop that can be reached on foot at low tide. The small island is entirely taken up by a 17th-century fort, now rather overgrown but still in good shape, with several cannons in place. If you want to walk across, check the tides in advance, since the island is accessible by foot for no longer than an hour. Despite the presence of a couple of rusty iron ladders in front of the fort, the best way to climb up to the island is through a gap in the coral overhang, which can be reached by walking around the right side of the island for about 100m. Look out for the many starfish and marine other creatures that inhabit the pools between the two islands at low tide.

MOSSURIL BAY

The mainland opposite Ilha de Moçambique, though relatively little visited by travellers, is well worth exploring. As with the island itself, settlements such as Lumbo, Mossuril, Cabaceira Grande and Cabaceira Pequina are steeped in history, while the sleepy town of Chocas Mar is a gateway to a succession of idyllic beaches running east on either side of the peninsula that terminates 10km further east at the superb new Coral Lodge 15.41. Most sites on the mainland can be visited in isolation as a day trip from the island, but it is also worth thinking about dedicating a few days to the area.

GETTING AROUND

By car The easiest way to explore this area is in a private vehicle, following an unsurfaced road that runs northward from the 45km **EN105** at almost the exact midway point between Monapo and Ilha de Moçambique. From here it is 21km to Mossuril and another 12km to Chocas Mar along a road that can be tackled in pretty much any vehicle.

The Cabaceiras lie to the east of Chocas Mar along a very sandy road that may require 4x4. It's about 3km from Chocas Mar to the unsignposted junction south to Cabaceira Grande, then another 2km to the village itself, along a dirt track that you shouldn't have any problem navigating if you got as far as the junction. The junction for Cabaceira Pequina is another 5km past this, just before the entrance to Coral Lodge, but although it is only 1.5km from here to the village, the road may be impassable at high tide and will most likely require 4x4 at other times.

By chapa Using public transport, there are fairly regular chapas between Lumbo (on the mainland opposite Ilha de Moçambique) and Mossuril, or you could hop on any vehicle travelling between Lumbo and Monapo, hop off at the junction, and wait there. Chapas between Mossuril and Chocas Mar are somewhat less frequent, but they do exist. There is no chapa transport from Chocas Mar to the Cabaceiras, but it is possible to catch a cheap public **boat** (an erratic service dependent on tides) across the 5km channel between Ilha de Moçambique and either of the Cabaceiras, or to Mossuril. You could also arrange a more costly private boat transfer through Ruby Backpackers (see page 289) or Genito's Campsite (see page 301). If you want to spend a night or two in the area, it is only a 3km walk from Cabaceira Pequina to the Carrusca Resort or Genito's Campsite.

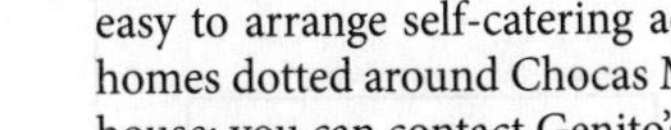

WHERE TO STAY In addition to the formal options listed below, it is usually quite easy to arrange self-catering accommodation in one of the many private holiday homes dotted around Chocas Mar. Expect to pay around US$55–60 per night for a house; you can contact Genito's Campsite below for further details.

Exclusive

Coral Lodge 15.41 (10 chalets) 266 60003; m 82 902 3612; e info@corallodge1541.com; www.corallodge1541.com. Officially opened in June 2010, this stunning new 5-star lodge under new management sets new standards for the northern Mozambican mainland. The location alone is marvellous, overlooking a quiet creek & a bone-white beach in a private reserve on the far tip of the peninsula east of Chocas Mar. The large thatched chalets have a roof fan, 4-poster beds with nets & silent built-in AC, mini-bar, large sitting area, en-suite bathroom with tub & shower, & simple but stylish décor with an ethnic feel. Other features include an infinity pool with views across to the Fortaleza de São Sebastião (only 3km distant as the crow flies), a quality seafood restaurant & a health spa using local products, while the dive centre is the only one in this part of Mozambique to offer wreck & reef dives, snorkelling, canoeing, *dhow* excursions to Ilha de Moçambique & historic walks to nearby Cabaceira Pequina. *US$565/850 sgl/dbl inclusive of all meals, house wines & most other drinks, & all non-motorised activities & tours.*

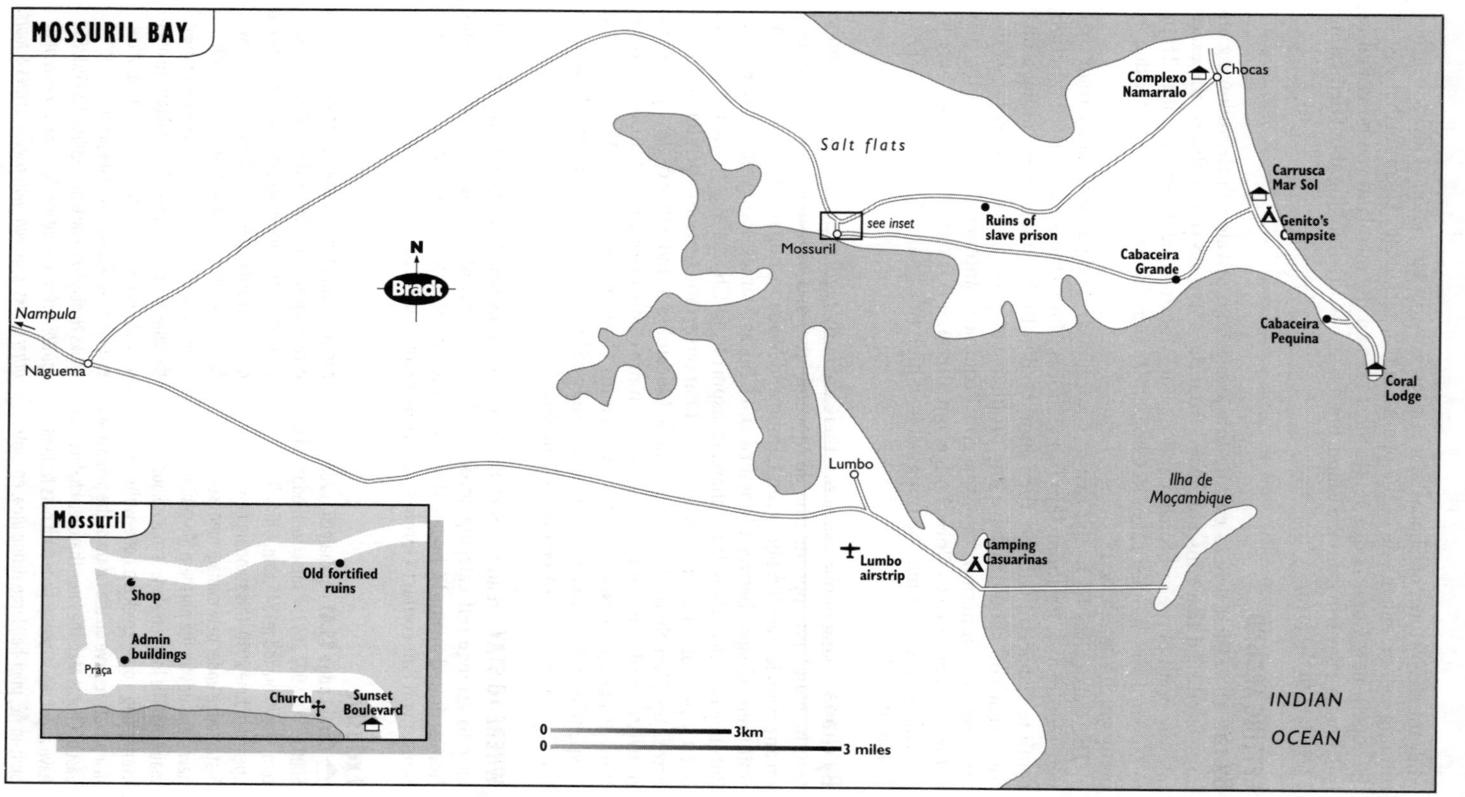
MOSSURIL BAY
Complexo Namarralo
Chocas
Salt flats
Carrusca Mar Sol
Genito's Campsite
see inset
Ruins of slave prison
Mossuril
Cabaceira Grande
N
Bradt
Nampula
Naguema
Cabaceira Pequina
Coral Lodge
Lumbo
Ilha de Moçambique
Camping Casuarinas
Lumbo airstrip
Mossuril
Old fortified ruins
Shop
Admin buildings
Praça
Church
Sunset Boulevard
0
3km
0
3 miles
INDIAN OCEAN

Mid-range

Carrusca Mar Sol (7 units) 262 13302; m 82 516 0173; e anibalcarrusca@hotmail.com. Situated 4km east of Chocas Mar along the road towards Cabaceira Pequina, this wonderful retreat has an idyllic location on a sandy rise overlooking a lovely white beach, a highly praised seafood restaurant, & the choice of small houses sleeping 2 or larger houses sleeping 4, the latter with AC, nets, barbecue area & a large balcony with hammocks. Camping is permitted. *US$35 small dbl or US$80 4-sleeper.*

Complexo Namarralo (8 rooms) 256 60049; m 82 673 0590. This peaceful complex is situated in Chocas Mar about 100m to the left of the main circle as you enter town, & a similar distance from the sea. Accommodation is in simple thatched rondawels with twin beds, en-suite hot shower & screened private balcony with seating. The terrace restaurant has a seafood dominated menu with most dishes falling in the US$6–8 range. *US$45 dbl.*

Budget

Sunset Boulevard m 82 7411907; e info@hotelsunsetboulevard.com; www.hotelsunsetboulevard.com. The only accommodation in Mossuril, this community-run guesthouse stands in 3ha gardens about 200m from the sea. To get there, follow the main road into Mossuril to where it terminates at a traffic circle, turn left next to the district government office & continue for about 800m passing a church to your right. Most of the staff graduated at the College of Tourism in Cabaceira, so service is slicker than you might expect. The restaurant has a reputation for good seafood, Macua dance performances can be arranged with notice, & accommodation is in simple but clean rooms using common bucket showers & toilets. *US$15 dbl.*

Genito's Campsite (1 room) m 82 667 6773; e genitomolava@hotmail.com. Situated next to Carrusca Mar Sol, this consists of one very basic reed hut with sandy floor & dorm beds, & a campsite. The location is great & food can be arranged on demand. It's advisable make contact in advance. *US$5.50 pp for a bed or US$3.50 camping.*

WHAT TO SEE AND DO

Lumbo The coastal terminus of the railway to Malawi prior to the construction of a new branch line to Nacala in 1947, the scattered settlement of Lumbo stands on the mainland side of the 3.5km motor bridge to Ilha de Moçambique. About 5km from the bridge and signposted along the main road towards Nampula is a war cemetery containing the graves of 80 soldiers killed at Lumbo fighting the Germans in 1918. It is also the site of the only airstrip in the area.

Mossuril This small town on the mainland about 10km northwest of Ilha de Moçambique was the main regional centre of the Muslim-dominated slave trade in the 19th century. The town itself houses few relicts of that era, though there are a few discarded cannons on the main circle overlooking the mangrove-lined bay, and the large church about 500m to the east certainly looks like it was built in the 19th century or earlier. The coast around Mossuril, though not as beautiful as around Chocas Mar, is also quite attractive, and some striking salt flats flank the road as you enter the town from the north.

Mossuril is the home of **Belmoz** (*m 82 389 7749; e belmoz@gmail.com; http://web.mac.com/belmoz*), a unique eco-friendly Belgian–Mozambican enterprise that produces a variety of organic products (fruit brandies, aloe cosmetics and digestives, etc) using local materials. Their products can be bought at a shop called Heroina in Mossuril or at Missanga Craft Shop on Ilha de Moçambique.

Two significant slaving-era ruins lie on the right side of the road from Mossuril to Chocas Mar. The first, a fortress-like structure 600m past the main circle, comprises a compound of 3–4m-high coral rag walls, with what appears to be a sealed turreted entrance on one corner, and a well built inside it. The second and less substantial ruin, situated about 2.5km further towards Chocas Mar, is reputedly the remains of an old slave prison and can be recognised by the twin turrets close to the road.

Chocas Mar This pretty village has an idyllic location on a low coral cliff overlooking a beach as attractive as any in this part of the country. There are lots of private holiday cottages in the village, as well as a *complexo turístico* with rooms and a restaurant, but most travellers head on out of town to Carrusca Sol Mar, 4km east of town, or the stunning Coral Lodge 15.41.

Cabaceira Grande One of the earliest Portuguese settlements on the Mozambican mainland, Cabaceira is the site of what must be the oldest actively used church in sub-Saharan African, the well-preserved Nossa Senhora dos Remédios, constructed in 1579 for Pedro de Castro, the Captain of Sofala and Moçambique, which still hosts occasional services today. It is a rather bizarre apparition, standing perhaps 12m tall in buttressed isolation on the edge of this mangrove-lined backwater, and arguably of greater note for its antiquity than any great architectural merit, though the heavy wooden Goan-style door is very impressive and there is a gold-flecked altar similar to the one in the church attached to the island's Palace Museum.

Also of interest in Cabaceira Grande is the old **Governor's Palace**, reputedly built in the early 19th century as a summer retreat for the island's governor. Behind this, the former **Naval Academy of Cabaceira** has been restored as a Colégio de Turismo e Agricultura, which was founded by author Lisa St Aubin de Terán in 2004 and now trains up to 40 locals annually to work in the tourist sector (see *www.teranfoundation.org* or get hold of her book *Mozambique Mysteries* for more details). The attached **Dios Coqueiros** (Two Coconuts) is an inexpensive bar and restaurant staffed by college students.

Cabaceira Pequina Local legend has it that this tiny palm-fringed village, situated on a marshy spit about 3km north of Ilha de Moçambique, is where Vasco da Gama landed in 1498, and that it was also the capital of the mysterious Moussa Ben Mbiki, after whom Mozambique is named. True or not, Cabaceira Pequina is clearly a settlement of genuine antiquity, scattered with the ruins of Swahili-style houses that reputedly pre-date the Portuguese occupation, while its main well – still in use today – is said to be the very same one that da Gama drank from all those centuries ago.

NACALA

Some 70km north of Ilha de Moçambique as the crow flies, Nacala is a purpose-built port town situated at the southern end of Fernão Veloso Bay, which is the deepest natural harbour along the east coast of Africa. The construction of Nacala in 1947, and simultaneous opening of a new rail link to the 900km line through Nampula to Malawi, sealed the declining fortunes of Ilha de Moçambique, diverting the majority of oceanic and terrestrial transport away from the old capital. The importance of Nacala extends beyond Mozambique to Malawi and Zambia, which made extensive use of the so-called Nacala Corridor prior to the collapse of apartheid in 1994, and effectively bankrolled its maintenance during that period.

Now operated by a multi-national consortium with US, South African and Portuguese investors, Nacala is the third-busiest port in Mozambique, handling about 200 cargo ships annually. It is also the site of several manufacturing concerns, including a large cement factory, and its significance will most likely be boosted when the recently privatised and expanded airport outside town starts to receive international flights. One result of all this activity is that the town has grown immensely since its foundation: with a population estimated at 225,000 it is now the country's fifth largest.

For all that, Nacala is of little interest to travellers, certainly by comparison with Ilha de Moçambique, and this is reflected in the rather poor selection of places to stay and eat in town. For adventurous travellers, a possible goal for an excursion would be the tiny island of Somana, a few hundred metres offshore near the entrance of Nacala Bay, which supports one of the few remaining pre-Portuguese Swahili ruins in Mozambique, comprising the coral walls of a merchant's dwelling and an associated cistern. A far more enticing prospect than Nacala itself is Fernão Veloso, a short drive out of town and a very attractive area for beach and watersports enthusiasts; the protected deep bay is perfect for snorkelling and diving, providing a tempting weekend getaway spot for residents of Nampula.

GETTING THERE AND AWAY

By car Nacala and Nampula are connected by the surfaced eastern 200km of the **EN8**, a good road that can be covered in two hours or so.

By chapa There are regular chapas between Nacala and Nampula, and less frequent ones between Nacala and Ilha de Moçambique. They leave from outside the TDM office in the Cidade Baixa and outside the petrol stations in the Cidade Alta (see *Orientation*, below). If you're heading to Fernão Veloso, then you may be able to get a chapa from the TDM office, but your best bet is to head to the market and look there; the journey takes around 45 minutes and costs US$0.20.

By train The rail link between Nampula and Nacala has been refurbished in anticipation of increased freight traffic, but no passenger services run along the line.

By air The upcoming international airport outside town should open to scheduled flights by 2012.

ORIENTATION The town has a split personality: the main residential area, known as Cidade Alta (uptown) and made up of a mixture of mud huts with some concrete buildings, is on top of the hill overlooking the bay, while the Cidade Baixa (downtown) is a more business-oriented concrete town near the docks at the bottom of the hill. The two are linked by a long curving avenue. Chapas around town seem to follow a loop from the TDM office in Baixa, up the avenue, around the market in Alta, back to the petrol stations and then back down the avenue again.

WHERE TO STAY If you are stuck for budget accommodation in town, the choice is between the **Residencial Canal** and **Residencial Bella Vista**, both of which are tucked away in the Cidade Alta and have rooms for around US$20.

Upmarket

Hotel Maiaia (30 rooms) 265 26827/43; m 82 601 5440; e inturhoteis@teledata.mz. Owned by the same group as the Hotel Omuhipiti on Ilha (& clearly continuing the habit of giving hotels unpronounceable names), this central hotel is of a similar standard. A decent restaurant with terrace is attached. *US$55/63 sgl/dbl or US$63/93 sgl/dbl suite; all rates B&B.*

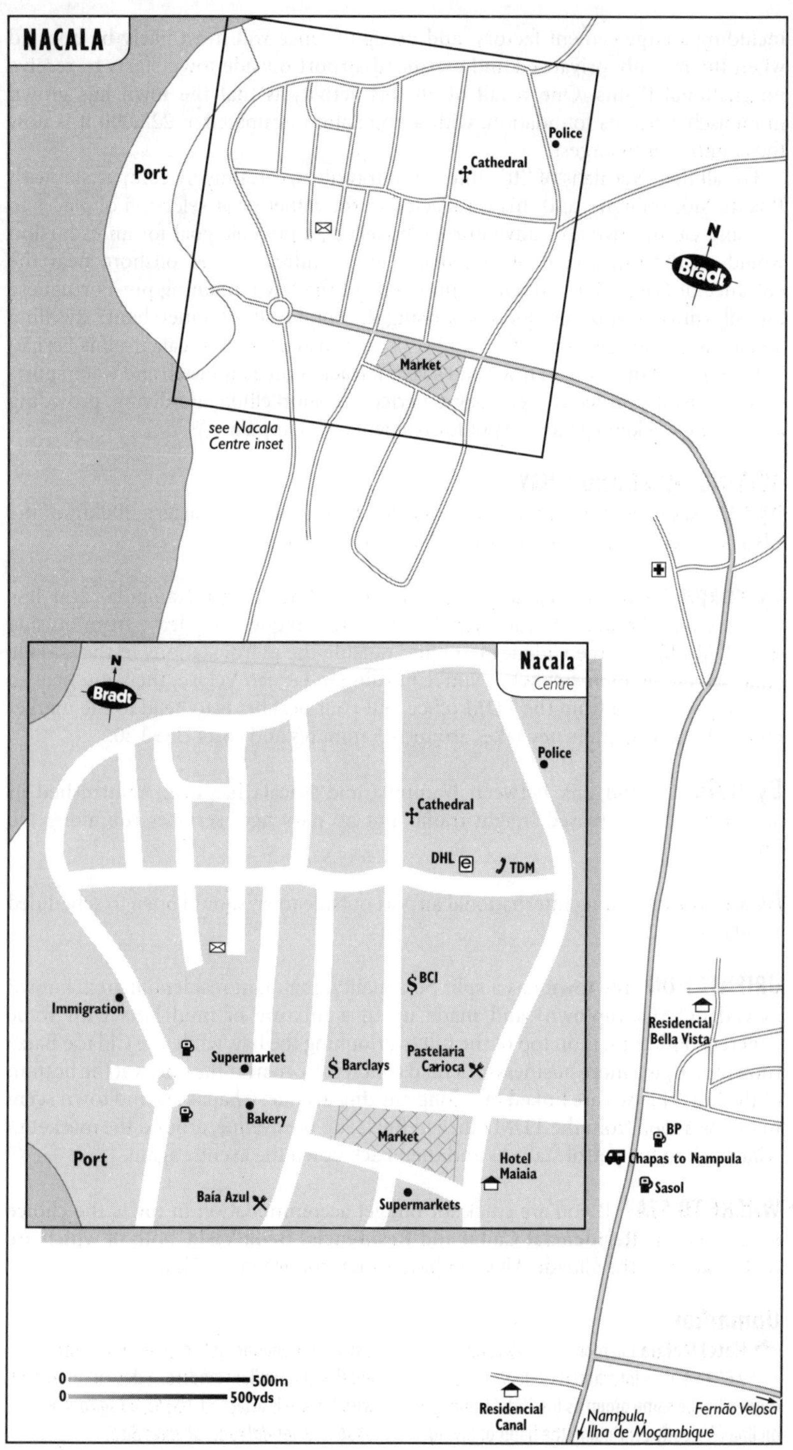

NACALA
Port
Police
Cathedral
Market
see Nacala Centre inset
Nacala
Centre
Police
Cathedral
DHL
TDM
BCI
Immigration
Supermarket
Barclays
Pastelaria Carioca
Bakery
Market
Port
Hotel Maiaia
Baía Azul
Supermarkets
Residencial Bella Vista
BP
Chapas to Nampula
Sasol
0 500m
0 500yds
Residencial Canal
Nampula, Ilha de Moçambique
Fernão Velosa

Mid-range

Libélula m 82 304 2909 or 82 306 6473; e info@divelibelula.com; www.divelibelula.com. By far the nicest place to stay in the vicinity of Nacala is this dive-oriented lodge set on an escarpment above a small private beach on Fernão Veloso Bay about 10km from the town centre. Recently taken over by friendly English–South African owner-managers, it offers a varied range of accommodation, from en-suite A-frames & stone cottages to dormitories & camping space. Facilities include a swimming pool, on-site dive centre offering various snorkel & dive packages, a restaurant serving tasty meals for around US$8, DSTV in the lounge, & a book exchange. Using public transport, you'll need to walk the last 2km of dirt road or ring in advance for a lift from Nacala (bear in mind that locals often still refer to it by the older names of Fim do Mundo or Bay Diving). *US$50/55 en-suite sgl/dbl; US$30 dbl sharing ablutions; US$12 pp dorm bed; US$8 pp camping.*

Complexo Turístico Napala (14 rooms) 265 20608; m 82 601 2760. This pleasant enough but rather soulless complex is situated above the beach at the tip of Fernão Veloso. *Dbl rondawels with AC cost US$57/73 sgl/dbl.*

Complexo Turístico Maharenque (7 rooms) 265 20737; m 82 322 6551; e ctnherenque@tdm.co.mz. Close to the Napala (see above) & very similar in standard. *US$73 dbl.*

WHERE TO EAT

Baía Azul Just down near the market, this is probably the best restaurant in town. Sadly it doesn't actually have views of the bay, but there is a dance floor.

Pastelaria Carioca Has the usual range of pastries & drinks, although they don't have any chairs & tables to eat at.

OTHER PRACTICALITIES

Banks Nacala's lack of interest in naming roads makes it difficult to give street addresses, but the main banks are all marked on the map and have ATMs.

Hospital 26 520880.

Internet Available at the TDM and DHL offices in the town centre.

Shopping The market itself is good for fruit and vegetables, and there are several grocery shops running down the main road to the dock.

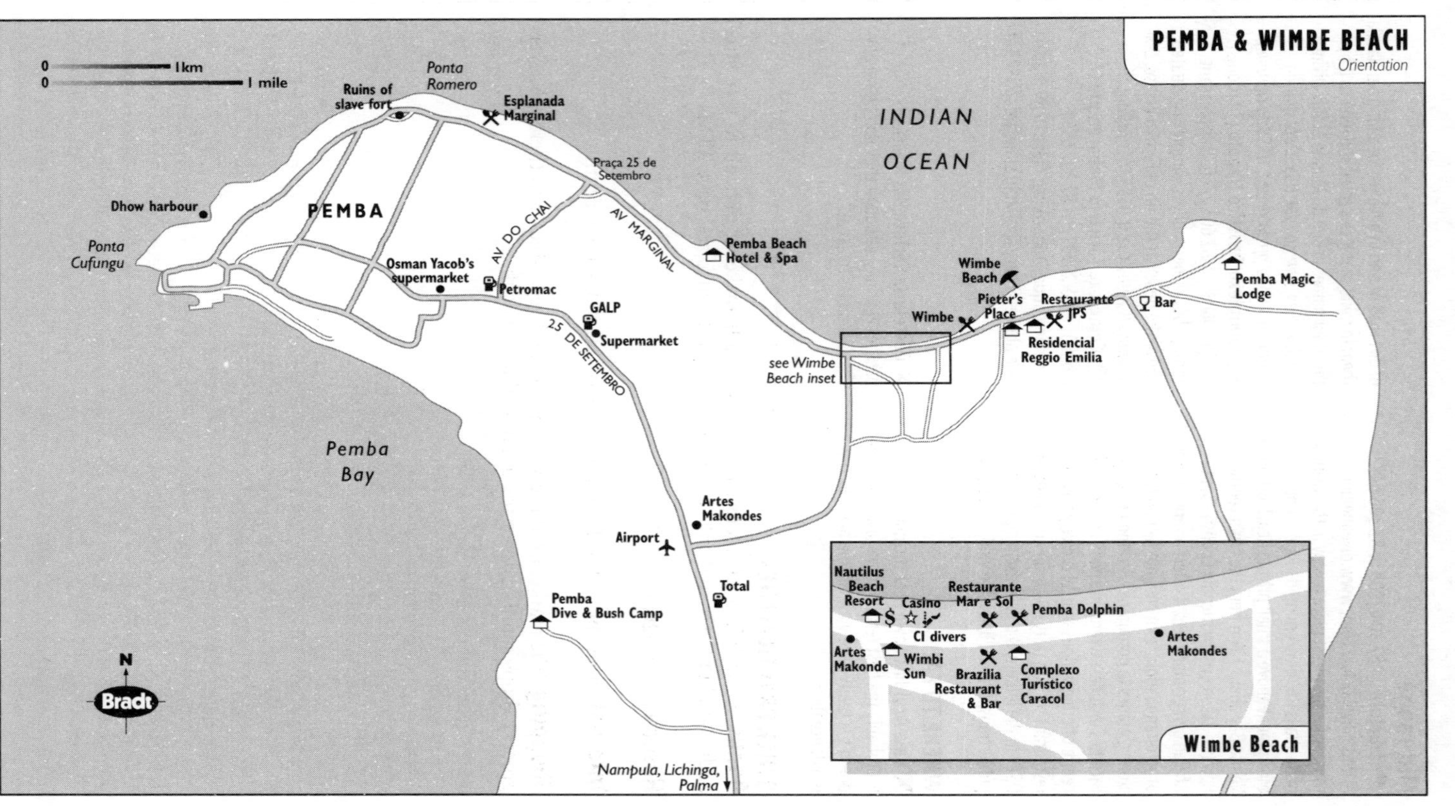
PEMBA & WIMBE BEACH
Orientation
0 1km
0 1 mile
INDIAN OCEAN
Ponta Romero
Ruins of slave fort
Esplanada Marginal
Praça 25 de Setembro
Dhow harbour
PEMBA
Ponta Cufungu
AV DO CHAI
AV MARGINAL
Pemba Beach Hotel & Spa
Osman Yacob's supermarket
Petromac
GALP
Supermarket
25 DE SETEMBRO
Wimbe Beach
Pieter's Place
Restaurante JPS
Wimbe
Bar
Pemba Magic Lodge
Residencial Reggio Emilia
see Wimbe Beach inset
Pemba Bay
Artes Makondes
Airport
Total
Pemba Dive & Bush Camp
Nampula, Lichinga, Palma
N
Bradt
Nautilus Beach Resort
Casino
Restaurante Mar e Sol
Pemba Dolphin
CI divers
Artes Makonde
Wimbi Sun
Brazilia Restaurant & Bar
Complexo Turístico Caracol
Artes Makondes
Wimbe Beach

18

Pemba and the Northeast

Pemba is the capital of Cabo Delgado ('Cape Thin'), Mozambique's most northeasterly province, bounded by Tanzania to the north, a long Indian Ocean coastline to the east, the Lúrio River to the south and Niassa Province to the west. The most important Mozambican port north of Nacala, it is also the site of northern Mozambique's only international airport, which nets it a growing amount of fly-in tourism from South Africa. However, while Pemba is significant as a travel hub, and pleasant enough as Mozambican towns go, the greater attraction for most visitors is surrounding Pemba Bay, where beaches such as Wimbe and Murrébué offer a good range of marine activities, including diving, snorkelling, kite-surfing and seasonal whale-watching. Further afield, Pemba is also the usual springboard for fly-in safaris to the Niassa Reserve (see page 356) in the province of the same name, and the Quirimba Archipelago (see page 323), site of the historic town of Ibo and some of the country's finest beach lodges.

Few people explore the Cabo Delgado mainland beyond Pemba unless they are in transit somewhere further afield. Montepuez, for instance, is of interest solely as the starting point of the tough road crossing west to Lichinga via Marrupa. The attractive small ports of Mocímboa da Praia and Palma lie along the coastal overland route north to Mtwara in southeast Tanzania. And Mueda, the unofficial capital of the Makonde Plateau, a relatively cool highland area inhabited by the Makonde people, is the last substantial Mozambican town along the newly bridged (and preferable) inland route to Newala in the same country.

The main ethnic groups in Cabo Delgado Province are the Makonde, the Macua and the Mwani, and the total population is now approaching the two million mark.

MACUA FACE MASKS

In Pemba, Ibo and elsewhere in Cabo Delgado, you'll frequently see Macua women wandering around with what appear to be white masks, the result of plastering their faces with *musiro,* a paste created by grinding the bark of the *Olax dissitiflora* tree in water. Unlike adornments in many other parts of Africa, these masks have no ritual significance. The white paste is merely a skin softener, serving a similar purpose to the face masks used in private by many Western women, but also protecting the skin against the sun when working outdoors. It is conventional for a bride to apply *musiro* to her entire body before her wedding, and married women sometimes wear it to demonstrate their status, especially when their husband is away for a long period. Interestingly, there's a similar custom in the Comoros islands, 200km away in the Indian Ocean.

PEMBA

This attractive old port is situated on the northwest tip of the peninsula that forms the southern entrance to Pemba Bay. The town itself is of less interest than its location, a large, deep, semi-enclosed natural harbour on a stretch of coast renowned for its wide, sandy and clean palm-lined beaches, protected by a coral reef that guarantees safe swimming as well as good snorkelling. The area's enormous potential as a tourist resort has been partially realised in recent years, but by most standards it remains somewhat off the beaten track, and it's likely to stay that way for the foreseeable future.

Pemba is a town of several parts. The modern CBD, focused on the junction of Avenida 25 de Setembro and Avenida Eduardo Mondlane, is undeniably on the bland side, but well equipped with shops, banks and restaurants. About 500m west of this, adjacent to the port, the old colonial town centre comprises a small grid of potholed roads lined with some run-down but mostly still attractive colonial buildings. Altogether different in character, running northward from Avenida 25 de Setembro, the neat reed-hut village called Paquitequete sprawls across an area of sandy ground that sometimes floods at high tide.

Facing seaward from the entrance of Pemba Bay, about 5km east of the town centre, is Wimbe (or Wimbi) Beach. While it was once a separate entity, these days Wimbe is linked to Pemba by a near-continuous belt of suburbia. A tourist resort in the colonial era, it never entirely shut down even during the civil war, and in the past few years has enjoyed a genuine resurgence, so that the waterfront is now lined with small hotels, restaurants, dive shops and other tourist-oriented facilities. The beach itself is very pleasant and can be quite busy during the weekends – refreshingly it's not frequented just by expats, but is one of the few places in the country where Mozambican tourists can be seen in large numbers. For those seeking a quieter beach experience, Murrébué, about 12km out of town, is currently a hotspot of low-key tourist development.

The best time to visit Pemba is from April to October, when the cooling trade winds blow. In the rainy season, the monsoon blows from the northeast, which can make the beach very unpleasant. Pemba is the most easterly place using Central African Time (the same as South Africa) so daybreak is very early (04.15 in midsummer) and the sun sets before 18.00 most of the year.

HISTORY Little information is available about Pemba Bay prior to the 20th century. The ruins of an Arabic-style fortress on Ponta Romero, at the north end of the

CASHEW APPLES

Cashew nuts are widely available and cheap throughout Mozambique, but Pemba is a good place to look out for the same tree's fruit – sometimes known as the cashew apple (*maça do caju*) or by its South American name *marañón*. Shaped like a pear, sweet smelling, and with a yellow or red waxen casing, the fruit is slightly astringent and quite refreshing, though you probably won't want to eat more than one at a sitting. In the spirit of health and safety, it should be noted that the greenish shell of the nut contains a toxin that is a skin irritant, so it's best not to chew that (and if you're allergic to nuts it might be best not to try it at all). In northern Mozambique and southern Tanzania, sun-dried cashew apples reconstituted with water form the basis of a strong liquor known as *gongo* or *água ardente* (fire water).

reed town, are said to be a relict of an early 19th-century slave-trade depot. This fort, presumably, was no longer operational by 1856, when Portugal granted land concessions to 36 settlers in an unsuccessful attempt to establish an agricultural centre on the same site. The modern town was founded in 1904, as an administrative centre for the Niassa Company, and named Porto Amélia after Queen Maria Amélia, a British-born French princess who married the Portuguese king Don Carlos I in 1886 and served as Queen Consort of Portugal for two years between the assassination of her husband in 1908 and the overthrow of the monarchy in 1910.

By the late 1920s the old town centre had more or less taken its present shape, and supported a population of over 1,500. After the dissolution of the Niassa Company in 1929, Porto Amélia continued to serve as the capital of Cabo Delgado, though it was renamed Pemba after independence in 1975. The town was largely untouched during the liberation war and civil war, despite its strategic location in one of the country's most unsettled provinces, and emerged from the wars looking less run-down than most other Mozambican towns (though it has arguably made up for this in the meantime). Today, it is ranked the ninth-largest town in Mozambique, with an estimated population of 160,000.

GETTING THERE AND AWAY

By air Most international visitors to Pemba arrive at the international airport about 3km from the town centre. **LAM** flies here from Maputo daily except Thursdays, with connecting flights to Dar es Salaam and Johannesburg on the same days. **South African Airlink** (*www.saairlink.co.za*) operates a twice-weekly direct three-hour flight from Johannesburg to Pemba. The airport lies on EN106, and while there aren't any direct chapas as such, any vehicle heading into Pemba town will stop if you flag it down. If you're staying at one of the more expensive hotels, see if they have a pick-up service. Alternatively, taxis to the town centre or Wimbe cost around US$4. The LAM office is on Avenida 25 de Setembro (*27 221 251*).

By car Coming from the south, Pemba is 440km from Nampula along the **EN8** and **EN106** via Namialo and Metoro. It's good tarmac all the way, and you should get through in about five hours in a private vehicle.

By bus, chapa and taxi The best **bus** service is Grupo Mecula, which takes around seven hours, costs US$6 per person, and leaves in either direction at around 05.00 daily. There is also a daily bus to Nacala, costing the same and leaving at same time, but travellers bound to/from Ilha de Moçambique will need to change vehicles at Namialo.

The Grupo Mecula terminal is tucked away near the fire station just off Avenida 25 de Setembro. But these and all other **chapas** out of Pemba run along Avenida 25 de Setembro from the junction with Avenida Eduardo Mondlane, so if you wait outside the mCel office before 05.00, you should be able to select a chapa heading in the direction you want.

You could walk between the town centre and Wimbe, but it's a fair old hike and absolutely not recommended after dusk. **Taxis** can be found near the roundabout at the junction of Avenida Eduardo Mondlane and Avenida25 de Setembro. Fares range from US$3–10 depending on where exactly you are headed (Russell's Place is more than twice as far as Pemba Beach Hotel) and time of day (prices rise late at night or early in the morning).

For further details of transport to Montepuez, Mocímboa da Praia and Ibo, see the individual *Getting there and away* sections for these places, pages 314, 320 and 325.

WHERE TO STAY

Exclusive

Londo Lodge (6 units) 272 29034; m 82 699 5070; e info@londolodge.com; www.londolodge.com. Situated on the northern shore of Pemba Bay, 15mins by boat from the Pemba Beach Hotel, this boutique lodge is easily the most alluring option near Pemba, with a sense of style & exclusivity to match the best lodges on the Quirimbas. It is set in a patch of indigenous coastal scrub on a coral cliff overlooking a small private beach whose incline (unlike most in Mozambique) is so steep and well protected you can usually enjoy excellent snorkelling in crystal clear water right from the shore. The arches & open spaces of the airy main building show a strong Swahili architectural influence, & there is a swimming pool and sea-facing deck where you can enjoy superlative seafood lunches & dinners. Accommodation is in huge individual octagonal villas with thatched roof, cane & bamboo furniture, outdoor showers & private balconies overlooking the sea. This place has 'honeymoon' written all over it, but a private dive centre offering a full range of marine activities makes it equally attractive to keen divers, snorkelers & anglers. *US$700/1000 sgl/dbl including all meals, drinks, non-motorised activities & airport transfers.*

Upmarket

Pemba Beach Hotel & Spa (103 rooms) Av Marginal; 272 21770; e pembabeach@raniresorts.com; www.pembabeachresort.com. Set in a vast beachfront compound about halfway between the town centre & Wimbe Beach, this 5-star resort is the largest & smartest hotel on this side of Pemba Bay. The architecture displays Arabic & Mediterranean influences, with terracotta buildings laid out spaciously in green palm-studded lawns that lead down to an idyllic beach. Facilities include a world-class spa, on-site dive centre offering a range of marine activities, 2 swimming pools, 2 restaurants, gym, gift shop, a superb buffet b/fast & free Wi-Fi throughout. Spacious tiled rooms come with king-size bed, AC, DSTV, balcony & large bathroom with separate tub & shower. The only thing that lets down an otherwise excellent & well-run hotel is the inexplicably abysmal front-desk staff. *US$248/330 sgl/dbl B&B with slight low-season discounts; suites from US$500.*

Mid-range

Pemba Dive & Bush Camp (13 units) 272 29525; m 82 661 1530 or 82 669 7050; e pembadive@gmail.com; www.pembadivecamp.com. Also known as Nacole Jardim, this lovely bush camp is set in dense coastal scrub on mangrove-lined Praia do Nacole about 5km southeast of the town centre as the crow flies. It's a very chilled spot, with a great macuti-roofed beachfront bar, plenty of hammocks & a host of free activities & amenities including offshore snorkelling, canoeing, jogging, birdwatching, guided nature walks, drumming sessions, DSTV, & an internet café, communal kitchen. There is also a DAN & PADI-registered dive centre offering courses & single-dive excursions to the reefs around Wimbi, Londo & further afield, 3–4 day courses & snorkelling with dolphins. The Potbelly Restaurant serves b/fast, lunch & dinner. It lies about 2km from the EN106 along a dirt track signposted 1km further out of town than the airport. Those without transport can arrange a free transfer from the airport. Accommodation is in screened en-suite dbl or 4-bed chalets with safe, fan & ethnic decor or cheaper backpacker rooms using common showers, & camping is permitted. Rates upon application only.

Ulala Lodge m 82 741 5104 or 82 710 9117; e contact@ulala-lodge.com; www.ulala-lodge.com. Attractively located on sandy Murrébué Beach about 20mins' drive from town, this new beachfront lodge offers earthy accommodation in en-suite bungalows with teak decks, macuti thatch roofs, king-size or twin beds with walk-in nets & a private terrace. The beach is ideal for swimming, snorkelling or long walks, & the restaurant serves seafood set menus. To get there follow the EN106 out of town for about 10km then turn left onto the Mecufi road, left again at the blue sign reading 'Distrito de Mecufi', then right at a crossroad with white stones & a street lamp, & left after about

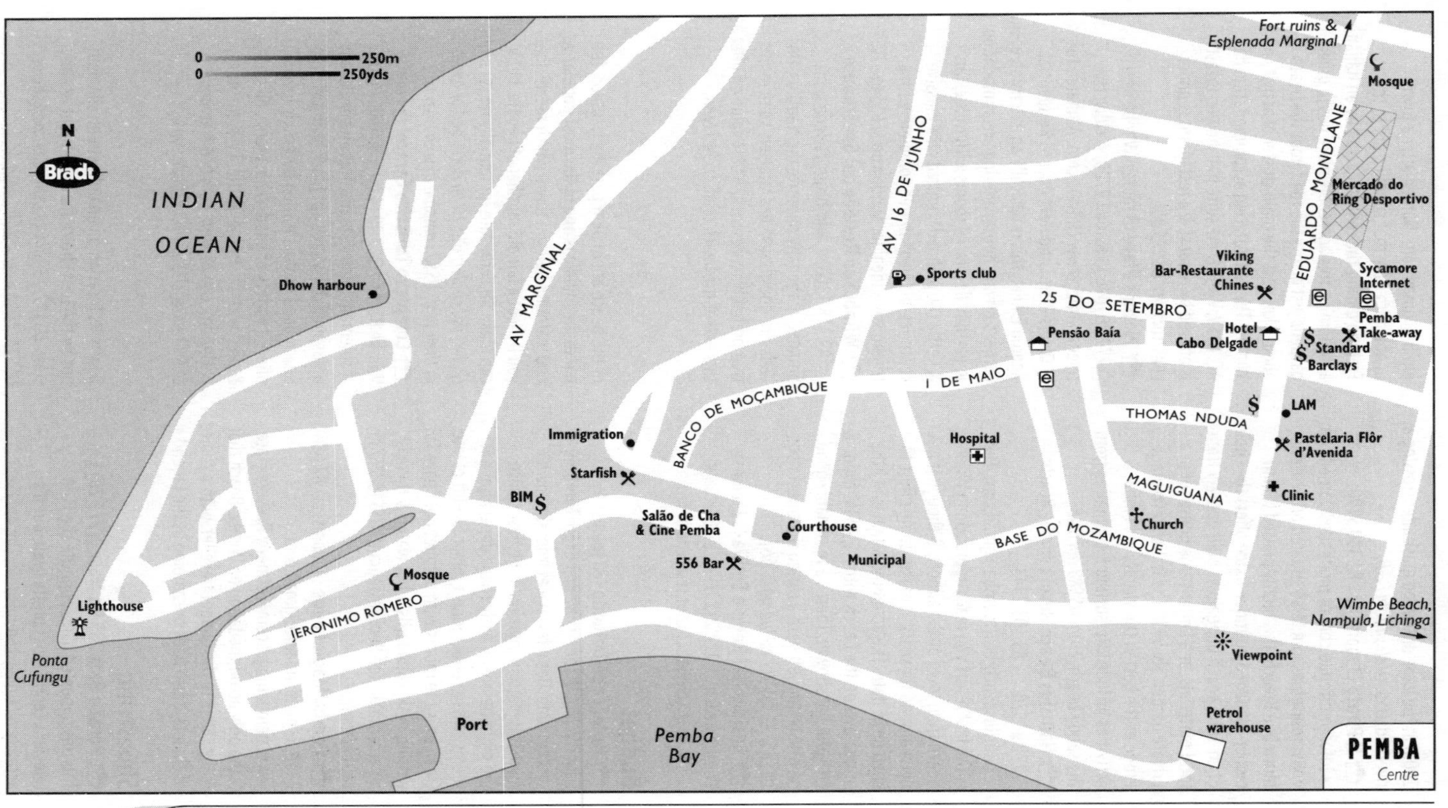

PEMBA
Centre
Fort ruins & Esplenada Marginal
Mosque
Mercado do Ring Desportivo
EDUARDO MONDLANE
Sycamore Internet
Pemba Take-away
Standard
Barclays
Viking Bar-Restaurante Chines
Hotel Cabo Delgade
LAM
Pastelaria Flôr d'Avenida
Clinic
Wimbe Beach, Nampula, Lichinga
THOMAS NDUDA
MAGUIGUANA
Church
Viewpoint
Petrol warehouse
25 DO SETEMBRO
Pensão Baía
BASE DO MOZAMBIQUE
1 DE MAIO
Hospital
Sports club
AV 16 DE JUNHO
Municipal
Courthouse
BANCO DE MOÇAMBIQUE
556 Bar
Salão de Cha & Cine Pemba
Pemba Bay
Immigration
Starfish
AV MARGINAL
BIM
Port
Mosque
JERONIMO ROMERO
0 250m
0 250yds
Dhow harbour
INDIAN OCEAN
Lighthouse
Ponta Cufungu
N
Bradt

200m at the large driftwood mask after crossing a riverbed. *US$70/80 sgl/dbl B&B.*

Il Pirata (3 rooms) m 82 380 5790; e info@murrebue.com or piratekites@gmail.com; www.murrebue.com. Also situated on peaceful Murrébué Breach, this highly praised Italian owner-managed boutique lodge offers the choice of en-suite beach bungalows built entirely from local materials, or a larger stone house set in a private garden above it. The Italian restaurant is one of the best in the vicinity of Pemba, & activities include kite-surfing & swimming from the sandy beach. *From US$88 dbl B&B.*

Nautilus Beach Resort Wimbe Beach; t 272 21520; m 83 303 2543; e nautilusbeachresortpemba@gmail.com. This is the first resort you reach approaching Wimbe Beach from town or the airport, & though it has been around for years, it makes some effort to keep up to date. The accommodation is in little bungalows on the beach with AC, DSTV, fridge & en-suite hot shower. There's a reasonably good on-site restaurant with a casino right next door. *US$65/72 sgl/dbl excluding b/fast.*

Residencial Reggio Emilia (12 rooms) Wimbe Beach; t 272 21297; m 82 888 0800; e c.forna@teledata.mz or residencial.regio.emilia@gmail.com. Named after a town in northern Italy that supplied aid to the Frelimo during the civil war & run by an Italian agronomist, this agreeable place lies in green gardens just across the road from the beach about 1km past the main cluster of activity on Wimbe. The self-catering accommodation has AC, DTSV, Wi-Fi & en-suite hot shower. B/fast is offered by request & a restaurant is under construction. *US$75 dbl.*

Pieter's Place (3 rooms) Wimbe Beach t 272 20102; m 82 682 2700; e cidivers@teledata.mz; www.cidivers.com. Affiliated to CI Divers & situated next door to Residencial Reggio Emilia, this is basically an extension of the owner's private house, offering accommodation in earthily decorated rooms with fridge, fan & kettle (AC planned) centred on a massive centuries-old baobab tree complete with a treehouse – ideal for sundowners. *US$45–70.*

Wimbi Sun Residencial Guesthouse m 82 318 1300; e wimbisun@teledata.mz. Situated diagonally opposite the Nautilus, this well-run guesthouse has large en-suite rooms that probably represent the best value on offer at this end of the beach road. *US$45 twin.*

Budget

Hotel Cabo Delgado (60 rooms) Av Eduardo Mondlane; m 82 303 6156. This long-serving hotel lies a few paces from the town's main intersection, making it the best choice the night before an early chapa departure, & it seems to have undergone a minor facelift of late. Clean en-suite rooms with parquet floor have TV, writing desk, cupboards & hot water, & there is an acceptable 1st-floor restaurant. *US$16/25/35 sgl/dbl/suite.*

Pemba Magic Lodge (4 rooms) m 82 686 2730; e pembamagic@gmail.com; www.pembamagic.com. Formerly Russel's Place, & the only accommodation on Wimbe Beach that really caters to the budget traveller, with a choice of chalets, dorm beds or camping at the far end of the beach about 3km past the Nautilus. The bar in the middle is one of the most popular w/end watering holes in town, which means that you'll meet a fair old number of people, but it can make for some late (potentially noisy) nights. *US$40 dbl chalet; US$10 pp dorm bed or camping in their tent; US$7 camping in your own tent.*

Complexo Turístico Caracol (24 units) Wimbe Bach; t 272 20142; m 82 688 7430; e sulemane@teledata.mz. This architecturally uninspired dbl-storey apt block facing Wimbe Beach has a useful location for beach-lovers & offers a variety of good-value rooms, all clean & tiled with AC, fridge, kettle, TV & en-suite bathroom. *US$28 with 1 dbl bed & veranda; US$50 suite; US$57–63 2-bedroom apt.*

Shoestring

Pensão Baía 289 R 1 Maio; t 272 20153. This unsignposted place opposite the TDM telecoms centre looks pretty grim, but it's actually relatively comfortable. The only real flaw is its location on an unlit street, so might not be the best choice for a late night or early start. *US$12/15 sgl/dbl using common showers; US$15/18 ensuite sgl/dbl with AC.*

Camping The best options are Pemba Magic Lodge and Pemba Beach Camp, both of which charge US$10 per person.

WHERE TO EAT

Restaurant Quirimbas 272 21770; b/fast, lunch & dinner daily. The more formal of 2 restaurants in the Pemba Beach Hotel, this is in the main building. *Serves set menus & light meals in the US$10–20 range.*

Clube Naval 272 21770; 10.00–24.00 daily. Set in the grounds of the Pemba Beach Hotel next to the dive centre, this unpretentious and breezy beachfront restaurant serves good filling seafood & other meals. *From US$10.*

Pastelaria Flôr D'Avenida Av Eduardo Mondlane; 272 20514. Very popular with expats, this terrace café is a great spot for a pastry & freshly brewed coffee, but also serves a good selection of light meals all day & night. *US$5–6.*

556 Bar Rua Numero 3; 272 21487; 11.00–late daily. Situated on a cliff overlooking the harbour just behind the Casa da Justica, this typical South African sports bar serves very good steaks & seafood. Satellite TV makes it a popular venue for big rugby matches & other international fixtures. *US$6–15.*

Pemba Take-Away Av 25 de Setembro. In former days the meeting place of choice for the expat community, this has now rather been overshadowed by the increased attractions of Wimbe, but still does good cheeseburgers & other light meals. *US$2–5.*

Viking Bar-Restaurante Chines Av 25 de Setembro; m 82 226 5520; 09.00–late daily. Despite the typically Mozambican wood-and-thatch exterior, this is a genuine Chinese eatery – a rarity on Mozambique – serving varied menu of meat, chicken, prawn & vegetarian dishes. Good value. *US$3–5.*

Starfish R Base do Mozambique; m 82 703 7951; e starfishpemba@gmail.com; 08.30–16.30 Mon–Fri. Situated opposite the immigration office, this clifftop coffee shop with outdoor seating has a great view over the harbour & the excellent coffee is complemented by a selection of wraps, salads & platters. *US$6–8.*

Esplanada Marginal Av Marginal; m 82 397 2659; 11.00–late daily. This beachfront terrace bar-restaurant at the north end of the reed town is a great place for a sundowner & it also serves a no-nonsense menu of seafood & chicken grills. *Around US$5.*

Canaia's Place m 82 64 30 610, (direct) or 83 309 6990 (Kaskazini). Also known as *Nipuro na Canaia*, this authentic local eatery in Nanhimbe, close to Wimbe Beach, prepares delicious traditional Macua meals accompanied by singing & drumming local children. You can pre-book with Kaskazini; US$25 pp includes return transfers from your hotel.

Pemba Dolphin Restaurant This popular stilted eatery of Wimbe Beach has a good cocktail menu & a varied selection. *Seafood, meat & pizzas for around US$6.*

Wimbe Restaurant Another well-known Wimbe eatery, this serves a typical selection of Mozambican dishes, with grilled seafood the speciality. Fri–Sun are disco nights. *Around US$5.*

OTHER PRACTICALITIES

Banks and ATMs All the usual banks have branches with ATMs in the town centre, mostly along Avenida Eduardo Mondlane. The only ATM on Wimbe is the BIM Millennium in the car park of the Nautilus Beach Resort.

Car rental Kaskazini (see *Travel information*, page 313) has a fleet of 4x4s available for rental. Alternatively, try Moti Rent-A-Car (*265 26070; e motimoz@teledata.mz*), which charges around US$50 per day for a sedan or US$95 for a 4x4.

Hospital Also on Rua 1 Maio opposite the police station (*27 220 348*). The private Cabo Delgado clinic on Rua Modesta Neva is in the old Hotel VIP (*27 221272/452; f 27 221447*).

Internet The best options are the TDM and Skynet, both of which stand on the corner of avenidas Eduardo Mondlane and 25 de Setembro.

Police The police station is on Rua 1 Maio on the corner with Rua Base Beira (☎ *27 221 006*). There is also one next door to the Wimbi Sun.

Post office On Avenida 25 de Setembro, just up from the junction with Avenida Eduardo Mondlane. There is also one opposite the port entrance on Rua numero 1.

Shopping The best market for fruit and vegetables is the one just down from the traffic circle (known as the **Mercado do Ring Desportivo**), although it is also worth checking out the **Mercado Municipal** in the old town. The biggest supermarket is **Osman Yacob's** on Avenida 25 de Setembro, although there are a number of others dotted around town, notably along Rua Jerónimo Romero in the old town. For imported good, fresh meat and delicatessen-type fare, Starfish (see *Where to eat*, page 311) has the best selection in town.

MAKONDE CARVERS

The Makonde of northeastern Mozambique and southeastern Tanzania are among Africa's best-known craftsmen, and their intricate carvings follow a tradition dating back several hundred years. Makonde society is strongly matrilineal, and the carvings in their purest form celebrate a cult of femininity. The carvers are always male and the carvings are mother figures carried for protection. Oral history links the origin of the carving tradition to the Makonde's original appearance on the plateau that bears their name. The progenitor of the first Makonde, so tradition goes, was a genderless being living alone in the bush who one day carved a statue in the shape of a woman, left it outside its hut overnight, and awoke to find it transformed into flesh and blood. The carver, apparently also transformed from his formerly genderless state, married the woman and they conceived a child, which died three days after its birth. They moved to higher ground, and again conceived, and again the child died after three days. When they finally moved to the top of the plateau, the woman gave birth to a child who survived and became the first Makonde.

In their purest form, the intricate, stylised carvings of the Makonde relate to this ancestral cult of womanhood, and are carried only by men, as a good luck charm. Traditional carvings almost always depict a female figure, sometimes surrounded by children. The large demonic masks that are also carved by the Makonde, more so perhaps in Mozambique than in Tanzania, are central to the traditional sindimba stilt dance, which is performed by men and women together. Makonde sculptures were practically unknown outside of Tanzania and Mozambique until a carving workshop was established in suburban Dar es Salaam during the 1950s, but today there are also workshops in Nampula and Pemba in Mozambique. Subsequently, like any dynamic art form, Makonde sculpture has been responsive to external influences and subject to changes in fashion, with new styles of carvings becoming increasingly abstract and incorporating wider moral and social themes. Today, the finest examples of the genre fetch prices in excess of US$5,000 from international collectors.

Tour operators and travel information An excellent tour operator, booking agent and general travel outlet called **Kaskazini** (m *82 309 6990*; e *info@kaskazani.com; www.kaskazini.com*; ⌚ *08.00-16.00 Mon–Fri, 08.30-12.00 Sat*) is based at the Pemba Beach Hotel. The flexible hands-on staff are a fine source of information about the various attractions in Cabo Delgado, and the website is well worth a visit as well. Kaskazini can organise most things in Cabo Delgado, Nampula and Niassa provinces, from accommodation and flight bookings to a full tour with driver-guide. They organise Mapiko dances too.

WHAT TO SEE AND DO

The most popular excursion from Pemba is to Ibo and the other islands of the Quirimba Archipelago, which are covered in the next chapter. Other local sites of interest are as follows.

Around town There's not a huge amount to do in Pemba itself, but it is a pleasant town to explore haphazardly. The old quarter, down by the docks, has some rather dilapidated colonial buildings. The reed huts of Paquitequete also make for interesting meandering, and the beach is lively with kids playing football, though you need to watch your step – hygiene here revolves around the sea. The fishing boats leave from around the lighthouse on Ponta Cufungu, and watching them return in the afternoons with the day's catch is interesting enough. Paquitequete served as an Arab slave-trade depot in the early 19th century, and you can still see the remains of a small fortified hexagonal building – said locally to be an old slave prison – within a traffic island on Avenida Marginal at Ponta Romero, about 250m northwest of the intersection with Avenida Eduardo Mondlane.

The sprawling **Mercado de Mbanguia** is an interesting place to wander around – keep an eye open for the string made by cutting old tyres into short strips – although it's probably best avoided after dark. There is a Makonde carving collective (**Artes Makondes**) along similar lines to the one in Nampula, based here, but rather than just the one outlet they have four. The main collective is on Avenida do Chai, but there are other outlets on Avenida 25 de Setembro (next to the Catholic cathedral), at the airport and next to the Caracol on Wimbe Beach.

Marine activities Wimbe is pretty much an archetypal beach resort, where activities all revolve around the sea. The diving off Wimbe is among the best on the east African coast, particularly below about 20m, and there are three dive operators to choose from. Snorkelling is also excellent, especially in the Londo area in the north of the bay. You can also hire boats for cruises or fishing trips through Kaskazini (see above).

CI Divers ☎ 27 220102; m 82 68 22 700; e cidivers@teledata.mz; www.cidivers.com. The oldest of the operators (the owner has been based here for some 15 years) & an established PADI training centre. It's also active in environmental protection of the area. Sgl dives from US$48, PADI Open Water Course US$420.

Pemba Beach Dive Centre ☎ 272 21770, ext 6010; www.pembabeachresort.com. Based at Pemba Beach Hotel's Clube Naval this offers sgl dives for US$60 upwards & PADI Open Water Courses for US$450, as well as snorkelling excursions (US$30) & whale-watching cruises for US$60 in season (Jul–Oct).

Pemba Dive ☎ 272 29525; m 82 661 1530 or 82 669 7050; e pembadive@gmail.com; www.pembadivecamp.com. Based at Pemba Beach Camp, this operation has been going around 8 years. It is the cheapest option in town, charging US$40/70 for sgl/back-to-back dives, or US$165 for a course of 5.

Lake Nikwita Situated about 45km north of Pemba, this perennial lake has a scenic location, in a patch of coastal bush studded with baobabs, and it supports a varied selection of resident and migratory waterbirds. It's best to get there early if birding is your main interest, and you can also arrange to be poled onto the water in a local dugout canoe. Kaskazini arranges half-day excursions there for US$45 per person, inclusive of a bush breakfast and a stop at the colourfully painted church at Mieze. Alternatively, self-drivers need to head north for about 40km along the Quissanga road to Metugé, from where it is another 5km to the lake along rough tracks (if in doubt, ask locals to point you towards '*lago*')

MONTEPUEZ

Founded in 1904 as a regional administrative centre for the Niassa Company, Montepuez is the second-largest town in Cabo Delgado, with a population of 80,000. It shares its name with a river that rises in the mountains to the east and eventually joins the Indian Ocean just south of Ilha do Ibo, and it is also the name of a form of grey marble found in the region. The town was the setting of a terrible massacre in 2000, after 500 Renamo supporters, demonstrating against what they claimed were fraudulent results in the previous year's elections, occupied the district administration, police station and jail for 24 hours on 9 November. Seven police officers and 14 protesters died in the clash, and the surviving policemen retaliated by detaining all alleged demonstrators on 21 November, and cramming them into a tiny cell where at least 83 people died of asphyxiation. Despite this, Montepuez today is a peaceful town, set attractively among granite inselbergs, and with something of a dead-end feel about it, though this may change following the discovery of rich ruby deposits in the vicinity in 2009.

GETTING THERE AND AWAY Montepuez lies 240km west of Pemba along the EN106 and EN242. It is a good surfaced road and self-drivers should get through within three hours. Chapas to and from Pemba leave from the large square next to the market. The journey takes around three hours and cost around US$4. For details of travel west to Marrupa and the Niassa Reserve, see box *The EN242 from Pemba to Lichinga,* page 359, and be aware that the filling stations here are the last reliable fuelling points before Marrupa.

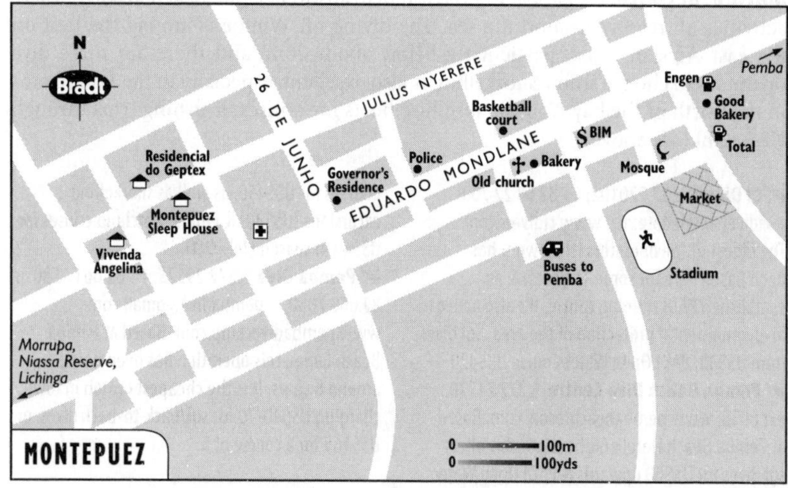

WHERE TO STAY AND EAT

Montepuez Sleep House (7 rooms) Av Julius Nyerere. The smartest option around, this was full when we were last in town, but the en-suite rooms with AC are reputedly very pleasant. The bar & restaurant has indoor & outdoor seating, & can be recommended for its tasty Mozambican-style chicken & seafood grills in the US$5–7 range. *Rooms US$60 dbl.*

Residencial do Geptex (15 rooms) Av Julius Nyerere; 272 51114. Diagonally opposite Montepuez Sleep House, this place consists of a row of dingy but otherwise adequate en-suite rooms with no running water. Difficult to take issue with at the price. *US$9/11 twin/dbl.*

Vivenda Angelina Av Julius Nyerere. A block away from the 2 places listed above, this falls between them in terms of quality & price. The dbl rooms using shared bathrooms are recommended, assuming you can locate the elusive owner or caretaker. *US$14 dbl.*

OTHER PRACTICALITIES

Banks and ATMs The only ATM is at the BIM Millennium half a block south of Avenida Eduardo Mondlane. Westbound travellers should be aware this will be their last opportunity to draw cash before Lichinga.

Shopping A few decent supermarkets line Avenida Eduardo Mondlane, a good market lies two blocks south of this, and an excellent bakery can be found on the road leading down to it.

TOWARDS TANZANIA

The Tanzanian border at the Ruvuma mouth lies about 250km north of Pemba as the crow flies, and it is probably fair to say that most travellers who pass through to the far north of Cabo Delgado are *en route* to or from there. There are two through-routes to Tanzania, both of which entail following the EN6 inland of Pemba for about 80km to the small junction town of Sunate, then turning north onto the EN243 and following it for 220km to Diaca. From here, the more established coastal route passes through the substantial port of Mocímboa da Praia and the smaller town of Palma to Namuiranga, where a ferry service crosses the Ruvuma mouth to Mwambo, 30km south of Mtwara, the largest port in southern Tanzania. In recent years, however, this ferry has proved unreliable and I have had several reports of travellers being asked to pay absurd sums of money (in the order of US$500) for the crossing. For this reason, a far better bet is the route via Mueda and Mocímboa da Ruvuma to the Tanzanian town of Newala, crossing the Ruvuma on the brand-new Unity Bridge, which officially opened in May 2010.

MACOMIA This small junction town lies on the EN243 about 200km northwest of Pemba and 150km southwest of Mocímboa da Praia. In itself it's an unprepossessing place, bustling and no-nonsense, and of interest to travellers solely on account of its position. For northbound travellers coming from Pemba, it lies at the end of the good surfaced road to which you'll have become accustomed, and it is also where the EN528 to coastal Pangane branches off the main road. For that reason, you may end up getting stuck here in transit.

Getting there and away The EN106/243 coming from Pemba is surfaced and well maintained in its entirety, and private vehicles should get through in about 2½ hours. North of Macomia, the EN243 is more erratic and there are some rough patches, so bank on an average driving time of around 50km per hour, certainly along the 100km stretch to Dacia. The main **buses** between the north and the south

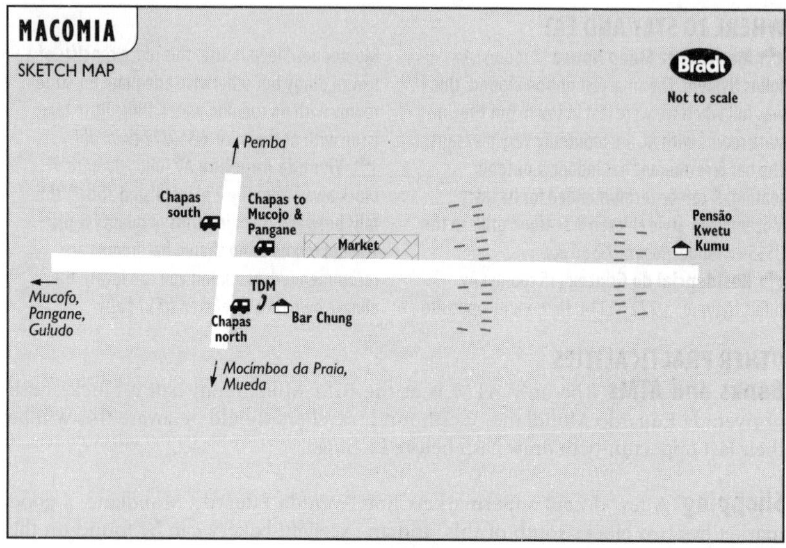

all pass through Macomia, stopping at the market next to the junction for around 20 minutes to give the drivers a break and to drop and pick up passengers. Most buses come past between 09.00 and 11.00. From here to Pemba will cost US$4, and take around three hours. To Mueda and Mocímboa da Praia costs about US$5 and takes up to five hours.

 Where to stay and eat

Bar Chung On the corner of the square & run by an old Chinese chap who always seems to have changed, this seems to be the closest Macomia has to a nightspot, & is a popular place to eat. Rooms are nice & clean & surprisingly cheap. *US$5.*

Pensão Caminho do Norte Also close to the junction, this has basic but clean rooms & generator electricity until 22.00. *US$10*

CHAI Lying about 40km north of Macomia and 60km south of Dacia along a stretch of road that is in dire need of upgrading, Chai is a town that you'll pass through almost without noticing, but if you mention it to Mozambicans you'll find that it holds a very special place in the nation's history. It was here, on 25 September 1964, that the first shot of the revolution was fired, when Frelimo, then still led by Eduardo Mondlane, attacked the town's administrative headquarters. The Frelimo battle plan for the raid can be seen in the Revolutionary Museum in Maputo (see page 121). The only local memorial to this pivotal event is a small mural roughly in the centre of town by one of Mozambique's most celebrated artists, Malangatana Ngwenya, a Frelimo veteran arrested by the Portuguese security police a year after this raid took place, and who now serves as a UNESCO goodwill ambassador. Oddly, the mural doesn't depict the raid on Chai, but the Mueda Massacre.

MUEDA Mueda is the principal town on the Mozambican part of the Makonde Plateau, the only part of the country that still remained unconquered by Portugal at the start of World War I. Even after the plateau was quelled in 1919, the Makonde people after whom it is named retained a tradition of resistance. This was intensified after an infamous massacre on 16 June 1960, when Portuguese soldiers fired on an officially sanctioned meeting of peasant farmers in Mueda, killing an estimated 600 people. Partly in reaction to this massacre – though also because of their proximity to independent Tanzania – the Makonde gave Frelimo strong support during the war of liberation. Most of the plateau was under Frelimo control after 1964, though Mueda itself remained in Portuguese hands. After the operation known as Gordian Knot, in which 350,000 Portuguese soldiers drove Frelimo underground in Cabo Delgado, roughly 300,000 people in the Mueda area were resettled into *aldeamentos*, collective villages that were wired off to prevent contact with Frelimo.

CROSSING INTO TANZANIA

The biggest travel news in this part of Mozambique was the long-awaited opening of the Unity Bridge, the first road bridge across the Ruvuma to southern Tanzania, which finally occurred in May 2010. The bridge crosses the river at Negomane, linking Mueda to the Tanzanian town of Newala, and for self-drivers it has rendered obsolete the established coastal cross-border route between Palma and Mtwara using a decidedly iffy ferry.

The road distance between Mueda and the Unity Bridge is about 170km, and from there it is another 60km to Newala, passing through some spectacular scenery as you descend into the Ruvuma Valley then climb back onto the plateau on the Tanzanian side. This stretch of road doesn't come close to matching the bridge in the modernity stakes, and parts can be quite tricky in the rainy season, even with high clearance, though this is likely to change when planned upgrades are complete. For the time being, however, expect the drive from Mueda to Newala to take around five to six hours, allowing for border formalities.

There is a low-key immigration office (more accurately, tent) at the Mozambique side of the bridge. The Tanzanian immigration shack lies about 10km from the bridge at the village of Masuguru and is signposted to the left. There is no customs on the Tanzanian side at present, so carnets need to be processed in Mtwara. Expect facilities to improve as the route becomes more popular. If you need accommodation in Newala, two places stand out, namely the Country Lodge (*en-suite rooms with net, fan & TV for around US$25*) and the cheaper Plateau Lodge (*en-suite rooms in the US$8–10 range*). There is also plenty of accommodation in Masasi.

There is still no public transport between Mueda and Newala via the Unity Bridge, though this will surely come as soon as the road has been upgraded. Until it does, however, backpackers must still cross between Mozambique and Tanzania along the old coastal route from Palma to Mtwara. Coming from Palma, the 40km to the Namoto border post takes two hours by chapa, along a road that is as bad as the surrounding scenery is beautiful. The immigration office here is easy-going, and there's a little shop selling water, sweets and such. Once formalities are complete, the same chapa will continue to the banks of the Ruvuma River, where you can expect a bit of a feeding frenzy among the motorboat pilots and moneychangers! If you have leftover Mozambican money, this is your last chance to get rid of it, though do be aware that the rate on offer is rather poor. The passenger launch across the river takes about 20 minutes and costs around US$1 per person. Pick-up trucks wait on the Tanzanian side to take you to Mtwara, stopping first at the border post at Singa.

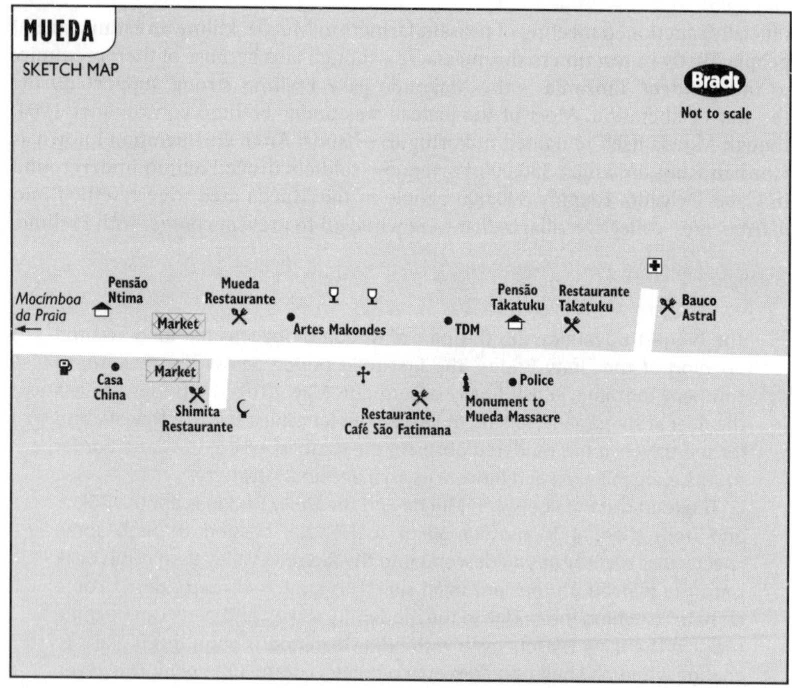

Needless to say, the fact that many of these were arbitrarily placed in arid areas did little to help Portugal win the hearts of Cabo Delgado's people.

Mueda today is about as close as it gets to a one-street town, with little to see aside from a small memorial to the massacre, and the mass grave in which its victims were buried. Set at an altitude of around 800m, the town has an unexpectedly bracing climate – a refreshing contrast to the sticky coast – and the surrounding area is very scenic. There's also a small Artes Makondes hut, though this really doesn't bear comparison to the larger co-operatives in Pemba and Nampula. If you explore a little, then you may find some Makonde carvers sitting outside their houses, but this is one of those occasions when the journey is its own reward, with the views as you approach the escarpment ringing the plateau possessing a real 'Lost World' atmosphere.

One word of warning – while you'll be able to change US dollars or Tanzanian shillings) at the small Barclays Bank, there is no ATM in Mueda. The electricity supply is decidedly on the spotty side too.

Getting there and away Mueda lies about 350km from Pemba and the road is tarred for most of the way, but with sporadic rough patches, so self-drivers should expect it to take at least five hours. **Chapas** to and from Pemba leave daily from the market, but the best transport option is the daily **Grupo Mecula** bus which departs in either direction at 05.00. The trip to Mocímboa da Praia costs around US$2.50 and takes around four hours, while Pemba is about US$5 and will take six hours.

Where to stay and eat There are a few basic guesthouses along Rua 1 de Maio, all offering basic accommodation with shared bathrooms for less than US$10. These are the good-value Pensão Ntima and slightly lesser Pensão Takatuku and

Motel Sanzala. If you don't eat at your hotel, the Shimita Restaurante and Mueda Restaurante face each other across the same road, and serve whatever they happen to have that day.

MOCÍMBOA DA PRAIA Mocímboa da Praia is the last established overnight stop for travellers heading to Tanzania, though its significance in this respect will surely diminish as a result of the recent opening of the Unity Bridge at Negomane, between Mueda and Newala. It has a rather lawless frontier feel about it (the 2005 elections were marred by violence), but is otherwise quite appealing, in many ways reminiscent of a warmer Lichinga, and its location along the main trade route between Pemba and southern Tanzania ensures it bustles with commercial activity. There is also a fishing harbour, unique in Mozambique, from where hundreds of boats leave at around 05.00 in the extraordinary colours of sunrise.

On a more practical note, you'll find that a surprising amount of English is spoken in Mocímboa da Praia, thanks to the number of Tanzanians and Somalians living there. It's also the site of Mozambique's northernmost post office. There is a Barclays Bank with an ATM. The only internet access is at Chez Natalie Lodge. The town is not on the national energy grid but should be linked to it by mid-2011

MAPIKO DANCES

The area between Mueda and Mocímboa da Praia is a good base for exploring Makonde culture, the highlight of which is the traditional *mapiko* dances that are held at practically every village in the region as part of the *likumbi* (male initiation/circumcision) season of December to January. This is one of the most elaborate masked-dance traditions in east or southern Africa, associated not only with initiation rituals, but also reflecting on broader aspects of Makonde social life and human nature, as well as tackling more contemporary concerns. Indeed, during the liberation war, the Makonde – whose homeland was a staunch Frelimo stronghold – invented several new masquerades dealing directly with the hardships they faced under the last oppressive decade of Portuguese rule.

The term *mapiko* is the plural of *lipiko*, the central figure in the dance, representing a malicious spirit that the community must protect itself against. Every person involved in a dance performance will drape his body in cloths until it is completely disguised, before donning an outsized wooden *lipiko* mask distinguished by its wild hair and grotesquely distorted facial features. Only men are allowed to perform the dance, and the masks cannot be viewed by women or by uncircumcised boys except when the dance is under way. These *lipiko* masks are also among the most collectible of traditional African artworks, which means that many fine examples have been exported to foreign collections, though an interesting selection can be seen in the ethnological museum in Nampula.

If you want to see the dancers in action, it shouldn't be too difficult to locate an event in the countryside between Mueda and Mocímboa da Praia during the *likumbi* season – just listen out for the drums, especially on a Saturday or Sunday afternoon. At other times of year, bespoke dances can be arranged with advance notice: Chez Natalie Lodge in Mocímboa da Praia (see page 322) and Kaskazini in Pemba (see page 317) are useful contacts.

Getting there and away Mocímboa da Praia lies about 360km from Pemba and the road is tarred for most of the way, but with sporadic rough patches, so self-drivers should expect it to take at least five hours. Chapas between Mocímboa da Praia and Mueda, Pemba and Nampula leave daily from opposite the Exito filling station, and include a daily Grupo Mecula bus to Pemba. The trip to Mueda costs around US$2.50 and takes around four hours, while Pemba is US$5 and will take six hours.

If you're heading to the border, plan for an even earlier start – chapas leave for Palma from between 02.00 and 03.00 in the morning. While you will be able to get something after this, you may not be able to get a connection on from the border. Chapas to the border cost US$10 and the journey takes up to five hours.

Where to stay and eat If you want a meal anywhere other than at Natalie's, it's a good idea to pop in and order in advance, agreeing, a time when you can come and eat The menus here won't stray far from chicken or fish with chips.

Chez Natalie Lodge t 272 81067/92; m 82 439 6080; e Natalie.bockel@gmail.com. Slightly out of town (around 30mins' walk from the town centre – just follow the signposts), this ever popular owner-managed lodge overlooks the mangroves that fringe Mocímboa. The chalets are nice & roomy, & they have camping facilities as well. The restaurant can serve well-made traditional Mozambican fare, & there are also self-catering facilities, internet access & free use of bicycles. *US$8.50 pp camping; US$52 chalet with 1 dbl & 2 sgl beds.*

Pensão Residencial Magid Av Samora Machel; t 27 281 099. The walls are brightly painted, & the rooms look OK; it serves food as well. *Rooms US$10.*

Restaurante Estrella Vermelha Av Samora Machel. Probably the best 'local' restaurant in town, & the pick for movers & shakers such as the village chief & district administrator. Don't expect much range in the menu, but what there is should be tasty.

Take Away Shakista Down in concrete town, & hence a bit of a walk from the 2 *pensões*, this place is decorated with pictures of pizzas & other delectable-looking items that don't appear on the menu.

PALMA The small but beautiful town of Palma, situated about 60km north of Mocímboa da Praia, lies on an attractive natural harbour that is thought once to have been a mouth of the Ruvuma River. The government buildings and hospital are up on the hill with a staggeringly beautiful view overlooking a coconut-palm-fringed lagoon and private residences by the sea. Palma is very quiet – most traffic bypasses it heading straight between Mocímboa and the border. If you are looking for transport to either, you'll need to wait in the high part of town. The reed town is down below between the hill and the beach, and it's here that you're most likely to find accommodation, although it will be in the houses of local people – there is apparently no *pensão* in either the alta (upper) or baixa (lower) areas of Palma.

19

The Quirimbas

The most important tourist attraction in the far north of Mozambique is the Quirimba Archipelago, which consists of 32 small offshore islands strung out along the 250km of Indian Ocean coastline that stretches northwards from Pemba to the small town of Palma. It is an area of great scenic beauty, boasting high levels of marine and terrestrial biodiversity, some of the most significant unspoilt reef ecosystems anywhere in the Indian Ocean, and a rich history and culture whose blend of indigenous African and exotic Arabic and Portuguese influences is epitomised by the historic town of Ibo on the island of the same name. In 2002, the most southerly 11 islands, together with the surrounding waters and a large tract of the facing mainland, were gazetted as the 7,506 km^2 Quirimbas National Park, of which some 20% comprises marine habitats while the remainder is terrestrial. In 2008, the entire archipelago was nominated as a tentative UNESCO World Heritage Site.

The closest thing to a tourist hub in the Quirimbas, and the only island that is reasonably accessible to travellers on a budget, is Ibo, which lies within the national park and is best known for the tiny but fascinating old town that shares its name. Elsewhere in the archipelago, honeymoon-friendly idylls such as Matemo, Medjumbe and Quilálea host some of Mozambique's finest and most exclusive beach resorts, all of them connected to Pemba by daily light aircraft flights. Ibo aside, the island retreats of the Quirimbas are aimed squarely at the fly-in 'barefoot luxury' market, so for practical purposes this chapter also includes a smattering of comparably upmarket beach lodges that technically lie outside the Quirimbas, as well as the handful of tourist developments that exist within (or close to) the vast mainland sector of the national park.

The archipelago itself is a classic fringing reef, but one that runs along the Mozambican coast for hundreds of kilometres. The individual islands are essentially those points where the reef protrudes above sea level, and the waters that separate them from the mainland are very shallow. Indeed, as seen from the air – as most visitors first see it – this entire coastline forms a beguiling network of dark green mangroves and narrow channels, bright azure shallows whose sandy floor is clearly visible through the translucent waters, and small wooded islets fringed by white beaches and rows of coconut palms. The substrate of these islands is composed of coral rag – coral and sand that has been bonded into a pockmarked black rock that is razor sharp (don't try to walk over it in bare feet) and yet brittle enough to break off with ease.

The islands are mostly lushly vegetated, and the surrounding shallows support extensive mangrove swamps and a wide range of wading birds, including an important breeding colony of sooty terns. Wandering across the intertidal areas is highly recommended (though be sure to wear a stout pair of sandals), as the pools host the likes of octopus, sea cucumber, lobster and mantis shrimp. The sandy beaches on seven of the 11 islands within the national park are used as breeding sites

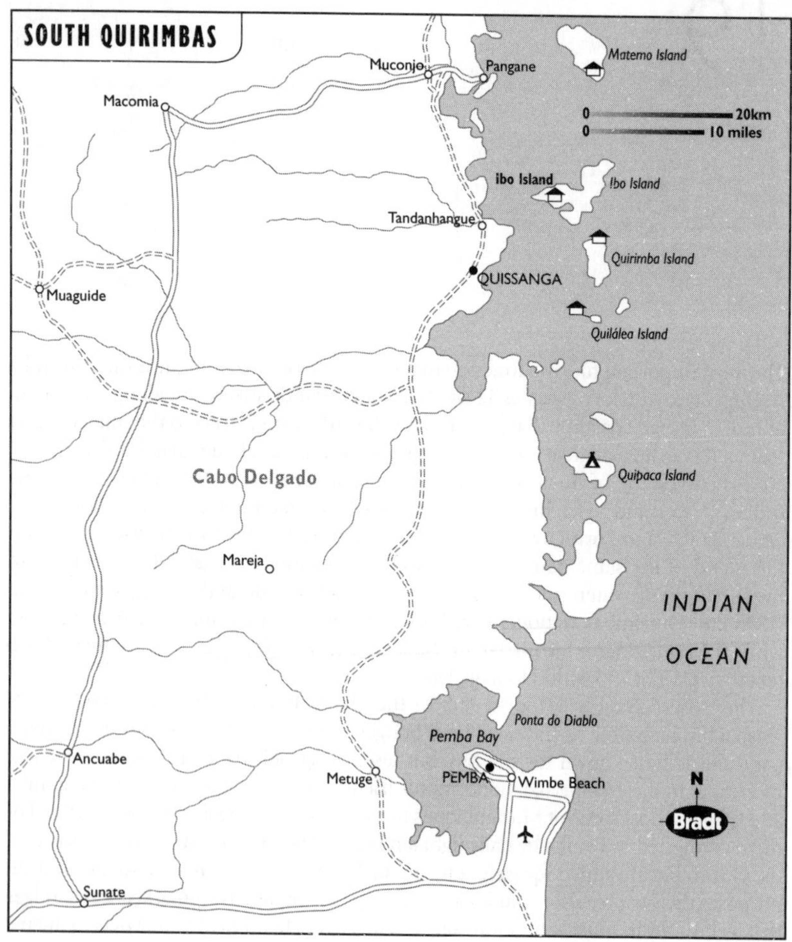

by hawksbill, green and olive ridley turtles, and loggerhead and leatherback turtles are also present in these waters. Several other species listed as threatened by the IUCN are resident or regular migratory visitors, among them the dugong, bottlenose dolphin, humpback whale, and grey-nurse, great white and whale shark. The offshore reefs support an incredible wealth of marine wildlife, including 52 coral and 375 fish species, making for some of the country's finest diving and snorkelling.

Most of the islands are inhabited and, while there is some industrial-scale agriculture on Quirimba Island (where the same family farmed coconuts for close on a century prior to selling up a few years back), the predominant occupation is subsistence fishing, not only by Mozambicans but also by itinerant semi-nomadic Tanzanian fishermen, who move from island to island every month or so, drying their catch and sending it in big sacks to market in Mtwara or Pemba.

HISTORY

Little is known about the history of the Quirimbas prior to the arrival of the Portuguese, but they were certainly occupied by Arabic traders by the 13th century, and possibly even as early as the 7th century. They are assumed to have formed an important link in the medieval coastal trade network between Kilwa and Sofala. The Quirimbas were originally known to the Portuguese as the Maluane Islands, after a type of cloth manufactured in the vicinity from pre-Portuguese times until well into the 17th century.

When the Portuguese first landed in the archipelago, the main trading centre was on Quirimba Island, immediately south of Ibo. In 1507, when the more northerly island city of Kilwa was occupied by Portugal, many of its Muslim merchants fled to Quirimba and continued operating from there, refusing to enter into trade with the Christian Portuguese. As a result, Portugal attacked Quirimba in 1522, killing about 60 of its Muslim residents and looting large amounts of ivory and other merchandise before they burned the town down. This massacre had little long-term effect in subduing the Muslim trade, however, so Portugal switched tactics and attempted to gain control over the islands by leasing them to Portuguese citizens.

By the end of the 16th century, seven of the nine largest islands in the archipelago were ruled by Portuguese traders and the other two by Muslims. Islanders were forced to pay a tribute of 5% of their produce to the island's ruler, as well as a tithe to the Church. By this time, the most important island in the archipelago was Ibo, said locally to be an acronym of the Portuguese Ilha Bem Organizado (Well-Organised Island), a claim we've been unable to verify elsewhere. A description dating from 1609 reveals that Ibo was substantially fortified, and that the islands were reasonably prosperous and a major source of food supplies for Ilha de Moçambique. By the 18th century, *prazos* had been established on all the main islands, and the archipelago was lorded over by two *mazungo* (white-skinned) families, the Meneses and Morues.

Ibo came into its own in the second half of the 18th century as the major supplier of slaves to the sugar-plantation owners of France's Indian Ocean islands. Portugal resented the prosperity of the islands' independent traders and, fearing that the archipelago might fall into Omani or French hands, granted Ibo municipal status in 1763. By the end of the 18th century, Ibo is thought to have been the second most important Portuguese trading centre after Ilha de Moçambique. It was still a major trading and administrative centre when it was leased to the Niassa Company in 1897 but, as it transpired, the shallow, narrow approach to the island wasn't suitable for modern ships. In 1904, the Niassa Company relocated its base to Porto Amélia (Pemba), three-quarters of Ibo's population followed, the islands faded into economic insignificance, and its old towns fell into gradual decline.

IBO

Situated on the island of the same name, the small town of Ibo ranks among Mozambique's most ancient settlements. Founded prior to the Portuguese era, it was the most important coastal port after Ilha de Moçambique up until the turn of the 20th century. By mainstream tourism standards, Ibo today is also one of southern Africa's best-kept travel secrets. Tourist facilities are limited, though steadily improving, and access is not exactly straightforward (unless, of course, you fly from Pemba, which takes all of 20 minutes). Yet for the select few visitors who do make it, wandering around the timeworn alleys of Ibo's old town and interacting with its fewer than 4,000 inhabitants invariably forms a highlight of their time in Mozambique.

The old town of Ibo, though run-down, is utterly compelling: a strangely haunting backwater that vaguely recalls Kilwa Kivinje on the south coast of Tanzania. As the UNESCO World Heritage Site tentative list notes: 'The architectural character of the stone-built town, created through several hundreds of years, is remarkable for its homogeneity … the town, the fortifications and many fine buildings are an outstanding example of architecture in which local Swahili traditions, Portuguese influences and Indian and Arab influences are all intertwined.'

Today, many of the palaces and villas built in Ibo's 19th-century heyday have been abandoned and lapsed into disrepair, with clay tiles falling from the roofs, walls layered in moss and foundations undermined by the vast sprawling tendrils of strangler figs. The exposed rag coral walls and fading whitewash of the crumbling buildings give the town a washed-out pastel air that is strangely at odds with the deep blue tropical sky and the bright red flame trees, and the lush greenery that lines the streets in which mangrove kingfishers sing at dawn.

If there is an obvious point of comparison, it is Ilha de Moçambique, but Ibo is far from being a miniature of Ilha – which may have been the Portuguese capital for four centuries, but is more evocative of the Muslim world than of anything European. Paradoxically Ibo, which was frequently a base for clandestine Muslim trade during the Portuguese era, has an uncluttered and overwhelmingly Mediterranean character, its wide roads lined with opulent high-roofed buildings boasting classical façades and expansive balconies supported by thick pillars. And while Ibo is also in a more advanced state of decay than Moçambique, this is steadily changing. An idea of Ibo's past grandeur can be seen at the Ibo Island Lodge, where three previously ruined mansions have been lovingly and sensitively restored to their former glory, and several other buildings are also in various stages of rehabilitation.

CONSERVATION ON THE QUIRIMBAS

The first survey work of the Quirimbas was carried out between 1996 and 1998 by Frontier-Mozambique, a project based on Ilha Quirimba and run by the Society for Environmental Exploration in conjunction with the Tropical Marine Department of the University of York in the UK, the Mozambican Department of the Environment (MICOA), the Mozambican Department of Fisheries (IDPPE) and the University of Eduardo Mondlane.

The project of a national park in the Quirimbas had – because of the region's very high biodiversity, great scenic beauty and important history – been under intermittent discussion since the 1970s. However, it was only in 2000 that the first protected marine area was established in the Quirimbas in the form of the Quilálea Marine Sanctuary, which was set up around the islands of Quilálea and Sencar (55km and 75km north of Pemba respectively) by a private company and endorsed by the government. In June 2002, at the request of 40 local community leaders, the 7,506km^2 Quirimba National Park was created to encompass both the southern half of the archipelago and a 5,984km^2 tract of the facing mainland. The park's marine sector extends over 1,522 km^2 and stretches 100km along the coast, from just north of Pemba to just south of Medjumbe Island. The park's headquarters are on Ibo Island.

The Worldwide Fund for Nature or WWF (*www.wwf.org*) is heavily involved in the Quirimba Park, and its website is a good source of information. The overall goal of the park, in this beautiful but ecologically fragile area, is 'to conserve the diversity, abundance and ecological integrity of all physical and biological resources in the park area, so that they may be enjoyed and used productively by present and future generations'. Nor is nature the only beneficiary. One of the park's six associated aims involves contributing to 'the economic and social well-

A number of organisations and investors have identified the importance of Ibo's history, culture and biodiversity, and community and conservation projects are already under way. A new community tourism programme, an agricultural market garden project, a silversmiths' programme and several other planned community-based alternative-enterprise projects will be operated and managed by Ibo Island Lodge (see page 328), and can be visited by the lodge's guests as well as by other visitors.

GETTING THERE AND AWAY

By air The easy way to get to Ibo is by air. **CFA** runs at least one daily flight connecting Pemba to Ibo and all other islands with lodges, though times and schedules are very flexible depending on the bookings for that day. Bookings can be made through their Pemba office (*272 20553;* m *82 575 2125;* e *raniaviation@teledata.mz; www.cfa.co.za*) or though Kaskazini (see page 317) and depending on your exact routing are mostly around US$120 one-way. The flights take up to 20 minutes and will be a visual delight in clear weather.

By boat A cheaper direct possibility between Pemba and Ibo is to catch a ride with the cargo boat operated by Pensão Cinco Portas (see page 330), which does a weekly supply run in either direction, stopping to offload at the Quililea Island Marine Sanctuary. The boat leaves Pemba for Ibo every Saturday morning and returns on Wednesday, one-way passage costs US$35 per person, and the trip takes

being of the park's ancestral inhabitants by promoting sustainable resource use strategies, by developing ecologically sensitive livelihood options and by prioritising their interests in the economic opportunities deriving from the establishment of the park'.

Park management currently runs largely on NGO funding, but the long-term goal is for park fees and other tourist revenue – of which 70% goes towards park management, another 20% to local communities and only 10% to state coffers – to make it financially self-sufficient. This goal, it has to be said, is a long way from being realised, as annual tourist arrivals currently stand at around 3,500 people, most them staying on Ibo or Matemo. However, ambitious plans for further development of community-based tourism on the oft-neglected mainland sector of the park have led to projections of 20,000 visitors annually by 2017.

Another player in the conservation of the island's natural and cultural assets is Ibo Island Lodge, which has aimed to provide clear community benefits since its inception. To this end they established a series of projects run from the Ibo Island Conservation Centre. These include a long-term programme teaching English language to the communities on Ibo, and the creation of alternative-enterprise projects such as a market garden scheme, whereby locals can produce sellable crops in their own gardens, the development of Ibo Island Coffee as a premium brand, and the development of the island's ancient silversmithing industry. There are also plans for the creation of a network of island guides to lead culture and heritage experiences. Another project is to record from oral and other sources the fascinating history of the island. More can be found out about these projects by checking Ibo Island Lodge's website (*www.iboisland.com*).

about 12 hours. They can also arrange combined car and boat transfers from Pemba via Tandanhangue for US$50 per person.

By *dhow* and chapa The more convoluted but cheaper option entails a combination of road transport and dhow, and you'd best resign yourself to a long bumpy ride. ***Dhows*** to Ibo leave from the fishing village of Tandanhangue, which lies on the coast north of Pemba a short distance past Quissanga. In the dry season, the shortest route to Tandanhangue involves following the **EN106** east out of Pemba for a few kilometres then turning right onto the direct coastal road running north through Metugé and Mahala. This route covers a distance 125km and takes three to four hours in a private vehicle. The better but longer (250km) inland route, which you'd be forced to use in the rainy season, involves following the surfaced EN106 and **EN243** via Senate to Muaguide, then turning right onto an all-weather dirt road through Bilibiza to connect with the coastal road at Mahala, where you need to turn left for Quissanga. Either way, a 4x4 is a must, and there is safe parking at Tandanhangue (expect to pay around US$2 per day to the guard).

Chapas run from Pemba to Quissanga and Tandanhangue, and while there will be at least one a day, it is possible that there will only be the one on the day you are travelling, so be at the chapa point in Pemba before 05.00. Be prepared for a long, hot, dusty and rough journey. The trip costs US$5.50 and takes a good five to six hours, longer in the rains.

Like so many coastal towns in Mozambique, Quissanga splits into two halves – the administrative block up on the hill and the main fishing village down in the mangroves. If you are heading to Tandanhangue, you need to take the turning north at the administrative block. Once at Tandanhangue, there should be a *dhow* waiting on the shore where the chapa drops you, though if the tides work against you, you may be in for a wait of a few hours. The journey is breathtakingly beautiful – the only sounds are the creaking of the mast, the wind in the sails, the water lapping around the boat and the birds calling from the mangroves. It costs US$5.50 and will take up to three hours depending on the sea and winds. The *dhow* will drop you on the beach in front of the Fortim de São José. Note that Miti Miwiri (see page 330) also offers boat transfers from Tandanhangue by prior arrangement, costing US$40 for up to four people.

It is possible to walk from Tandanhangue to Ibo at certain times of tide. It should only be attempted on low spring tides and you *must* take a local guide – if you stray off the path then you will very quickly find yourself trapped in knee-deep mud, with a very real risk of being stuck there until someone comes along who can help you out, or the tide comes in.

WHERE TO STAY

Exclusive

Ibo Island Lodge (9 rooms) +27 21 702 0285 (South Africa) or 269 6049 (lodge); e info@iboisland.com; www.iboisland.com. The western waterfront was the most exclusive address in town during Ibo's glory days, dominated by a trio of 19th-century mansions that fell into ruin & decay as the town faded. Two of these mansions, Villa Niassa & Villa Bella Vista, both of which served as governors' palaces at some point in their history, have now been sensitively rehabilitated & restored as Ibo Island Lodge, & the third mansion, Villa Paradiso, should be added to the lodge during the lifespan of this edition. The rooms have lofty ceilings, & are spacious, cool, & filled with restored colonial-era or locally made hardwood furniture. The rooftop restaurant-bar is a perfect place to watch the sun go down over the bay & the mangrove forest beyond. There is also a lovely large garden, planted with frangipani, bougainvillea

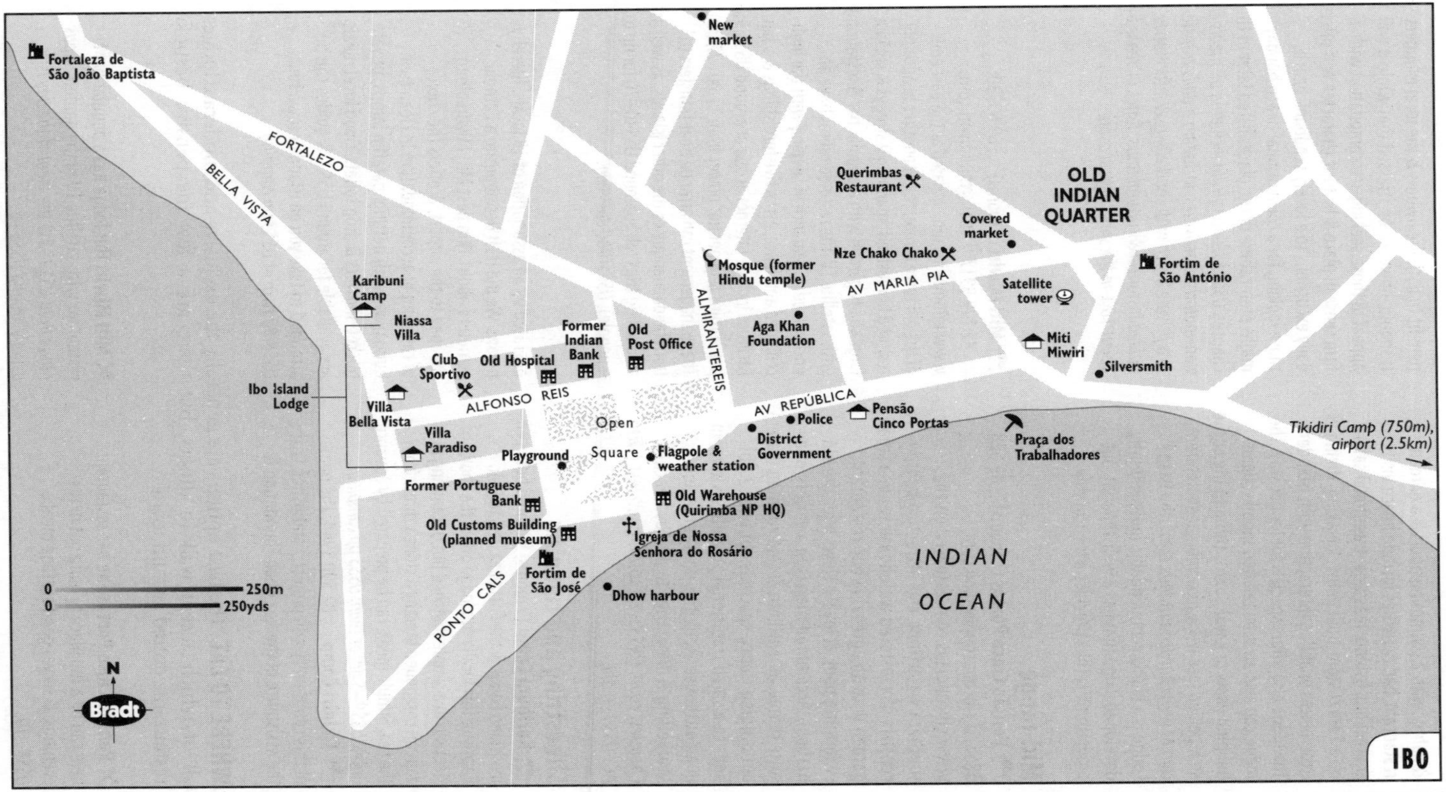

IBO
Fortaleza de São João Baptista
New market
FORTALEZO
BELLA VISTA
Querimbas Restaurant
OLD INDIAN QUARTER
Covered market
Nze Chako Chako
Mosque (former Hindu temple)
ALMIRANTEREIS
AV MARIA PIA
Fortim de São António
Satellite tower
Karibuni Camp
Niassa Villa
Former Indian Bank
Old Post Office
Aga Khan Foundation
Miti Miwiri
Club Sportivo
Old Hospital
Silversmith
Ibo Island Lodge
Villa Bella Vista
ALFONSO REIS
AV REPÚBLICA
Police
Pensão Cinco Portas
Villa Paradiso
Open Square
District Government
Tikidiri Camp (750m), airport (2.5km)
Praça dos Trabalhadores
Playground
Flagpole & weather station
Former Portuguese Bank
Old Warehouse (Quirimba NP HQ)
Old Customs Building (planned museum)
Igreja de Nossa Senhora do Rosário
INDIAN OCEAN
Fortim de São José
Dhow harbour
PONTO CALS
0 250m
0 250yds
N
Bradt

& palms, with 2 swimming pools & a garden restaurant-bar. Activities include beach visits, snorkelling, fishing, massage, traditional safaris on a 14m custom-built *dhow*, kayaking, diving, & experiences enabling interaction with islanders. The lodge also offers specials for longer stay. The lodge can also arrange tailored mobile island-hopping *dhow* or kayak safaris through the entire archipelago (see *www.mozambiquedhowsafaris.com* or *www.kayakquirimbas.com*). Ibo Island Lodge is a highly commendable independently developed lodge that has a well-thought-out programme & thus provides a measurable benefit to both the owners & the local islanders. It should, however, be stressed that while it will appeal to those seeking accommodation with a firm sense of place & historic character, & it offers daily excursions to a lovely sandbank beach, those looking for a conventional beach holiday might prefer some of the places listed later in the chapter. *US$435/670 sgl/dbl including all meals & non-motorised activities, including a daily transfer to a private beach with snorkelling, & informative guided historical & cultural tours. Rates increase by about 10% in the short high season.*

Mid-range

Pensão Cinco Portas (7 rooms) 82 628 6858; e cincoportas@yahoo.com; www.cincoportas.com. Situated on the southern waterfront, this attractive *pensão* consists of a restored warehouse set in a small garden with an agreeable bar-restaurant, swimming pool, & lovely views over the old harbour. Accommodation is in a variety of en-suite rooms, all with fan & cold running water, but ranging from a spacious apt with 2 dbl beds to a small traditional Swahili-style room in an outhouse. Activities on offer include snorkelling & *dhow* trips to nearby beaches. *Cheapest room US$35/60 sgl/dbl; priciest (with AC) US$120 dbl.*

Miti Miwiri (9 rooms) 269 60530; m 82 729 8917; e mail@mitimiwiri.com; www.mitimiwiri.com. Situated at the east end of the old town centre, this is another beautifully restored homestead, spanning 2 storeys & set in a large shady garden with a popular bar & restaurant with satellite TV. The restored rooms have an uncluttered appearance in keeping with the high-ceilinged ambience, attractive furnishings & a fan. Facilities include internet access at around US$1.50 per 30mins & generator power from 17.00–22.00. The management can arrange boat transfers to/from Tandanhangue or the other islands, as well as snorkelling trips (all at around US$40–70 for up to 4 people). *US$50/60 dbl/twin.*

Shoestring and camping

Karibuni Camp (5 rooms) Situated between Ibo Island Lodge & the Fortaleza de São João Baptista, this locally run lodge offers the choice of sleeping in a simple thatched hut or camping in a green compound literally a stone's throw from the sea. Simple meals can be prepared by advance order. *US$9–5 dbl or twin; US$3 pp camping.*

Tikidiri Camp m 82 590 3944. The name of this community-run project, established with the assistance of the Aga Khan Foundation & operated by an association of 18 locals, literally means 'We did it'. It lies opposite a Catholic cemetery about 1km past Miti Miwiri along the road to the airport, & offers the choice of camping or accommodation in clean twin bungalows with netting, paraffin lamps, private bucket-showers & drop toilets. Good local meals are available for around US$2, & guides can be arranged to take you on island or town tours. *US$8.50 twin or US$3 pp camping.*

WHERE TO EAT The best options are generally the exclusive and moderate lodges, all of which accept walk-in diners, but there are a few inexpensive bespoke restaurants dotted around town.

Pensão Cinco Portas The bar-restaurant here can be a fun place to hang out in the evenings, & serves good seafood meals. *US$8–10.*

Miti Miwiri This lodge has a popular bar & restaurant with satellite TV in the garden. *Tapas range from US$2–3 & the meal of the day is usually around US$5–6.*

✕ Club Sportivo Situated behind Ibo Island Lodge, this quiet local bar serves typical Mozambican fare including good seafood. Meals are best ordered a couple of hours in advance, but if you don't get around to it, there is a full bar to amuse you while you wait for the food to be prepared. *US$3–5.*

✕ Nze Chako Chako This no-frills eatery in the old Indian quarter serves inexpensive local meals as well as beer and tea.

✕ Quirimbas Restaurant Another good & inexpensive local eatery, this is set along the road connecting the Old Indian quarter to the market.

WHAT TO SEE AND DO Ibo's magic lies in the feeling of history that radiates from the walls of the old town, particularly around dusk, when you can almost feel the ghosts brushing past you as you walk the streets and alleys. Laid out in a rough triangle with the Fortaleza de São João Baptista forming the northwestern apex and the Fortim de São José and Fortim de São António at the base, the old town is so small that there is little need to follow a prescribed route around it, but for convenience's sake, the information below is organised along a circuit that starts at the western waterfront, near Ibo Island Lodge, then runs east along Avenida República to Fortim de São António, before returning east along Avenida Maria Pia to the Fortim de São António. If you prefer a guided tour, these are offered free to people staying at Ibo Island Lodge, and can also be arranged at a small fee through the island's other lodges and camps.

As in the case in several other old Mozambican towns, it is hard to establish the age of many of Ibo's buildings. The dates on tiles and a few buildings seem to place much of the town centre in the early 19th century, a few buildings are older still, and it seems unlikely that many post-date the relocation of the Niassa Company's headquarters to Porto Amélia (Pemba) in 1904. Relics of pre-Portuguese times reputedly exist, including two ancient mosques and an Arab fortress, but if so they are difficult to locate, though recent excavations at the Fortaleza de São João Baptista have revealed the ruins of a Swahili house that pre-dates the fort's construction. A more surprising relict of pre-Portuguese times is the wild coffee shrubs, descended from plants brought by Arab traders, that have been growing on both Ibo and Quirimba for centuries. (One of the projects identified at Ibo Island Lodge is to establish the coffee as a recognisable brand and help islanders set up their own businesses growing and marketing it.)

A trio of striking mansions, now incorporated into Ibo Island Lodge, line the western waterfront. All three date to the late 19th century or earlier: **Villa Niassa** was originally the governor's palace but later became the headquarters of the Niassa Company, **Villa Bella Vista** served as a governor's palace some time after that, while **Villa Paradiso** was built as the home of a rich merchant and later became an Indian restaurant.

A block east of the waterfront, Avenida República opens out to become **Praça dos Heróis Moçambicanos**, a central square surrounded by several of the island's oldest buildings. These include the former **Portuguese Bank** on the southwest side, the former **Indian Bank**, **Old Hospital** and **Old Post Office** on the north, and a **former warehouse** (now housing the Quirimba National Park headquarters and a carpentry co-operative) on the southeast side – all dating from the 19th century.

On the south side of the praça, the large whitewashed **Igreja de Nossa Senhora do Rosário** (also sometimes known as Igreja de São João) still holds monthly services for the few dozen Christians who remain on the island. The pedigree of this church is somewhat uncertain. According to one source, it was built in 1580, a date lent some credibility by Dominican missionary records claiming some 16,000 converts in the Quirimbas by 1593. Other sources suggest a construction date of 1760, while inscriptions recording the church's wealthy benefactors place it c1800. The architectural style recalls the 18th-century cathedrals at Inhambane and Quelimane, and it is very possible that the present church was built at around that time on the site of an older predecessor. Beside the church are about 15 children's graves.

Next to the church, the **old customs building**, constructed in 1879, retains the ornate filigree railings typical of Indian buildings of that period. After closing as a customs house, it served as the town archive for several decades, and many papers dating from the late 19th century through to World War II are reputedly still stored inside. Closed for renovations in 2010, it will most likely reopen as a museum during the lifespan of this edition. Alongside the old customs building, overlooking the semi-fortified southern waterfront, the moderately proportioned and architecturally mundane **Fortim de São José** was the first Portuguese-built fort on Ibo, dating to 1760, three years before the town was granted municipal status. It was used as a slave prison following the construction of the Fortaleza de São João Baptista, and eventually fell into disuse. Renovations are under way at the time of writing.

Following Avenida República east, you pass several interesting buildings to your right, many of them old waterfront administrative buildings and warehouses, while to the left are a few rather dilapidated old mansions. About 500m past the main praça, the undistinguished **Praça dos Trabalhadores** offers a view over the dhow harbour, and another 200m or so brings you an excellent **silversmith co-operative**, where you can watch the artisans at work and, if you like, buy some of their products. Turn left here and after another 200m you'll reach the **Fortim de São António**, which lies at the back of the town near the market. Built in 1847, this neat little fort offers a good view over the town from the tower, and the site was reputedly chosen because it has access to a natural tunnel that runs underground for about 1.5km to emerge near the airstrip. It was closed for renovations in 2010 but should reopen in 2011.

From here, Avenida Maria Pia runs west through the **old Indian Quarter**, site of the little-used covered market and a number of small shops, eateries and bars that generate the closest thing on Ibo to a feeling of commercial buzz. About 500m west of this, a short diversion north along Avenida Almirante Reis leads to the most interesting of the town's **mosques**, whose hybridised appearance is explained by the fact it was converted from a Hindu temple in 1975. This building, like the almost disused church, serves to remind us that while much of the architecture on Ibo is Portuguese or Indian, the town today is inhabited almost entirely by indigenous Africans, 99% of whom are Muslim.

Follow Avenida do Fortaleza for another 1km northwest from here, and you will emerge in front of its most interesting and best-preserved building, the recently restored and whitewashed **Fortaleza de São João Baptista**, a large, star-shaped fort, complete with a dozen or so cannons and ringed by a grove of tall palms. Built in 1791 to protect the island from a French invasion from the island of Réunion, this fort was used as a prison into the 1970s, which explains the broken soft-drink bottles that line the tops of the walls. During the liberation war of 1965–75, it seems that Ibo and its fort became the Mozambican equivalent to South Africa's Robben Island (where Nelson Mandela and other political prisoners were detained at the height of apartheid). Some deeply disturbing stories relate to this period: locals say that the ramparts are haunted by the ghosts of political prisoners who drowned or died of disease after being locked into crowded waterlogged cells where they had no choice but to drink the same water in which all the cell's occupants were forced to defecate and urinate. The fort no longer has any formal use, but it is very well maintained and its entrance is occupied by some traditional silversmiths who'll happily allow you to watch them at work without expecting you to buy anything.

OTHER ACTIVITIES As with the rest of the Quirimbas, Ibo is a useful base for marine activities, though the island itself lacks a real swimming beach on account of the high density of mangroves. There is currently no diving operation on the island, but dives can sometimes be arranged through nearby Matemo Island Resort. Snorkelling excursions can be arranged through any of the moderate or upmarket lodges in Ibo, as can dhow trips to beaches on other islands. The fishing is also very good. In addition, Ibo Island Lodge operates fully guided and catered adventure and luxury tailor-made dhow and kayak safaris, hopping between the very best of the islands south and north of Ibo – see the listing on page 328 for contact details.

Out of town, Ibo Island also has some good walking possibilities, and bicycles can be rented outside Miti Miwiri for around US$5 per day. A short walk out of town is the cemetery along the airport road, where you'll find graves with inscriptions in several languages. Further afield, the dilapidated Majuca Lighthouse was established in 1873 on a separate seaward islet called Majuca, which lies about 5km east of Ibo town and can be reached on foot at low tide. This walk takes up to two hours in either direction, leading out past the Fortaleza de São João Baptista, then following the mangrove- and palm-lined northern shore past tidal flats that often support large flocks of waders and marine birds.

The dominant cultural group on Ibo, as in the rest of the Quirimbas, is the Mwani ('People of the Sea'), whose Kimwani (or Kimuane) tongue shares about 60% of its vocabulary with KiSwahili and, like that language, shows many unambiguous Arabic influences. Mwani culture combines Islamic beliefs with a strong core of typically ebullient African traditions, and the night air is often filled with the sound of drumming associated with initiation, funereal, wedding and other ceremonies. Sometimes the drumming might signal the start of a traditional procession through the streets, but more often you will need to ask around to see traditional Mwani dances. For those interested in traditional and contemporary Mozambican arts and culture, a good time to visit is over 24–5 June, when the Fiesta do Ibo is held to coincide with Independence Day. Another big event locally is New Year's Day, when the entire village jumps into the sea in a ritual cleansing ceremony known as *Tomar de Banho* (literally 'Bath-taking').

OTHER ISLANDS OF THE QUIRIMBAS

Although Ibo is the most important of the Quirimbas historically, and the only one that caters to travellers of all budgets, the chain comprises another 31 islands, of which about half a dozen host idyllic upmarket resorts that cater both to sun-worshippers and to those pursuing more active marine adventures. The southernmost 11 islands in the chain, including Quipaco, Mefunvo, Quirimba, Ibo, Quilálea and Matemo, are now protected within Quirimba National Park, while more northerly islands such as Medjumbe, Tambuze, Metundo, Vamizi, Rongui and Tecomaji are not formally protected, though several function as something close to a private sanctuary. The market for these resorts is almost entirely fly-in, which makes the area quite difficult to explore independently or on a budget, the one exception being Matemo Island, where there is a community camp aimed at backpackers, and transport from Ibo can be arranged through Miti Miwiri (see page 330). Running from south to north, the islands that are of greatest interest to visitors are as follows:

ILHA QUIPACO The most southerly of the archipelago's major islands, Quipaco lies about 40km north of Pemba as the crow flies. It has never boasted much in the way of a settlement due to the scarcity of fresh water. The shallow ocean between here and

Ponta do Diablo is known for its good game fishing and a private camp is reputedly under construction (Kaskazini in Pemba will know as and when it opens).

ILHA QUISIVA This 3km² island was settled by the Portuguese in the late 16th century, and later became the main outpost of the Moraes family, who owned five of the Quirimba islands and dominated local trade in the early 18th century. The significant fortified Portuguese ruins on the island are said locally to date to the time of Vasco da Gama, but it seems unlikely they are quite that old, and there are also the remains of some old plantation houses. The sandy spit that protrudes westward from the main island is great for swimming. Quisiva is currently under development by the Seasons in Africa chain as an ultra-exclusive beach retreat due to open in 2011.

ILHAS QUILÁLEA AND SENCAR These two islands comprise the terrestrial portion of the Quilálea Marine Sanctuary, a pioneering private reserve that was established in 2000 as the archipelago's first protected marine area but now officially forms part of the national park. Since the sanctuary's inception, local fishing has been banned within it, leading to a great increase in marine life. Turtles nest on the beaches, dugongs are sometimes sighted, and humpback whales shelter in the channel from July to January before journeying south. More than 375 different species of fish have been identified in the sanctuary area, giving snorkelers a rare and colourful treat. The shores of Quilálea are particularly rich in seashells. You can stroll round the whole of tiny (35ha) uninhabited Quilálea in well under an hour. A lodge, built on the site of one of the old itinerant fishing camps, opened in 2002 but is currently closed following a change in ownership.

ILHA QUIRIMBA Situated immediately south of Ibo, Quirimba is one of the larger islands in the chain, and is mostly covered by coconut plantations. It was the site of the archipelago's most important trade outpost in the pre-Portuguese era, and it remains one of the more densely settled islands, with a population estimated at 4,000. Farmed by the same German family since the 1920s, the island once hosted a popular lodge, but this has been closed for some years now.

ILHA MATEMO The second-largest island in the chain at 24km², Matemo lies to the north of Ibo just within the boundaries of the national park. It was almost certainly settled when the Portuguese first sailed into the Indian Ocean, and its population was boosted when the infamous Zimba raids of the late 16th century encouraged the mainland Muslim community associated with the making of Maluane cloth to take refuge on the island. Today, there are two large villages on the island, along with Portuguese ruins dating to the time when Matemo's plantations were major suppliers of food to Ilha de Moçambique. Characterised by sweeping sandy beaches, lush vegetation and palm groves, it is now the site of the upmarket Matemo Island Resort as well as the more low-key community-run Dadi Lodge.

ILHA DAS ROLAS Only ten minutes' boat trip from Matemo in calm weather, this tiny island has no fresh water whatsoever, and the small encampment there is used only by itinerant fishermen and their families, who cross to the mainland for water when they're in residence. It has an almost bipolar feel – the southern end is a spit of sand, bereft of any form of vegetation, while the northern end has low, rough scrub. There is a fairly large intertidal area that makes for good

DUGONGS AND MERMAIDS *Dr Mark Whittington*

I was research co-ordinator on the Frontier-Mozambique Project that conducted the first surveys of the Quirimba Archipelago, and one of our objectives was to establish the numbers of dugong in the area. One of the techniques for establishing whether a particular marine species was present in the islands was to conduct interviews with local fishermen. I would show them the UNFAO (United Nations Food and Agriculture Organisation) field guide for commercial fish species in Mozambican coastal waters and point to the various illustrations to see if they were recognised. During one of these interviews they said, 'This book is incomplete: it doesn't mention mermaids. You must report this to the Ministry of Fisheries …'

At this my interpreter, a government scientist from Maputo, rolled his eyes and turned to the page showing the dugong, but they were very clear – they knew what a dugong was and they knew what a mermaid was, and the two were quite distinct. For a few minutes we discussed their understandings of mermaids and it was remarkably clear-cut – they knew of the social hierarchy of mermaids, how they behaved and what their food sources were. Before moving on to more mundane topics, I asked them one final question: 'Are mermaids beautiful?' They discussed this among themselves before coming back with, 'No, not really. Their hair is rather lank and stringy.'

beachcombing. It has recently been recolonised as a breeding site by hawksbill turtles, who are resident in the surrounding reefs. Rolas is regarded as perhaps the best snorkelling site in the Quirimbas, and it is also good for diving.

ILHA MEDJUMBE Site of the exclusive Medjumbe Island Lodge, this tiny islet (1.1km by 350m) north of Matemo hosts a variety of bird species including the black heron, while the offshore waters contain marlin, sailfish, dogtooth tuna, mackerel, various species of kingfish, and bonefish. The diving is spectacular.

ILHAS VAMIZI, MACALOE AND RONGUI Outside the Quirimba National Park, the Maluane Project was initiated in 1998 to protect an ecologically diverse area of coast that comprises this trio of islands, the surrounding coastal waters, and a 330km^2 wildlife reserve on the facing mainland. The project is supported by the Zoological Society of London and the Mozambican government, and has strong environmental and community links. The objective is to conserve and develop a stretch of coast whose marine wildlife includes turtles, humpback whales, whale sharks, dugongs, dolphins, manta rays and giant clams. It is of particular significance for its pristine reefs, which comprise 30 different genera of coral and support 350 species of reef fish.

The mainland section of the reserve is essentially an extension of the terrestrial sector of Quirimba National Park, and it supports a similar selection of species, including elephant, lion, buffalo, hippo, leopard, African wild dog, various antelope and monkey species, and a huge variety of birds. The long-term goal is that the reserve will be sustained by tourist revenue, part of which will be dedicated to associated communities, to which end an upmarket lodge has already been constructed in Vamizi. It is likely that lodges will eventually be built on the other two islands, as well as on the mainland part of the reserve.

GETTING THERE AND AWAY

By air As with Ibo, the easiest way to visit those islands that have tourist facilities is by air. **CFA** operates a daily service connecting all the islands' airstrips to each other and to Pemba, though times and schedules are very flexible depending on the bookings for that day. See page 327 for contact details.

By boat For charter boats between the islands, speak to Miti Miwiri in Ibo, which regularly takes travellers to the community campsite on Matemo and could presumably head out to islands further afield of you are prepared to pay for it.

By *dhow* Quirimba Island can be reached with relative ease by *dhow*, since regular boats run there from Quissanga (again, see the Ibo section for details of getting there). As with everything in the archipelago, the boat's timetable will be dictated by the tides and winds, but the crossing usually takes up to two hours and it will cost around US$5–6 per person. There may also be boats travelling between Ibo and Quirimba, but you'll have to ask around on Ibo to find out. Somewhat incredibly, it's also possible to walk from Ibo to Quirimba. If you're mad enough to try this then you need to do it at low spring tides, you *must* take a guide and you should be prepared for a four- to five-hour walk that starts in the mangroves and ends in a wade across the small channel that separates the bottom of Ibo and the top of Quirimba.

WHERE TO STAY

Exclusive As with the island descriptions above, the listings below follow the chain of islands from south to north. It is worth noting that the status of several island lodges is unclear at the time of writing: Quilálea and Quirimba Lodge are closed following changes of ownership, the lodges on Quipaco and Quisiva are both under development, and there is also talk of new lodges opening on Macaloe and Rongui as part of the Maluane Project. If you want to keep tabs on developments, visit our update website (*http://updates.bradtguides.com/mozambique*) or get in touch with Kaskazini (*www.kaskazini.com*).

Quisiva Island Sanctuary (14 units) Ilha Quisiva; +27 (0)13 750 2358 (South Africa); e info@seasonsinafrica.com; www.quisiva.com. Under development at the time of writing, this new lodge looks to be luxurious even by the standards of the Quirimbas, offering accommodation in 14 large villas set above a low coral cliff overlooking a sand spit that protrudes westward into the sea. The full range of marine activities will be on offer, & rates are likely to be at the very top end of the scale.

Quilálea Island Resort This lodge on Ilha Quilálea opened in Nov 2002 & has been highly rated by both tour operators & guests, who called it 'a jewel in Africa' & 'an instant classic'. The house reef is just a few flipper-strokes from the beach & activities include big-game fishing, PADI dive courses & excursions to other islands. Access is via plane from Pemba to Quirimba Island & thence by boat to Quilálea. Closed at the time of writing, it is likely to reopen as part of the Azura chain during the lifespan of this edition – see www.azura-retreats.com for details.

Quirimba Lodge The lodge opened on Ilha Quirimba in 1998, making it the 1st on the archipelago. It's closed at the moment, & we have no idea when it will reopen. It's got a lovely site – peaceful & shaded with a stunning view of the sunrises over the Indian Ocean.

Matemo Island Resort (24 units) Ilha Matemo; 213 01618; e enquiries@raniresorts.com; www.matemoresort.com. This sumptuous lodge has accommodation in large chalets with macuti thatch roofs & timber floors strung along a lovely beach that offers good swimming & snorkelling at high tide. All chalets have dbl bed with walk-in nets, hardwood furnishings, DSTV, AC, fan, en-suite bathroom with tub & shower, mini-bar & private veranda only a 50m barefoot stumble from the beach. Facilities include a large freshwater swimming pool, a superb restaurant serving seafood-dominated buffets, & a dive centre offering diving & snorkelling excursions to Ilha das Rolas & elsewhere, along with a full range of watersports, sunset cruises & daily excursions to Ibo town & to other islands. *US$920–1,050 dbl depending on season, inclusive of all meals, house wines, non-motorised activities &marine reserve fees.*

Medjumbe Island Resort (13 units) Ilha Medjumbe; 213 01618; e enquiries@raniresorts.com; www.matemoresort.com. Under the same management as Matemo but smaller, pricier & very popular with honeymooners, Medjumbe lies on a tiny island with a pristine white beach & plentiful sites for diving & snorkelling. Accommodation is of similar standard to Matemo, comprising a widely spaced row of beachfront chalets, but every unit has a private jacuzzi/plunge pool set in an open-air deck, as well as a private outdoor shower. The seafood-dominated meals are superb & a full range of marine activities is offered. *US$1,030–1,200 dbl depending on season, inclusive of all meals, house wines, non-motorised activities & marine reserve fees.*

Vamizi Island Lodge (10 rooms) Ilha Vamizi; + 44 (0)1285 762217 (UK); e enquiries@vamizi.com; www.vamizi.com. This ultra-exclusive lodge, the only one currently operating in the community-based sanctuary managed by the Maluane Project, has more of a bush aesthetic. The spacious chalets, strung out along a wide sandy beach, have a floor plan of 170m^2, king-size 4-poster beds with walk-in nets & paddle fans, a safe, complimentary mini-bar, & stylish marble bathrooms built with local materials. The beach here is one of the most important turtle-breeding sites in Mozambique, & the island is also home to an endemic dwarf python & the bizarre giant coconut crab. Snorkelling & diving on the pristine offshore reefs is spectacular, & other activities include fishing, kayaking, *dhow* trips & forest walks. The food has been praised as among the best anywhere in Mozambique. *US$1,215/1,620 sgl/dbl all-inclusive, with significant low-season discounts.*

Budget and camping To say that the choice of budget accommodation other than on Ibo is limited would be a understatement. The only formal possibility is Dadi Lodge, listed below, but it is also true that travellers could quite easily find a room in a local house on any of the inhabited islands, especially were they to carry a tent as a fallback.

Dadi Lodge (4 units) Matemo Island; contact through Miti Miwiri on Ibo. Set in the village of Palusansa (aka First Village), this community-run lodge offers accommodation in basic A-frames, & also allows camping & provides simple meals. Miti Miwiri can arrange transfers at US$60 for up to 4 people. *Rooms US$12 pp.*

THE QUIRIMBAS MAINLAND

The mainland sector of Quirimbas National Park, though often neglected in tourist literature, is a truly vast entity, protecting some 5,984km^2 of predominantly miombo woodland stretching 150km inland from the Indian Ocean to the east bank of the Messala River. Our ecological knowledge of the park is still limited, but it is known to support significant numbers of lion, leopard, spotted hyena, buffalo, plains zebra, sable antelope, eland, greater kudu, waterbuck, bushbuck, reedbuck, red duiker, suni, bushpig, warthog, samango monkey, vervet monkey and yellow baboon. The elephant population, estimated at 2,000, is thought to be partially migratory, with some seasonal movement to the more westerly Niassa Reserve, but a WWF study of eight collared individuals undertaken in 2009 was unable to establish this for certain. The park is also home to a substantial population of the endangered and African wild dog, with a minimum of six packs and 60 individuals thought to be present, though once again it is unclear whether this should be considered as an eastern extension of the Niassa-Selous population.

An estimated 90,000 people live within the park, mostly along the road corridors and coastline, and another 30,000 inhabit the 10km-wide buffer zone that surrounds it. Although there is some conflict between the Quirimbas's human and animal inhabitants (elephants in particular often raid local subsistence farms), the park was established largely at the request of these local communities. And while tourist development of the park's mainland is still in its infancy, the few options that exist are all to some extent community-driven, a trend that will almost certainly continue as further lodges and camps are added.

WHERE TO STAY

Mareja Lodge (5 rooms) 272 20684; m 82 705 8860; e info@mareja.com; www.mareja.com. This lodge is set on the eponymous community-based Mareja Reserve, which protects a varied habitat of riverine, palm & upland forests, as well as coastal savanna & inselbergs, set within the mainland portion of Quirimba National Park. Elephant, kudu, bushbuck, sable antelope, lion & leopard are resident, & African wild dog pass through from time to time. The project aims to train locals as rangers & has had success in limiting illegal hunting & logging in the area, thus providing a safe zone for local wildlife to thrive. Accommodation is in a restored colonial farmhouse abandoned after independence & sleeps up to 10, & camping is permitted. Meals can be provided if ordered in advance, while activities include guided walks, game drives, birdwatching & community dances. The drive from Pemba to Mareja Lodge takes up to 3 hours, using 1 of 2 routes. The shorter (70km) coastal route along the Quissanga road via Metugé requires 4x4 throughout & can be impassable during the rainy season. The longer route through the interior entails following the surfaced EN243 towards Mocímboa da Praia as far as Nanduli (about 100km from Pemba), then turning right onto a dirt road & following it for another 40km to the lodge. Transfers can be arranged through Kaskazini in Pemba. *US$20 pp bed, US$10 pp camping.*

Guludo Beach Camp (9 units) 269 60569; m 82 723 4470; enquiries@guludo.com; www.guludo.com. Founded on 'fair trade tourism' principles & operated in conjunction with a UK-registered charity, this small honeymoon-friendly lodge overlooks what was voted the world's 14th-best deserted beach by the UK newspaper *The Observer* & the 13th-best location in the world by *Sabado Magazine* in Lisbon – a long unspoilt stretch of white sand fringed with palm trees. Accommodation is in spacious beachfront tented or adobe bandas with macuti roofs & a barefoot luxury ambience. The restaurant serves food bought daily from local fishermen, & activities include diving, snorkelling, village visits, seasonal whale watching, sunset cruises & visits to Ibo. An important & impressive aspect of the lodge is its support of local community projects, & it is also actively involved in marine research. The lodge is situated at the northern end of the park more or less opposite Matemo Island & about 15km south of Mucojo. Most people fly here from Pemba

NUARRO LODGE

Set on Memba Bay about 100km south of Pemba and 50km north of Nacala, this isolated upmarket lodge is not actually situated within the Quirimbas, but it is similarly geared towards honeymooners, divers and marine enthusiasts seeking an exclusive beachfront retreat. Accommodation is in 12 vast beachfront chalets with king-size bed, walk-in nets, indoor and outdoor showers, a lounge area, and a large wooden veranda and sun deck. The lodge has a private dive centre that also offers snorkelling, sea kayaking, dhow trips to Ilha de Moçambique and Lúrio Falls, walking and cycling eco-trails, birdwatching and cultural village tours. Rates are US$445/590 single/double inclusive of meals and non-motorised activities. For further details contact m 82 304 4049 or 82 301 4294; e trienke@nuarro.com; www.nuarro.com.

GIANT COCONUT CRAB

Looking for all the world like a refugee from an improbable science fiction B-movie, the giant coconut crab is the world's largest terrestrial crustacean, attaining a mass of 5kg, a length of up to 50cm, and a leg span of 1m. The foremost of its five leg-pairs terminates in deadly pincers capable of scything straight through a wooden broomstick, or of lifting an object six times its body weight. Pairs two to four, meanwhile, are tipped by smaller pincers that enable the crab to clasp tightly onto the trunks of the vertical palm trees it habitually ascends.

The first recorded description of this massive decapod was penned by the 17th-century Dutch naturalist Georgius Rumphius, who noted that it was 'always on land, without ever getting into the water' and that 'it climbs Coconut Trees, and pinches off the nuts, and then searches under the tree for the ones that were thrown down'. More than a century later, the 'monstrous' terrestrial crab and 'wonderful strength' of its pincers so captured the imagination of Charles Darwin that he devoted a full page of his landmark *Voyage of the Beagle* to describing how an associate 'confined one in a strong tin box ... the lid being secured with wire; but the crab turned down the edges and escaped [and] actually punched many small holes through the tin!'

Darwin was the first to document the crab's ability to break open a coconut using its mighty pincers: 'The crab begins by tearing the husk, fibre by fibre, always from that end under which the three eye-holes are situated; when this is completed, the crab commences hammering with its heavy claws on one of the eye-holes till an opening is made. Then turning round its body, by the aid of its posterior and narrow pair of pincers it extracts the white albuminous substance.'

Unusually for a crustacean, the coconut crab only reaches sexual maturity at the venerable age of five years, and some individuals live to be at least 30. The young are amphibious but the adult is a confirmed landlubber that would drown were it to be submerged for any time. Several idiosyncrasies are associated with this terrestrial lifestyle. It has an acute sense of smell thanks to a 'nose' that most closely resembles those of terrestrial insects, a textbook example of convergent evolution.

Its remarkable capacity to climb smooth palm trunks to a height of 6m is encapsulated by Dr Karen Burns's evocative recollection of a 'big adult coconut crab dining on a dead rat that he had hauled high up onto a tree limb leopard-style'. Then there is its magpie-like propensity for wandering back to its daytime lair with a booty of shiny household objects, as alluded to in its German name palmendieb (palm thief) as well as in the Latin binomial *Birgus latro* (robber crab).

(landing at Matemo's airstrip for a boat transfer) but the road here is in good condition & a land transfer from Pemba is a lot cheaper than flying. *US$520–790 dbl depending on season & type of room, inclusive of meals & most non-motorised activities.*

Meluco Community Project Contact Kaskazini (see page 317) for details. This dusty small town lies in the western sector of the Quirimbas National Park, about 50km west of Muaguide on the EN243. Basic accommodation is available at Casa Anna Maria, & the surrounding countryside offers wonderful walks (with newly trained guides) to the top of several inselbergs offering stunning views. There is also a chance of wildlife encounters & birdlife is abundant.

Taratibu Bush Camp (3 units) Contact Kaskazini (see page 317) for details. The only other place to stay in the mainland part of Quirimba National Park, this fantastically remote camp comprises 3 self-catering chalets alongside a river & below a trio of dramatic inselbergs, one of which has an impressive baobab forest on its crown. The chalets are very comfortable, to the standard of a South African national park rest camp, & have an en-suite hot showers. Guided walks are the main activity, with elephant & greater kudu common in the dry season, & the surrounding woodland & rivers host an immense variety of birds. Access is by 4x4 only & bookings are essential. It lies about 3hrs' drive from Pemba, following the EN242 west to within about 30km of Montepuez, then heading north along a dirt track (full directions can be obtained upon booking), so could be visited *en route* to the Niassa Reserve (see page 356), though a stopover of at least 2 nights is recommended.

PANGANE

Situated about 50km east of the EN243 north, this remote Mwani fishing village – *sans* electricity, mobile phone reception or internet – boasts an extremely pleasant white beach, set on a spit of land that points out towards Ilha Macaloe, and a long-standing reputation as a good place to get away from it all. It lies less than 10km north of the Quirimba National Park boundary, and the area still supports significant (but elusive) populations of large mammals such as buffalo, elephant and lion. But the focus of attention here is the beach, which offers a range of seaside activities – it's easy to hire a boat to explore the surrounding reefs or to any of the Quirimba islands – and offers stunning sunsets over the fishing boats moored off the sprawling village. Pangane is one of the few places in this part of the country that caters to backpackers, and it is relatively accessible on public transport, particularly for people who are already heading north from Pemba towards the Tanzanian border.

GETTING THERE AND AWAY

By car Coming from Pemba, you first need to follow the surfaced **EN106/243** towards Mueda as far as Macomia. Here, you must turn right onto the **EN528**, the first 40km of which, as far as Mucojo, is hard dirt, variable in quality but overall quite easy to drive. The shorter 12km section between Mucojo and Pangane is more challenging, veering from rutted dirt road to sand track, and trying to do it in anything other than a 4x4 is foolish.

By chapa A trickle of chapas runs along the EN528, leaving from the same junction as buses north and south; some only go as far as Mucojo, while others continue to Pangane. The cost will be the same, around US$4, and the journey time to Mucojo is around four hours. Pangane itself is another hour or so's drive, and while you could walk it in theory, it will entail around 10km over rough road that turns into a sand track around halfway.

WHERE TO STAY AND EAT

Campamento Pangane (Aka Hashim's Camp) This locally owned campsite is sited at the end of the village, at the narrowest point of the spit. If it wasn't for the reed wall you'd be able to see the sea on both sides at once. Given some notice they can produce good seafood dishes, & fabulous garlic & lemon piri-piri. They also have 3 chalets for hire, should you not have your tent with you. Hashim the owner works at the fish-processing factory in the village. *US$12/17 sgl/dbl; US$6 camping.*

Casa Suki In the centre of the village, with small but pleasant enough rooms, though they can get very hot during the summer nights. *Rooms US$8.*

20

Niassa Province

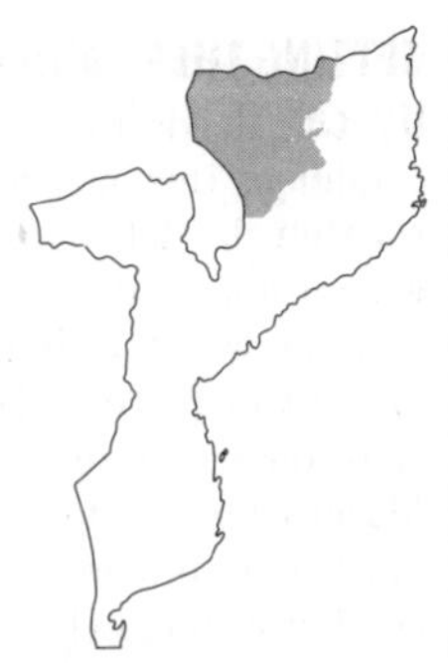

Niassa is Mozambique's driest, most remote, poorest and least densely populated province. It's also one of the most beautiful, with scenery ranging from the mountains of the Rift Valley to the shores of Lago Niassa (Lake Malawi). Samora Machel used to treat the province as a dumping ground for people who weren't entirely behind Frelimo after independence, and it is still known as 'Ponte Final' among officials, for whom a posting there is regarded as career dead-end. This partly explains why Niassa was the birthplace of Renamo (albeit with Rhodesian midwifery) and why the opposition party still enjoys strong support here.

Niassa has the smallest population (1,027,000) in the largest area (129,056km^2) of any Mozambican province, and the villages tend to be based along the roads and around the lake. Most travellers only see a small part of the province, skirting through Cuamba *en route* between Nampula and Malawi, but its real highlights lie further north. The shores of Lago Niassa provide a peaceful counterpoint to the busier Malawian side of the same lake, and the provincial capital Lichinga is a breezy montane town where you might finally find a use for the sweater that your mum made you bring along 'just in case it gets cold at night'. For wildlife enthusiasts, there is also the vast and remote Niassa Reserve, which extends over 42,000km^2 along the border with Tanzania.

CUAMBA

The most important route focus in northwest Mozambique, Cuamba is the western terminus of the railway line (and road) to Nampula (for Pemba and Ilha de Moçambique), the main roads north to Lichinga and Lago Niassa, a quieter route southeast via Gurué to Quelimane, and several crossing points west into Malawi. Formerly called Nova Freixo (New Ash), it has a population of around 102,000, making it one of the largest towns in the Mozambican interior. Set along the Muanda River at an altitude of 575m below a horseshoe of attractive mountains, it is not the most inspiring of places, being relatively dry, dusty and chilly, and rather quiet despite its status as a university town (the Catholic University's Department of Agriculture is based here).

Situated about 10km northeast of the town centre, Serra Mitucué rises to 1,803m above the surrounding plains, and is the source of several streams, including a tributary of the Muanda that has been dammed at Chefe Namacôma to form a kilometre-long serpentine lake that provides hydro-electric power to the town. The dam is quite high up on the eastern side of the massif, and the hike from the base takes two hours. Guides and directions can be obtained from the Hotel Vision 2000 or Pensão São Miguel, and the staff at the latter can also rent out bicycles for the day.

GETTING THERE AND AWAY

By car Roads to and from Cuamba are mostly unsurfaced and in quite poor condition. This includes the rough but staggeringly beautiful **EN8** east to Nampula via Mutuali, Malema and Ribáuè, a 360km stretch that may require 4x4 after rain and will most likely entail a full day's driving (if you want to break it up, Malema is your best bet, with the choice of staying over at the inexpensive Pensão Malema or the pricier Complexo Malaya). At Mutuali, about 65km east of Cuamba, a 100km road runs south to Gurué. Northwest of Cuamba, a 140km stretch of the EN8 runs to the Malawian border town of Mandimba, from where the **EN249** runs for about 145km north to the provincial capital Lichinga. Though it is unsurfaced, this road is in pretty good nick and can be covered in about five hours in a private vehicle.

By chapa and train Most **chapas** leave from around railway station at the southern end of town. Chapas to Mandimba cost US$5 and take about three hours, while chapas to Lichinga cost US$10 and take about six hours. Direct pick-ups to Gurué leave at 05.00 and cost US$7, but it is also possible to take the **train** as far as Mutuali and catch road transport from there. No chapas run to Nampula – the road is too bad – and most people use the train. Coming from Nampula by train, you can be sure there will be chapas to the border towns of Mandimba and Entrélagos waiting for your arrival.

For details of the passenger train between Cuamba and Nampula, see the *Getting there and away* section for Nampula, page 273.

WHERE TO STAY

Mid-range

Quinto Timbwa (25 rooms) 2km out of town off the Mandimba Rd; m 82 300 0752. This unexpected gem, set in a patch of indigenous bush overlooking a small artificial lake, is the best place to stay for those with private transport & a possibility for those without, as it is only a 25min walk from the railway/chapa station, & well signposted. Accommodation ranges from small twin rooms with fan & shared bathroom to cottages with sitting room, TV, AC, fridge & en-suite bathroom with hot shower & tub. The restaurant, reached via a wooden bridge over the lake, serves very acceptable meals for around US$4–6, & an unusually hearty b/fast is included in all room rates. *US$20 dbl using common shower; US$35–45 en-suite dbl.*

Hotel Vision 2000 (20 rooms) Av 3 de Fevereiro; 271 62632; e book@vision-2000.biz; www.vision-2000.biz. The closest thing to an international hotel in Cuamba, this long-serving central institution has clean, comfortable en-suite rooms with AC & TV. The terrace bar & restaurant serves a predictable selection of chicken, fish & curry dishes in the US$3–6 range. *US$50/75 B&B sgl/dbl.*

Budget

Pensão Cariacó (22 rooms) Av 5 Novembro; 271 62595/62685. A decent budget hotel set around a green courtyard about 5mins' walk from the railway station. The rooms are nothing to shout about but seem good value (at least unless you have just crossed from Malawi) & the pricier rooms come with private bathrooms &/or TV. Secure parking. *US$10/16 sgl/dbl; US$20–25 en-suite dbl.*

Pensão São Miguel Av 3 de Fevereiro. A couple of doors down from Vision 2000, the São Miguel has quiet but slightly frayed rooms, some with en-suite bathroom, TV & fridge. It also has secure parking & an adequate restaurant. Feels overpriced. *US$15 dbl with shared ablutions or US$25/30 en-suite sgl/dbl.*

WHERE TO EAT There isn't a huge range of places aside from the hotels, of which the Vision 2000 (*06.00–22.00 daily*) and the superior but less central Quinto Timbwa

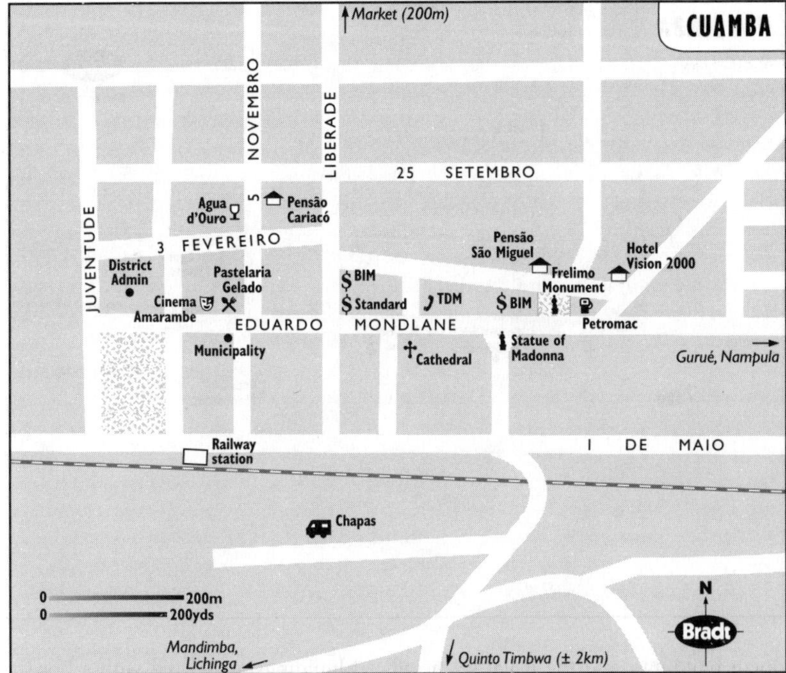

stand out. Alternatively the **Agua d'Ouro** (opposite the cathedral) looks like a nice place to while away a few hours in the evening, although it's more of a bar than a restaurant. Next door to the cinema, the **Pastelaria Gelado** serves a good range of pastries, drinks and sandwiches, and it has a small supermarket. In the middle of the park on Avenida 3 de Fevereiro, the **Quiosque Deucan** serves snacks and small meals during the day. The market is very small and has a limited range of fresh fruit and vegetables.

OTHER PRACTICALITIES

Banks and ATMs There are two branches of BIM Millennium as well as a Standard Bank, all with ATMs.

Hospital To the left-hand side of the square, in front of the railway station.

Internet TDM used to have one PC with an internet connection in the same building as the post office, but it appeared to be closed on last inspection.

Post office In the centre of town, just over from the statue of the Madonna.

Security The disused airstrip south of the town centre is an army barracks, and best avoided or you risk a protracted run-in with the police.

MANDIMBA AND MASSANGULO

Situated at the west of the EN8 about 140km from Cuamba, Mandimba is the most popular and probably the best road crossing between Mozambique and Malawi. There's not much to the twin itself, just a block or two of slightly run-

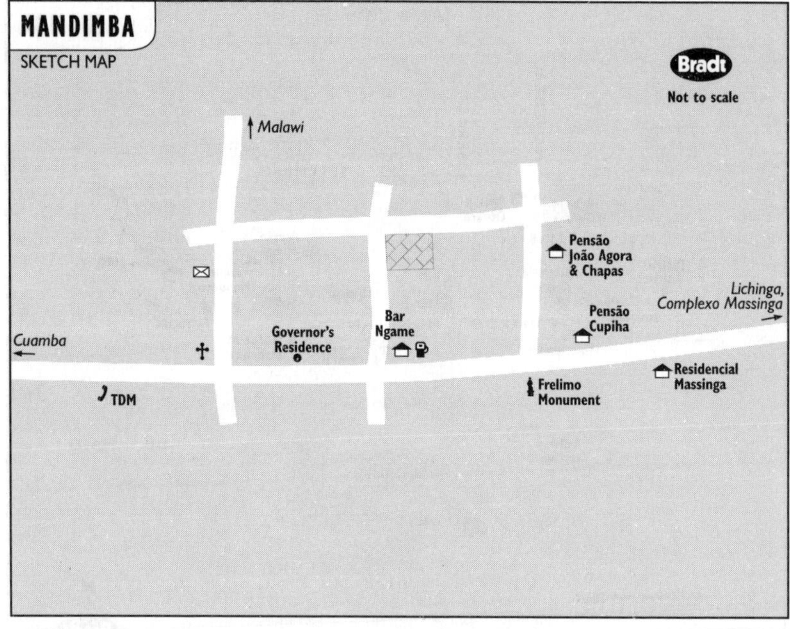

down buildings, and the usual set of official buildings associated with a border town. If you are heading to or from Malawi you'll find that taxis are bicycles along similar lines to those in Quelimane – the fee for a lift along the 4km road between Mandimba and the Malawian border is around US$1. Alternatively you can walk, or just hang around at the junction in town and try to hitch.

On the Malawian side of the border, a hugely attractive 35km road winds downhill to Mangochi, a substantial town with plenty of accommodation set on the west bank of the Shore River, and there is plenty of transport from there on to the evergreen resorts of Monkey Bay and Cape Maclear in Lake Malawi National Park.

Roughly 65km north of Mandimba, Massangulo is a characterful small town about 2km east of the main Cuamba–Lichinga road. It is situated at the base of a pretty mountain, and centred on the oldest Catholic mission in the region, whose extraordinary church was evidently built without cement. Massangulo could be an attractive place to spend a couple of nights, particularly if you like walking, though there is no formal accommodation as far as we can ascertain. Most vehicles heading between Cuamba and Lichinga don't divert to Massangulo, but you can ask to be dropped at the signposted turn-off and walk from there.

WHERE TO STAY AND EAT

Complexo Massinga (11 rooms) m 82 300 0778. The largest & nicest of a few adequate lodgings in Mandimba, a block or 2 north of the border junction along the road to Lichinga. Accommodation is a series of clean, well-appointed rondawels. There's also a restaurant serving meals for around US$3–5, an open-air disco & secure parking. *US$13 en-suite dbl; US$25 with TV & AC.*

LICHINGA

Founded in 1931 with the name of Vila Cabral, Lichinga is the capital of Niassa Province, the main domestic gateway to the Mozambican shore of Lago Niassa, and the country's eighth-largest city, with a rapidly growing population currently estimated at 165,000. It is the main population centre for the Yao people, who also live in bordering parts of Malawi, and whose long Muslim tradition dates back to their involvement in the 19th-century slave trade.

Set on a plateau that forms part of the eastern Rift Valley escarpment above Lago Niassa, Lichinga lies at an altitude of around 1,350m, and has a refreshingly breezy climate. The well-watered and fertile soils around town support the unusual combination of exotic pine plantations and more characteristic tropical vegetation such as mango trees and leafy plantains.

Lichinga has a markedly different atmosphere from any other large town in Mozambique, and without being in any way spectacular, has a relaxed, temperate mood that might end up enticing you to stay slightly longer than you had planned.

GETTING THERE AND AWAY

By air There is an **airport** about 7km north of the city centre, off the road to Metangula, and **LAM** (*Av FPLM; 27 120434*) flies there from Maputo several times a week.

By road The main routes in and out of Lichinga are the 145km unsurfaced **EN249** south to Mandimba, the adequately surfaced 110km EN249 north to the lakeshore port of Metangula, and the magnificently nippy **EN242**, which is surfaced for 310km east to Marrupa. All these roads can be driven in an ordinary saloon car. There are plenty of **chapas** in both directions along the EN249, leaving from the station next to the market, and it's not uncommon for lorries looking for passengers to swing by there as well. Chapas to Metangula or Mandimba cost around US$5 each.

WHERE TO STAY

Upmarket

Girassol Lichinga (72 rooms) Av Filipe Samuel Magaia; 271 21280; m 82 300 3676; e girassollichinga@visabeira.co.mz; www.girassolhoteis.co.mz. This 4-star hotel in the centre of the city caters mainly to business travellers, but is also the most comfortable option for tourists. The tiled en-suite rooms are very spacious if perhaps a little under-furnished, but they all come with DSTV, combination hot tub/shower & free Wi-Fi. There is a good ground-floor restaurant. *US$68/76 sgl/dbl; suites from US$100; all rates B&B.*

Mid-range

Pensão Ponte Final (14 rooms) Av Filipe Samuel Magaia; 271 20912; m 82 304 3632. This comfortable lodge on the verge of the city centre has clean en-suite motel-style rooms with TV, hot water & fridge. Facilities include a restaurant & secure parking. *US$20/26 sgl/dbl including a cursory b/fast.*

Residencial 2+1 (25 rooms) Av Primeira; 271 21632; m 82 088 0880. Recognisable from afar thanks to the bright orange exterior, this pleasant & popular new hotel has clean en-suite rooms with DSTV, fan, AC & hot shower. *US$34/43 sgl/dbl.*

Pousada Lichinga (16 rooms) Av Filipe Samuel Magaia; 271 20176. This central stalwart, a few doors up from the Girassol, is adequate but nothing special, despite recent renovations, & feels overpriced for what you get. *US$26/30 sgl/dbl with shared ablutions; US$30/33 en-suite sgl/dbl.*

Budget

Pensão Mangazi de José Chissanga Nacuinja 271 20592; m 84 271 5632. Magnificently named & tucked away on a street off the market, this place is only a 1min walk from the chapas, & pretty good value, the higher-priced rooms having firm beds & en-suite bathrooms. *US$10 sgl using shared ablutions; US$20 en-suite sgl.*

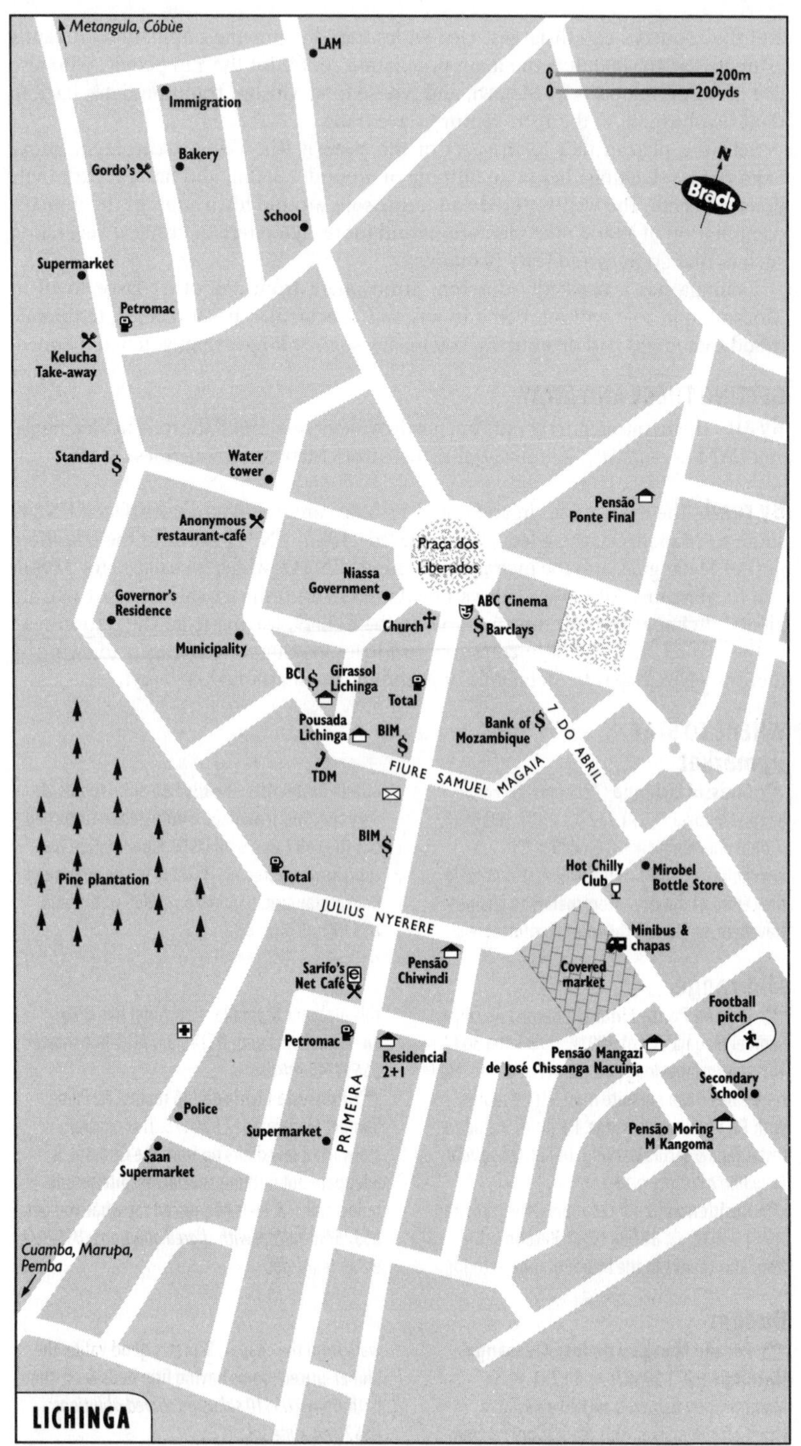
Metangula, Cóbùe
LAM
0 200m
0 200yds
Bradt
N
Immigration
Bakery
Gordo's
School
Supermarket
Petromac
Kelucha Take-away
Standard
Water tower
Anonymous restaurant-café
Praça dos Liberados
Pensão Ponte Final
Niassa Government
ABC Cinema
Church
Barclays
Governor's Residence
Municipality
BCI
Girassol Lichinga
Total
Bank of Mozambique
7 DO ABRIL
Pousada Lichinga
BIM
TDM
FIURE SAMUEL MAGAIA
BIM
Hot Chilly Club
Mirobel Bottle Store
Total
Pine plantation
JULIUS NYERERE
Minibus & chapas
Sarifo's Net Café
Pensão Chiwindi
Covered market
Football pitch
Petromac
Residencial 2+1
Pensão Mangazi de José Chissanga Nacuinja
PRIMEIRA
Secondary School
Police
Supermarket
Pensão Moring M Kangoma
Saan Supermarket
Cuamba, Marupa, Pemba
LICHINGA

Shoestring

Pensão Moring M Kangoma (25 rooms) m 82 551 2659. Also just around the corner from the chapa station, this rabbit warren of a place is as basic as it gets, but the dingy cell-like rooms seem clean & have nets. *US$5/7 sgl/dbl.*

WHERE TO EAT AND DRINK

Sarifo's Net Café Av Primeira; 07.00–21.00 daily. Situated diagonally opposite the Residencial 2+1, this place could reasonably bill itself as the 3-in-1: internet café with free Wi-Fi, cafe/bakery serving fresh sweet & savoury pastries & sandwiches, & bona-fide restaurant serving a standard range of Mozambican fish, meat & chicken dishes, along with pizzas & burgers. There's indoor & outdoor seating, & very pleasant feel about the place – recommended. *US$2–6.*

Girassol Lichinga (see page 345) 07.00–22.00 daily. This hotel restaurant is the smartest in town, & arguably the best. The food is a bit overpriced, but servings are generous & few other central options stay open in the evening. *Mains US$11–15.*

Gordo's It'd be easy to miss this place, tucked away in what could easily be mistaken for a backstreet garage in the northwest end of the town centre, but the food's good & cheap.

Anonymous restaurant-café Av Filipe Samuel Magaia. Opposite the water tower & easily recognised by the orange exterior with a Manica beer sign, this looks more like a bar than a restaurant or cafe, & it is certainly well stocked booze-wise. *Also serves a selection of inexpensive meals such as fish & chips for around US$3.*

Hot Chilly Club Av Julius Nyerere. One of a cluster of bars in the Feira Popular next to the market, this distinguishes itself from the pack by having satellite TV & pool tables.

OTHER PRACTICALITIES

Banks and ATMs All the main banks are represented in Lichinga, including Barclays, Standard, BIM Millennium and BCI, and most branches have ATMs within a block of the central Praça do Liberados.

Internet The best option is Sarifo's Net Café, which has computers for browsing as well as Wi-Fi.

Hospital On Avenida Trabalho (*27 120 211*).

Post office Opposite the BIM Millennium on the corner of Avenidas Filipe Samuel Magaia and Primeira.

Police There is a police station on Avenida Trabalho opposite the hospital and another one on Avenida Primeira just down from Praça dos Liberados (*21 120 751*).

Shopping If you are self-catering, there are several supermarkets to choose from. The best is probably the Supermercado Saan on Avenida Trabalho opposite the hospital, but there are a few others along Avenida Primeira and Avenida Filipe Samuel Magaia. The central market has a better than average selection of vegetables, fruit and meat on offer.

LAGO NIASSA (LAKE MALAWI)

Better known to outsiders as Lake Malawi, Lago Niassa is the third-largest lake in Africa (and ninth largest in the world), running for 585km from north to south, and up to 75km wide from east to west. By any name, it is a remarkable body of water, lying at the southern end of the Rift Valley system, the immense geological scar that cuts through Africa all the way from the Red Sea to the Zambezi Valley. Up to 700m deep, it is hemmed in by the dramatic mountains of the Rift Valley escarpment, which tower more than a kilometre above its surface in places. Known for its thrillingly clear water and relatively low pollution levels, it probably harbours a greater variety of fish than any other lake in the world, including hundreds of endemic cichlid species.

The bulk of Lake Niassa lies within Malawi, but the northeastern waters are territorially part of Tanzania, while some 200km of the eastern shore falls within the Mozambican province that shares its name. The Mozambican part of the lake is poorly developed for tourism by comparison with Malawian resorts such as Nkhata Bay and Cape Maclear, but it is no less beautiful, and its westward orientation is ideal for catching the sunsets for which the region is famed. Furthermore, there

CICHLIDS OF LAGO NIASSA

The staggering diversity of Africa's terrestrial fauna is old news, but few people are aware that it also harbours the greatest freshwater fish diversity of any continent. And nowhere does this diversity reach such heights as in Lago Niassa, whose 850 described fish species – with more awaiting formal discovery – exceed the number of known freshwater species in Europe and North America combined

Lago Niassa's fish diversity is the product of the most dramatic incidence of explosive speciation known to evolutionists. The majority of these fish species are cichlids – pronounced 'sicklids' – a perch-like family of freshwater fishes called Cichlidae that ranges through the Middle East, Madagascar, Asia and South and Central America. It is in Africa's three largest lakes, however, that this widespread family has undergone an unprecedented explosion of evolutionarily recent speciation that has resulted in it constituting an estimated 5% of the world's vertebrate species.

The cichlids of Africa's great lakes are generally divided into a few major groupings, often referred to by scientists by names used locally in Malawi and/ or Mozambique. These include the small plankton-eating *utaka*, the large, pike-like and generally predatory *ncheni*, the bottom-feeding *chisawasawa* and the algae-eating *mbuna*. People who have travelled in any part of Africa close to a lake will almost certainly have dined on one or other of the tilapia (or closely related *oreochromis*) cichlids, large *ncheni* that make excellent eating and are known locally as *chambo*. To aquarium keepers, snorkelers and scuba divers, however, the most noteworthy African cichlids are the *mbuna*, a spectacularly colourful group of small fish of which some 300 species are known from Lake Malawi alone.

The *mbun*a of Lago Niassa first attracted scientific interest in the 1950s, when they formed the subject of Dr Geoffrey Fryer's classic study of adaptive radiation. This term is used to describe the explosion of a single stock species into a variety of closely related forms, each of which evolves specialised modifications that allow it to exploit an ecological niche quite different from that occupied by the common ancestral stock. This phenomenon is most likely to occur when an adaptable species colonises an environment where several food sources are going unused, for instance on a newly formed volcanic island or lake. The most celebrated incidence of adaptive radiation – the one that led Charles Darwin to propose the theory of evolution through natural selection – occurred on the Galapagos Islands, where a variety of finch species evolved from one common seed-eating ancestor to fill several very different ecological niches.

is a genuine sense of adventure attached to exploring this off-the-beaten-track corner of Mozambique, though the lakeshore does now host a couple of superb eco-friendly upmarket destinations in the form of the award-winning Manda Wilderness Community Conservation Area and the newer and less well-known Mbuna Bay Lodge (see page 351).

There are three main points of access to the Mozambican shore of Lago Niassa. Starting in the south, Meponda lies almost directly east of Lichinga along a good 65km road, so is the easiest place to get to from the provincial capital. Metangula has better facilities than Meponda but is roughly 110km from Lichinga, albeit along a road that is now surfaced in its entirety. The more remote village of Cóbuè lies another 100km north of Metangula, along a road that can be tricky in parts, but its proximity to Malawi's popular Likoma Island makes it a good point to cross between Malawi and Mozambique.

The explosive speciation that has occurred among Africa's cichlids is like Darwin's finches amplified a hundredfold. The many hundreds of cichlid species in Lake Tanganyika and Lago Niassa evolved from a handful of river cichlids that entered the lakes when they formed about two to three million years ago. (No less remarkable is the probability that the 200 or so cichlids in Lake Victoria all evolved from a few common ancestors over the 10,000–15,000 years since the lake last dried up.) In all three lakes, specialised cichlid species have evolved to exploit practically every conceivable food source: algae, plankton, insects, fish, molluscs and other fishes. Somewhat macabrely, the so-called kiss-of-death cichlids feed by sucking eggs and hatchlings from the mouths of mouth-brooding cichlids. No less striking is the diverse array in size, coloration and mating behaviour displayed across different species. In addition to being a case study in adaptive radiation, the cichlids of the great lakes are routinely cited as a classic example of parallel evolution – in other words, many similar adaptations appear to have occurred independently in all three lakes.

Why this should have occurred with the cichlids rather than any of several other fish families is a question that is likely to keep ichthyologists occupied for decades. One factor is cichlids are exceptionally quick to mature, and thus have a rapid turnover of generations. Their anatomy also appears to be unusually genetically malleable, with skull, body, tooth and gut structures readily modifying over relatively few generations.

This capacity to colonise new freshwater habitats is boosted by a degree of parental care rare in other fish – the mouth-brooders, which include all but one of the cichlid species of Lago Niassa, hold their eggs and fry in their mouth until they are large enough to fend for themselves. Bearing in mind that the separation of breeding populations lies at the core of speciation, there is also mounting evidence to suggest that cichlids have a unique capacity to erect non-physical barriers between emergent species – possibly linked to a correlation between colour morphs and food preferences in diverging populations.

Africa's lake cichlids are never likely to rival its terrestrial wildlife as a tourist attraction. All the same, snorkelling and diving in Lago Niassa is both thrilling in itself, and a humbling introduction to what has justifiably been described as a 'unique evolutionary showcase'.

NIASSA OR MALAWI?

The original local name for Lago Niassa is something of a mystery. The name Niassa (or Nyasa) probably dates to 1859, when the explorer David Livingstone reached the lakeshore and mistakenly applied the generic local term for lake (Nyasa or Nyanza) to his discovery. Throughout the colonial era, the lake was officially known as Nyasa or Niassa, and the country we now know as Malawi was called Nyasaland. In 1964, however, Nyasaland gained independence from Britain under the leadership of Dr Hastings Banda, who retitled both the country and the lake Malawi.

Several explanations have been put forward for this. Banda himself once claimed that Malawi is an adaptation of 'Maravi', the name of a (possibly unrelated) lake depicted on JBB d'Anville's famous 18th-century map of southern Africa. Maravi is also the name of an iron-smelting empire that flourished in the region in the 15th century, and is widely seen as the precursor to the modern-day Chewa people of south-central Malawi. Another story is that Maravi is a local word meaning 'flaming water', a reference to the dazzling sunrises and sunsets that frequently illuminate the lake's surface.

Whatever the truth, while Malawians and and most outsiders now know the lake as Malawi, this name has never been favoured in the other two countries that share its waters, so it is still officially and colloquially known as Lake Nyasa in Tanzania and Lago Niassa in Mozambique.

The more adventurous traveller might be interested to know that there are walking paths between Meponda, Metangula and Cóbuè (though the sandy paths are not particularly suitable for cycling). The stretch from Meponda to Metangula, for instance, will take about three days for a good walker, who should carry enough food and water to last the whole trip. If you're looking for inspiration, the admirable English doctor Peg Cumberland has walked the entire length of the coast innumerable times since 2004, with nothing but a backpack of medicine to treat locals who have no access to proper medical facilities. Known locally as Dr Peg, she has also trained about 400 locals as volunteer health carers, and was awarded an MBE in the New Year Honours List for 2010.

MEPONDA The closest lakeshore settlement to Lichinga, Meponda is little more than a glorified village whose few concrete buildings are mostly derelict. It lies on an attractive sandy beach that arcs for a kilometre or more below low wooded hills, and although there's nowhere formal to stay at present, you could sleep on the beach. A company called **Lúrio Empreendimentos** (271 28010; e *lempreendimentos@teledata.mz*) in Lichinga plans to open a restaurant and campsite here in September 2011, with rooms to follow by the end of the year. Chapas from Lichinga to Meponda cost US$2 and take up to two hours.

METANGULA The largest settlement on the Mozambican shore of Lago Niassa (which *truly* isn't saying a great deal), Metangula is of ignominious historical significance as the most important port on the eastern lakeshore when the slave trade was at its height in the mid-19th century. Back then, it effectively served as the eastern counterpart to Nkhotakota (Malawi), the base of the notorious Jumbe dynasty, founded in 1845 by coastal Arabs who shipped many thousands of coast-bound slaves across the lake to Metangula annually over the next five decades. So far as can be ascertained, few relics of those times survive in Metangula today, though the area remains predominantly Muslim while the more northerly part of the Mozambican lakeshore is mainly Christian.

Although it's the administrative centre for Lago district and the site of the country's only inland naval base, Metangula has a very out-of-the-way feel about it, and it comes across more like an amorphous sprawling village than a proper town. In the main administrative area, centred around a long oval of roads atop a hilly peninsula, a few ambitious but rather run-down government buildings rub shoulders with boarded-up shops and open green patches that could by no stretch of the imagination be called gardens. Between this and the main Lichinga–Cóbùe road is the low-rise commercial and residencial centre, where a good market, a couple of pensões and a museum are set amid mud-and-thatch houses. On the plus side, this small peninsular town is surrounded by the lake on three sides, seems very relaxed and friendly, and plenty of English is spoken.

Rumours that an upmarket lodge would be built at the tip of the village during the lifespan of the last edition have yet to translate into reality. But motorised visitors seeking good-quality accommodation near Metangula are now catered for by the superb Mbuna Bay Lodge, which lies on an isolated bay about 15km out of town. For more budget-conscious travellers, the place to head for is the smaller village of Chiwanga (also spelt Chuanga), which has a lovely lakeshore location about 8km along the road to Cóbùe, and a couple of decent accommodation options. Note that neither Metangula nor Chiwanga has a bank or ATM, but travellers coming from Malawi will have no problem changing excess kwacha here. More surprisingly, as we went to print we were informed that Metangula now has an internet café, based in the old cathedral.

Getting there and away

By car Lichinga is connected to Metangula by a good surfaced 110km road, about 90 minutes' drive and very do-able in a saloon car, though there are a couple of moderately potholed stretches.

By chapa Regular chapas between Lichinga and Metangula cost around US$3.50 and take up to three hours.

By boat Metangula is now the only Mozambican port visited by the MV *Ilala*, a comfortable and affordable Malawian boat that has been plying the lake waters between Monkey Bay and Chilumba since 1952. On its northward leg, the boat usually stops at Metangula early on Saturday morning, and it comes past again at around midday Tuesday for the southbound leg, though delays are commonplace. If you are entering Mozambique this way, note that the immigration office at Metangula does not currently issue Mozambican visas, and if you arrive without one, expect to be given a rough time before being planted on the next chapa to Lichinga to get one there. Unless this changes, or you have bought a visa in advance, better to disembark the *Ilala* at Likoma and cross from there to Cóbùe, where visas can be issued.

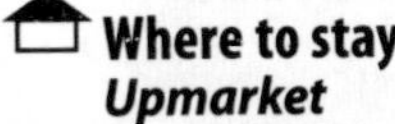

Where to stay

Upmarket

Mbuna Bay Lodge (8 rooms) 82 536 7781; e colongueretreat@hotmail.com; www.mbunabay.ch. Situated at Nkholongue village 15km north of Metangula, this Swiss-built lodge stands on a long sandy beach lined with baobabs & mango trees below the brachystegia-

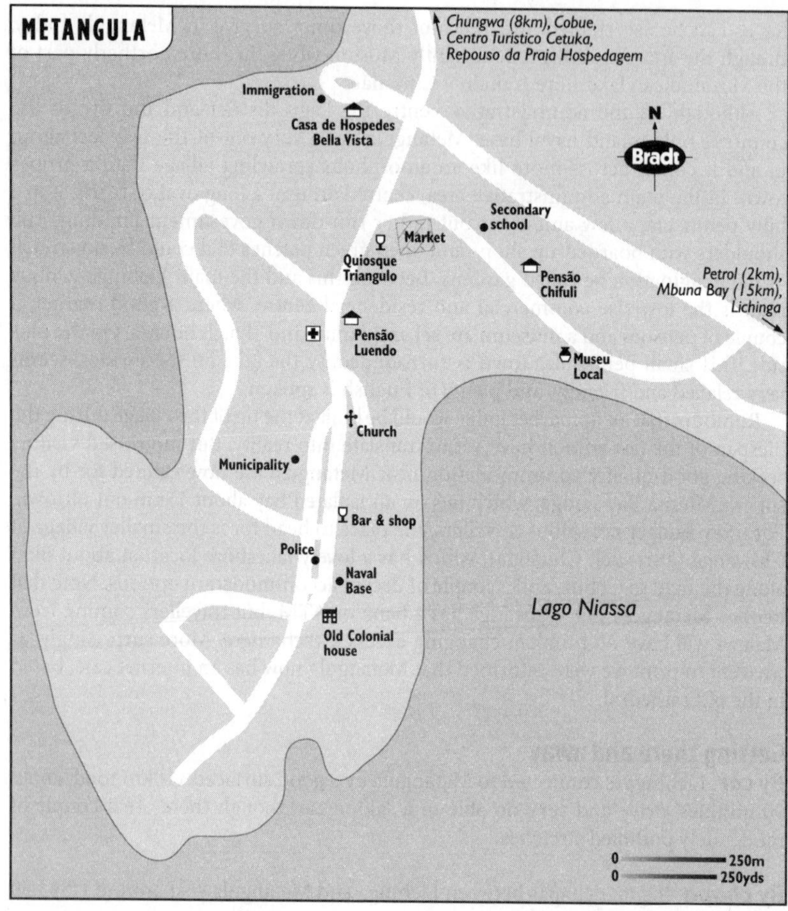

covered slopes of the Rift Valley wall. A very eco-friendly set-up, it operates on solar electricity only, employs almost all its staff from the nearby village, serves imaginative vegetarian meals made mainly with organic ingredients grown on site, & allocates a significant portion of proceeds to community development projects including construction of a clinic & primary school. In addition to a swimming beach, the rocky area offshore is good for snorkelling (plenty of colourful *mbuna* fish & the occasional otter); other activities include kayaking, community visits to the local chief & a traditional doctor, yoga, a 2hr hike to the top of Mt Chifuli, or a guided lakeshore ramble to Metangula. The en-suite bamboo-&-thatch beach houses are spacious, characterful & very comfortable, with king-size beds under a walk-in net, as well as verandas with hammocks. There are also some more functional brick houses using outdoor hot showers. Coming from Lichinga, the turn-off is signposted to the left about 2km before you arrive in Metangula; from there it is another 12km on rocky sloping roads to the lodge itself (if in doubt, ask anybody to point you towards Nkholongue. *US$125/165 sgl/dbl in beach house; US$95/125 in brick house; all rates FB with some activities included.*

Budget

Centro Turístico Cetuka (8 rooms) m 82 291 2012. Situated on the beach in Chiwanga, 8km north of Metangula, this pleasant, good-value complex has a helpful English-speaking owner, adequate en-suite rooms, camping space & a decent restaurant serving fish-based meals for around US$6. It is poorly signposted: coming along the Cóbùe road from the direction of Metangula, turn left about 10m past the first sign for 'Praia do Chuanga', follow this road for about 600m, turn left immediately after crossing a small concrete bridge, from where it is another 50m or so to the entrance. If you don't have a vehicle you could walk here from Metangula, but it's a feat of endurance in the lakeshore heat, so you might prefer to try for a rare chapa. *US$11 dbl; US$8 per tent.*

Repouso da Praia Hospedagem (12 rooms) 271 20431; m 82 629 9780. Situated in Chiwanga directly behind Cetuka, this is not quite so nice as its neighbour & lacks a beachfront location, but the basic rooms are clean & pretty good value. A bar & restaurant are attached. *US$6/8 sgl/dbl.*

Shoestring

Casa de Hospedes Bella Vista (8 rooms) m 82 739 2403. Situated next to the beachfront immigration office at the northern end of Metangula town, this place has very basic rooms with ³/₄ beds. *US$3 per room.*

Pensão Chifuli (10 rooms) Set in a quiet compound near the market, this has rather stuffy rooms with dbl or ³/₄ bed, net & standing fan. *US$5 per room.*

Where to eat and drink If you stay at Mbuna Bay or Chiwanga, you'll most likely want to eat at your hotel. Unsurprisingly, there are no tourist-orientated restaurants in Metangula itself, but you will find some local restaurants in the market. For a cold beer, try the Quiosque Triangulo near the market. You could also try to track down the **Chilenge Restaurant** (m *82 757 5740*), which has been recommended by a local and is reputedly in the administrative area near the police station.

What to see Metangula and Chiwanga are agreeable enough places to while away a day or two but aside from the museum described below and the beach at Chiwanga, neither boasts much in the way of formal attractions. If you're looking for a guide to take you on hikes to Mount Chifuli or to a nearby waterfall, or want to go fishing in a local dugout canoe, ask near the market for a guide called Lourenço Thawe.

Museu local (*07.00–12.00 Tue–Sun, 13.30–17.00 Tue–Sat; entrance free*) Opened in 2008, this small but well-organised local history museum is housed in the former Escola Primaria João de Deus, a historic red-and-white building in the heart of Metangula. Exhibitions cover the history and cultures of Lago district from the Stone Age to the present. Archeological artefacts from recent excavations include stone tools from Micuio, 5km south of Metangula, Iron Age pots found in nearby Mount Chifuli, and material containing the oldest evidence of sorghum cultivation in Africa. Other displays explore the region's role in the 19th-century slave trade and the associated arrival of Islam, as well as the spread of Christianity from the UMCA mission on Likoma Island, established in 1886 as part of a drive to end the slave trade. A separate exhibition looks at the exotic origins of crops such as maize, cassava, sweet potato and tomato, and at indigenous edible plants. There's also an oral history archive, where you can read or listen to 95 recordings of individual biographies, folk tales and songs, and a photo wall of locals who contributed to this collection.

CÓBÙE The village of Cóbùe lies on the mainland opposite Likoma Island, and is heavily influenced by its proximity to this Malawian territory. Kwachas are more useful here than meticais, English is quite widely spoken, mobile phones are on the Malawian network, and until recently it was one of the ports serviced by the

MV *Ilala*. Cóbùe is a lovely part of the world – very remote and quiet, and the only electricity comes from private generators – but the main reason you'd visit is *en route* between Malawi and Mozambique (the crossing is very straightforward, and this is the one place on the lake where Mozambican visas are issued).

Besides the scenery, which is gorgeous, the only thing to see in Cóbùe is the surprisingly big Catholic church, which has been roofless since it was attacked in the civil war, but is still used on Sundays. About 7km south of the village is the small fishing village of Mbueca, site of Mchena Wede Backpackers and a great place to experience traditional lakeshore living. Cóbùe is also the springboard for visits to Nkwichi Lodge in the Manda Wilderness Area (see opposite)

Getting there and away

By car The 100km dirt road from Metangula clings to the lakeshore north for about 10km, just past Chiwanga, before it ascends the brachystegia-strewn slopes of the Rift Valley escarpment inland, then descends back to the lakeshore as it enters Cóbùe. It's a tough drive, alternately rutted and sandy in parts, and there are some steep slopes to contend with, but a 4x4 or strong pick-up should get through in three hours. The wild scenery serves as compensation for the bumpy ride, and you can expect to see some wildlife – most likely baboons and a variety of birds – along the roadside.

By chapa Chapas along this road mostly amount to pick-up trucks that cram as many people in the back as possible, then a few more, but you should be able to organise a (dusty) lift without too much sweat. Ask around at any of the lodges and expect to pay around US$3–4 per person.

By boat The *Ilala* no longer stops at Cóbùe, but you can disembark at Likoma and catch a local boat across from there. These usually leave once daily, at around 07.00, and the fare is nominal, but they may not leave if there are insufficient passengers and you are unwilling to pay enough to make it worth the captain's while to make a special crossing.

The *Dangalilia* is a local boat service that runs between Metangula and Aldeia Ngofi twice weekly, stopping by request at all villages in between, including Chiwanga, Mbueca and Cóbùe. The *Dangalilia* administration in Metangula can be contacted at ☎ 82 791 5520. It does the northbound run on Monday and Thursday, leaving Metangula in the early morning and arriving at Cóbùe in the early afternoon, and the southbound leg on Tuesday and Friday.

Where to stay and eat

Mchenga Wede Backpackers m 82 431 5013; e info@mbunabay.ch. Set up & run by the local manager of Mbuna Bay, Mchenga Wede is a very relaxed lakeshore lodge set in the tiny fishing village of Mbueca about 7km south of Cóbùe market. There is accommodation in cosy reed-&-thatch huts, a campsite, a restaurant serving fresh fish & chicken dishes for US$10, a bar, & a range of activities on offer, including swimming, snorkelling, birdwatching, hiking, village tours & a visit to a nearby river where crocodiles are resident. You can get to Mbueca on the *Dangalila*, or by walking along the rocky lakeshore south from Cóbùe in 4–5hrs, or by asking a chapa between Cóbùe and Metangula to drop you at the village of Manda Mbuzi, & following a 2hr footpath from there. Alternatively, ask around in Cóbùe for Senhor Bandali, who can set up transport there. *US$15 pp room; US$10 pp camping.*

Khango Beach (6 rooms) m +265 99 385 3638 (Malawi). Situated on the beach facing Likoma, close to where the *Ilala* used to drop passengers, this place offers basic accommodation in twin reed huts using common ablutions. Basic meals available. *US$8 twin; US$4 per tent camping.*

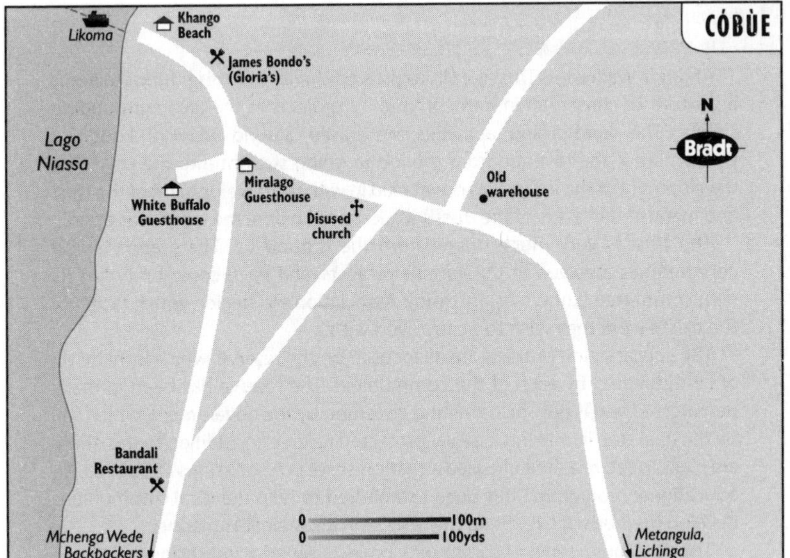

White Buffalo Guesthouse (8 rooms) Also known by its local name Nyati Yoyela, this block of lakeshore rooms includes one that is substantially bigger than the others & contains a dbl bed. It's well looked after, but wasn't taking visitors at the time of research as all rooms were semi-permanently occupied by employees of a mining company.

Miralago Guesthouse (6 rooms) Just up the hill from the White Buffalo, this has slightly bigger rooms, with 3/4 bed, electricity & mosquito nets. *US$6 per room.*

James Bondo's Also known as Gloria's (depending on whether the husband or the wife is running it that day), this is down on the beach. The food is basic but good, & there's the usual range of soft drinks & beers available. He's willing to change meticais for kwacha should you need them.

MANDA WILDERNESS AREA Established in 1999 on a mountainous peninsula between Metangula and Cóbùe, the multiple award-winning Manda Wilderness Project is a 1,200km² game reserve managed in trust for local communities comprising some 20,000 Nyanja people. It protects a patchwork of habitats, including brachystegia woodland and riverine forest, savanna, swamps, streams and mountains, all running down to the lovely beaches and crystal-clear waters of Lago Niassa. Game viewing is done on foot or from a canoe, and the most frequently seen large mammals are zebra, monkeys and otters, though others present include lions and wild dogs. Though it falls within Mozambique, Manda operates mostly as an extension to the safari circuits in Malawi and Zambia, and can be reached by boat from Likoma or Cóbùe, or by charter flight from anywhere in the region.

Where to stay

Nkwichi Lodge (6 chalets) m 82 709 7920; e info@mandawilderness.org; www.mandawilderness.org. Sited about 10km south of Cóbùe, this is the only lodge in the reserve itself, & can cater for only 14 guests in 6 individual chalets. The site itself is stunning – the chalets are widely spread on a rocky peninsula flanked by a lovely white beach & dense brachystegia woodland, & are built from locally available materials & designed to blend into their surroundings, incorporating granite outcrops as part of the structure. Each has its own private bathroom with shower & bath, & there is a central dbl-floored restaurant, bar & library.

MANDA WILDERNESS COMMUNITY TRUST

The Manda Wilderness Trust is a UK-registered charity that raises funds towards a mixture of conservation and community projects in the area surrounding Cóbùe. The fund-raising activities are based around Nkwichi Lodge, a proportion of the revenue from the lodge going straight into the trust. The development of the lodge was dovetailed in with the development of the trust and many of the facets of the trust's work started before the lodge was open.

The trust is very much driven from the ground up. There are 15 local communities involved in the various projects, and each community has its own committee (known as an 'Umoji Association') to decide which facets of the trust's work they wish to be involved with.

The conservation projects are all focused on the reserve, which is made up of land donated by each of the communities. The reserve has been formally demarcated and is now just awaiting gazetting by the government, which will be the final step in making it a fully protected reserve. In addition to this, there are plans to set up a similarly sized aquatic reserve in association with US Aid. An educational programme has been established to help the local communities develop methods of exploiting the reserve in a sustainable manner.

The trust runs a series of community projects aimed at improving facilities in each village, with each Umoji Association deciding what is most needed in its village. Thus far the trust has contributed to the construction of six schools with a further four or five planned, a maize mill to enable villagers to grind their own produce, and a clinic based in Cóbùe with equipment supplied from the UK and training carried out by a local NGO. To help bring the communities together, the trust has organised a local football league, supplying kit, goalposts, fees for referees and the possibility of arranging training schemes in the future.

A third strand, slightly smaller at the moment, is the agricultural project. The aim of this is to introduce local farmers to permaculture and find methods by which the local diet can be improved. Each Umoji Association selects up to five villagers who attend a training course at the lodge's farm. The training courses cover the importance of proper nutrition, soil conservation, planting and care of seeds and plants, pest control and the importance of healthy soil to the potential for selling excess produce in local markets.

The success of the trust can be gauged by the interest being shown by the Mozambican national government – in August 2005 11 directors of the provincial governments visited the reserve and the trust, and in June 2006 President Guebuza visited Cóbùe, the first time in Mozambique's history that its president had visited Niassa Province.

There's plenty to keep you busy, from tracking animals to activities on the lake such as canoeing, snorkelling or sailing, & you also have the option of visiting some of the local communities to see how the project has benefited them. There again, you can just sit in a hammock. The whole set-up is hugely impressive, & serves as a perfect example of how a lodge could & should be developed. *From US$375/580 sgl/dbl including all meals & non-motorised activities.*

NIASSA RESERVE

Situated in the remote north of Mozambique bordering Tanzania, Niassa Reserve is Africa's third-largest wildlife sanctuary, extending over 42,000km² – that's twice as large as the Kruger Park, almost three times the size of the Serengeti, or (to place it in a non-African context) comparable in area to Denmark or the state of Massachusetts. Niassa is also one of Africa's most under-publicised and unvisited safari destinations, serviced by just one exclusive wilderness camp on the forested banks of the picturesque Lugenda River, and while the reserve's isolation has held back development, it has also allowed it to retain an untrammelled feel that is increasingly rare in modern Africa. Scenically, Niassa is hugely impressive, dominated by the Lugenda River, whose shallow perennial flow is hemmed in by wide sandbanks and a ribbon of lush riparian forest. Away from the river, there are vast tracts of miombo woodland studded with bulbous fleshy grey baobabs, and immense granite inselbergs that rise majestically into the deep blue African sky, hundreds of metres above the surrounding plains.

It should be stated clearly that Niassa is not a suitable safari destination for those seeking a quick 'Big Five' fix. True, all but one of this much-hyped quintet is present here in significant numbers (the exception being rhinos, who were poached to extinction in the 1980s) but the only near-certainty in the course of a standard three-to-four-day visit would be elephant. What Niassa offers is an altogether more holistic wilderness experience, one in which the reserve's mesmerising scenic qualities and wonderfully rich birdlife figure as prominently as its mammalian wildlife. This is also one of those rare reserves where activities need not be dominated by motorised game drives: guided game walks offer the opportunity to experience the African bush as its inhabitants do, on foot, without the constant roar of an engine providing an unwanted aural backdrop; while canoeing on the river – past spluttering hippos, drinking elephants and a splendid array of birds – is utterly entrancing. In short, Niassa offers as untrammelled an African bush experience as still exists in the 21st century.

HISTORY AND CONSERVATION The Niassa Reserve was established in 1954 to protect the dry and thinly inhabited territory that lies between the Ruvuma and Lugenda rivers, but it was effectively abandoned between 1975 and 1988 as a result of the civil war. The reserve's modern boundaries were established in 1998 and include the original 22,000km^2 core zone between the rivers, along with some 20,000km^2 of buffer zones. It was also in 1998 that the Mozambican government entered into an innovative partnership with the Sociedade para a Gestão e Desenvolvimento da Reserva do Niassa (SRN), a private organisation that retains exclusive rights to manage and develop the reserve. The SRN subsequently divided the reserve into 17 management zones, of which six currently operate as hunting and/or photographic safari concessions (the most important being Block L7, aka Luwire Concession, which is the site of Lugenda Wilderness Camp, the only functioning tourist facility not dedicated to hunting), while the other nine are to be made available on a similar basis.

The Niassa Reserve is one of two core components in the Selous-Niassa Transfrontier Conservation Area (SNTCA), the other being the Selous Game Reserve, which extends over 47,000km^2 of southern Tanzania. The SNTCA also incorporates Tanzania's Mikumi National Park, Udzungwa National Park and Kilombero Game Protected Area, all of which border the Selous, and its ecological integrity was greatly boosted in 1999 with the creation of the 17,030km^2 Selous-Niassa Corridor Reserve, which extends southward from the Selous border to share 175km of international Ruvuma frontage with the Niassa Reserve. All told, the SNTCA can now lay claim to being Africa's largest contiguously protected chunk of untrammelled bush, extending over a total area exceeding 150,000 km^2. And it harbours some of Africa's most prodigious wildlife, including at least 5% of the global population of African elephant, around 20% of the world's free-ranging African wild dogs, and what are quite probably the largest existing populations of lion, buffalo, hippo and sable antelope.

Some 30,000 people inhabit the Niassa Reserve and its immediate boundaries, a third of them in the district capital Mecula, which lies within the eastern section of the core reserve below Serra Mecula. Despite this low density, the interests of the reserve's human and wildlife populations are often at odds. The greatest problem exists along the rivers, which are heavily fished, not only by local Mozambicans but also by people hopping over the border from Tanzania. A certain amount of snaring occurs along and away from the river, and occasional instances of commercial poaching have been reported, but the good news is that this appears to occur at sustainable levels and estimated numbers of most key species have remained stable or risen over the 12-year tenure of the SRN, which currently provides employment for more than 200 locals. And the risks faced by people living in and around the reserve should not be ignored: at least 11 people have been killed in lion attacks since 2002, while elephants frequently raid smallholdings for crops, and crocodiles lurk in the rivers. In the long term, it is to be hoped that tourist revenue will alleviate these risks by generating further work opportunities and income for local communities.

GEOGRAPHY AND VEGETATION The Niassa Reserve accounts for about a third of Niassa Province's surface area, and also extends eastwards into Cabo Delgado. It lies within the drainage basin of the Ruvuma River, which flows east for more than 300km along the reserve's northern border with Tanzania. The most important of several tributaries, and in many respects the lifeblood of Niassa, is the Lugenda River, which flows along the southeastern boundary between the core area and buffer reserve to its confluence with the Ruvuma. The Ruvuma and Lugenda are both large sand-bed rivers with a strong perennial flow, and their mutual watershed feeds numerous other seasonal rivers that flow only during the rainy season of late October to May. Although the eastern border of Niassa is a full 200km from the coast, the terrain is essentially low-lying, with a base altitude of 100m at the Lugenda–Ruvuma confluence, rising to around 600m in parts of the west. These flattish dry plains are interrupted – to thrillingly dramatic effect – by a liberal scattering of black granitic inselbergs that rise hundreds of metres above the canopy to give the reserve its unique scenic quality. The tallest mountain in the reserve is Serra Mecula, which rises to a prominent 1,441m peak above the town of the same name.

Some 95% of the Niassa Reserve consists of miombo woodland, which can be divided into two broad types. Dominant in the southwest is tall closed brachystegia-dominated woodland, while elsewhere there tends to be a more open cover of mixed broadleaved woodland including various brachystegia, julbernadia, combretum and terminalia species. The two main rivers support a ribbon of evergreen riparian woodland and riverine thickets, and patches of acacia woodland are often associated with the clayey soils close to the rivers. Niche habitats include roughly 1km^2 of montane forest in half a dozen scattered patches on the upper slopes of the Serra Mecula, the rocky cliffs and slopes associated with the reserve's trademark granite outcrops, and seasonally flooded grassy depressions called dambos, whose boundaries are often demarcated by a ring of waterberry trees.

WILDLIFE Wildlife in Niassa tends to be less visible than in some other more iconic African reserves, but there is plenty of it around. The most recent published figures, based on 2004 estimates, are 7,000 buffalo, 2,500 bushbuck, 3,500 Lichtenstein's hartebeest, 5,000 warthog, 3,500 plains zebra and around 1,000–1,500 of each of impala, greater kudu, waterbuck, wildebeest and reedbuck. Three of these animals are represented by subspecies endemic to this part of Africa: Niassa wildebeest (slightly larger than other subspecies), Crawshay's zebra (lacks the shadow stripes of other southern zebra subspecies) and Johnston's impala (slightly smaller than most subspecies). More recent estimates place the elephant population close to 20,000, while yellow baboon, vervet monkey and blue monkey are all quite common, with the latter mostly restricted to riverine woodland. The reserve evidently supports one of the world's largest populations of sable antelope, estimated at 13,500 in 2004.

In practical terms, impala, waterbuck and greater kudu are common around Lugenda Wilderness Camp (see page 360) throughout the year, as are warthog and elephant. Hippos belch and wallow in the river near camp, while pairs of dainty klipspringer antelope bound around the boulder-strewn slopes. As the dry season takes its grip, larger concentrations of ungulates gather along the river, and sightings of zebra, wildebeest, buffalo, Lichtenstein's hartebeest and sable antelope become more frequent. Unusually, predators are most visible in the early part of the dry season, when the lush vegetation encourages them to follow game-viewing tracks as they patrol their territories or search for prey. Lion sightings are not quite an everyday occurrence, but the reserve harbours a healthy population of 800–1,000, according to a recent survey undertaken by Colleen and Keith Begg. It's one of the better places to look for African wild dog (see box below), and 20 other carnivore species have been recorded, of which leopard, genet and civet are all quite commonly observed on night drives.

BIRDLIFE The birding in Niassa is excellent. Some of the more interesting everyday species that enjoy high visibility are purple-crested turaco, green woodhoopoe, lilac-breasted roller, brown-hooded kingfisher, brown-headed parrot, African grey hornbill, black-collared barbet (the unusual streaky-breasted *zombae* race), white-fronted bee-eater, collared palm thrush, black-headed oriole and African paradise-flycatcher. It is a good place to see a bunch of miombo specials, including racquet-

WILD DOGS IN SELOUS-NIASSA

The second most endangered of Africa's large carnivores (after the ultra-localised Ethiopian wolf) is the African wild dog *Lycaon pictus*, a fascinating pack animal that was once so abundant it was listed as vermin in many of the 40 countries through which it ranged. Today, this beleaguered creature is IUCN red-listed as Endangered, largely as a result of human persecution and susceptibility to canid diseases spread by domestic dogs, and the non-captive global population is estimated to stand at 4,000–6,000 individuals. The importance of Selous-Niassa to the survival of African wild dogs would be difficult to overstate. It has long been known that the Selous harbours the world's largest African wild dog population: surveys undertaken in the 1990s indicated that every part of the reserve fell within the home range of at least one pack, from which a total population of between 800 and 1,300 was extrapolated. Until recently, little was known about wild dog numbers in Niassa, but a survey undertaken by Colleen and Keith Begg over 2004–6 documented 336 individual wild dogs in 39 packs, and the reserve's population is now estimated at around 450. On a continental level, this means that Niassa ranks immediately below Selous in terms of wild dog numbers, and the total population of the SNTCA probably stands at 1,200-1,500.

tailed roller, pale-billed hornbill, miombo pied barbet, Stierling's wren-warbler, Arnot's chat and Shelley's sunbird, while riverine forest and thicket support the likes of Pel's fishing owl, trumpeter hornbill, brown-throated barbet, Böhm's bee-eater, broad-billed roller, Livingstone's flycatcher and black-throated wattle-eye. Niassa is probably the best site in Mozambique for birds of prey: bateleur and African fish eagle are among the more conspicuous large raptors, while the inselbergs support cliff-nesting species such as Verreaux's (black) eagle, augur buzzard, lanner falcon and the very localised Taita falcon, and the massive crowned eagle and handsome Dickinson's kestrel are frequently seen in the riparian forest.

One disappointment is that the river supports so few waterbirds, possibly as a result of overfishing – you might well see saddle-billed and woolly-necked storks, possibly African skimmer, but there are very few waterfowl, waders or lapwings. Get your timing right, however, and the most alluring avian attraction of Niassa has to be the Angola pitta, a spectacularly coloured but very seldom observed species that usually renders itself conspicuous by call around Lugenda Wilderness Camp during its brief mating season over two to three weeks in November.

GETTING THERE AND AWAY

By air Niassa is a very long way from anywhere by road, and most visitors fly there on a charter from Pemba or the Quirimbas as part of a package based at Lugenda Wilderness Camp.

By car It is perfectly possible to drive there from Pemba or Lichinga, assuming that you have 4x4 and some time at your disposal. The main urban springboard for self-drive visits is Marrupa, which lies about 100km south of the Kiboko entrance gate along a well-maintained unsurfaced road that can be covered in two hours. This road continues north to Mecula across what is the only bridge across the Lugenda into the core area of Niassa Reserve. The Kiboko entrance gate closes at 17.00 and you maybe refused entry if you arrive later, so try to set off from Marrupa before 14.30.

There are three main approaches to Marrupa. The best is the surfaced **EN242** running 310km east from Lichinga, but travellers coming from the coast will more likely use the EN242 west, a somewhat more challenging dirt road that may require 4x4 and leads to Pemba after 440km west of Pemba. Both roads are covered in the boxed text *Pemba to Lichinga on the EN242* (see opposite page). Another option, coming from the south, is the **EN248**, an adequate but unsurfaced 250km road running northeast from Cuamba. If you use this route, the mission at Maúa and the even more remote mission at Nipepe both have beautiful churches decorated in traditional style.

WHERE TO STAY Tourism development in Niassa is still very much in its infancy. There are several hunting camps in some concessions, but at present the only formal option for less bloodthirsty visitors is Lichinga Wilderness Camp, which will hopefully soon extend its accommodation network with the construction of four fly camps elsewhere in the Luwire Concession. It seems likely that other concessions will be developed for tourism during the lifespan of this edition. Also under development is a new community campsite aimed at self-drivers. Until this is up and running, you can camp at the staff headquarters, which has a reasonable toilet block but few other facilities.

Lugenda Wilderness Camp (8 rooms) 213 01618; e enquiries@raniresorts.com; www.lugenda.com. The only tourist facility in Niassa at present is this exclusive riverfront camp set within a portion of the 7,500km2 Luwire Concession used solely for photographic safaris. The camp is set in a strip of riverine running along the south bank of the Lugenda, immediately below an impressive granite outcrop & offering more distant views to Serra Mecula. Accommodation is in luxurious permanent tents with king-size beds, walk-in nets, private balconies, large en-suite bathrooms with hot shower & generator electricity from around 06.00–11.00 & 17.00–21.00. The camp supports plenty of wildlife, including blue & vervet monkey, a multitude of woodland birds (including mewling flocks of trumpeter hornbills,

PEMBA TO LICHINGA ON THE EN242

One of the longest and most remote roads in Mozambique, the EN242 is of interest to self-drive visitors firstly as the most direct route between the coastal port of Pemba (see page 308) in Cabo Delgado and the highland town of Lichinga in Niassa, and secondly as the main access road to the Niassa Reserve. The 750km journey from Pemba to Lichinga breaks up into three distinct phases, and while it could be covered in one long day with a very early start and a modicum of luck, it is probably more realistic to bank on overnighting somewhere *en route*, ideally the small town of Montepuez.

The first stretch is the 240km run from Pemba to Montepuez, which involves following the EN106 west for about 120km to the junction town of Metore, which is where the westbound road becomes the EN242. This is a good tar road the whole way, passing through rather unmemorable scenery and a few equally undistinguished small towns, and you should easily get through within three hours. Montepuez, the largest town along this road, has a fair selection of places to sleep and eat, covered in greater detail on pages 314–15.

The shortest stretch on paper – around 180–200km, depending on which map you believe, and how many unintended diversions you take – is the unsurfaced road between Montepuez and Marrupa. It is also the longest and most difficult stretch in practice, carrying perhaps half a dozen vehicles along a road that frequently amounts to little more than a pair of sandy tyre tracks running through the dense brachystegia woodland typical of this region (an experience reminiscent of how travel was in most of Mozambique shortly after the civil war). This area is fantastically remote, with only a few tiny villages as urban punctuation, and you might well see some wildlife on the way. You shouldn't require 4x4 in the dry season, but it could come in handy, and you will definitely need good clearance and a powerful engine, and may want to deflate tyres in places. The worst stretch of road at the time of writing is about 60–35km before Marrupa, where there are several river crossings that could go horribly wrong if you misjudge the best track to use – if in doubt, get out of the car and ask local advice before attempting anything iffy. In the rainy season, 4x4 will be absolutely essential.

Marrupa itself is a district capital and the junction town for the Niassa Reserve (Kiboko Gate lies 100km to the north along a fair dirt road). It's a more substantial place than you might expect, with a large market, a few adequate restaurants, and reputedly one hard-to-track-down and very basic pensão. More to the point, it is also the improbable start/end point of what is arguably the finest road anywhere in Mozambique, a nippy 310km stretch of pristine surfaced bliss that can easily have you arrive in Lichinga within three hours, assuming you are not too distracted by the memorable mountain scenery.

SERRA JECI (NJESI PLATEAU)

Keith Barnes & Josh Engel (www.tropicalbirding.com)

Like Mount Namuli (see pages 269–72), this remote area on northwest Niassa offers some incredible birding. The same warnings for Mount Namuli apply here – bring plenty of provisions, 4x4 vehicles, and learn some Portuguese to maximise your experience. The most enticing species of this area are long-billed forest warbler (formerly called long-tailed or Moreau's tailorbird) and red-capped forest warbler (formerly called African tailorbird), otherwise only spotted in very small areas of Tanzania. There are many other species that could turn up here, such as Chapin's apalis or Winifred's warbler ... or perhaps something completely unknown.

The long-billed forest warbler is perhaps one of the rarest birds in all of Africa, Once thought extinct until surveys in the 1980s rediscovered the species in the Amani area of the East Usambaras in Tanzania. Birds from the population on the Serra Jeci were only seen again in 2001, when a team from the University of Cape Town rediscovered them here. Continued surveys suggest the entire world population comprises a few hundred birds, and given the massive geographical distances between the two populations one may question whether they are best treated as the same species, and both may be extremely rare and critically endangered.

Besides the forest warblers, there is a long list of tempting birds found in and around Serra Jeci, including Stierling's and speckle-throated woodpeckers, cinnamon-breasted tit, spotted creeper, and olive-headed and Bertram's weavers. The Serra Jeci area remains extremely little known, and given the correct provisions it is worth spending several days exploring the region.

& breeding Angola pittas in November) & the occasional transient elephant or hippo. There's a swimming pool overlooking the river, a lounge with a good selection of field guides & other interpretive material, & excellent meals which are usually eaten at a communal table with staff & other guests. Rates are inclusive of activities such as game drives, guided walks, short canoeing trips, birdwatching excursions & rock climbing. By advance arrangement, the camp can also be used as a springboard for stays at one or more of 4 small fly camps currently under development deeper in the reserve, or for exciting wilderness hikes and canoeing trips of several days' duration. Closed December–May. *US$900 dbl inclusive of all meals, activities, house wines & most other drinks, laundry & park fees.*

Mussomo Community Campsite Currently under development by the same management as Lugenda, this community-owned camp on the north bank of the Lugenda, opposite Kiboko Gate, will be aimed at self-sufficient self-drive visitors. Facilities are likely to include simple ablution blocks, a barbecue area with firewood supplied, & a dining area. Guides will need to bring all food, drinks & fuel with them. Rates are likely to be *US$20 pp per night.*

Appendix 1

LANGUAGE

Mozambicans speak Portuguese in a more sing-songy way than the Portuguese themselves, and their speech is much easier to understand than the guttural string of consonants Europeans use. There are two renderings of the verb 'to be'. *Ser* (*sou, és, é, somos, são*) is more or less for characteristics or permanent states, and *estar* (*estou, estás, está, estamos, estão*) for temporary states. Many words can be guessed from English or Spanish, and some Spanish-speakers get along quite well with a mixture of *português* and *espanhol*, popularly known as *portanhol*. Examples include many words ending with -ion in English and -on in Spanish which are similar in Portuguese but end in -ão (plural usually -ões) – *televisão, razão* (reason), *verão* (summer).

Take care, though, for some similar Spanish and Portuguese words have completely different meanings: *niño* (Spanish = child) versus *ninho* (Portuguese = nest); *pretender* means 'intend' rather than 'pretend' (*fingir*); and it is best not to describe an ordinary man as *ordinário* as this implies he is common or vulgar.

Asterisks (*) denote words derived in or specific to Mozambique or Africa.

I would strongly recommend that, in addition to a phrasebook, you get a good pocket Portuguese dictionary. While phrasebooks have a place in the early stages of learning a language, their limitations very soon become a hindrance to both the learning process and simple communication. A good pocket dictionary is a useful tool – we use the *Oxford Portuguese Mini-Dictionary*, although there are other equally good ones out there.

PRONUNCIATION

ã + a followed by m	nasal (similar to 'ang')
c	ss before i or e; k elsewhere
ç	ss
cc	ks
ch	sh
g	soft j before i or e; hard g elsewhere
j	soft j (as in French)
lh	ly (as in Spanish ll)
nh	ny (as Spanish ñ)
o or ô	oo when unstressed
o or ó	o when stressed (as in hot)
ou	o sound (as in both or window)
õ + o followed by m	nasal (similar to 'ong').
qu	k before i or e; kw elsewhere
s	z or sh (at end of syllable)
x	sh or s
z	soft j

Double vowels are pronounced separately:

compreendo	*compree-endo*
cooperação	*coo-operassaoo*

VOCABULARY

Greetings

Good morning	*Bom dia*
Good afternoon	*Boa tarde*
Good evening	*Boa noite* (meeting at night as well as taking leave)
Hello	*Hola*
Goodbye	*Até logo* (until later)
What is your name?	*Como se chama?*
My name is	*Chamo-me* [*shamow mu*]
How are you?	*Como está* [*komo shta*]?
I am well	*Estou bem* [*shtow be(ng)*] (or a reply to *como está* might be *bom, obrigado/boa, obrigada* = I am good, thank you)

Basic phrases

please	*se faz favor* (or *por favor*)
thank you	*obrigado/a* (I'm obliged)
you're welcome	*de nada* (ie: 'it's nothing' – reply to thank you)
There is no …	*Não há* (or *falta*) …
Excuse me	*Di sculpe* (or *Perdone me*)
Give me	*De me*
I like to …	*eu gosto de …*
I would like …	*(eu) queria …*
How?	*Como?*
How much?	*Quanto?*
How much (cost)?	*Quanto custa/é isso?*
What?	*(O) Quê?*
What's this (called)?	*Como se chama isso?*
Who?	*Quem?*
When?	*Quando?*
Where?	*Onde?*
From where?	*Donde?* (contraction of *de onde*)
Where is … ?	*Onde fica /é / está … ?*
Do you know?	*Você sabe?*
I don't know	*Não sei*
I don't understand	*Não compreendo* (also *não percebo*)
yes	*sim*
no	*não*
perhaps	*talvez [talvej]*
good	*bom/boa* (m/f)

Food and drink

bean	*feijão* (*feijoada* = a dish of rice, beans and pork)
beef	*carne de vaca*
beer	*cerveja*
bon appétit	*bom apetito*
bread	*pão*

breakfast	*matabicho* (* lit. 'kill beast')
cake	*bolo*
cassava, manioc	*mandioca*
chicken	*frango* (as food)
chips, French fries	*batatas fritas*
coffee	*café*
dinner	*jantar*
drink (noun)	*uma bebida*
drink (verb)	*beber*
eggs	*ovos*
fish	*peixe* [*payshy*] or *pescado* (as food)
fizzy soft drink	*refresco*
juice, squash	*sumo*
lunch	*almoço*
maize beer	*byalwa (*)*
maize, mealies	*milho*
maize porridge	*vuswa (*)* or *nsima* (* in the north, *nsheema*)
meat	*carne*
milk	*leite*
pasta	*massa* (NB *pasta* = file or briefcase)
pork	*carne de porco*
potato	*batata*
restaurant	*restaurante*
rice	*arroz*
rum (local)	*cachaça*
snack	*merenda* or *lanche* (elevenses)
spirits	*aguardente*
sweet potato	*batata doce*
tea	*chá*
to eat	*comer*
water	*água*

Other useful words

a little (not much)	*pouco/a*
a lot (very, much)	*muito/a*
aeroplane	*avião*
after	*depois (de)*
bank	*banco*
bathroom, toilet	*casa de banho*
battery (dry)	*pilha*
bed	*cama*
before	*antes (de)*
block (of buildings)	*quarteirão*
boarding house	*pensão*
book	*livro*
bus	*machimbombo* (*) *autocarro* (Portuguese)
car	*carro*
casualty department	*banco de socorros*
change	*câmbio*
child	*criança*
church	*igreja*
city, town	*cidade*
cold/hot water	*água fria/quente*
(hard) currency	*devisas*
day	*dia*
diarrhoea	*diarréia*
doctor	*médico*
dry season	*estação seca*
enough	*bastante*
fever	*febre*
film (roll of)	*película*
hill	*colina*
hospital	*hospital*
hotel	*hotel*
house	*casa*
hut	*palhota*
ill	*doente*

lake	*lago*	road	*estrada* [*shtrada*]
large	*grande*	sea	*mar*
lorry, truck	*camião*	shop	*loja*
malaria	*malária, paludismo*	small	*pequenho/a*
market	*mercado*	street, road, highway	*rua*
money	*dinheiro*	swamp, marsh	*pântano*
mosque	*mesquita*	today	*hoje*
mosquito net	*mosquiteiro*	tomorrow	*amanhã*
mountain	*montanha*	to hurt (or ache)	*doer*
never	*nunca*	to swim	*nadar*
night	*noite* [*noyty*]	toilet paper	*papel higiênico*
nightclub	*boite* [*booat(y)*]	too much	*demais/demasiado/a*
nothing	*nada*	train	*comboio*
now	*agora*	travellers' cheques	*cheques de viagem*
on the beach	*na praia*	village	*aldeia*
railway	*caminho de ferro* (n)	yesterday	*ontem*
	ferroviário/a (adj)	you	*você* (polite, formal),
rain	*chuva*		*tu* (familiar)
river	*rio*		

NUMBERS Each part of a cardinal number is changed to ordinal when referring to a place in a sequence (eg: 2,112th = two thousandth hundredth tenth second), so it is simpler to call the 11th floor of a building *andar numero onze* than *o décimo primeiro andar*, for instance. For days of the month only the first is an ordinal number (first of May, but two of May etc). Therefore, one can get by with only the cardinal numbers and *primeiro/a* (= first).

1	*um/uma*	21	*vinte e um/uma*
2	*dois/duas*	30	*trinta*
3	*três*	40	*quarenta*
4	*quatro*	50	*cinquenta*
5	*cinco*	60	*sessenta*
6	*seis*	70	*setenta*
7	*sete*	80	*oitenta*
8	*oito*	90	*noventa*
9	*nove*	100	*cem*
10	*dez*	1,000	*mil*
11	*onze*	1,000,000	*milhão*
20	*vinte*		

Appendix 2

FURTHER INFORMATION

Note that many of the books below are difficult to locate through mainstream bookshops but most can be ordered new or secondhand through online booksellers such as amazon.com or amazon.co.uk.

HISTORY AND BACKGROUND

Newitt, Malyn *A History of Mozambique* C Hurst & Co Publishers, 1994. This is probably the best single-volume history of an African country that I've ever come across. Clocking in at more than 600 pages, it is authoritative, stimulating and highly readable, though coverage ends in the mid-1990s, Still, nobody with a passing interest in Mozambique's colourful history should visit the country without reading it.

For those requiring greater detail on a particular period, books that I found to be both useful and readable included the following:

Axelson, Eric *Portuguese in East Africa 1488–1600* Wits University Press, 1973
Axelson, Eric *Portuguese in East Africa 1600–1700* Wits University Press, 1960
Axelson, Eric *Portugal and the Scramble for Africa 1875–1891* Wits University Press, 1967
Beach, David *The Shona and Zimbabwe 900–1850* Heinemann, 1980. A recommended read for its wider coverage of the Karonga Kingdoms and Manomotapa.
Isaacman, Allen and Barbara *Mozambique: From Colonialism to Revolution 1900–1982* Westview Press, 1983.

Some of the better books covering more recent events in Mozambique are the following:

Finnegan, William *A Complicated War: The Harrowing of Mozambique* University of California Press, 1992.
Hanlon, Joseph *Mozambique: Who Calls the Shots?* James Currey, 1991.
Main, Michael *Zambezi: Journey of a River* Southern Book Publishers, 1990. An eminently readable introduction to practically every aspect of southern Africa's largest watercourse, with solidly researched material on the region's history and a wealth of obscure anecdotal detail about some of the more eccentric characters who have been associated with the Zambezi.
Minter, William *Apartheid's Contras: An Inquiry into the Roots of War in Angola and Mozambique* Booksurge, 2008.
Vine, Alex *Renamo: From Terrorism to Democracy in Mozambique* James Currey, revised and updated edition, 1996.
World Biographical Series No 78: Mozambique (edited by Colin Darch & Calisto Pacheleke) Clio Press, 1987. The definitive annotated bibliography of books about Mozambique.

TRAVELOGUES

Crook, Sally *Viva Mozambique* Starling Books, 1997. A personal account of the author's six years of living and working in the country.

Green, Lawrence *Harbours of Delight* Howard Timmins, 1969. A lively and anecdotal travelogue covering most of Africa's main harbours.

Kirkman, James *Men and Monuments on the East African Coast* Willmer Brothers, 1964. An excellent survey of the important old buildings of the Swahili coast.

Middleton, Nick *Kalashnikovs and Zombie Cucumbers: Travels in Mozambique* Phoenix, 1994. Something of a companion piece to Swift's book – though infinitely better – this book offers a similar snapshot of Mozambique 20 years on, during the closing stages of the civil war and shortly after the signing of the 1992 Peace Accord. Hanging out with NGO workers rather than generals, Middleton punctuates his languid and often very funny travelogue with some pithy insights into the detrimental effects of the Western aid industry, a clear background to the civil war, and some fascinating stuff on the occultism that lies close to the surface of rural life in Mozambique.

St Aubin de Terán, Lisa *Mozambique Mysteries* Virago, 2007. This autobiographical account of the establishment of a tourism college at Mossuril (on the mainland opposite Ilha de Moçambique), though a little self-absorbed, contains plenty of interesting material.

Swift, Kerry *Mozambique and the Future* Don Nelson Publishers, 1974. According to the cover blurb, its author was the last journalist to conduct a comprehensive tour of Mozambique before the 1974 coup in Portugal. Notwithstanding a few reservations about assertions such as 'South Africa ... appears to be sincere in her promises of sovereign independence for the Homelands', not to mention the author's evident admiration for the gung-ho antics of the Portuguese officers he encounters along the way, this book does offer an interesting and plausible on-the-spot snapshot of Mozambique during the closing stages of the liberation war.

FIELD GUIDES Any of several field guides to the mammals of southern Africa will be close to comprehensive for Mozambique. For birders, several field guides to southern African birds are available, and these include all species recorded in Mozambique south of the Zambezi.

Hemstra, Phil and Elaine *Coastal Fishes of Southern Africa* National Inquiry Services Centre, 2007. Probably the best one-volume guide to the region's marine fish.

Newman, Kenneth *Birds of Southern Africa* (2010 edition) Struik, South Africa. Recently revised, this classic bird guide remains arguably the most useful book of its type in the field.

Richmond, Matthew *Field Guide to the Seashores of Eastern Africa* SIDA, SAREC & University of Dar es Salaam, 2002. Distinctly rucksack sized.

Sinclair, Ian, Hockey, Phil and Tarboton, Warwick *Sasol Birds of Southern Africa* (2002 edition) Struik, South Africa. This is also very good, indeed many South Africa birders now prefer it to Newman's.

Sinclair, Ian and Ryan, Peter *Birds of Africa: South of the Sahara* (2010 edition) Struik, South Africa. Worth carrying for serious birders heading north of the Zambezi, an area for which coverage in the two guides listed above is incomplete.

Stuart, Chris and Tilde *Field Guide to the Larger Mammals Africa* (2006 edition) Struik, South Africa, 1988. Good all-round guide for a country still finding its feet as a safari destination.

HEALTH

Wilson-Howarth, Dr Jane, and Ellis, Dr Matthew *Your Child Abroad: A Travel Health Guide* Bradt Travel Guides, 2005.

Wilson-Howarth, Dr Jane, *The Essential Guide To Travel Health: Don't Let Bugs, Bites and Bowels Spoil Your Trip* Cadogan, 2009.

WEBSITES Particularly recommended to independent travellers is the website www.mozguide.com maintained by Mozambique travel guru Mike Slater.

The following websites all contain Mozambique-related news stories in English, as well as links to other sites relevant to Mozambique.

www.mozambique.mz
www.allafrica.com/mozambique
www.mozambiquenews.com

Bradt Travel Guides

www.bradtguides.com

Africa

Access Africa: Safaris for People with Limited Mobility £16.99
Africa Overland £16.99
Algeria £15.99
Angola £17.99
Botswana £16.99
Cameroon £15.99
Cape Verde Islands £14.99
Congo £15.99
Eritrea £15.99
Ethiopia £16.99
Ghana £15.99
Kenya Highlights £15.99
Madagascar £16.99
Malawi £15.99
Mali £14.99
Mauritius, Rodrigues & Réunion £15.99
Mozambique £15.99
Namibia £15.99
Niger £14.99
Nigeria £17.99
North Africa: Roman Coast £15.99
Rwanda £15.99
São Tomé & Príncipe £14.99
Seychelles £14.99
Sierra Leone £16.99
Sudan £15.99
Tanzania, Northern £14.99
Tanzania £17.99
Uganda £16.99
Zambia £17.99
Zanzibar £14.99
Zimbabwe £15.99

The Americas and the Caribbean

Alaska £15.99
Amazon, The £14.99
Argentina £15.99
Bahia £14.99
Cayman Islands £14.99
Colombia £16.99
Dominica £14.99
Grenada, Carriacou & Petite Martinique £14.99
Guyana £14.99
Nova Scotia £14.99
Panama £14.99
Paraguay £14.99
Turks & Caicos Islands £14.99
Uruguay £14.99
USA by Rail £14.99
Venezuela £16.99
Yukon £14.99

British Isles

Britain from the Rails £14.99
Eccentric Britain £13.99
Eccentric London £13.99
Slow: Cotswolds £14.99
Slow: Devon & Exmoor £14.99
Slow: Norfolk & Suffolk £14.99
Slow: North Yorkshire £14.99
Slow: Sussex & South Downs National Park £14.99

Europe

Abruzzo £14.99
Albania £15.99
Armenia £15.99
Azores £14.99
Baltic Cities £14.99
Belarus £15.99
Bosnia & Herzegovina £14.99
Bratislava £9.99
Budapest £9.99
Bulgaria £13.99
Cork £6.99
Croatia £13.99
Cross-Channel France: Nord-Pas de Calais £13.99
Cyprus see North Cyprus
Dresden £7.99
Estonia £14.99
Faroe Islands £15.99
Georgia £15.99
Greece: The Peloponnese £14.99
Helsinki £7.99
Hungary £15.99
Iceland £14.99
Kosovo £15.99
Lapland £13.99
Latvia £13.99
Lille £9.99
Lithuania £14.99
Luxembourg £13.99
Macedonia £15.99
Malta & Gozo £12.99
Montenegro £14.99
North Cyprus £12.99
Riga £6.99
Serbia £15.99
Slovakia £14.99
Slovenia £13.99
Spitsbergen £16.99
Switzerland Without a Car £14.99
Transylvania £14.99
Ukraine £15.99
Zagreb £6.99

Middle East, Asia and Australasia

Bangladesh £15.99
Borneo £17.99
Eastern Turkey £16.99
Iran £15.99
Iraq: Then & Now £15.99
Israel £15.99
Kazakhstan £15.99
Kyrgyzstan £15.99
Lake Baikal £15.99
Maldives £15.99
Mongolia £16.99
North Korea £14.99
Oman £15.99
Shangri-La: A Travel Guide to the Himalayan Dream £14.99
Sri Lanka £15.99
Syria £15.99
Taiwan £16.99
Tibet £13.99
Yemen £14.99

Wildlife

Antarctica: Guide to the Wildlife £15.99
Arctic: Guide to Coastal Wildlife £15.99
Australian Wildlife £14.99
Central & Eastern European Wildlife £15.99
Chinese Wildlife £16.99
East African Wildlife £19.99
Galápagos Wildlife £15.99
Madagascar Wildlife £16.99
New Zealand Wildlife £14.99
North Atlantic Wildlife £16.99
Pantanal Wildlife £16.99
Peruvian Wildlife £15.99
Southern African Wildlife £18.95
Sri Lankan Wildlife £15.99

Pictorials and other guides

100 Animals to See Before They Die £16.99
100 Bizarre Animals £16.99
Eccentric Australia £12.99
Northern Lights £6.99
Wildlife and Conservation Volunteering: The Complete Guide £13.99

WIN A FREE BRADT GUIDE

READER QUESTIONNAIRE

Send in your completed questionnaire and enter our monthly draw for the chance to win a Bradt guide of your choice.

To take up our special reader offer of 40% off, please visit our website at www.bradtguides.com/freeguide or answer the questions below and return to us with the order form overleaf.

(Forms may be posted or faxed to us.)

Have you used any other Bradt guides? If so, which titles? ....

....

What other publishers' travel guides do you use regularly? ....

....

Where did you buy this guidebook? ....

What was the main purpose of your trip to Mozambique (or for what other reason did you read our guide)? eg: holiday/business/charity ....

....

How long did you travel for? (circle one)

weekend/long weekend   1–2 weeks   3–4 weeks   4 weeks plus

Which countries did you visit in connection with this trip? ....

....

Did you travel with a tour operator?' If so, which one? ....

....

What other destinations would you like to see covered by a Bradt guide?

....

If you could make one improvement to this guide, what would it be?

....

Age (circle relevant category) 16–25   26–45   46–60   60+

Male/Female (delete as appropriate)

Home country ....

Please send us any comments about this guide (or others on our list).

....

....

....

Bradt Travel Guides

IDC House, The Vale, Chalfont St Peter, Bucks SL9 9RZ, UK

t +44 (0)1753 893444 f +44 (0)1753 892333

e info@bradtguides.com

www.bradtguides.com

TAKE 40% OFF YOUR NEXT BRADT GUIDE!

Order Form

To take advantage of this special offer visit www.bradtguides.com/freeguide and enter our monthly giveaway, or fill in the order form below, complete the questionnaire overleaf and send it to Bradt Travel Guides by post or fax.

Please send me one copy of the following guide at 40% off the UK retail price

No	*Title*	*Retail price*	*40% price*
1	....	....	....

Please send the following additional guides at full UK retail price

No	*Title*	*Retail price*	*Total*
...	....	....	....
...	....	....	....
...	....	....	....

Sub total ....

Post & packing ....

(Free shipping UK, £1 per book Europe, £3 per book rest of world)

Total ....

Name ....

Address ....

Tel .... Email ....

☐ I enclose a cheque for £........ made payable to Bradt Travel Guides Ltd

☐ I would like to pay by credit card. Number: ....

Expiry date: .../........ 3-digit security code (on reverse of card) .....

Issue no (debit cards only) .....

☐ Please sign me up to Bradt's monthly enewsletter, Bradtpackers' News.

☐ I would be happy for you to use my name and comments in Bradt marketing material.

Send your order on this form, with the completed questionnaire, to:

Bradt Travel Guides
IDC House, The Vale, Chalfont St Peter, Bucks SL9 9RZ, UK
t +44 (0)1753 893444 f +44 (0)1753 892333
e info@bradtguides.com www.bradtguides.com

Index

Entries in **bold** indicate main entries; those in *italics* indicate maps

accommodation 59–60
air travel 55
Alto Molócuè 264, *265*
Angoche 279–82, *280*
antelope 27–8
art 23–4
at a glance 2
ATMs 54

background information **2–24**
Banhine National Park 148–9
bargaining 63
Barra Beach 171–3
Barraco dos Assassinatos 171
Bazaruto National Park 187–91
Beira **197–209**, *199*, *204–5*
  accommodation 200–2
  banking 203
  cinema 203
  Corridor 211
  getting there and away 198–200
  golf 203
  history 197–8
  internet 206
  orientation 200
  restaurants 202–3
  shopping 206
  sightseeing 206–9
  swimming pools 206
Bella Vista 132–3
Benguerra Island *see Bazaruto National Park*
Bilene 142–4, *143*
bilharzia 79–81
binoculars 52
birds 30–2, 231, 233, 237
boat travel 55
Bobole 142
bookshops 119
Boroma Mission 247–8
bribery 48
budgeting 54–5
buses 58–9

Cabaceira Grande 302
Cabaceira Pequina 302
Cahora Bassa Dam 245–7
Caia 236
camping gear 51–2
Capatu Forestry Concession 235
car importation 44
car rental 58
Casa dos Noivos 272
Cascata de Namuli 272
cashew apples 308
Catembe 131–2
central Mozambique 193–250, *194–5*
Chai 318
chapas 58–9
charities 69–70
Chidenguele 153
children, travel with 49–50
Chimanimani National Reserve 223–5
Chimoio 212–16, *214*
Chimoio and the Manica Highlands *210*, 211–24
Chinhamapere Rock Art Site 220
Chinizuia Forest 237
cichlids 348–9
civil war 16
climate 4, 39
clothing 52
Cóbùe 353–5, *355*
Colonial period 12–15
conservation 326–7
crab, giant coconut 339
credit cards 54
crime 46–8
crocodile 28, 32
Cuamba 341–43, *343*
culture 23–4

dapple-throat 272
diarrhoea 77–8
disabled travellers 50–1
diving 85–92
documents 56

dog, African wild 26, 359
dolphins 34–5
drinks 62–3
driving 56–7
dugong 35, 335

early history 4–7
East African Coast 1530–1600 8–9
East African Coast 1600–1800 9–10
eating 61–2
economy 18–21
electricity 53
embassies 43

field guides 368
fines 48
first-aid kit 76–7
fish 35–6
flights 43–4
foreign exchange 44, 53–4
further reading 367–8

gay travellers 49
general information 1–93
geography 3–4
getting around 55–8
getting there and away 43–6
Gilé National Reserve 264–6
Gorongosa and the Caia Road 227–38
Gorongosa National Park *226*, 227–32
government 18
Great Limpopo Transfrontier Park *see Limpopo National Park*
Guludo Beach Camp 338–9
Gurué 266–72, *267*

health 71–83
highlights 39–40
hippo 28
history 4–18
hitching 60
HIV/AIDS 81

Ibo 325–33, *329*
Ilha de Moçambique *284*, 285–98, *294*
  accommodation 288–90
  banking 291
  boat trips 291
  Fortaleza de São Sebastião 293–5
  getting there and away 288
  history 286–8, 292, 295
  internet 291
  Maritime Museum 296
  Palace Museum 295–6
  restaurants 290
  Sacred Art Museum 296–7
  São Paulo Palace 295–6
Ilha de Moçambique *continued*
  shopping 291
  sightseeing 292–7
  slave trade 287
  snorkelling 291
Ilha de Xefina 125
Ilha Portuguesa 131
Inchope 235
Independent Mozambique 15–18
Inhaca Island 127–31
Inhambane 155–62, *159*
Inhambane and Surrounds 155–74, *156*
Inhassoro 184–7, *185*
insect bites 80
internet 67

Kruger National Park (South Africa) 126, 144–7

Lago Niassa 347–56, 350
Lake Chicamba 217
Lake Malawi *see Lago Niassa*
Lake Nikwita 316
Lake Poelela 153
land mines 48–9
language 22–3
language 363–6
leopard 26
liberation war 14
Lichinga 344–7, *346*
Limpopo National Park 144–8
Limpopo Valley and Coast South of Inhambane 141–54
lion 26, 28
literature 24
lizards 33
Lugenda Wilderness Camp 360–2
luggage 50–1
Lumbo 300

Machampane Luxury Camp 146
Machel, Samora 14, 16
Macomia 317–18, *318*
Macua face masks 306
Makonde carvers 314
malaria 73–5
Maluane Project 335–6, 337
mammals 26–9, 34–5
Manda Wilderness 356
Mandimba 343–4, *344*
Manica 217–21, *219*
Manyikeni Ruins 182
Mapiko dances 321
maps 53
Maputaland 127–40, 128
Maputo **99–126**, *100*, *106*, *113*
  accommodation 107–9

Maputo *continued*
airlines 118
airport 104
ATMs 119
Baixa 122
banks 119
book shops 119
Casa de Ferro 124
Centre Cultural Franco-Mozambicain 110, 116, 124
chapa 105
cinemas 116
Costa do Sol 112, 125
day trips out of 124–6
embassies 119
entertainment 115–17
football 116
Fortalezada Nossa Senhora da Conceição 121, 123
Geological Museum 121, 122
getting there and away 104–5
handicrafts 118
harbour 123
history 102–4
hospitals 119
Ilha de Xefina 125
internet 118–19
Jardim Tunduru 123
maps 119
markets 117
Matola 125
medical 119–20
money 119
Mucapana Safari Park 125
Museu da Revoluçao 121
Museu Nacional da Moeda 121, 123
Museu Nacional des Artes 121
Natural History Museum 120–1, 122
nightlife 114–15
Núcleo de Arte 121
Old Town 123
passports 116
phone 118
Polana 122
police 115, 116, 119
post 118
Praça dos Trabalhadores 123
railway station 123
restaurants 110–14
safety 115
shopping 117–18
sightseeing 120–6
supermarkets 117–18
taxis 105
theatres 116
tours 105
Vila Algarve 122

Maputo *continued*
walks 122–4
Maputo Special Reserve 133–5
Mareja Lodge 338
marine life 34–7
Marracuene 141–2
Marromeu Buffalo Reserve 237–8
Marrupa 361
Mary Livingstone's grave 236–7
Massangulo 344
Matemo Island 333, 336–7
Matola 125
Maxixe 162–4,*163*
medical facilities 77
Medjumbe Island 335, 337
Meluco Community Project 339–40
Meponda 350
Metangula 350–53, *352*
Milange 273, *273*
Moçimboa da Praia 321–22
Mocuba 262–4, *263*
Mondlane, Eduardo 14
money 53–5
money belt 52
monkeys 27, 28
Montepuez 316–17, *316*, 361
Moribane Forest Reserve 223–4
Morrungulo 173–4
Mossuril 301
Mossuril Bay 298–302, *300*
Mount Binga 223, 224
Mount Gorongosa 232–4
Mount Namuli 269–72
Mount Tsetsera 224–5
Mozambique in the 19th century 10–12
Mozambique Island *see* Ilha de Moçambique
Mphingwe Camp 236
Mucapana Safari Park 125
Mueda 318–21, *320*
music 24

Nacala 302–4, *304*
Namialo 282, *283*
Nampula *274*, 275–83
natural history 25–37
newspapers 66
Niassa Province 341–62
Niassa Reserve 356–62
Njesi Plateau *see Serra Jeci*
northern Mozambique 251–362, *252–3*
Nuarro Lodge 338

overland borders 44–6

Palma 322
Pangane 340
Pansy Island 191

Parque Nacional de Banhine *see Banhine National Park*
Parque Nacional de Bazaruto *see Bazaruto National Park*
Parque Nacional de Gorongosa *see Gorongosa National Park*
Parque Nacional de Quirimba *see Quirimbas*
Parque Nacional de Zinave *see Zinave National Park*
Parque Nacional do Limpopo *see Limpopo National Park*
Pemba *306*, 308–16, *311*
Pemba and the northeast 307–22
Penhalonga 221–22
people 21–2
photography 64–6
police 56
politics 18
Ponta da Linga Linga 173–4
Ponta do Ouro 136–40, 137
Ponta Malongane 135–6
Ponta Mamoli 135–6
Portuguese 363–6
Portuguese occupation 7–8
post 67
practical information 39–70
Praia do Xai-Xai *150*, 152–3
Primeiras Archipelago 282
provinces 3
public holidays 62–3

Quelimane 255–61, *258*
Quilálea Marine Sanctuary 333, 336
Quipaco Island 333
Quirimba National Park *see Quirimbas*
Quirimbas 323–40, *324*
Quisiva Island 333, 336
Quissico 153

rabies 81–2
radio 66
rail travel 55
ray, manta 165
red tape 42–3
religion 23
reptiles 32–3, 34
Reserva Nacional de Chimanimani *see Chimanimani National Reserve*
responsible tourism 67–8
rhinos 29
Rio Elefantes Canoeing Trail 147
road travel 55–8
Ruvuma ferry 317, 319

Salamanga 132–3
Santa Carolina Island *see Bazaruto National Park*
Segundas Archipelago 282
Sena Railway Bridge 238
Serra Jeci 362
Shingwedzi 4x4 Eco-Trail 147
shopping 63–4
SIM card 42
skin infections 78, 79
snakebite 82–3
snakes 32–3
snorkelling 92–3
Sofala 210
Songo *see Cahora Bassa Dam*
southern Mozambique 95–191, *96–7*
sun, protection from 73

Tanzania, border crossing 319
Taratibu Bush Camp 340
telephone 52, 66–7
television 66
Tete (province) 239–49
Tete (town) *240*, 241–44
tickbite fever 82
Tofinho 164–71, *166*
Tofo 164–71, *166*
tour operators 40–2
tourist information 40
travel clinics 75–6
travelling positively 68–70
turtles 34

Unity Bridge (Ruvuma River) 317, 319

vaccinations 71–3
Vamizi Island 335–6, 337
vegetation 25–6
Vila Gorongosa 235
Vilankulo 175–84, *178*
Vilankulo, Inhassoro and Bazaruto National Park 175–91, *176*
visas 42

water 77
whale shark 165
whales 34
when to visit 39
wild dog 359
Wimbe Beach *see Pemba*
women travellers 49

Xai-Xai 148–52, *150*

Zalala Beach 261
Zambézia 255–73
Závora 153
Zinave National Park 148–9
Zongoene 153
Zumbo 248–9